MW00678167

Interrupt Handling Functions

See also *TSR Functions*.

Keyboard Functions

Memory Resident Functions

See *TSR Functions*.

Mouse Functions

Numeric Functions

See under *Utility Functions*.

(continued on inside back cover)

Computer users are not all alike.
Neither are SYBEX books.

We know our customers have a variety of needs. They've told us so. And because we've listened, we've developed several distinct types of books to meet the needs of each of our customers. What are you looking for in computer help?

If you're looking for the basics, try the **ABC's** series. You'll find short, unintimidating tutorials and helpful illustrations. For a more visual approach, select **Teach Yourself**, featuring screen-by-screen illustrations of how to use your latest software purchase.

Mastering and **Understanding** titles offer you a step-by-step introduction, plus an in-depth examination of intermediate-level features, to use as you progress.

Our **Up & Running** series is designed for computer-literate consumers who want a no-nonsense overview of new programs. Just 20 basic lessons, and you're on your way.

We also publish two types of reference books. Our **Instant References** provide quick access to each of a program's commands and functions. SYBEX **Encyclopedias** and **Desktop References** provide a *comprehensive reference* and explanation of all of the commands, features and functions of the subject software.

Sometimes a subject requires a special treatment that our standard series don't provide. So you'll find we have titles like **Advanced Techniques, Handbooks, Tips & Tricks,** and others that are specifically tailored to satisfy a unique need.

We carefully select our authors for their in-depth understanding of the software they're writing about, as well as their ability to write clearly and communicate effectively. Each manuscript is thoroughly reviewed by our technical staff to ensure its complete accuracy. Our production department makes sure it's easy to use. All of this adds up to the highest quality books available, consistently appearing on best-seller charts worldwide.

You'll find SYBEX publishes a variety of books on every popular software package. Looking for computer help? Help Yourself to SYBEX.

For a complete catalog of our publications:

SYBEX Inc.
2021 Challenger Drive, Alameda, CA 94501
Tel: (510) 523-8233/(800) 227-2346 Telex: 336311
Fax: (510) 523-2373

Systems Programming
in Microsoft C

Systems Programming
in Microsoft® C

Second Edition

Michael J. Young

SYBEX®

San Francisco ■ Paris ■ Düsseldorf ■ Soest

Acquisitions Editor: Dianne King
Project Editor: Barbara Dahl
Copy Editor: Bradley B. Hess
Technical Editor: Jon Forrest
Production Editor: Carolina Montilla
Word Processors: Ann Dunn, Susan Trybull
Book Designer and Chapter Art: Charlotte Carter
Layout Artist: Alissa Feinberg
Typesetter: Deborah Maizels
Proofreader: Lisa Haden
Cover Designer: Thomas Ingalls + Associates
Cover Photographer: David Bishop

Library of Congress Card Number: 91-66290
ISBN: 0-7821-1026-6

Manufactured in the United States of America
10 9 8 7 6 5 4 3 2 1

ACKNOWLEDGMENTS

As always I enjoyed writing this book for SYBEX. I thank Rudolph Langer, editor-in-chief, and Dianne King, acquisitions editor, for their outstanding support. I especially enjoyed working with Bradley Hess, who edited the entire book and enhanced the clarity and consistency of the manuscript. I also thank the other people at SYBEX who worked on the project. Finally, I am grateful to Microsoft Corporation for supplying the software used to develop the functions and programs.

CONTENTS AT A GLANCE

TABLE OF CONTENTS ─────────────

Chapter 6: AN INTERACTIVE SCREEN DESIGNER 199

Chapter 7: DEVICE-INDEPENDENT GRAPHICS FUNCTIONS 241

Chapter 8: INTERRUPT HANDLERS 283

Chapter 12:   UTILITY FUNCTIONS   451

INTRODUCTION

This is a book for Microsoft C programmers that is written to meet two distinct needs. First, for the applications programmer, it contains an extensive collection of ready-to-use functions that can be immediately incorporated into a C program, and that significantly extend the Microsoft C runtime library. Second, for the systems programmer, it provides complete source code listings and detailed explanations for each of the functions to exemplify many of the advanced features of Microsoft C, and to show how to make optimal use of this language for systems-level programming.

The functions and techniques presented in this book can be used with either the Microsoft C optimizing compiler *or* Microsoft QuickC; the differences between these two compilers are briefly described later in the introduction.

The text clearly distinguishes documentation on the *use* of the functions from descriptions of the *inner workings* of these functions. The application programmer interested primarily in *using* the functions may safely skip the sections on the inner workings. It is not necessary to understand how the functions are implemented in order to use them effectively; in fact, the functions were designed to provide a simple programmer interface and to hide the details of their implementation from the calling program.

For the programmer who is interested in the advanced features of Microsoft C and who wants to use this language as a systems programming tool, Chapter 1 provides an overview of such features as memory models, interfacing with assembly language, calling system services, and using Microsoft C interrupt functions. The routines in the remainder of the book illustrate many interesting methods, pitfalls, tricks, and caveats. For this programmer, the functions may serve more as programming examples and the starting point for custom routines, rather than as a ready-to-run package.

The software tools presented in the book have been carefully developed for the Microsoft C environment, and take advantage of many of the unique features of this compiler. The functions are designed to be easy to use, to fill the gaps in the Microsoft C runtime library, and to provide practical and important services for application programs. Many of the functions are currently in use in applications developed by the author, and have proven their usefulness and reliability. You may find that the collection of functions presented in this book are all that you need to develop a broad range of sophisticated applications (you may also need one or more special-purpose function libraries for performing tasks such as managing indexed files).

The book contains a diverse collection of functions. They share, however, a common purpose: to extend the power of Microsoft C by giving an application program direct access to many important software and hardware resources available in MS-DOS machines. The standard C library is quite generic; it was designed to be portable from system to system. Consequently, it fails to take advantage of many of the most significant features of the MS-DOS environment. Microsoft C adds a number of MS-DOS specific functions, and the software tools in this book add many more.

AN OVERVIEW OF THE CHAPTERS

You should begin by reading the first three sections of Chapter 1, which describe the basic steps for preparing and using the functions presented in the subsequent chapters. If you are interested in systems-level programming you should also read the remaining sections in this chapter, which discuss advanced techniques in Microsoft C programming, and provide important background information for the explanations of the workings of the functions throughout the book.

Once you have read the desired sections of Chapter 1, you can read the other chapters in any order, since they are largely self-sufficient. However, you should read a given chapter through from the beginning, since many important concepts are explained only when they are first encountered.

The listings in the book are liberally commented. You can read these listings to gain an understanding of the implementation details. The descriptions of the functions in the text focus on the general flow of logic and the basic strategies behind the coding details. Also, although there are no formal exercises, the book offers many suggestions for enhancements of the routines.

Chapter 1: Techniques

Chapter 1 focuses on the basic techniques that will be used throughout the remainder of the book. The chapter begins by describing the organization of the functions presented in the subsequent chapters. It then outlines the methods for using these functions in an application program, and presents the detailed steps for preparing the functions and example programs from the listings in the book.

The remainder of Chapter 1 discusses advanced techniques in Microsoft C programming that are used in the development of the functions. Specifically, it explains how to use C memory models, how to interface C programs with assembly language functions, how to call the system services available in MS-DOS machines, and how to write interrupt handling functions in the C language.

Chapter 2: Keyboard and Console Functions

Chapter 2 begins the presentation of the library of systems functions that form the core of the book. This chapter presents two modules of functions: routines for managing the keyboard, and routines for improving the performance and modifying the behavior of input and output through the console.

Chapter 3: Printer Functions

Chapter 3 presents a module of functions for managing the printer. Using these functions, you can determine whether the printer is on-line and ready to receive output; you can direct output to any printer in a system with multiple printers; you can print data at specific row and column positions on the printed page; you can submit a file to the DOS PRINT queue, so that it will print in the background; and you can perform many other printing tasks.

Chapter 4: File Management Functions

Chapter 4 presents a set of functions for managing directories, volume labels, and files. These functions allow you to rename a directory or volume label, to get or set the modification date of a file, to open up to 255 file handles at one time (circumventing the DOS 20 file handle limit), and to perform other disk-related tasks.

Chapter 5: Video Functions

The module presented in Chapter 5 contains a comprehensive set of video functions that allow you to create fast and attractive video displays, and to manage the display of screens and windows generated using the interactive screen designer of Chapter 6. The routines use direct video memory access to provide optimal speed and flexibility.

Chapter 6: An Interactive Screen Designer

Using the program presented in Chapter 6, you can create and save screen designs, and subsequently display these screens from your C program using the video functions of Chapter 5. The program allows you to draw screens that appear exactly as they will be displayed, provides immediate access to all normal and semi-graphic characters in the IBM set, and offers a full set of character and block editing commands for efficiently manipulating screen data. The commented source code for this program also serves to illustrate the use of many of the video functions.

Chapter 7: Device-Independent Graphics Functions

Chapter 7 presents a basic but comprehensive package of graphics functions that illustrate many low-level programming techniques in Microsoft C. The function interface is designed to remain independent of the specific graphics mode, and the module is written to facilitate adding new graphics functions and support for additional graphics modes. The module therefore forms a good platform for developing a custom graphics library and for supporting a wide variety of graphics devices.

Chapter 8: Interrupt Handlers

Unlike many high-level languages, Microsoft C is ideally suited for writing interrupt handlers. The interrupt mechanism is an important resource in MS-DOS machines, and by installing interrupt service routines, your program can execute tasks in the background, gain control over break-key and critical-error conditions, and perform other useful services. Chapter 8 demonstrates how to write both hardware and software interrupt handlers in Microsoft C, and the functions presented in this chapter make it easy to install clock tick service routines, control-break handlers, and critical-error functions.

Chapter 9: Memory Resident Programs

Memory resident programs are one of the most popular and successful devices for expanding the power of MS-DOS. Developing a memory resident program involves a myriad of low-level details and normally requires assembly language. The functions in Chapter 9, however, allow you to convert a normal Microsoft C program to a memory resident utility with a single function call. Also, these functions permit you to specify a hotkey to activate your program, and make it possible for your resident program to use MS-DOS services (which are employed by many of the standard C library functions, such as **printf**).

Chapter 10: An Expanded Memory Interface

The expanded memory specification is an increasingly popular and important mechanism for enlarging the amount of memory available to an MS-DOS application. The functions in Chapter 10 provide a simplified high-level interface that makes it easy to allocate and access expanded memory pages from a Microsoft C program.

Chapter 11: A Mouse Interface

Chapter 11 presents a comprehensive set of functions for managing a mouse. These functions support the Microsoft, Logitech, or compatible mouse, and allow you to implement a full mouse interface for your application program without using additional programming tools.

Chapter 12: Utility Functions

Chapter 12 completes the presentation of the library of functions for Microsoft C. This chapter presents a diverse set of routines. Many of these functions provide support for the other function modules in the book; others offer unique services that do not fit into any of the categories presented in the previous chapters.

Appendix A: Alphabetical Summary of the Functions

Appendix A provides concise reference information on all of the function modules and individual functions in the book. Once you have read the lengthier descriptions in the text, this appendix will serve as a convenient reference guide.

Appendix B: Setting Up a Library File

Appendix B describes the methods for creating and maintaining a library file that contains all of the functions in the book. A library file provides the most compact and convenient vehicle for linking these routines to your Microsoft C program.

Appendix C: Extended Keyboard Codes

Appendix C provides a concise table of the codes that are used to recognize a wide variety of keystrokes and key combinations that can by typed on standard and enhanced IBM-compatible keyboards.

Bibliography

The Bibliography lists many useful books and programmer's magazines that cover topics on C programming and the MS-DOS environment.

Endpapers

Finally, the inside covers of the book list all of the functions presented in the book, according to the types of services they provide. This list provides a convenient method for finding an appropriate function for your program.

REQUIRED TOOLS AND BACKGROUND

To prepare the functions presented in this book you will need *either* the Microsoft optimizing C compiler, version 5.0 or later, *or* Microsoft

QuickC, version 1.0 or later. Note that if you purchase the Microsoft C optimizing compiler, QuickC is included in the package. Note also that QuickC provides both a compiler that can be run in the traditional fashion from the DOS command line, *and* an integrated development environment. The integrated environment allows you to edit, compile, run, and debug programs within windows, using a set of commands and pull-down menus. The optimizing compiler generates smaller and more efficient programs than QuickC; however, it is not required in order to take full advantage of the functions given in this book.

Throughout the book, the expression *Microsoft C compiler* is used as a general term to refer to *both* the optimizing C compiler *and* to QuickC. The text explains any differences between the optimizing compiler and QuickC, and between QuickC versions 1.0, 2.0, and later.

You will also need the Microsoft Macro Assembler, version 5.0 or later, to prepare the functions written in assembly language. Note, however, that you do not need the assembler to *call* these functions from your C program; therefore, if you have obtained the companion disk set described at the end of the introduction, you can make full use of all of the functions in the book without employing the macro assembler.

The functions and programs in this book were all tested using the Microsoft C compiler versions 5.0, 5.1, and 6.0, QuickC versions 1.0 and 2.0, and the Microsoft Macro Assembler version 5.1. The functions will run under all versions of MS-DOS and PC-DOS 2.0 or later, and in the DOS compatibility environment of OS/2 (except for the PRINT queue functions).

The primary background required to take advantage of this book is a basic understanding of the C programming language. Common C constructs are presented without explanation, although more advanced methods, and features unique to the Microsoft C system, are thoroughly explained.

You do not need to be an advanced C programmer, however. As stated previously, the book addresses two levels of needs, and even a beginning programmer will soon feel the need for functions that extend the Microsoft C library. Once the functions in this book have been entered and compiled, they can be called as easily as the standard library functions, without attention to the manner in which they are written. Furthermore, beginning programmers using QuickC will notice it is an excellent learning medium, and will rapidly find themselves becoming experienced through use of this environment.

Readers with an intermediate level of experience in C programming will be able to understand the inner workings of the functions at a deeper level. Advanced C and assembler systems programmers will be especially interested in the explanations and examples of the unique features of Microsoft C, some of which greatly facilitate systems-level programming.

There are many books available on C that can facilitate the learning process. Among the numerous general books on C programming, I recommend the following:

The C Programming Language, by Kernighan and Ritchie, is the classic definition of the language, and is a precise and succinct exposition.

C: A Reference Manual, by Harbinson and Steel, is a more verbose and current treatment, and contains useful information on the standards and extensions to C that are being defined by the ANSI committee on the standardization of the C language.

For an introduction to C programming that focuses specifically on the QuickC environment, I recommend *Mastering QuickC* by Stan Kelly-Bootle.

For further advanced information on programming in Microsoft C and assembly language under MS-DOS, you can consult my book *Inside DOS: A Programmer's Guide.* Also, I have written a book for the Turbo C compiler from Borland, which is similar to the present title and is called *Systems Programming in Turbo C.* Finally, if you are interested in developing programs for the protected mode of OS/2 (the functions in the present book will run only under the real mode), see one of my introductory books on OS/2 programming: *Programmer's Guide to OS/2* or *Programmer's Guide to the OS/2 Presentation Manager.*

All of the books mentioned in this section are cited in the Bibliography.

COMPANION DISK SET

For programmers who would like to avoid typing in the source files in this book, and who want to make immediate use of all the functions and utilities, a companion disk set is available. The three disks in this set include all the source code listings from the book and a set of ready-to-link library files. A separate library file is provided for each memory model; each of these files contains all the function modules in the book. See the Disk Offer in the back of the book for more information on these products and for complete ordering instructions.

Techniques

CHAPTER **1**

This chapter discusses the basic techniques for using the library of functions presented in the book, and also introduces some of the advanced techniques and concepts in Microsoft C programming that will be used in the development of these functions. Before reading and exploring the topics in this chapter, you should have installed the Microsoft C compiler— either the optimizing compiler, version 5.0 or later, or the QuickC integrated environment or command line system—and you should be familiar with its basic operations. (This book assumes a familiarity with the C language and the use of the Microsoft C compiler; if you need further background information on either of these topics, see the Bibliography for the titles of introductory books.)

The chapter begins with a description of the overall organization of the functions in this book, followed by a summary of the methods for preparing and using these functions in a C program. It then discusses how to work with Microsoft C memory models and how to interface C programs with assembly language functions. Finally, it describes the general techniques for accessing system services (those provided by MS-DOS and the BIOS), and the methods for writing interrupt handling routines in the C language.

HOW THE FUNCTIONS ARE ORGANIZED

The functions in this book are organized as a collection of separate *modules*. The term module refers to a set of related functions, data structures, and constant definitions. The functions in a given module all have names that begin with a three letter prefix identifying the module to which they belong. The following are the function modules presented in the book:

Prefix	Chapter	Purpose
Kbd	2	Manage the keyboard.
Ioc	2	Manage console I/O.
Prt	3	Manage the printer.
Fil	4	Manage disks, directories, and files.
Scr	5	Perform text mode screen I/O.
Buf	5	Manage a logical screen buffer for displaying data in a window.

Gra	7	Generate graphics screen output.
Int	8	Handle hardware and software interrupts.
Tsr	9	Install and manage memory resident programs.
Ems	10	Allocate and manage expanded memory.
Mou	11	Manage a mouse.
Uty	12	Perform utility services.

For example, the function **KbdGetC** belongs to the **Kbd** module, and serves to read a character from the keyboard, and the function **ScrPutS** belongs to the **Scr** module, and writes a string to a specific position on the screen.

Each module is implemented as a collection of related files. For example, the **Kbd** module consists of the following files:

Kbd module file	**Contents**
KBD.C	Source code for the functions written in C; private data declarations and constant definitions.
KBDA.ASM	Source code for the functions written in assembly language; private data declarations and constant definitions.
KBD.H	Prototypes for all public functions; all public data declarations and constant definitions.

Additionally, the book provides a set of example programs for each module that demonstrate the use of the functions in that module. For instance, the **Kbd** module is accompanied by the following example programs:

```
KBDDEM01.C
KBDDEM02.C
KBDDEM03.C
KBDDEM04.C
KBDDEM05.C
KBDDEM06.C
```

Also, as you will see in a following section, for each example program both a MAKE file (a script for preparing the program with the Microsoft

MAKE or NMAKE utility), and a QuickC program list (which allows you to generate a MAKE file for the QuickC integrated environment) are provided.

For certain modules (specifically, the **Kbd**, **Scr**, **Tsr**, and **Uty** modules), one or more of the functions are written in assembly language. Note, however, that both the C source file and the assembly language file are considered to belong to the same module, as that term is used in this book.

Note also that the functions in this book are designed to support the notion of code and data *abstraction*, or *encapsulation*. According to this ideal, the details of the implementation and the internal data structures of a function are hidden from the user of the function (that is, from the calling program). The user is presented a simple public interface, does not need to know the inner workings of the function, and should not directly access its internal data. Code and data abstraction represents a sort of division of labor: the systems programmer writes the functions, and the application programmer uses them. The systems programmer is thus free to change the implementation of the functions at any time, as long as the public interface (the calling protocol and any shared variables) remains constant.

Accordingly, the function and variable declarations and constant definitions that are used only by the module functions themselves are declared *within* the module source file. Furthermore, these private functions and data items are declared using the **static** keyword, which renders them inaccessible to other source files. (Data declared within assembly language files are kept private by excluding the PUBLIC statement.)

In contrast, all function and data declarations and constant definitions that are shared with the calling program are placed within the header file. Also, public functions and data items are declared *without* the **static** keyword, which automatically makes them available to other source files. (In the assembly language files, all public items are declared with a PUBLIC statement.) For example, the header file EMS.H contains the declarations for all of the **Ems** module functions that can be called by an application program, as well as declarations for all variables and definitions of all constants that can be accessed by the calling program. The module source files (.C and .ASM) thus represent the private portion of the function module, and the header file (.H) represents the publicly accessible interface.

USING THE FUNCTIONS

To use one of the functions presented in this book you must *import* the function into your application program using the following three simple steps:

1. Include the appropriate header file. As you have seen, the header files are named according to the three letter prefix for the associated module. For example, if you want to call the function **KbdReady**, you must include the header file KBD.H, and if you want to call **ScrGetS**, you must include SCR.H. *It is absolutely essential to include the appropriate header file*: the functions will not work properly unless you do so. One important reason for including the proper header file is that it contains full prototypes for all functions in the module that can be called externally. Such prototypes inform the compiler of the data types of the functions and their parameters. This information, for example, allows the compiler to generate the proper call instruction for a **far** function, and causes it to properly convert a **near** address to a **far** address for a parameter declared as a **far** pointer (see the section "Using Memory Models" later in the chapter).

2. Call the desired function as documented in this book.

3. Link the program with the appropriate object file or files. The object files required for each module are listed in the description of that module in Appendix B. The example programs that illustrate the modules are accompanied by MAKE files—these list the required object files as well. For example, if you call the function **KbdGetShift**, you must link your program with KBD.OBJ (the object file generated from KBD.C) and UTYA.OBJ (the object file generated from UTYA.ASM). UTYA.OBJ is required since the source file KBD.C contains several calls to functions defined in the file UTYA.ASM.

Note that the third step can be greatly simplified by placing the code for all function modules in a single library file. The linker will then be able to find referenced code within any module without the need to specify each required object file on the linker command line. The process of preparing such a library file is described in Appendix B.

The example programs, MAKE files, and QuickC program lists presented in the subsequent chapters of the book illustrate the exact methods for using the function modules. Also, the section "Preparing the Functions and Example Programs," later in the chapter, provides further details.

Handling Errors

Many (but not all) of the functions presented in this book supply the calling program with an error code indicating whether the function was successful. A zero error code value always means that the function was successful, and a nonzero value always means that an error occurred. Error codes are transmitted to the calling program using one of the following two mechanisms:

1. The function may simply return the error code directly to the calling program. For example, **KbdInsert** returns 0 if successful or 1 if an error occurred. The return value can be tested as in the following example:

```
int Error;
   .
   .
   .
Error = KbdInsert (65, 0);

if (Error)
    /* then KbdInsert failed; call error */
    /* handler. */
```

This method of supplying an error code is suitable for a function that does not need to return a value other than the error status.

2. The function may return a *special value* indicating that an error occurred; it then assigns the actual error code to a global error variable. For example, the function **EmsAlloc** normally returns a pointer to the base of the allocated memory. If the function fails, however, it returns the value NULL and assigns the actual error code to the global variable **EmsError**, which is defined in the header file EMS.H and is therefore accessible to

the calling program. The calling program can test the error status as follows:

```
char far *PtrEms;

if ((PtrEms = EmsAlloc (4)) == NULL)
    switch (EmsError)
        {
        case NOTINSTALLED:
            /* EMS memory not installed; */
            /* call error handler. */

        case ALLOCATED:
            /* EMS memory already */
            /* allocated;*/
            /* call error handler. */
        .
        .
        .
```

This method of supplying an error code is suitable for a function that normally needs to return a value other than an error code. The special value indicating an error must be within the range of possible return values, but not within the range of meaningful values.

The error reporting protocol is documented for each function, both in the description of the function in the text and in the function summary given in Appendix A. Note that when a function can supply more than one nonzero error code, the module header file defines descriptive constants for these codes (such as NOTINSTALLED and ALLOCATED, defined in the file EMS.H and used in the example just given).

PREPARING THE FUNCTIONS AND EXAMPLE PROGRAMS

As mentioned previously in the chapter, the book presents one or more example programs for each of the function modules. Furthermore, for each example program, the book provides a script for preparing the program with the Microsoft MAKE or NMAKE utility (a *MAKE file*, with a .M file extension), and a program list for preparing the program within the QuickC integrated environment. A given MAKE file — or QuickC program list—not only prepares the associated example program, but also automatically compiles or assembles all module source files that have been newly entered or modified. For example, the following MAKE file is provided for preparing the fifth **Kbd** module example program, KBDDEM05.C:

```
KBDDEM05.OBJ : KBDDEM05.C KBD.H
     cl /c /W2 /Zp KBDDEM05.C

KBD.OBJ : KBD.C KBD.H
     cl /c /W2 /Zp KBD.C

UTYA.OBJ : UTYA.ASM
     masm /MX UTYA.ASM;

KBDDEM05.EXE : KBDDEM05.OBJ KBD.OBJ UTYA.OBJ
     link /NOI /NOD KBDDEM05+KBD+UTYA,,NUL,SLIBCER;
```

This MAKE file first compiles the example program KBDDEM05.C (*if* it is necessary to bring the object file up to date with the C source file and header file). Since KBDDEM05.C calls functions found in the file KBD.C (**KbdSetShift** and **KbdGetShift**), the MAKE script next generates the object file KBD.OBJ. Furthermore, since the KBD.C file calls several functions in the UTYA.ASM file, the MAKE script also prepares the object file KBDA.OBJ. Finally, it invokes the linker to bind together all of the object files that have just been brought up to date, generating the executable file KBDDEM05.EXE. See your compiler documentation for more information on the operation of the MAKE utility.

The following is a brief summary of the command line flags used in the MAKE files throughout this book:

Flag	Utility	Effect
/c	CL	Compiles the program without running the linker.
/W2	CL	Provides an intermediate level of compiler warnings, including warnings for data conversions and mismatches (in type or number) between the parameters passed to a function and the function prototype (also generates a warning if the prototype is missing).

/Zp	CL	Packs all structures; that is, each structure field is placed on the first available byte address rather than being aligned on even addresses (packing is important when using structures to exchange data with the operating system, as do several of the modules in the book).
/MX	MASM	Preserves case in public and external names (if you omit this option, the assembler converts these names to uppercase letters; you must include this flag if you select the linker **/NOI** option).
/NOI	LINK	Causes the linker to distinguish between uppercase and lowercase letters (often used with C programs, since C is a case sensitive language; if you select this option, you must also choose the **/MX** assembler option).
/NOD	LINK	Prevents the linker from searching the default C library (the compiler writes the default name of this library to the object file).

Note that if your C runtime libraries use the standard names (for example, SLIBCE.LIB for the small model library), you do not need to choose the **/NOD** option, and you do not need to specify the C library name, in the LINK command line. If, however, your libraries do not use the default names, you must specify the **/NOD** flag and include the name of the library, as in the MAKE files given in this book. (These MAKE files specify the library SLIBCER.LIB, which was the name of the small model C library in the system used to prepare the functions and example programs; the *R* was added to the library names to distinguish the real mode MS-DOS library versions from the OS/2 protected mode versions.) If you do not use the default names, specify the actual name of the appropriate C library in your MAKE files.

Using QuickC and C 6.0

If you are preparing the function modules with the QuickC command line compiler, you can use the MAKE files provided in the book by simply substituting the **qcl** command for each **cl** command. All of the command line flags work correctly with the QuickC compiler and linker. Also, all of the functions and programs listed in the book may be prepared using the QuickC command line compiler.

If you are using the standard Microsoft MAKE utility (MAKE.EXE, supplied with the optimizing C compiler *prior* to version 6.0 and the macro assembler), you need to specify only the name of the MAKE file when invoking the MAKE utility. For example, the following line would cause the MAKE utility to prepare the example program KBDDEMO1.EXE:

```
MAKE KBDDEMO1.M
```

If, however, you are using the NMAKE program supplied with QuickC and the optimizing compiler version 6.0 or later, you must specify both the name of the MAKE file (with the **/f** flag) *and* the name of the target program you want to prepare. For example, you would use the following command to build the program KBDDEMO1.EXE:

```
NMAKE /f KBDDEMO1.M KBDDEMO1.EXE
```

If you want to prepare an example program within the QuickC integrated environment, you can use the QuickC program list that is provided with the program. For example, the following program list is provided for the example program KBDDEM05.C (this list is thus equivalent to the MAKE file shown previously in this section):

```
KBDDEM05.C
KBD.C
UTYA.OBJ
```

Once you have started the QuickC integrated environment (by typing QC) and have loaded the desired example program, you can prepare this program, and any required function modules, through the following steps:

1. Enter the Make menu and select the Set Program List item. (For QuickC version 1.0 you enter the File menu to select this item.)

2. QuickC will request a file name; enter the name of the example program (without the .C extension). QuickC will then ask whether to create a MAKE file (with the .MAK extension); you should respond affirmatively.

3. Next, enter all file names exactly as they appear in the program list, and select the Save List box to cause QuickC to generate and save the MAKE file.

4. To prepare and run the application using the MAKE file just generated, enter the Make menu and select the Build Program item, or the Run menu and select Go (under QuickC version 1.0, enter the Run menu and select Start or Compile).

Note that the QuickC integrated environment searches the C library to resolve any references to C library functions that are not in the Quick-C core library. It assumes that this library has the standard name. For example, if you are preparing a small memory model program, it will look for the library SLIBCE.LIB (which must be in the path specified by the LIB environment variable). If you have given this library a different name, you must add the *full path name* of your library (including the .LIB extension) to the program list. (Note that under the QuickC version 1.0 integrated environment, all programs are compiled using the medium-memory model, and therefore QuickC will search for the library MLIBCE.LIB.)

Note also that assembly language files cannot be assembled within the QuickC integrated environment. Accordingly, these files are specified as object files (such as UTYA.OBJ in the example just given). You must use the macro assembler to prepare these object files *prior* to entering Quick-C, as in the following command:

```
masm /MX UTYA.ASM;
```

Alternatively, since QuickC version 2.0 now supports inline assembly language, you could convert the assembly language source files into C source files containing inline assembler instructions. Such programs can be compiled only in the QuickC integrated environment or with the QuickC command line compiler (the optimizing compiler does not support inline assembly language). See the compiler documentation for more information on inline assembly language.

All of the programs in the book can be prepared in the QuickC environment (except EMSDEMO2.C, given in Chapter 10, if you are using QuickC version 1.0). Several programs, however, should not be run within this environment (namely, the memory resident applications of Chapter 9).

Creating a Library File

As mentioned earlier in the chapter, the easiest way to prepare the example programs is to place the object code for all function modules in a single library file, using the methods given in Appendix B. Once you have created such a library file, you can prepare a program that uses any of the functions contained in this library with a single command. For example, if the object code for the function has been placed in a library file named MSCTOOLS.LIB, you could prepare the example program KBDDEM05.C using the following command:

```
cl /W2 /Zp KBDDEM05.C /link /NOD SLIBCER.LIB MSCTOOLS.LIB
```

Note that if your C library bears the standard name, SLIBCE.LIB, you can omit the **/link /NOD SLIBCER.LIB** portion of the command line.

As you work through the book, you can add functions to the library file as they are needed. Alternatively, if you have obtained the Companion Diskette Set, which includes library files for all memory models, you can immediately use any of the functions in the book by simply linking your application program with the library file for the current memory model.

▌USING MEMORY MODELS

Microsoft C, as well as most other C compilers written for the 8086 family of processors, classifies data pointers and functions as **near** or **far**, according to the addressing mode that is used for the object. This classification has important implications for systems programming, and stems from the addressing method used by the 8086 family of processors. In the 8086 family, data and code addresses consist of a 16-bit *segment* address and a 16-bit *offset* from that segment. (Since the 16-bit offset can specify a value no larger than 64 kilobytes, 64 kilobytes is the maximum size for a code or data segment.)

If all data objects in a particular program module are contained within the same segment, it is not necessary to maintain the segment address for each variable, and therefore data pointers need be only 16 bits long (and segment registers do not have to be reloaded each time a data object is accessed). Likewise, if all functions are within the same segment, function addresses need be only 16 bits long, and function calls do not have to reload the code segment register (that is, **near** calls and returns are used). Such data pointers and functions are classified as **near**.

If, however, a particular program stores its data objects in more than one segment, then data pointers must contain both the segment address as well as the offset, and therefore need to be 32 bits long. Similarly, if the functions in a program are contained in more than a single segment, function addresses must be 32 bits long, and function calls and returns need to load and restore the code segment register (that is, **far** calls and returns are used). These data pointers and functions are classified as **far**, and are typically used for programs that contain more than 64 kilobytes of code or 64 kilobytes of data.

The overhead associated with **near** objects (in terms of code size and execution speed) is less than that for **far** objects. To allow the programmer to use the most efficient addressing modes possible, the Microsoft optimizing C compiler and QuickC provide four distinct memory models: *small*, *medium*, *compact*, and *large*. (Microsoft C also provides a *huge* memory model, which is not available under QuickC version 1.0; see the compiler documentation for an explanation of this model.) These models are selected through the /AX command line parameter, where X is the first letter of the desired model (S, M, C, or L). The model that is selected determines the default types for both data pointers and functions (that is, **near** or **far**), and the overall organization of the program segments in memory. Table 1.1 summarizes the data pointer and function types, and the default segment layout, for each of these memory models.

Table 1.1: Characteristics of the four Microsoft C memory models

Memory Model	CL or QCL Flag	Data Pointers	Function Calls	Default Segments
small	/AS	near (16 bit)	near	1 for code 1 for data
medium	/AM	near (16 bit)	far	multiple for code 1 for data
compact	/AC	far (32 bit)	near	1 for code multiple for data
large	/AL	far (32 bit)	far	multiple for code multiple for data

Note that the MAKE files in this book do not specify a memory model, and therefore generate small-model programs since this model is the default for the Microsoft optimizing C (CL) and QuickC (QCL) command line compilers. If you want to call any of the functions presented in the book from a compact, medium, or large model program, you must recompile the C source code for the functions, specifying the same model as the calling program (by means of the /AX flag). As you will see in the next section, the assembly language source files are designed so that the functions they contain can be called from *any* model C program; you therefore do not need to modify or reassemble these files if you change memory models.

Note also that programs compiled within the QuickC version 1.0 integrated environment always use the medium memory model; you therefore cannot adjust memory models within this environment.

Once a memory model has been selected, you can override the default address types of individual data pointers or functions by using the **near** or **far** keywords as declaration modifiers. For example, the expression

```
char far *Video;
```

creates a **far** (32 bit) pointer, regardless of the memory model. Such pointers are useful in small data models for accessing memory in a segment other than the default C data segment (such as video memory), and are illustrated in many of the functions and example programs in this book.

Note that if you compile a C program within the QuickC integrated environment (version 2.0) that uses a **far** pointer to access an address outside of the program, you must disable the Pointer Check option (through the Options/Make/Compiler Flags menu item). Otherwise, the resulting program will generate a runtime message when the address instruction is executed.

The following function declaration illustrates two additional uses for the **far** keyword:

```
void far FarFunction (char far *FarParm);
```

First, the **far** keyword placed before the function name forces this function to be called with a **far** call, *regardless of the current memory model*. (If **FarFunction** is written in a small code C program, the function type specified at the beginning of the actual function must also contain the **far** keyword so that the compiler knows to generate a **far** return instruction. If **FarFunction** is written in assembly language, it should be declared as a PROC FAR, or it should follow the .MODEL MEDIUM or .MODEL LARGE assembler directive.)

Second, the **far** keyword placed before the parameter **FarParm** specifies that it is a **far** pointer. Accordingly, the compiler will automatically convert a **near** address you pass as a parameter to the appropriate **far** address.

As you will see in the next section, declaring an assembly language function—and any address parameter that it receives—using the **far** keyword, allows you to call this function without modification from any memory model C program.

This section has provided only a brief introduction to Microsoft C memory models; see the Microsoft C *User's Guide* for a more complete discussion (this guide also explains the *huge* memory model and the **huge** keyword, and describes how to create custom memory models).

■ INTERFACING WITH ASSEMBLY LANGUAGE

Occasionally it is necessary or preferable to write a function in assembly language rather than in the C language. Examples include functions that require direct access to machine registers or the ability to call specific machine language instructions (such as RET 2, MOVSB, and CLI). You may also need to use assembly language for routines that have critical timing constraints (such as the CGA video functions given in Chapter 5), or for routines that must be extremely efficient.

This section briefly describes the anatomy of an assembly language source file, and explains how to write assembly language functions that can be called by a C program compiled under *any* memory model. For more information on basic assembly language programming, see the introductory book by Lafore cited in the Bibliography; for detailed information on interfacing C and assembly language, see Chapter 2 of *MS-DOS Advanced Programming*, also listed in the Bibliography.

Figure 1.1 illustrates a simple assembly language source file (the function it contains, **KbdReady**, is explained in Chapter 2). The file begins with the directive

```
.MODEL LARGE
```

which causes the assembler to use a memory model that matches the large memory model employed by the C compiler. The most important effect of this directive for the functions given in the book is that

```
 1: .MODEL LARGE
 2: .CODE
 3:
 4: PUBLIC _KbdReady
 5: _KbdReady PROC
 6: ;
 7: ;       Prototype:
 8: ;            int far KbdReady
 9: ;                 (void)
10: ;
11: ;    This function returns a non-zero value if a key is ready to be read, or
12: ;    zero if the BIOS keyboard buffer is empty.
13:
14:        mov   ah, 01            ;Specify the BIOS keyboard status function.
15:        int   16h               ;Invoke BIOS keyboard services.
16:        jz    a01               ;ZF set means keyboard buffer empty.
17:        mov   ax, 1             ;ZF not set; key is ready; therefore return 1.
18:        ret
19: a01:
20:        mov   ax, 0             ;Return 0 indicating no key ready.
21:        ret
22:
23: _KbdReady ENDP
24:
25: END
```

Figure 1.1: A simple assembly language source file

the assembler will generate **far** return statements for all subsequent procedures defined in the file. Accordingly, all assembly language functions must be declared within the calling C program using the **far** keyword, so that the C compiler will use a **far** call to invoke the function *regardless of the current memory model*. Accordingly, the function in Figure 1.1 is declared in the KBD.H header file as follows:

```
int far KbdReady (void);
```

Line 2 of Figure 1.1 contains the directive

```
.CODE
```

which tells the assembler that the subsequent statements will define code. This directive remains in effect until the end of the file, or until you issue another directive, such as .DATA, which informs the assembler that subsequent statements will define data (the .CODE or .DATA directive must follow a .MODEL directive).

The definition of the function **KbdReady** begins on line 4 with the statement

```
PUBLIC _KbdReady
```

The PUBLIC directive allows you to call the function from other source files (this statement would be omitted if the function were called only within the assembler source file). Note that you must add an underscore to the beginning of the function name as it appears in the C program (the C compiler adds this character to external symbols when it writes them to the object file).

The beginning of the actual function code is indicated by the directive (line 5)

```
_KbdReady PROC
```

and the end of the function code is marked by the directive (line 23)

```
_KbdReady ENDP
```

Note that the function returns a value to the C program by assigning it to register AX (lines 17 and 20). Finally, the end of the assembly language source file is indicated by the END statement on line 25.

Figure 1.2 lists a slightly more complex assembly language function (**UtyFarNearCopy**, described in Chapter 12), which illustrates several additional techniques. First, this function accepts a set of parameters from the calling program, which the C compiler pushes on the program stack immediately before calling the function (they are pushed in the reverse order from the order in which they are listed in the function call). The assembly language function accesses these parameters through the following techniques:

▌ Lines 25 through 33 define a structure with a field of the appropriate size for each parameter (plus fields for the return address and base pointer, which are also pushed on the stack). Note that these parameters must appear in the structure in the same order in which they are listed in the function call. Note also that the structure does not reserve memory, but rather serves only as a convenient template to access the parameters on the stack.

▌ At the beginning of the code, the base pointer register (BP) is assigned the current value of the top of the stack (SP) so that it can be used to address the parameters on the stack. For example, the last parameter could subsequently be addressed through the expression

```
[bp].fcnCount
```

```
 1: .MODEL LARGE
 2: .CODE
 3:
 4: Frame        equ     [bp]                    ;Base for accessing stack frame.
 5:
 6: PUBLIC _UtyFarNearCopy
 7: ;
 8: ;      Prototype
 9: ;          void far UtyFarNearCopy
10: ;              (char far *TargetAddr,
11: ;              unsigned SourceSeg,
12: ;              unsigned SourceOff,
13: ;              unsigned Count);
14: ;
15: ;          This function copies 'Count' bytes from the far memory location
16: ;          that has the segment address 'SourceSeg' and the offset address
17: ;          'SourceOff' to the program target buffer specified by 'TargetAddr'
18: ;          It is useful for copying data from another segment to a program
19: ;          buffer in a small data model C program (the compiler automatically
20: ;          converts a near pointer passed as the first parameter to a far
21: ;          pointer).
22: ;
23: _UtyFarNearCopy PROC
24:
25: fncFrame       struc                         ;Template to access stack frame.
26: fncBasePtr     dw       ?                    ;Position of saved BP register.
27: fncRetAd       dd       ?                    ;Return address.
28: fncTargetOff   dw       ?                    ;Target offset.
29: fncTargetSeg   dw       ?                    ;Target segment address.
30: fncSourceSeg   dw       ?                    ;Source segment.
31: fncSourceOff   dw       ?                    ;Source offset.
32: fncCount       dw       ?                    ;Number of copies.
33: fncFrame       ends
34:
35:                                              ;Standard initialization.
36:        push  bp                              ;Set up base pointer to access frame.
37:        mov   bp, sp
38:
39:        push  di                              ;Save C register variables.
40:        push  si
41:        push  ds                              ;Save C data segment register.
42:
43:        mov   ax, Frame.fncSourceSeg          ;Place source segment in DS.
44:        mov   ds, ax
45:        mov   si, Frame.fncSourceOff          ;Place source offset in SI.
46:
47:        mov   ax, Frame.fncTargetSeg          ;Place target segment in ES.
48:        mov   es, ax
49:        mov   di, Frame.fncTargetOff          ;Place target offset in DI.
50:
51:        mov   cx, Frame.fncCount              ;Place number of bytes to move in CX.
52:
53:        cld                                   ;Move from low to high addresses.
54:
55:        rep   movsb                           ;Byte-by-byte string transfer.
```

Figure 1.2: A more complex assembly language source file

```
56:
57:        pop    ds
58:        pop    si                              ;Restore registers.
59:        pop    di
60:        mov    sp, bp
61:        pop    bp
62:        ret                                    ;Return to C program.
63:
64: _UtyFarNearCopy ENDP
65:
66: END
```

Figure 1.2: A more complex assembly language source file (continued)

▌ To make the notation more readable, the identifier **Frame** (signifying the base of the stack frame) is set equal to **[bp]** (through the **equ** statement on line 4). Accordingly, parameters can be referenced through structure notation similar to that used by high-level languages, as in the expression

```
mov cx, Frame.fncCount
```

The function in Figure 1.2 also shows how to pass an address to an assembler function from a C program compiled under any memory model. By declaring the address parameter as a **far** pointer within the calling C program, the assembler function always receives a valid **far** address regardless of the current memory model (as mentioned in a previous section, the C compiler automatically converts a **near** address to a **far** address, provided you have included the function prototype). The assembly language function can therefore process the address uniformly without regard to the memory model used by the calling program.

Accordingly, the first parameter passed to **UtyFarNearCopy** is declared as a **far** character pointer in the UTY.H header file, as follows:

```
char far *TargetAddr
```

Note that the assembler function defines two adjacent fields in the stack frame structure that correspond to this parameter (lines 28 and 29), so that it can access the segment and offset portions of the **far** address as individual values.

Finally, Figure 1.2 illustrates that an assembler function must save and restore certain registers if it alters them. Specifically, the function must preserve the values contained in the SI, DI, SP, BP, DS, CS, and SS registers.

USING SYSTEM SERVICES

Many of the functions presented in this book make use of the services offered by the MS-DOS operating system, and by the BIOS (basic input/output system) provided in the read-only memory of MS-DOS machines. These services are invoked through the interrupt instruction, and information is typically exchanged between the program and the service routine through machine registers. For example, the following assembly language code invokes the MS-DOS service for obtaining the current disk drive:

```
Drive db ?          ;Stores number of current drive.
    .
    .
    .
mov ah, 19h         ;Place function number in AH.
int 21h             ;Invoke interrupt 21h.
mov Drive, al       ;Save drive number returned in AL.
```

Invoking interrupt number 21h transfers control to the main MS-DOS function dispatcher. The value 19h, loaded into register AH prior to the interrupt instruction, tells DOS which service you want to obtain; DOS then returns the number of the current drive in register AL (0 is drive A, 1 is drive B, and so on).

Since the C language does not provide the interrupt instruction, you must generate interrupts through a C library function such as **int86** or **int86x**. For example, you can invoke the same interrupt given in the assembly language example through the following C instructions:

```
unsigned char Drive;    /* Stores number of current */
                        /* drive.                   */
union REGS Reg;         /* Holds register values.   */
    .
    .
    .
Reg.h.ah = 0x19;            /* Place function number */
                           /* in AH.                 */
int86 (0x21, &Reg, &Reg); /* Invoke interrupt 21h.  */
Drive = Reg.h.al;          /* Save drive number.     */
```

The function **int86** first loads the values contained in the REGS union passed as the second parameter into the corresponding machine registers. It next invokes the interrupt specified by the first parameter.

Upon return from the interrupt service, it loads the current values of the registers (some of which may have been modified by the interrupt service) into the REGS union passed as the third parameter (if you do not need to retain the values your program has loaded into the registers, the second and third parameters may be the address of the *same* structure, as in this example).

The REGS union passed to **int86** contains fields for the general purpose registers (AX, BX, CX, DX, as well as the half registers such as AH), registers SI and DI, and the carry flag. If you need to load values into segment registers when invoking an interrupt service, or to retrieve values from these registers, you can use the function **int86x**, which accepts a pointer to an SREGS structure containing a field for each segment register (DS, ES, SS, and CS). For example, the following code invokes the MS-DOS service for reading a file, and requires that you place the segment address of the receiving buffer into register DS:

```
union REGS Reg;
struct SREGS SReg;
.
.
.
Reg.h.ah = 0x3f;            /* Place function        */
                            /* number in AH.         */
Reg.x.bx = Handle;          /* Place file handle     */
                            /* in BX.                */
Reg.x.cx = Number;          /* Number of bytes to    */
                            /* read.                 */
SReg.ds = FP_SEG (Buf);     /* Segment address of    */
                            /* target.               */
Reg.x.dx = FP_OFF (Buf);    /* Offset address of     */
                            /* target.               */
int86x (0x21, &Reg, &Reg, &SReg); /* Invoke          */
                                  /* interrupt 21h. */

if (Reg.x.cflag)            /* Carry flag is set on  */
                            /* error.                */
                            /* then call error handler. */
```

For a complete explanation of the techniques for invoking the MS-DOS and BIOS services, and for descriptions of each service, see the book *Inside DOS: A Programmer's Guide* (cited in the Bibliography).

USING INTERRUPT FUNCTIONS

Both the Microsoft C optimizing compiler (beginning with version 5.0) and QuickC allow you to declare functions using the **interrupt** keyword. When this keyword is added to a function declaration, the compiler generates a special function format designed specifically for interrupt service routines. Interrupt service routines are programs that are invoked either by hardware interrupts (caused, for example, by pressing a key or the tick of the system clock), or by the software INT instruction (in an assembly language program, or through C library functions such as **int86**). These routines are often made resident in memory (see Chapter 9), and may receive control at any time during the execution of the program running in the foreground.

In general, interrupt service routines have some special requirements that are not met by normal C functions; therefore, they have typically been written in assembly language. Microsoft C **interrupt** functions, however, meet most of these requirements, and can often be used in place of assembly language procedures. Chapters 8 and 9 provide many examples of C **interrupt** functions.

The following are the primary features that distinguish a function declared with the **interrupt** keyword from a normal C function:

- The function loads the correct value into the DS register to permit access to data in the C data segment. (When a normal C function begins running, the DS register has been correctly set by the C startup routine; an **interrupt** function, however, may receive control while another program is running, and therefore the initial value of the DS register is unpredictable.)

- The function saves and restores all of the machine registers, except SS. The compiler places code within the **interrupt** function that pushes the registers onto the stack before your instructions begin executing, and then pops the registers off the stack immediately before the function returns.

- The compiler does *not* include a call to the C stack check routine at the beginning of the function. If an **interrupt** function receives control while another program is running, it borrows the stack of the interrupted program rather than using the C program stack; in this case, the stack check routine would fail. (For this reason, you should not call C library functions—which include calls to the stack check routine—from an **interrupt** function that may be activated within the context of another program. If you call conventional C functions that you have written, you must disable stack checking for these functions through the **#pragma check_stack (off)** line in your source file, or by means of the **/Gs** command line flag.)

■ You can easily read the register values saved *from* the interrupted program, and can set the register values that will be restored to the interrupted program by declaring appropriate parameters. This technique is explained shortly.

■ The function returns with an IRET instruction rather than a RET instruction (since it is invoked by a INT instruction— or a by hardware interrupt—rather than through a CALL instruction).

The most confusing aspect of Microsoft C **interrupt** functions is their unconventional use of the parameters you declare when writing the function. Normally, parameters are used to access the values pushed on the stack by the calling program before it calls the function. With **interrupt** functions, however, the parameters are used to access the *register values that have been pushed on the stack when the function begins executing* (**interrupt** functions are not normally passed parameters). For example, the following is the declaration of an **interrupt** function that would allow you to access all of the registers saved on the stack:

```
void interrupt far IntHandler (unsigned ES, unsigned DS,
                               unsigned DI, unsigned SI,
                               unsigned BP, unsigned SP,
                               unsigned BX, unsigned DX,
                               unsigned CX, unsigned AX,
                               unsigned IP, unsigned CS,
                               unsigned Flags);
```

As an example of using one of these parameters, the instruction

```
SavedAX = AX;
```

placed within the function **IntHandler** would obtain and save the value of the AX register from the interrupted program, which has been saved on the stack. Likewise, the instruction

```
AX = 0;
```

would modify the value of the AX register saved on the stack. Since the register values saved on the stack are popped back into the appropriate registers immediately before the **interrupt** function returns, the altered value of the AX register would be returned to the interrupted program. Note that parameters such as **AX** *do not access the current value of the registers.*

You can give these parameters any names you want; it is only the position of a given parameter within the parameter list that determines which register value it accesses. Also, if you do not need to access the saved register values within an **interrupt** function, you do not need to declare parameters for this function. For example, the following is a valid **interrupt** function declaration:

```
void interrupt far IntHandler (void);
```

Furthermore, you do not need to declare all 13 parameters, only those up to and including the last register you want to access. For example, the following interrupt function (which is presented and explained in Chapter 9) needs to access only the value of register AX that will be restored to the interrupted program; therefore, it declares only those parameters through the position of register AX in the parameter list (the previous parameters are not used but must be included as place holders):

```
static void interrupt far NewInt24
    (unsigned ES, unsigned DS,
    unsigned DI, unsigned SI,
    unsigned BP, unsigned SP,
    unsigned BX, unsigned DX,
    unsigned CX, unsigned AX)
    {
    AX = 0;

    } /* end NewInt24 */
```

The best way to further explore the anatomy of an **interrupt** function is to write some very simple ones, and then examine the assembler code generated when you select the /Fa, /Fl, or /Fc command line option. Also, see Chapter 8 for additional general information on writing interrupt handling routines.

Keyboard and
Console Functions

C HAPTER 2

Now that you have explored many of the advanced features of Microsoft C in the first chapter, this and the remaining chapters present a collection of systems functions that you can call from a Microsoft C program. These functions are designed both to illustrate advanced programming techniques and to provide a ready-to-use collection of routines that significantly enhance the C runtime library and allow you to make optimal use of the environment of MS-DOS machines. The systems-level programmer interested mainly in learning new methods may want to focus on the "How the function works" sections; the applications programmer interested primarily in *using* the functions may safely skip these sections and concentrate instead on the "How to use the function" sections.

Note that the routines are grouped into modules of related functions, each one typically focusing on a particular device or type of service. See the first section of Chapter 1 for a general description of the organization and use of the functions in this book. See also Appendix A for a summary of each function: its purpose, calling protocol, return value, and the files that must be included and linked.

This chapter presents two function modules: routines for the keyboard (KBD.C and KBDA.ASM), and routines to control I/O through the console (IOC.C).

KEYBOARD FUNCTIONS

The module of functions for managing the keyboard (the **Kbd** function module) consists of both a C file and an assembly language file. The C file is named KBD.C, and is listed in Figure 2.1. The assembly language file is named KBDA.ASM, and is listed in Figure 2.2. To use a function contained in either of these two files, you must include KBD.H (Figure 2.3) in your C source program; this header file contains all required function and constant definitions. Also, you must link the program with the appropriate object file (KBD.OBJ or KBDA.OBJ, depending upon whether the function is contained in the C or the assembler source file); alternatively, you can use a library file as described in Chapter 1 and in Appendix B. The functions in this module allow you to perform the following operations:

▮ Read both the ASCII value and the extended code of a key entered from the keyboard (**KbdGetC**).

```
#include <DOS.H>

#include "KBD.H"
#include "UTY.H"

#pragma check_stack (off)        /* Turn off stack checks so that functions   */
                                 /* can be called from interrupt routines.    */

int KbdGetShift (void)
/*
    This function returns the BIOS shift status word.
*/
    {
    /* Far pointer to shift flag in BIOS data area.                           */
    unsigned far *PtrShiftFlag = (unsigned far *)0x00400017;

    return (*PtrShiftFlag);

    } /* end KbdGetShift */


void KbdSetShift (int ShiftStat)
/*
    This function sets the BIOS shift status word.
*/
    {
    /* Far pointer to shift flag in BIOS data area.                           */
    int far *PtrShiftFlag = (int far *)0x00400017;

    *PtrShiftFlag = ShiftStat;

    } /* end KbdSetShift */


/*** Declarations for KbdInsert. ********************************************/

/* Pointer to keyboard buffer head offset:                                  */
static unsigned far *PtrHeadOffset = (unsigned far *)0x0040001A;

/* Pointer to keyboard buffer tail offset:                                  */
static unsigned far *PtrTailOffset = (unsigned far *)0x0040001C;

/* Pointer to character in keyboard buffer:                                 */
static unsigned far *PtrBuffer     = (unsigned far *)0x00400000;


int KbdInsert (char AscCode, char ExtCode)
/*
    This function inserts the specified key code into the tail of the BIOS
    keyboard buffer.  The key code is specified by the two parameters as
    follows:
        AscCode:  The ASCII code for the key, or 0 if the keystroke does
                  not have an ASCII value
        ExtCode:  The extended key code.
    The function returns zero if the key was successfully inserted, or a
    nonzero value if the keyboard buffer is full.
```

Figure 2.1: KBD.C: C Functions for managing the keyboard

```
*/
          {
          unsigned int TailOffset;      /* Stores offset to keyboard buffer tail.*/
          int Enabled;                  /* Stores state of interrupt flag.       */

          Enabled = UtyEnabled ();      /* Store original state of interrupts.   */
          UtyDisable ();                /* Unconditionally disable interrupts.   */

          /* Get new offset of keyboard buffer tail.                             */
          TailOffset = *PtrTailOffset + 2;
          if (TailOffset > 0x003d)
             TailOffset = 0x001e;

          /* If new tail offset == head offset, buffer is full.                  */
          if (TailOffset == *PtrHeadOffset)
             return (1);                /* Return value of 1 indicates an error. */

          /* Write character at OLD tail offset.                                 */
          FP_OFF (PtrBuffer) = *PtrTailOffset;
          *PtrBuffer = AscCode | (ExtCode << 8);

          /* Adjust BIOS tail offset variable to new value.                      */
          *PtrTailOffset = TailOffset;

          /* Preserve the original condition of the interrupt flag.              */
          if (Enabled)
              UtyEnable ();

          return (0);                   /* Return value of 0 indicates success.  */

          } /* end KbdInsert */
```

Figure 2.1: KBD.C: C Functions for managing the keyboard (continued)

- Determine whether a key is ready to be read (**KbdReady**).

- Flush all characters from the system keyboard buffer (**KbdFlush**).

- Get and set the status of shift keys, such as Caps Lock and Num Lock (**KbdGetShift** and **KbdSetShift**).

- Insert one or more characters directly into the system keyboard buffer so that the characters will be read as if the user had typed them on the keyboard (**KbdInsert**).

```
.MODEL LARGE
.CODE
PUBLIC _KbdFlush
_KbdFlush PROC
;
;       Prototype:
;              void far KbdFlush
;                  (void)
;
;       This function flushes the keyboard buffer maintained by the BIOS.
;
b01:
     mov   ah, 01          ;Specify the BIOS keyboard status function.
     int   16h             ;Invoke BIOS keyboard services.
     jz    b02             ;If ZF is set, buffer is empty.
                           ;ZF not set;  must remove one or more keys.
     mov   ah, 00          ;Specify the BIOS read key function.
     int   16h             ;Invoke BIOS keyboard services.
     jmp   b01             ;Return to test for empty keyboard buffer.
b02:
     ret                   ;Buffer is empty;  return to C program.

_KbdFlush ENDP
PUBLIC _KbdGetC
_KbdGetC PROC
;
;       Prototype:
;              int far KbdGetC
;                  (void)
;
;       This function reads a key using the BIOS.  The return value contains:
;              High order byte:    Extended code.
;              Low order byte:     ASCII value.

     mov   ah, 0           ;Specify BIOS read key service.
     int   16h             ;Invoke BIOS keyboard services.
     ret

_KbdGetC ENDP


PUBLIC _KbdReady
_KbdReady PROC
;
;       Prototype:
;              int far KbdReady
;                  (void)
;
```

Figure 2.2: KBDA.ASM: Assembler functions for managing the keyboard

```
;       This function returns a non-zero value if a key is ready to be read, or
;       zero if the BIOS keyboard buffer is empty.

        mov  ah, 01                 ;Specify the BIOS keyboard status function.
        int  16h                    ;Invoke BIOS keyboard services.
        jz   a01                    ;ZF set means keyboard buffer empty.
        mov  ax, 1                  ;ZF not set;  key is ready;  therefore return 1.
        ret
a01:
        mov  ax, 0                  ;Return 0 indicating no key ready.
        ret

_KbdReady ENDP
END
```

Figure 2.2: KBDA.ASM: Assembler functions for managing the keyboard (continued)

```
#define RIGHTSHIFT          0x0001
#define LEFTSHIFT           0x0002
#define CONTROL             0x0004
#define ALT                 0x0008
#define SCROLLSTATE         0x0010
#define NUMLOCKSTATE        0x0020
#define CAPLOCKSTATE        0x0040
#define INSERTSTATE         0x0080
#define CTRLNUMLKSTATE      0x0800
#define SCROLLLOCK          0x1000
#define NUMLOCK             0x2000
#define CAPSLOCK            0x4000
#define INSERT              0x8000


int  KbdGetShift  (void);
int  KbdInsert    (char AscCode, char ExtCode);
void KbdSetShift  (int ShiftStat);

void far KbdFlush (void);                           /* Assembler functions:  */
int  far KbdGetC  (void);
int  far KbdReady (void);
```

Figure 2.3: KBD.H: Header file that must be included in your program to call the **Kbd** functions

KbdGetC

Using KbdGetC

KbdGetC, which has the prototype

```
int far KbdGetC
    (void)
```

is a general purpose function for reading a single key from the keyboard. When the user types a key, the system (specifically, the BIOS) places the code for this keystroke into a keyboard buffer. **KbdGetC** causes the system to remove the next available keystroke from this buffer (keys are removed in the same order in which they are entered). If the buffer is currently empty, **KbdGetC** does not return until a key has been typed.

There are several functions in the standard C library for reading keys (for example, **getchar**, **getch**, and **getche**). **KbdGetc**, however, has the following unique set of properties:

■ If a key has not already been entered (stored in the BIOS keyboard buffer), then this function *waits* for keyboard input. (You can first call the function **KbdReady**, described next, to determine whether a key is available.)

■ The function returns immediately after the key is pressed; in contrast to the C function **getchar**, the user does *not* need to press Enter to return control to the program.

■ The key is not echoed on the screen.

■ The function returns the ASCII value of the key pressed in the low-order byte of the integer return value. If the key does not have an ASCII value (for example, function keys), then 0 is returned in the low order byte.

■ The function returns the *extended code* of the key in the high-order byte of the return value. The extended code is useful for identifying a key or key combination that does not have an ASCII value, such as F3, Alt-F1, or an arrow key (see Appendix C for a list of these codes). Note that the C library functions simply return 0 for these non-ASCII keystrokes, and require a second function call to obtain the extended code. **KbdGetC** always returns both values with a single call.

▮ **KbdGetC** treats Ctrl-C as a normal character. (With **getchar**, for example, Ctrl-C causes activation of a break handler that normally terminates the program.)

▮ The input always comes from the keyboard, and can not be redirected from another device.

The character cannot be read directly from the value returned by **KbdGetC**. Rather, either the low-order byte must be extracted to obtain the ASCII value, as in the expression

```
KbdGetC() & 0x00ff
```

or the high-order byte must be extracted to obtain the extended code, as in the expression

```
KbdGetC() >> 8
```

To detect *any* key or key combination, first test the ASCII value. If it is nonzero, then process the key based on its ASCII value; if it is zero, then test the extended code to determine the keystroke that has been entered.

The program KBDDEM01.C, shown in Figure 2.4, demonstrates several uses for **KbdGetC**. First, it calls this function, discarding the return value, as a convenient method for creating a pause in program execution. Next, the program goes into a loop that repeatedly calls **Kbd-GetC**, displaying both the ASCII value and the extended code for each key that is entered. The loop is terminated when the Esc key is pressed. Note that since the program calls a function belonging to the **Kbd** module, it includes the required header file, KBD.H.

Figure 2.5 provides a MAKE file (KBDDEM01.M), which you can use to automate the process of compiling and linking the example program when employing the optimizing C compiler. Figure 2.6 provides the list of files which you should enter into the Program List when using the QuickC integrated environment. Since KBDDEM01.C calls the function **KbdGetC**, which is located in the file KBDA.ASM, you must link the program with the object file KBDA.OBJ. (See the description of using the MAKE files in the section "Preparing the Functions and Example Programs" in Chapter 1.)

*How KbdGetC
Works*

KbdGetC is located in the assembly language file KBDA.ASM, listed in Figure 2.2. This function simply invokes the BIOS keyboard service

```
#include <STDIO.H>
#include "KBD.H"

void main (void)
    {
    int Ch;

    /* Use KbdGetC to create a pause.                              */
    printf ("Press any key to begin ...");
    KbdGetC ();

    /* Use KbdGetC to get both ASCII and Extended Codes.           */
    printf ("\n\nASCII Code        Extended Code\n");
    printf ("(press <Esc> to end)\n\n");
    do
        {
        Ch = KbdGetC ();
        printf ("\n%5d%18d", Ch & 0x00ff,Ch >> 8);
        }
    while ((Ch & 0x00ff) != 0x1b);                    /* Test for <Esc>. */

    } /* end main */
```

Figure 2.4: KBDDEM01.C: A program demonstrating the function **KbdGetC**

for reading a key, which is requested by placing 0 in register AH and generating interrupt number 16h. The BIOS service returns the key value in register AX, formatted as described above. Note that since the apropriate return value (the keyboard code) is automatically placed in re-gister AX (which assembler functions use for returning values), **KbdGetC** immediately returns control without explicitly loading the return value. See the book *MS-DOS Advanced Programming* (cited in the Bibliography) for a complete description of the services provided by the BIOS.

```
KBDDEM01.OBJ : KBDDEM01.C KBD.H
     cl /c /W2 /Zp KBDDEM01.C

KBDA.OBJ : KBDA.ASM
     masm /MX KBDA.ASM;

KDBDEM01.EXE : KBDDEM01.OBJ KBDA.OBJ
     link /NOI /NOD /NOD KBDDEM01+KBDA,,NUL,SLIBCER;
```

Figure 2.5: KBDDEM01.M: A MAKE file for KBDDEM01.C

```
KBDDEM01.C
KBDA.OBJ
```

Figure 2.6: A QuickC program list for preparing KBDDEM01.C

KbdReady

Using KbdReady

You can call the function **KbdReady** to determine whether a key has been typed by the user and is ready to be read. This function has the prototype

```
int far KbdReady
    (void)
```

It returns a non-zero value if the BIOS keyboard buffer contains at least one key, and it returns zero if the buffer is currently empty.

If **KbdReady** returns a non-zero value, indicating that a key is available, a subsequent call to **KbdGetC** will immediately return this key, removing it from the keyboard buffer. Remember that if a key is *not* available, **KbdGetC** will not return control until a key has been entered, suspending program execution for an indefinite period. Accordingly, you can use the **KbdReady** function to avoid blocking the program while waiting for keyboard input. If **KbdReady** indicates that a key is ready, the program can call **KbdGetC** to quickly read this key; otherwise, the program can perform another task and call **KbdReady** again at a later time.

The program KBDDEM02.C, listed in Figure 2.7, demonstrates how you can call **KbdReady** at regular intervals to poll the status of the keyboard, while performing useful work between calls to this function. The program consists of a single loop; with each repetition it prints a message and generates a 0.5 second delay (by calling **UtyPause**, described in Chapter 12) to simulate performing a program task. (At this point an actual application could execute an operation such as sending a character to the printer or calculating a value.) The loop also

```
#include <STDIO.H>
#include <PROCESS.H>
#include "KBD.H"
#include "UTY.H"

void main (void)
    {
    for (;;)
        {
        /* Perform a program task.                                  */
        printf ("Press <Esc> to terminate program.\n");
        UtyPause (0.5);                      /* Generate a 0.5 second pause. */

        /* If a keystroke is available, read it and test for <Esc>.  */
        if (KbdReady ())
            if ((KbdGetC () & 0x00ff) == 0x1b)
                exit (0);
        }

    } /* end main */
```

Figure 2.7: KBDDEM02.C: A program demonstrating the function **KbdReady**

contains a call to **KbdReady**; if this call indicates that a key is ready, the program calls **KbdGetC** to read the key. If the key is Esc, the program terminates. Note that the program includes the header files KBD.H and UTY.H, since it calls functions belonging to both the **Kbd** and **Uty** modules.

Figure 2.8 provides a MAKE file for preparing this program, and Figure 2.9 gives the program list for generating the program within the QuickC integrated environment. Because the program calls **KbdReady**, which is defined in the source file KBDA.ASM, and **UtyPause**, which is defined in the source file UTY.C, it must be linked with the correspond-

```
KBDDEM02.OBJ : KBDDEM02.C KBD.H
        cl /c /W2 /Zp KBDDEM02.C

KBDA.OBJ : KBDA.ASM
        masm /MX KBDA.ASM;

UTY.OBJ : UTY.C UTY.H
        cl /c /W2 /Zp UTY.C

UTYA.OBJ : UTYA.ASM
        masm /MX UTYA.ASM;

SCR.OBJ : SCR.C SCR.H
        cl /c /W2 /Zp SCR.C

KBDDEM02.EXE : KBDDEM02.OBJ KBDA.OBJ UTY.OBJ UTYA.OBJ SCR.OBJ
        link /NOI /NOD KBDDEM02+KBDA+UTY+UTYA+SCR,,NUL,SLIBCER;
```

Figure 2.8: KBDDEM02.C: KBDDEM02.M: A MAKE file for KBDDEM02.C

```
KBDDEM02.C
KBDA.OBJ
UTY.C
UTYA.OBJ
SCR.C
```

Figure 2.9: A QuickC program list for preparing KBDDEM02.C

ing object files, KBDA.OBJ and UTY.OBJ. Note, however, that it must also be linked with UTYA.OBJ and SCR.OBJ, since UTY.C contains calls to functions within these two object files.

How KbdReady Works

KbdReady is contained in the assembly language source file listed in Figure 2.2. **KbdReady** first invokes the BIOS service that returns the status of the keyboard; this service is accessed by loading 0 into register AX and issuing interrupt 16h. If a key is available, the BIOS clears the zero flag (ZF), and if a key is not available, the BIOS sets the zero flag. Accordingly, if ZF is set, **KbdReady** returns a value of 0, and if ZF is clear, it returns a value of 1.

KbdFlush

Using KbdFlush

The keyboard buffer is maintained by the BIOS at an address in low memory (starting at the address 0040h:001Eh), and can hold up to 15 characters. Normally, characters remain in this buffer until they are requested by a program. Sometimes, however, it is useful to make sure that the keyboard buffer is empty. For example, if your program asks the user whether or not to delete a file, you want to make sure that a *y* character you read was actually entered *after* the message appeared, and is not some character entered at a prior time still sitting in the buffer. Calling **KbdFlush** simply empties the BIOS buffer and discards any characters it contains. The prototype for this function is

```
void far KbdFlush
    (void)
```

The file KBDDEM03.C in Figure 2.10 illustrates the effect of **Kbd-Flush**. The program invites the user to enter some characters and then creates a 10 second pause by calling **UtyPause (10.0)**. During this time, all characters that the user types go into the BIOS keyboard buffer (until it is full). Next, **KbdFlush** is called to flush all keystrokes from the keyboard buffer. Finally, to demonstrate that the buffer has been emptied, the program contains a loop that would read and display any characters contained in the buffer. When the program is run, no characters appear, indicating that **KbdFlush** successfully flushed all keystrokes entered into the buffer. (If you remove the call to **KbdFlush**, the characters typed during the 10 second pause appear on the screen immediately after the pause.)

Note, however, that emptying the BIOS keyboard buffer does *not* remove characters stored internally by buffered C input functions such as **getchar**. For example, when **getchar** is called to read a single character, the user may enter an entire line (**getchar** does not return control until the user presses Enter). Only the first character, however, will be returned to the program; the remaining characters are stored by **getchar**, and will be returned on subsequent calls to this function. Since these characters have already been removed from the BIOS buffer, calling **KbdFlush** will not eliminate them. Therefore, **KbdFlush** is best used in conjunction with routines that read characters directly from the BIOS, without buffering, such as **KbdGetC** described previously in the chapter.

```
#include <STDIO.H>
#include "KBD.H"
#include "UTY.H"

void main (void)
    {
    /* Wait for 10 seconds to allow user to type characters.      */
    printf ("You have 10 seconds to enter characters: ");
    UtyPause (10.0);

    /* Empty the BIOS keyboard buffer;  try removing this function call.  */
    KbdFlush ();

    /* Display contents of keyboard buffer.                        */
    printf ("\nDelay over;  contents of keyboard buffer:  ");
    while (KbdReady ())
            putchar (KbdGetC () & 0x00ff);

    } /* end main */
```

Figure 2.10: KBDDEM03.C: A program demonstrating the function **KbdFlush**

The BIOS keyboard buffer is explained in greater detail in the section on the **KbdInsert** function, at the end of the chapter. Figure 2.11 provides a MAKE file and Figure 2.12 gives a QuickC program list for preparing this example program.

How KbdFlush Works

KbdFlush is contained in the assembly language file (KBDA.ASM) of Figure 2.2. This function uses the two BIOS keyboard services accessed through interrupt 16h that have already been explained: service 01 for determining whether a key is available, and service 00 for reading and removing a key from the buffer. **KbdFlush** consists of a loop that repeatedly removes keys from the keyboard buffer (using service 00) as long as there is a key available (determined by invoking service 01). **KbdFlush** returns when the buffer is empty.

```
KBDDEM03.OBJ : KBDDEM03.C KBD.H
     cl /c /W2 /Zp KBDDEM03.C

KBDA.OBJ : KBDA.ASM
     masm /MX KBDA.ASM;

UTY.OBJ : UTY.C UTY.H
     cl /c /W2 /Zp UTY.C

UTYA.OBJ : UTYA.ASM
     masm /MX UTYA.ASM;

SCR.OBJ : SCR.C SCR.H
     cl /c /W2 /Zp SCR.C

KBDDEM03.EXE : KBDDEM03.OBJ KBDA.OBJ UTY.OBJ UTYA.OBJ SCR.OBJ
     link /NOI /NOD KBDDEM03+KBDA+UTY+UTYA+SCR,,NUL,SLIBCER;
```

Figure 2.11: KBDDEM03.M: A MAKE file for KBDDEM03.C

```
KBDDEM03.C
KBDA.OBJ
UTY.C
UTYA.OBJ
SCR.C
```

Figure 2.12: A QuickC program list for preparing KBDDEM03.C

KbdGetShift

*Using
KbdGetShift*

The **KbdGetShift** function, which has the prototype

```
int KbdGetShift
    (void)
```

returns the current status of the *shift keys* (such as Caps Lock or Ins) on the IBM-compatible keyboards. Each bit of the integer that this function returns indicates a specific shift state, as given in Table 2.1.

Note that codes indicating that a key is *depressed* signify that the user is currently holding down the key. Codes indicating that a key is *active* refer to keys that toggle particular states on and off (for example, Ins or Caps Lock): if the bit is on, then the corresponding state is currently active whether or not the key is actually depressed. By calling **KbdGetShift**, a program can respond to the current state of shift keys. For example, an

Table 2.1: Encoding of the shift keys

Bit	Shift Key State
0	Right-Shift depressed
1	Left-Shift depressed
2	Ctrl depressed
3	Alt depressed
4	Scroll Lock active
5	Num Lock active
6	Caps Lock active
7	Ins active
8 - 10	Not used
11	Ctrl-Num Lock (*suspend key*) active
12	Scroll Lock depressed
13	Num Lock depressed
14	Caps Lock depressed
15	Ins depressed

editor can process the arrow keys in a manner that depends upon the current state of the Scroll Lock key, and it can switch between insert mode and overwrite mode depending upon the state of the Ins key. Also, a program can maintain a continuous display of the current status of keys such as Num Lock and Caps Lock by monitoring the shift flags. Finally, as you will see in Chapter 9, a memory resident utility can use a specific combination of shift keys as a signal that it should become active (this key combination is known as the *hotkey*).

To simplify access to the individual bits of the integer returned by this function, the header file KBD.H provides a set of constant definitions that can be used as bit masks. For example, the constant INSERT can be used in conjunction with the **&** (AND) operator to determine whether the insert state is currently active, as follows:

```
if (KbdGetShift () & INSERT)
        /* then insert state is active */
```

The program KBDDEM04.C, listed in Figure 2.13, demonstrates the use of **KbdGetShift**. The program first clears the screen and displays a set of titles (by means of **ScrClear** and **ScrPutS**, which are presented in Chapter 5). It then goes into a loop that repeatedly reads the shift key status using **KbdGetShift**, and then displays the results for each key. Note that the string for the appropriate status (e.g., "Down" or "Up") is selected by "ANDing" the returned value with the appropriate bit mask constant, and applying the C *ternary* operator, **?** :. The loop is terminated by the user pressing Esc. (If **KbdReady** returns a nonzero value, indicating that a key has been pressed, then the key is read with **KbdGetC**; note that unlike some languages, C guarantees that the second part of an AND expression will not be evaluated if the first part evaluates false.) Figure 2.14 lists a MAKE file, and Figure 2.15 a QuickC program list, for automating the generation of the executable program.

How KbdGetShift Works

KbdGetShift is contained in the C source file KBD.C, listed in Figure 2.1. This function works by simply reading and returning the keyboard shift status word maintained by the BIOS at memory location 0040h:0017 h (note that a *word* is a 16-bit value). The method used for accessing this value is employed by many routines in this book for reading or writing specific memory locations outside of the C data segment.

First, a variable is declared as a **far** (that is, 32-bit) pointer to the appropriate data type (**KbdGetShift** declares **PtrShiftFlag** as a **far** pointer

```
#include "KBD.H"
#include "SCR.H"

void main ()
    {
    int ShiftStat;
    unsigned char Row = 0;

    ScrClear (0,0,24,79);                       /* Clear screen and print titles. */
    ScrPutS ("Shift Key Status",0x0f,Row++,0);
    ScrPutS ("Press <Esc> to end",0x0f,Row++,0);
    Row = 4;
    ScrPutS ("Right Shift",0x0f,Row++,0);
    ScrPutS ("Left Shift",0x0f,Row++,0);
    ScrPutS ("Control",0x0f,Row++,0);
    ScrPutS ("Alt",0x0f,Row++,0);
    ScrPutS ("Scroll Lock State",0x0f,Row++,0);
    ScrPutS ("Num Lock State",0x0f,Row++,0);
    ScrPutS ("Caps Lock State",0x0f,Row++,0);
    ScrPutS ("Insert State",0x0f,Row++,0);
    ScrPutS ("Control-Num Lock State",0x0f,Row++,0);
    ScrPutS ("Scroll Lock",0x0f,Row++,0);
    ScrPutS ("Num Lock",0x0f,Row++,0);
    ScrPutS ("Caps Lock",0x0f,Row++,0);
    ScrPutS ("Insert",0x0f,Row++,0);

    for (;;)                                    /* Read and display shift status.*/
        {
                                                /* Test if Esc has been pressed. */
        if (KbdReady () && (KbdGetC () & 0x00ff) == 27)
            break;
        ShiftStat = KbdGetShift ();             /* Get shift status.             */
        Row = 4;                                /* Update status display.        */
        ScrPutS (ShiftStat&RIGHTSHIFT?   "Down":"Up  ",0x0f,Row++,25);
        ScrPutS (ShiftStat&LEFTSHIFT?    "Down":"Up  ",0x0f,Row++,25);
        ScrPutS (ShiftStat&CONTROL?      "Down":"Up  ",0x0f,Row++,25);
        ScrPutS (ShiftStat&ALT?          "Down":"Up  ",0x0f,Row++,25);
        ScrPutS (ShiftStat&SCROLLSTATE?  "On ":"Off",0x0f,Row++,25);
        ScrPutS (ShiftStat&NUMLOCKSTATE? "On ":"Off",0x0f,Row++,25);
        ScrPutS (ShiftStat&CAPLOCKSTATE? "On ":"Off",0x0f,Row++,25);
        ScrPutS (ShiftStat&INSERTSTATE?  "On ":"Off",0x0f,Row++,25);
        ScrPutS (ShiftStat&CTRLNUMLKSTATE?"On ":"Off",0x0f,Row++,25);
        ScrPutS (ShiftStat&SCROLLLOCK?   "Down":"Up  ",0x0f,Row++,25);
        ScrPutS (ShiftStat&NUMLOCK?      "Down":"Up  ",0x0f,Row++,25);
        ScrPutS (ShiftStat&CAPSLOCK?     "Down":"Up  ",0x0f,Row++,25);
        ScrPutS (ShiftStat&INSERT?       "Down":"Up  ",0x0f,Row++,25);
        }

    } /* end main */
```

Figure 2.13: KBDDEM04.C: A program demonstrating the function **KbdGetShift**

to an unsigned integer, which is a 16-bit value). This pointer variable is then assigned the address of the memory location that is to be accessed. The address is specified as a 32 bit value containing the segment address in the high-order 16 bits and the offset address in the low-order 16 bits and is cast to the appropriate **far** pointer type (**PtrShiftFlag** is assigned the value **(unsigned far *)0x00400017**, which represents the address of the BIOS shift status word). Finally, the actual memory location is ac-

```
KBDDEM04.OBJ : KBDDEM04.C KBD.H
     cl /c /W2 /Zp KBDDEM04.C

KBD.OBJ : KBD.C KBD.H
     cl /c /W2 /Zp KBD.C

KBDA.OBJ : KBDA.ASM
     masm /MX KBDA.ASM;

SCR.OBJ : SCR.C SCR.H
     cl /c /W2 /Zp SCR.C

UTYA.OBJ : UTYA.ASM
     masm /MX UTYA.ASM;

KBDDEM04.EXE : KBDDEM04.OBJ KBD.OBJ KBDA.OBJ SCR.OBJ UTYA.OBJ
     link /NOI /NOD KBDDEM04+KBD+KBDA+SCR+UTYA,,NUL,SLIBCER;
```

Figure 2.14: KBDDEM04.M: A MAKE file for KBDDEM04.C

cessed by using the *indirection* operator (*****) on the **far** pointer (the value of
the shift flag is returned through the expression ***PtrShiftFlag**).

KbdSetShift

*Using
KbdSetShift*

KbdSetShift effectively changes the current status of one or more of
the shift keys, according to the bit mask that is passed as a parameter.
The prototype for this function is

```
KbdSetShift
        (int ShiftStat)
```

where **ShiftStat** is the desired shift status word, encoded as shown in
Table 2.1. This function is generally less useful than **KbdGetShift**, and

```
KBDDEM04.C
KBD.C
KBDA.OBJ
SCR.C
UTYA.OBJ
```

Figure 2.15: A QuickC program list for preparing KBDDEM04.C

should be used cautiously since it directly changes the internal record of the status of the shift keys, which is normally altered only when the user actually presses keys. As a result of using this function, the internal status information can become out of synchrony with the physical state of the keyboard, and the BIOS and application programs can become confused.

One useful application for this function is to switch on the Caps Lock active state, prior to accepting user input into a field that requires all capital letters. The program KBDDEM05.C, listed in Figure 2.16, uses **KbdSetShift** to activate the Caps Lock state. Note that **KbdGetShift** is first called to get the current shift status so that only the Caps Lock state bit is altered. Note also that whereas testing a bit required the AND (&) operator, setting a bit requires the OR (|) operator. Figure 2.17 lists a MAKE file, and Figure 2.18 a QuickC program list for preparing the executable file.

Another use for this function is to turn on the Num Lock active state for a calculator or other numerical entry application in order to automatically activate the numerical keypad on a standard PC or AT keyboard. The results of this function can be amusing, and you may discover some other practical uses.

How KbdSetShift Works

KbdSetShift fools the BIOS by directly altering the shift status word it maintains at memory location 0040h:0017h. The technique used to access this absolute memory address is identical to that employed by **KbdGetShift**, except that the memory location is written to rather than read.

```
#include "KBD.H"

void main (void)
    {
    KbdSetShift (KbdGetShift () | CAPLOCKSTATE);        /* Turn on Caps Lock */

    } /* end main */
```

Figure 2.16: KBDDEM05.C: A program demonstrating the function **KbdSetShift**

```
KBDDEM05.OBJ : KBDDEM05.C KBD.H
      cl /c /W2 /Zp KBDDEM05.C

KBD.OBJ : KBD.C KBD.H
      cl /c /W2 /Zp KBD.C

UTYA.OBJ : UTYA.ASM
      masm /MX UTYA.ASM;

KBDDEM05.EXE : KBDDEM05.OBJ KBD.OBJ UTYA.OBJ
      link /NOI /NOD KBDDEM05+KBD+UTYA,,NUL,SLIBCER;
```

Figure 2.17: KBDDEM05.M: A MAKE file for KBDDEM05.C

KbdInsert

Using KbdInsert

The **KbdInsert** function has the prototype

```
int KbdInsert
      (char AscCode,
      char ExtCode)
```

and inserts a keystroke directly into the BIOS keyboard buffer. The parameter **AscCode** specifies the ASCII code for the key, and **ExtCode** the extended code. Both of these codes are described in the section on **KbdGetC** at the beginning of the chapter; they are also discussed in Appendix C. Normally, keys are inserted into the buffer only by the BIOS in response to keyboard activity. **KbdInsert**, however, circumvents the normal mechanism and places a key directly into the buffer; this keystroke becomes indistinguishable from one that the user has entered through the keyboard, and will subsequently be read by a program as if it were typed by the user. (As you will see in the next section, the BIOS

```
KBDDEM05.C
KBD.C
UTYA.OBJ
```

Figure 2.18: A QuickC program list for preparing KBDDEM05.C

inserts new keys at the *tail* of the buffer and removes keys from the *head* of the buffer; keys are thus removed in the same order in which they were inserted. **KbdInsert** also inserts a key at the tail of the buffer, so that if the buffer already contains keystrokes, the new key will be read last, just as if it were typed.)

If the key is successfully inserted, **KbdInsert** returns zero. If, however, the buffer is full and the key could not be inserted, **KbdInsert** returns a nonzero value.

Inserting keystrokes directly into the keyboard buffer is a useful technique for a keyboard macro program that replaces a single keystroke with a sequence of keys. Such utilities normally run as memory resident background processes (described in Chapter 9), and the foreground program receives the keys as if they were typed by the user. Note that **KbdInsert** assumes that the keyboard buffer is located at the standard address (discussed in the next section); this function will not work properly if a utility has been installed that moves the keyboard buffer to another address.

Figure 2.19 lists the program KBDDEM06.C, which demonstrates the effect of the function **KbdInsert**. This program calls **KbdInsert** repeatedly to insert each of the characters in the string "Hello" directly into the keyboard buffer. Since KBDDEM06.C does not read the keyboard, the inserted characters remain in the BIOS buffer during the execution of the program. However, as soon as the program terminates and control returns to DOS, the string "Hello" instantly appears at the command prompt as if they had been typed. Figure 2.20 provides a MAKE file, and Figure 2.21 a QuickC program list.

```
#include "KBD.H"

void main (void)
    {
    static char *Message = "Hello";

    /* Insert message into the BIOS keyboard buffer.        */
    while (*Message)
        KbdInsert (*Message++,0);

    } /* end main */
```

Figure 2.19: KBDDEM06.C: A program demonstrating the function **KbdInsert**

```
KBDDEM06.OBJ : KBDDEM06.C KBD.H
     cl /c /W2 /Zp KBDDEM06.C

KBD.OBJ : KBD.C KBD.H
     cl /c /W2 /Zp KBD.C

UTYA.OBJ : UTYA.ASM
     masm /MX UTYA.ASM;

KBDDEM06.EXE : KBDDEM06.OBJ KBD.OBJ UTYA.OBJ
     link /NOI /NOD KBDDEM06+KBD+UTYA,,NUL,SLIBCER;
```

Figure 2.20: KBDDEM06.M: A MAKE file for KBDDEM06.C

How KbdInsert Works

Figure 2.22 provides a memory map of the BIOS keyboard buffer. The data structure illustrated in this figure is contained within the BIOS data area, which begins at segment address 0040h; the addresses in the figure are offsets with respect to this segment. Thus, for example, the full address of the start of the keyboard buffer is 0040h:001Eh. Note that the BIOS maintains a pointer to the head of the buffer (containing the next character to be removed), and a pointer to the tail (the location where the next character will be inserted). The keyboard buffer itself is 32 bytes long, providing space for 16 keystroke entries (each keystroke entry requires two bytes: the ASCII value is stored in the low-order byte and the extended code in the high-order byte). The buffer illustrated in Figure 2.22 contains the three keystrokes *ABC* (entered in this order; the *A* was the first key entered and will be the first key removed and passed to a program reading the keyboard).

The BIOS keyboard buffer is treated as a *circular queue*. A circular queue stores data on a first-in-first-out basis. When a queue element is added or removed, the tail or head pointer is incremented to the *next highest* address; when the highest address is reached, the pointer is assigned the lowest address. Conceptually, therefore, the queue forms a circle in which the first and last entries are connected.

Figure 2.23 illustrates the keyboard buffer as a circular queue. Part A shows an empty queue; when the queue is empty, *the head pointer and*

```
KBDDEM06.C
KBD.C
UTYA.OBJ
```

Figure 2.21: A QuickC program list for preparing KBDDEM06.C

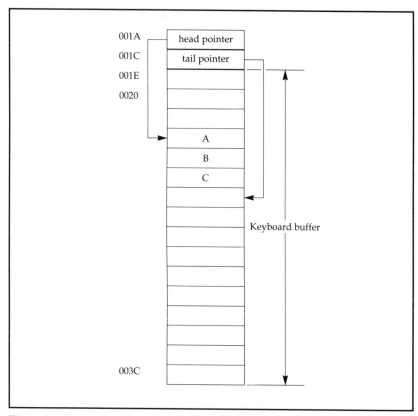

Figure 2.22: A memory map of the BIOS keyboard buffer

tail pointer are equal. Part B shows the queue after the three keystrokes ABC have been entered (in this order). Part C shows the queue after the maximum number of characters (15) have been entered. Note that when a character is inserted into the queue, the new character is *first* written to the position currently indicated by the tail pointer, and *then* the tail pointer is incremented to point to the next position (or set to the point to the first position if the end of the queue has been reached). Although the queue in Part C seems to contain room for an additional character, if another character were added, the tail and head pointers would become equal, which is a state indicating an empty queue. Accordingly, even though the queue contains 16 positions, it can hold only 15 keystrokes (one position must be reserved to indicate an empty queue; if an external flag were used to indicate the empty state, then the queue could be used to store 16 keystrokes).

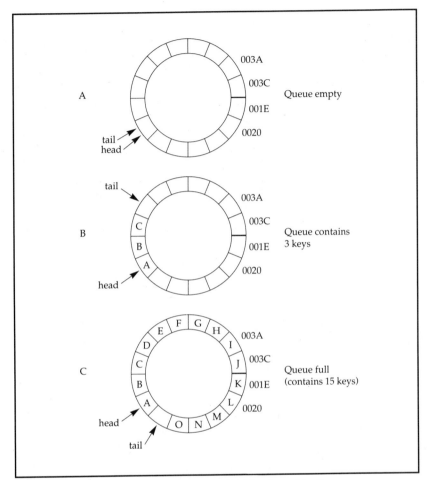

Figure 2.23: Entering characters into the BIOS keyboard buffer

Figure 2.24 shows the queue illustrated in part C of Figure 2.23 after three keys (*A*, *B*, and *C*) have been read by a program and removed from the queue. When a key is read, the BIOS returns the key currently pointed to by the head pointer (provided the queue is not empty); it then increments the head pointer to point to the next position (or sets it to the first position if the end of the queue has been reached). Conceptually, therefore, both the head and tail pointers are always moved around the circular queue illustrated in Figures 2.23 and 2.24 in a clockwise direction.

The function **KbdInsert** is contained in the C source file KBD.C, listed in Figure 2.1. This function determines whether the queue is full

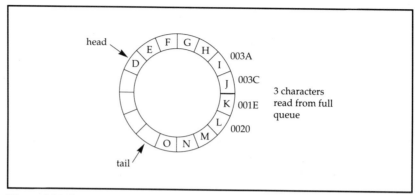

Figure 2.24: Removing characters from the BIOS keyboard buffer

by calculating the *next* position of the tail (expressed as an offset with respect to the BIOS data segment at 0040h). The current position of the tail is obtained from the tail pointer maintained by the BIOS at address 0040h:001Ch; the next position is derived by adding 2 to the current off-set (and adjusting the value to the beginning of the buffer if the resulting offset exceeds the highest buffer address).

If the next position of the tail pointer is at the offset stored in the head pointer (at address 0040h:001Ah), then the queue is empty, and **KbdInsert** immediately returns 0. If, however, there is room in the queue, **KbdInsert** writes the ASCII and extended codes at the original position of the tail, and then adjusts the tail to the new position that it calculated when testing for a full condition.

Note that **KbdInsert** also calls several functions in the utility (**Uty**) module to make certain that hardware interrupts are disabled while it manipulates the keyboard buffer. Each time the user presses a key, the keyboard generates a hardware interrupt (number 09h), which activates the BIOS routine for inserting the key into the keyboard buffer. Hardware interrupts must therefore be disabled to prevent both **KbdInsert** and the BIOS from attempting to access the keyboard data structures at the same time.

Before accessing the keyboard data, **KbdInsert** calls **UtyEnabled** to determine the existing state of the hardware interrupts (**UtyEnabled** returns a nonzero value if interrupts are enabled, or zero if they are disabled). It then calls **UtyDisable** to disable the hardware interrupts (if the interrupts are already disabled this function has no effect). Finally, before the **KbdInsert** returns, it restores the original state of the interrupts by calling **UtyEnable** if the interrupts were originally enabled. These **Uty** functions are explained in Chapter 12.

CONSOLE I/O FUNCTIONS

The two final functions discussed in this chapter, **IocRawMode** and **IocCookMode**, can be used to modify the behavior and enhance the performance of input and output through the *console*. Under MS-DOS, the console consists of the monitor and the keyboard. These two functions are listed in the module IOC.C, in Figure 2.25. The required header file, IOC.H, is in Figure 2.26.

```
#include <DOS.H>

#pragma check_stack (off)       /* Turn off stack checks so that functions */
                                /* can be called from interrupt routines.  */

void IocRawMode (void)
/*
    This function places the console device in the raw mode.
*/
    {
    union REGS Reg;

    Reg.x.ax = 0x4400;          /* DOS get device information service.   */
    Reg.x.bx = 2;               /* Standard Error handle.                */
    int86 (0x21,&Reg,&Reg);     /* DOS services interrupt.               */

    Reg.x.ax = 0x4401;          /* DOS set device information service.   */
    Reg.x.bx = 2;               /* Standard Error handle.                */
    Reg.h.dh = 0;               /* 0 out DH.                             */
    Reg.h.dl |= 0x20;           /* Turn on raw mode bit (#5).            */
    int86 (0x21,&Reg,&Reg);     /* DOS services interrupt.               */

    } /* end IocRawMode */


void IocCookMode (void)
/*
    This function places the console device in the cooked mode.
*/
    {
    union REGS Reg;

    Reg.x.ax = 0x4400;          /* DOS get device information service.   */
    Reg.x.bx = 2;               /* Standard Error handle.                */
    int86 (0x21,&Reg,&Reg);     /* DOS services interrupt.               */

    Reg.x.ax = 0x4401;          /* DOS set device information service.   */
    Reg.x.bx = 2;               /* Standard Error handle.                */
    Reg.x.dx &= 0x00df;         /* Turn off raw mode bit and 0 out DH.   */
    int86 (0x21,&Reg,&Reg);     /* DOS services interrupt.               */

    } /* end IocCookMode */
```

Figure 2.25: IOC.C: The I/O device control functions

```
void IocRawMode (void);
void IocCookMode (void);
```

Figure 2.26: IOC.H: Header file for IOC.C

Using IocRawMode and IocCookMode

The standard MS-DOS device drivers that manage input and output for character devices (i.e., the console, printer, and serial port) operate in one of two modes: *raw* (also known as *binary*), or *cooked* (also known as *ASCII*). When DOS opens these devices, it places them by default in the cooked mode. When the console device is in the cooked mode, it exhibits the following features:

- Input and output characters are checked for Ctrl-S, Ctrl-P, and Ctrl-C.

- Input characters are echoed to the monitor.

- Output tabs are expanded into spaces.

- Input data is buffered and may be edited using the usual DOS function keys.

- Control characters are echoed as a caret and a letter. For example, Ctrl-D echoes as **^D**.

The problem with console output, which is routed through an MS-DOS device driver, is that it is very slow. However, by placing the console in raw mode, the above features are disabled, and performance is significantly enhanced. A benchmark program (given in Chapter 8 of *MS-DOS Advanced Programming*, cited in the Bibliography), demonstrated a speed increase in console output of approximately 35 percent when the console was put into the raw mode.

The function **IocRawMode**, which has the prototype

```
void IocRawMode
    (void)
```

puts the console into the raw mode. The function **IocCookMode**, which has the prototype

```
void IocCookMode
     (void)
```

restores the default cooked mode. If your program displays a large amount of data on the screen using DOS services (which are employed by standard C functions such as **printf**), you can first call **IocRawMode** to increase the speed of screen display. However, before your program terminates you should call **IocCookMode** to restore the cooked mode, or programs subsequently run may behave strangely (for example, tabs may display as little circles rather than being expanded into spaces).

How IocRawMode and IocCookMode Work

MS-DOS provides a family of services for communicating directly with device drivers (*IOCTL* functions); these services are all accessed through interrupt 21h, with 44h in register AH. The individual services in this family are requested by placing specific values in register AL. **IocRawMode** and **IocCookMode** use both the "get device information" service (AL = 0), and the "set device information" service (AL = 1).

IocRawMode and **IocCookMode** both begin by obtaining the current device information word for the console. This word is obtained by placing the file handle for the device in register BX and invoking interrupt 21h with 44h in AH and 0 in AL. DOS returns the device information word in register DX. Note that file handle 2 (standard error) was used to access the console. Either file handle 0 (standard input) or handle 1 (standard output) could have been used instead, since they also refer to the console device; however, these two handles are subject to redirection by the user and therefore may be associated with the wrong device.

When bit number 5 of the device information word is on, the device is in raw mode. Therefore, **IocRawMode** turns this bit on, and **IocCookMode** turns the bit off. By first reading the current information and changing only bit 5, the remainder of the device information remains unaltered. Once the bit is set appropriately, both functions invoke the DOS "set device information" service to effect the mode change. Note that when using this DOS service, register DL must be 0 (therefore the high-order byte of the device information cannot be changed).

Printer Functions

C HAPTER 3

This chapter presents the module of printer functions. These functions are divided into three groups: a group of low-level services that control one or more printers directly through the BIOS; a set of functions to facilitate printing formatted reports by printing characters and strings at absolute row and column positions on the page; and a group of functions for managing the MS-DOS PRINT queue that allow your program to print files in the background while the main application continues to run in the foreground.

Figure 3.1 lists the module PRT.C, which contains the set of printer management functions. To use these functions in your C program, you must include the file PRT.H, Figure 3.2, and link your program with the object module PRT.OBJ.

LOW-LEVEL PRINTER CONTROL FUNCTIONS

The five functions in this section are designed to control the operation of one or more printers. All of these functions directly call low-level BIOS services or manipulate BIOS data maintained in low memory, and allow you to perform the following general operations:

- Determine the number of printers currently installed (**PrtInstalled**).
- Switch output among printers in systems with multiple printers attached (**PrtSwap**).
- Change the delay used by the system before displaying an error message (**PrtTimeout**).
- Determine if the printer is ready for output (**PrtReady**).
- Initialize the printer port (**PrtInit**).

```
#include <STDIO.H>
#include <DOS.H>
#include <STRING.H>
#include <STDLIB.H>
#include "PRT.H"

#pragma check_stack (off)          /* Turn off stack checks so that functions  */
                                   /* can be called from interrupt routines.   */

/************************ BIOS Level Functions ************************/

int PrtInstalled ()
/*
    This function returns the number of printers installed.
*/
    {
    union REGS Reg;

    int86 (0x11, &Reg, &Reg);              /* BIOS equipment list service.    */

    return ((Reg.x.ax & 0xc000) >> 14);   /* Return bits 15 and 14.          */

    } /* end PrtInstalled */


int PrtSwap (int PrtNumber)
/*
    This function swaps the printer currently associated with LPT1 with
    printer number 2 or 3, as specified by 'PrtNumber'.  The function returns
    zero if successful, or a nonzero value if an error occurred.
*/
    {
    int Hold;                    /* Temporary storage for printer port address.*/
    /* Pointer to port address of base printer:                              */
    int far *PtrBasePrinter = (int far *)0x00400008;
    int far *PtrNewPrinter;  /* Pointer to port address of new printer.       */

    /* Check valid printer numbers (1 is ineffective but benign).            */
    if (PrtNumber < 1 || PrtNumber > 3)
        return (1);               /* 1 return value indicates an error.       */

    /* Swap printer port addresses maintained by the BIOS.                   */
    PtrNewPrinter = PtrBasePrinter + (PrtNumber-1);
    Hold = *PtrBasePrinter;
    *PtrBasePrinter = *PtrNewPrinter;
    *PtrNewPrinter = Hold;

    return (0);                  /* No error.                                 */

    } /* end PrtSwap */
void PrtTimeout (unsigned char Seconds)
/*
    This function sets the timeout count used by the BIOS printer error
    handler.
*/
    {
    unsigned char far *PtrTimeout = (unsigned char far *)0x00400078;

    *PtrTimeout = ++Seconds;

    } /* end PrtTimeout */
```

Figure 3.1: PRT.C: Functions for managing the printer

```
int PrtReady ()
/*
      This function returns the 'selected' bit of the printer status byte.  It
      obtains the value via BIOS interrupt 17h.  This bit generally indicates
      that the printer is ready to receive characters without error, and using
      this function prior to writing to the printer can avoid the usual
      "Abort, Retry, Ignore?" message when attempting to write to a printer
      that is offline.  Test this function with your system, since the exact
      coding of the status bits seems to vary with different BIOS and printer
      combinations.
*/
      {
      union REGS Reg;

      Reg.h.ah = 2;                   /* BIOS service 2: return printer status.*/
      Reg.x.dx = 0;                   /* First printer port.                   */
      int86 (0x17, &Reg, &Reg);       /* BIOS printer services.                */
      return (Reg.h.ah & 0x10);       /* Mask all bits except 'selected' bit.  */

      } /* end PrtReady */


void PrtInit ()
/*
      This function initializes the printer port for the printer associated
      with LPT1.
*/
      {
      union REGS Reg;

      Reg.h.ah = 1;                   /* BIOS initialize printer port function.*/
      Reg.x.dx = 0;                   /* First printer port.                   */
      int86 (0x17, &Reg, &Reg);       /* BIOS printer services.                */

      } /* end PrtInit */


/*************************** DOS Level Functions ***************************/

void PrtPutC (int Ch)
/*
      This function sends character 'Ch' to the printer.
      Warning:  this function should not be used in conjuntion with
      PrtPosition unless it is used to send a control code that does NOT move
      the printer head (otherwise the internal record of the current printer
      row and column maintained by PrtPosition and PrtNewPage would become
      invalid).
*/
      {
      putc (Ch,stdprn);          /* Standard C macro:  buffered output to LPT1.*/

      } /* end PrtPutC */


void PrtPutS (char *String)
/*
      This function sends NULL-terminated 'String' to the printer.

      Warning:  this function should not be used in conjuntion with
      PrtPosition unless it is used to send a string of control characters that
      do NOT move the printer head (otherwise the internal record of the
      current printer row and column maintained by PrtPosition and PrtNewPage
      would become invalid).
```

Figure 3.1: PRT.C: Functions for managing the printer (continued)

```
*/
        {
    while (*String)                         /* Loop until NULL termination.    */
            PrtPutC (*String++);

    } /* end PrtPutS */


                         /* Private data for page position printing functions.  */
static int CurRow = 1;
static int CurCol = 1;

int PrtPosition (char *String,int Row,int Col)
/*
    This function prints NULL terminated 'String' beginning at the position
    specified by 'Row' and 'Column'.  The following rules must be observed:

    o  The string must NOT contain control characters (i.e., any characters
       that do not advance the print head a single column).  To send control
       codes, use 'PrtPutC' or 'PrtPutS'.
    o  The string must not contain tab characters!
    o  The string must not contain newline characters.  To advance to a new
       line, use a subsequent call specifying the desired Row.  Do not send
       more characters than can fit on the current line.
    o  To generate a new page and reset the row and column numbers, use
       'PrtNewPage'.  Do not send more lines than can fit on a single page.
    o  If the requested print position is to the left or above the current
       position, the function returns an error code of 1.  If no error
       occurs, a 0 is returned.
*/
        {
                             /* Test for valid Row and Col.                     */
    if (Row < CurRow || Row == CurRow && Col < CurCol)
        return (1);
    while (Row - CurRow)     /* Print CR/LF until reaching desired row.    */
            {
        PrtPutC (13);
        PrtPutC (10);
        ++CurRow;
        CurCol = 1;
            }
    while (Col - CurCol)     /* Print spaces until reaching desired column.*/
            {
        PrtPutC (32);
        ++CurCol;
            }
    while (*String)          /* Print the string until the NULL.           */
            {
        PrtPutC (*String++);
        ++CurCol;
            }
    return (0);              /* Return 0 for no error.                      */

    } /* end PrtPosition */


void PrtNewPage (int FormFeed)
/*
    This function produces a formfeed if 'FormFeed' is non-zero, resets the
    internal row and column counters, and flushes printer output.
```

Figure 3.1: PRT.C: Functions for managing the printer (continued)

```
*/
     {
     if (FormFeed)
          {
          PrtPutC (13);                /* Carriage return.            */
          PrtPutC (12);                /* Form feed.                  */
          .}
     CurRow = CurCol = 1;       /* Reset current row and column.     */
     fflush (stdprn);           /* Flush 'fputc' buffer.             */

     } /* end PrtNewPage */


/*********************** DOS PRINT Queue Functions ************************/


int PrtQueState ()
/*
     This function returns the installed state of the DOS PRINT queue.  The
     following values are returned (defined in PRT.H):

          NOERROR (= 0) PRINT is installed.
          NOTINST       PRINT is not installed but may be installed.
          CANTINST      PRINT is not installed and cannot be installed.
          WRONGDOS      Wrong version of DOS.
*/
     {
     union REGS Reg;

     /* Check for appropriate version of MS-DOS.                      */
     if (_osmajor < 3 || _osmajor >= 10)
          return (WRONGDOS);

     Reg.h.ah = 1;                /* DOS PRINT queue family of services. */
     Reg.h.al = 0;                /* Get queue status service.           */
     int86 (0x2f, &Reg, &Reg);    /* Invoke "Multiplex" interrupt.       */

     /* Branch according to status returned in AL.                    */
     switch (Reg.h.al)
          {
          case 0:
               return (NOTINST);
          case 1:
               return (CANTINST);
          case 0xff:
               return (NOERROR);
          default:
               return (Reg.h.al);
          }

     } /* end PrtQueState */

#pragma pack (1)                 /* Tell QuickC to pack structure.      */

static struct                    /* Submit packet used by PrtQueSubmit. */
     {
     char Level;
     char far *FileName;
     }
near SubmitPack = {'\0'};
```

Figure 3.1: PRT.C: Functions for managing the printer (continued)

```
int PrtQueSubmit (char far *FileName)
/*
    This function submits the file whose path is contained in the string
    'FileName' to the DOS PRINT queue.  Global filename characters are NOT
    allowed.
*/
    {
    union REGS Reg;
    int ErrorCode;

    if (ErrorCode = PrtQueState ())      /* Test that queue is installed.  */
        return (ErrorCode);

    SubmitPack.FileName = FileName;      /* Assign address of file name.   */

    Reg.x.dx = (unsigned int)&SubmitPack;  /* Address of submit packet.    */
    Reg.h.ah = 1;                          /* Queue services.              */
    Reg.h.al = 1;                          /* Submit file service.         */
    int86 (0x2f, &Reg, &Reg);              /* 'Multiplex' interrupt.       */
    ErrorCode = Reg.x.ax;                  /* Error code returned in AX.   */
    if (ErrorCode <= 15)                   /* Check for valid error code.  */
        return (ErrorCode);
    else
        return (NOERROR);

    } /* end PrtQueSubmit */


static char near Buf [65];             /* DOS work area used by PrtQueCancel.  */

int PrtQueCancel (char *FileName)
/*
    This function cancels the file(s) specified by the path contained in
    FileName from the DOS PRINT queue.  Global filename characters ARE
    allowed.  FileName must be a NULL-terminated string.
*/
    {
    union REGS Reg;
    int ErrorCode;

    if (ErrorCode = PrtQueState ())      /* Test that queue is installed.  */
        return (ErrorCode);

    strcpy (Buf, FileName);                /* FileName better be NULL-terminated! */
    Reg.x.dx = (unsigned int)Buf;          /* Pass address of file name string.   */
    Reg.h.ah = 1;                          /* Queue services.              */
    Reg.h.al = 2;                          /* Cancel file service.         */
    int86 (0x2f, &Reg, &Reg);              /* Invoke "Multiplex" interrupt. */

    ErrorCode = Reg.x.ax;                  /* Error code returned in AX.   */
    if (ErrorCode <= 15)                   /* Check for valid error code.  */
        return (ErrorCode);
    else
        return (NOERROR);

    } /* end PrtQueCancel */
```

Figure 3.1: PRT.C: Functions for managing the printer (continued)

```
int PrtQueCancelAll (void)
/*
      This function cancels ALL files from the DOS PRINT queue.
*/
      {
      union REGS Reg;
      int ErrorCode;

      if (ErrorCode = PrtQueState ())      /* Test that queue is installed.  */
            return (ErrorCode);
      Reg.h.ah = 1;                        /* Queue services.                */
      Reg.h.al = 3;                        /* Cancel ALL files service.      */
      int86 (0x2f, &Reg, &Reg);            /* 'Multiplex' interrupt.         */

      ErrorCode = Reg.x.ax;                /* Error code returned in AX.     */
      if (ErrorCode <= 15)                 /* Check for valid error code.    */
            return (ErrorCode);
      else
            return (NOERROR);

      } /* end PrtQueCancelAll */
```

Figure 3.1: PRT.C: Functions for managing the printer (continued)

PrtInstalled

Using PrtInstalled

The function **PrtInstalled**, which has the prototype

```
int PrtInstalled
      (void)
```

simply returns the number of printers that are attached to the computer. Note, however, that this information is obtained at initialization time, and reflects the number of parallel *ports* that are detected by the system; a given port may or may not have a functional printer attached. Also, printers attached to serial ports will not be included. Therefore, if the program requires an accurate count of the number of actual printers, it is best to obtain the number from the user. See the program listed in Figure 3.7 (described later in the chapter) for an example of using this function.

```
/* Prt... function prototypes.                                         */

int  PrtInstalled   (void);
int  PrtSwap        (int PrtNumber);
void PrtTimeout     (unsigned char Seconds);
int  PrtReady       (void);
void PrtInit        (void);
void PrtPutC        (int Ch);
void PrtPutS        (char *String);
int  PrtPosition    (char *String,int Row,int Col);
void PrtNewPage     (int FormFeed);
int  PrtQueState    (void);
int  PrtQueSubmit   (char far *FileName);
int  PrtQueCancel   (char *FileName);
int  PrtQueCancelAll (void);

/* Constants for DOS PRINT Queue errors.                               */

#ifndef NOERROR
#define NOERROR        0         /* No error.                          */
#endif

                                 /* Codes 1-15 are the general errors  */
                                 /* returned by the DOS services.      */
#define BADFUNC        1         /* Invalid function.                  */
#define NOFILE         2         /* File not found.                    */
#define NOPATH         3         /* Path not found.                    */
#define MAXOPEN        4         /* Too many open files.               */
#define NOACCESS       5         /* Access denied.                     */
#define QUEFULL        8         /* Queue full.                        */
#define BUSY           9         /* Busy.                              */
#define MAXNAME        12        /* Name too long.                     */
#define BADDRIVE       15        /* Invalid drive.                     */
#define NOTINST        20        /* PRINT not installed, OK to install. */
#define CANTINST       21        /* PRINT not installed, can't install. */
#ifndef WRONGDOS
#define WRONGDOS       22        /* Wrong version of MS-DOS.           */
#endif
```

Figure 3.2: PRT.H: Header file that should be included in your program when calling functions in the PRT.C module

How PrtInstalled Works

PrtInstalled works by invoking the BIOS equipment determination service, interrupt 11h. This service returns a word in register AX that indicates the installed equipment detected by the BIOS at system initialization. This word is known as the *equipment flag*, and is encoded as shown in Table 3.1. (The equipment flag is also stored at memory location 0040h:0010h, where it may be directly modified in order to change the system's internal record of installed devices. Such a modification might be necessary, for example, when changing from a monochrome adapter to a color adapter in a system with two adapters, or with a single adapter that supports both modes.)

Table 3.1: Encoding of the Equipment Flag

Bit	Meaning
15,14:	Number of attached printers.
13:	Not used.
12:	Game I/O attached (if bit = 1).
11,10,9:	Number of RS-232 adapters.
8:	Not used.
7,6:	Number of diskette drives. The following codes specify the number of diskette drives, but *only if bit 0 of the equipment flag is 1*:

	Code	Number of drives
	00	1
	01	2
	10	3
	11	4

Bit	Meaning
5,4:	Initial video mode:

	Value	Mode
	00	Not used.
	01	40×25 CGA card.
	10	80×25 CGA card.
	11	80×24 monochrome card.

Bit	Meaning
3,2:	RAM on motherboard:

	Code	Amount of RAM
	00	16K
	01	32K
	10	48K
	11	64K

Bit	Meaning
1:	Not used.
0:	One or more diskette drives are present (see bits 7,6 for the actual number).

After invoking interrupt 11h, **PrtInstalled** isolates the bits that indicate the number of printers (15 and 14) by masking and shifting, and then returns the resulting value.

PrtSwap

Using PrtSwap

IBM-compatible computers allow you to install up to three parallel printers. MS -DOS printer services permit access to any one of these three printers by writing to the DOS devices LPT1 (equivalent to PRN), LPT2, or LPT3. (If you are writing to the printer by directly invoking the BIOS printer services through interrupt 17 h, you specify one of these three printers by passing a value of 0, 1, or 2; LPT1 is equivalent to printer 0, LPT2 to printer 1, and LPT3 to printer 2.)

Many programs (including the BIOS print-screen routine) automatically write printer output to device LPT1 (or to printer 0, as it is known to the BIOS), and neither DOS nor the BIOS provide services to redirect this output to one of the other two parallel ports. It might be nice, for example, to be able to temporarily redirect all output for LPT1, associated with a dot matrix printer, to a daisy-wheel printer normally accessed as LPT2.

The function **PrtSwap** allows you to swap the printer currently associated with LPT1 with the printer currently associated with either LPT2 or LPT3. (From the perspective of the BIOS, output to printer 0 goes to the printer port formerly accessed as printer 1 or 2, and output to printer 1 or 2 goes to the printer port formerly accessed as printer 0.) The prototype for this function is

```
int PrtSwap
     (int PrtNumber)
```

where **PrtNumber** is either 2 or 3 depending upon which printers you want to swap. Specifically, a value of 2 would switch the printers associated with LPT1 and LPT2, and a value of 3 would switch the printers associated with LPT1 and LPT3. (Passing a value of 1 would be harmless but would do nothing, since it would simply switch the printer attached to LPT1 with itself.) As an example, if you have two or three printers attached to your system, the function call

```
PrtSwap (2);
```

would cause all subsequent writes directed to LPT1 to go to the printer that was formerly associated with LPT2, and all output to LPT2 to go to the printer previously attached to LPT1. The effect of this function call is illustrated in Figure 3.3. To restore the former printer association, simply issue this *same* function call again: **PrtSwap (2)**.

If a value other than 1, 2, or 3 is passed, **PrtSwap** returns an error code of 1; otherwise, it returns 0. For a program demonstrating the use of this function, see the listing in Figure 3.7 (described later in the chapter).

How PrtSwap Works

The BIOS maintains a list of the physical port addresses of all printers installed (up to 3). This list is labeled PRINTER_BASE, and is located beginning at address 0040h:0008h in the BIOS data area. Each port address is one word long (that is, a 16-bit value). Writes to LPT1 (or BIOS printer 0) end up going to the first port address in this list, writes to LPT2 (or BIOS printer 1) to the second port address in the list, and so on. Therefore, swapping the printer associated with LPT1 with the printer associated with either LPT2 or LPT3 is a simple matter of switching the port addresses maintained in this list. The function uses Microsoft C **far** pointers to access the absolute memory locations outside of the C data segment, and is straightforward.

PrtTimeout

Using PrtTimeout

When the system is attempting to send characters to the printer and the printer is currently offline (that is, not *selected*), it will display the familiar message

```
Not ready error writing device PRN
Abort, Retry, Ignore?
```

This message is not displayed immediately, but only after a delay known as a *timeout*. The delay gives the user time to prepare the printer if it is not ready immediately after issuing a print command. The default timeout delay is 20 seconds. The function **PrtTimeout** allows you to specify another timeout value. Its prototype is

```
void PrtTimeout
    (unsigned char Seconds)
```

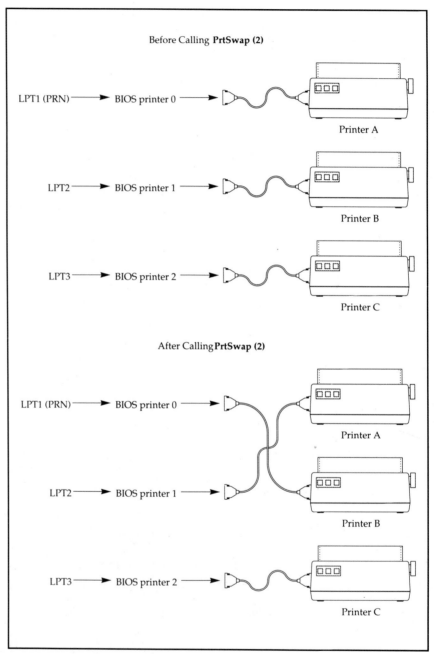

Figure 3.3: Swapping printers by calling PrtSwap (2)

where **Seconds**, the desired delay, can be a value between 0 and 255. Note, however, that a timeout delay is used only for certain errors (*not selected* errors, which are those that occur, for example, when the *selected* button on the printer is off). For other errors (for example, *I/O errors* that occur when the power switch is off), the following message is displayed immediately, without a delay period:

```
Write fault error writing device PRN
Abort, Retry, Ignore?
```

PrtTimeout affects only the printer associated with LPT1 (remember, however, that the function **PrtSwap** can effectively connect another printer to LPT1). See Figure 3.7 (described later in the chapter) for an example of the use of this function.

How PrtTimeout Works

The BIOS maintains a list of one byte timeout counters, one for each of the three possible printers, beginning at memory location 0040h:0078h. **PrtTimeout** works by directly altering the first of these values, thereby setting the timeout value for the printer accessed through LPT1. Note that the seconds value is first incremented; this is necessary because the BIOS routine uses the value as a counter, *first* decrementing the number and *then* comparing it to 0. If **PrtTimeout** did not increment the number of seconds, then a request for 0 seconds would actually result in a delay of 255 seconds (0 minus 1 produces an unsigned byte value of 255).

PrtReady

Using PrtReady

PrtReady, which has the prototype

```
int PrtReady
     (void)
```

returns a non-zero value only if the printer is currently ready to receive output. You should call this function immediately before sending output to the printer, to avoid one of the "Abort, Retry, Ignore?" error messages described above. (See Chapter 8 for a method of handling these critical errors once they happen.) Note that this function affects only the printer currently associated with LPT1. Figure 3.7 (described later in the chapter) demonstrates the use of this function in the context of a program.

How PrtReady Works

PrtReady invokes the BIOS printer services interrupt 17 h, function 2, which returns the current printer status in register AH. The bits of this status byte have the following meanings when they are turned on:

Bit	Meaning when Bit is Set
7	Printer not busy
6	Acknowledge
5	Printer out of paper
4	Printer selected
3	Printer has an I/O error
2, 1	Unused
0	Timeout

The best general indicator that the printer is currently ready to receive output seems to be the *selected* bit (number 4), and therefore **PrtReady** returns this single bit. (The *I/O error* bit, number 3, could also be used; however, with some printers this bit does *not* indicate an error when the selected button is off.) Note that the BIOS service allows you to specify a particular printer by placing either 0, 1, or 2 in register DX; **PrtReady** passes a 0 to select the printer currently associated with LPT1.

PrtInit

Using PrtInit

Calling **PrtInit**, which has the prototype

```
void PrtInit
    (void)
```

initializes the printer port that is currently associated with LPT1. Initialization empties the printer buffer, sets the printer line counter to the top-of-form position, and clears any control codes that have been sent to the printer through software. Calling this function is a good method for bringing the printer to a known state before sending control codes and beginning a new printing job. Be sure, however, not to call **PrtInit** while there are still data in the printer buffer that you want to print, since the function will completely clear this buffer. The function is demonstrated in Figure 3.7 (described later in the chapter).

How PrtInit Works

PrtInit works by invoking the BIOS printer services interrupt 17 h, function number 1. This BIOS service initializes the printer port specified by the value placed in register DX (0, 1, or 2). **PrtInit** passes a 0 to initialize the printer associated with LPT1.

REPORT PRINTING FUNCTIONS

The four functions in this section are an integrated set of services for sending characters or strings to the printer, and for formatting printed reports. These functions allow you to do the following:

▌ Send a single character or control code to the printer (**PrtPutC**).

▌ Send a NULL terminated string of characters or control codes to the printer (**PrtPutS**).

▌ Print a string at a specific row and column on a printed report (**PrtPosition**).

▌ Generate a new page, flushing the C buffer and resetting the internal row and column counters (**PrtNewPage**).

PrtPutC

Using PrtPutC

The **PrtPutC** function has the prototype

```
void PrtPutC
     (int Ch)
```

and sends character **Ch** to LPT1. Note that **PrtPutC** should *not* be used in conjunction with **PrtPosition**, unless it is called to send a control code that does not move the printer head; otherwise, the internal record of the current position of the printer head maintained by **PrtPosition** and **PrtNewPage** would become invalid. The use of this function is demonstrated in Figure 3.4 (described later in the chapter).

How PrtPutC Works

The C language supports two levels of file I/O: low-level functions such as **open** and **write** that directly generate operating-system calls, and high-level functions such as **fopen** and **putc** that store characters in internal buffers. **PrtPutC** uses the high level function **putc** (actually a macro that calls a function) to take advantage of the buffering. (You might try rewriting this routine calling the low-level **write** function, and comparing the results.) The printer is accessed through the standard preopened file stream **stdprn**; therefore, the function module does not need to call **fopen** and **fclose** to open and close the printer device.

Note that the C macro **putc** accesses the printer through MS-DOS I/O services. Why was **PrtPutC** designed to send data to the printer through MS-DOS when it would be more efficient to write directly to the printer through the BIOS services (such as those used in the control functions described above)? Aside from the benefits of the buffering provided by **putc**, the primary reason for choosing to route printer output through MS-DOS is to take advantage of the critical-error handling features that the operating system provides. Critical errors (for example, the paper jamming or the ribbon coming to an end) are common during printing operations. If **PrtPutC** used the BIOS printer services, it would have to provide its own error handling routine. However, if DOS services are used, then the operating system will automatically invoke a standard, general purpose critical error handler that you can install when your program begins running. See Chapter 8 for information on writing critical error handlers.

All of the other functions in this module call **PrtPutC** to print individual characters. Note also that since **PrtPutC** uses the standard printer stream, **stdprn**, it automatically writes to LPT1. However, to write to other printers you can simply use the **PrtSwap** function described earlier in the chapter.

PrtPutS

Using PrtPutS

PrtPutS, which has the prototype

```
void PrtPutS
     (char *String)
```

prints the NULL-terminated string given by the parameter **String** at the current position of the printer head. The same warning given for **PrtPutC** applies to this function: you should not use **PrtPutS** in conjunction with **PrtPosition**, unless you are sending a sequence of control codes that *do not move the printer head* (for example, a sequence of codes for switching into near letter-quality print).

Although **PrtPutS** does not have the internal formatting features of **fprintf**, remember that you can first use the C function **sprintf** to write data to a buffer with full formatting control, and then print the buffer with **PrtPutS**. **PrtPutS** is demonstrated in Figures 3.4 and 3.7 (described later in the chapter).

How PrtPutS Works

PrtPutS simply scans through the string that it is passed until it reaches the NULL termination, sending each character to the printer using **PrtPutC**.

PrtPosition

*Using
PrtPosition*

The function **PrtPosition**, which has the prototype

```
int PrtPosition
    (char *String,
    int Row,
    int Col)
```

prints the string given by **String** at the position on the page specified by **Row** and **Col**; rows and columns are numbered beginning with 1. This function greatly facilitates designing and printing reports, or printing information onto preprinted forms. If successful, **PrtPosition** returns 0; if an error occurs, it returns 1.

To design a new report, either lay out the information on a printer chart (which has a grid indicating the row and column of each character), or go into a text editor or word processor that indicates the row and column of the cursor and design the report interactively. In either case, once you know the row and column starting position of each field, you can easily write the code using **PrtPosition** to position and print each field. Remember that you can first format any numeric or other data into a buffer using **sprintf**, and then print the entire buffer employing **PrtPosition**.

To print information onto a preprinted form (such as a tax return form), you can use a utility that prints a matrix of row and column numbers directly onto a sample form. Such a program is listed in Figure 3.4 (which also serves to illustrate the use of **PrtPutC** and **PrtPutS**). Simply place a sample form in the printer at the desired starting position and run the utility; it will print numbers on the form that will allow you to identify the starting row and column of each field that needs to be printed. Note how this program uses **sprintf** combined with **PrtPutS** to accomplish formatted printing. You may adjust the program for the size of the form by modifying the constants NUMROWS and NUMCOLS. Figure 3.5 provides a MAKE file, and Figure 3.6 a QuickC program list for preparing this utility.

The following are a set of guidelines for using **PrtPosition**:

■ You must call the function **PrtNewPage** (described later in the chapter), before printing each new page, in order to reset the internal row and column counters used by **PrtPosition**.

```
#include <STDIO.H>
#include "PRT.H"

#define NUMROWS 60
#define NUMCOLS 80

void main (void)
    {
    int Row, Col;
    char Buf [4];
                            /* Print matrix of row and column numbers on form. */
    for (Row = 1;Row <= NUMROWS;++Row)
        {
        if (Row % 2)                              /* Odd rows.              */
            {
            sprintf (Buf,"%3d",Row);
            PrtPutS (Buf);
            for (Col = 4; Col <= NUMCOLS; ++Col)
                if (Col % 10 == 0)
                    PrtPutC ((Col % 100) / 10 + '0');
                else
                    PrtPutC (' ');
            }
        else                                      /* Even rows.             */
            for (Col = 1;Col <= NUMCOLS;++Col)
                PrtPutC (Col % 10 + '0');

        PrtPutC ('\r');      /* Terminating carriage return / linefeed.    */
        PrtPutC ('\n');
        }

    } /* end main */
```

Figure 3.4: PRTDEM01.C: A program that generates a number grid for designing reports

```
PRTDEM01.OBJ : PRTDEM01.C PRT.H
     cl /c /W2 /Zp PRTDEM01.C

PRT.OBJ : PRT.C PRT.H
     cl /c /W2 /Zp PRT.C

PRTDEM01.EXE :  PRTDEM01.OBJ PRT.OBJ
     link /NOI /NOD PRTDEM01+PRT,,NUL,SLIBCER;
```

Figure 3.5: PRTDEM01.M: A MAKE file for PRTDEM01.C

```
PRTDEM01.C
PRT.C
```

Figure 3.6: A QuickC program list for preparing PRTDEM01.C

▌ You cannot move backwards! In other words, the requested row and column cannot be above or to the left of the current printer head position. If you attempt to move the printer head backwards, the function returns an error code of 1; otherwise, it returns 0.

▌ You are responsible for not trying to print more columns or rows than can fit on the printed page; there is no error checking for such attempts, and the results are unpredictable.

▌ Each call to **PrtPosition** should print on only a single line. Do not embed newline characters in the string; rather, generate a new line by calling the function again, passing it the number of the next row.

▌ *Each character in the string must advance the printer head exactly one column.* Therefore, do not embed tab, control, or backspace characters. To send control codes that do not move the print head, use **PrtPutC** or **PrtPutS**.

The use of **PrtPosition** is illustrated in Figure 3.7, described later in the chapter.

How PrtPosition Works

PrtPosition stores the current position of the printer head in the external static integers **CurRow** and **CurCol**. These values are set to 1 with each call to **PrtNewPage**. **PrtPosition** first checks that the requested row and column would not attempt to move the printer head backwards, returning 1 if this error is discovered. It then positions and prints the string in three steps:

▌ It prints carriage return/linefeed pairs until reaching the desired row (if any are required).

▌ It prints spaces until reaching the requested column (if any are required).

▌ It prints characters from the string until it reaches the NULL termination.

All printing is accomplished through **PrtPutC**, and a 0 is returned on successful completion.

PrtNewPage

*Using
PrtNewPage*

You should call **PrtNewPage** before printing each new page. This function resets the internal row and column counters used by **PrtPutC** and flushes the C buffer holding output for the printer. The prototype is

```
void PrtNewPage
     (int FormFeed)
```

If **FormFeed** is nonzero, then a form feed is generated. When you call **PrtNewPage** before printing the first page, you can pass a value of 0 to avoid an initial form feed, which wastes a sheet of paper. This function is demonstrated in Figure 3.7, described later in the chapter.

*How
PrtNewPage
Works*

PrtNewPage simply prints a carriage return and a form feed if its parameter is nonzero, assigns 1 to the row and column counters, and then calls the C function **fflush** to flush all output to the printer that might be waiting in the buffer maintained by **putc**.

A Printer Function Demonstration

The program PRTDEM02.C, listed in Figure 3.7, readies the printer and prints a sample report. It manages to use all of the printer functions that have been discussed so far, except **PrtPutC**. Since this program uses functions from both the keyboard module and the printer module, it includes the header files KBD.H and PRT.H.

The program first calls **PrtInstalled** to determine the number of printers that are installed. If the number of printers is two or three, it allows the user to select a printer to receive output. The function **PrtSwap** is then used to swap the printer addresses, so that all subsequent printer functions will control or send output to the selected printer.

Next, the program calls **PrtTimeout** to change the system error message delay from the default of 20 seconds down to a value of 10 seconds. Subsequently, all *not selected* errors will be reported more promptly.

Before proceeding, the program makes sure that the selected printer is prepared to receive output. Control enters a polling loop, which executes until **PrtReady** returns a value indicating that the printer is ready. At this point a more robust program would give the user the option to exit the

```c
#include <STDIO.H>
#include <PROCESS.H>
#include "PRT.H"
#include "KBD.H"

static void Header (void);              /* Prototype for local function.  */
static int Row;                         /* NEXT row to be printed.        */

void main (void)
    {
    int NumberPrt;                      /* Number of printers installed.  */
    int PrtSelected;                    /* Printer selected for output.   */
    int i;

    NumberPrt = PrtInstalled ();  /* Obtain number of printers installed. */
    if (NumberPrt == 0)
        {
        printf ("No printer installed\n");
        exit (1);
        }
    else if (NumberPrt > 1)         /* Let user choose a printer.         */
        {
        KbdFlush ();                        /* Rid spurious input.        */
        printf ("Which printer do you want to recieve output?\n");
        printf ("     (1)  LPT1\n");
        printf ("     (2)  LPT2\n");
        if (NumberPrt == 3)
            printf ("     (3)  LPT3\n");
        printf ("Enter Choice: ");
        do
            PrtSelected = (KbdGetC ()&0x00ff) - '0';
        while (PrtSelected < 1 || PrtSelected > NumberPrt);

        PrtSwap (PrtSelected);              /* Remap the printers.        */
        }

    printf ("\nPrinting report...");

    PrtTimeout (10);    /* Set the timeout delay to half the default      */
                        /* delay of 20 seconds.                           */

    while (!PrtReady ())            /* Make sure printer is ready.         */
        {
        printf ("\nReady printer and press any key to continue ...");
        KbdGetC ();
        }

    PrtInit ();                         /* Initialize printer.            */

    PrtPutS ("\x1b\x49\x33");       /* Send control code sequence for near */
                                    /* letter quality (Okidata).           */
    PrtNewPage (0);             /* Initialize a new page without formfeed. */
    Header ();                  /* Print first header.                     */
```

Figure 3.7: PRTDEM02.C: A program demonstrating the printer management functions

```
        for (i = 1; i <= 80; ++i)/* Process 80 detail lines as a demonstration.*/
            {
            if (Row > 55)
                {
                PrtNewPage (1);                    /* New page with a formfeed.  */
                Header ();                         /* Print another header.      */
                }
            PrtPosition ("Field One",Row,1);
            PrtPosition ("Field Two",Row,23);
            PrtPosition ("Field Three",Row,44);
            PrtPosition ("Field Four",Row++,67);
            }
        PrtPosition ("End of Report",++Row,1);
        PrtNewPage (1);                            /* Force out last page.        */

        if (NumberPrt > 1)                         /* Restore the printer mapping.*/
            PrtSwap (PrtSelected);

        } /* end main */


static void Header (void)
        {
        PrtPosition ("S A M P L E    R E P O R T",1,27);
        PrtPosition ("Heading One",3,1);
        PrtPosition ("Heading Two",3,23);
        PrtPosition ("Heading Three",3,44);
        PrtPosition ("Heading Four",3,67);
        PrtPosition ("-----------",4,1);
        PrtPosition ("-----------",4,23);
        PrtPosition ("-------------",4,44);
        PrtPosition ("-----------",4,67);
        Row = 6;

        } /* end Header */
```

Figure 3.7: PRTDEM02.C: A program demonstrating the printer management functions (continued)

program gracefully, or perhaps select another printer, if the problem cannot be remedied. The current implementation would require the user to press the Ctrl-Break key combination to abort the program if the printer cannot be readied. (Exiting a program using a break key does not normally permit the program to save data or perform other final tasks. One method for allowing the user to safely exit through a break key is to install a break-key handler as described in Chapter 8.)

The program next initializes the selected printer port by calling **PrtInit**. This function will clear any previous control codes that have been sent to the printer and reset the printer's line counter to the top-of-form position. The printer is now ready to receive a new set of control codes, and to start printing at the top of a new page. **PrtInit** should never be called *after* sending output to the printer since it will immediately erase any data still sitting in the printer buffer waiting to be printed (even in this program there is some danger that data may be waiting in the printer buffer from a previous program).

Before entering the main printing loop, **PrtNewPage** is called to initialize the internal counters used by **PrtPosition**, and the header routine is called to print the report heading on the first page and initialize the line counter, **Row**. Note that **PrtNewPage** is passed a zero to avoid an unnecessary line feed at the beginning of the report.

The main loop begins by testing whether the number of lines that have been printed exceeds the maximum lines per page. If the maximum has been exceeded, then the program calls **PrtNewPage** to prepare for a new page, and passes it a value of 1 to generate a form feed. Both the main loop and the header routine print strings at specific positions on the page using **PrtPosition**. (The report was initially laid out using a text editor.)

The main loop terminates after printing 80 lines. **PrtNewPage** is now called once more, both to flush all remaining data from the C buffer to the printer, and to eject the report from the printer with a final form feed. Finally, if **PrtSwap** was called at the beginning of the program, it is now called once again using the *same* parameter, in order to reswap the printer port addresses back to their original arrangement.

A MAKE file for this program is listed in Figure 3.8, and a QuickC program list in Figure 3.9.

```
PRTDEM02.OBJ : PRTDEM02.C PRT.H
    cl /c /W2 /Zp PRTDEM02.C

PRT.OBJ : PRT.C PRT.H
    cl /c /W2 /Zp PRT.C

KBDA.OBJ : KBDA.ASM
    masm /MX KBDA.ASM;

PRTDEM02.EXE :  PRTDEM02.OBJ PRT.OBJ KBDA.ASM
    link /NOI /NOD PRTDEM02+PRT+KBDA,,NUL,SLIBCER;
```

Figure 3.8: PRTDEM02.M: A MAKE file for PRTDEM02.C

```
PRTDEM02.C
PRT.C
KBDA.OBJ
```

Figure 3.9:A QuickC program list for preparing PRTDEM02.C

MS-DOS PRINT QUEUE MANAGEMENT FUNCTIONS

The MS-DOS PRINT program installs itself as a memory-resident application, places files in a queue waiting to be printed, and continues to send data to the printer while other programs run in the foreground. With DOS versions prior to 3.0, this queue was accessible only from the command line through the PRINT command. Beginning with version 3.0, however, the queue can be managed from within an application program through the services of interrupt 2Fh. Note that the PRINT program provided in the DOS-compatibility mode of OS/2 is not a memory resident program and therefore does *not* provide print queue services to application programs.

The functions in this section are designed to manage the DOS PRINT queue from within a Microsoft C program. By accessing the DOS PRINT queue, your program can do the following:

- Determine whether the DOS PRINT queue is installed (**PrtQueState**).

- Submit a file to the DOS queue so that the system can print it in the background while your program continues to run (**PrtQueSubmit**).

- Remove a specific file (**PrtQueCancel**), or all files (**PrtQueCancelAll**), from the queue.

PrtQueState

*Using
PrtQueState*

The **PrtQueState** function has the prototype

```
int PrtQueState
    (void)
```

and returns one of four possible values indicating the current status of
the DOS PRINT queue:

■ NOERROR, which equals zero and signifies that the DOS
  program PRINT.COM is installed and ready.

■ NOTINST, meaning that queue is not currently installed but
  may be installed.

■ CANTINST, if the queue is not installed but for some reason
  cannot be installed.

■ WRONGDOS, if the operating system version is less than 3.0.
  This value is also returned if the version number is equal to
  or greater than 10; the DOS-compatibility mode of OS/2
  returns a version number of 10 or greater, and, as mentioned
  previously, this environment does not provide PRINT queue
  services through interrupt 2Fh.

These constants are defined in the header file PRT.H, shown in
Figure 3.2. This function should be called prior to using any of the
other queue management functions to make sure that the resident portion of the PRINT program is properly installed.

If **PrtQueState** returns NOTINST, and the presence of the queue is required for your program, the user must terminate the program, type the
DOS PRINT command (no files need be specified to simply install
PRINT.COM in memory), and restart the program. Don't even think
about loading PRINT.COM from within your program as a child
process, for the following reason: The file PRINT.COM would successfully load itself above your application and remain resident in memory.
However, when your program terminate and release the memory it oc-
cupy, a large gap would be left in memory.

PrtQueState is demonstrated in Figure 3.10, described later in the
chapter.

How PrtQueState Works

PrtQueState first checks that an appropriate version of DOS is installed by testing the value of the predefined C variable **_osmajor**. This variable contains the major DOS version number (1, 2, 3, 4, and so on). If the version is incorrect, **PrtQueState** immediately returns the value WRONGDOS.

All of the **print** queue functions that are described in this section work by using the MS-DOS PRINT services available through interrupt 2Fh. Interrupt 2Fh is known as the *multiplex* interrupt, and is intended to provide access to multiple sets of interrupt service routines, where each set of routines is accessed by placing a particular value in register AH when invoking the interrupt. The family of routines that access the DOS PRINT program is requested by placing 1 in AH. Each of the individual routines within this family is requested by placing a specific value in register AL.

PrtQueState places 1 in AH and 0 in AL to request the service that returns the installed state of the program PRINT.COM. This DOS service returns one of three possible values in register AL:

- 0 if PRINT.COM is not installed but *may* be installed.
- 1 if PRINT.COM *cannot* be installed.
- FFh if PRINT.COM is already installed and ready to go.

PrtQueState tests register AL and returns the appropriate value. If something has gone wrong and AL contains an unexpected value, the **default** branch of the **switch** statement simply returns the aberrant value.

PrtQueSubmit

Using PrtQueSubmit

The **PrtQueSubmit** function has the prototype

```
int PrtQueSubmit
    (char far *FileName)
```

and adds the file specified by the string **FileName** to the DOS PRINT queue, so that this file will begin printing in the background while your program continues to run. **FileName** can contain a full path name, including drive and directory, but must specify only a single file; the wildcard characters * and ? cannot be used. Under certain versions of DOS, you *must* specify the complete path name.

Note: Even though this function takes a **far** pointer as an argument, a normal pointer or address may be passed in any memory model, since the compiler will automatically convert a **near** pointer to **far**, as long as the function prototype occurs in the file before the function call. (Be sure to include the PRT.H file!)

If successful, **PrtQueSubmit** will return NOERROR; otherwise it will return one of the error codes defined in the header file PRT.H (Figure 3.2). This function is demonstrated in Figure 3.10, described later in the chapter.

How PrtQueSubmit Works

PrtQueSubmit first calls **PrtQueState** to make sure that the PRINT program is installed (in case the programmer forgot to perform this check). If **PrtQueState** returns a nonzero value, indicating that PRINT.COM is not properly installed, **PrtQueSubmit** immediately returns, passing back the received error code. (Since NOERROR equals 0, a nonzero return value signifies that an error has occurred.)

PrtQueSubmit uses the MS-DOS "submit file" service, invoked by placing 1 in AH and 1 in AL, and generating interrupt 2Fh (explained in the **PrtQueState** section). This particular service requires that the segment:offset address of a *submit packet* be passed in registers DS:DX. The submit packet must contain a 0 followed by a **far** pointer to a NULL terminated string specifying the path name of the file submitted. In the PRT.C module, the submit packet is defined immediately above the function **PrtQueSubmit** as an external static structure, **SubmitPack**. **PrtQueSubmit** first assigns the address of the file name that it has been passed to the address field of **SubmitPack**, as follows (both of these values are **far** pointers, as required):

```
SubmitPack.FileName = FileName;
```

It then places the offset address of the submit packet into register DX (note that for large data models, the segment portion of this address would be removed by truncation when the address is cast to an integer). For all memory models, DS already contains the correct segment address of **SubmitPack**. (Note that **SubmitPack** is declared using the **near** keyword to make sure that in large data model programs it is placed within the default data segment. This default data segment may be addressed through register DS.)

After invoking the interrupt, **PrtQueSubmit** tests the value of register AX. If an error occurs, the DOS service returns an error code value between 1 and 15 (the error codes defined in Figure 3.2 in the range from 1 to 15 are those returned by DOS). Unfortunately, if the operation is successful, DOS does not return a special value, such as 0, but rather seems to leave AX with a large, undefined value. Therefore, **PrtQueSubmit** assumes that if the value in AX is less than or equal to 15, an error occurred, and it passes back the error code. Otherwise, it assumes that since the AX value is not a valid error code, no error occurred, and it returns NOERROR.

PrtQueCancel

Using PrtQueCancel

This function has the prototype

```
int PrtQueCancel
        (char *FileName)
```

and removes the file specified by the string **FileName** from the PRINT queue. **FileName** may contain a full path name, and may also include the wildcard characters * and ? so that multiple files may be removed. On successful completion **PrtQueCancel** returns NOERROR; if an error occurred, it returns one of the codes defined in PRT.H (Figure 3.2).

How PrtQueCancel Works

PrtQueCancel is quite similar to **PrtQueSubmit**. It also begins with a call to **PrtQueState** to make sure that PRINT.COM is properly installed, and likewise invokes interrupt 2Fh, with a value of 1 in register AH. However, the specific DOS service that cancels a file in the queue is selected by placing 2 in register AL. Also, instead of requiring the address of a submit packet in registers DS:DX, this service needs the address of the actual string containing the file name. **PrtQueCancel** first copies the string from the parameter FileName into an external static buffer, **Buf**. It then assigns the offset address of **Buf** to register DX, places the appropriate values in AH and AL, and invokes the interrupt. The error return mechanism is identical to that used by **PrtQueSubmit**.

Why does **PrtQueCancel** use the variable **Buf**? Why can't it simply assign the address of the parameter **FileName** directly to register DX, as follows?

```
Reg.x.dx = FileName;
```

The two reasons are worth discussing, since the first points out a danger in using this DOS service, and the second illustrates an important principle in writing code that is independent of the specific memory model.

The first reason for copying the parameter into **Buf**, is that DOS makes free use of the buffer as a work area. Specifically, if the file name contains the wildcard character *, then DOS expands this character into a string of ? characters, writing directly into your buffer! Therefore a buffer that is larger than the actual string is required to avoid memory corruption.

The second reason for copying the string into a variable defined within the current file is that the DS register must contain the segment address of the string. In large data model programs, however, the file name string may be contained in a segment other than the segment in DS (that is, the offset portion of the parameter **FileName** may not be an offset with respect to the segment address in DS). Rather than temporarily adjusting the value of the DS register (by calling **int86x** rather than **int86**), the string is simply copied into a variable known to be in the default data segment (which is addressable through DS).

PrtQueCancelAll

Using PrtQueCancelAll

PrtQueCancelAll, which has the prototype

```
int PrtQueCancelAll
    (void)
```

cancels *all* files that are waiting to be printed in the DOS queue. If successful, it returns NOERROR; otherwise, it returns one of the error codes defined in PRT.H (Figure 3.2).

*How
PrtQueCancelAll
Works*

PrtQueCancelAll also begins by checking the DOS PRINT queue status through a call to **PrtQueState**. It then simply invokes the DOS "cancel all files" service by placing 1 in AH and 3 in AL, and invoking interrupt 2Fh. Error codes are returned in the same manner as the **PrtQueCancel** and **PrtQueSubmit** functions.

A Demonstration of the PRINT Queue Functions

The program listed in Figure 3.10 demonstrates several of the PRINT queue functions described in the preceding sections. The program first opens a test file, writes a single line to this file, and then closes the file, using standard high-level C library file functions.

The program then proceeds to print this file by submitting it to the DOS PRINT queue. First, it calls **PrtQueState** to verify that PRINT.COM is installed, quitting with an appropriate error message if it is not. Note that there is a **default** branch in the **switch** statement in case something goes wrong with the function call and an unexpected value is returned. Second, the program calls **PrtQueSubmit**, passing it the name of the file that was just created. The program then branches according to the return code, again providing a **default** branch to cover unexpected or unlikely error codes.

The actual advantage of using the DOS PRINT queue, which is not significant in this trivial demonstration, is that the program does not need to wait while the file is being printed, but can continue to run while the file prints in the background. An editor program, for example, could print a file while the user continues to edit another file. Also, this set of utilities could be used within a memory resident C utility to allow instant access to the DOS print queue from within any program (see Chapter 9).

Figure 3.11 contains a MAKE file and Figure 3.12 provides a QuickC program list for this program.

```
#include <STDIO.H>
#include <PROCESS.H>
#include "PRT.H"

void main (void)
     {
     FILE *TestFile;               /* File pointer to create test file.  */
     int ErrorCode;                /* 'Prt' function error code.         */

                                   /* Create a test file.                */
     if ((TestFile = fopen ("@DEMO@.@@@","w")) == NULL)
          {
          printf ("Cannot create demo file\n");
          exit (1);
          }
                                   /* Write some data to the test file.  */
     fprintf (TestFile,"This is a single line written to the demo file\n");
     fclose (TestFile);            /* Close the test file.               */

     ErrorCode = PrtQueState ();
     switch (ErrorCode)           /* Test if PRINT.COM is installed.     */
          {
          case NOERROR:
               break;

          case NOTINST:
               printf ("Must install DOS PRINT before running program\n");
               exit (1);

          case CANTINST:
               printf ("DOS PRINT cannot be used\n");
               exit (1);

          case WRONGDOS:
               printf ("Must use MS-DOS or PC-DOS version 3.0 or higher\n");
               exit (1);

          default:
               printf ("Error %d accessing DOS PRINT queue\n", ErrorCode);
               exit (1);
          }
                         /* Submit the test file to the DOS print queue.  */
     ErrorCode = PrtQueSubmit ("@DEMO@.@@@");

     switch (ErrorCode)
          {
          case NOERROR:
               exit (0);

          case NOFILE:
          case NOPATH:
               printf ("File has disappeared!\n");
               exit (1);

          default:
               printf ("Error %d submitting file to DOS PRINT queue\n",
                       ErrorCode);
               exit (1);
          }

     } /* end main */
```

Figure 3.10: PRTDEM03.C: A demonstration of the PRINT queue functions

```
PRTDEM03.OBJ : PRTDEM03.C PRT.H
     cl /c /W2 /Zp PRTDEM03.C

PRT.OBJ : PRT.C PRT.H
     cl /c /W2 /Zp PRT.C

PRTDEM03.EXE :  PRTDEM03.OBJ PRT.OBJ
     link /NOI /NOD PRTDEM03+PRT,,NUL,SLIBCER;
```

Figure 3.11: PRTDEM03.M: A MAKE file for PRTDEM03.C

```
PRTDEM03.C
PRT.C
```

Figure 3.12: A QuickC program list for preparing PRTDEM03.C

File Management
Functions

C HAPTER 4

This chapter presents a set of special-purpose functions for managing files, directories, and volume labels. The functions are contained in the module FIL.C, listed in Figure 4.1. To use these functions in your C program, you must include the file FIL.H (Figure 4.2) in your source listing, and link the program with the object file FIL.OBJ. These routines allow you to do the following:

- Rename a directory (**FilRenameDir**).

- Get, rename, or remove a hard disk or diskette volume label (**FilGetVolid, FilSetVolid, FilDelVolid**).

- Get or set the modification date and time of a file (**FilGetTime, FilSetTime**).

- Open up to 255 file handles simultaneously, circumventing the DOS 20 file handle limit (**FilOpen, FilHandle**).

- Read or write file data to or from a memory location outside the program's default data segment (**FilReadFar, FilWriteFar**).

FilRenameDir

*Using
FilRenameDir*

The **FilRenameDir** function has the prototype

```
int FilRenameDir
        (char *OldDir,
        char *NewDir)
```

and changes the name of the directory **OldDir** to **NewDir**. **OldDir** may contain a drive specification but may *not* contain a path. Thus, the following are legal directory values for **OldDir**:

```
ACE
B:ACE
```

The following, however, is an illegal value for **OldDir**:

```
\CARDS\ACE
```

If no drive is specified, the current drive is assumed; the directory is always the current directory of the specified drive. **NewDir** may contain *only* a file name; the drive and directory are automatically the same as that of **OldDir**.

```c
#include <STDIO.H>
#include <DOS.H>
#include <FCNTL.H>
#include <IO.H>
#include <CTYPE.H>
#include <PROCESS.H>
#include <STDLIB.H>
#include <SYS\TYPES.H>
#include <SYS\STAT.H>

#define MODFILE
#include "FIL.H"

#pragma pack (1)                   /* Tell QuickC to pack structures.     */
#pragma check_stack (off)          /* Turn off stack checks so that functions */
                                   /* can be called from interrupt routines.  */

                        /* Extended File Control Block structures for   */
                        /* FilRenameDir, FilGetVolid, & FilSetVolid.    */
static struct
    {
    unsigned char ExtCode;         /* Flag indicating extended FCB.       */
    char Res1 [5];                 /* Reserved field.                     */
    unsigned char Code;            /* File attribute code.                */
    unsigned char OldDrive;        /* Drive for old name.                 */
    char OldName [11];             /* Old directory name or volume ID.    */
    char Res2 [5];                 /* Reserved field.                     */
    char NewName [11];             /* New directory name or volume ID.    */
    char Res3 [9];                 /* Reserved field.                     */
    }
DirFcb = {'\xff',"",'\x10'},                      /* For FilRenameDir.    */
VolFcb = {'\xff',"",'\x08','\0',"???????????"};   /* For FilGet/SetVolid. */


int FilRenameDir (char *OldDir,char *NewDir)
/*
    This function renames the directory 'OldDir' to the name 'NewDir'.
*/
    {
    register int i;
    int ErrorCode;
    union REGS Reg;

    if (OldDir [1] == ':')              /* Colon indicates a drive specifier.   */
        {
        DirFcb.OldDrive = toupper (OldDir [0]) - 64;
        OldDir += 2;
        }
    else    /* No drive on command line;  therefore specify default drive.*/
        DirFcb.OldDrive = 0;

    for (i = 0; i < 11; ++i) /* Copy old and new drives to file control    */
                             /* block, blank padding on right.             */
```

Figure 4.1: FIL.C: Functions for managing files, directories, and volume labels

```
                   {
                   if (*OldDir == '\0')
                        DirFcb.OldName [i] = ' ';
                   else
                        DirFcb.OldName [i] = *OldDir++;
                   if (*NewDir == '\0')
                        DirFcb.NewName [i] = ' ';
                   else
                        DirFcb.NewName [i] = *NewDir++;
                   }
          Reg.x.dx = (unsigned int)&DirFcb;    /* Address of file control block.  */
          Reg.h.ah = 0x17;                     /* DOS rename file service.        */
          int86 (0x21, &Reg, &Reg);            /* DOS service interrupt.          */

          ErrorCode = Reg.h.al;                /* Error code returned in AL.      */
          if (ErrorCode == 0)
                   {
                   FilError = NOERROR;
                   return (NOERROR);
                   }
          else
                   {
                   FilError = NODIR;
                   return (NODIR);
                   }

          } /* end FilRenameDir */

                                    /* Disk transfer area used by FilGetVolid  */
                                    /* and FilSetVolid.                        */
static struct
          {
          char Res1 [8];            /* Reserved field.                         */
          char OldVolid [11];       /* Filled in by DOS.                       */
          char Res2 [5];            /* Reserved field.                         */
          char NewVolid [11];       /* Used only by FilSetVolid.               */
          char Res3 [9];            /* Reserved field.                         */
          }
Dta;


char *FilGetVolid (unsigned char Drive)
/*
          This function returns the volume label for the disk drive given by
          'Drive'.
                   Drive:    0 = Default drive.
                             1 = Drive A:
                             2 = Drive B:
                             etc.

*/
          {
          int ErrorCode;
          union REGS Reg;
                                             /* Set the default DTA.           */
          Reg.x.dx = (unsigned int)&Dta;     /* Pass address of 'Dta'.         */
          Reg.h.ah = 0x1a;                   /* DOS set DTA function.          */
          int86 (0x21, &Reg, &Reg);          /* DOS service interrupt.         */
```

Figure 4.1: FIL.C: Functions for managing files, directories, and volume labels (continued)

```
                                                  /* Search for directory entry having */
                                                  /* a volume ID attribute.            */
        VolFcb.OldDrive = Drive;                  /* Fill in 'Drive' field of FCB.     */
        Reg.x.dx = (unsigned int)&VolFcb;  /* Pass address of FCB.              */
        Reg.h.ah = 0x11;                          /* 'Search for first entry' service. */
        int86 (0x21, &Reg, &Reg);                 /* DOS service interrupt.            */

        ErrorCode = Reg.h.al;                     /* Error returned in AL.             */
        if (ErrorCode == 0)
            {
            FilError = NOERROR;
            return (Dta.OldVolid);
            }
        else
            {
            FilError =  NOVOL;
            return (NULL);
            }

        } /* end FilGetVolid */


int FilSetVolid (unsigned char Drive, char *Volid)
/*
    This function sets the volume label for drive given by 'Drive' to the
    name 'Volid'.
*/
        {
        register int i;
        int ErrorCode;
        union REGS Reg;

        if (FilGetVolid (Drive) == NULL)          /* No volume label exists.           */
            {                                      /* Create a new one.                 */
            for (i = 0; i < 11; ++i)               /* Copy volume name to FCB,          */
                if (*Volid == '\0')                /* blank padding.                    */
                    VolFcb.OldName [i] = ' ';
                else
                    VolFcb.OldName [i] = *Volid++;
            Reg.x.dx = (unsigned int)&VolFcb;  /* Pass address of FCB.              */
            Reg.h.ah = 0x16;                       /* DOS create file service.          */
            int86 (0x21, &Reg, &Reg);              /* DOS service interrupt.            */

            ErrorCode = Reg.h.al;                  /* Error returned in AL.             */
            if (ErrorCode == 0)
                {
                FilError = NOERROR;
                return (NOERROR);
                }
            else
                {
                FilError = NOCREAT;
                return (NOCREAT);
                }

            }
```

Figure 4.1: FIL.C: Functions for managing files, directories, and volume labels (continued)

```
        else                                    /* Volume label exists;       */
                                                /* Therefore rename it.        */
            {                                   /* Copy new name to DTA, blank */
            for (i = 0; i < 11; ++i)            /* padding.                    */
                if (*Volid == '\0')
                    Dta.NewVolid [i] = ' ';
                else
                    Dta.NewVolid [i] = *Volid++;
            Reg.x.dx = (unsigned int)&Dta;      /* Pass address of DTA.        */
            Reg.h.ah = 0x17;                    /* DOS rename file service.    */
            int86 (0x21, &Reg, &Reg);           /* DOS services interrupt.     */

            ErrorCode = Reg.h.al;               /* Error returned in AL.       */
            if (ErrorCode == 0)
                {
                FilError = NOERROR;
                return (NOERROR);
                }
            else
                {
                FilError = NOREN;
                return (NOREN);
                }
            }

        } /* end FilSetVolid */


int FilDelVolid (unsigned char Drive)
/*
    This function removes the volume label from drive specified by 'Drive'.
*/
    {
    int ErrorCode;
    union REGS Reg;

    if (FilGetVolid (Drive) == NULL)            /* No volume label exists.     */
        {                                       /* Return error.               */
        FilError = NOVOL;
        return (NOVOL);
        }
    else                                        /* Volume label exists;        */
                                                /* Therefore delete it.        */
        {                                       /* Pass address of DTA.        */
        Reg.x.dx = (unsigned int)&Dta;          /* DOS delete file service.    */
        Reg.h.ah = 0x13;                        /* DOS services interrupt.     */
        int86 (0x21, &Reg, &Reg);

        ErrorCode = Reg.h.al;                   /* Error returned in AL.       */
        if (ErrorCode == 0)
                {
                FilError = NOERROR;
                return (NOERROR);
                }
    else
        {
        FilError = NODEL;
        return (NODEL);
        }
        }
    } /* end FilDelVolid */
```

Figure 4.1: FIL.C: Functions for managing files, directories, and volume labels (continued)

```
                                    /* Structures for FilGetTime and FilSetTime. */
static struct                   /* File date.                              */
    {
    unsigned Day   : 5;
    unsigned Month : 4;
    unsigned Year  : 7;         /* Year minus 1980.                        */
    }
FileDate;

static struct                   /* File time.                              */
    {
    unsigned TwoSeconds : 5;    /* Number of seconds / 2.                  */
    unsigned Minutes    : 6;
    unsigned Hours      : 5;
    }
FileTime;


int FilGetTime (char *FilePath,char *Date,char *Time)
/*
    This function writes the modification data and time for file given by
    'FilePath' to the strings 'Date' and 'Time'.
*/
    {
    int Handle;

    if ((Handle = open (FilePath,O_RDONLY)) == -1)  /* First open the file.*/
        {
        FilError = NOOPEN;
        return (NOOPEN);
        }
    /* Call Microsoft C function.                                          */
    if (_dos_getftime (Handle, (unsigned *)&FileDate, (unsigned *)&FileTime))
        {
        close (Handle);             /* Close file and return.             */
        FilError = NOACC;                                                  */
        return (NOACC);
        }
                                    /* Format the returned date and time.  */
    sprintf (Date,"%02d/%02d/%02d",FileDate.Month,FileDate.Day,
            FileDate.Year + 80);
    sprintf (Time,"%02d:%02d",FileTime.Hours,FileTime.Minutes);

    close (Handle);                 /* Close file and return.             */

    FilError = NOERROR;
    return (NOERROR);

    } /* end FilGetTime */


int FilSetTime (char *FilePath,char *Date,char *Time)
/*
```

Figure 4.1: FIL.C: Functions for managing files, directories, and volume labels (continued)

```
    This function sets the date and time of the file matching the path
    given by 'FilePath' according to the strings 'Date' and 'Time.'  'Date'
    must have the format 'mm/dd/yy' or 'mm-dd-yy', and 'Time' must have the
    format 'hh:mm', in 24 hour time.  Note that all digits, including 0's,
    must be filled in (e.g., "09/05/87").  No checking is made for invalid
    dates (e.g. "09/31/87") or times (e.g. "25:65").  The following error
    codes may be returned:

        NOERROR   No problem.
        NOOPEN    Could not open the file to get the required handle.
        BADDATE   Invalid date format.
        BADTIME   Invalid time format.
        NOACC     Cannot access file to set time.
*/

{
int Handle;

if ((Handle = open (FilePath,O_RDONLY)) == -1)        /* First open file.  */
    {
    close (Handle);
    FilError = NOOPEN;
    return (NOOPEN);
    }
if ((FileDate.Month = atoi (Date)) == 0)              /* Convert month.     */
    {
    close (Handle);
    FilError = BADDATE;
    return (BADDATE);
    }
if ((FileDate.Day = atoi (Date+3)) == 0)              /* Convert day.       */
    {
    close (Handle);
    FilError = BADDATE;
    return (BADDATE);
    }
if ((FileDate.Year = atoi (Date+6)) == 0)             /* Convert year.      */
    {
    close (Handle);
    FilError = BADDATE;
    return (BADDATE);
    }
FileDate.Year -= 80;
if ((FileTime.Hours = atoi (Time)) == 0)              /* Convert hours.     */
    {
    close (Handle);
    FilError = BADTIME;
    return (BADTIME);
    }
if ((FileTime.Minutes = atoi (Time+3)) == 0)          /* Convert minutes.   */
    {
    close (Handle);
    FilError = BADTIME;
    return (BADTIME);
    }
FileTime.TwoSeconds = 0;                              /* Set seconds to 0. */
```

Figure 4.1: FIL.C: Functions for managing files, directories, and volume labels (continued)

```
              /* Call Microsoft C function.                          */
              if (_dos_setftime (Handle, *(unsigned *)&FileDate,
                                 *(unsigned *)&FileTime))
                  {                               /* Error occurred.        */
                  close (Handle);                 /* Close file and return. */
                  FilError = NOACC;
                  return (NOACC);
                  }
              else
                  {                               /* No error.              */
                  close (Handle);                 /* Close file and return. */
                  FilError = NOERROR;
                  return (NOERROR);
                  }

              }  /* end FilSetTime */


/*************** Functions for opening up to 255 file handles **************/

int FilOpen (char *FilePath,int Access,int Permiss)
/*
      This function returns a file number which must be passed by the
      application to 'FilHandle' immediately prior to calling a standard
      low-level C file handle function.  If an error is encountered, it
      returns -1 and sets 'FilError' to an error code.  Possible values of
      'FilError' are:

              NOERROR   No problem.
              NOOPEN    An error occurred when opening the file (test the global
                        C variable 'errno' for more information).
*/
      {
      unsigned char far *FtPtr;      /* Far pointer to the PSP file table   */
                                     /* entry for handle 5.                 */

      FP_SEG (FtPtr) = _psp;         /* Assign file table address.          */
      FP_OFF (FtPtr) = 0x1d;

      *FtPtr = 0xff;                 /* Mark this handle free.              */
      if (open (FilePath,Access,Permiss) == -1)   /* Now open the file.     */
          {
          FilError = NOOPEN;
          return (-1);
          }
      FilError = NOERROR;
      return (*FtPtr);     /* Return the internal DOS file number to be used */
                           /* to refer to the file in subsequent functions.  */

      }  /* end FilOpen */


int FilHandle (int FileNumber)
/*
      This function takes the 'FileNumber' which was passed to the application
      by 'FilOpen' and places it in the DOS file table entry for handle 5, so
      that the next low-level function call that is passed handle 5 will
      access the appropriate file.  For convenience, this function returns the
      file handle value of 5 so that the function call can be used as a
      parameter to the C file handle function.
*/
```

Figure 4.1: FIL.C: Functions for managing files, directories, and volume labels (continued)

```
            {
            unsigned char far *FtPtr;      /* Far pointer to the PSP file table  */
                                           /* entry for handle 5.                */

            FP_SEG (FtPtr) = _psp;         /* Assign file table address.         */
            FP_OFF (FtPtr) = 0x1d;
            *FtPtr = (unsigned char)FileNumber; /* Place file number in file table.*/
            return (5);                    /* Return handle 5.                   */

            } /* end FilHandle */


/** Functions for transferring data between files and far memory locations.**/


int FilReadFar (int Handle,char far *Buf,int Number)
/*
            This function reads file data directly into a 'far' buffer (a buffer
            located outside the default C data segment).  It is useful for reading
            data into an arbitrary memory location (such as video memory) in small
            data model C programs.  It returns and sets 'FilError' to one of the
            following two values:

                  NOERROR       Function was successful.
                  READERROR     Error occurred while reading file.
*/
            {
            union REGS Reg;
            struct SREGS SReg;

            Reg.x.bx = Handle;             /* File handle.                       */
            Reg.x.cx = Number;             /* Number of bytes to read.           */
            SReg.ds = FP_SEG (Buf);        /* Segment address of target buffer*/
            Reg.x.dx = FP_OFF (Buf);       /* Offset address of target buffer.   */
            Reg.x.ax = 0x3f00;             /* Specify DOS read service.          */
            int86x (0x21, &Reg, &Reg, &SReg); /* Invoke DOS services.            */

            if (Reg.x.cflag)               /* Carry flag is set on error.        */
                  {
                  FilError = READERROR;
                  return (READERROR);
                  }

            FilError = NOERROR;
            return (NOERROR);

            } /* end FilReadFar */


int FilWriteFar (int Handle,char far *Buf,int Number)
/*
            This function writes data to a file directly from a 'far' buffer (a
            buffer located outside the default C data segment).  It is useful for
            writing data from an arbitrary memory location (such as video memory) in
            small data model C programs.  It returns and sets 'FilError' to one of
            the following two values:

                  NOERROR       Function was successful.
                  WRITEERROR    Error occurred while writing to file.
*/
```

Figure 4.1: FIL.C: Functions for managing files, directories, and volume labels (continued)

```
    {
    union REGS Reg;
    struct SREGS SReg;

    Reg.x.bx = Handle;                  /* File handle.                   */
    Reg.x.cx = Number;                  /* Number of bytes to write.      */
    SReg.ds = FP_SEG (Buf);             /* Segment address of source buffer*/
    Reg.x.dx = FP_OFF (Buf);            /* Offset address of source buffer.*/
    Reg.x.ax = 0x4000;                  /* Specify DOS write service.     */
    int86x (0x21, &Reg, &Reg, &SReg);   /* Invoke DOS services.           */

    if (Reg.x.cflag)                    /* Carry flag is set on error.    */
        {
        FilError = WRITEERROR;
        return (WRITEERROR);
        }

    FilError = NOERROR;
    return (NOERROR);

    } /* end FilWriteFar */
```

Figure 4.1: FIL.C: Functions for managing files, directories, and volume labels (continued)

```
    int FilRenameDir (char *OldDir,char *NewDir);
    char *FilGetVolid (unsigned char Drive);
    int FilSetVolid (unsigned char Drive, char *Volid);
    int FilDelVolid (unsigned char Drive);
    int FilGetTime (char *FilePath,char *Date,char *Time);
    int FilSetTime (char *FilePath,char *Date,char *Time);
    int FilReadFar (int Handle,char far *Buf,int Number);
    int FilWriteFar (int Handle,char far *Buf,int Number);
    int FilOpen (char *FilePath,int Access,int Permiss);
    int FilHandle (int FileNumber);

    #ifdef MODFILE
    int FilError;                  /* Global file module error flag.           */
    #else
    extern int FilError;
    #endif

                                   /* Error return constants.                  */
    #ifndef NOERROR
    #define NOERROR      0   /* No Error.                                       */
    #endif
    #define NODIR        1   /* Directory not found/other rename error.         */
    #define NOVOL        2   /* Volume label not found.                         */
    #define NOCREAT      3   /* Cannot create new volume label.                 */
    #define NOREN        4   /* Cannot rename volume label.                     */
    #define NODEL        5   /* Cannot delete volume label.                     */
    #define NOOPEN       6   /* 'FilGetTime','FilSetTime', or 'FilOpen' can't   */
                             /* open file.                                      */
    #define NOACC        7   /* 'FilGetTime'/'FilSetTime' can't access file.    */
    #define BADDATE      8   /* Invalid date format for 'FilSetTime'.           */
    #define BADTIME      9   /* Invalid time format for 'FilSetTime'.           */
    #define READERROR   10   /* 'FilReadFar' read failure.                      */
    #define WRITEERROR  11   /* 'FilWriteFar' write error.                      */
```

Figure 4.2: FIL.H: Header file that must be included in your program to call functions in FIL.C

If the function is successful, it returns the value NOERROR. (Error codes are defined in FIL.H, listed in Figure 4.2.) Otherwise, it returns the code NODIR, which usually indicates that the old directory was not found, or that the name contained in **NewDir** is used by an existing directory or file. In addition to returning an error code, **FilRenameDir** also assigns the error code to the global variable **FilError**, which is defined in FIL.H and can therefore be accessed by your program. Note that not all of the functions in this module directly return the error code; all of them, however, return a special value indicating that an error occurred and assign the error code to **FilError**.

Figure 4.3 contains a short program that makes use of **FilRenameDir**, and allows you to rename a directory from the command line. Figure 4.4 provides a MAKE file, and Figure 4.5 a QuickC program list for preparing this example program.

How FilRenameDir Works

FilRenameDir uses the MS-DOS service to rename a file, which is invoked by placing 17h in register AH and generating interrupt 21h. Under MS-DOS, a directory is actually a file with a special attribute. This DOS service requires that the address of an *extended file control block* be passed in registers DS:DX. The extended file control block is used to

```
#include <STDIO.H>
#include <PROCESS.H>
#include "FIL.H"

void main (int argc, char *argv[])
    {
    if (argc != 3)
        {
        printf ("usage:  RENDIR [drive:]olddir newdir\n");
        exit (1);
        }
    switch (FilRenameDir (argv [1], argv [2]))
        {
        case NOERROR:
            printf ("Rename successful\n");
            exit (0);
        case NODIR:
            printf ("FilRenameDir error\n");
            exit (1);
        }

    } /* end main */
```

Figure 4.3: FILDEM01.C: A program demonstrating the function
FilRenameDir

```
FILDEM01.OBJ : FILDEM01.C FIL.H
     cl /c /W2 /Zp FILDEM01.C

FIL.OBJ : FIL.C FIL.H
     cl /c /W2 /Zp FIL.C

FILDEM01.EXE : FILDEM01.OBJ FIL.OBJ
     link /NOI /NOD FILDEM01+FIL,,NUL,SLIBCER;
```

Figure 4.4: FILDEM01.M: A MAKE file for FILDEM01.C

```
FILDEM01.C
FIL.C
```

Figure 4.5: A QuickC program list for preparing FILDEM01.C

provide DOS information on the old and new directory names, and is
defined in this module as the static structure **DirFcb**. Two of the fields
of this structure are preassigned: **ExtCode** with the value FFh, a flag that
indicates an extended file control block, and **Code** with the value 10h,
which indicates that the names belong to directories (not data files).

FilRenameDir first checks whether **OldDir** contains a drive specifier
(indicated by a colon in the second position of the string). If a drive is
found, it is converted to a number (1 = A, 2 = B, and so on), and is assigned to the file control block field **OldDrive**. If no drive is found, 0 is
assigned to **OldDrive**, which indicates the default drive. Next, the
remainder of **OldDrive** and **NewDrive** are copied into the appropriate
fields of the file control block, and the offset address of **DirFcb** is assigned to DX (the segment address is already contained in DS). After the
function number 17 h is placed in AH, control passes to DOS by invoking interrupt 21h.

DOS function 17 h returns 0 in register AL if no error occurred, and
FFh in AL if there was an error. **FilRenameDir** tests the value placed in
AL, assigns an appropriate error code to **FilError**, and also returns the
error code to the calling program.

FilGetVolid

Using FilGetVolid

FilGetVolid has the prototype

```
char *FilGetVolid
     (int Drive)
```

and returns the volume label for the drive specified by the parameter **Drive**, where 0 is the default drive, 1 is drive A, 2 is drive B, and so on. (A volume label is a name assigned to a disk or diskette.) If a volume label is found for this drive, the function returns the address of a string containing the label, and sets the global variable **FilError** to NOERROR. If there is no label for the specified drive, **FilGetVolid** returns NULL, and sets **FilError** to NOVOL. (NULL is defined in STDIO.H, and the error code constants are defined in FIL.H, Figure 4.2.) Note that the string containing the volume label will be clobbered with subsequent calls to either **FilGetVolid** or **FilSetVolid**, and therefore it might be necessary to copy it into a safe area if it will be required later in the program.

The program listed in Figure 4.6 demonstrates the use of **FilGetVolid**. This program finds the volume label for the drive specified by the first

```
#include <STDIO.H>
#include <CTYPE.H>
#include "FIL.H"

void main (int argc,char *argv[])
     {
     char *Volid;
     unsigned char Drive;

     if (argc == 1)                 /* No drive on command line; therefore  */
          Drive = 0;                /* specify default drive.               */
     else
                                    /* Convert drive letter to number.      */
          Drive = toupper (argv[1][0]) - 64;

                                    /* Get volume ID.                       */
     if ((Volid = FilGetVolid (Drive)) == NULL)
          printf ("No volume ID was found\n");
     else
          printf ("The volume ID for the specified drive is %s\n",Volid);

     } /* end main */
```

Figure 4.6: FILDEM02.C: A program demonstrating the function **FilGetVolid**

parameter on the command line. The drive letter is converted to the appropriate number (A = 1, and so on) and passed to **FilGetVolid**; or, if there is no parameter, 0 is passed to indicate the default drive. Figure 4.7 lists a MAKE file, and Figure 4.8 provides a QuickC program list.

How FilGetVolid Works

The method used by **FilGetVolid** to obtain a volume label requires two DOS services, and is somewhat confusing. First, **FilGetVolid** must invoke DOS function 1Ah in order to set the default disk transfer area (DTA) to the structure **Dta**, which is defined immediately above the function as a static structure. The address of this new DTA is passed in registers DS:DX. The DTA is used by certain DOS file services (the file control block read and write functions) to transfer data to and from files, and DOS must be apprised of its current location. Here, however, the DTA is used for a special purpose to be described shortly.

FilGetVolid now uses DOS service 11h to search for a volume label. This service will find the first file matching the specifications that the programmer places in an extended file control block (explained above, under **FilRenameDir**), the address of which is passed in registers DS:DX. Note that under MS-DOS a volume label is simply a file with a special attribute. The static structure **VolFcb**, defined at the beginning of the program, is used for the file control block. Note that several fields are preassigned: **ExtCode** to FFh, which earmarks an extended file control

```
FILDEM02.OBJ : FILDEM02.C FIL.H
    cl /c /W2 /Zp FILDEM02.C

FIL.OBJ : FIL.C FIL.H        `
    cl /c /W2 /Zp FIL.C

FILDEM02.EXE : FILDEM02.OBJ FIL.OBJ
    link /NOI /NOD FILDEM02+FIL,,NUL,SLIBCER;
```

Figure 4.7: FILDEM02.M: A MAKE file for FILDEM02.C

```
FILDEM02.C
FIL.C
```

Figure 4.8: A QuickC program list for preparing FILDEM02.C

block, **Code** to 08h, which is the file attribute for a volume label, and **OldName** to a series of **?** characters, which matches any name. Thus, this file control block specifies *any* file that has the attribute of being a volume label. The only field now missing is **OldDrive** (this field is some-what misnamed for this function, but the field is shared by **FilRenameDir**). Accordingly, **FilGetVolid** now assigns this field the value of the parameter **Drive**. Next, it places the address of the file control block (**&VolFcb**) into register DX (actually, into the **x.dx** field of the structure **Reg**), and proceeds to invoke interrupt 21h, service 11h.

If DOS manages to find a matching file, it returns 0 in register AL, and otherwise returns FFh in AL. This is the point where the default disk transfer area becomes important. If DOS does find a volume label, it places this label in the default disk transfer area, which is currently assigned to the structure **Dta**. The label is put in the field labeled **OldVolid** within this structure. (Other fields in the structure are also assigned, creating a *valid unopened extended file control block*. See the DOS technical reference for details.) Thus, **FilGetVolid** returns the address of the **OldVolid** field if a label was found (and sets **FilError** to NOERROR), or returns NULL if no label was found (and sets **FilError** to NOVOL).

FilSetVolid

Using FilSetVolid

The **FilSetVolid** function has the prototype

```
int FilSetVolid
     (int Drive,
      char *Volid)
```

and sets the volume label of the drive specified by the parameter **Drive** to the string **Volid**. **Drive** should be 1 for drive A:, 2 for drive B:, and so on; a value of 0 indicates the current logged drive. **Volid** is a string up to 11 characters in length. The function returns NOERROR if successful, and otherwise returns either NOCREAT if it was unable to create a new volume label, or NOREN if it was unable to rename an existing volume label. (Error constants are also assigned to the global error variable **FilError**; they are defined in FIL.H, Figure 4.2.)

The program in Figure 4.9 illustrates the use of **FilSetVolid**. This program allows the user to set the volume label from the command line. If only one parameter is passed (that is, **argc** is 2), it is assumed to be a volume label for the default drive. If two parameters are passed (that is, **argc** is 3), then the first parameter is assumed to be a volume label and the second parameter a letter specifying a drive. Assuming that the program is converted to an executable file having the name SETVOL.EXE, the syntax would be as follows:

```
SETVOL volname [drive]
```

where the optional parameter **drive** is the letter of the drive, such as **A**, **B**, or **C**. Note that the program converts the letter drive designation to

```
#include <STDIO.H>
#include <CTYPE.H>
#include <PROCESS.H>
#include "FIL.H"

void main (int argc,char *argv[])
    {
    unsigned char Drive;

    switch (argc)
        {
        case 2:                 /* No drive on command line;  therefore  */
            Drive = 0;          /* specify default drive.                */
            break;

        case 3:                 /* Convert drive letter to number.       */
            Drive = toupper (argv [2][0]) - 64;
            break;

        default:                /* Invalid number of arguments.          */
            printf ("Usage:  SETVOL volname [drive]\n");
            exit (1);
        }
                                /* Set the volume label.                 */
    switch (FilSetVolid (Drive,argv [1]))
        {
        case NOERROR:
            printf ("Volume label set\n");
            break;

        case NOCREAT:
            printf ("Cannot create new volume label\n");
            exit (1);

        case NOREN:
            printf ("Cannot rename volume label\n");
            exit (1);
        }

    } /* end main */
```

Figure 4.9: FILDEM03.C: A program demonstrating the function **FilSetVolid**

the appropriate numerical value before calling **FilSetVolid**. Figure 4.10 provides a MAKE file and Figure 4.11 a QuickC program list for preparing the executable file.

How FilSetVolid Works

FilSetVolid first calls **FilGetVolid** to determine whether a volume label already exits. If no volume label exists (that is, **FilGetVolid** returns NULL), then it must create a new one, using the DOS "create file" service, number 16h. (Remember that a volume label is simply a file with a special attribute.) First, it copies the parameter **Volid** into the **OldName** field of the file control block **VolFcb**, padding this field on the right with blanks if necessary. As explained in the section on How **FilGetVolid** Works, the other required fields of **VolFcb** have already been initialized, and the **OldDrive** field gets set through the call to **FilGetVolid**. The function now moves the address of the file control block into the **Reg** field for register DX and invokes interrupt 21h, service number 16h. On function return, the appropriate error code is assigned to **FilError** and is also returned directly to the calling program.

If, however, a volume label already exists, then it must be renamed using DOS service 17 h (the same service that is used by **FilRenameDir**). Since the function **FilGetVolid** was just called successfully, all of the fields of the structure **Dta** have been assigned by DOS (see the explanation of **FilGetVolid**), except for the field **NewVolid**. Accordingly, the

```
FILDEM03.OBJ : FILDEM03.C FIL.H
     cl /c /W2 /Zp FILDEM03.C

FIL.OBJ : FIL.C FIL.H
     cl /c /W2 /Zp FIL.C

FILDEM03.EXE : FILDEM03.OBJ FIL.OBJ
     link /NOI /NOD FILDEM03+FIL,,NUL,SLIBCER;
```

Figure 4.10: FILDEM03.M: A MAKE file for the program FILDEM03.C

```
FILDEM03.C
FIL.C
```

Figure 4.11: A QuickC program list for preparing FILDEM03.C

parameter **Volid** is now transferred to **Dta.NewVolid**, and blanks are padded on the right as necessary. Next, the offset address of **Dta** is transferred to the register DX field of **Reg**, and interrupt 21h, service 17 h is generated. Again, on function return, the appropriate error code is assigned to the global error variable and also returned directly to the calling program.

FilDelVolid

Using FilDelVolid

The function **FilDelVolid** has the prototype

```
int FilDelVolid
        (int Drive)
```

and removes the volume label from the drive specified by **Drive**, where 0 refers to the default drive, 1 to drive A, 2 to drive B, and so on. This function returns NOERROR if successful, NOVOL if no volume label is found, or NODEL if it encounters an error when deleting an existing label. (Error constants are also assigned to the global error variable **FilError**; they are defined in FIL.H, Figure 4.2.)

Figure 4.12 lists a short program that employs **FilDelVolid** to remove a volume label from the drive specified on the command line (as a letter). If no parameter is passed, then the program passes a 0 to **FilDelVolid** to specify the current default drive. Figure 4.13 is a MAKE file and Figure 4.14 a QuickC program list for processing this program.

How FilDelVolid Works

FilDelVolid first calls **FilGetVolid** to determine whether a volume label exists for the specified drive, and to fill in the fields of **Dta** if the label exists. If there is no volume label, it immediately returns the error code NOVOL. Otherwise, it proceeds to delete the label using the DOS "delete file" service, number 13h. As mentioned in the explanations of the previous two functions, when DOS successfully finds a file (through DOS service 11h called by **FilGetVolid**) it automatically fills in most of the fields of the disk transfer address structure **Dta**. Therefore, since **FilDelVolid** first calls **FilGetVolid**, it need only pass DOS the address

```
#include <STDIO.H>
#include <CTYPE.H>
#include <PROCESS.H>
#include "FIL.H"

void main (int argc,char *argv[])
    {
    unsigned char Drive;

    switch (argc)
        {
        case 1:                 /* No drive on command line;  therefore    */
            Drive = 0;          /* specify default drive.                   */
            break;

        case 2:                 /* Convert drive letter to number.         */
            Drive = toupper (argv [1][0]) - 64;
            break;

        default:                /* Invalid number of arguments.            */
            printf ("Usage:  DELVOL [drive]\n");
            exit (1);
        }

    switch (FilDelVolid (Drive))            /* Delete volume label.    */
        {
        case NOERROR:
            printf ("Volume label deleted\n");
            break;

        case NOVOL:
            printf ("Cannot find volume label\n");
            exit (1);

        case NODEL:
            printf ("Cannot delete volume label\n");
            exit (1);
        }

    } /* end main */
```

Figure 4.12: FILDEM04.C: A program that uses **FilDelVolid** to remove a volume label

```
FILDEM04.OBJ : FILDEM04.C FIL.H
     cl /c /W2 /Zp FILDEM04.C

FIL.OBJ : FIL.C FIL.H
     cl /c /W2 /Zp FIL.C

FILDEM04.EXE : FILDEM04.OBJ FIL.OBJ
     link /NOI /NOD FILDEM04+FIL,,NUL,SLIBCER;
```

Figure 4.13: A MAKE file for FILDEM04.C

```
FILDEM04.C
FIL.C
```

Figure 4.14: A QuickC program list for preparing FILDEM04.C

of **Dta** (in register DX) and invoke interrupt 21h, service 13h. This DOS service returns 0 in register AL if successful, and FFh if an error occurs. Accordingly, **FilDelVolid** returns either NOERROR for success, or NODEL for failure.

FilGetTime

Using FilGetTime

FilGetTime, which has the prototype

```
int FilGetTime
    (char *FilePath,
    char *Date,
    char *Time)
```

obtains the modification date and time for the file specified by **FilePath** (which may include a full path name). Unlike the Microsoft C function **_dos_getftime**, which returns numeric values, this function formats the values as strings. The date is written to the string pointed to by the parameter **Date**, in the format mm/dd/yy, and therefore the receiving string needs to be at least nine bytes long (the string is NULL terminated). The time is written as hh:mm within the string pointed to by **Time**, which needs to be at least six bytes long. If successful, the function returns NOERROR; otherwise it returns NOOPEN if it was unable to open the file, or NOACC if it was unable to obtain the file time. (Error constants are also assigned to the global error variable **FilError**; they are defined in FIL.H, Figure 4.2.)

The program listed in Figure 4.15 demonstrates the use of this function, obtaining the file name from the command line, and printing the file modification date and time exactly as they are returned from

FilGetTime. Figures 4.16 and 4.17 provide the usual MAKE file and QuickC program list.

How FilGetTime Works

FilGetTime first opens the file using the low-level standard C library function **open**. (It opens the file in read-only mode to prevent difficulties in case the file has the read-only attribute.) It then calls the Microsoft C library function **_dos_getftime**, which has the prototype

```
int _dos_getftime
     (int handle,
      unsigned *date,
      unsigned *time)
```

```
#include <STDIO.H>
#include <PROCESS.H>
#include "FIL.H"

void main (int argc,char *argv[])
    {
    char Date [9], Time [6];      /* Buffers to hold values loaded by    */
                                  /* 'FilGetTime'.                       */
    if (argc != 2)                /* Invalid number of arguments.        */
        {
        printf ("Usage: GETTIME filepath\n");
        exit (1);
        }
    if (FilGetTime (argv [1],Date,Time))    /* Get file date and time.   */
        {
        printf ("Can't get file date.\n");
        exit (1);
        }
    printf ("File: %s     Date: %s     Time: %s\n",argv [1],Date,Time);

    } /* end main */
```

Figure 4.15: FILDEM05.C: A program demonstrating the function **FilGetTime**

```
FILDEM05.OBJ : FILDEM05.C FIL.H
     cl /c /W2 /Zp FILDEM05.C

FIL.OBJ : FIL.C FIL.H
     cl /c /W2 /Zp FIL.C

FILDEM05.EXE : FILDEM05.OBJ FIL.OBJ
     link /NOI /NOD FILDEM05+FIL,,NUL,SLIBCER;
```

Figure 4.16: FILDEM05.M: A MAKE file for FILDEM05.C

```
FILDEM05.C
FIL.C
```

Figure 4.17: A QuickC program list for preparing FILDEM05.C

passing it the handle that was obtained by opening the file. The function **_dos_getftime** assigns the modification date—encoded as a two-byte numeric value—to the variable pointed to by the second parameter, and it assigns the modification time—also encoded as a two-byte numeric value—to the variable pointed to by the third parameter. The date and time are encoded using the standard MS-DOS formats. The module FIL.C defines two structures that allow access to the individual time and date values. The date is stored in the structure **FileDate**, which is defined as follows:

```
static struct
    {
    unsigned Day    : 5;
    unsigned Month  : 4;
    unsigned Year   : 7;
    }
FileDate;
```

Note that the overall size of this structure is 16 bits (the individual elements are known as *bit fields*, which are sets of adjacent bits within a single integer). The structure conforms to the DOS date formatting scheme, in which the low-order 5 bits contain the number of the day of the month, the next four bits the number of the month, and the high-order 7 bits the year (which is equal to the numeric value of the year minus 1980).

The time is stored in the structure **FileTime**, which is defined as follows:

```
static struct
    {
    unsigned TwoSeconds : 5;
    unsigned Minutes    : 6;
    unsigned Hours      : 5;
    }
FileTime;
```

Note that the field **TwoSeconds** contains the number of seconds divided by two (a value between 0 and 29; this field does not contain the full number of seconds, since 31 is the maximum number that can be encoded in 5 bits).

Once **FilGetTime** has obtained the numeric values for the date and time the file was last modified, it uses **sprintf** to format these numbers onto the target strings, and then closes the file.

FilSetTime

Using FilSetTime

The prototype for **FilSetTime** is

```
int FilSetTime
        (char *FilePath,
        char *Date,
        char *Time)
```

This function sets the modification date and time for the file specified by **FilePath**, which may include a full path name but *not* the global file name characters **?** and *****. Unlike the Microsoft C function **_dos_setftime**, which receives numeric values, **FilSetTime** accepts the date and time as strings. The parameter **Date** must point to a string containing the desired date, in the format mm/dd/yy. Any other separator can be used instead of the slash (/), but all digits, including 0's, must be present; for example 09/03/87 is acceptable, but 9/3/87 is not. The string containing the time must be in the format hh:mm, in 24 hour time. Again, other separator characters can be substituted for the colon (:), but *all* digits must be included. The function checks for bad formats, but does not check for impossible dates or times, such as 09/31/87. On success, NOERROR is returned; otherwise, the function returns NOOPEN if the file could not be opened, BADDATE or BADTIME if the date or time formats are invalid, or NOACC if the file modification date could not be changed. (Error constants are also assigned to the global error variable **FilError**; they are defined in FIL.H, Figure 4.2.)

The program in Figure 4.18 demonstrates the use of the **FilSetTime** function, and provides a convenient utility for changing the modification date and time of a file. This program is useful for working with

```
#include <STDIO.H>
#include <DOS.H>
#include <PROCESS.H>
#include "FIL.H"

void main (int argc,char *argv[])
    {
    struct dosdate_t DosDate;
    struct dostime_t DosTime;
    char Date [9];
    char Time [6];
    char *DatePtr;
    char *TimePtr;

    switch (argc)
        {
        case 2:                               /* No date or time specified.  */
            _dos_getdate (&DosDate);
            sprintf (Date,"%02d/%02d/%02d",DosDate.month, DosDate.day,
                    DosDate.year-1900);
            DatePtr = Date;
            _dos_gettime (&DosTime);
            sprintf (Time,"%02d:%02d",DosTime.hour,DosTime.minute);
            TimePtr = Time;
            break;

        case 3:                               /* No time specified.          */
            DatePtr = argv [2];
            _dos_gettime (&DosTime);
            sprintf (Time,"%02d:%02d",DosTime.hour,DosTime.minute);
            TimePtr = Time;
            break;

        case 4:                               /* Both date and time specified.  */
            DatePtr = argv [2];
            TimePtr = argv [3];
            break;

        default:                              /* Invalid number of arguments.  */
            printf ("Usage:  TOUCH filename [date] [time]\n");
            exit (1);
        }

                                              /* Set file date and time.     */
    switch (FilSetTime (argv [1],DatePtr,TimePtr))
        {
        case NOERROR:
            printf ("File Date/Time modified\n");
            break;

        case NOOPEN:
            printf ("Could not open %s.\n",argv [1]);
            exit (1);

        case BADDATE:
            printf ("Invalid date format.\n");
            exit (1);
```

Figure 4.18: FILDEM06.C: A utility that uses the function **FilSetTime** to set a file's modification
        date and time

FILE MANAGEMENT FUNCTIONS

```
        case BADTIME:
            printf ("Invalid time format.\n");
            exit (1);

        case NOACC:
            printf ("Could not access %s.\n",argv [1]);
            exit (1);
    }

} /* end main */
```

Figure 4.18: FILDEM06.C: A utility that uses the function **FilSetTime** to set a file's modification date and time (continued)

MAKE files, and it allows you either to specify a particular date and time, or to use the current values. If the program is compiled to an executable file named TOUCH.EXE, the proper syntax would be as follows:

TOUCH filename [date] [time]

The file name parameter is required; the date and time parameters are optional. You may omit the time parameter *or* you may omit both the date and time parameters; you may not, however, omit the date and include the time. The program substitutes the *current* date or time if the corresponding parameter is missing, using the Microsoft C function **_dos_ getdate** or **_dos_ gettime**.

As an enhancement, you might modify this utility to accept the global file name characters * and ? to modify the date and time of an entire set of files (the Microsoft C library functions **_dos_findfirst** and **_dos_findnext** can be used to find the files matching the specification). Figures 4.19 and 4.20 provide a MAKE file and a QuickC program list.

How FilSetTime Works

Like **FilGetTime**, **FilSetTime** first opens the file using **open**, and saves the file handle. It employs the Microsoft C function **_dos_setftime**, which has the prototype

```
int _dos_setftime
        (int handle,
         unsigned date,
         unsigned time)
```

```
FILDEM06.OBJ : FILDEM06.C FIL.H
     cl /c /W2 /Zp FILDEM06.C

FIL.OBJ : FIL.C FIL.H
     cl /c /W2 /Zp FIL.C

FILDEM06.EXE : FILDEM06.OBJ FIL.OBJ
     link /NOI /NOD FILDEM06+FIL,,NUL,SLIBCER;
```

Figure 4.19: FILDEM06.C: A MAKE file for preparing the program

```
FILDEM06.C
FIL.C
```

Figure 4.20: A QuickC program list for preparing FILDEM06.C

The first parameter is the handle of the file that is to have its modification date and time set. The second parameter is the date, encoded in the standard DOS format described in the section on **FilGetTime**, and the third parameter is the time, similarly encoded. Accordingly, **FilSetTime** uses the same structures, **FileDate** and **FileTime**, employed by **FilGetTime**.

FilSetTime uses the standard C library function **atoi** to convert the date and time strings passed as parameters (**Date** and **Time**) to integers, and assigns these values to the appropriate fields of the **FileDate** and **FileTime** structures. The values contained in **FileDate** and **FileTime** are then passed to **_dos_setftime** to set the file's modification date and time. Note that the function **atoi** returns a value of 0 either if the string honestly evaluates to 0, or if the string cannot be converted to an integer; in either case, a 0 return value indicates an invalid string, and **FilSetTime** returns either BADDATE or BADTIME. If an error occurs while setting the file date and time, **_dos_setftime** returns a non-zero value, and **FilSetTime** returns the error code NOACC; otherwise, **FilSetTime** returns NOERROR (these values are also assigned to the global variable **FilError**). Whether or not an error occurs, the file is closed before the function returns.

FilOpen and FilHandle

Using FilOpen and FilHandle

One of the most notorious limitations of MS-DOS versions through 3.2 is that a program cannot have more than 20 file handles open simultaneously. (DOS interrupt 21h, function 67 h removes this limitation, but is available *only* with version 3.3 or later). However, by using the two functions **FilOpen** and **FilHandle**, your program can open up to 255 handles at the same time, under all versions of DOS beginning with 2.0. As these two functions are implemented, they allow you to use the low-level C file functions, such as **read** or **write**, but not the high-level *stream* functions such as **fprintf** or **fwrite**. **FilOpen** and **FilHandle**, however, could be converted for use with the stream functions; this task is left as an exercise for the reader. The following are the required steps for using these functions to circumvent the MS-DOS limit of 20 file handles.

The first step is to specify the desired number of handles in the configuration file (the maximum is 255). For example, if you want to be able to open 31 handles simultaneously, place the following line in CONFIG.SYS:

```
FILES = 31
```

Second, open each file by calling the function **FilOpen**, saving the integer that is returned. This integer will be called a *file number* (to clearly distinguish it from a file *handle*), and must be used to perform any further operations with the file, as will be shown later. You may open up to the total number of files specified in the configuration file; however, if you are using **FilOpen**, *do not use any other C file opening functions*, such as **open**, **sopen**, **creat**, or **fopen**. The prototype for **FilOpen** is

```
int FilOpen
    (char *FilePath,
    int Access,
    int Permiss)
```

The three parameters are the same three that are passed to the standard C function **open**. (See the documentation on **open** in the Microsoft C *Run-Time Library Reference* for an explanation of these parameters.) **Permiss** is required to specify a file permission only if O_CREAT is included in **Access**; if **Permiss** is not needed, you may simply pass a dummy value such as 0 to prevent the compiler from reporting that you have supplied too few parameters. If **FilOpen** encounters an error, it returns -1 and sets **FilError** to NOOPEN; otherwise it returns the file number and sets **FilError** to NOERROR. The following example opens a single file and saves the file number:

```
int FileNumber;
    .
    .
    .
FileNumber = FilOpen (FileName,O_RDWR |
    O_CREAT,S_IREAD | S_IWRITE);
```

Or, if you want to check for an error, use the following expression:

```
if ((FileNumber = FilOpen (FileName,O_RDWR | O_CREAT,
    S_IREAD | S_IWRITE)) == -1)
    /* then call error routine */
```

The third step is to freely use normal low-level C file functions such as **read**, **write**, **tell**, **lseek**, and **close**. However, rather than passing a file handle to these functions (remember, you haven't saved any file handles), you must *first* call **FilHandle**, passing it the file number for the appropriate file, and *then* pass the value returned by **FilHandle** to the C function. The prototype for **FilHandle** is

```
int FilHandle
    (int FileNumber)
```

This process may sound complex, but by nesting the call to **FilHandle** inside the call to the C function, it is the height of simplicity. For example, to write to the file opened above, you could use the expression

```
write (FilHandle (FileNumber), Buffer, BufferSize);
```

where the expression **FilHandle (FileNumber)** is used in place of a normal file handle.

The program in Figure 4.21 demonstrates the **FilOpen** and **FilHandle** functions by opening 31 file handles simultaneously. There are 5 preopened standard handles, and the program creates 26 test files, all of which are open at the same time. The program first executes 26 repetitions of a loop, each of which generates a unique file name and then opens the file using **FilOpen**. The 26 file numbers are stored in an array of 26 integers, **FileNumber**. At the end of this loop there are 31 open file handles. The program then goes into a second loop that writes a line of data to each file using the low-level C function **write**, passing this function the expression

```
FilHandle (FileNumber [i])
```

instead of a file handle. Finally, the program executes a loop that closes the 26 new files using the C **close** function. When the program terminates, you will notice that there are 26 new files on your disk, named TESTA, TESTB, ...,TESTZ.

Note that if you run this program from the command line, you must specify at least 31 files in the configuration file, as explained previously in this section; if, however, you run it within the QuickC environment,

```
#include <STDIO.H>
#include <SYS\TYPES.H>
#include <SYS\STAT.H>
#include <IO.H>
#include <FCNTL.H>
#include <PROCESS.H>
#include "FIL.H"

void main (void)
     {
     register int i;
     int FileNumber [26];
     static char FileName [6] = "TESTx";
     static char TestString [] = "ABCDEFGHIJKLMNOPQRSTUVWXYZ";

     for (i=0;i<26;++i)        /* Create 26 files just to show that they    */
          {                    /* can be open all at once.                  */
          FileName [4] = (char)('A' + i);
          if ((FileNumber [i] = FilOpen (FileName,O_RDWR | O_CREAT,
                                        S_IREAD | S_IWRITE)) == -1)
               {
               printf ("Error opening files\n");
               exit (1);
               }
          }
                                        /* At this point 31 files are open! */

                                        /* Write a string to each file.     */
     for (i = 0; i < 26; ++i)
          write (FilHandle (FileNumber [i]), TestString, sizeof (TestString));

     for (i = 0; i < 26; ++i)            /* Close the 26 files.              */
          close (FilHandle (FileNumber [i]));

     } /* end main */
```

Figure 4.21: FILDEM07.C: A program demonstrating the functions **FilOpen** and **FilHandle**

you must request a greater number of files to provide additional handles for the files opened by QuickC. Figures 4.22 and 4.23 provide a
MAKE file and a QuickC program list for this program.

How FilOpen and FilHandle Work

When MS-DOS loads a program, it sets up a *file table* in the program
segment prefix for that program (or PSP, a 100h byte preamble to your
program containing a variety of important information). Each time you
open a file handle, DOS places its own internal *file number* in the first
available entry of the file table. DOS does not pass this number to your
program; rather, it passes your program an index into the file table,
which points to the actual file number. This index is known as a *file
handle*, and since there is room for only twenty entries in the file table,
there can be only twenty file handles. Basically, **FilOpen** and **FilHandle**
work by using the actual DOS file numbers (of which there can be up to
255), rather than the file handles (of which there can be only 20).

Note that under MS-DOS version 3.3 and later, you can invoke interrupt 21h, function 67 h, to force the system to create an extended file
handle list, which allows the application to open the requested number
of files (up to the limit set by the FILES= command in the configuration
file). The **FilOpen** and **FilHandle** functions, however, can be used
under any version of DOS, beginning with 2.0.

```
FILDEM07.OBJ : FILDEM07.C FIL.H
     cl /c /W2 /Zp FILDEM07.C

FIL.OBJ : FIL.C FIL.H
     cl /c /W2 /Zp FIL.C

FILDEM07.EXE : FILDEM07.OBJ FIL.OBJ
     link /NOI /NOD FILDEM07+FIL,,NUL,SLIBCER;
```

Figure 4.22: FILDEM07.M: A MAKE file for FILDEM07.C

```
FILDEM07.C
FIL.C
```

Figure 4.23: A QuickC program list for preparing FILDEM07.C

FilOpen first initializes a **far** character pointer to point to entry number 5 of the file table (that is, the entry corresponding to handle 5). Why entry 5? Entries 0 through 4 are used by the standard preopened file handles (standard input, output, error, auxiliary device, and printer). **FilOpen** now assigns a value of FFh to this file table position, since FFh is the value used by DOS to mark a free entry in the table. It next calls **open**, which requests that DOS open a file and return a handle. Since DOS always uses the *first* available position in the file table, it is certain that it will place its internal number in entry 5, and therefore return handle 5. **FilOpen** is not interested in the file handle (which it already knows will be 5!); rather, it obtains the internal DOS *file number* by reading directly from the file table, and returns this value to the calling program. The calling program now saves this file number and uses it as explained above.

The story continues when your program is about to perform a file operation, and calls **FilHandle**. The parameter passed to **FilHandle** is the same internal DOS file number that was obtained by **FilOpen**. **FilHandle** now takes this number and places it back in entry number 5 of the file table (again, using a **far** pointer). Therefore, when DOS performs the next operation on file handle 5, it will go to entry 5 of the file table and will find there the internal file number for just the desired file. **FilHandle** then returns 5 for the convenience of the calling pro-gram, which can simply substitute the call to **FilHandle** for a file handle parameter to a C file function.

If you have followed the above strategy, which is not as complex as it seems, you can see that this method allows opening up to 255 files simultaneously using only one file handle!

FilReadFar and FilWriteFar

*Using
FilReadFar and
FilWriteFar*

The functions **FilReadFar** and **FilWriteFar** allow you to exchange data directly between a file and a **far** memory location. A **far** memory location is an area in memory outside of the program's default data segment, which must be addressed using a **far** pointer. (A **far** pointer is 32 bits long, and contains both the offset and segment addresses. Pointers for locations within the program's default data segment need store only the offset, since the DS register already holds the appropriate segment address; such pointers are known as **near** pointers, and are only 16 bits long). In small and medium memory model programs, however, functions such as **read** and **write** accept only **near** pointers. Accordingly, you cannot use these functions for transferring file data to or from **far** memory locations (rather, you would have to use a local buffer to effect the read or write operation, and then transfer the data to or from the **far** address using a function such as **movedata**).

FilReadFar has the prototype

```
int FilReadFar
      (int Handle,
       char far *Buf,
       int Number)
```

and reads the specified number of bytes (**Number**) from a file into the memory buffer addressed by the **far** pointer **Buf**. The file is designated by passing its handle as the first parameter; the file must therefore have been opened using a low-level file function such as **open**. Note that **FilReadFar** is passed the same parameters as the standard C function **read**. **FilReadFar** returns (and assigns to **FilError**) the value NOERROR if successful, or the value READERROR if an error occurs.

FilWriteFar has the prototype

```
int FilWriteFar
      (int Handle,
       char far *Buf,
       int Number)
```

and writes the specified number of bytes (**Number**) from the memory location addressed by the **far** pointer **Buf** to the file whose handle is passed as the first parameter. Note that **FilWriteFar** is analogous to the standard C function **write**. **FilWriteFar** returns (and assigns to **FilError**) the value NOERROR if successful, or the value WRITEERROR if an error occurs.

FilReadFar and **FilWriteFar** can be used in conjunction with the other low-level C file functions, such as **open**, **creat**, **close**, **tell**, and **lseek**.

Figure 4.24 lists a program that demonstrates the use of **FilReadFar** and **FilWriteFar** to transfer screen data directly between a file and the computer's video memory. (Video memory is a buffer contained on the video adapter card; the video hardware automatically displays on the screen all data contained in this buffer.) Video memory must be addressed using a **far** pointer, since it lies well outside the program's data segment. The example program first uses the **ScrGetMode** function to

Video Functions

CHAPTER **5**

determine the exact **far** location of video memory (**ScrGetMode** is explained in Chapter 5; as you will see, in monochrome text mode, video memory begins at address B000h:0000h, and in color text mode, at address B800h:0000h). Next, the program calls the C function **creat** to create a file and then calls **FilWriteFar** to write the current contents of video memory to this file. Performing this step saves the entire current screen image.

The program subsequently calls **ScrClear** and **ScrSetCur** to clear the screen and to position the cursor at the upper-left corner (these functions are explained in Chapter 5). After calling **KbdGetC** to generate a pause, the program proceeds to restore the original screen image by calling **FilReadFar** to read the screen data stored in the file directly into video memory. A MAKE file is provided in Figure 4.25, and a QuickC program list in Figure 4.26.

```
#include <STDIO.H>
#include <SYS\TYPES.H>
#include <SYS\STAT.H>
#include <IO.H>
#include "FIL.H"
#include "SCR.H"
#include "KBD.H"

void main (void)
    {
    struct Mode Mode;
    char far *PtrVideo;
    int FileHandle;

    printf ("Press any key to save contents of the screen in a file...");
    KbdGetC ();

    ScrGetMode (&Mode);
    if (Mode.VideoMode == 7)
        PtrVideo = (char far *)0xb0000000;
    else
        PtrVideo = (char far *)0xb8000000;

    FileHandle = creat ("@SCR@.@@@", S_IWRITE);
    FilWriteFar (FileHandle,PtrVideo,4000);
    ScrClear (0,0,24,79);
    ScrSetCur (0,0,0);
    printf ("Press any key to display screen contents saved in the file...");
    KbdGetC ();

    lseek (FileHandle, 0L, 0);

    FilReadFar (FileHandle,PtrVideo,4000);
    close (FileHandle);

    } /* end main */
```

Figure 4.24: FILDEM08.C: A program demonstrating the functions **FilReadFar** and **FilWriteFar**

How FilReadFar and FilWriteFar Work

FilReadFar works by invoking DOS function 0Fh, which reads from a file or device. Before issuing this interrupt, you must place the segment:offset address of the buffer to receive the data into registers DS:DX. Accordingly, **FilReadFar** uses the **int86x** C function rather than **int86** so that it can set the DS register to the segment address of the target buffer before the interrupt is issued (**int86** and **int86x** are described in Chapter 1). The DOS read function sets the carry flag if an error occurs; **FilReadFar** therefore tests the carry flag (through the structure field **Reg.x.cflag**) after control returns from DOS, and returns the error code READERRROR if the flag is set.

The function **FilWriteFar** is similar to **FilReadFar**, except that it invokes DOS function 40h, which writes to a file or device.

```
FILDEM08.OBJ : FILDEM08.C FIL.H KBD.H SCR.H
      cl /c /W2 /Zp FILDEM08.C

FIL.OBJ : FIL.C FIL.H
      cl /c /W2 /Zp FIL.C

KBDA.OBJ : KBDA.ASM
      masm /MX KBDA.ASM;

SCR.OBJ : SCR.C SCR.H
      cl /c /W2 /Zp SCR.C

FILDEM08.EXE : FILDEM08.OBJ FIL.OBJ KBDA.OBJ SCR.OBJ
      link /NOI /NOD FILDEM08+FIL+KBDA+SCR,,NUL,SLIBCER;
```

Figure 4.25: FILDEM08.M: A MAKE file for FILEDEM08.C

```
FILDEM08.C
FIL.C
KBDA.OBJ
SCR.C
```

Figure 4.26: A QuickC program list for preparing FILDEM08.C

This chapter presents a complete and integrated set of functions for creating fast and attractive screen displays, and for managing the display of windows, on IBM-compatible computers. Chapter 6 continues the treatment of video programming by presenting an interactive editor for creating screens and windows that can be displayed using the functions in this chapter. Also, Chapter 7 presents a set of device-independent graphics functions for producing bit-mapped screen images.

The standard C library offers only primitive methods for producing video output. Functions such as **printf** simply write a stream of characters in teletype fashion at the current cursor position, using the existing display attribute (explained later). Also, these functions route their output through the operating system and are thus incredibly slow. By employing the low-level BIOS services, and by writing directly to video memory, the functions in this chapter not only offer much finer control over video display, but are also orders of magnitude faster than **printf**. In a benchmark presented in the book *MS-DOS Advanced Programming* (see Bibliography), a video display task that took **printf** 52.95 seconds was accomplished in 0.22 seconds using a function that writes directly to video memory, such as those presented here.

The video functions in this chapter are contained in two separate modules: the **Scr** module and the **Buf** module. The **Scr** module (SCR.C and SCRA.ASM) includes the general purpose video routines. The **Buf** module (BUF.C) is comprised of a set of special-purpose functions that collect video output in a buffer larger than the physical screen, and then display this buffer through a window, a portion at a time.

GENERAL PURPOSE VIDEO FUNCTIONS

The functions in this section are designed specifically to take advantage of the display capabilities of the IBM-PC and PS/2 family of computers. Using this set of routines, you can perform the following tasks:

- Obtain or set the current video mode (**ScrGetMode** and **ScrSetMode**).
- Get or set the cursor position and cursor shape, or hide the cursor (**ScrGetCur, ScrSetCur, ScrGetStyle, ScrSetStyle**).

■ Save and restore the current video display on a stack, so that windows can overlay the screen, windows can be moved, and multiple windows can be stacked (**ScrPush, ScrPop**).

■ Read screen data from a file (generated by the screen designer of Chapter 6) into a program buffer (**ScrReadWindow**).

■ Rapidly display screen data from any portion of a video data buffer to a specified position on the screen (**ScrPutWindow**).

■ Display a string instantly on the screen, at a given position, using any video display attribute (**ScrPutS**).

■ Display any size box, at a given position on the screen, using one of four line styles (**ScrPutBox**).

■ Clear a portion of the screen (**ScrClear**).

■ Read a string from a given position on the screen, echoing output using any video attribute, with optional uppercase conversion or automatic field exit (**ScrGetS**).

■ Modify the video display attribute over a section of the screen, without altering existing screen data (**ScrPutAttr**).

■ Determine the type of video adapter (or adapters) currently installed, and the video modes supported (**ScrTypes**).

■ Switch the display between the monochrome screen and the color screen in a system with two monitors installed (**ScrMonoCard** and **ScrColorCard**).

The video functions are designed to work well together, and they form a comprehensive library of routines that will meet the needs of most video-intensive applications. Many examples are given in this chapter to illustrate the use of groups of these functions; the functions are also demonstrated in Chapters 6 and 9.

The functions in this chapter, as well as the screen designer in Chapter 6, should work uniformly with a wide variety of display types, including standard monochrome, Hercules compatible monochrome, EGA, and the VGA and MCGA standards introduced with the PS/2 family of machines. They will also work with many of the compatible CGA (color graphics adapter) displays that are currently available. However, with the original IBM CGA, many of the routines will produce a "snow" or "sparkle" effect; therefore, the last part of this section discusses how the functions can be modified to work with this adapter type.

Note that if you are using QuickC version 1.0 the video functions work best when the calling program is run from the DOS command prompt, rather than being executed within the integrated environment. As you will see, many of these functions directly modify the screen, making it difficult for QuickC version 1.0 to segregate its own video output from that generated by the program. If you are building a program with QuickC 1.0, select the .Exe output option from the Run/Compile/Output Options menu; this setting causes QuickC to prepare a freestanding program that can be run from the DOS command prompt. The video functions all work properly within the QuickC version 2.0 integrated environment.

The C video functions are contained in the file SCR.C, listed in Figure 5.1, and the assembler functions in the file SCRA.ASM, listed in Figure 5.2. To call any of these functions from your C program, you must include the file SCR.H, listed in Figure 5.3, and link your program with the object file SCR.OBJ or SCRA.OBJ, as well as the file KBD.OBJ (produced from KBD.C, presented in Chapter 2).

ScrGetMode and ScrSetMode

*Using
ScrGetMode and
ScrSetMode*

Call **ScrGetMode**, which has the prototype

```
void ScrGetMode
     (struct Mode *ModePtr)
```

to obtain information on the current video mode. You should pass this function the address of a **struct Mode** variable that you have declared in your program. This structure type is defined in SCR.H as follows:

```
struct Mode
     {
     int VideoMode;
     int Columns;
     int VideoPage;
     };
```

ScrGetMode returns information by writing directly to the three fields of this structure. The field **VideoMode** is assigned the current video

```
#include <DOS.H>
#include <STDIO.H>
#include <STDLIB.H>
#include <MEMORY.H>
#include <CTYPE.H>

#include "KBD.H"
#include "SCR.H"

#pragma check_stack (off)        /* Turn off stack checks so that functions  */
                                 /* can be called from interrupt routines.   */

void ScrGetMode (struct Mode *ModePtr)
/*
    This function gets the current video mode, number of display columns,
    and video page.
*/
    {
    union REGS Reg;

    Reg.h.ah = 15;                        /* BIOS get video mode service.   */
    int86 (0x10, &Reg, &Reg);            /* BIOS video services.           */
    ModePtr->VideoMode = Reg.h.al;       /* AL returns mode.               */
    ModePtr->Columns = Reg.h.ah;         /* AH returns number of columns.  */
    ModePtr->VideoPage = Reg.h.bh;       /* BH returns active page.        */

    } /* end ScrGetMode */


void ScrSetMode (struct Mode *ModePtr)
/*
    This function sets the video mode and display page.  Note that the
    'Columns' field is not used and need not be set, since this value is
    implicit in the mode.
*/
    {
    union REGS Reg;

    Reg.h.ah = 0;                        /* BIOS set mode service.         */
    Reg.h.al = (unsigned char)ModePtr->VideoMode;  /* BL specifies mode.   */
    int86 (0x10,&Reg,&Reg);              /* BIOS video services.           */

    Reg.h.ah = 5;                        /* BIOS set active page service.  */
    Reg.h.al = (unsigned char)ModePtr->VideoPage;  /* AL specifies page.   */
    int86 (0x10,&Reg,&Reg);              /* BIOS video services.           */

    } /* end ScrSetMode */


void ScrGetCur (int *Row,int *Col,int Page)
/*
    This function assigns the current cursor position to the variables
    pointed to by Row and Col, for video page Page.
*/
    {
    union REGS Reg;
```

Figure 5.1: SCR.C: The set of C video functions

```
                Reg.h.bh = (unsigned char)Page;   /* BH specifies page.            */
                Reg.h.ah = 3;                     /* Service to get cursor position. */
                int86 (0x10,&Reg,&Reg);           /* BIOS video services.          */

                *Row = Reg.h.dh;                  /* DH returns row.               */
                *Col = Reg.h.dl;                  /* DL returns column.            */

                } /* end ScrGetCur */


        void ScrSetCur (int Row,int Col,int Page)
        /*
            This function positions the cursor as specified by 'Row' and 'Col', for
            video page 'Page'.
        */
                {
                union REGS Reg;

                Reg.h.bh = (unsigned char)Page;   /* BH specifies video page.      */
                Reg.h.dh = (unsigned char)Row;    /* DH specifies cursor row.      */
                Reg.h.dl = (unsigned char)Col;    /* DL specifies cursor column.   */
                Reg.h.ah = 2;                     /* BIOS set cursor position service.*/
                int86 (0x10, &Reg, &Reg);         /* BIOS video services.          */

                } /* end ScrSetCur */


        void ScrGetStyle (int *StartLine,int *StopLine)
        /*
            This function assigns the current cursor starting and stopping lines to
            the variable pointed to by 'StartLine' and 'StopLine'.  These parameters
            determine the current cursor shape or "style".
        */
                {
                union REGS Reg;

                Reg.h.bh = 0;                     /* BH specifies video page.      */
                Reg.h.ah = 3;                     /* Service to get cursor position/style. */
                int86 (0x10,&Reg,&Reg);           /* BIOS video services.          */
                *StartLine = Reg.h.ch;            /* CH returns cursor start line. */
                *StopLine = Reg.h.cl;             /* CL returns cursor stop line.  */

                } /* end ScrGetStyle */


        void ScrSetStyle (int StartLine,int StopLine)
        /*
            This function sets the cursor shape according to the values passed in
            StartLine and StopLine.
        */
                {
                union REGS Reg;

                Reg.h.ch = (unsigned char)StartLine; /* CH specifies start line.   */
                Reg.h.cl = (unsigned char)StopLine;  /* CL specifies stop line.    */
                Reg.h.ah = 1;                        /* BIOS set cursor type function. */
                int86 (0x10,&Reg,&Reg);              /* BIOS video services.       */

                } /* end ScrSetStyle */
```

Figure 5.1: SCR.C: The set of C video functions (continued)

```
/************************** ScrPush/ScrPop *****************************/

#define MAXSCREENS 10

static char *BufPtAr [MAXSCREENS];    /* Elements of this array point to   */
                                      /* the screen storage buffers on the */
                                      /* screen stack.                     */
static int BufIdx = -1;               /* Index to 'BufPtAr'.               */

int ScrPush (void)
/*
    This function saves the contents of the current screen on the screen
    stack.
*/
    {
    int VideoSeg;                     /* Stores video segment address.      */
    unsigned char far *PtrVideoMode = (unsigned char far *)0x00400049;
    char far *FarPtrCh;               /* Temporary far pointer.             */

    if (++BufIdx >= MAXSCREENS)       /* Test if maximum stack size exceeded. */
        return (MAXTOOSMALL);
                                      /* Allocate heap memory for one screen. */
    if ((BufPtAr [BufIdx] = malloc (4000)) == NULL)
        {
        --BufIdx;                     /* Out of heap memory.                */
        return (NOHEAP);
        }

    /* Determine video segment address according to video mode.           */
    VideoSeg = (*PtrVideoMode == 7) ? 0xb000 : 0xb800;

    FarPtrCh = (char far *)BufPtAr [BufIdx];  /* Get far address of buffer.*/

                                      /* Transfer video memory.           */
    movedata (VideoSeg,0,FP_SEG (FarPtrCh),FP_OFF (FarPtrCh),4000);

    return (NOERROR);

    } /* end ScrPush */


int ScrPop (int Remove)
/*
    This function restores the most recently saved screen on the screen
    stack, and removes the screen from the stack IF 'Remove' is non-zero.
*/
    {
    int VideoSeg;                     /* Stores video segment address.      */
    unsigned char far *PtrVideoMode = (unsigned char far *)0x00400049;
    char far *FarPtrCh;               /* Temporary far pointer.             */

    if (BufIdx < 0)                                /* No screens to restore. */
        return (STACKEMPTY);

    /* Determine video segment address according to video mode.           */
    VideoSeg = (*PtrVideoMode == 7) ? 0xb000 : 0xb800;

    FarPtrCh = (char far *)BufPtAr [BufIdx];  /* Get far address of buffer.*/
```

Figure 5.1: SCR.C: The set of C video functions (continued)

```
                                                   /* Transfer video memory.    */
          movedata (FP_SEG (FarPtrCh),FP_OFF (FarPtrCh),VideoSeg,0,4000);

          if (Remove)                              /* Remove screen from stack. */
              free (BufPtAr [BufIdx--]);

          return (NOERROR);

          } /* end ScrPop */

/*******************************************************************************/

#include <FCNTL.H>
#include <IO.H>

int ScrReadWindow (char *Buffer,char *FileName)
/*
     This function reads the 4000 byte screen image file specified by
     'FileName' (may contain a full path), into the buffer pointed to by
     'Buffer.'
*/
     {
     int FileHandle;
                                                   /* Open file.             */
     if ((FileHandle = open (FileName,O_RDONLY|O_BINARY)) == -1)
         return (OPENERR);

     if (read (FileHandle,Buffer,4000) != 4000)     /* Read screen data.    */
         return (READERR);

     if (close (FileHandle) == -1)                  /* Close file.          */
         return (CLOSERR);

     return (NOERROR);

     }  /* end ScrReadWindow */


void ScrPutWindow (char *Buffer,int SourceStartRow,int SourceStartCol,
                   int SourceEndRow,int SourceEndCol,int TargetRow,
                   int TargetCol)
/*
     This function displays the rectangular area of the screen data buffer
     'Buffer' specified by 'SourceStartRow', 'SourceStartCol', 'SourceEndRow',
     and 'SourceEndCol' at the beginning position on the screen given by
     'TargetRow', and 'TargetCol'.
*/
     {
     register int Row, SourceOff;
     int VideoSeg, VideoOff, BytesPerRow;
     unsigned char far *PtrVideoMode = (unsigned char far *)0x00400049;
     char far *FarPtrBuffer;       /* Temporary far pointer.                  */

                     /* Calculate offset of first character in buffer.         */
     SourceOff = FP_OFF (Buffer) + SourceStartRow * 160 + SourceStartCol * 2;
```

Figure 5.1: SCR.C: The set of C video functions (continued)

```
            /* Determine video segment address according to video mode.    */
        VideoSeg = (*PtrVideoMode == 7) ? 0xb000 : 0xb800;

                        /* Calculate offset of first character in video memory. */
        VideoOff = TargetRow * 160 + TargetCol * 2;
                        /* Calculate number of bytes per row.             */
        BytesPerRow = (SourceEndCol - SourceStartCol + 1) * 2;

        FarPtrBuffer = (char far *)Buffer;        /* Get far address of buffer.*/

                        /* Move data to video memory row by row.          */
        for (Row = 1; Row <= SourceEndRow - SourceStartRow + 1 ; ++Row)
            {
            movedata (FP_SEG (FarPtrBuffer),SourceOff,VideoSeg,VideoOff,
                    BytesPerRow);
            SourceOff += 160;        /* Increment offset in buffer.        */
            VideoOff += 160;        /* Increment offset in video memory.   */
            }

        } /* end ScrPutWindow */


void ScrPutS (char *String,unsigned char Attr,
            unsigned char Row,unsigned char Col)
/*
        This function displays null terminated 'String' with video attribute
        'Attr', beginning at the position given by 'Row' and 'Col'.
*/
        {
        register unsigned char A;            /* Fast register storage for Attr. */
        unsigned char far *PtrVideoMode = (unsigned char far *)0x00400049;
        unsigned char far *Video;            /* Far pointer to video memory.   */

        A = Attr;                            /* Store attribute in register.   */

        /* Calculate far pointer to video memory.                          */
        FP_SEG (Video) = (*PtrVideoMode == 7) ? 0xb000 : 0xb800;
        FP_OFF (Video) = Row * 160 + Col * 2;

        while (*String)            /* Write characters from string until null. */
            {
            *Video++ = *String++;
            *Video++ = A;
            }

        } /* end ScrPutS */


void ScrPutBox (int ULR,int ULC,int LRR,int LRC,int Style)
/*
        This function displays a box on the screen starting at row and column
        'ULR' and 'ULC' and ending at row and column 'LRR' and 'LRC'. 'Style'
        selects the line style, and may be between 0 and 3.
*/
        {
        register int i;          /* Loop counter.                    */
        int Delta1, Delta2;      /* Bytes between lines.             */
                                 /* Store the box characters for each style. */
```

Figure 5.1: SCR.C: The set of C video functions (continued)

```
        static char ulc [] = {218,201,213,214};
        static char urc [] = {191,187,184,183};
        static char llc [] = {192,200,212,211};
        static char lrc [] = {217,188,190,189};
        static char hl  [] = {196,205,205,196};
        static char vl  [] = {179,186,179,186};
        char far *Video;          /* Far pointer to video memory.        */
        unsigned char far *PtrVideoMode = (unsigned char far *)0x00400049;

        Delta1 = (LRC - ULC) * 2;        /* Bytes between 2 vertical lines. */
        Delta2 = 160 - Delta1;           /* Bytes between right vertical    */
                                         /* line and left vertical line of  */
                                         /* next row.                       */

        /* Initialize far pointer to video memory, upper left corner of box. */
        FP_SEG (Video) = (*PtrVideoMode == 7) ? 0xb000 : 0xb800;
        FP_OFF (Video) = ULR*160+ULC*2;

        *Video = ulc [Style];               /* Draw upper left corner.    */
        Video += 2;                         /* Skip attribute byte.       */
        for (i = 1; i <= LRC - ULC - 1; ++i)   /* Draw top horizontal line.  */
            {
            *Video = hl [Style];
            Video += 2;
            }
        *Video = urc [Style];               /* Draw upper right corner.   */
        Video += Delta2;
        for (i = 1; i <= LRR - ULR - 1; ++i)   /* Draw both vertical lines.  */
            {
            *Video = vl [Style];            /* Left vertical line.        */
            Video += Delta1;
            *Video = vl [Style];            /* Right vertical line.       */
            Video += Delta2;
            }
        *Video = llc [Style];               /* Draw lower left corner.    */
        Video += 2;
        for (i = 1; i <= LRC - ULC - 1; ++i)   /* Draw bottom horizontal line.*/
            {
            *Video = hl [Style];
            Video += 2;
            }
        *Video = lrc [Style];               /* Draw lower right corner.   */

        } /* end ScrPutBox */


void ScrClear (unsigned char StartRow,unsigned char StartCol,
                unsigned char StopRow,unsigned char StopCol)
/*
    This function clears the rectangular section of the screen specified
    by the four parameters.
*/
        {
        union REGS Reg;
```

Figure 5.1: SCR.C: The set of C video functions (continued)

```
            Reg.h.bh = 0x07;          /* Use normal, white on black video attribute.*/
            Reg.h.ch = StartRow;      /* CH specifies start row.                     */
            Reg.h.cl = StartCol;      /* CL specifies start column.                  */
            Reg.h.dh = StopRow;       /* DH specifies stop row.                      */
            Reg.h.dl = StopCol;       /* DL specifies stop column.                   */
            Reg.x.ax = 0x0600;        /* BIOS scroll page up function.               */
            int86 (0x10,&Reg,&Reg);   /* Invoke BIOS video services.                 */

            } /* end ScrClear */


    int ScrGetS (char *Buffer,int Attr,int Row,int Col,int Length,int Mode)
    /*
            This function reads characters into 'Buffer', echoing the input starting
            at 'Row' and 'Column', using video attribute 'Attr'.  Characters are
            read until an exit key (CR, Esc, or arrow) is encountered, or until the
            number read is one less than the specified buffer size, 'Length'.  If
            the first key pressed is an exit key, the buffer is unaltered.
            Otherwise, the buffer is initially filled with blanks and terminated
            with a null; therefore, the resulting string will be blank padded on the
            right.  The terminating exit key is not placed into the buffer.  The
            'Length' parameter should equal the 'sizeof' the receiving buffer.

            The 'Mode' parameter can specify one or more of the following features
            (constants defined in SCR.H):

                NOFEAT:   No 'Mode' features specified.
                AUTOEXIT: Exit field automatically when buffer is full.
                UPPER:    Convert all letters to upper case.

            The function returns one of the following codes indicating the field
            exit key pressed by the user:

                -1    <Esc>
                 0    <Cr>
                 1    <Left-Arrow>
                 2    <Right-Arrow>
                 3    <Up-Arrow>
                 4    <Down-Arrow>
                 5    Automatic exit (last character entered and AUTOEXIT selected).

    */
            {
            register int CurCol,i;       /* Current column/loop index.             */
            int far *Video;              /* Far pointer to video memory.           */
            int Key;                     /* Stores input key value.                */
            int FirstChar = 1;           /* Flag to indicate the first character.  */
            char *ChPt;                  /* For filling buffer with blanks.        */
            int far *IntFP;              /* For writing blanks to screen.          */
            unsigned char far *PtrVideoMode = (unsigned char far *)0x00400049;

            CurCol = Col;                              /* Initialize current column.   */

            /* Initialize far pointer to video memory.                                */
            FP_SEG (Video) = (*PtrVideoMode == 7) ? 0xb000 : 0xb800;
            FP_OFF (Video) = Row*160+Col*2;

            ScrSetCur (Row,CurCol,0);  /* Place cursor at first character position.*/
```

Figure 5.1: SCR.C: The set of C video functions (continued)

```
        for (;;)                        /* Keyboard read loop.            */
        switch (Key = KbdGetC ())
             {
             case 0x011b:                    /* Escape.                   */
                  return (-1);
             case 0x4b00:                    /* Left arrow.               */
                  return (1);
             case 0x4d00:                    /* Right arrow.              */
                  return (2);
             case 0x4800:                    /* Up arrow.                 */
                  return (3);
             case 0x5000:                    /* Down arrow.               */
                  return (4);
             case 0x1c0d:                    /* Return.                   */
                  return (0);
             case 0x0e08:                    /* Backspace.                */
                  if (CurCol > Col)          /* Process if right of first column.*/
                       {
                       ScrSetCur (Row,--CurCol,0);    /* Move cursor back.     */
                       *--Video = (Attr << 8) | ' ';  /* Write blanks.         */
                       *--Buffer = ' ';
                       }
                  break;
             default:
                  if (CurCol >= Col + Length - 1)     /* Test end of buffer.     */
                       break;
                  if ((Key & 0x00ff) == 0)        /* Test for non-ASCII character*/
                       break;
                  if (Mode & UPPER)               /* Upper case conversion.    */
                       Key = toupper (Key & 0x00ff);
                  else
                       Key &= 0x00ff;             /* Remove extended code.     */
                                    /* Place key in video memory and buffer. */
                  *Video++ = (Attr << 8) | Key;
                  *Buffer++ = (char)Key;
                  ScrSetCur (Row,++CurCol,0);   /* Update cursor position.   */
                  if (FirstChar)        /* Blank fill buffer on first character. */
                       {
                       FirstChar = 0;
                       ChPt = Buffer;
                       IntFP = Video;
                       for (i = 1; i <= Length - 2; ++i)
                            {
                            *ChPt++ = ' ';
                            *IntFP++ = (Attr << 8) | ' ';
                            }
                       *ChPt = '\0';
                       }
                                              /* Test for auto-exit.     */
                  if ((CurCol >= Col + Length - 1) && (Mode & AUTOEXIT))
                       return (5);              /* Code for autoexit.      */
                  break;

             } /* end switch */

        } /* end ScrGetS */
```

Figure 5.1: SCR.C: The set of C video functions (continued)

```
void ScrPutAttr (int Attr,int StartRow,int StartCol,int StopRow,int StopCol)
/*
    This function displays the video display attribute 'Attr' on the
    rectangular area of the screen specified by the last four parameters,
    without altering existing screen data.
*/
    {
    register int Row,Col;                /* Row and column counters.        */
    int CharPerRow,Delta;
    char far *Video;                     /* Far pointer to video memory.    */
    unsigned char far *PtrVideoMode = (unsigned char far *)0x00400049;

    /* Initialize far pointer to first attribute in video memory.           */
    FP_SEG (Video) = (*PtrVideoMode == 7) ? 0xb000 : 0xb800;
    FP_OFF (Video) = (StartRow*160+StartCol*2)+1;

                                 /* Calculate characters per row.           */
    CharPerRow = StopCol - StartCol + 1;

                                 /* Calculate increment value between rows. */
    Delta = 160 - (StopCol - StartCol + 1) * 2;

                                 /* Transfer attributes row by row.         */
    for (Row = 1; Row <= StopRow - StartRow + 1; ++Row)
        {
        for (Col = 1; Col <= CharPerRow; ++Col) /* Display a row.           */
            {
            *Video = (char)Attr;         /* Write the attribute.            */
            Video += 2;                  /* Increment to next attribute.    */
            }

        Video += Delta;                  /* Increment to next row.          */
        }

    } /* end ScrPutAttr */

void ScrMonoCard (void)
/*
    This function activates the monochrome adapter card on a system with
    both a color card/monitor and a monochrome card/monitor.
*/
    {
    struct Mode ModeStruct;   /* Used to specify video mode for ScrSetMode. */
                              /* Pointer to the BIOS equipment flag:        */
    unsigned far *PtrEquipFlag = (unsigned far *)0x00400010;

    *PtrEquipFlag |= 0x0030;   /* Set BIOS equipment flag to mono adapter.  */
    ModeStruct.VideoMode = 7;  /* Specify monochrome text mode.             */
    ModeStruct.VideoPage = 0;  /* Specify video page 0.                     */
    ScrSetMode (&ModeStruct);  /* Set the video mode.                       */

    } /* end ScrMonoCard */
```

Figure 5.1: SCR.C: The set of C video functions (continued)

```
    void ScrColorCard (void)
    /*
         This function activates the color adapter card on a system with
         both a color card/monitor and a monochrome card/monitor.
    */
         {
         struct Mode ModeStruct;   /* Used to specify video mode for ScrSetMode. */
                                   /* Pointer to the BIOS equipment flag:        */
         unsigned far *PtrEquipFlag = (unsigned far *)0x00400010;

         *PtrEquipFlag &= 0xffcf;       /* Set video adapter bits to indicate   */
         *PtrEquipFlag |= 0x0020;       /* an 80 column color card.             */
         ModeStruct.VideoMode = 3;      /* Specify 80 column color text mode.   */
         ModeStruct.VideoPage = 0;      /* Specify video page 0.                */
         ScrSetMode (&ModeStruct);      /* Set the video mode.                  */

         } /* end ScrColorCard */
```

Figure 5.1: SCR.C: The set of C video functions (continued)

mode number. Table 5.1 lists the video mode numbers for IBM PC, PC AT, and PS/2 machines.

The field **Columns** is assigned the current number of text columns, and the field **VideoPage** is assigned the current video page. Monochrome adapters have only page 0; standard color graphics adapters have pages 0–3 in 80-column text modes, and pages 0–7 in 40-column text modes. The default *active* page (that is, currently displayed) is 0. However, using BIOS services you can write to any video page and then instantly display that page by making it active (using **ScrSetMode**). The functions in this chapter, which must work uniformly with monochrome or color adapters, do not use multiple video pages.

Call the function **ScrSetMode**, which has the prototype

```
    void ScrSetMode
        (struct Mode *ModePtr)
```

to set the current video mode and active display page. Again, you must declare a structure of type **struct Mode** in your program. Set the field **VideoMode** to the desired video mode, and the field **VideoPage** to the desired video page, and pass the address of the structure to **ScrSetMode**. Note that you do not need to set the field **Columns**, since the num-ber of columns is implicit in the chosen video mode, and the value of this field will have no effect.

Note also that **ScrGetMode** and **ScrSetMode** do not detect or permit you to switch into the Hercules monochrome graphics mode. As you will see, these two functions rely on the services of the system

```
          .MODEL LARGE

          ;Return values for _ScrTypes:
                                              ;MODES SUPPORTED:
          VMDA        equ     01              ;7.
          VHGC        equ     02              ;Hercules 720 x 348 mono. graphics.
          VCGA        equ     04              ;0, 1, 2, 3, 4, 5, 6.
          VEGAM       equ     08              ;7, F.
          VEGAC       equ     16              ;0, 1, 2, 3, 4, 5, 6, D, E, 10.
          VPS2        equ     32              ;Call int 10h, function 1bh to get
                                              ;list of supported modes.
          .DATA
          Video       dw      ?               ;_ScrTypes:  holds adapter types.

          .CODE

          PUBLIC _ScrTypes
          ;
          ;       Prototype:
          ;               int far ScrTypes
          ;                       (void);
          ;
          ;       This function returns a code indicating the video adapter type or
          ;       types currently installed (possible return values are defined at the
          ;       beginning of this file).
          ;
          _ScrTypes PROC
                      mov     video, 0        ;Initialize video flag w/ no attributes.

                                              ;*** Test for MDA. ***
                                              ;Test for 6845 monochrome registers.
                      mov     dx, 03b4h       ;Index register.
                      mov     al, 0fh         ;Select register 0fh.
                      out     dx, al          ;Write to index register.
                      mov     dx, 03b5h       ;Data register.
                      in      al, dx          ;Read register 0fh.
                      mov     ah, al          ;Store value read in AH.
                      mov     al, 99h         ;Write a number to the register.
                      out     dx, al
                      mov     cx, 512         ;Pause.
          a01:
                      loop    a01
                      in      al, dx          ;Now read the register back.
                      xchg    ah, al          ;Restore saved register value.
                      out     dx, al
                      cmp     ah, 99h         ;Compare value read to value written.
                      jne     a02             ;No MDA;  go on to test for CGA.
                      or      video, VMDA     ;Set MDA bit.
          a02:                                ;CGA test.
                                              ;Test for 6845 CGA registers.
                      mov     dx, 03d4h       ;Index register.
                      mov     al, 0fh         ;Select register 0fh.
                      out     dx, al          ;Write to index register.
                      mov     dx, 03d5h       ;Data register.
                      in      al, dx          ;Read register 0fh.
                      mov     ah, al          ;Store in AH.
                      mov     al, 99h         ;Write a number to the register.
                      out     dx, al
                      mov     cx, 512         ;Pause.
```

Figure 5.2: SCRA.ASM: The set of assembly language video functions

```
a03:
            loop     a03
            in       al, dx              ;Now read the register back.
            xchg     ah, al              ;Restore saved register value.
            out      dx, al
            cmp      ah, 99h             ;Compare value read to value written.
            jne      a04                 ;No CGA;  go on to test for Hercules.
            or       video, VCGA         ;Set CGA bit.
a04:                                     ;** Test for HERCULES. **
                                         ;This routine supplied courtesy of
                                         ;Hercules Computer Technology.
            mov      dx, 03bah           ;Display status port.
            xor      bl, bl              ;Clear counter.
            in       al, dx              ;Read port.
            and      al, 80h             ;Mask off all bits except 7.
            mov      ah, al              ;Save bit 7 in AH.
            mov      cx, 8000h           ;Set loop counter.
a05:
            in       al, dx              ;Read port again.
            and      al, 80h             ;Mask out bit 7.
            cmp      al, ah              ;Test if bit has changed.
            je       a06                 ;Bit not yet changed.
            inc      bl                  ;Bit changed, increment counter.
            cmp      bl, 10              ;Want to see it change 10 times.
            jb       a06                 ;Need to see more changes.
            or       video, VHGC         ;Yes, it is a HCG.
            jmp      a07                 ;Go on to EGA test.
a06:
            loop     a05                 ;Continue testing for changes.

a07:                                     ;** Test for EGA. **
            mov      bh, 0ffh            ;Impossible return value.
            mov      ah, 12h             ;BIOS alternate select function.
            mov      bl, 10h             ;Request EGA information.
            int      10h                 ;BIOS video services interrupt.
            cmp      bh, 0               ;Test for EGA/color.
            jne      a08
            or       video, VEGAC
            jmp      a09
a08:                                     ;Test for EGA/monochrome.
            cmp      bh, 1
            jne      a09
            or       video, VEGAM
a09:                                     ;** Test for PS/2 display **
            mov      ah, 1ah             ;BIOS video display combination service.
            mov      al, 0               ;Return display combination subfunction.
            int      10h
            cmp      al, 1ah             ;Test whether function is supported.
            jne      a10                 ;Function not supported.
            or       video, VPS2         ;PS/2 functions supported.
a10:                                     ;Exit point.
            mov      ax, video
            ret

_ScrTypes ENDP

END
```

Figure 5.2: SCRA.ASM: The set of assembly language video functions (continued)

```
/*********************** ScrGetMode & ScrSetMode *************************/

struct Mode
     {
     int VideoMode;
     int Columns;
     int VideoPage;
     };

void ScrGetMode (struct Mode *ModePtr);
void ScrSetMode (struct Mode *ModePtr);

/*************************** Cursor Functions ****************************/

void ScrGetCur (int *Row,int *Col,int Page);
void ScrSetCur (int Row,int Col,int Page);
void ScrGetStyle (int *StartLine,int *StopLine);
void ScrSetStyle (int StartLine,int Stopline);

/************************** ScrPush & ScrPop ****************************/

                          /* Error return constants.                    */
#ifndef NOERROR
#define NOERROR      0    /* No Error.                                  */
#endif
#define MAXTOOSMALL 1     /* Request to push more than MAXSCREENS times. */
#define NOHEAP      2     /* Out of heap memory.                        */
#define STACKEMPTY  3     /* No screen has been pushed.                 */

int ScrPush (void);
int ScrPop (int Remove);

/*************************** ScrReadWindow *****************************/

#define OPENERR    1      /* Error opening screen file.                 */
#define READERR    2      /* Error reading screen file.                 */
#define CLOSERR    3      /* Error closing screen file.                 */

int ScrReadWindow (char *Buffer,char *FileName);

/*************************** Other Functions ****************************/

void ScrPutWindow (char *Buffer,int SourceStartRow,int SourceStartCol,
                   int SourceEndRow,int SourceEndCol,int TargetRow,
                   int TargetCol);
void ScrPutS (char *String,unsigned char Attr,
              unsigned char Row,unsigned char Col);
void ScrPutBox (int ULR,int ULC,int LRR,int LRC,int style);
void ScrClear (unsigned char StartRow,unsigned char StartCol,
               unsigned char StopRow,unsigned char StopCol);
int ScrGetS (char *Buffer,int Attr,int Row,int Col,int Length,int Mode);
void ScrPutAttr (int Attr,int StartRow,int StartCol,int StopRow,int StopCol);
void ScrMonoCard (void);
void ScrColorCard (void);
                                  /* Assembler function:         */
int far ScrTypes (void);
```

Figure 5.3: SCR.H: Header file that must be included in your program to use the functions of
         SCR.C or SCRA.ASM

```
/******************** Other Constant Definitions ****************************/
                                     /* VIDEO DISPLAY ATTRIUBTES.            */
#define BLINK        0x80            /* Blinking.                            */
                                     /* COLOR ATTRIBUTES:                    */
#define BG_R         0x40            /* Red background.                      */
#define BG_G         0x20            /* Green background.                    */
#define BG_B         0x10            /* Blue background.                     */
#define FG_I         0x08            /* Lightens foreground color.           */
#define FG_R         0x04            /* Red foreground.                      */
#define FG_G         0x02            /* Green foreground.                    */
#define FG_B         0x01            /* Blue foreground.                     */
                                     /* MONOCHROME ATTRIBUTES:               */
#define BG           0x70            /* Turns on the background.             */
#define INTENSE      0x08            /* Adds high intensity to foreground.   */
#define FG_NORM      0x07            /* Turns on the normal foregound.       */
#define FG_UL        0x01            /* Turns on the underlined foreground.  */

                                     /* Constants for ScrGetS 'Mode' parameter. */
#define NOFEAT       0x0000          /* Turn off all 'mode' features.        */
#define AUTOEXIT     0x0001          /* Exit field automatically on full buffer. */
#define UPPER        0x0002          /* Convert all letters to upper case.   */

                                     /* Bit masks for video adapter types    */
                                     /* returned by ScrTypes.                 */

                                     /* MODES SUPPORTED:                     */
#define  VMDA     1                  /* 7.                                   */
#define  VHGC     2                  /* Hercules 720 x 348 mono.graphics.    */
#define  VCGA     4                  /* 0, 1, 2, 3, 4, 5, 6.                 */
#define  VEGAM    8                  /* 7, F.                                */
#define  VEGAC    16                 /* 0, 1, 2, 3, 4, 5, 6, D, E, 10.       */
#define  VPS2     32                 /* Call int 10h, function 1bh to get    */
                                     /* list of supported modes.             */
```

Figure 5.3: SCR.H: Header file that must be included in your program to use the functions of SCR.C or SCRA.ASM (continued)

BIOS, which supports only the standard video modes provided by IBM-compatible adapters. You can use the function **ScrTypes** (described later in this chapter) to detect the presence of a Hercules card. Also, you can activate the Hercules graphics mode using the **GraInit** function, presented in Chapter 7.

The program shell SCRDEM01.C, listed in Figure 5.4, illustrates a typical method for using these two functions to save the current video mode and place the monitor in an 80-column text mode at the beginning of a program, and then restore the former video mode at the end of a program. (Note that saving and restoring the current video mode is especially important for memory resident applications; see Chapter 9 for more information on using these functions within a memory resident utility.)

SCRDEM01.C declares two **Mode** structures: **OldMode** for obtaining and restoring the former video mode, and **NewMode** for setting the new video mode. First, **ScrGetMode** is called to obtain the existing mode.

Table 5.1: Video mode numbers

Mode	Characters or Pixels	Description
00h	40 × 25	B&W text
01h	40 × 25	Color text
02h	80 × 25	B&W text
03h	80 × 25	Color text
04h	320 × 200	4-color graphics, 2 color palettes
05h	320 × 200	B&W graphics
06h	640 × 200	B&W graphics
07h	80 × 25	Monochrome text
08h	160 × 200	16-color graphics (PCjr)
09h	320 × 200	16-color graphics (PCjr)
0Ah	640 × 200	4-color graphics (PCjr)
0Dh	320 × 200	16-color graphics (EGA & VGA)
0Eh	640 × 200	16-color graphics (EGA & VGA)
0Fh	640 × 350	Monochrome graphics (EGA, VGA, & MCGA)
10h	640 × 350	4-color (EGA with 64K video RAM) or 16-color (EGA with128K video RAM & VGA) graphics
11h	640 × 480	2-color graphics (VGA & MCGA)
12h	640 × 480	16-color graphics (VGA)
13h	320 × 200	256-color graphics (VGA & MCGA)

To make sure that the display is in an 80-column text mode, the program now tests the existing mode contained in **OldMode.VideoMode**. If the mode is 07 h (monochrome text), 02h (80-column B&W text), or 03h (80-column color text), then no change is necessary. If the mode is 0Fh (a monochrome monitor in the EGA monochrome graphics mode), then the monitor is placed in mode 07 h. If, however, the mode is some other

```
#include <STDIO.H>
#include "SCR.H"
#include "KBD.H"

void main (void)
    {
    struct Mode OldMode, NewMode;

    ScrGetMode (&OldMode);                   /* Save old video mode.              */

    switch (OldMode.VideoMode)
        {
        case 2:                              /* Standard 80 column b&w text.      */
        case 3:                              /* Standard 80 column color text.    */
        case 7:                              /* Standard 80 column mono text.      */
            break;

        case 15:                             /* EGA/VGA monochrome graphics.      */
            NewMode.VideoMode = 7;           /* Put in mono text mode.            */
            NewMode.VideoPage = 0;           /* Specify video page 0.             */
            ScrSetMode (&NewMode);
            break;

        default:                             /* Must be a color card, not in      */
            NewMode.VideoMode = 3;           /* mode 3; therefore put in mode 3.  */
            NewMode.VideoPage = 0;           /* Activate video page 0.            */
            ScrSetMode (&NewMode);
            break;
        }

    printf ("Press any key to continue...");
    KbdGetC ();

    /*          M A I N   B O D Y   O F   P R O G R A M   H E R E                 */

    /* End of Program.                                                            */

    ScrSetMode (&OldMode);                   /* Restore old video mode.           */

    } /* end main */
```

Figure 5.4: SCRDEM01.C: A program illustrating the functions **ScrGetMode** and **ScrSetMode**

value, then the monitor must be color, and the adapter is switched into mode 03h.

Figure 5.5 provides a MAKE file for preparing this program, and Figure 5.6 a QuickC program list.

How ScrGetMode and ScrSetMode Work

Both of these functions make use of the BIOS video services accessed through interrupt 10h. **ScrGetMode** invokes function 15 (by placing 15 in register AH), which returns the current video mode, number of columns, and display page. Function 15 returns the current video mode in register AL, the number of columns in AH, and the active video page

```
SCRDEM01.OBJ : SCRDEM01.C SCR.H
    cl /c /W2 /Zp SCRDEM01.C

SCR.OBJ : SCR.C SCR.H
    cl /c /W2 /Zp SCR.C

KBDA.OBJ : KBDA.ASM
    masm /MX KBDA.ASM;

SCRDEM01.EXE : SCRDEM01.OBJ SCR.OBJ KBDA.OBJ
    link /NOI /NOD SCRDEM01+SCR+KBDA,,NUL,SLIBCER;
```

Figure 5.5: SCRDEM01.M: A MAKE file for SCRDEM01.C

```
SCRDEM01.C
SCR.C
KBDA.OBJ
```

Figure 5.6: A QuickC program list for preparing SCRDEM01.C

in BH. **ScrGetMode** simply assigns each of these values to the appropriate field of the **Mode** structure addressed through the parameter **ModePtr**.

ScrSetMode works in a similar fashion, except that it must use two separate BIOS services: function 0 to set the video mode, and function 5 to set the current display page.

ScrGetCur and ScrSetCur

Using ScrGetCur and ScrSetCur

ScrGetCur, which has the prototype

```
void ScrGetCur
    (int *Row,
     int *Col,
     int Page)
```

obtains the current cursor position for the specified video page. Note that you should pass this function the *addresses* of the integers that are to receive the current row and column values. Rows are numbered from 0 to 24, starting at the top of the screen, and columns from 0 to 79 (or 0 to 39 in a 40-column mode), starting at the left of the screen. The **Page** parameter specifies the video display page (as described in the previous section) and will usually be 0.

The function **ScrSetCur** has the prototype

```
void ScrSetCur
     (int Row,
      int Col,
      int Page)
```

and sets the cursor to the position specified by the parameters **Row** and **Col**, for the display page given by **Page** (usually 0). Note that assigning an impossible position (such as **ScrSetCur (24,80,0)**) generally makes the cursor disappear.

These functions are demonstrated in Figure 5.7, discussed later in the chapter.

How ScrGetCur and ScrSetCur Work

These two functions also use the BIOS video services accessed through interrupt 10h. **ScrGetCur** uses function number 3 to read the current cursor position, and **ScrSetCur** uses function number 2 to set the cursor position.

ScrGetStyle and ScrSetStyle

Using ScrGetStyle and ScrSetStyle

Many programs use the cursor shape (or "style") to convey information to the user. For example, an editor may use one shape to indicate the insert mode and another shape to signify the overwrite mode. The cursor shape is specified in terms of the horizontal line of pixels where the cursor begins, and the line where it ends. The lines are numbered beginning with 0 at the top; on a monochrome system the lines range from 0 to 13, and on a color system they range from 0 to 7. The default cursor uses only the bottom two lines of pixels (thus, on a monochrome system the default starting line is 12 and the default ending line is 13, and on a color system the default starting line is 6 and the default ending line is 7).

ScrGetStyle has the prototype

```
void ScrGetStyle
     (int *StartLine,
      int *StopLine)
```

where **StartLine** and **StopLine** are the addresses of the variables that are to receive the values for the current beginning and ending lines used to form the cursor.

ScrSetStyle has the prototype

```
void ScrSetStyle
     (int StartLine,
      int StopLine)
```

where **StartLine** and **StopLine** are the desired cursor beginning and ending lines. Note that if the starting line is *greater* than the ending line, a two-part cursor will result. Also, if either of these two values is assigned a value of 32 or larger, the cursor will generally disappear. (Thus, there are two methods for hiding the cursor: assigning it a position beyond the screen coordinates using **ScrSetCur**, or setting the start and stop lines to 32. Since the result of either of these methods is somewhat unpredictable, it might be best to use *both* techniques to make sure the deed is done.)

Notice that you do not need to pass a page value to either of these functions, since the cursor shape (unlike the cursor position) is always the same for all video pages. Note also that it is not possible to disable the blinking of the PC cursor through a software routine. Your program, however, can hide the cursor using one of the methods discussed above, and then generate its own nonblinking cursor.

The program listed in Figure 5.7 demonstrates all four of the cursor control functions just discussed. This program shell uses these functions to save and restore the existing cursor position and style, and to set the cursor position and style for the application. Note that to create a full-size cursor, it tests the current video mode to determine the appropriate starting and ending values for the type of monitor.

The MAKE file for this program, and the QuickC program list are found in Figures 5.8 and 5.9.

```
#include <STDIO.H>
#include "SCR.H"
#include "KBD.H"

void main (void)
     {
     int OldRow, OldCol;
     int OldStart, OldStop;
     struct Mode CrtMode;

     ScrGetStyle (&OldStart,&OldStop);    /* Save current cursor style.     */
     ScrGetCur (&OldRow,&OldCol,0);       /* Save current cursor position.  */
     ScrGetMode (&CrtMode);               /* Get video mode.                */

     if (CrtMode.VideoMode == 7)    /* Create a full sized cursor.          */
         ScrSetStyle (0,12);        /* Monochrome monitor.                  */
     else
         ScrSetStyle (0,7);         /* Color monitor.                       */

     ScrSetCur (5,10,0);               /* Set initial cursor position.      */


     printf ("Press any key to continue...");
     KbdGetC ();

     /*      M A I N   B O D Y   O F   P R O G R A M   H E R E              */


     ScrSetStyle (OldStart,OldStop);    /* Restore old cursor style.        */
     ScrSetCur (OldRow,OldCol,0);       /* Restore old cursor position.     */

     } /* end main */
```

Figure 5.7: SCRDEM02.C: A program demonstrating the functions **ScrGetCur, ScrSetCur,**
ScrGetStyle, and **ScrSetStyle**

```
SCRDEM02.OBJ : SCRDEM02.C SCR.H
     cl /c /W2 /Zp SCRDEM02.C

SCR.OBJ : SCR.C SCR.H
     cl /c /W2 /Zp SCR.C

KBDA.OBJ : KBDA.ASM
     masm /MX KBDA.ASM;

SCRDEM02.EXE : SCRDEM02.OBJ SCR.OBJ KBDA.OBJ
     link /NOI /NOD SCRDEM02+SCR+KBDA,,NUL,SLIBCER;
```

Figure 5.8: SCRDEM02.M: A MAKE file for SCRDEM02.C

How ScrGetStyle and ScrSetStyle Work

ScrGetStyle uses the BIOS "read cursor position" service, accessed by placing 3 in register AH and the video page number in BH, and generating interrupt 10h. **ScrGetStyle** specifies video page 0; however,

```
SCRDEM02.C
SCR.C
KBDA.OBJ
```

Figure 5.9: A QuickC program list for preparing SCRDEM02.C

the cursor style is the same for all pages. In addition to returning the cursor position (which is disregarded here), this BIOS service returns the current starting and ending cursor lines in registers CH and CL.

ScrSetStyle calls the BIOS "set cursor type" service by placing 1 in register AH, the starting and ending line values in registers CH and CL, and generating interrupt 10h.

ScrPush and ScrPop

Using ScrPush and ScrPop

The functions **ScrPush and ScrPop** allow you to save and restore the contents of multiple screen displays. Each time you call **ScrPush** the entire current screen is saved on a stack; each time you call **ScrPop** the *last* screen that was saved is restored. The functions thus allow you to display a window or a full screen of data on top of an existing screen, and then later restore the original screen contents. Since multiple screens can be saved, the functions also allow you to stack several overlapping windows, and then remove them one at a time. Finally, as demonstrated later in the chapter, the **ScrPop** function facilitates moving a window across the screen.

ScrPush has the prototype

```
int ScrPush
    (void)
```

and simply pushes the current screen contents on top of a stack. You should call this function immediately before overwriting the current display if you hope to be able to restore the contents of the screen at a later time. If the function is successful, it returns NOERROR. Otherwise, it returns either MAXTOOSMALL if you have attempted to push more than 10 screens (the current limit, which can be altered as explained below), or NOHEAP if the program has run out of dynamic allocation memory. (The error codes are defined in SCR.H, Figure 5.3.)

ScrPop has the prototype

```
int ScrPop
        (int Remove)
```

and always restores the most recently pushed window that is still on the screen stack. If the parameter **Remove** is given a non-zero value, then the screen will be restored and also removed from the screen stack, so that it cannot be restored again. If, however, **Remove** is 0, then the screen will be restored to the monitor, but will *not* be removed from the stack. (Thus, the next call to **ScrPop** will restore the same screen. This feature is useful for efficiently moving windows as demonstrated in Figure 5.14, described later in the chapter). If successful, the function returns NOERROR. Otherwise, it returns STACKEMPTY, indicating that there are no more screens on the stack to restore (that is, **ScrPop** was called without a corresponding call to **ScrPush**).

These functions are demonstrated in Figures 5.8, 5.14, 5.18, and 5.21, which are described later in the chapter.

How ScrPush and ScrPop Work

The functions **ScrPush** and **ScrPop** form a module within a module. They share two external variables (declared **static** so that they are hidden from other files): **BufPtAr**, an array of character pointers, and **BufIdx**, an index to this array initialized to −1. The members of the **BufPtAr** array point to a collection of 4000 byte buffers that constitute the stack of saved screens, and **BufIdx** contains the index of the top of this stack. (Note that video memory must contain 4000 bytes to encode a 25-row by 80-column screen, since there are 2000 characters and 2000 video display attributes. The first byte of video memory is the ASCII code for the first character on the first row of the screen, and the second byte is the attribute for this character. The next two bytes contain the ASCII code and attribute for the second character on the first row, and so on.)

Each time **ScrPush** is called, it increments **BufIdx** to access the next member of the **BufPtAr** array, and tests to make sure that **BufIdx** has not exceeded the maximum number of array elements (MAXSCREENS, which you must increase if you want to be able to push more than 10 screens). Next, **ScrPush** calls the main C memory allocator, **malloc**, to provide storage for the next saved screen, and assigns the address of the allocated buffer to the current member of **BufPtAr**. Before transferring data, it must test the video mode in order to determine the correct segment address of video memory. (The starting segment address for monochrome systems is 0xb000 and for color systems is 0xb800.) Once this segment address is obtained, **ScrPush** uses the C library function **movedata** to effect the transfer of the 4000 bytes of data in video memory to the 4000-byte storage buffer. The function **movedata** is useful since it allows specification of both the segment and offset address values of the source and destination, and can thus be used to transfer data between different segments in any memory model program. To obtain the segment address of the destination array, **Bufptar [BufIdx]** is cast to a **far** pointer and the resulting value is stored in **FarPtrCh**. The Microsoft C macros FP_SEG and FP_OFF are then used to extract the segment and offset values from **FarPtrCh**.

See *MS-DOS Advanced Programming*, Chapter 8, for a complete explanation of the structure of video memory, and its use for generating screen output.

When **ScrPop** is called, it first tests whether the stack index **BufIdx** is less than 0 (it might be −1), which would indicate that the stack of saved screens is empty. If the stack contains at least one screen, **ScrPop** restores the screen to video memory using the same process described above except that the source and destination parameters passed to **movedata** are reversed. Finally, if the **Remove** parameter is set to a nonzero value, it frees the memory occupied by the restored screen with the C library function **free**, and then decrements the stack index **BufIdx**.

ScrReadWindow

*Using
ScrReadWindow*

Using the interactive editor presented in Chapter 6, you can create a full display screen, and then save it on disk as a screen data file. This file is an exact image of video memory, and is precisely 4000 bytes long (80 × 25 characters plus 80 × 25 display attributes). The function **ScrReadWindow** allows you to read one of these data files directly into a 4000 byte buffer that you have declared in your program. Once the block of screen data is contained in an internal buffer, all or selected portions of it can be displayed instantly using the function **ScrPutWindow** (which will be described next).

The prototype for **ScrReadWindow** is

```
int ScrReadWindow
        (char *Buffer,
         char *FileName)
```

where **Buffer** is the address of your 4000-byte character array, and **File-Name** specifies the name of the screen data file as it was saved by the screen designing utility (a full path name is allowed). If the function is successful, it returns NOERROR; otherwise it returns OPENERR if it could not open the file, READERR if it encountered an error while reading the file, or CLOSERR if it could not close the file.

This function is demonstrated in Figures 5.10 and 5.14, described later in the chapter.

How ScrReadWindow Works

ScrReadWindow uses the standard low-level C file functions **open**, **read**, and **close**. These routines are selected since the buffering provided by the high-level C functions (such as **fopen**) offers no advantage for this routine. (Buffering is helpful for repeated, small, sequential disk accesses, while this routine requests a single block transfer.) Note that the file mode parameter must contain the O_BINARY option to prevent translation of the input data.

An Enhancement

If your program uses many screens, it would be inefficient to store each screen in a separate data file. It would be faster and use less disk space to concatenate all the screens into a single file, which would be opened only *once* the first time the function is called, and then access individual screens using the C function **lseek**. It is left as a exercise for the interested reader to modify **ScrReadWindow** to support a multiple screen file. Note that the individual screen files generated by the editor can easily be concatenated using the DOS COPY command; for example:

```
copy SCR1.SCR+SCR2.SCR COMBSCR.SCR /b
```

ScrPutWindow

Using
ScrPutWindow

Once an internal 4000-byte buffer contains the data for a screen, **Scr-PutWindow** may be used to display any portion of this buffer at a specified position on the screen. This function is ideal for displaying entire screens or individual windows that cover only a portion of the screen, and the results are truly instantaneous (writing screens with this function is approximately 250 times faster than using **printf**!).

The prototype is

```
void ScrPutWindow
     (char *Buffer,
      int SourceStartRow,
      int SourceStartCol,
      int SourceEndRow,
      int SourceEndCol,
      int TargetRow,
      int TargetCol)
```

Buffer contains the address of your screen data buffer. The next four parameters specify the rectangular block within this buffer that you want to display: **SourceStartRow** and **SourceStartCol** are the beginning row and column numbers, and **SourceEndRow** and **SourceEndCol** are the ending row and column numbers. Finally, **TargetRow** and **TargetCol** specify the starting position on the screen where you would like to display the data (that is, the upper left corner of the rectangular block of data written to the screen; note that the existing screen data in areas of the screen not actually covered by this block are left intact). For example, the following line would display the entire screen of data contained in the buffer **ScrBuf**:

```
ScrPutWindow (ScrBuf,0,0,24,79,0,0);
```

As another example, the following line would display the upper right quadrant of data contained in **ScrBuf** in the center of the screen:

```
ScrPutWindow (ScrBuf,0,40,11,79,6,20);
```

Note that rows and columns are numbered beginning with 0. Also, you are responsible for making sure that the window will actually fit on the screen given the specified starting position. For example, the call

```
ScrPutWindow (ScrBuf,0,0,24,79,12,40)
```

attempts to display an entire screen of data starting at the center of the screen, and the results will be disappointing.

After you have created a screen using the screen designer described in Chapter 6, there are two methods for getting the data into an internal buffer in your program so that it can be displayed via **ScrPutWindow**. The first method, described above, is to read the data at runtime from a screen file directly into your buffer. The second method is to *initialize* the buffer at compile time with the appropriate screen data. The second method results in faster screens and does not require additional files on the runtime disk; however, it uses more space in the program's data segment (4000 bytes per screen), making the program larger and slower to load (it also adds steps and slows the compiling process). The best compromise might be to read seldom used screens from the disk, but initialize the most frequently used and important displays.

To facilitate initializing a screen data buffer, the screen designer has an option that will generate a file containing the code necessary to initialize a 4000-byte character array. This file consists of 4000 decimal numbers separated by commas and can be included directly in your program. For example, if the resulting file is called SCR01.INC, you could initialize **ScrBuf** as follows:

```
char ScrBuf [4000] =
     {
     #include "SCR01.INC"
     };
```

The program in Figure 5.10 demonstrates **ScrPutWindow**, as well as several of the video functions described previously. This program first uses **ScrReadWindow** to read a screen data file (TEST.SCR) into the buffer **WinBuf**. The file TEST.SCR is shown in Figure 5.11, exactly as it would appear in the screen editor (or if the entire screen were displayed at once). If **ScrReadWindow** returns with an error, the program bails out by calling the **UtyQuit** function, described in Chapter 12. The program now saves the current screen contents by calling **ScrPush**, and uses **ScrPutWindow** to display the upper left window of TEST.SCR. After positioning the cursor through **ScrSetCur**, it pauses for user input with a call to **KbdGetC**. In a similar fashion, it displays two more of the windows from TEST.SCR, saving the previous screen contents each time and shifting the location of each window so that it will overlap the underlying window. Finally, the program removes the windows one at a time by calling **ScrPop**, pausing for user input between each window removal. (The fourth window is used in the program of Figure 5.14.)

```c
#include <STDIO.H>
#include "SCR.H"
#include "KBD.H"
#include "UTY.H"

char WinBuf [4000];

void main (void)
    {
    int ErrorCode;                  /* Holds error code.             */
    char Message [41];              /* For formatting error message. */
    int Row, Col;                   /* Cursor position.              */

    if ((ErrorCode = ScrReadWindow (WinBuf,"TEST.SCR")) != NOERROR)
        {
        sprintf (Message, "ScrReadWindow error %d",ErrorCode);
        UtyQuit (Message,__FILE__,__LINE__);
        }

    ScrPush ();                                 /* Display window number 1.  */
    Row = Col = 0;
    ScrPutWindow (WinBuf,0,0,11,39,Row,Col);
    ScrSetCur (Row+5,Col+35,0);
    KbdGetC ();

    ScrPush ();                                 /* Display window number 2.  */
    ScrPutWindow (WinBuf,0,40,11,79,(Row += 2),(Col += 4));
    ScrSetCur (Row + 5,Col + 35,0);
    KbdGetC ();

    ScrPush ();                                 /* Display window number 3.  */
    ScrPutWindow (WinBuf,12,0,23,39,(Row+=2),(Col+=4));
    ScrSetCur (Row + 5,Col + 35,0);
    KbdGetC ();

    ScrPop (1);                                 /* Pop window 3.             */
    ScrSetCur ((Row -= 2) + 5,(Col -= 4) + 35,0);
    KbdGetC ();

    ScrPop (1);                                 /* Pop window 2.             */
    ScrSetCur ((Row -= 2) + 5,(Col -= 4) + 35,0);
    KbdGetC ();

    ScrPop (1);                                 /* Pop window 1.             */

    ScrSetCur (23,0,0);

    } /* end main */
```

Figure 5.10: SCRDEM03.C: A program demonstrating the stacking of windows, using the functions **ScrPutWindow, ScrReadWindow, ScrPush, ScrPop,** and **ScrSetCur**

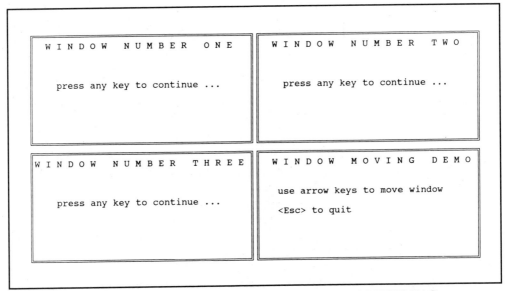

Figure 5.11: TEST.SCR: The screen data file read by SCRDEM03.C and SCRDEM04.C

Figures 5.12 and 5.13 provide a MAKE file for this program and a QuickC program list.

As another example, the program in Figure 5.14 demonstrates how the functions discussed so far can be used to allow the user to move a

```
SCRDEM03.OBJ : SCRDEM03.C SCR.H
      cl /c /W2 /Zp SCRDEM03.C

SCR.OBJ : SCR.C SCR.H
      cl /c /W2 /Zp SCR.C

KBDA.OBJ : KBDA.ASM
      masm /MX KBDA.ASM;

UTY.OBJ : UTY.C UTY.H
      cl /c /W2 /Zp UTY.C

UTYA.OBJ : UTYA.ASM
      masm /MX utya.asm;

SCRDEM03.EXE : SCRDEM03.OBJ SCR.OBJ KBDA.OBJ UTY.OBJ UTYA.OBJ
      link /NOI /NOD SCRDEM03+SCR+KBDA+UTY+UTYA,,NUL,SLIBCER;
```

Figure 5.12: SCRDEM03.M: A MAKE file for SCRDEM03.C

```
SCRDEM03.C
SCR.C
KBDA.OBJ
UTY.C
UTYA.OBJ
```

Figure 5.13: A QuickC program list for preparing SCRDEM03.C

window across the screen. Like the preceding example, this program begins by reading the screen data file TEST.SCR into the internal buffer **WinBuf**. It then saves the current screen contents using **ScrPush** and displays the window stored in the *lower right* quadrant of **WinBuf** at the *upper left* corner of the screen (note that the existing screen data in areas of the screen not covered by this window are left intact). The program now reads the keyboard and responds to arrow keys by restoring the original screen with **ScrPop** and then redisplaying the window at a position that is offset one row or column in the appropriate direction (thus, each time an arrow key is pressed the window is moved a distance of one row or column). The important detail in this process is that **ScrPop** is called with the parameter **Remove** set to 0, so that the screen that was originally saved remains on the stack. Otherwise, it would be necessary to call **ScrPush** with each movement of the window, and the process would be considerably slower.

Figure 5.15 lists a MAKE file for preparing SCRDEM04.C, and Figure 5.16 contains a QuickC program list.

*How
ScrPutWindow
Works*

ScrPutWindow is quite similar to **ScrPush** and **ScrPop**, except that only a *portion* of video memory is transferred. This function therefore cannot use a single block move since the bytes of data that it transfers are not necessarily contiguous. Rather, it must move the data row by row, with a separate call to **movedata** for each row. It must also calculate the offsets within the source buffer (**SourceOff**) and within video memory (**VideoOff**), according to the requested row and column positions passed as parameters (in **ScrPush** and **ScrPop** these offsets were always 0). Before transferring the data, the function must also calculate the number of bytes that need to be moved for each row, as well as the total number of rows.

```c
#include <STDIO.H>
#include <PROCESS.H>
#include "SCR.H"
#include "KBD.H"
#include "UTY.H"

char WinBuf [4000];

void main (void)
    {
    register int Row, Col;          /* Position of window.         */
    int ErrorCode;                  /* ScrReadWindow error code.   */
    char Message [41];              /* For formatting error message. */

                                    /* Read the window data.       */
    if ((ErrorCode = ScrReadWindow (WinBuf,"TEST.SCR")) != NOERROR)
        {
        sprintf (Message, "ScrReadWindow error %d",ErrorCode);
        UtyQuit (Message,__FILE__,__LINE__);
        }

    ScrPush ();                     /* Save the screen data.       */
    Row = Col = 0;                  /* Set initial window position. */
    ScrPutWindow (WinBuf,12,40,23,79,Row,Col);  /* Display the window. */

    for (;;)                        /* Loop to process the arrow keys. */
        switch (KbdGetC ())
            {
            case 0x011b:                    /* Escape.             */
                exit (0);                   /* Quit program.       */

            case 0x4b00:                    /* Left arrow.         */
                if (Col > 0)
                    {
                    ScrPop (0);
                    ScrPutWindow (WinBuf,12,40,23,79,Row,--Col);
                    }
                break;

            case 0x4d00:                    /* Right arrow.        */
                if (Col + 39 < 79)
                    {
                    ScrPop (0);
                    ScrPutWindow (WinBuf,12,40,23,79,Row,++Col);
                    }
                break;

            case 0x4800:                    /* Up arrow.           */
                if (Row > 0)
                    {
                    ScrPop (0);
                    ScrPutWindow (WinBuf,12,40,23,79,--Row,Col);
                    }
                break;
```

Figure 5.14: SCRDEM04.C: A program that demonstrates moving a window, using the functions **ScrReadWindow**, **ScrPutWindow**, **ScrPush**, and **ScrPop**

```
        case 0x5000:                    /* Down arrow.            */
            if (Row+11 < 24)
                {
                ScrPop (0);
                ScrPutWindow (WinBuf,12,40,23,79,++Row,Col);
                }
            break;

        } /* end switch */

} /* end main */
```

Figure 5.14: SCRDEM04.C: A program that demonstrates moving a window, using the functions **ScrReadWindow**, **ScrPutWindow**, **ScrPush**, and **ScrPop** (continued)

```
SCRDEM04.OBJ : SCRDEM04.C SCR.H
    cl /c /W2 /Zp SCRDEM04.C

SCR.OBJ : SCR.C SCR.H
    cl /c /W2 /Zp SCR.C

KBDA.OBJ : KBDA.ASM
    masm /MX KBDA.ASM;

UTY.OBJ : UTY.C UTY.H
    cl /c /W2 /Zp UTY.C

UTYA.OBJ : UTYA.ASM
    masm /MX utya.asm;

SCRDEM04.EXE : SCRDEM04.OBJ SCR.OBJ KBDA.OBJ UTY.OBJ UTYA.OBJ
    link /NOI /NOD SCRDEM04+SCR+KBDA+UTY+UTYA,,NUL,SLIBCER;
```

Figure 5.15: SCRDEM04.M: A MAKE file for SCRDEM04.C

```
SCRDEM04.C
SCR.C
KBDA.OBJ
UTY.C
UTYA.OBJ
```

Figure 5.16: A QuickC program list for preparing SCRDEM04.C

ScrPutS

Using ScrPutS

Whereas **ScrPutWindow** is designed to display large blocks of screen data, the purpose of **ScrPutS** is to display individual strings at specific locations on the screen. A typical programming sequence would be to use **ScrPutWindow** to display an entire screen or window, containing the borders, titles, and other constant data, and then to use **ScrPutS** to display messages and other changing data at specific positions on the screen consistent with the screen design.

The prototype for this function is

```
void ScrPutS
      (char *String,
      int Attr,
      int Row,
      int Col)
```

The parameter **String** points to the NULL-terminated string that you want to display. The parameters **Row** and **Col** specify the starting row and column where the string is to be displayed. The parameter **Attr** gives the video display attribute.

The effect of the video attribute parameter on the displayed characters depends upon whether the system is monochrome (that is, the video mode is 7), or color (that is, the video mode is *not* 7). The attribute value can range from 0 to 255. The meanings of these 256 values for both color and monochrome systems are listed exhaustively in the IBM technical references (for the PC, PC AT, and so on—see the Bibliography), and in other handbooks. However, there is some logic to the manner in which the individual bits are encoded, thus you do not need to look up the code for each desired attribute combination. A set of constant definitions are defined in the file SCR.H (Figure 5.3), which you can use to derive any of the possible display attributes by combining the individual constants with the logical OR operator (|).

Any color or monochrome attribute value can be made to generate blinking by combining the attribute and the constant BLINK with the logical OR operator.

The following constants are defined in SCR.H for specifying video attributes on *color* systems:

Constant	Meaning
BG_R	Red background
BG_G	Green background
BG_B	Blue background
FG_I	Lightens foreground color
FG_R	Red foreground
FG_G	Green foreground
FG_B	Blue foreground

These attribute constants can be used to specify any one of eight background colors and any one of 16 foreground colors. Since each of the three primary colors—red, green, and blue—can be either on or off, eight basic colors are possible. The foreground, however, also has an intensity bit (FG_I) that optionally lightens the basic foreground color, thus providing another eight possible foreground colors. The foreground and background colors you can specify with these constants are listed in Table 5.2. This table lists the possible foreground colors separately from the possible background colors; when specifying an attribute, you should combine all desired foreground and background constants in a *single* expression. For example, the expression

```
BG_R | FG_B
```

selects a red background and a blue foreground. The expression

```
FG_R | BLINK
```

chooses a red, blinking foreground on a black background (*no* background color is selected). To produce a color other than red, green, or blue, you must understand something of the way the primary colors combine (or consult Table 5.2). For example,

```
FG_B | FG_R
```

generates a magenta foreground on a black background, and

```
FG_I | FG_R | FG_G | BG_G | BG_B
```

Table 5.2: Color video attribute values

BACKGROUND COLORS	
Expression	**Background Color**
(no background constants)	Black
BG_R	Red
BG_G	Green
BG_B	Blue
BG_R | BG_G	Yellow
BG_R | BG_B	Magenta
BG_G | BG_B	Cyan
BG_R | BG_G | BG_B	White
FOREGROUND COLORS	
Expression	**Foreground Color**
(no foreground constants)	Black
FG_R	Red
FG_G	Green
FG_B	Blue
FG_R | FG_G	Yellow
FG_R | FG_B	Magenta
FG_G | FG_B	Cyan
FG_R | FG_G | FG_B	White
FG_I	Dark Grey
FG_I | FG_R	Light Red
FG_I | FG_G	Light Green
FG_I | FG_B	Light Blue
FG_I | FG_R | FG_G	Light Yellow
FG_I | FG_R | FG_B	Light Magenta
FG_I | FG_G | FG_B	Light Cyan
FG_I | FG_R | FG_G | FG_B	Bright White

produces a light yellow foreground on a cyan background.

Note that the colors listed in Table 5.2 are those generated on a standard color graphics adapter (CGA). EGA and VGA adapters use these same colors by default (that is, these colors are in effect when the BIOS first switches into a color text mode); however, the colors corresponding to given attribute values can be modified by writing to the adapter's palette registers (see Wilton 1987, cited in the Bibliography).

The following are the constants defined in SCR.H for specifying *monochrome* display attributes:

Constant	Meaning
BG	Turns on the background.
INTENSE	Adds high intensity to foreground.
FG_NORM	Turns on the normal (that is, *not* underlined) foreground.
FG_UL	Turns on the underlined foreground.

Using these four constants (plus the BLINK constant), you can generate any monochrome attribute. Remember that individual attributes are combined by joining the appropriate constants with the logical OR operator. For example, the following expression specifies a normal, blinking foreground:

```
FG_NORM | BLINK
```

Observe the following guidelines for using these constants to generate monochrome attributes:

- There is one type of background, BG, but two types of foreground, FG_NORM and FG_UL. Only one type of foreground may be selected, depending on whether or not underlining is desired (combining the foreground attributes with the OR operator would simply produce a normal foreground).

- If neither the background (BG), nor a foreground (FG_NORM or FG_UL) is selected, then the characters will be black on black (that is, invisible).

- If only a foreground is selected, then the characters will be white on black (either normal or underlined).

- If only the background is selected, then the characters will be black on white (that is, reverse video). The intensity bit selected in combination with reverse video makes a visible difference only with certain video adapters.

▎ If *both* the background *and* a foreground are selected, then the foreground takes precedence and the characters will be white on black. (Thus, it is impossible to have reverse video and underlined characters, since this would necessitate selecting both the background and a foreground).

A final note: although **ScrPutS** allow only a simple string to be passed, and does not provide data formatting facilities like **printf**, remember that you can first format numeric and other data types onto the string using the **sprintf** function, and then display the string enjoying the speed and control of **ScrPutS**. The function **ScrPutS** is demonstrated in Figures 5.18 and 5.21, discussed later in the chapter.

How ScrPutS Works

ScrPutS begins by storing the attribute parameter (**Attr**) in a register variable, since this value must be poked into memory for each character in the string. (If it is stored in a register, only one **mov** operation is required for each character; if it remains on the stack, two moves are required.) Next, the function determines the correct segment address of video memory, and calculates the offset of the first character in the string from the beginning of this segment; these two values are then used to initialize the **far** pointer **Video** which will be used to write the characters and attributes. Finally, **ScrPutS** goes into a loop that writes each character of the string directly to the appropriate position in video memory, followed by the attribute.

An Enhancement

As **ScrPutS** is implemented, it allows you to specify only a single attribute for all the characters of the string. An enhanced version might allow a separate attribute to be assigned to each character. (A distinct attribute could be embedded in the string after each character, and another parameter passed to indicate the presence of these attribute codes. This design would be similar to the BIOS "write string" function 13h of interrupt 10h, which is present only in the AT and on EGA and VGA adapters.) This enhancement is left as an exercise for the interested reader.

ScrPutBox

Using ScrPutBox

The function **ScrPutBox** can be used to draw a rectangular box directly on the screen. It has the prototype

```
void ScrPutBox
    (int ULR,
    int ULC,
    int LRR,
    int LRC,
    int Style)
```

where ULR and ULC are the row and column of the upper left corner of the desired box, and LRR and LRC are the row and column of the lower right corner. The parameter **Style** specifies one of four styles, numbered from 0 to 3. These styles are illustrated in Figure 5.17.

Boxes can certainly be generated using the interactive screen editor and then displayed via **ScrPutWindow**; **ScrPutBox**, however, provides an alternative method for creating simple boxes. You can use this function to display pop-up windows by performing the following series of operations:

▌ Save the contents of the current screen using **ScrPush**.

▌ Draw the box that is to form the outline of the window by means of **ScrPutBox**.

▌ Clear the inside of the box with the function **ScrClear**, to be presented next.

▌ Write any messages to the window via the function **ScrPutS**.

▌ Read any data from the user through the function **ScrGetS**, to be described shortly.

▌ Remove the window and restore the original screen by calling **ScrPop**.

This sequence of steps is illustrated by the example programs in Figures 5.18 and 5.19, described later in the chapter.

Note that there is no parameter specifying a display attribute. In fact, the **ScrPutBox** draws the box without changing any of the attribute values of the current screen.

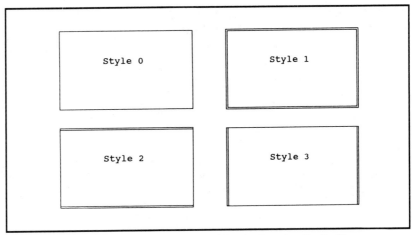

Figure 5.17: The four box styles generated by the function **ScrPutBox**

How ScrPutBox Works

Like most of the functions in this module, **ScrPutBox** achieves its performance by writing directly to video memory. The function stores the codes for the special IBM box drawing characters in static character arrays so that it can easily fetch the appropriate character for the selected style. For example, the expression **ulc [Style]** would have the value of the correct character for the upper left corner of a box having the style that has been chosen.

ScrPutBox begins by initializing the **far** pointer to video memory, **Video**, to the address of the upper left corner of the box, using the same technique for finding the segment and offset values illustrated in several of the functions described previously. After each character is written, **Video** is incremented by *two* in order to skip over the attribute byte. Thus, the existing attributes in video memory are left unchanged. (An enhanced version of this function might allow specification of the display attribute—another project for the ambitious reader.) The box characters are drawn in the following sequence:

1. The upper left corner.

2. The top horizontal line.

3. The upper right corner.

4. Both vertical lines are drawn simultaneously. Note that **Delta1** is the number of bytes in video memory between the

left vertical line and the right vertical line. **Delta2** is the number of bytes that must be skipped to go from the right vertical line all the way to the left vertical line on the next row.

5. The lower left corner.

6. The lower horizontal line.

7. The lower right corner.

ScrClear

Using ScrClear

The function **ScrClear** has the prototype

```
void ScrClear
     (int StartRow,
      int StartCol,
      int StopRow,
      int StopCol)
```

and simply clears the specified area of the screen. **StartRow** and **StartCol** give the upper left corner of this area, and **StopRow** and **StopCol** the lower right corner. This function is demonstrated in the programs of Figures 5.18 and 5.21, described later in the chapter.

How ScrClear Works

ScrClear uses the BIOS "scroll active page up" service number 6 of interrupt 10h. Normally, this function scrolls up the specified area of the screen, by the number of lines contained in register AL. However, if AL is 0, the entire area will be blanked. The upper left row and column of the area to clear is placed in registers CH and CL, and the lower right row and column in registers DH and DL. The video display attribute that the BIOS is to place in the blanked section is given in register BH (**ScrClear** uses the value 0x07, for normal white on black).

ScrGetS

Using ScrGetS

ScrGetS is a very useful function for obtaining user input from the context of a carefully designed screen or window. There are several problems with the standard C library functions for reading keyboard input, such as **gets** and **scanf**. First, these functions do not allow you to keep the echoed characters contained within a specific section of the screen; as a result, the user can easily mess up the screen design. Second, they do not allow specification of the attribute to be used for echoing characters.

ScrGetS has the prototype

```
int ScrGetS
    (char *Buffer,
    int Attr,
    int Row,
    int Col,
    int Length,
    int Mode)
```

The parameter **Buffer** should contain the address of the character array to receive the input string. **Attr** specifies the video display attribute, and **Row** and **Col** give the starting position of the characters echoed to the screen. (See the complete discussion of display attributes under **ScrPutS**). The **Length** parameter specifies the maximum number of characters that are read, including the NULL termination (therefore, the user is allowed to enter the number of characters given by **Length**, less one). The final parameter, **Mode**, is used to select one of several options to be discussed shortly.

ScrGetS reads and echoes characters until either an exit key (Enter, Esc, or an arrow key) is encountered, or until the number of characters read is one less than the specified buffer size. If the first key read is an exit key, the buffer is not altered; otherwise, the buffer is initially filled with blanks and terminated with a NULL character. (Therefore, regardless of the number of characters entered by the user, the returned string always has a length—which includes the NULL—equal to the **Length** parameter, and is blank padded on the right. This feature is useful for receiving the fixed length fields of a data file, where sort keys and fields are often compared over their entire lengths, and not just up to the first NULL character.) The terminating exit key is *not* placed in the buffer. **ScrGetS** returns one of the following codes to indicate the key used to exit the field:

Return value	Exit key
−1	Esc
0	Enter
1	Left arrow (←)
2	Right arrow (→)
3	Up arrow (↑)
4	Down arrow (↓)
5	Automatic exit (see below)

The calling program can use this return information in a variety of ways. For example, Esc (−1) might indicate that the user wants to abort the process, and the arrow key codes could be used to allow the user to navigate from field to field on a data input screen.

Special features can be selected through the **Mode** parameter. The file SCR.H provides a set of constant definitions for these features. NOFEAT specifies no additional features. AUTOEXIT causes **ScrGetS** to return immediately, without the user pressing Enter, when the maximum number of characters has been entered. UPPER causes all alphabetical characters to be converted to uppercase. These two features may be combined by passing the expression

```
AUTOEXIT | UPPER
```

How can numeric data be entered? **ScrGetS** does not have the built in numeric conversion features of **scanf**; however, it is convenient to enter all data as simple strings, and *then* convert any numeric values within your program using a standard C library function such as **atof**, **atoi**, or **sscanf**. Note also that you can eliminate the echoing of characters simply by specifying a display attribute of 0 (black characters on a black background!).

The program in Figure 5.18 demonstrates **ScrGetS** as well as several of the other screen functions that have been presented, and illustrates a typical sequence of operations for displaying a pop-up window, receiving user input through the window, and then restoring the original screen. The program first saves the screen by calling **ScrPush**.

```
#include "SCR.H"
#include "KBD.H"

void main (void)
     {
     char Name [14];                      /* Stores a name.              */
     char Number [2];                     /* Stores a number.            */
     char Sort [5];                       /* Stores an upper-case sort code.*/

     ScrPush ();                          /* Save screen data.           */
     ScrPutBox (0,0,11,39,3);             /* Display a box.              */
     ScrClear (1,1,10,38);
     ScrPutS ("Window Data Entry",0x0f,1,10);       /* Display labels in box.*/
     ScrPutS ("Enter your first name:",0x0f,3,2);
     ScrPutS ("            ",0x70,3,25);
     ScrPutS ("Enter a number (0-9):",0x0f,5,2);
     ScrPutS (" ",0x70,5,25);
     ScrPutS ("Enter a sort code:",0x0f,7,2);
     ScrPutS ("     ",0x70,7,25);

     ScrGetS (Name,0x70,3,25,sizeof (Name),NOFEAT); /* Read data from user. */
     ScrGetS (Number,0x70,5,25,sizeof (Number),AUTOEXIT);
     ScrGetS (Sort,0x70,7,25,sizeof (Sort),UPPER);

     ScrPop (1);                          /* Restore the screen.         */
     ScrSetCur (23,0,0);                  /* Position cursor at bottom of screen. */

     } /* end main */
```

Figure 5.18: SCRDEM05.C: A program that displays a pop-up window and reads user input

It then draws the window frame and clears the inside of this frame using **ScrPutBox** and **ScrClear**. It now displays a title and a series of prompts via the function **ScrPutS**. Note that it also displays reverse video blank characters to clearly mark the fields where the user will be entering data. After displaying all required information, the program accepts user input from the three fields, illustrating the use of the automatic exit feature for entering a single digit, and uppercase conversion for entering a sort key. When the last field is exited, the screen is restored with a call to **ScrPop**.

Figures 5.19 and 5.20 offer the customary MAKE file and QuickC program list.

How ScrGetS Works

Like many of the other functions in this module, **ScrGetS** also begins by initializing a **far** pointer (**Video**) to point to the position in video memory that is to receive the first character. Note that in this case **Video** is an *integer* pointer so that it can access both a character and its associated attribute through a single indirection. The function also initializes the screen column marker, **CurCol**, to the column to receive the

```
SCRDEM05.OBJ : SCRDEM05.C SCR.H
     cl /c /W2 /Zp SCRDEM05.C

SCR.OBJ : SCR.C SCR.H
     cl /c /W2 /Zp SCR.C

KBDA.OBJ : KBDA.ASM
     masm /MX KBDA.ASM;

SCRDEM05.EXE : SCRDEM05.OBJ SCR.OBJ KBDA.OBJ
     link /NOI /NOD SCRDEM05+SCR+KBDA,,NUL,SLIBCER;
```

Figure 5.19: SCRDEM05.M: A MAKE file for SCRDEM05.C

```
SCRDEM05.C
SCR.C
KBDA.OBJ
```

Figure 5.20: A QuickC program list for preparing SCRDEM05.C

first echoed character, and places the cursor at this same column position on the specified starting row. **ScrGetS** now goes into a loop to read and respond to characters entered from the keyboard.

If any of the exit keys is entered, the function immediately returns the appropriate code to the calling program.

If a backspace key is entered *and* the current column (**CurCol**) has advanced beyond the starting column (**Col**), the following steps are performed. First, **CurCol** is decremented and the cursor is moved back to the new position. Next, **Video** is decremented to the prior position in video memory and a space is written at this location. Finally, the buffer pointer (**Buffer**) is decremented and a space is written into the buffer to erase the prior character. Note that the word written to video memory is composed of both the character and the attribute, and is formed by shifting the attribute parameter left one byte and combining the result with the character using the logical OR operator, as follows:

```
(Attr << 8) | ' '
```

If the **default** arm of the **switch** statement is reached, then either the user has entered some non-ASCII key (a meaningless control code), which will cause the function to loop back for another key, or the user has entered a key with a valid ASCII code that must be echoed and inserted into the buffer. The **default** branch first tests for the end of the buffer. If the end has been reached, then the function loops back for another key (even though no more characters can be entered into the buffer, the routine must still wait for the user to enter an exit key or a backspace). Since it is now known that the key has a valid ASCII code, the upper byte (containing the extended keyboard code, described in Chapter 2 and Appendix C) is removed. Also, if the UPPER option is in effect, the character is converted to upper case at this time. The pointers **Video** and **Buffer** are now incremented, the character is written to both video memory and the buffer, and the cursor position is updated (**ScrSetCur**). Next, the flag **FirstChar** is tested to see if this is the first character entered. If this is the first character, the function goes into a routine that initializes the buffer with blanks and places a NULL at the end. Finally, if the AUTOEXIT option is in effect and the buffer is full, the routine immediately returns, passing back a code of 5.

ScrPutAttr

Using ScrPutAttr   The function **ScrPutAttr** can be used to modify the video display attribute of any section of the screen, without altering the existing screen characters. For example, the function could allow the user to move a highlight bar (an area displaying the reverse video attribute) over different menu items on the screen in order to select an item. The prototype is

```
void ScrPutAttr
    (int Attr,
    int StartRow,
    int StartCol,
    int StopRow,
    int StopCol)
```

where **Attr** is the desired video display attribute, and the next four parameters specify the rectangular area of the screen to receive the attribute.

Figure 5.21 presents a program that demonstrates the use of **ScrPutAttr** to move a highlight bar across a menu of three items, allowing the user to select the highlighted item by pressing Enter. The program displays and removes a pop-up window using the same method employed by the example in Figure 5.18. The main part of the program consists of a

```
#include <PROCESS.H>
#include "SCR.H"
#include "KBD.H"

void main (void)
    {
    register int Row;                              /* Position of highlight.  */

    ScrPush ();                                    /* Save screen data.       */
    ScrPutBox (0,0,11,39,2);                       /* Display a box.          */
    ScrClear (1,1,10,38);                          /* Clear inside of box.    */
    ScrPutS ("M E N U",0x0f,1,16);                 /* Display labels in box.  */
    ScrPutS ("Program Part One",0x0f,3,12);
    ScrPutS ("Program Part Two",0x0f,5,12);
    ScrPutS ("Program Part Three",0x0f,7,11);
    ScrPutS ("Exit Program",0x0f,9,14);
    ScrPutS ("Select Item & Press Enter",0x70,11,7);

    Row = 3;                                       /* Place highlight on      */
    ScrPutAttr (0x70,Row,11,Row,28);               /* first item.             */
    for (;;)
        switch (KbdGetC ())                        /* Read arrow keys.        */
            {
            case 0x4800:                           /* Up arrow.               */
                if (Row > 3)
                    {
                    ScrPutAttr (0x0f,Row,11,Row,28);
                    Row -= 2;
                    ScrPutAttr (0x70,Row,11,Row,28);
                    }
                break;

            case 0x5000:                           /* Down arrow.             */
                if (Row < 9)
                    {
                    ScrPutAttr (0x0f,Row,11,Row,28);
                    Row += 2;
                    ScrPutAttr (0x70,Row,11,Row,28);
                    }
                break;

            case 0x1c0d:                           /* Return.                 */
                switch (Row)
                    {
                    case 3:
                    case 5:
                    case 7:
                        break;
                    case 9:
                        ScrPop (1);
                        ScrSetCur (23,0,0);
                        exit (0);
                    }
                break;

            } /* end switch */

    } /* end main */
```

Figure 5.21: SCRDEM06.C: A program that uses **ScrPutAttr** to highlight menu items

loop that responds to an ↑, ↓, or Enter key. The arrow key arms of the **switch** statement restore the normal video attribute to the current row, update the row counter (**Row**), and then display the reverse video attribute at the new row position. The branch for the Enter key executes the currently highlighted menu item, which is found from the value of **Row**. (Only the Exit Program menu item actually does anything.)

Figure 5.22 provides a MAKE file for preparing this example program, and Figure 5.23 contains a QuickC program list.

How ScrPutAttr Works

ScrPutAttr first initializes a **far** character pointer to video memory (**Video**) using the usual method (see the section "How ScrPutS Works"), except that 1 is added to the offset value so that **Video** points to the *attribute* at the first position, and not to the character. Next, the function calculates the number of characters per row (**CharPerRow**), and the number of bytes in video memory between the last column and the beginning of the first column on the next row (**Delta**). Finally, the attribute value is poked into video memory row by row. Note that after each attribute, 2 must be added to **Video** to skip to the next attribute, and after each row, **Delta** must be added.

```
SCRDEM06.OBJ : SCRDEM06.C SCR.H
        cl /c /W2 /Zp SCRDEM06.C

SCR.OBJ : SCR.C SCR.H
        cl /c /W2 /Zp SCR.C

KBDA.OBJ : KBDA.ASM
        masm /MX KBDA.ASM;

SCRDEM06.EXE : SCRDEM06.OBJ SCR.OBJ KBDA.OBJ
        link /NOI /NOD SCRDEM06+SCR+KBDA,,NUL,SLIBCER;
```

Figure 5.22: SCRDEM06.M: A MAKE file for SCRDEM06.C

```
SCRDEM06.C
SCR.C
KBDA.OBJ
```

Figure 5.23: A QuickC program list for preparing SCRDEM06.C

ScrTypes

ScrTypes has the prototype

```
int far ScrTypes
       (void)
```

and returns a code indicating the video adapter type or types currently installed in the machine. This code allows you to determine the video modes that are supported by the hardware. Table 5.3 lists the codes that may be returned by this function, their meanings, and the corresponding video modes that are supported (see the description of the video modes in Table 5.1). The constants for the return codes are defined in SCR.H (Figure 5.3); since each code corresponds to a single bit in the returned value, more than one code may be returned. **ScrTypes** will indicate more than one adapter type in two different situations. First, the machine may have both a monochrome display adapter (a standard

Table 5.3: Video adapter codes returned by **ScrTypes**

Code Returned	Meaning	Modes Supported
VMDA	Monochrome display adapter	7
VHGC	Hercules graphics card	720 × 348 monochrome graphics
VCGA	Color graphics adapter	00h, 01h, 02h, 03h, 04h, 05h, 06h
VEGAM	Enhanced graphics adapter / monochrome monitor	07h, 0Fh
VEGAC	Enhanced graphics adapter / color monitor	00h, 01h, 02h, 03h, 04h, 05h, 06h, 0Dh, 0Eh, 10h
VPS2	PS/2 video BIOS supported	Call interrupt 10h, function 1Bh, to get a complete list of supported modes

MDA, a Hercules card, or an EGA adapter configured for a monochrome monitor) *and* a color display adapter (standard CGA, EGA, MCGA, or VGA) installed at the same time.

Second, **ScrTypes** will return more than one adapter type if an adapter is installed that provides compatibility with a previous adapter model. For example, a Hercules graphics card fully supports the monochrome text mode provided by the standard monochrome display adapter; accordingly, if a Hercules adapter is installed, **ScrTypes** returns both VHGC and VMDA. Also, if the machine contains an EGA adapter, **ScrTypes** returns the values VEGAC and VCGA, since an EGA adapter supports all of the CGA video modes in addition to providing a set of new modes.

Note that if the machine contains two adapters (attached to two monitors) you cannot simply call the function **ScrSetMode** to immediately switch into any of the video modes indicated by **ScrTypes**, since only one adapter is active at a given time. See the following section on **ScrMonoCard** and **ScrColorCard** for a description of the techniques for activating alternate video adapters.

To test for a particular code, you can use the AND operator on the returned value, as in the following example:

```
if (ScrTypes () & VEGAM)
        /* then modes 07h and 0Fh are available */
```

Note that if the value VPS2 is included in the returned byte, then the PS/2 video BIOS functions are supported. In this case you should call interrupt 10h, function 1Bh, for a complete list of the supported video modes (see the BIOS interface technical reference cited in the Bibliography for details).

The program in Figure 5.24 calls **ScrTypes** and prints a list of the adapter types that are detected, together with the supported video modes for each adapter. Figure 5.25 provides a MAKE file, and Figure 5.26 a QuickC program list.

How ScrTypes Works

ScrTypes is contained in the assembly language source file of Figure 5.3 (SCRA.ASM). This function performs the following sequence of steps:

1. The function determines whether a monochrome display adapter is installed by performing a presence test for the 6845

```
#include <STDIO.H>
#include "SCR.H"

void main (void)
     {
     int VideoTypes;

     VideoTypes = ScrTypes ();           /* Get installed video adapter types. */

                                         /* Print them out.                    */

     printf ("VIDEO ADAPTER TYPE        MODES SUPPORTED (in hex)\n");
     printf ("------------------        ------------------------\n");
     printf (!(VideoTypes & VMDA)        ? "" :
             "MDA                       7\n");
     printf (!(VideoTypes & VHGC)        ? "" :
             "Hercules graphics         7, 720 x 348 monochrome graphics\n");
     printf (!(VideoTypes & VCGA)        ? "" :
             "CGA                       0, 1, 2, 3, 4, 5, 6\n");
     printf (!(VideoTypes & VEGAM)       ? "" :
             "EGA MONOCHROME            7, F\n");
     printf (!(VideoTypes & VEGAC)       ? "" :
             "EGA COLOR                 0, 1, 2, 3, 4, 5, 6, D, E, 10\n");
     printf (!(VideoTypes & VPS2)        ? "" :
             "PS/2:  VGA or MCGA        Invoke interrupt 10h, function 1Bh,\n"
             "                          for a complete list of supported modes.\n"

     } /* end main */
```

Figure 5.24: SCRDEM07.C: A program that calls **ScrTypes** to obtain a list of installed adapter types

```
SCRDEM07.OBJ : SCRDEM07.C SCR.H
     cl /c /W2 /Zp SCRDEM07.C

SCRA.OBJ : SCRA.ASM
     masm /MX SCRA.ASM;

SCRDEM07.EXE : SCRDEM07.OBJ SCRA.OBJ
     link /NOI /NOD SCRDEM07+SCRA,,NUL,SLIBCER;
```

Figure 5.25: SCRDEM07.M: A MAKE file for SCRDEM07.C

```
SCRDEM07.C
SCRA.OBJ
```

Figure 5.26: A QuickC program list for preparing SCRDEM07.C

video controller registers that are used by this adapter. The routine attempts to write to the data register at address 3B5h; if the value can be successfully read back, then the register is present and the monochrome adapter must be installed.

2. The function then performs a similar test for the color graphics adapter (the data register for this adapter is located at address 3D5h).

3. The function tests for the presence of a Hercules graphics adapter. This test (supplied courtesy of Hercules Computer Technology) determines whether bit 7 of the "display mode status" port (3BAh) changes at least 10 times during the execution of a loop (8000h repetitions). On a Hercules card this bit goes low with each vertical retrace (see the section "Modifications for the Color Graphics Adapter"), while IBM cards do not use the bit.

4. The function tests for an EGA adapter by calling BIOS interrupt 10h, function 12 (the "alternate select" function). This service returns 0 in register BH if an EGA adapter attached to a color monitor (an enhanced display) is present. It returns 1 in register BH if an EGA adapter attached to a monochrome monitor is present. If neither 0 nor 1 is returned in BH, then an EGA system is not installed.

5. The function determines whether the PS/2 video BIOS services are supported by calling interrupt 10h, function 1Ah ("read/write display combination code"), passing a subfunction code of 00h in AL (to read the display combination). If this function is supported, it returns 1Ah in register AL. In this case, **ScrTypes** sets the VPS2 bit of the return value; when your program receives this value, it can call interrupt 10h, function 1Ah, to determine the active and secondary display adapters, and it can call interrupt 10h, function 1Bh, to obtain a complete list of all supported video modes (as well as other detailed video information). See the description of these functions in the IBM BIOS interface reference cited in the Bibliography.

ScrMonoCard and ScrColorCard

*Using
ScrMonoCard
and ScrColorCard*

As mentioned in the previous section, you can have both a monochrome adapter and monitor *and* a color adapter and monitor installed in the same machine. Only one of these adapters, however, is *active* at a given time. The active adapter is the one currently managed by the BIOS video services. All video output displayed through the BIOS (or through C functions such as **printf**, which ultimately invoke the BIOS) is directed to the active adapter. Also, the BIOS services can be used to activate only those video modes supported by the active adapter. For example, you cannot use the function **ScrSetMode** (which invokes the BIOS) to switch into video mode 07 h (monochrome text) if the color adapter is currently active.

The functions **ScrMonoCard** and **ScrColorCard**, however, permit you to set the active adapter. **ScrMonoCard**, which has the prototype

```
void ScrMonoCard
     (void)
```

activates the monochrome adapter, switching into monochrome text mode (video mode 07 h). **ScrColorCard**, which has the prototype

```
void ScrColorCard
     (void)
```

activates the color adapter and switches into 80-column color text mode (video mode 03h).

Note that **ScrMonoCard** performs the same task as the MS-DOS command

```
mode mono
```

and **ScrColorCard** has the same effect as the MS-DOS command

```
mode co80
```

The advantage of these two functions is that they allow you to conveniently switch modes from within an application program. You can use them to select an active adapter on a system with two adapters (and two monitors), or to display data on both monitors by calling the two functions alternately. Note that when calling one of these functions, the existing screen data is erased from the monitor that is being activated; data remains intact, however, on the monitor that is losing the active status.

The program in Figure 5.27 demonstrates the effect of **ScrMonoCard** and **ScrColorCard**. This program first calls **ScrTypes** to determine whether the system has both a monochrome and a color adapter attached (by testing the VCGA and VMDA bits in the return value). Provided both types of adapter are installed, the program then calls **ScrGetMode** to ascertain the adapter that is currently active (**MonoActive** is set to 1 if the monochrome adapter is active, or to 0 if the color adapter is active). It then enters a loop that repeatedly calls **printf** (with a delay between calls generated by **UtyPause**) to display a string on the currently active monitor. If the user presses Enter, however, the program calls either **ScrMonoCard** or **ScrColorCard** to switch active adapters; the messages then begin appearing on the newly activated monitor.

Figure 5.28 provides a MAKE file, and Figure 5.29 contains a QuickC program list.

See Chapter 7 for a description of the techniques for switching into the Hercules graphics mode on a system with a Hercules-compatible adapter type (indicated by **ScrTypes** returning VHGC).

*How
ScrMonoCard
and
ScrColorCard
Work*

Chapter 3 described the BIOS equipment flag that is returned by the interrupt 11h equipment determination service. This flag is stored at address 0040h:0010h, and may be directly modified by a program. The function **ScrMonoCard** first modifies the *initial video mode* bits of the equipment flag (bits 5 and 4) to the value 11 (binary). The bits contained in this word are listed in Table 3.1. The value 11 (binary) indicates an 80-column monochrome text mode. More importantly, it signals the BIOS that a monochrome adapter is installed and active. Once these bits are set to make sure that they indicate a monochrome card, **ScrMonoCard** calls **ScrSetMode** to switch into monochrome text mode (mode 7; if the video mode bits were *not* set to the binary value 11 the BIOS would refuse to change into monochrome text mode).

The function **ScrColorCard** works in an analogous manner, except that the video mode bits in the equipment flag are set to the binary value 10 to indicate a color card, and the video mode is then set to 80-column color text (mode 3).

Modifications for the Color Graphics Adapter

With the standard IBM color graphics adapter (CGA), the routines in this chapter that read or write directly to video memory will cause a "snow" effect to appear on the monitor. This effect occurs when both

```
#include <STDIO.H>
#include <PROCESS.H>
#include "SCR.H"
#include "KBD.H"
#include "UTY.H"

void main (void)
    {
    int VideoTypes;            /* Stores video adapter types.          */
    int MonoActive;            /* Flag indicating monochrome display active. */
    struct Mode ModeStruct;    /* Holds video mode information.        */

                               /* Test whether system has two monitors. */
    VideoTypes = ScrTypes ();
    if (!(VideoTypes & VCGA && VideoTypes & VMDA))
        {
        fprintf (stderr,"Cannot run program.\nYou must have both a color"
                        " and a monochrome monitor installed.\n");
        exit (1);
        }

                               /* Find initial video mode.             */
    ScrGetMode (&ModeStruct);
    MonoActive = ModeStruct.VideoMode == 7;

    for (;;)                   /* Loop to display message, read keyboard. */
        {
        printf ("Press Enter to switch monitors, or Esc to end program.\n");

        UtyPause (0.5);        /* Generate 1/2 second delay.           */

        if (KbdReady ())       /* Test whether key entered.            */
            switch (KbdGetC () & 0x00ff)
                {
                case 0x1b:
                    exit (0);

                case 0x0d:
                    if (MonoActive)
                        ScrColorCard ();  /* Switch to color monitor. */
                    else
                        ScrMonoCard ();   /* Switch to mono monitor.  */
                    MonoActive ^= 1;      /* Toggle flag.             */
                    break;
                }

        } /* end for loop */

    } /* end main */
```

Figure 5.27: SCRDEM08.C: A program that switches between active adapters by calling **Scr-MonoCard** and **ScrColorCard**

```
SCRDEM08.OBJ : SCRDEM08.C SCR.H KBD.H UTY.H
     cl /c /W2 /Zp SCRDEM08.C

SCR.OBJ : SCR.C SCR.H
     cl /c /W2 /Zp SCR.C

SCRA.OBJ : SCRA.ASM
     masm /MX SCRA.ASM;

KBDA.OBJ : KBDA.ASM
     masm /MX KBDA.ASM;

UTY.OBJ : UTY.C UTY.H
     cl /c /W2 /Zp UTY.C

UTYA.OBJ : UTYA.ASM
     masm /MX UTYA.ASM;

SCRDEM08.EXE : SCRDEM08.OBJ SCR.OBJ SCRA.OBJ KBDA.OBJ UTY.OBJ UTYA.OBJ
     link /NOI /NOD SCRDEM08+SCR+SCRA+KBDA+UTY+UTYA,,NUL,SLIBCER;
```

Figure 5.28: SCRDEM08.M: A MAKE file for SCRDEM08.C

the CPU and the video hardware attempt to access video memory simultaneously. This section shows how these routines can be modified to prevent snow. The versions of these routines written specifically for CGA systems, however, are considerably slower than the general versions given in this chapter, and should not be used unless there is a known display problem. It is not advisable to rely on a software test for the CGA, since many hardware compatible versions of this adapter do *not* display snow. Therefore, it is best to query the user through an installation procedure.

Although routines modified for the CGA are slower than the unmodified versions, they are still considerably faster than the standard BIOS or DOS services. For example, in the benchmark mentioned at the beginning of the chapter, writing ten screens of data was accomplished by a DOS routine in approximately 53 seconds, by the BIOS in 35 seconds, by direct video access in .38 seconds, and by direct video access modified for the CGA in 2.53 seconds.

```
SCRDEM08.C
SCR.C
SCRA.OBJ
KBDA.OBJ
UTY.C
UTYA.OBJ
```

Figure 5.29: A QuickC program list for preparing SCRDEM08.C

Because of the precise timing involved, CGA display routines virtually demand assembly language. Since assembly language is somewhat beyond the scope of this book, and on account of the decreasing importance of the original CGA adapter, separate CGA routines are not provided for all the applicable functions in the chapter. However, the following discussion and example routines provide sufficient information to allow the interested reader to write a CGA version for any of the video routines.

The only functions that require modification are those that directly read from or write to video memory. To prevent snow, it is necessary to perform reads or writes only during those times when the monitor beam is blanked. There are two such times: after the electron beam has completed scanning a line and is moving back across the screen (*horizontal retrace*), and after the beam has completed the bottom line and is returning to the top of the screen (*vertical retrace*). Horizontal retrace is extremely fast and allows the transfer of only a single byte; vertical retrace, however, is relatively slow, and permits the transfer of more than 400 bytes.

The video functions may be divided into two categories: first, those that transfer small quantities of data (no more than one row, or 160 bytes), and second, those that transfer large blocks of data (more than a single row). The functions that transfer small quantities of data are **ScrPutS**, **ScrPutBox**, and **ScrGetS**; the functions that transfer blocks of data are **ScrPush**, **ScrPop**, **ScrPutWindow**, and **ScrPutAttr**. A different strategy will be used for each of these two categories, and an example assembler routine will be presented to demonstrate each strategy.

Small Data Transfers

Figure 5.30 contains the assembly language listing for the function **ScrPutSCga**. This function is a version of **ScrPutS**, written specifically for CGA adapters that create snow. The file conforms to the assembly language interface discussed in Chapter 1, so that it may be called from a Microsoft C program.

ScrPutSCga is typical of functions that display a small quantity of data, and the basic strategy used is to wait for the beginning of a horizontal retrace period before transferring each byte of data to video memory. The reason for not using the vertical retrace period is that it is likely that all the data could be transferred using horizontal retrace periods, *before* the next vertical retrace even begins. (The period *between* vertical retrace periods is sufficient to transfer nearly 200 bytes, one at a time during horizontal retraces.)

```
 1: .MODEL LARGE
 2: .CODE
 3:
 4: PUBLIC _ScrPutSCga
 5: ;
 6: ;            Prototype:
 7: ;
 8: ;            void far ScrPutSCga (char far *String,unsigned char Attr,
 9: ;                             unsigned char Row,unsigned char Col);
10: ;
11: ;            This procedure is a special version of 'ScrPutS' designed
12: ;            especially for Color Graphics Adapters that produce "snow" when
13: ;            writing to video memory.
14: ;
15: _ScrPutSCga PROC
16:
17: h_retrace   macro                        ;Pauses until the beginning of a
18:             local    m01, m02            ;horizontal retrace.
19: m01:        in       al, dx              ;Loop to complete any retrace period
20:             test     al, 1               ;in progress.
21:             jnz      m01
22: m02:        in       al, dx              ;Loop until start of a new horizontal
23:             test     al, 1               ;retrace.
24:             jz       m02
25:             endm
26:
27: sframe      struc                        ;Template to access stack frame.
28: BasePtr     dw       ?                   ;Position of saved BP register.
29: RetAd       dd       ?                   ;Return address.
30: StringAdd   dd       ?                   ;String address.
31: Attrib      dw       ?                   ;Display attribute.
32: Row         dw       ?                   ;Starting row.
33: Col         dw       ?                   ;Starting column.
34: sframe      ends
35:
36: frame       equ      [bp]                ;Base for accessing stack frame.
37:
38:                                          ;Standard initialization.
39:             push     bp                  ;Set up base pointer to access frame.
40:             mov      bp, sp
41:             push     di                  ;Save C register variables.
42:             push     si
43:             push     ds                  ;Save C data segment.
44:
45:             lds      si, frame.StringAdd;Load DS:SI with far address of start
46:                                          ;of string.
47:
48:             mov      ax, 0b800h          ;Set ES to CGA buffer.
49:             mov      es, ax
50:                                          ;Starting offset =
51:                                          ;    (Row * 160) + (Col * 2)
52:             mov      di, frame.Row       ;Place row in DI and multiply by 160.
53:             mov      ax, di
54:             mov      cl, 7
55:             shl      di, cl
56:             mov      cl, 5
57:             shl      ax, cl
58:             add      di, ax
```

Figure 5.30: The assembly language function **ScrPutSCga**

```
59:
60:                 mov     ax, frame.Col        ;Multiply Col by 2.
61:                 shl     ax, 1
62:                 add     di, ax               ;Add (Col * 2) to DI.
63:
64:                                              ;Attribute in BH.
65:                 mov     bh, byte ptr frame.Attrib
66:                 mov     dx, 03dah            ;CRT status register.
67: a01:
68:                 cmp     byte ptr [si], 0     ;Test for null termination.
69:                 je      a02
70:                 mov     bl, [si]             ;Move next character to BL.
71:                 inc     si
72:                 cli                          ;Disable interrupts.
73:                 h_retrace                    ;Wait for horizontal retrace.
74:                 mov     es:[di], bl          ;Move ASCII.
75:                 inc     di
76:                 h_retrace                    ;Wait again.
77:                 mov     es:[di], bh          ;Move ATTRIBUTE.
78:                 sti                          ;Restore interrupts.
79:                 inc     di                   ;Increment offset in video memory.
80:                 jmp     a01                  ;Go back for another character.
81: a02:
82:                 pop     ds                   ;Restore registers.
83:                 pop     si
84:                 pop     di
85:                 mov     sp, bp
86:                 pop     bp
87:                 ret                          ;Return to C program.
88:
89: _ScrPutSCga ENDP
90:
91: END
```

Figure 5.30: The assembly language function **ScrPutSCga** (continued)

The function **ScrPutSCga** begins by setting registers DS:SI to point to
the beginning of the source string (line 45). It next sets ES to point to the
color video memory segment. (Therefore, this function will not work on
a monochrome system!) Like its C counterparts, it now calculates the
starting offset in video memory, and places the result in DI (lines 52–62).
The display attribute is stored in BH.

On a CGA adapter during a horizontal retrace, bit 0 of the port at I/O
address 03DAh is *on*. This port address is stored in DX and the routine
enters the main loop that writes each character to video memory (lines
67–80). The test for the end of the string is at the head of the loop. Following this test, the next character from the string is loaded into register
BL (to prepare it for a rapid transfer to video memory at the correct
time), and the pointer to the string (SI) is incremented.

Lines 72 through 78 contain the timing-critical part of the loop. First,
the interrupts are disabled, since a hardware interrupt occurring at this
time could ruin the synchronization of the data transfers with horizontal retraces. Next, the macro **h_retrace** causes the program to wait until

the beginning of a new horizontal retrace. The program then has time to transfer the one-byte character to video memory. Before transferring the attribute it must invoke **h_retrace** again. After both bytes are safely moved, the interrupts are reenabled. Note that the macro **h_retrace** (lines 17–25) contains two polling loops. The first loop waits until the end of a horizontal retrace in case one is active (otherwise, the program could proceed in the middle of a retrace, which would probably not allow sufficient time for the transfer). The second loop waits until the beginning of a new horizontal retrace.

Large Data Transfers

The function **ScrPutWindow** is typical of one that transfers a large block of data. Figure 5.31 lists the assembly language version of this function, **ScrPutWinCga**, designed specifically to prevent snow on the CGA adapter. The routine is basically a translation of the C version, with many assembly language housekeeping details. Like the C version, it transfers the data row by row; however, unlike the C program, the main loop (lines 96 –134) moves two rows with each repetition and contains the special synchronization logic.

The basic strategy employed by this function is to move one entire row during vertical retrace, and then while waiting for the next vertical retrace period, to move another row byte by byte, during horizontal retrace periods. Thus, the routine makes optimal use of both parts of the vertical retrace cycle: when vertical retrace is *active* it uses the fastest possible technique to transfer a block of data (that is, the **rep movsb** instruction); when vertical retrace is inactive, rather than simply waiting in a idle state it makes the best use of this time by transferring another row by the slower single byte method.

Note that the number of bytes transferred during vertical retrace and during horizontal retrace change, depending upon the dimensions of the window, and are unlikely to be optimal. However, no more than one row can be transferred in a single block move since data on adjoining rows are not necessarily contiguous in video memory. For functions that transfer *all* of video memory (which is a single contiguous block in memory), you can experiment with different values to find the optimal number of bytes to transfer during each stage. You might start with transferring approximately 400 bytes during vertical retrace, and 150 bytes between vertical retraces (one by one during horizontal retraces).

```
 1: .MODEL LARGE
 2: .CODE
 3:
 4: PUBLIC _ScrPutWinCga
 5: ;
 6: ;              Prototype:
 7: ;
 8: ;              void far ScrPutWinCga (char far *Buffer,int SourceStartRow,
 9: ;                            int SourceStartCol,int SourceEndRow,
10: ;                            int SourceEndCol,int TargetRow,
11: ;                            int TargetCol);
12: ;
13: ;              This procedure is a special version of 'ScrPutWindow' designed
14: ;              especially for Color Graphics Adapters that produce "snow" when
15: ;              writing to video memory.
16: ;
17: _ScrPutWinCga PROC
18:
19: sframe      struc                      ;Template to access stack frame.
20: BasePtr     dw      ?                  ;Position of saved BP register.
21: RetAd       dd      ?                  ;Return address.
22: buf_ad      dd      ?                  ;Address of source buffer.
23: ulr_s       dw      ?                  ;Upper-left row source.
24: ulc_s       dw      ?                  ;Upper-left column source.
25: lrr_s       dw      ?                  ;Lower-right row source.
26: lrc_s       dw      ?                  ;Lower-right column source.
27: ulr_d       dw      ?                  ;Upper-left row destination.
28: ulc_d       dw      ?                  ;Upper-left column destination.
29: sframe      ends
30:
31: frame       equ     [bp]               ;Base for accessing stack frame.
32:
33:                                        ;Standard initialization.
34:             push    bp                 ;Set up base pointer to access frame.
35:             mov     bp, sp
36:             push    di                 ;Save C register variables.
37:             push    si
38:             push    ds                 ;Save C data segment.
39:
40:             lds     si, frame.buf_ad   ;Load DS:SI with address of source
41:                                        ;buffer.
42:
43:                                        ;Calculate source buffer offset in BX
44:                                        ;     = (row * 160) + (col * 2)
45:             mov     ax, frame.ulr_s    ;Multiply starting row by 160.
46:             mov     bx, ax
47:             mov     cl, 7
48:             shl     ax, cl
49:             mov     cl, 5
50:             shl     bx, cl
51:             add     bx, ax
52:
53:             mov     ax, frame.ulc_s    ;Multiply starting column by 2.
54:             shl     ax, 1
55:             add     bx, ax             ;Total offset in BX.
56:
57:             add     si, bx             ;Add offset to SI;  SI now contains
58:                                        ;offset in source buffer.
```

Figure 5.31: The assembly language function **ScrPutWinCga**

```
 59:
 60:              mov      ax, 0b800h         ;Set ES to CGA video buffer.
 61:              mov      es, ax
 62:
 63:                                          ;Calculate video memory offset
 64:                                          ;     = (row * 160) + (col * 2)
 65:              mov      di, frame.ulr_d    ;Place row in DI and multiply by 160.
 66:              mov      ax, di
 67:              mov      cl, 7
 68:              shl      di, cl
 69:              mov      cl, 5
 70:              shl      ax, cl
 71:              add      di, ax
 72:
 73:              mov      ax, frame.ulc_d    ;Multiply col by 2.
 74:              shl      ax, 1
 75:              add      di, ax             ;Add (col * 2) to DI.
 76:                                          ;DI now contains video memory offset.
 77:
 78:                                          ;Calculate number of rows in BL.
 79:              mov      bl, byte ptr frame.lrr_s
 80:              sub      bl, byte ptr frame.ulr_s
 81:              inc      bl
 82:                                          ;Calculate number of bytes/row in BH.
 83:              mov      bh, byte ptr frame.lrc_s
 84:              sub      bh, byte ptr frame.ulc_s
 85:              inc      bh
 86:              shl      bh, 1
 87:
 88:              mov      ah, 160            ;Calculate SI, DI increment in AH.
 89:              sub      ah, bh
 90:
 91:              mov      dx, 3dah           ;Keep crt status register in DX.
 92:
 93:              cld
 94:              mov      ch, 0              ;Only need LSB of CX.
 95:
 96: b01:         mov      cl, bh             ;Load bytes/row into CX.
 97:
 98:                                          ;Pause until the beginning of a
 99:                                          ;vertical retrace.
100: b02:         in       al, dx             ;Loop to complete any retrace period
101:              test     al, 8              ;in progress.
102:              jnz      b02
103: b03:         in       al, dx             ;Loop until start of a new vertical
104:              test     al, 8              ;retrace.
105:              jz       b03
106:
107:              rep      movsb              ;Move entire row in vert. retrace.
108:              mov      cl, ah             ;AH stores SI, DI increment value.
109:              add      si, cx             ;Adjust SI, DI to start of next row.
110:              add      di, cx
111:              dec      bl                 ;Decrement row counter.
112:              jz       b06                ;Quit if no more rows.
113:
```

Figure 5.31: The assembly language function **ScrPutWinCga** (continued)

```
114:                                      ;Move another row, byte by byte,
115:                                      ;before next vertical retrace.
116:                                      ;Pause until the beginning of a
117:                                      ;horizontal retrace.
118:          mov     cl, bh              ;Loop to complete any retrace period
119: b04:     in      al, dx              ;in progress.
120:          test    al, 1
121:          jnz     b04
122:          cli                         ;Don't want an interrupt now.
123: b05:     in      al, dx              ;Loop until start of a new horizontal
124:          test    al, 1               ;retrace.
125:          jz      b05
126:          movsb                       ;Move one byte.
127:          sti                         ;Byte transferred, so interrupts ok.
128:          loop    b04                 ;Loop until entire row is moved.
129:          mov     cl, ah
130:          add     si, cx              ;Adjust SI, DI to start of next row.
131:          add     di, cx
132:          dec     bl                  ;Decrement row counter.
133:          jz      b06                 ;Quit if no more rows.
134:          jmp     b01                 ;Go back to move another row during
135:                                      ;the next vertical retrace.
136: b06:
137:          pop     ds                  ;Restore registers.
138:          pop     si
139:          pop     di
140:          mov     sp, bp
141:          pop     bp
142:          ret                         ;Return to C program.
143:
144: _ScrPutWinCga ENDP
145:
146: END
```

Figure 5.31: The assembly language function **ScrPutWinCga** (continued)

BUFFER FUNCTIONS

If you are using the set of video functions that have been presented so far in this chapter, your screen displays are probably carefully designed, with borders, titles, prompts, messages, and data input fields all at specific locations on the screen. This type of design is easy to maintain for data entry screens, and for screens displaying constant information. However, what happens if you want to display a report with an unknown number of lines that cannot fit on a single screen? The usual method is to simply write a stream of characters to the screen, allowing the entire screen contents to scroll up once the last line has been reached. This method, of course, completely destroys your carefully designed screen; also, once data have scrolled off the screen they are gone forever, so that the user cannot recall a previous line.

The set of functions presented in this section offer two great advantages for displaying reports or other data of indeterminate length, within the context of a windowed screen. First, the functions allow you to confine output to a single window, without affecting other screen areas. Second, since the functions store all screen data in an internal buffer, they allow the user to recall previous pages of data. Conceptually, although the report is larger than the window and cannot be viewed in its entirety at one time, the user can move the buffer up and down behind the window so that any portion of the report can be brought into view.

Using the set of buffer functions described in this section you can perform the following operations:

▮ Define a window on the screen through which you will view the contents of the buffer (**BufInit**).

▮ Store lines of data in a buffer that can be much larger than the physical screen size (**BufNextLine**).

▮ Display a given portion of the buffer through the defined window (**BufShow**).

▮ Obtain the address of any line stored in the buffer (**BufGet**).

▮ Free the memory held by the buffer when you have finished displaying its contents (**BufFree**).

The buffer functions are listed in the file BUF.C of Figure 5.32. To call these functions from your C program, you must include the file BUF.H, Figure 5.33, and link your program with the object files BUF.OBJ, SCR.OBJ, and KBDA.OBJ (Chapter 2).

BufInit

Using BufInit

Before using the buffer functions to store and display a given set of data, you must call **BufInit** to initialize the system and associate the internal buffer with a window on the screen. The prototype is

```
void BufInit
      (int StartRow,
       int StartCol,
       int StopRow,
       int StopCol)
```

```
#include <STDIO.H>
#include <PROCESS.H>
#include <MALLOC.H>
#define MODFILE
#include "BUF.H"
#include "SCR.H"
#include "KBD.H"

#pragma check_stack (off)          /* Turn of stack checks so that functions  */
                                   /* can be called from interrupt routines.  */

#define MAXLINES 75
static char *LinePtAr [MAXLINES];
static unsigned char ULR,ULC,LRR,LRC;
static int LinesPerWin;
static int CharPerLine;

void BufInit (int StartRow,int StartCol,int StopRow,int StopCol)
/*
    This function initializes the buffer display system of functions.  It
    does not set BufError or return a value.
*/
    {
    ULR = (unsigned char)StartRow;      /* Save dimensions of window.  */
    ULC = (unsigned char)StartCol;
    LRR = (unsigned char)StopRow;
    LRC = (unsigned char)StopCol;
    LinesPerWin = LRR - ULR + 1;
    CharPerLine = LRC - ULC + 2;
    LastLine = -1;                      /* Initialize global variable.  */

    } /* end BufInit */


char *BufNextLine (void)
/*
    This function adds another line to the internal buffer.  If successful,
    it sets BufError to NOERROR and returns the starting address of the line.
    If an error occurs, it returns the value NULL after setting BufError to
    one of the following values:

    TOOMANYLINES       The number of lines has exceeded MAXLINES.
    OUTOFMEMORY        No more heap memory is available.
*/
    {
    if (++LastLine >= MAXLINES)                 /* Test for buffer size limit. */
        {
        BufError = TOOMANYLINES;
        return (NULL);
        }
    if (LastLine % LinesPerWin == 0)                  /* Time to allocate. */
        {
        if ((LinePtAr [LastLine] =
            (char *)malloc (LinesPerWin * CharPerLine)) == NULL)
            {
            BufError = OUTOFMEMORY;
            return (NULL);
            }
        }
```

Figure 5.32: BUF.C: The buffer functions for storing and displaying data

```
        else
             LinePtAr [LastLine] = LinePtAr [LastLine - 1] + CharPerLine;

        BufError = NOERROR;
        return (LinePtAr [LastLine]);

        } /* end BufNextLine */


void BufShow (int StartLine)
/*
     This function displays the buffer, beginning with the line having the
     index specified by 'StartLine';  it does not set BufError or return a
     value.
*/
     {
     register int Line,Row;

     ScrClear (ULR,ULC,LRR,LRC);                    /* First clear the window.   */
     Row = ULR;
                                                    /* Print the lines.          */
     for (Line = StartLine;
          Line < StartLine + LinesPerWin && Line <= LastLine;
          ++Line)
          ScrPutS (LinePtAr [Line],0x0f,(unsigned char)Row++,ULC);

     } /* end BufShow */


char *BufGetLine (int Line)
/*
     This function returns the address of buffer line number 'Line'.  If
     successful, it sets 'BufError' to NOERROR;  if the requested line is out
     of range, it sets 'BufError' to LINEOUTOFRANGE and returns NULL.
*/
     {
     if (Line <= LastLine)
          {
          BufError = NOERROR;
          return (LinePtAr [Line]);
          }
     else
          {
          BufError = LINEOUTOFRANGE;
          return (NULL);
          }
     } /* end BufGetLine */


void BufFree (void)
/*
     This function frees the buffer memory.  It does not set BufError or
     return an error code.
*/
     {
     int i;

     for (i = 0; i <= LastLine; i += LinesPerWin)
          free (LinePtAr [i]);

     } /* end BufFree */
```

Figure 5.32: BUF.C: The buffer functions for storing and displaying data (continued)

```
void BufInit (int StartRow,int StartCol,int StopRow,int StopCol);
char *BufNextLine (void);
void BufFree (void);
void BufShow (int StartLine);
char *BufGetLine (int Line);

#ifdef MODFILE
int BufError;
int LastLine;
#else
extern int LastLine;
extern int BufError;
#endif

                               /* Error return constants.              */
#ifndef NOERROR
#define NOERROR          0     /* No Error.                            */
#endif
#define TOOMANYLINES     1     /* The number of lines has exceeded MAXLINES.*/
#define OUTOFMEMORY      2     /* No more heap memory is available.    */
#define LINEOUTOFRANGE   3     /* Line passed to BufGet is out of range.  */
```

Figure 5.33: BUF.H: Header file that you must include in your program in order to call the functions of BUF.C

The first two parameters specify the upper left corner of the window on the screen through which you want to view the buffer, and the second two parameters specify the lower right corner of this window. The width of the window determines the maximum length of a line that can be stored in the buffer; the number of lines, however, is limited only by the available heap space.

Note that these functions provide only a single buffer; therefore only one set of data can be stored at a given time. You must call **BufInit** before storing a set of data, and **BufFree** (described below) after you are done displaying the data. These functions are demonstrated in Figure 5.34, described later in the chapter.

How BufInit Works

BufInit stores the coordinates of the window that will be used to display the buffer (so that these values do not need to be passed by the other buffer function calls). It also calculates and stores the number of lines in a single window (**LinesPerWin**), and the number of characters per window line (**CharPerLine**; note that the number of characters is one greater than the width of the window to allow room for a terminating NULL). All these variables are declared externally so that they will persist between function calls, and are made **static** so that they are private to the file.

BufNextLine

*Using
BufNextLine*

Each time you call **BufNextLine**, which has the prototype

```
char *BufNextLine
    (void)
```

it allocates another line in the internal buffer, and returns its address. If the function is successful, it sets the global variable **BufError** to NOERROR before returning the address. If an error occurs, it returns the value NULL, after setting **BufError** to TOOMANYLINES if the maximum number of lines allowed by the module has been exceeded, or to OUTOFMEMORY if heap memory has been exhausted.

You can then use this address to copy your next line of data into the buffer. You can perform the copying through C functions such as **sprintf**, **strcpy**, or **strncpy**; **sprintf** is especially useful for formatting data. For example, the following expression might be used to "print" your next line of data to the buffer:

```
sprintf (BufNextLine(), "%-25s%8.2f", emp.name,
    emp.salary);
```

This expression is exactly analogous to sending a line to the screen or printer, except that the line is collected in an internal buffer rather than being displayed. (**BufNextLine** is also analogous to the Pascal command **writeln**, since a new line is implicit in the function call without the need for an explicit newline character.)

To allow your program to determine how many lines have actually been allocated and stored in the buffer, **BufNextLine** maintains the global variable **LastLine** (declared in BUF.H and therefore accessible to your program). Buffer lines are numbered beginning from 0, so that after the first time you call **BufNextLine**, **LastLine** will equal 0, and after the second call it will be 1, and so on. Note than it is a grievous error to attempt to store a line longer than the width of the buffer that you specified in the call to **BufInit**.

The **BufNextLine** function is demonstrated in Figure 5.34, described later in the chapter. The next function, **BufShow**, is used to actually display the buffer on the screen.

*How
BufNextLine
Works*

BufNextLine begins by incrementing the global line counter (**Last-Line**) and testing whether the maximum number of lines that can be allocated has been exceeded. If your program encounters this error, you must increase the constant MAXLINES, defined in BUF.C (Figure 5.32).

The address of each line in the buffer is stored internally by this module in the array of character pointers **LinePtAr**. Each time **BufNextLine** is called, it stores the address of the next buffer line in the next free member of **LinePtAr**. The memory used to store the buffer lines is obtained from the heap by calling the main C allocator **malloc**. However, it would be inefficient to call the allocator each time **BufNextLine** is called; therefore, memory is allocated in blocks that are large enough to store one entire window of data, and **malloc** is called only when this allocation unit is exhausted. Therefore, if the current buffer line is a multiple of the number of lines per window (that is, **LastLine % LinesPerWin == 0**), the function must allocate more memory; otherwise, it simply calculates and returns the address of the next line within the block that is already allocated:

```
LinePtAr [LastLine-1] + CharPerLine
```

BufShow

Using BufShow

The function **BufShow** displays a section of the internal buffer within the window on the screen that was specified with the call to **BufInit**. The prototype is

```
void BufShow
     (int StartLine)
```

where **StartLine** is the number of the first buffer line to display. This line will be displayed on the first line of the window, and **BufShow** will automatically display as many subsequent buffer lines as can fit within the window (up to and including **LastLine**). If you pass a value for **StartLine** that is greater than **LastLine**, then the window will simply be blanked. This function is demonstrated in Figure 5.34, described later in the chapter.

*How BufShow
Works*

BufShow first clears the window with a call to **ScrClear**. It then prints lines from the buffer into the window using **ScrPutS**. It begins by printing the buffer line indexed by **StartLine** on the first row of the window, and continues printing lines on subsequent rows until either of the following occurs:

▌ There are no more lines in the buffer (that is, **LastLine** has been exceeded).

▌ The last row of the window on the screen is reached.

BufGetLine

Using BufGetLine

This **BufGetLine** function has the prototype

```
char *BufGetLine
     (int Line)
```

and returns the address of the line in the internal buffer having the number given by **Line**. The parameter **Line** must be a value between 0 and **LastLine**. If a number is passed outside of this range, the function returns NULL and sets the global variable **BufError** to LINEOUTOFRANGE. If the function is successful, it sets **BufError** to NOERROR. **BufGetLine** is useful for retrieving the contents of a line that has been copied to the buffer at some prior point in the program.

*How BufGetLine
Works*

BufGetLine simply returns the address stored in the element of **LinePtAr** that is indexed by the requested line. To avoid the need for this function, **LinePtAr** could have been declared as a globally available variable in BUF.H, so that the user could directly access the desired buffer address. However, in the spirit of data encapsulation (a concept discussed in Chapter 1) **LinePtAr** is kept private to the buffer module.

BufFree

Using BufFree

BufFree, which has the prototype

```
void BufFree
    (void)
```

should be called after you are done displaying the lines of data stored in the buffer, in order to free memory in the program heap for the use of other functions. Note that it is vital that this function be called once, and only once, after each call to **BufInit**.

How BufFree Works

BufFree cycles through all of the blocks of heap memory that have been allocated by **BufNextLine**, and frees them using the standard C library function **free**.

An Example

The program in Figure 5.34 demonstrates the use of the buffer functions. This program generates a 50-line dummy report, which it stores in the buffer and then displays a portion at a time through a window on the screen, allowing the user to move up and down through the buffer by means of the arrow keys. The program performs the following series of steps, which typify the technique for using the buffer functions:

1. A box is displayed on the screen to serve as a border for the window, using **ScrPutBox**.

2. The program calls **BufInit**, passing it the dimensions of a window that is just within the border.

3. The report is now "printed" into the buffer, calling **BufNextLine** for each line, and using **sprintf** to format the data. For a more typical report, of course, the actual number of lines is not known in advance.

```
#include <STDIO.H>
#include <PROCESS.H>
#include "BUF.H"
#include "SCR.H"
#include "KBD.H"

void main (void)
    {
    register int i;                     /* Loop index.                      */
    int CurLine = 0;                    /* Number of top line displayed.    */

    ScrPutBox (0,0,12,79,3);            /* Draw a box.                      */

    BufInit (1,1,11,78);                /* Initialize buffer module,        */
                                        /* specifying size of window.       */

                                        /* Write data to buffer.            */
    for (i = 0; i < 50; ++i)
        sprintf (BufNextLine (),"This is line number %d of the report.",i);

    BufShow (CurLine);                  /* Display first screen of buffer.  */

    for (;;)                            /* Display different areas of buffer*/
        switch (KbdGetC ())             /* in response to arrow keys.       */
            {
            case 0x11b:                 /* Escape.                          */
                BufFree ();             /* Release buffer memory.           */
                ScrSetCur (23,0,0);     /* Set cursor at bottom of screen.  */
                exit (0);               /* Terminate program.               */

            case 0x4800:                /* Up arrow.                        */
                if (CurLine > 0)
                    BufShow (--CurLine);
                break;

            case 0x5000:                /* Down arrow.                      */
                if (CurLine < LastLine)
                    BufShow (++CurLine);
                break;

            } /* end switch */

    } /* end main */
```

Figure 5.34: BUFDEMO1.C: A program that uses the buffer function to display a report through a window

4. The program now displays the first 11 lines of the buffer (the height of the window), using **BufShow**, with the parameter **CurLine** set to 0.

5. Control now passes into a loop that reads the up and down arrow keys, and the Esc key.

6. The ↑ key causes the program to decrement **CurLine** if it is greater than 0, and then to display the buffer beginning one line up.

7. The ↓ causes the program to increment **CurLine** if it is less than **LastLine**, and then to display the buffer beginning one line down.

8. Finally, if the Esc key is pressed, the program calls **BufFree** to free the allocated memory, adjusts the cursor, and terminates.

Figure 5.35 contains a MAKE file, and Figure 5.36 a QuickC program list.

```
BUFDEM01.OBJ : BUFDEM01.C BUF.H
     cl /c /W2 /Zp BUFDEM01.C

BUF.OBJ : BUF.C BUF.H
     cl /c /W2 /Zp BUF.C

SCR.OBJ : SCR.C SCR.H
     cl /c /W2 /Zp SCR.C

KBDA.OBJ : KBDA.ASM
     masm /MX KBDA.ASM;

BUFDEM01.EXE : BUFDEM01.OBJ BUF.OBJ SCR.OBJ KBDA.OBJ
     link /NOI /NOD BUFDEM01+BUF+SCR+KBDA,,NUL,SLIBCER
```

Figure 5.35: BUFDEM01.M: A MAKE file for BUFDEM01.C

```
BUFDEM01.C
BUF.C
SCR.C
KBDA.OBJ
```

Figure 5.36: A QuickC program list for preparing BUFDEM01.C

Enhancements

The following are two possible enhancements that could be made to the buffer routines, and are left as exercises for the reader.

First, the routines could be modified to allow multiple internal buffers, so that several reports could be viewed simultaneously in different windows.

Second, the use of heap memory by these functions is somewhat extravagant. For the sake of simplicity, a fixed block of memory is allocated to each line (equal to the width of the window plus one byte for a terminating NULL), regardless of the actual length of the string that is copied into the buffer. A more miserly strategy would allocate only enough memory to encompass the actual size of the string (measured by a function such as **strlen**).

An Interactive
Screen Designer

CHAPTER **6**

This chapter presents the complete C source code for an interactive screen designing utility. The program not only serves to demonstrate the use of many of the video functions given in the previous chapter, but also provides a convenient tool for creating screens and windows that can be displayed with this set of functions. The screen designer allows you to perform the following basic operations:

- Create full screens or collections of windows that appear exactly as they will be displayed by your program.

- Directly access any of the 254 characters available in text modes. In addition to the standard ASCII characters, this set includes many characters for drawing lines, boxes, and textures, as well as foreign language and mathematical symbols.

- Use any of the monochrome or color display attributes available in IBM-compatible systems.

- Manipulate the screen design using a set of block editing commands.

- Save the screen in a file that is a 4000 byte image of video memory. This file can then be reloaded by the screen designer to perform further editing, or be read by a program into a buffer (via **ScrReadWindow**) and then displayed using **ScrPutWindow**.

- Directly generate an **include** file that can be used to initialize a C program buffer at compile time. The screen data can then be immediately displayed using **ScrPutWindow**, without the need to store screens on disk and read them at runtime.

The editor allows you to determine the row and column position of any field on the screen. Therefore, once your program displays a screen or window, you can easily write messages to specific locations or accept data from specific fields by using the functions **ScrPutS** and **ScrGetS**, presented in Chapter 5.

This chapter first summarizes the procedure for compiling and linking the source code and explains how to use the program, so that you can get it running as quickly as possible. Next, it discusses the design goals that shaped the implementation of the program, and then describes how the program works. Finally, the chapter concludes with some suggestions for enhancements you might want to add to the source code.

■ COMPILING AND LINKING THE PROGRAM

The Companion Diskette Set described at the end of this book contains the executable as well as source versions of the screen designer. If you have obtained these diskettes, then you are ready to start using the program and may want to skip to the next section. Otherwise, you can follow the suggestions offered here to process the source code file.

The source code for the screen designer is given in Figure 6.1. This program contains many special purpose internal functions, and also calls external functions from the **Scr**, **Kbd**, and **Uty** modules, which are presented in other chapters. It is therefore necessary to import these modules by including the appropriate header files and linking with the required object files. Figure 6.2 provides a MAKE file that will compile the program, update the object modules, and perform the linking step. Figure 6.3 gives a QuickC program list, which you can use if you want to prepare the program within the QuickC environment.

By examining the MAKE file, you can see the source files that need to be on the disk when preparing the program: SCRGEN.C, SCR.C (Chapter 5), KBD.C (Chapter 2), KBDA.ASM (Chapter 2), UTY.C (Chapter 12), and UTYA.ASM (Chapter 12). The corresponding header files (SCR.H, KBD.H, and UTY.H) also need to be present.

The program includes an additional header file: SCRGEN.INC. This file contains the screen data necessary to initialize the buffer **Scr**, and consists of 4000 decimal numbers separated by commas. Although you can easily produce such a file using the screen designer itself, the screen designer does not yet exist! The solution to this quandary is to use the following bootstrap approach:

1. Before compiling the program the first time, remove the **Scr** array initialization. Specifically, replace the lines

    ```
    char Scr [4000] =
        {
        #include "SCRGEN.INC"
        };
    ```

    with the single line

    ```
    char Scr [4000];
    ```

```
#include <STDIO.H>              /* Include files for Microsoft C library.   */
#include <DOS.H>
#include <CONIO.H>
#include <PROCESS.H>
#include <IO.H>
#include <FCNTL.H>
#include <STRING.H>
#include <SYS\TYPES.H>
#include <SYS\STAT.H>

#include "SCR.H"                /* Include files for imported modules.      */
#include "KBD.H"
#include "UTY.H"

void OpenMessage (void);        /* Displays opening message.                */
void Menu (void);               /* Display Alt key menu.                    */
void HelpScreen (void);         /* Display help screen.                     */
void SelectChar (void);         /* Select character to "draw" on screen.    */
void SelectAttr (void);         /* Select current display attribute.        */
void MonoAttr (void);           /* Monochrome attribute routine.            */
void ColorAttr (void);          /* Color attribute routine.                 */
void ReadFile (void);           /* Read in a screen file.                   */
void WriteFile (void);          /* Save current screen in file.             */
void IncFile (void);            /* Generate a C include file for screen.    */
void DisplayStat (void);        /* Display row, column, key information.     */
void InitBuf (void);            /* Initialize video image buffer.           */
void ShowVideo (void);          /* Display the video image buffer on screen. */
void ShowBlock (void);          /* Display marked block.                    */
void CpyMovBlock (int Move);    /* Copies or moves marked block to cursor pos */
void DeleteBlock (void);        /* Clear marked block area of screen.       */

char Scr [4000] =               /* Buffer containing data for display screen. */
    {
    #include "SCRGEN.INC"
    };

typedef int ROW [80];           /* One row of screen data.                  */
ROW far *Video;                 /* Pointer to access video memory.          */
int Buffer [25][80];            /* Video image buffer.                      */
char far *FarPtrBuffer;         /* 'Far' address of 'Buffer'.               */
int HoldBuf [25][80];           /* Temporary storage for video data.        */
int Row = 0;                    /* Current row screen.                      */
int Col = 0;                    /* Current column on screen.                */
int AttrChar = 0x0720;          /* Stores the current attribute and character.*/
char FileName [50];             /* Stores file name for reading & writing.   */
int BlockStartRow = -1;         /* UL row of marked block.                  */
int BlockStartCol = -1;         /* UL column of marked block.               */
int BlockEndRow = -1;           /* LR row of marked block.                  */
int BlockEndCol = -1;           /* LR column of marked block.               */
int Modified = 0;               /* Flag indicates that buffer is modified.   */
int MenuDisplayed = 0;          /* Flag indicates Alt menu is on screen.    */
int BlockShown = 0;             /* Flag indicates block is displayed.       */
void main (void)
    {
    int Key;                    /* Extended code/ASCII value of key read.   */
    int Code;                   /* Stores return code for KbdGetC.          */
    unsigned char far *PtrVideoMode = (unsigned char far *)0x00400049;
```

Figure 6.1: SCRGEN.C: Source listing for the interactive screen editor

```
                              /* Initialize file name w/ blanks.        */
              UtyBlank (FileName, sizeof (FileName));

                    /* Initialize far pointer to first character in video memory. */
              FP_SEG (Video) = (*PtrVideoMode == 7) ? 0xb000 : 0xb800;
              FP_OFF (Video) = 0;

              FarPtrBuffer = (char far *)Buffer;  /* Get 'far' address of 'Buffer'. */

              ScrClear (0,0,24,79);     /* Clear the whole screen.              */
              InitBuf ();               /* Initialize the screen image buffer.  */
              ScrSetCur (Row,Col,0);    /* Place cursor at first position.       */
              OpenMessage ();           /* Display opening message.             */

              for (;;)                  /* Begin keyboard read loop.            */
                  {
                  if (KbdGetShift () & ALT)        /* Alt key is pressed.       */
                      {
                      if (!MenuDisplayed)          /* Menu not already displayed. */
                          {
                          Menu ();                 /* Display Alt key menu.     */
                          MenuDisplayed = 1;       /* Turn on flag.             */
                          }
                      }
                  else if (MenuDisplayed)
                      {                 /* Alt key released and menu is displayed. */
                      ShowVideo ();              /* Restore the screen.         */
                      MenuDisplayed = 0;         /* Turn off flag.              */
                      }
                  if (KbdReady ())      /* Test if a key has been pressed.      */
                      switch (Key = KbdGetC ())
                          {
                          case 0x011b:          /* Escape pressed.              */
                              break;            /* Do not process.              */

                          case 0x4838:          /* Up arrow-Shift.              */
                              Video  [Row][Col] = AttrChar; /* Write "draw" char */
                              Buffer [Row][Col] = AttrChar;
                              Modified = 1;
                                                /* Note:  control drops through. */
                          case 0x4800:          /* Up arrow.                    */
                              if (Row > 0)
                                  ScrSetCur (--Row,Col,0); /* Update cursor.    */
                              break;

                          case 0x5032:          /* Down arrow-Shift.            */
                              Video  [Row][Col] = AttrChar; /* Write "draw" char */
                              Buffer [Row][Col] = AttrChar;
                              Modified = 1;
                                                /* Note:  control drops through. */
                          case 0x5000:          /* Down arrow.                  */
                              if (Row < 24)
                                  ScrSetCur (++Row,Col,0); /* Update cursor.    */
                              break;

                          case 0x4b34:          /* Left arrow-Shift.            */
                              Video  [Row][Col] = AttrChar; /* Write "draw" char */
                              Buffer [Row][Col] = AttrChar;
                              Modified = 1;
```

Figure 6.1: SCRGEN.C: Source listing for the interactive screen editor (continued)

```
                                /* Note:  control drops through.  */
        case 0x4b00:            /* Left arrow.                     */
            if (Col > 0)
                ScrSetCur (Row,--Col,0); /* Update cursor.    */
            break;

        case 0x4d36:            /* Right arrow-Shift.              */
            Video  [Row][Col] = AttrChar; /* Write "draw" char */
            Buffer [Row][Col] = AttrChar;
            Modified = 1;
                                /* Note:  control drops through.  */
        case 0x4d00:            /* Right arrow.                    */
            if (Col < 79)
                ScrSetCur (Row,++Col,0); /* Update cursor.    */
            break;

        case 0x4700:            /* <Home> pressed.                 */
        case 0x4737:
            ScrSetCur (Row,Col=0,0);      /* Update cursor.    */
            break;

        case 0x4f00:            /* <End> pressed.                  */
        case 0x4f31:
            ScrSetCur (Row,Col=79,0);     /* Update cursor.    */
            break;

        case 0x4900:            /* <PgUp> pressed.                 */
        case 0x4939:
            ScrSetCur (Row=0,Col,0);      /* Update cursor.    */
            break;

        case 0x5100:            /* <PgDn> pressed.                 */
        case 0x5133:
            ScrSetCur (Row=24,Col,0);     /* Update cursor.    */
            break;

        case 0x2300:            /* Alt-H pressed.                  */
            HelpScreen ();      /* Display help screen.            */
            ScrSetCur (Row,Col,0);   /* Restore cursor.        */
            ShowVideo ();            /* Restore screen.        */
            break;

        case 0x2e00:            /* Alt-C pressed.                  */
            SelectChar ();      /* Select "draw" character.        */
            ScrSetCur (Row,Col,0);   /* Restore the cursor.    */
            ShowVideo ();  /* Restore the screen.               */
            break;

        case 0x1e00:            /* Alt-A pressed.                  */
            SelectAttr ();      /* Select attribute.               */
            ScrSetCur (Row,Col,0);   /* Restore the cursor.    */
            ShowVideo ();  /* Restore the screen.               */
            break;

        case 0x1300:            /* Alt-R pressed.                  */
            ReadFile ();   /* Read screen file.                   */
            ScrSetCur (Row,Col,0);   /* Restore the cursor.    */
            ShowVideo ();  /* Restore the screen.               */
            break;
```

Figure 6.1: SCRGEN.C: Source listing for the interactive screen editor (continued)

```
            case 0x1100:        /* Alt-W pressed.                    */
                WriteFile (); /* Save current screen file.           */
                ScrSetCur (Row,Col,0);    /* Restore the cursor.     */
                ShowVideo ();  /* Restore the screen.                */
                break;

            case 0x1700:        /* Alt-I pressed.                    */
                IncFile ();     /* Generate "include" file.          */
                ScrSetCur (Row,Col,0);    /* Restore the cursor.     */
                ShowVideo ();  /* Restore the screen.                */
                break;

            case 0x1f00:        /* Alt-S pressed.                    */
                DisplayStat ();/* Display status information.        */
                ScrSetCur (Row,Col,0);    /* Restore the cursor.     */
                ShowVideo ();  /* Restore the screen.                */
                break;

            case 0x2d00:        /* Alt-X pressed = exit.             */
                if (Modified)  /* Test if data would be lost.        */
                    {
                    ScrClear (0,0,4,79);
                    ScrPutBox (0,0,4,79,1);
                    ScrPutS ("Buffer is modified.  Enter Y to save"
                             ", N to loose edits, or ESC cancel:",
                             0x0f,2,4);
                    ScrSetCur (2,75,0);
                    do
                        {                   /* Get user's response.  */
                        switch (KbdGetC () & 0x00ff)
                            {
                            case 'y':
                            case 'Y':
                                WriteFile ();  /* Save file.   */
                                if (Modified)  /* User pressed */
                                    {          /* Escape -- go */
                                    Code = 0; /* back to prog */
                                    break;
                                    }     /* Else drop through.*/
                            case 'n':
                            case 'N':          /* Go ahead and exit.*/
                                ScrClear (0,0,24,79);
                                exit (0);
                            case 0x1b:      /* Escape -- go     */
                                Code = 0; /* back to program.  */
                                ShowVideo ();
                                break;
                            default:           /* Invalid key --    */
                                Code = 1; /* get another one.  */
                                break;
                            }
                        }
                    }
```

Figure 6.1: SCRGEN.C: Source listing for the interactive screen editor (continued)

```
                              while (Code);
                           }
                     else        /* Simple exit if buffer not modified.   */
                           {
                           ScrClear (0,0,24,79);
                           exit (0);
                           }
                     ScrSetCur (Row,Col,0);   /* Restore cursor.          */
                     break;

               case 0x3002:    /* Control-B: mark block beginning.   */
                     BlockStartRow = Row; /* Assign current start pos. */
                     BlockStartCol = Col;
                     ShowBlock ();  /* Mark the block on screen.      */
                     break;

               case 0x1205:    /* Control-E: mark block end.         */
                     BlockEndRow = Row;  /* Assign current end pos.    */
                     BlockEndCol = Col;
                     ShowBlock ();
                     break;

               case 0x2e03:              /* Control-C: copy block to   */
                     CpyMovBlock (0);     /* current cursor position.   */
                     break;

               case 0x320d:              /* Control-M: move block to   */
                     CpyMovBlock (1);     /* current cursor position.   */
                     break;

               case 0x2308:              /* Control-H: toggle block display. */
                     if (BlockShown)      /* If it's on, turn it off.   */
                           {
                           BlockShown = 0;
                           ShowVideo ();
                           }
                     else                 /* If it's off, turn it on.   */
                           ShowBlock ();
                     break;

               case 0x2004:              /* Control-D: clear marked block. */
                     DeleteBlock ();
                     break;

               case 0x0e08:              /* Backspace.                 */
                     if (Col > 0)         /* Test if possible.          */
                           {
                           ScrSetCur (Row,--Col,0); /* Update cursor.   */
                               /* Write space with current attribute.  */
                           Video  [Row][Col] = (AttrChar & 0xff00) | ' ';
                           Buffer [Row][Col] = (AttrChar & 0xff00) | ' ';
                           }
                     break;

               default:                  /* Non-ASCII key or character.  */
                     if ((Key = Key&0x00ff) == 0)  /* Non-ASCII key.      */
                           break;
```

Figure 6.1: SCRGEN.C: Source listing for the interactive screen editor (continued)

```
                                        /* Write the attribute and character.    */
                        Video  [Row][Col] = (AttrChar & 0xff00) | Key;
                        Buffer [Row][Col] = (AttrChar & 0xff00) | Key;
                        Modified = 1;
                        if (Col < 79)
                                ScrSetCur (Row,++Col,0); /* Update cursor.    */
                        break;

                } /* end switch */

        } /* end forever loop */

} /* end main */


void OpenMessage ()          /* Display opening message.                      */
        {
        ScrPutBox (7,15,12,62,2);
        ScrPutS ("C Screen Generator",0x0f,8,30);
        ScrPutS ("Copyright (C) 1988  Michael J. Young",0x07,9,21);
        ScrPutS ("press Alt key for menu",0x0f,11,28);

                                /* Pause until key entered or Alt pressed. */
        while (!KbdReady () && !(KbdGetShift () & ALT))
                ;
        ScrClear (7,15,12,62);              /* Remove display and return.    */
        return;

        } /* end OpenMessage */


void Menu ()                 /* Display Alt key menu.                         */
        {
        unsigned char Row = -1;

        ScrClear (0,0,16,31);
        ScrPutBox (0,0,16,31,0);
        ScrPutS ("Alt-H    Help window",0x0f,Row+=2,2);
        ScrPutS ("Alt-C    select Character",0x0f,Row+=2,2);
        ScrPutS ("Alt-A    select Attribute",0x0f,Row+=2,2);
        ScrPutS ("Alt-R    Read file",0x0f,Row+=2,2);
        ScrPutS ("Alt-W    Write screen file",0x0f,Row+=2,2);
        ScrPutS ("Alt-I    make 'Include' file",0x0f,Row+=2,2);
        ScrPutS ("Alt-S    display Status",0x0f,Row+=2,2);
        ScrPutS ("Alt-X    eXit program",0x0f,Row+=2,2);

        } /* end Menu */


void HelpScreen ()                                  /* Display help screen.    */
        {
        ScrSetCur (25,80,0);
        ScrPutWindow (Scr,0,0,24,49,0,0);
        KbdGetC ();                                 /* Pause for a keystroke.  */

        } /* end HelpScreen */
```

Figure 6.1: SCRGEN.C: Source listing for the interactive screen editor (continued)

```
    void SelectChar ()                /* Select character to "draw" on screen.       */
        {
        register int r, c;            /* Row and column counters.                    */
        int SelRow, SelCol;           /* Position of character chosen by user.       */
        int Ch;                       /* For printing the characters.                */

        ScrSetCur (25,80,0);                      /* Hide the cursor.                 */
        ScrClear (0,0,18,72);                     /* Clear window.                    */
        ScrPutBox (0,0,18,72,1);                  /* Draw window border.              */
                                                  /* Print titles.                    */
        ScrPutS ("Select Drawing Character",0x0f,1,23);
        ScrPutS ("<Arrow> keys move highlight.",0x0f,15,22);
        ScrPutS ("Press <Esc> to select highlighted character",0x0f,16,14);
        ScrPutS ("or <Space Bar> to select <Space> character.",0x0f,17,14);

        if ((AttrChar&0x00ff) == ' ') /* If current character is blank, place         */
            {                         /* the cursor at the first character.          */
            SelRow = 3;
            SelCol = 3;
            }
                                          /* Draw the 253 visible characters.         */
        for (Ch = 1,c = 3; c <= 69; c += 3)    /* 23 columns.                         */
            for (r = 3; r <= 13; ++r,++Ch)     /* by 11 rows.                         */
                {
                if (Ch == ' ')            /* Skip blank character.                   */
                    ++Ch;
                              /* Write character;  attributes alternate between       */
                              /* high and low intensity.                             */
                Video [r][c] = (r % 2 ? 0x0700 : 0x0f00) | Ch;
                                          /* Look for current character:              */
                if (Ch == (AttrChar & 0x00ff))
                    {
                    SelRow = r;           /* Save row, and column of                 */
                    SelCol = c;           /* current character.                      */
                    }
                }
                                  /* Hightlight current character.                    */
        ScrPutAttr (0x70,SelRow,SelCol - 1,SelRow,SelCol + 1);

        for (;;)              /* Accept input to allow user to choose character.      */
            switch (KbdGetC ())
                {
                case 0x4800:              /* Up arrow.                                */
                    if (SelRow > 3)       /* Check bounds of char. on screen.         */
                        {                 /* Update highlight and cursor position.    */
                        ScrPutAttr (SelRow % 2 ? 0x07 : 0x0f,SelRow,
                                    SelCol - 1,SelRow,SelCol + 1);

                        --SelRow;
                        ScrPutAttr (0x70,SelRow,SelCol - 1,SelRow,
                                    SelCol + 1);
                        }
                    break;
                case 0x5000:              /* Down arrow.                              */
                    if (SelRow < 13)      /* Check bounds of char. on screen.         */
                        {                 /* Update highlight and cursor position.    */
                        ScrPutAttr (SelRow % 2 ? 0x07 : 0x0f,SelRow,
                                    SelCol - 1,SelRow,SelCol + 1);

                        ++SelRow;
                        ScrPutAttr (0x70,SelRow,SelCol - 1,SelRow,
                                    SelCol + 1);
```

Figure 6.1: SCRGEN.C: Source listing for the interactive screen editor (continued)

```
                          }
                        break;

              case 0x4b00:              /* Left arrow.                     */
                  if (SelCol > 3)       /* Check bounds of char. on screen. */
                        (              /* Update highlight and cursor position. */
                          ScrPutAttr (SelRow % 2 ? 0x07 : 0x0f,SelRow,
                                      SelCol-1,SelRow,SelCol + 1);
                          SelCol -= 3;
                          ScrPutAttr (0x70,SelRow,SelCol - 1,SelRow,
                                      SelCol + 1);
                          }
                        break;

              case 0x4d00:              /* Right arrow.                    */
                  if (SelCol < 69)      /* Check bounds of char. on screen. */
                        (              /* Update highlight and cursor position. */
                          ScrPutAttr (SelRow % 2 ? 0x07 : 0x0f,SelRow,
                                      SelCol - 1,SelRow,SelCol + 1);
                          SelCol += 3;
                          ScrPutAttr (0x70,SelRow,SelCol - 1,SelRow,
                                      SelCol + 1);
                          }
                        break;

              case 0x011b:              /* Escape.                         */
                  /* Assign the selected character to the current          */
                  /* attribute and character variable.                     */
                  AttrChar = (AttrChar & 0xff00) | (Video [SelRow][SelCol]
                             & 0x00ff);
                  return;

              case 0x3920:              /* Space bar pressed.              */
                  /* Space is now the current character.                   */
                  AttrChar = (AttrChar & 0xff00) | ' ';
                  return;

              } /* end Switch */

        } /* end SelectChar */


void SelectAttr ()                /* Select current display attribute.     */
        (
        ScrSetCur (25,80,0);                     /* Hide the cursor.        */
        ScrClear (0,0,14,39);                    /* Clear window.           */
        ScrPutBox (0,0,14,39,1);                 /* Draw window border.     */
        ScrPutBox (4,9,6,30,1);                  /* Draw inner box.         */
        ScrPutS ("foreground",0x0f,5,15);        /* Print labels.           */
        ScrPutS ("+  toggle blinking",0x0f,11,10);

        if (FP_SEG (Video) == 0xb000)    /* Branch to appropriate routine.  */
             MonoAttr ();                /* Monochrome routine.             */
        else
             ColorAttr ();               /* Color routine.                  */

        return;

        } /* end SelectAttr */
```

Figure 6.1: SCRGEN.C: Source listing for the interactive screen editor (continued)

```
void MonoAttr ()                    /* Monochrome attribute routine.      */
{
    char Buf [30];                  /* For formatting titles.             */
    unsigned char Blink;            /* Blinking attribute.                */
                                    /* Table of all monochrome attributes.*/
    static unsigned char AttrTab [] =
        {
        0x07,           /* Normal.                                        */
        0x0f,           /* High intensity.                                */
        0x01,           /* Underlined.                                    */
        0x09,           /* High intensity, underlined.                    */
        0x70,           /* Reverse video.                                 */
        };
                                    /* Length of attribute table.         */
    static int TabLen = sizeof (AttrTab) / sizeof (unsigned char);
    int TabIdx;
                                    /* Find the index for the current attribute. */
    for (TabIdx=0; TabIdx < TabLen; ++TabIdx)
        if (((AttrChar & 0x7fff) >> 8) == AttrTab [TabIdx])
            break;

    if (TabIdx >= TabLen)           /* Attribute not found; therefore assign */
        TabIdx = 0;                 /* index of normal attribute.         */
                                    /* Isolate current blinking attribute: */
    Blink = (unsigned char)(AttrChar & 0x8000) >> 8;
                                                       /* Print titles.    */
    ScrPutS ("SELECT MONOCHROME ATTRIBUTE",0x70,2,6);
    sprintf (Buf,"%c%c select attribute",27,26);       /* Format arrows.   */
    ScrPutS (Buf,0x0f,10,10);

    for (;;)
        {                                   /* Display current attribute.  */
        ScrPutAttr (AttrTab [TabIdx] | Blink,5,10,5,29);
        switch (KbdGetC ())                 /* Read keys from keyboard.    */
            {
            case 0x4b00:                    /* Left arrow.                 */
                /* If index at first entry, wrap around to last.          */
                if (TabIdx == 0)
                    TabIdx = TabLen - 1;
                else
                    --TabIdx;               /* Go to prior entry in table. */
                break;

            case 0x4d00:                    /* Right arrow.                */
                /* If index at last entry, wrap around to first.          */
                if (TabIdx == TabLen - 1)
                    TabIdx = 0;
                else
                    ++TabIdx;               /* Go to next entry in table.  */
                break;

            case 0x4e2b:                    /* Gray +.                     */
                Blink ^= 0x80;              /* Toggle blinking attribute.  */
                break;

            case 0x011b:                    /* Escape.                     */
                                            /* Assign the selected attribute. */
                AttrChar = (AttrChar & 0x00ff) |
                    ((AttrTab [TabIdx] | Blink) << 8);
                return;
```

Figure 6.1: SCRGEN.C: Source listing for the interactive screen editor (continued)

```
                    } /* end switch */

               } /* end forever loop */

          } /* end MonoAttr */


    void ColorAttr ()              /* Color attribute routine.          */
          {
          char Buf [30];           /* For formatting titles.            */
          unsigned char Attr;      /* One byte temporary storage for attribute. */

                                   /* Print titles.                     */
          ScrPutS ("SELECT COLOR ATTRIBUTE",0x70,2,9);
          sprintf (Buf,"%c%c select foreground",27,26);  /* Format arrow chars. */
          ScrPutS (Buf,0x0f,9,10);
          sprintf (Buf,"%c%c select background",24,25);  /* Format arrow chars. */
          ScrPutS (Buf,0x0f,10,10);
          Attr = (unsigned char)(AttrChar >> 8); /* Initialize selected attribute*/
                                   /* to current attribute.             */
          for (;;)
               {
               ScrPutAttr (Attr,5,10,5,29);   /* Display selected attribute.     */
               switch (KbdGetC ())            /* Read keys from user.            */
                    {
                    case 0x4800:              /* Up arrow.                       */
                                              /* Increment background bits.      */
                         Attr = (Attr & 0x80) | (Attr + 0x10 & 0x7f);
                         break;

                    case 0x5000:              /* Down arrow.                     */
                                              /* Decrement background bits.      */
                         Attr = (Attr & 0x80) | (Attr - 0x10 & 0x7f);
                         break;

                    case 0x4b00:              /* Left arrow.                     */
                                              /* Decrement foreground bits.      */
                         Attr = (Attr & 0xf0) | (Attr - 1 & 0x0f);
                         break;

                    case 0x4d00:              /* Right arrow.                    */
                                              /* Increment foreground bits.      */
                         Attr = (Attr & 0xf0) | (Attr + 1 & 0x0f);
                         break;

                    case 0x4e2b:              /* Gray +.                         */
                         Attr ^= 0x80;        /* Toggle blinking bit.            */
                         break;

                    case 0x011b:              /* Escape.                         */
                         /* Assign selected attribute to current attribute.      */
                         AttrChar = (AttrChar & 0x00ff) | (Attr << 8);
                         return;

                    } /* end switch */

               } /* end forever loop */

          } /* end ColorAttr */
```

Figure 6.1: SCRGEN.C: Source listing for the interactive screen editor (continued)

```
    void ReadFile ()                    /* Read in a 4000 byte screen data file.    */
        {
        int Code;                       /* Return code for 'ScrGetC'.               */
        int Handle;                     /* Low-level file handle.                   */

        ScrClear (0,0,5,79);                        /* Clear screen for window.     */
        ScrPutBox (0,0,5,79,1);                     /* Draw border for window.      */
        if (Modified)                   /* Test if screen data would be lost.       */
            {
            ScrPutS ("Buffer is modified.  Save? (y/n):",0x0f,2,3);
            ScrSetCur (2,37,0);
            switch (KbdGetC () & 0x00ff)
                {
                case 'n':       /* Only an explicit 'n' will cause go ahead. */
                case 'N':
                    ScrClear (1,1,4,78);
                    break;
                default:
                    WriteFile ();               /* Save current screen data.    */
                    ScrClear (0,0,5,79);
                    ScrPutBox (0,0,5,79,1);
                    break;
                }
            }
        ScrPutS ("Name of file to READ:",0x0f,2,3);  /* Print prompt.              */
        ScrPutS (FileName,0x70,2,26);               /* Print existing file name.    */

        do          /* Get file name;  allow user to exit only w/ CR and Esc.       */
            {
            while ((Code = ScrGetS (FileName,0x70,2,26,sizeof(FileName),NOFEAT))
                    != -1 && Code != 0)
                ;
            if (Code == -1)                         /* Exit if user pressed escape.*/
                return;
            if ((Handle = open (FileName,O_RDONLY | O_BINARY)) == -1)
                {                       /* File open error.                         */
                ScrPutS ("file not found",0x8f,3,32);
                Code = 1;               /* Go back for another file name.           */
                }
            }
        while (Code);
        read (Handle,(char *)Buffer,4000);          /* Low-level block read.        */
        close (Handle);
        Modified = 0;
        return;

        } /* end ReadFile */


    void WriteFile ()               /* Save the current screen data in a file.      */
        {
        int Code;                       /* Return code for ScrGetS.                 */
        int Handle;                     /* Low-level file handle.                   */

        ScrClear (0,0,5,79);                        /* Clear screen for window.     */
        ScrPutBox (0,0,5,79,1);                     /* Draw border for window.      */
        ScrPutS ("Name of file to WRITE:",0x0f,2,3); /* Print prompt.               */
        ScrPutS (FileName,0x70,2,26);               /* Print existing file name.    */
```

Figure 6.1: SCRGEN.C: Source listing for the interactive screen editor (continued)

```
        do
            {       /* Get file name;  allow user to exit only w/ CR and Esc.   */
            while ((Code = ScrGetS (FileName,0x70,2,26,sizeof(FileName),NOFEAT))
                    != -1 && Code != 0)
                ;
            if (Code == -1)                             /* Exit if user pressed escape.*/
                return;
                                                        /* Open an EXISTING file.      */
            if ((Handle = open (FileName,O_RDWR | O_BINARY)) != -1)
                {                               /* No error, therefore file exists. */
                ScrPutS ("File already exists;  overwrite? (y/n):",0x8f,3,17);
                ScrSetCur (3,57,0);
                switch (KbdGetC() & 0x00ff)
                    {
                    case 'y': /* Only an explicit 'y' will overwrite file.  */
                    case 'Y':
                        Code = 0;
                        break;
                    default:  /* User doesn't want to overwrite;          */
                              /* therefore close file, blank name and go   */
                              /* back for another name.                    */
                        close (Handle);
                        UtyBlank (FileName,sizeof (FileName));
                        ScrPutS (FileName,0x70,2,26);
                        ScrPutS (UtyRepeat (78,' '),0x0f,3,1);
                        Code = 1;
                        break;
                    }
                }                               /* File does not exist; therefore  */
                                                /* create a new one.               */
            else if ((Handle = open (FileName,O_RDWR | O_BINARY | O_CREAT,
                    S_IREAD | S_IWRITE)) == -1)
                {
                ScrPutS ("Error creating file",0x8f,3,28);
                Code = 1;
                }
            }
        while (Code);

        write (Handle,(char *)Buffer,4000);
        close (Handle);
        Modified = 0;
        return;

        } /* end WriteFile */


void IncFile ()                 /* Generate a C include file for screen.   */
    {
    register int c;             /* Column counter.                         */
    register int i;             /* Loop index.                             */
    FILE *FilePtr;              /* High-level file pointer.                */
    char IFileName [44];        /* Name for include file.                  */
    int Code;                   /* Return code from ScrGetC.               */
    unsigned char *BufferPtr;   /* Pointer to screen image buffer.         */
    char Buf [4];               /* For formatting the output numbers.      */
```

Figure 6.1: SCRGEN.C: Source listing for the interactive screen editor (continued)

```
ScrClear (0,0,5,79);                            /* Clear screen for window.  */
ScrPutBox (0,0,5,79,1);                         /* Draw border for window.   */
ScrPutS ("Name of INCLUDE FILE to generate:",0x0f,2,2);      /* Prompt. */
ScrPutS (UtyRepeat (43,' '),0x70,2,36);
do
        {    /* Get file name;  allow user to exit only w/ CR and Esc.   */
        while ((Code = ScrGetS (IFileName,0x70,2,36,sizeof (IFileName),
            NOFEAT)) != -1 && Code != 0)
            ;
        if (Code == -1)                         /* Exit if user pressed escape.*/
            return;
        /* First open file for read only simply to find if it exists.   */
        if ((FilePtr = fopen (IFileName,"rb")) == NULL)
            {
            /* File does not exist;  therefore, create it.              */
            if ((FilePtr = fopen (IFileName,"wb")) == NULL)
                {
                ScrPutS ("Error creating file",0x8f,3,28);
                Code = 1;
                }
            }
        else
            {
            /* File exists, therefore close pointer and reopen for      */
            /* writing (destroys existing file) if user chooses to.     */
            fclose (FilePtr);
            ScrPutS ("File already exists;  overwrite? (y/n):",0x8f,3,17);
            ScrSetCur (3,57,0);
            switch (KbdGetC () & 0x00ff)
                {
                case 'y':
                case 'Y':               /* Open file for writing.       */
                    if ((FilePtr = fopen (IFileName,"wb")) == NULL)
                        {
                                        /* Erase message.      */
                        ScrPutS (UtyRepeat (78,' '),0x0f,3,1);
                        ScrPutS ("Error opening file ",0x8f,3,28);
                        Code = 1; /* Go back for another file name.     */
                        }
                    break;

                default:  /* User does not want to overwrite, therefore */
                          /* blank file name and go back for another.   */
                    UtyBlank (IFileName,sizeof (IFileName));
                    ScrPutS (IFileName,0x70,2,36);
                    ScrPutS (UtyRepeat (78,' '),0x0f,3,1);
                    Code = 1;
                    break;

                } /* end switch */

            } /* end existing file */

        } /* end do */
```

Figure 6.1: SCRGEN.C: Source listing for the interactive screen editor (continued)

```
            while (Code);

            c = -1;                                    /* Initialize column counter.    */
            BufferPtr = (unsigned char *)Buffer;    /* Initialize buffer pointer.    */
            for (i = 1; i <= 4000; ++i)    /* Write 4000 bytes from screen image  */
                {                                  /* buffer to the file.           */
                if (c > -1)
                    if (c <= 75)      /* Write newline if needed, and comma.  */
                            putc (',',FilePtr);
                        else
                            {
                            fputs ("\r\n",FilePtr);
                            c = -1;
                            }
                sprintf (Buf,"%1d",*BufferPtr++);  /* Format the character as a   */
                fputs (Buf,FilePtr);               /* decimal number into the     */
                c += strlen (Buf) + 1;             /* minimum sized field.        */

                } /* end for */

            fputs ("\r\n",FilePtr);  /* Write final CR-LF characters.           */

            fclose (FilePtr);

            } /* end IncFile */


    void DisplayStat () /* Display current row, column, and shift key status.   */
            {
            char Buf [3];
            int ShiftStat;

            ScrClear (0,0,10,40);
            ScrPutBox (0,0,10,40,1);
            ScrPutS ("S T A T U S    I N F O R M A T I O N",0x0f,1,3);
            ScrPutS ("Current Row",0x0f,3,7);
            sprintf (Buf,"%2d",Row);
            ScrPutS (Buf,0x70,3,28);
            ScrPutS ("Current Column",0x0f,4,7);
            sprintf (Buf,"%2d",Col);
            ScrPutS (Buf,0x70,4,28);
            ScrPutS ("Num Lock",0x0f,6,7);
            ScrPutS ("Caps Lock",0x0f,7,7);
            ScrPutS ("Scroll Lock",0x0f,8,7);
            do
                {
                ShiftStat = KbdGetShift ();                /* Get shift status word. */
                ScrPutS (ShiftStat & NUMLOCKSTATE ?  "ON " : "OFF",0x70,6,28);
                ScrPutS (ShiftStat & CAPLOCKSTATE ?  "ON " : "OFF",0x70,7,28);
                ScrPutS (ShiftStat & SCROLLSTATE  ?  "ON " : "OFF",0x70,8,28);
                }
            while (!KbdReady ());          /* Continue until any key is pressed.   */
            KbdGetC ();                    /* Get rid of that key.                 */
            return;

            } /* end DisplayStat */
```

Figure 6.1: SCRGEN.C: Source listing for the interactive screen editor (continued)

```
void InitBuf ()      /* Initialize the video image buffer with the current   */
     {               /* screen contents.                                      */

     /* Transfer data FROM video memory TO video image 'Buffer'.             */
     movedata (FP_SEG (Video),0,
               FP_SEG (FarPtrBuffer),FP_OFF (FarPtrBuffer),4000);

     } /* end InitBuf */


void ShowVideo ()                /* Display the video image buffer on screen.  */
     {
     if (BlockShown)             /* Must preserve any currently marked block.  */
          ShowBlock ();          /* First displays video image, then redraws   */
                                 /* the marked block.                          */

     else                        /* No block marked;  just go ahead and        */
          {                      /* transfer the data.                         */
          /* Transfer data FROM video image 'Buffer' TO video memory.          */
          movedata (FP_SEG (FarPtrBuffer),FP_OFF (FarPtrBuffer),
                    FP_SEG (Video),0,4000);
          }

     } /* end ShowVideo */

/*************************** block functions *****************************/

void Buf2Hold (int Clear); /* Move block from video image buffer to hold buf*/
void Hold2Buf (void);      /* Move block from hold to video image buffer.    */

void ShowBlock ()                /* Draw the current marked block on screen.   */
     {
     register int r,c;
     unsigned char Attr;

     BlockShown = 0;             /* First erase any old block markings.         */
     ShowVideo ();

     /* Check if the current start and end positions are valid.               */
     if (BlockStartRow == -1 || BlockEndRow == -1)
          return;
     if (BlockStartRow > BlockEndRow || BlockStartCol > BlockEndCol)
          return;

     BlockShown = 1;                                 /* Switch on global flag. */

     for (r = BlockStartRow; r <= BlockEndRow; ++r)  /* Loop through block. */
          for (c = BlockStartCol; c <= BlockEndCol; ++c)
               {
               if (FP_SEG (Video) == 0xb000)
                    {                                /* Monochrome routine.    */
                    switch ((Video [r][c] & 0x7f00) >> 8)
                         {                           /* Reverse the current    */
                         case 0x07:                  /* attribute to make      */
                         case 0x0f:                  /* block visible.         */
                         case 0x01:
                         case 0x09:
                              Attr = 0x70;
                              break;
```

Figure 6.1: SCRGEN.C: Source listing for the interactive screen editor (continued)

```
                               case 0x70:
                                    Attr = 0x07;
                                    break;
                               }
                  else                                  /* Color routine.       */
                       {
                       /* Exclusive OR the current attribute to make the block */
                       /* stand out.                                           */
                       Attr = (unsigned char)((Video [r][c] ^ 0xffff) >> 8)
                             & 0x7f;
                       }
                  /* Write the resulting attribute to video memory.      */
                       Video [r][c] = (Video [r][c] & 0x80ff) | (Attr << 8);
                  }

          } /* end ShowBlock */


void CpyMovBlock (int Move)      /* Copy or move marked block to current    */
     {                          /* cursor position depending on value of Move */
     if (!BlockShown)            /* First make sure a block is marked.     */
          return;
     Buf2Hold (Move);               /* Transfer the block to hold buffer.    */
     Hold2Buf ();    /* Transfer the block from hold buffer to screen image. */
     ShowBlock ();   /* Display the screen image buffer.                     */
     Modified = 1;   /* Mark buffer as modified.                             */

     } /* end CpyMovBlock */


void Buf2Hold (int Clear)       /* Copies data from video image 'Buffer' to  */
     {                          /* hold buffer, deleting source if 'Clear'<>1.*/

     register int c,tc;   /* Buffer column and target column:  vary the     */
                          /* fastest, therefore use register variables.     */
     int r,tr;            /* Buffer row and target row.                     */

     /* Transfer as much of block as will fit starting at target position.  */
     for (r = BlockStartRow,tr = Row; r <= BlockEndRow && tr <= 24; ++r,++tr)
          for (c = BlockStartCol,tc = Col; c <= BlockEndCol && tc <= 79;
               ++c,++tc)
               {
               HoldBuf [tr][tc] = Buffer [r][c];  /* Transfer character/attr*/
               if (Clear)                   /* For move operation, fill    */
                    Buffer [r][c] = 0x0720;  /* image buffer block w/ space.*/
               }

     } /* end Buf2Hold */


void Hold2Buf ()        /* Transfers data from the hold buffer to screen image */
     {                  /* 'Buffer'.                                           */

     register int r,c;                        /* Row and column counters.    */
```

Figure 6.1: SCRGEN.C: Source listing for the interactive screen editor (continued)

```
                      /* First modify the current marked block delimiters.   */
        BlockEndRow = Row + BlockEndRow - BlockStartRow;
        if (BlockEndRow > 24)
             BlockEndRow = 24;

        BlockStartRow = Row;

        BlockEndCol = Col + BlockEndCol - BlockStartCol;
        if (BlockEndCol > 79)
             BlockEndCol = 79;

        BlockStartCol = Col;

        for (r = Row; r <= BlockEndRow; ++r)      /* Transfer the entire block.  */
             for (c = Col; c <= BlockEndCol; ++c)
                  Buffer [r][c] = HoldBuf [r][c];

        } /* end Hold2Buf */


void DeleteBlock ()                /* Erases the current marked block.       */
     {
     register int r,c;             /* Row and column counters.               */

     if (!BlockShown)              /* Return if no block is marked.          */
          return;

     /* Place space characters, normal attribute, in video image buffer.    */
     for (r = BlockStartRow; r <= BlockEndRow; ++r)
          for (c = BlockStartCol; c <= BlockEndCol; ++c)
               Buffer [r][c] = 0x0720;

     BlockShown = 0;               /* Hide the block since it is now deleted.  */
     ShowVideo ();                 /* Now transfer the new contents of the video */
                                   /* image buffer to the screen.              */
     Modified = 1;                 /* Marked buffer as modified.               */

     } /* end DeleteBlock */

/*************************** end of block functions ***************************/
```

Figure 6.1: SCRGEN.C: Source listing for the interactive screen editor (continued)

2. Generate the program using the MAKE file (after removing SCRGEN.INC from the first line of this file). You can now use all features of the program except the help screen (accessed through the command Alt-H), which will not be very helpful since it will only display a window of random characters.

3. Using the screen editor as described below, enter the help screen shown in Figure 6.4, and generate the include file SCRGEN.INC.

4. Replace the array initialization in the SCRGEN.C source file and recompile. The program will now be complete.

```
SCRGEN.OBJ : SCRGEN.C SCR.H KBD.H UTY.H SCRGEN.INC
    cl /c /W2 /Zp SCRGEN.C

SCR.OBJ : SCR.C SCR.H
    cl /c /W2 /Zp SCR.C

KBD.OBJ : KBD.C KBD.H
    cl /c /W2 /Zp KBD.C

KBDA.OBJ : KBDA.ASM
    masm /MX KBDA.ASM;

UTY.OBJ : UTY.C UTY.H
    cl /c /W2 /Zp UTY.C

UTYA.OBJ : UTYA.ASM
    masm /MX UTYA.ASM;

SCRGEN.EXE : SCRGEN.OBJ SCR.OBJ KBD.OBJ KBDA.OBJ UTY.OBJ UTYA.OBJ
    link /NOI /NOD SCRGEN+SCR+KBD+KBDA+UTY+UTYA,,NUL,SLIBCER;
```

Figure 6.2: SCRGEN.M: A MAKE file for preparing SCRGEN.C

USING THE SCREEN DESIGNER

When you load the program, you will be greeted by an opening message that vanishes as soon as any key is pressed, leaving a blank screen. Anything you enter on this screen becomes part of the buffer that you can save on disk and ultimately display from a C program. The screen designer always saves the entire screen contents in a single 4000 byte file (25 × 80 characters and an equal number of display attributes). Remember, however, that the video functions in Chapter 5 allow you to display *any portion* of this buffer. You can therefore use the program to design either a single full screen display, or as many smaller window displays as will fit on the screen. For example, it is often convenient to

```
SCRGEN.C
SCR.C
KBD.C
KBDA.OBJ
UTY.C
UTYA.OBJ
```

Figure 6.3: A QuickC program list for preparing SCRGEN.C

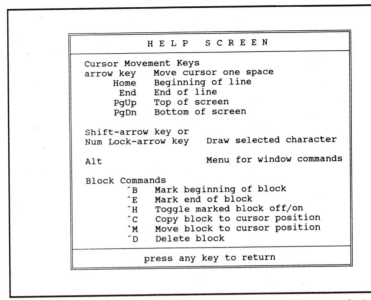

```
┌─────────────────────────────────────────────────┐
│  ┌───────────────────────────────────────────┐  │
│  │            H E L P   S C R E E N          │  │
│  ├───────────────────────────────────────────┤  │
│  │  Cursor Movement Keys                      │  │
│  │  arrow key    Move cursor one space        │  │
│  │       Home    Beginning of line            │  │
│  │        End    End of line                  │  │
│  │       PgUp    Top of screen                │  │
│  │       PgDn    Bottom of screen             │  │
│  │                                            │  │
│  │  Shift-arrow key or                        │  │
│  │  Num Lock-arrow key    Draw selected character │
│  │                                            │  │
│  │  Alt                   Menu for window commands │
│  │                                            │  │
│  │  Block Commands                            │  │
│  │         ^B   Mark beginning of block       │  │
│  │         ^E   Mark end of block             │  │
│  │         ^H   Toggle marked block off/on    │  │
│  │         ^C   Copy block to cursor position │  │
│  │         ^M   Move block to cursor position │  │
│  │         ^D   Delete block                  │  │
│  ├───────────────────────────────────────────┤  │
│  │          press any key to return           │  │
│  └───────────────────────────────────────────┘  │
└─────────────────────────────────────────────────┘
```

Figure 6.4: The data for the help screen as it appears in the screen designer

design and save four separate windows in a single screen file, and then display these windows individually (for instance, the screen file shown in Figure 5.11).

Cursor Movement

To begin creating a screen, you can simply enter text from the keyboard. Any character you type always overwrites the current character at that position. The cursor can be moved on the screen using the following keys:

Key	Cursor Movement
Arrow keys	One column/row in corresponding direction
Home	To beginning of current line
End	To end of current line
PgUp	To top of screen in current column
PgDn	To bottom of screen in current column

When moving the cursor with the arrow keys, make sure that the Num Lock state is off, and that the Shift key is not pressed (to prevent replication of the current drawing character, as explained in the section on Alt-C).

Block Commands

To facilitate the manipulation of the data displayed on the screen, a family of block commands is provided. These commands are all executed by pressing Ctrl in conjunction with a letter. The following block commands are available:

Key	Action
Ctrl-B	Mark *beginning* of block
Ctrl-E	Mark *end* of block
Ctrl-H	Toggle block-marking off and on (*hide* block)
Ctrl-C	*Copy* marked block-to cursor position
Ctrl-M	*Move* marked block to cursor position
Ctrl-D	*Delete* marked block

The first step is to mark the beginning and end of a rectangular block on the screen using Ctrl-B and Ctrl-E. The beginning and end can be marked in either order; nothing will appear on the screen, however, until both a beginning and an end have been marked. (Also, nothing will appear if the beginning position is placed below or to the right of the end position.) The block is marked by a reversal of video attributes. (On a monochrome system, light areas become black and black areas become light. On a color system, the foreground and background colors are altered.) You can now hide the block marking by pressing Ctrl-H (the block will no longer be marked on the screen; the program, however, will remember the position of the block). When Ctrl-H, Ctrl-B, or Ctrl-E are subsequently pressed, the block will again become marked on the screen. Ctrl-H thus toggles the marking off and on.

What can be done with a block once it is marked? There are three options. First, you can delete the block by pressing Ctrl-D, which simply clears the marked area of the screen, and then hides the block from view. Second, you can copy the block to another position on the screen by moving the cursor to the *upper left corner* of the desired position and pressing Ctrl-C. Finally, you can move the block to another position by placing the cursor at the upper left corner of the new position and pressing Ctrl-M, which will clear the original location of the block and place the block at the new location. Note that a copied or moved block always overwrites the data at the target position. Also, if there is insufficient room to place the entire block at the selected location, the block will be copied or moved only until the borders of the screen are encountered.

One typical use for the block commands is to center a title within a particular area on the screen. Simply type the title approximately in the center, mark it as a block, and then use the Ctrl-M command— repeatedly if necessary—to center the title. You do not need to remark the block each time, since when a block is copied or moved, the beginning and end positions move with it, and the block remains marked on the screen.

Menu Commands

The remaining commands are all activated by Alt-key combinations and are accessed through a pop-up menu. To display this menu and execute one of the commands, simply press the Alt-key, and a menu will immediately appear on the screen. To perform the desired command, type the appropriate letter while holding down Alt:

Key	Action
Alt-H	Display *help* window
Alt-C	Select drawing *character*
Alt-A	Select *attribute*
Alt-R	*Read* file
Alt-W	*Write* file
Alt-I	Generate **include** file
Alt-S	Display *status* information
Alt-X	*Exit* from program

As you are learning the system, the automatic Alt-key menu serves as a useful reminder. However, after you have learned the system, the menu can simply be ignored and will demand no extra keystrokes. A description of these commands follows.

Alt-H: Display Help Window

If you press Alt-H a window will be displayed that summarizes all of the keystrokes and commands that you can use when editing a screen (except the Alt-key commands, which are displayed automatically when you press Alt). To return to the program, press any key.

Alt-C: Select Drawing Character

The IBM keyboard allows you to repeat a character across the screen by simply holding down the key. When designing a screen, however, it is useful to be able to repeat a character in *any* direction. The screen editor allows you to select a character, and then replicate it across the screen in any direction. This feature is especially convenient for drawing lines or filling in textures using the special IBM graphics characters. It also allows ready access to the extended characters that cannot be typed directly from the keyboard (without looking up the ASCII codes).

Selecting the Character

When the program begins, the default "drawing" character is a space. To select another drawing character, press Alt-C. A pop-up window displaying a matrix of all 253 visible characters will immediately appear. Simply move the highlight bar using the arrow keys to the desired character and press Esc. The character is stored and the window disappears. You can also return to a blank as the drawing character by hitting the space bar while the window is displayed. Selecting the space character allows you to erase data as the cursor is moved in any direction on the screen.

Drawing the Character

Normally, the arrow keys simply move the cursor across the screen. However, if the shift key is held down while pressing an arrow key, *or* the Num Lock state is active, then the selected drawing character will be replicated as the cursor is moved in any direction. Experiment with this feature by selecting one of the line or texture characters, and then painting it on the screen in various directions. Using this method, you can design imaginative screens and windows.

Alt-A: Select Attribute

As discussed in Chapter 5, the IBM PC and PS/2 family of machines can display a character using any one of a variety of monochrome or color display attributes. The screen designer allows you to select the current display attribute by pressing Alt-A. Once an attribute is selected, it will be used for all subsequent characters written to the screen, until another attribute is chosen.

The procedure for selecting an attribute on a monochrome system is different from the procedure for choosing the foreground and background colors on a color system. When you type Alt-A, the program will automatically employ the appropriate routine and display the correct pop-up window based upon the type of adapter it detects.

Selecting a Monochrome Attribute

If you have a monochrome system, a window will appear containing an inner box displaying the current attribute. Use the left and right arrow keys to view other attributes, and press Esc to select the attribute that is shown. The + key near the numeric keypad toggles blinking on and off.

Selecting a Color Attribute

If you have a color system, a window will appear that displays the current background and foreground colors. You can view other foreground colors using the left and right arrow keys, and other background colors using the up and down arrow keys. The + key near the numeric keypad toggles blinking on and off, and the Esc key selects the attribute that is shown and removes the window.

Alt-R: Read File

You can read an existing screen data file into the buffer by pressing Alt-R, and then entering the file name when prompted (a full path can be specified). If you have already read or written a file, the name of this file will appear as a default; either press Enter to accept this name or type a new name. You can return to the program without performing the read operation by pressing Esc.

Alt-W: Write File

You can save the current contents of the screen buffer at any time by pressing Alt-W. A prompt for the file name will appear, and you can specify a full path name. If you have already read or written a file, the name of this file will appear; either press Enter to accept this name or type a new name. If you are about to overwrite an existing file, you will be warned, and can either continue or enter another name. You can return to the program without performing the write operation by pressing Esc. Be careful that you do not accidentally write a file instead of reading one, resulting in saving a blank screen on top of an existing screen data file!

Once a screen buffer has been saved in a file, you can read it back into the editor at any subsequent time to perform further editing (see Alt-R). You can also place this file on your program runtime disk and read it into an internal 4000-byte buffer prior to displaying the data on the screen. See the descriptions of the functions **ScrReadWindow** and **ScrPutWindow** in Chapter 5.

Alt-I: Generate include File

By pressing Alt-I you can generate an **include** file for a C program based on the current contents of the screen buffer. As described above and in Chapter 4, this file serves to initialize a 4000-byte character array in a C program at compile time. For example, if you generate an **include** file with the name SCR01.INC, then you can initialize the array **Scr01** in a C program using the following statement:

```
char Scr01 [] =
    {
    #include "SCR01.INC"
    };
```

You can then directly display the screen using the function **ScrPutWindow**, without the need to store the screen in a data file or read it at runtime. See Chapter 5 for details on using this function, and for a comparison of the **include** file method versus reading the data at runtime.

Again, you will be prompted for the file name, and will be warned if you are about to overwrite an existing file. You can return to the program without generating the **include** file by pressing Esc. Remember that generating an **include** file does *not* save the current screen buffer in a form that can be reread by the screen editor—be sure to use Alt-W to save your work.

Alt-S: Display Status Information

The Alt-S command displays the current row and column position of the cursor, and also the status of the Num Lock, Caps Lock, and Scroll Lock keys.

When using **ScrPutS** to display data or **ScrGetS** to read user input, you must specify the row and column position of the field on the screen. The following technique can help you identify the positions of all fields on a screen design. First, while in the screen editor, print the screen by pressing Shift-PrtSc. Next, place the cursor at the beginning of each field that you must access from your program, and press Alt-S. Finally, jot down the row and column numbers next to the field on the printout. The printed copy of the screen will make a handy reference while coding your program.

Another suggestion: The coordinates for a particular field may appear at many locations in the program. Rather than coding the specific row and column numbers as follows

```
ScrPutS ("Enter your name:",FG_NORM,10,5);
```

use **define** statements, for example:

```
#define S1F1R   10
#define S1F1C    5
    .
    .
    .
ScrPutS ("Enter your name:",FG_NORM,S1F1R,S1F1C);
```

If you modify the screen, it will thus be necessary to change the coordinates at only one place in the source code (or in a header file shared by several source listings).

The shift-key information is useful for an older keyboard that does not have lights indicating the current status of these keys. For example, you may wonder why the cursor keys are causing little faces to be written to the screen; the answer will be revealed by pressing Alt-S and noting that Num Lock is active (which causes replication of the drawing character).

Alt-X: Exit from Program

Pressing Alt-X will terminate the program. If you have entered any data that have not been saved, you will be warned about the imminent loss and will be given the opportunity to save the screen in a file.

DESIGN GOALS

Before discussing the inner workings of the program, this section reviews some of the general goals that determined the way the program was written, and provides a general explanation for many of the implementation details.

First, the program had to be short and simple enough to be presented within the context of a single chapter of a book. Therefore, some useful features have been left out. A few of these are presented at the end of the chapter as possible enhancements, and the program forms a good foundation for building additional functions.

Second, although the program length and complexity was constrained, it was designed to provide an immediately useful utility. In fact, the simplicity of the program offers several advantages. First, it is easy to learn. Second, it offers the programmer greater control and flexibility than more complex screen designing systems. It simply produces an image of the screen; the programmer can then choose the best way to accept input, define fields, and validate data.

Third, the program was designed to be used without printed reference material. All commands are defined either in the automatic Alt-key menu or in the help window. Therefore, once you have gained an overview of how the features work by reading this chapter, you should be able to use the program without looking up commands.

Finally, the program was designed to fully embody the principle of WYSIWYG (what you see is what you get). The screen is an exact image of what will be displayed by the program, and all 25 lines by 80 columns are available. Therefore, no status information is presented on the basic screen, and all information not part of the actual screen design is exchanged through pop-up windows.

HOW THE SCREEN DESIGNER WORKS

The program listing (SCRGEN.C, Figure 6.1) contains numerous comments, which explain many of the details of the implementation. This section therefore focuses on the basic structure of the code and elucidates some of the more general strategies.

The screen designer stores and manipulates all video data by maintaining two distinct buffers. The first buffer is video memory itself.

Video memory was described in Chapter 5, and its salient feature is that any character written here instantly appears on the screen. The second buffer, **Buffer**, is declared as an array of 25 by 80 integers, and stores only the data that is actually part of the screen design. Each time a character is entered into the screen, it is written simultaneously to *both* buffers. However, when pop-up windows are displayed or blocks are marked on the screen, the characters and attributes are written only to video memory. Thus, **Buffer** maintains a pure image of the actual screen design, while video memory is used to display the current screen design, as well as other information, to the user. After displaying a window or marking a block, it is easy to restore the screen simply by transferring the contents of **Buffer** directly to video memory. If only video memory had been used, it would have been necessary to continually save and restore the screen, a process that would have become very complex (especially for implementing the block functions).

Following the include statements and a set of function prototypes, the program declares all of the global variables (those that are shared by two or more functions). The screen image, **Buffer**, is declared as a two dimensional array of *integers* so that both a character and its associated attribute can be read or written with a single statement; for example

```
Buffer [Row][Col] = AttrChar;
```

Video memory is accessed through the **far** pointer **Video**. This variable is declared as a pointer to an array of 80 integers so that it can be used in a manner exactly analogous to **Buffer** (without having to remember the indirection symbol); for example,

```
Video [Row][Col] = AttrChar;
```

There are several other global variables used throughout the program. **Row** and **Col** always contain the value of the current cursor position on the designing screen. **AttrChar** contains the current display attribute in the high-order byte, and the selected "drawing" character in the low-order byte. (Maintaining both these values in the same integer makes it possible to write the drawing character and the current attribute with a single instruction, as shown above.) The flag **Modified** is set to 1 whenever the buffer is changed so that the user can be warned of impending data loss, and the flag **MenuDisplayed** indicates that the Alt-key menu is currently displayed. The remaining global variables and flags are described below, in the context of the functions that employ them.

The function **main** begins by blanking the global file name buffer, **FileName**, and initializing the **far** pointer **Video** to the address of video memory (the correct segment is determined by directly reading the video mode value maintained by the BIOS in low memory). It also obtains the **far** address of the video image array, **Buffer**; this address is required by the functions that transfer video data. The function **main** then clears the screen (**ScrClear**) and calls **InitBuf**, which initializes **Buffer**. After placing the cursor in the upper left corner of the screen (**ScrSetCur**) and displaying the opening message (**OpenMessage**), the program goes into the main keyboard reading loop (a perpetual loop created by the expression **for (;;)**).

The main loop begins by checking to see if the Alt key is pressed (**KbdGetShift**), and displays or removes the Alt-key menu as necessary. The menu is removed by calling **ShowVideo**, which restores the entire screen by transferring the video image maintained in **Buffer** directly to video memory. At this point the program reads the keyboard; however, rather than pausing for keyboard input, it first calls the function **KbdReady** to see if a key is ready. If no key is available, control immediately returns to the top of the loop so that the program can continue to monitor for the Alt key. If a key is ready, it is obtained using **KbdGetC**, and control passes into a large **switch** statement that branches according to the value of the keystroke.

If the Esc key is pressed, control returns immediately to the top of the loop. If the ↑ key is pressed in conjunction with Shift or Num Lock (**Key** = 0x4838), then the drawing character is written to both the video image buffer and to video memory, and the **Modified** flag is turned on. Note that there is no **break** statement at the end of this branch (a dangerous practice, but one that saves writing redundant code), so that control falls directly into the routine for a simple ↑ key (**Key** = 0x4800). The up-arrow routine merely updates the cursor position. The remaining three arrow keys are handled in the same manner.

The next section of the **switch** statement tests for the Home, End, PgUp, and PgDn keys, and updates the cursor position if any of these keys has been pressed. Note that these routines will be activated either if the key is pressed by itself or if the key is pressed in conjunction with Shift or Num Lock (for example, the code 0x4700 represents the Home key by itself, and 0x4737 represents the Home key with Shift or Num Lock; the Home key routine is therefore labeled with both these values). The next eight branches now test for the Alt-key combinations that activate the commands on the Alt-key menu. If any of these keys is detected, the appropriate function is called and then the cursor position and screen data are restored (**ScrSetCur** and **ShowVideo**). The exit key (Alt-X) routine first tests the **Modified** flag to see if data would be lost, and gives the user the opportunity to save the file if necessary (by calling **WriteFile**). It then clears the screen and exits, or returns to the program if the user opts not to terminate.

The next six branches of the **switch** statement contain the code for the block commands, which will be explained later (in the "Block Manipulation" section). Following these branches, the program tests for the Backspace key. If this key is detected and the cursor is not in the first column, the cursor is moved one column left and a space is written both to the buffer and to video memory. The space is written using the current attribute, which is obtained from the variable **AttrChar** by using the logical AND and logical OR operators as follows:

```
(AttrChar & 0xff00) | ' '
```

The final branch of the **switch** statement is the **default** label. If control has reached this point, then either the user has entered a key without an ASCII value (some meaningless control code), or the user has typed a character that needs to be written to the screen. If a non-ASCII key has been entered (that is, the low-order byte of **Key** is 0), then control passes immediately back to the top of the loop without moving the cursor. However, if a normal ASCII character has been typed, then the character is written to both the video image buffer and to video memory, and the cursor position is updated.

The procedures that are called from **main** can be divided into five categories, according to the functions they perform:

- Information display
- Character and attribute selection
- Reading or writing files
- Video data transfer
- Block manipulation

The following sections discuss the functions belonging to each of these categories.

Information Display

The functions that serve simply to display information are **Open-Message**, which prints the program opening message, **Menu**, which puts up the Alt-key menu, **HelpScreen**, which displays the help screen, and **DisplayStat**, which shows the current position of the cursor and the status of the shift keys. These functions demonstrate two basic methods for displaying pop-up windows on the screen.

All of the functions except **HelpScreen** first clear an area of the screen (**ScrClear**), draw a window border within this area (**ScrPutBox**), and then display each line of information with a separate call to **ScrPutS**.

The function **HelpScreen**, however, uses an alternative method that is suitable for a more complex window design. First, the window was designed using the screen editor itself (this screen is shown in Figure 6.4, which unfortunately cannot reveal the different video attributes), and the **include** file SCRGEN.INC was generated (through the Alt-I menu item of the screen generator). This **include** file was then used to initialize the array **Scr** at compile time. The help screen function displays the entire window with a single call to **ScrPutWindow**, passing the address of **Scr**.

Because of the double buffer system used by this program, none of these functions needs to save the current contents of the screen. The original screen is restored on function return by a simple call to **ShowVideo**, which transfers the contents of the video image buffer directly into video memory.

Character and Attribute Selection

The function **SelectChar** allows the user to select the current "drawing" character. This function displays a window by clearing the screen and drawing a box as described in the previous section. After writing the titles, it goes into a loop that prints each of the 253 visible ASCII characters in a 23-column by 11-row matrix. While it goes through this loop, it also searches for the position of the current character (contained in **AttrChar**) so that it can later place the selection highlight on this character (if the current character is a blank, then the highlight is placed on the *first* character). The position of the selection highlight is stored in

SelRow and **SelCol**. The expression that writes the characters to video memory

```
Video [r][c] = (r % 2 ? 0x7000 : 0x0f00) | Ch;
```

generates the normal attribute for odd rows, and the high intensity attribute for even rows, so that the division between touching characters is visible.

The function next displays the highlight (with **ScrPutAttr**) on the current drawing character and enters a keyboard loop. If the user presses an arrow key, **SelRow** and **SelCol** are appropriately updated and the highlight is moved. If the user presses Esc, then the highlighted character is read back from video memory and placed into the low-order byte of **AttrChar**, and the function returns. If, however, the space bar is pressed, then a space character is loaded into this byte.

The **SelectAttr** function displays a window, and then calls either the monochrome routine or the color routine for selecting the display attribute.

The monochrome routine (**MonoAttr**) uses a table containing the basic monochrome attributes (**AttrTab**). The routine first searches for the current attribute in this table and stores the index of the attribute in **TabIdx**. Next, the unsigned character **Blink** is assigned the value of the current blinking bit, which is bit number 15 of **AttrChar**. The main keyboard loop begins by displaying the attribute indexed by **TabIdx** in the center of the window, and then responds to several keys. The ← key decrements **TabIdx** and the → key increments it. Control then passes to the start of the loop which displays either the prior or the next attribute in the table. The user is thus able to move through the attribute table, seeing each attribute displayed. When the last entry is reached, the index wraps around to the first entry; when the first entry is reached, the index goes to the last. The + key toggles the value stored in the **Blink** variable by using the exclusive- OR operator. Finally, when Esc is pressed, the currently indexed attribute is placed in the high-order byte of **AttrChar** and the function returns.

The color routine (**ColorAttr**) is similar to the monochrome routine except that it must allow the independent selection of any of the eight background colors or 16 foreground colors, in addition to blinking. Therefore, the keyboard loop responds to the ← and → keys to select the foreground color, and to the ↑ and ↓ keys to select the background color. The color attribute byte is encoded as shown in Figure 6.5. The 16 foreground colors are encoded in bits 0 through 3, and the eight background colors are encoded in bits 4 through 6. The routine works by simply incrementing or decrementing the appropriate bits. For example, the following expression serves to increment the background bits,

```
Attr = (Attr & 0x80) | (Attr + 0x10 & 0x7f);
```

This expression increments bits 4, 5, and 6 of **Attr**, leaving the other bits unchanged. Note that these three bits can be incremented indefinitely, since when the maximum value is reached (7), the next increment causes the bits to overflow and return to 0. (They can be continuously decremented for the same reason.)

Reading and Writing Files

The function **ReadFile** reads a 4000-byte screen data file directly into the screen image array **Buffer**. Since it reads only a single block of data, it uses the low-level block file functions **open**, **read**, and **close**, rather than the high-level buffered functions. Before reading the file, however, it checks the **Modified** flag to see if the present buffer has been modified, since its contents are overwritten by the read operation. If the

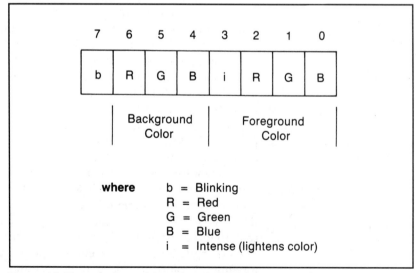

Figure 6.5: The encoding of the color attribute byte

buffer has been modified, the user is warned and given the opportunity to first save the data, which is accomplished by calling **WriteFile**. The user is then prompted for the file name, and is allowed to exit from the data entry field only by pressing either Esc or Enter. If Esc is pressed (that is, the return code is −1) then the function returns immediately; otherwise, the specified file is opened. Note that the file is opened in the binary mode (O_BINARY) so that the C library will not perform translation on the data. Finally, the data are read into **Buffer**, the file is closed, and the **Modified** flag is reset.

The function **WriteFile** saves the contents of the screen array **Buffer** in a screen data file, and is similar to **ReadFile**. However, the function contains some additional logic to warn the user if an existing file is about to be overwritten. It first attempts to open an existing file for reading and writing by calling **open**, which will normally return an error (−1) if the file does not exist. If **open** does *not* return an error, then the file already exists and the user is warned and given the opportunity to enter a new file name. If, however, **open** returns an error, then the file does not exist and therefore **open** is called again, this time passing it the O_CREAT flag, which will force the library routine to create a new file.

Finally, the function **IncFile** translates the contents of **Buffer** directly to an **include** file— a text file consisting of 4000 decimal numbers representing each character and attribute byte in **Buffer**, separated by commas. As demonstrated above and in Chapter 5, the **include** file is used to initialize an internal screen buffer in a C program at compile time, in order to provide the fastest possible display of screen data. Unlike the functions **ReadFile** and **WriteFile**, **IncFile** uses the high-level buffered routines **fopen**, **fputs**, **putc**, and **fclose** since it writes the data a few bytes at a time. It also warns the user if an existing file is about to be overwritten; however, the logic for the high-level functions is slightly different than the low-level functions. First, **fopen** is called for *reading* a file (by passing the access type "rb") merely to see if the file exists. If **fopen** returns an error (that is, NULL), the file does not exist and it is immediately reopened for writing (using the "wb" access type). If, however, **fopen** is successful, then the file exists; it is therefore closed, and the user is warned and given the option to enter a new file name. If the user chooses to go ahead, then the file is reopened for writing, which truncates the existing file to length 0. Note that the "b" in the access type is equivalent to the O_BINARY flag described above.

Once the file is opened, the character pointer **BufferPtr** is initialized to point to the beginning of **Buffer**, and the function enters a loop that formats each byte of **Buffer** as a decimal number and writes the string to the **include** file, inserting commas and newline characters (that is, carriage-return/line-feed pairs) as necessary. The numbers are formatted into the minimum-size field ("%1d") to minimize the size of the include file; also, the decimal radix is chosen since it is more compact than hexadecimal.

Video Data Transfer

The functions **InitBuf** and **ShowVideo** both use the C library function **movedata** to transfer the entire contents of video memory in a single block move.

InitBuf transfers the contents of video memory *into* **Buffer**. The purpose of this function is to initialize the contents of **Buffer** to blank characters having the normal video attribute (0x07). Rather than poking these values one at time into the buffer, the strategy is to let the BIOS perform this task on video memory by calling **ScrClear**, and then immediately call **InitBuf** to transfer the freshly cleared screen contents into **Buffer**. (Once you have the program running you could simply generate an **include** file for a blank screen, and then use this file to initialize **Buffer** at compile time.)

ShowVideo transfers the screen data in the opposite direction: *from* **Buffer** *to* video memory. This function is used to restore the screen after a window has been displayed, and to update the screen after a block transfer has been performed (it is also used to hide a marked block, as explained below). Before performing the transfer, however, it first checks to see if a block is currently marked on the screen, so that it does not inadvertently remove this marking. If a block is marked (the flag **BlockShown** is nonzero), then it calls **ShowBlock**, which first restores the screen (by another call to **ShowVideo** with **BlockShown** *false*), and then repaints the block in video memory.

Block Manipulation

The final set of functions manage the manipulation of blocks of data on the screen. These functions are **ShowBlock**, **CpyMovBlock**, **Buf2Hold**, **Hold2Buf**, and **DeleteBlock**.

The function **ShowBlock** marks the current block on the screen, as it is defined by the global variables **BlockStartRow**, **BlockStartCol**, **BlockEndRow**, and **BlockEndCol**. This function is called whenever these global variables are updated as a result of the user pressing Ctrl-B, or Ctrl-E; or when the block is currently unmarked on the screen and the user types Ctrl-H to make the block marking reappear.

ShowBlock first turns off the **BlockShown** flag, and calls **ShowVideo** to erase any existing block markings (the **BlockShown** flag must be off so that **ShowVideo** does not try to restore the block markings). It then checks the validity of the current values of the global variables **BlockStartRow**, **BlockStartCol**, and so on. If any of these equals −1, which is the initial value, then the user has not marked a complete block and the function returns immediately. The function also returns if the end of the block falls before the beginning. Next, **ShowBlock** turns the **BlockShown** flag back on, and enters a loop that modifies the display attribute in video memory for each character that falls within the marked block. If the monitor is monochrome, then all reverse video attributes (0x70) are changed to normal (0x07), and all other attributes are converted to reverse video. If, however, the monitor is color, then all attributes are combined with 0xff using the exclusive-OR operator, which reverses the value of each bit, thus providing visual contrast.

If its parameter is 0, the **CpyMovBlock** function copies the marked block to the current cursor position, leaving the original data intact. If the parameter is nonzero, then **CpyMovBlock** moves the block to the current cursor position, clearing the original area. The copy option is requested when the user types Ctrl-C, and the move option when the user types Ctrl-M. This function first checks the flag **BlockShown** to make sure that a block is currently marked on the screen, returning if it is not. It then calls **Buf2Hold**, to transfer the contents of the marked block from **Buffer** to a temporary holding buffer, **HoldBuf**. The **Move** parameter is passed directly to **Buf2Hold**; if this parameter is nonzero, then as each byte is moved into the holding buffer the original location in **Buffer** is blanked. Note that **Buf2Hold** copies only as much of the marked block as will fit at the target location by terminating the loop if the target row or column exceeds 24 or 79.

CpyMovBlock next calls **Hold2Buf** to transfer the contents of the hold buffer back to **Buffer**, starting at the current cursor position (always contained in the global variables **Row** and **Col**). **Hold2Buf** first updates the global block delimiters (**BlockStartRow**, and so on) so that the marked block will now be at the new location. It then uses these global variables in the loop that actually transfers the data. The reason a second holding buffer is used, rather than transferring the data directly from the source area of **Buffer** to the target area, is to resolve the problems that occur when the two areas overlap.

Finally, **DeleteBlock** is called when the user presses Ctrl-D. This function clears the marked block by cycling through each row and column, inserting a blank with a normal display attribute (0x07) at each character position. When this operation is complete, it sets the flag **BlockShown** to 0 and calls **ShowVideo**, which updates the video display and removes the block marking. Before returning, the **Modified** flag is set on to indicate that the buffer has changed.

SOME POSSIBLE ENHANCEMENTS

This final section presents some suggested enhancements for the reader who would like to build upon the screen designer source code. The enhancements described below pertain to character drawing, file I/O, and block operations, in addition to a few miscellaneous enhancements.

Character Drawing Enhancements

The first possible enhancement is a mode that would write only the selected attribute to the screen as the cursor is moved in any direction, without disturbing the existing screen data. This mode could be toggled on and off with a control key, such as Ctrl-A, and the cursor could assume a characteristic shape to indicate that the mode is active (use **ScrSetStyle**).

Another enhancement is a "box drawing" mode. First, one of the four basic box styles could be selected, and then the appropriate lines generated as the cursor is moved across the screen in any direction, with intersections and corners automatically generated. This feature would greatly facilitate designing attractive screens.

File I/O Enhancements

The following features would enhance the screen designer's file operations:

■ A screen file could be specified on the program command line, which would automatically be opened and displayed at program initialization.

■ Default extensions could be automatically appended to the names of files read or written: .SCR for screen data files, and .INC for include files.

■ When files are read, the program could display a window with a list of all screen files found in the current directory, and allow the user to choose one of them.

■ There could be a feature for saving screens as simple text files, consisting of 2000 characters without attributes, so that the data could be viewed by a text editor or be displayed by the TYPE command.

■ A data compression scheme could be used for saving and retrieving screen files. For example, repeated character-attribute pairs could be eliminated, or an encoding scheme, such as the Huffman algorithm, employed.

Block Command Enhancements

There are two additional block commands that would be useful and simple to implement. The first would assign the current attribute to the marked block, and the second would fill the marked block with the current character (the current attribute and character are those stored in the global variable **AttrChar**).

Miscellaneous Enhancements

Finally, there are several miscellaneous enhancements that could be added to the program:

- There could be a command to clear the entire buffer to prepare for editing a new screen (with an *Are you sure?* message if the current buffer has not been saved).

- There could be an "undo" command to reverse the effect of the last command.

- Special versions of the routines could be written to allow the program to run on the original CGA adapter without the "snow" effect. This topic is explored at the end of Chapter 5.

Device-Independent
Graphics Functions

C HAPTER 7

This chapter presents an integrated set of graphics functions that may be called by a Microsoft C program. The programmer interface provided by this module is designed to be independent of the current graphics hardware and video mode. The functions presently support the two-color graphics modes provided by Hercules compatible adapters, and by adapters compatible with the standard CGA (Color Graphics Adapter), EGA (Enhanced Graphics Adapter), and VGA (Video Graphics Array, provided with the PS/2 machines). By modifying some of the low-level routines, you can easily take advantage of higher resolution and multi-color graphics modes, without changing the programmer interface or the basic structure of the module.

This chapter describes each of the graphics functions individually. Many of the functions work intimately together and must be called in the correct order; also, important general concepts are often presented in the context of individual function descriptions. Therefore, it is important to read the chapter through from the beginning, rather than simply looking up specific functions. As in other chapters, the description of using the function is separate from the description of how the function works, which may safely be skipped if you are primarily interested in simply calling the routine from your program. The chapter concludes with a summary of possible enhancements that you might want to add to the graphics package.

The C source listing for the graphics module is contained in Figure 7.1, and the corresponding header file in Figure 7.2.

THE GRAPHICS FUNCTIONS

A primary feature of this set of graphics functions is that their use is almost entirely independent of both the currently active graphics mode and type of display adapter. Once you have determined the graphics modes that are available, and have selected a particular mode, the manner in which you call subsequent graphics display functions does not depend upon the selected mode. For example, if you call a function to display a square in the middle of the screen, the overall size, shape, and position of this square will not change significantly with different graphics modes. The resolution and color of the square may vary depending upon the features of the mode, and its proportions may change slightly with different monitors, but there is no need to recode

```
#include <CONIO.H>
#include <DOS.H>

#include "GRA.H"
#include "SCR.H"
#include "UTY.H"
                                        /* Local functions.              */
static void _Point (int _X, int _Y, int Attr);
static int _GetPoint (int _X, int _Y);
static void _Line (int _X1, int _Y1, int _X2, int _Y2, int Attr);
static void _Fill (int _X, int _Y, int Attr, int Bound);

                                        /* Data private to this module.  */
static float XMin = 0.0, YMin = 0.0;    /* World coordinates, initialized */
static float XMax = 8.0, YMax = 6.0;    /* to default values.            */
static int _XMax, _YMax;                /* Pixel limits, which depend on  */
                                        /* the current graphics mode.    */
static float XRatio, YRatio;            /* Ratio of pixel values to world */
                                        /* coordinate values.            */
static int CurrMode = NOMODE;           /* Current graphics mode,        */
                                        /* initialized to NO graphics mode. */

                                        /* Macro definitions.            */
#define XPIX(x)     ((int)((x - XMin) * XRatio + (x - XMin < 0 ? -0.5 : 0.5)))
#define YPIX(y)     (_YMax - (int)((y - YMin) * YRatio + (y-YMin<0?-0.5:0.5)))
#define BADX(x)     (x < 0 || x > _XMax)
#define BADY(y)     (y < 0 || y > _YMax)
#define MIN(x,y)    (x < y ? x : y)
#define MAX(x,y)    (x > y ? x : y)


/*************************** GraInit & GraQuit ****************************/

static struct Mode OldMode, NewMode;   /* For saving & setting CGA mode.  */
static unsigned OldEquipFlag;          /* For saving BIOS equipment flag. */
                                       /* Pointer to the BIOS equipment flag:*/
static unsigned far *PtrEquipFlag = (unsigned far *)0x00400010;

static unsigned char GraphTable [] =  /* Values to initialize 6845       */
    {                                 /* controller into Hercules        */
    0x35, 0x2d, 0x2e, 0x07,           /* Graphics mode.                  */
    0x5b, 0x02, 0x57, 0x57,
    0x02, 0x03, 0x00, 0x00
    };

static unsigned char TextTable [] =   /* Values to initialize 6845       */
    {                                 /* controller into Hercules        */
    0x61, 0x50, 0x52, 0x0f,           /* text mode.                      */
    0x19, 0x06, 0x19, 0x19,
    0x02, 0x0d, 0x0b, 0x0c
    };
```

Figure 7.1: GRA.C: A Microsoft C graphics package

```
int GraInit (int Mode)
/*
    This function switches to the requested graphics mode and initializes
    internal variables maintained by the module.  It must be called before
    using any of the graphics functions.
*/
    {
    register int i;
    int VideoTypes;              /* Stores the currently active adapter types. */

    VideoTypes = ScrTypes ();    /* Get adapter types supported by hardware.*/

    switch (Mode)
        {
        case CGAHIRES:           /* CGA one color 640 x 200 "high resolution". */
            if (!(VideoTypes & VCGA))/* Check that hardware supports CGA.*/
                return (WRONGMODE); /* Mode not supported by hardware.  */

            ScrGetMode (&OldMode);   /* Save old video mode.            */

                                     /* Save old equipment flag.        */
            OldEquipFlag = *PtrEquipFlag;
            *PtrEquipFlag &= 0xffcf; /* Set video adapter bits to       */
            *PtrEquipFlag |= 0x0020; /* indicate an 80 column color card.*/

                                     /* Set new mode.                   */
            NewMode.VideoMode = CGAHIRES;
            NewMode.VideoPage = 0;
            ScrSetMode (&NewMode);

            _XMax = 639;             /* Initialize pixel limits.        */
            _YMax = 199;

            CurrMode = CGAHIRES;     /* Set global mode flag.           */
            break;

        case HERC:
            if (!(VideoTypes & VHGC))/* Check for Hercules compatibility.*/
                return (WRONGMODE); /* Mode not supported by hardware.  */

            outp (0x03bf,1);         /* Enable configuration switch for */
                                     /* page 0 graphics.                */
            outp (0x03b8,2);         /* Set Display Mode Control Port    */
                                     /* for page 0 graphics, disabled.   */

            for (i = 0; i < 12; ++i) /* Initialize the 6845 with graphics*/
                {                    /* parameters from table.           */
                outp (0x03b4,i);                         /* Index reg.  */
                outp (0x03b5, GraphTable [i]);           /* Data reg.   */
                }

            UtyFarSetWord (0xb000,0,0,0x4000); /* Fill the 32k graphics  */
                                     /* page 0 with 0's.                 */
            outp (0x03b8,0x0a);      /* Enable graphics through Display  */
```

Figure 7.1: GRA.C: A Microsoft C graphics package (continued)

```
                                     /* mode controller port.       */
             _XMax = 719;            /* Initialize pixel limits.     */
             _YMax = 347;

             CurrMode = HERC;        /* Set global mode flag.        */
             break;

        default:
             return (BADMODE);       /* Requested mode not supported. */

        } /* end switch */

    XRatio = _XMax / (XMax - XMin);  /* Set global pixel to world    */
    YRatio = _YMax / (YMax - YMin);  /* coordinate unit ratios.      */
    return (NOERROR);

    } /* end GraInit */


int GraQuit (void)
/*
    This function switches back into text mode and resets the global mode
    flag to NOMODE.
*/
    {
    register int i;

    switch (CurrMode)
        {
        case NOMODE:
             return (NOGRAPH);

        case CGAHIRES:
             *PtrEquipFlag = OldEquipFlag;   /* Restore equipment flag. */
             ScrSetMode (&OldMode);          /* Restore video mode.     */
             break;

        case HERC:
             outp (0x03b8,0x20);        /* Set Display Mode Control Port */
                                        /* for text, disabled.           */
             for (i = 0; i < 12; ++i)   /* Initialize the 6845 with text */
                 {                      /* parameters from table.        */
                 outp (0x03b4,i);
                 outp (0x03b5, TextTable [i]);
                 }

             /* Fill text video memory with normal attribute spaces: */
             UtyFarSetWord (0xb000,0,0x0720,2000);

             outp (0x03b8,0x28);        /* Enable text through Display  */
                                        /* mode controller port.        */
             break;

        } /* end switch */
```

Figure 7.1: GRA.C: A Microsoft C graphics package (continued)

```
        CurrMode = NOMODE;                      /* Set flag to NO graphics mode set.*/
        return (NOERROR);

        } /* end GraQuit */


/************************ end GraInit & GraQuit****************************/


int GraClear (int Attr)
/*
        This function fills the current graphics screen with the requested
        attribute, which for this implementation should be either OFF (= 0) or
        ON (= 1).
*/
        {
        switch (CurrMode)
                {
                case NOMODE:
                        return (NOGRAPH);

                case CGAHIRES:
                        UtyFarSetWord (0xb800,0,Attr ? 0xffff : 0,0x2000);
                                                        /* Fill the 16k graphics  */
                        break;                          /* memory with 0's or 1's.*/

                case HERC:
                        UtyFarSetWord (0xb000,0,Attr ? 0xffff : 0,0x4000);
                                                        /* Fill the 32k graphics  */
                        break;                          /* page 0 with 0's or 1's.*/
                }

        return (NOERROR);

        } /* end GraClear */


int GraSetCoord (float XMinNew, float YMinNew, float XMaxNew, float YMaxNew)
/*
        This function sets the minimum and maximum world coordinate values for
        the graphics screen.
*/
        {
        if (XMinNew >= XMaxNew || YMinNew >= YMaxNew)       /* Test for validity.*/
                return (BADCOORD);

        XMin = XMinNew;                          /* Set internal variables.       */
        XMax = XMaxNew;
        YMin = YMinNew;
        YMax = YMaxNew;
        XRatio = _XMax / (XMax - XMin);     /* Calculate new pixel to world  */
        YRatio = _YMax / (YMax - YMin);     /* coordinate unit ratios.       */

        return (NOERROR);

        } /* end GraSetCoord */
```

Figure 7.1: GRA.C: A Microsoft C graphics package (continued)

```
void GraGetCoord (float *XMinPtr, float *YMinPtr, float *XMaxPtr,
                  float *YMaxPtr)
/*
    This function returns the current maximum and minimum world coordinates.
*/
    {
    *XMinPtr = XMin;
    *YMinPtr = YMin;
    *XMaxPtr = XMax;
    *YMaxPtr = YMax;

    } /* end GraGetCoord */


int GraPoint (float X, float Y, int Attr)
/*
    This function plots a single point with attribute 'Attr' at the location
    specified by the world coordinate values 'X' and 'Y'.
*/
    {
    if (CurrMode == NOMODE)          /* Test for a valid graphics mode.      */
        return (NOGRAPH);

    _Point (XPIX (X), YPIX (Y), Attr);       /* Convert world coordinates to*/
                                             /* pixel values and call low-  */
    return (NOERROR);                        /* level function.             */

    } /* GraPoint */


int GraGetPoint (float X, float Y)
/*
    This function returns the display attribute (either ON or OFF) of the
    point specified by the world coordinate values 'X' and 'Y'.
*/
    {
    int _X, _Y;                      /* For pixel values.                   */

    if (CurrMode == NOMODE)          /* Make sure graphics mode is active*/
        return (NOGRAPH);

    _X = XPIX (X);                   /* Convert world coordinates to    */
    _Y = YPIX (Y);                   /* pixel values.                   */

    if (BADX (_X) || BADY (_Y))      /* Test for pixels within valid    */
        return (OUTOFRANGE);         /* range.                          */

    if (_GetPoint (_X,_Y))           /* Call low-level function.        */
        return (ON);
    else
        return (OFF);
    } /* end GraGetPoint */


int GraLine (float X1, float Y1, float X2, float Y2, int Attr)
/*
    This function plots a line from 'X1','Y1' to 'X2', 'Y2' (given in world
    coordinates), using attribute 'Attr'.
```

Figure 7.1: GRA.C: A Microsoft C graphics package (continued)

```
*/
        {
        if (CurrMode == NOMODE)                 /* Test for valid graphics mode.    */
                return (NOGRAPH);

        /* Convert world coordinates to pixel values/call low-level function.  */
        _Line (XPIX (X1), YPIX (Y1), XPIX (X2), YPIX (Y2), Attr);

        return (NOERROR);

        } /* end GraLine */

int GraBox (float X1, float Y1, float X2, float Y2, int Attr)
/*
        This function draws a box with opposite corners given by the world
        coordinate values 'X1','Y1' and 'X2','Y2', using display attribute
        'Attr'.
*/
        {
        register int i;
        int _X1, _Y1, _X2, _Y2;         /* For pixel values.                */

        if (CurrMode == NOMODE)         /* Test for valid graphics mode.    */
                return (NOGRAPH);

        _X1 = XPIX (X1);                /* Convert world coordinates to pixel */
        _Y1 = YPIX (Y1);                /* values.                            */
        _X2 = XPIX (X2);
        _Y2 = YPIX (Y2);

        for (i = MIN (_X1,_X2); i <= MAX (_X1,_X2); ++i)  /* Draw horizontal  */
                {                                         /* lines.           */
                _Point (i,_Y1,Attr);    /* Low level point plotting function. */
                _Point (i,_Y2,Attr);
                }

        for (i = MIN (_Y1,_Y2)+1; i <= MAX (_Y1,_Y2)-1; ++i)  /* Draw vertical */
                {                                             /* lines.        */
                _Point (_X1,i,Attr);
                _Point (_X2,i,Attr);
                }

        return (NOERROR);

        } /* end GraBox */

#define SINDELTA 0.078459               /* Constants for GraCircle.         */
#define COSDELTA 0.996917

int GraCircle (float X, float Y, float R, int Attr, float Aspect)
/*
        This function draws an ellipse, with center at the world coordinate
        value 'X', 'Y' and radius 'R', with display attribute 'Attr' and
        aspect ratio 'Aspect'.
*/
        {
        register int Facet;             /* Counter for sides of the polygon. */
```

Figure 7.1: GRA.C: A Microsoft C graphics package (continued)

```
    int _X, _Y;                      /* Pixel coordinates of the center.     */
    float XRat, YRat;                /* World coordinate to pixel ratios.    */
    double CosTheta = 1.0;           /* Cosine of the angle theta.           */
    double SinTheta = 0.0;           /* Sine of the angle theta.             */
    int DeltaX;                      /* X and Y distances of line end points */
    int DeltaY = 0;                  /* from the center (in pixels).         */
    double CosOld, SinOld;           /* Storage for FORMER values.           */
    int DeltaXOld, DeltaYOld;

    if (CurrMode == NOMODE)          /* Test for valid graphics mode.        */
        return (NOGRAPH);

    _X = XPIX (X);                   /* Convert world coordinates of center  */
    _Y = YPIX (Y);                   /* to pixel values.                     */

    XRat = XRatio;                   /* Calculate world coordinate to pixel  */
    YRat = YRatio;                   /* ratios.                              */

    if (Aspect < 1.0)                /* Adjust ratios for aspect ratio.      */
        YRat *= Aspect;

    else if (Aspect > 1.0)
        XRat /= Aspect;

    DeltaX = (int)(R * XRat + 0.5);              /* X value of first endpoint. */

    for (Facet = 1; Facet <= 20; ++Facet)    /* Draw 20 * 4 = 80 sides.      */
        {
        CosOld = CosTheta;                       /* Store old values.         */
        SinOld = SinTheta;
        DeltaXOld = DeltaX;
        DeltaYOld = DeltaY;

        /* Calculate new sine and cosine values of theta.                    */
        CosTheta = CosOld * COSDELTA - SinOld * SINDELTA;
        SinTheta = SinOld * COSDELTA + CosOld * SINDELTA;

        /* Calculate new pixel coordinates of end of line segment.           */
        DeltaX = (int)(R * CosTheta * XRat + 0.5);
        DeltaY = (int)(R * SinTheta * YRat + 0.5);

        /* Draw 4 line segments.                                             */
        _Line (_X+DeltaXOld, _Y+DeltaYOld, _X+DeltaX, _Y+DeltaY, Attr);
        _Line (_X-DeltaXOld, _Y+DeltaYOld, _X-DeltaX, _Y+DeltaY, Attr);
        _Line (_X+DeltaXOld, _Y-DeltaYOld, _X+DeltaX, _Y-DeltaY, Attr);
        _Line (_X-DeltaXOld, _Y-DeltaYOld, _X-DeltaX, _Y-DeltaY, Attr);
        }

    return (NOERROR);

    } /* end GraCircle */
```

Figure 7.1: GRA.C: A Microsoft C graphics package (continued)

```
int GraFill (float X, float Y, int Attr, int Bound)
/*
    This function fills the area surrounding the point given by the world
    coordinates 'X' and 'Y' with attribute 'Attr', until a boundary having
    attribute 'Bound' is encountered.  Since the module currently
    supports only monochrome graphics, 'Attr' must equal 'Bound'.
*/
    {
    int _X, _Y;                         /* For pixel coordinates.          */

    if (CurrMode == NOMODE)             /* Test for valid graphics mode.   */
        return (NOGRAPH);

    _X = XPIX (X);                      /* Convert world coordinates to    */
    _Y = YPIX (Y);                      /* pixel values.                   */

    if (BADX (_X) || BADY (_Y))         /* Make sure point is on the screen.*/
        return (OUTOFRANGE);

    _Fill (_X, _Y, Attr, Bound);        /* Call low-level function.        */

    return (NOERROR);

    } /* end GraFill */


/***************************** local functions ****************************/

static unsigned char far *Video;

static void _Point (int _X, int _Y, int Attr)
/*
    This function plots the point specified by the pixel coordinates '_X'
    and '_Y' using attribute 'Attr'.
*/
    {
    if (BADX (_X) || BADY (_Y))         /* Clip out of range coordinates.  */
        return;

    switch (CurrMode)
        {
        case CGAHIRES:
            /* Set 'Video' to point to byte containing the point.          */
            FP_SEG (Video) = 0xb800;
            FP_OFF (Video) = 0x2000 * (_Y & 1) + 80 * (_Y >> 1) + (_X >>3);
            if (Attr == OFF)                 /* Modify the specific bit.    */
                *Video &= ~(0x80 >> (_X & 7));    /* Turn pixel off.        */

            else if (!(Attr & XOR))
                *Video |= 0x80 >> (_X & 7);       /* Turn pixel on.         */

            else if (Attr != XOR)
                *Video ^= 0x80 >> (_X & 7);       /* Toggle pixel.          */

            break;

        case HERC:
            /* Set 'Video' to point to byte containing the point.          */
```

Figure 7.1: GRA.C: A Microsoft C graphics package (continued)

```
                FP_SEG (Video) = 0xb000;
                FP_OFF (Video) = 0x2000 * (_Y & 3) + 90 * (_Y >> 2) + (_X >>3);

                if (Attr == OFF)                /* Modify the specific bit.  */
                    *Video &= ~(0x80 >> (_X & 7));     /* Turn pixel off.   */

                else if (!(Attr & XOR))
                    *Video |= 0x80 >> (_X & 7);          /* Turn pixel on.   */

                else if (Attr != XOR)
                    *Video ^= 0x80 >> (_X & 7);          /* Toggle pixel.    */

                break;

        } /* end switch */

    return;

    } /* end _Point */


static int _GetPoint (int _X, int _Y)
    {
    switch (CurrMode)
        {
        case CGAHIRES:
            /* Set 'Video' to point to byte containing the point.        */
            FP_SEG (Video) = 0xb800;
            FP_OFF (Video) = 0x2000 * (_Y & 1) + 80 * (_Y >> 1) + (_X >>3);

            /* Return the specific bit value.                            */
            return ((*Video & 0x80 >> (_X & 7)) != 0);

        case HERC:
            /* Set 'Video' to point to byte containing the point.        */
            FP_SEG (Video) = 0xb000;
            FP_OFF (Video) = 0x2000 * (_Y & 3) + 90 * (_Y >> 2) + (_X >>3);

            /* Return the specific bit value.                            */
            return ((*Video & 0x80 >> (_X & 7)) != 0);

        } /* end switch */
    } /* end _GetPoint */


static void _Line (int _X1, int _Y1, int _X2, int _Y2, int Attr)
/*
    This function draws a line from '_X1', '_Y1' to '_X2', '_Y2' (given in
    pixel coordinates), using display attribute 'Attr'.
*/
    {
    register int i, Delta;      /* 'Delta' is longest dimension of line. */
    int HalfDelta;              /* Error threshold.                      */
    int DeltaX, DeltaY;         /* Change in X and Y values over line.   */
    int ErrNumX=0, ErrNumY=0;   /* Numerators of line errors.            */
    int IncrX, IncrY;           /* Size of X and Y increments.           */

    if ((DeltaX = _X2 - _X1) > 0) /* Set X increment and convert 'DeltaX' */
        IncrX = 1;                /* to its absolute value.              */
```

Figure 7.1: GRA.C: A Microsoft C graphics package (continued)

```
            else if (DeltaX < 0)
                  {
                  DeltaX = -DeltaX;
                  IncrX = -1;
                  }
            else
                  IncrX = 0;

            if ((DeltaY = _Y2 - _Y1) > 0) /* Set Y increment and convert 'DeltaY'  */
                  IncrY = 1;               /* to its absolute value.               */

            else if (DeltaY < 0)
                  {
                  DeltaY = -DeltaY;
                  IncrY = -1;
                  }
            else
                  IncrY = 0;
                                           /* Set 'Delta' to longest line dimension.*/
            Delta = DeltaX > DeltaY ? DeltaX : DeltaY;

            HalfDelta =  Delta / 2;        /* Error threshold is half of 'Delta'.   */

            _Point (_X1, _Y1, Attr);       /* Double plot first point (see text).   */

            for (i = 1; i <= Delta+1; ++i)
                  {
                  _Point (_X1, _Y1, Attr);       /* Plot a point.                    */
                  ErrNumX += DeltaX;             /* Increment X error numerator.     */

                  if (ErrNumX > HalfDelta)       /* Test if error threshold exceeded.*/
                        {                        /* If exceeded, reset X error       */
                        ErrNumX -= Delta;        /* numerator and increment X        */
                        _X1 += IncrX;            /* dimension.                       */
                        }

                  ErrNumY += DeltaY;             /* Increment Y error numerator.     */

                  if (ErrNumY > HalfDelta)       /* Test if error threshold exceeded.*/
                        {                        /* If exceeded, reset Y error       */
                        ErrNumY -= Delta;        /* numerator and increment Y        */
                        _Y1 += IncrY;            /* dimension.                       */
                        }
                  }

            } /* end _Line */


static void _Fill (int _X, int _Y, int Attr, int Bound)
/*
      This function fills the area surrounding the point given by the pixel
      coordinates '_X' and '_Y' with display attribute 'Attr' until the
      attribute 'Bound' is encountered.
*/
      {
      register int LeftX, RightX;      /* Pixels to left/right of current pixel.*/
      int NewY;                        /* New Y pixel value.                    */
      int DeltaY; .                    /* Change in Y pixel value.              */
      int A;                           /* Stores display attribute.             */

      LeftX = _X;                      /* Initialize left and right pixel       */
      RightX = _X;                     /* values.                               */
```

Figure 7.1: GRA.C: A Microsoft C graphics package (continued)

```
/* Fill the LINE containing '_X' and '_Y', until edge of screen or    */
/* the boundary attribute is encountered.                             */

/* First, fill to LEFT of starting point.                             */
while (LeftX >= 0 && _GetPoint (LeftX,_Y) != Bound)
    {
    if (*Video == (Attr ? 0 : 0xff))
        {                        /* 'Video' was set by '_GetPoint'. If it*/
                                 /* is completely unfilled, then fill    */
        *Video = (Attr ? 0xff:0);/* an entire BYTE.                      */
        LeftX &= 0xfff8;         /* Move left to next byte boundary. */
        if (RightX == _X)        /* Move right the first time into   */
            RightX |= 0x0007;    /* this 'if' statement.             */
        }
    else                         /* Only part of byte was unfilled. */
        _Point (LeftX, _Y, Attr);/* Therefore fill only a single bit.*/
    --LeftX;                     /* Move to next pixel left.         */
    }
++RightX;                        /* Move to next pixel right.        */

/* Now fill to RIGHT of starting point.                               */
while (RightX <= _XMax && _GetPoint (RightX, _Y) != Bound)
    {
    if (*Video == (Attr ? 0 : 0xff))
        {                        /* 'Video' was set by '_GetPoint'. If it*/
                                 /* is completely unfilled, then fill    */
        *Video = (Attr ? 0xff:0);/* an entire BYTE.                      */
        RightX |= 0x0007;        /* Move right to next byte boundary.*/
        }
    else                         /* Only part of byte was unfilled. */
        _Point (RightX, _Y, Attr);   /* Therefore fill only a bit.  */

    ++RightX;                        /* Move to next pixel right.    */
    }

/* Now make series of recursive calls for intermediate vertical points */
/* to reduce maximum depth of recursion.                               */

_X = (LeftX + RightX) / 2;   /* _X assigned middle point on line.   */
DeltaY = -1;                 /* 'DeltaY' is -1, then 1.             */

while (DeltaY <= 1)
    {
    NewY = _Y + DeltaY;      /* Initialize 'NewY'.                  */

    /* Get furthest unfilled Y value into 'NewY'.                       */
    while (NewY <= _YMax && NewY >= 0 && _GetPoint (_X, NewY) != Bound)
        NewY += DeltaY;

    NewY = (_Y + NewY) / 2;  /* Assign 'NewY' the middle value.     */

    if (_GetPoint (_X, NewY) != Bound)      /* If new line not filled */
        _Fill (_X, NewY, Attr, Bound);      /* fill recursively.      */

    DeltaY += 2;
    }

/* Finally, recursively fill on both sides of original line.          */

NewY = _Y - 1;
```

Figure 7.1: GRA.C: A Microsoft C graphics package (continued)

```
    while (NewY <= _Y + 1)    /* First fill lower numbered lines, then  */
        {                      /* higher numbered lines.                 */
        _X = LeftX + 1;        /* Move X from left to right along original */
        while (_X < RightX)    /* line.                                  */
            {
            A = _GetPoint (_X, NewY);    /* Get attribute of adjacent    */
                                         /* point -- move right a BYTE   */
            if (*Video == (Attr ? 0xff:0))/* if adjacent byte filled.    */
                _X |= 0x0007;

            else if (A != Bound && !BADY (NewY))    /* Point not filled;  */
                _Fill (_X, NewY, Attr, Bound);      /* start filling at   */
                                                    /* this point.        */
            ++_X;              /* Move on to next X value.                */
            }

        NewY += 2;
        }

    } /* end _Fill */
```

Figure 7.1: GRA.C: A Microsoft C graphics package (continued)

```
                          /* Constants for active graphics mode.        */
#define NOMODE   -2       /* No graphics mode active.                   */
#define HERC     -1       /* Hercules page 0 graphics.                  */
#define CGAHIRES  6       /* CGA 640 x 200 two color graphics.          */

                          /* Constants for error return codes.          */
#define NOERROR      0    /* No error.                                  */
#define WRONGMODE    1    /* Requested mode not supported by hardware.  */
#define BADMODE      2    /* Invalid mode requested.                    */
#define NOGRAPH      3    /* Graphics mode not set.                     */
#define BADCOORD     4    /* Invalid coordinates passed.                */
#define OUTOFRANGE  -1    /* Requested point is out of range.           */

                          /* Display attribute for graphics pixels.     */
#define ON   0x01         /* Turn bit on (white).                       */
#define OFF  0x00         /* Turn bit off (black).                      */
#define XOR  0x80         /* Exclusive OR value w/ existing bit.        */

                          /* Function prototypes.                       */
int GraInit (int Mode);
int GraQuit (void);
int GraClear (int Attr);
int GraSetCoord (float XMinNew, float YMinNew, float XMaxNew, float YMaxNew);
void GraGetCoord (float *XMinPtr, float *YMinPtr, float *XMaxPtr,
                  float *YMaxPtr);
int GraPoint (float X, float Y, int Attr);
int GraGetPoint (float X, float Y);
int GraLine (float X1, float Y1, float X2, float Y2, int Attr);
int GraBox (float X1, float Y1, float X2, float Y2, int Attr);
int GraCircle (float X, float Y, float R, int Attr, float Aspect);
int GraFill (float X, float Y, int Attr, int Bound);
```

Figure 7.2: GRA.H: Header file to include in your program for calling the functions in GRA.C

the function call for each graphics mode. The manner in which this device independence is achieved is described later in the chapter.

Another important general feature is that although the module currently supports only two graphics modes, it is designed so that it can easily be enhanced to support additional modes. Therefore, some of the features of the functions do not have immediate relevance to the modes currently supported, but are provided with enhancement in mind. The module is short and simple enough to present in a single chapter, yet provides a good foundation for developing a full-featured graphics library. Suggestions for enhancements are offered throughout the following descriptions as well as at the end of the chapter.

The following is a summary of the functions contained in the graphics module:

- Switch into a selected graphics mode and initialize the graphics module (**GraInit**).
- Return to text mode (**GraQuit**).
- Erase the entire screen, filling it with the requested color (**GraClear**).
- Set and obtain the current world coordinate ranges for the graphics screen (**GraSetCoord** and **GraGetCoord**).
- Plot a single point with a specified color (**GraPoint**).
- Obtain the color of a given point on the screen (**GraGetPoint**).
- Draw a line in a chosen color (**GraLine**).
- Draw a rectangle in a chosen color (**GraBox**).
- Draw a circle or ellipse in a chosen color (**GraCircle**).
- Fill a bounded area of the screen with a selected color (**GraFill**).

GraInit and GraQuit

Using GraInit and GraQuit

Before using any of the graphics display functions in this module, you must call **GraInit**. The prototype for this function is

```
int GraInit
    (int Mode)
```

where **Mode** is the desired video mode. The two modes supported are CGAHIRES, the CGA high resolution graphics mode (640 × 200 pixels), and HERC, the Hercules monochrome graphics mode (720 × 348 pixels). You should first call **ScrTypes** (Chapter 5) to determine which mode or modes are available. If you pass a mode other than these two, **GraInit** returns BADMODE. If the requested mode is valid, but not supported by the hardware, WRONGMODE is returned. If successful, the function returns NOERROR. These constants are defined in GRA.H (Figure 7.2).

In addition to switching into the selected graphics mode, **GraInit** initializes a set of internal variables to values based upon the specific mode. If you call graphics display functions without first calling **GraInit**, then these functions will return an error message (NOGRAPH).

To return to the text mode, either at the end of your program or at any time your program requires normal textual display, you may call the function **GraQuit**. This function has the prototype

```
int GraQuit
    (void)
```

and automatically restores the appropriate color or monochrome text mode. It will return NOGRAPH if no graphics mode was active, and otherwise NOERROR. Once this function is called, it is not possible to use graphics functions until **GraInit** is called again.

A typical sequence for using the functions that have been described so far is illustrated in Figure 7.3. Figures 7.4 and 7.5 provide a MAKE file and a QuickC program list to demonstrate the method for compiling this program and importing the graphics routines.

How GraInit and GraQuit Work

GraInit first calls **ScrTypes** to obtain the currently available adapter types and saves the result in the variable **VideoTypes**. It next branches to one of two routines depending on the value of **Mode**, the requested video mode.

The routine for the CGA high resolution mode (CGAHIRES) first tests **VideoTypes** to verify that a CGA adapter is present, returning

```
#include <STDIO.H>
#include <PROCESS.H>

#include "GRA.H"
#include "SCR.H"
#include "KBD.H"

void main ()
    {
    int AdapterTypes;                   /* Stores modes supported.        */
    int Choice;                         /* Stores user mode selection.    */

    AdapterTypes = ScrTypes ();         /* Determine adapter(s) present.  */

    /* Select graphics mode and initialize graphics module.              */

    if (AdapterTypes & VCGA && AdapterTypes & VHGC)   /* Both adapters.  */
        {
        printf ("Which graphics adapter would you like to use?\n");
        printf ("    (1) Color Graphics Adapter.\n");
        printf ("    (2) Hercules Graphics Card.\n");
        printf ("Enter 1 or 2: ");
        do
            {
            Choice = (KbdGetC () & 0x00ff) - '0';
            }
        while (Choice < 1 || Choice > 2);

        if (Choice == 1)
            GraInit (CGAHIRES);
        else
            GraInit (HERC);
        }

    else if (AdapterTypes & VCGA)                    /* Only CGA adapter. */
        GraInit (CGAHIRES);

    else if (AdapterTypes & VHGC)                    /* Only HGC adapter. */
        GraInit (HERC);

    else                                /* No graphics adapter.  Therefore */
        {                               /* terminate gracefully.           */
        printf ("Must have either CGA or Hercules graphics adapter\n");
        exit (0);
        }

    /*    M A I N   G R A P H I C S   A P P L I C A T I O N   H E R E    */

    GraQuit ();                         /* Restore text mode before ending */
                                        /* program.                        */
    } /* end main */
```

Figure 7.3: GRADEMO1.C: A typical sequence for setting the graphics mode and then restoring the text mode

```
GRADEM01.OBJ : GRADEM01.C GRA.H SCR.H KBD.H
     cl /c /W2 /Zp GRADEM01.C

GRA.OBJ : GRA.C GRA.H
     cl /c /Zp GRA.C

SCR.OBJ : SCR.C SCR.H
     cl /c /W2 /Zp SCR.C

SCRA.OBJ : SCRA.ASM
     masm /MX SCRA.ASM;

KBDA.OBJ : KBDA.ASM
     masm /MX KBDA.ASM;

UTYA.OBJ : UTYA.ASM
     masm /MX UTYA.ASM;

GRADEM01.EXE : GRADEM01.OBJ GRA.OBJ SCR.OBJ SCRA.OBJ KBDA.OBJ UTYA.OBJ
     link /NOI /NOD GRADEM01+GRA+SCR+SCRA+KBDA+UTYA,,NUL,SLIBCER;
```

Figure 7.4: GRADEM01.M: A MAKE file for GRADEM01.C

WRONGMODE if it is not. Next, the existing mode is saved and the new mode is established through the following steps:

1. **ScrGetMode** is called to obtain the current video mode, which is stored in the structure **OldMode**.

2. The current value of the BIOS equipment flag is stored in the variable **OldEquipFlag**. This value is saved so that it can be restored by the function **GraQuit**.

3. Bits 5 and 4 of the BIOS equipment flag are set to 10 (binary), which signals the BIOS that a color graphics adapter is installed and currently active. This provision is necessary to make sure that the color card is active in a system with both a color and a monochrome adapter (otherwise, **ScrSetMode** will be unable to set the desired graphics mode).

4. **ScrSetMode** is called to switch into graphics mode (mode 6, CGA two-color graphics).

```
GRADEM01.C
GRA.C
SCR.C
SCRA.OBJ
KBDA.OBJ
UTYA.OBJ
```

Figure 7.5: A QuickC program list for preparing GRADEM01.C

See the description of the functions **ScrMonoCard** and **ScrColorCard** in Chapter 5 for an explanation of the role of the BIOS equipment flag in switching video modes. Note that for convenience, the constant CGAHIRES is defined to be equal to the actual mode number, 6. Finally, several global variables are set according to the selected mode: **_XMax** and **_YMax** are given the maximum numbers of horizontal and vertical pixels, and **CurrMode** is assigned the current mode.

The routine to establish the Hercules graphics mode (HERC) is not as simple as the CGA routine, since the IBM BIOS offers no support for Hercules graphics and it is necessary to program the video controller directly. This routine also tests **VideoTypes** for the required adapter, and assigns initial values to the global variables. Switching into graphics mode, however, is accomplished by writing to ports on the 6845 video controller chip and is performed in the following five stages:

1. Page 0 graphics is allowed by writing a value of 1 to the "configuration switch" at port address 3BFh. The Hercules card has two distinct pages of graphics memory: page 0, 32 kilobytes beginning at segment address B000h, and page 1, 32 kilobytes beginning at segment B800h. This module enables and uses only page 0 in order to avoid an address conflict in case the computer also contains a standard CGA card (which uses a block of memory beginning at the same address as Hercules page 1).

2. The adapter is switched to a graphics mode, but the video display is disabled, by writing 2 to port 3B8h (the display is disabled to avoid video "noise" while performing the remaining operations).

3. The first twelve 6845 data registers are loaded with the appropriate parameters to establish the graphics mode. These registers are all accessed through a single port address by first loading an index value into the port at address 3B4h to select a data register, and then writing to the data register port at address 3B5h. The 12 parameters are stored in the array of bytes **GraphTable**, and are loaded one at time.

4. The graphics page is cleared by using the function **UtySetFar** to load 0's into the 32K of graphics memory beginning at segment B000h. (This function allows fast initialization of a block of memory at a **far** address with a given word, and is described in Chapter 12.)

5. Finally, the video display is enabled in the graphics mode by writing 0Ah to port 3B8h.

Before terminating, the function calculates two more global variables, **XRatio** and **YRatio**, which contain the ratio of number of pixels to the current world coordinate units (the concept of world coordinates is explained later in the chapter). Having these two values already calculated facilitates many of the conversions that are performed in the display functions.

The function **GraQuit** performs two tasks: it switches back into text mode and it sets the global variable **CurrMode** back to the value NOMODE. If the system is not currently in a graphics mode (**CurrMode** equals NOMODE), the function immediately returns the error code NOGRAPH. To restore text mode from CGA graphics, **GraQuit** sets the BIOS equipment flag back to the value saved by **GraInit** (in **OldEquip-Flag**) and calls **ScrSetMode**, passing this function the address of the structure containing the former video mode (**OldMode**).

The method for switching a Hercules adapter back to text mode is similar to the procedure for activating the graphics mode, and consists of the following four steps:

1. The adapter is switched to text mode and the display disabled by writing 0x20 to port 3B8h.

2. The data registers are loaded with the appropriate parameters for text mode, which are stored in the array **TextTable**.

3. The screen is cleared by writing 2000 blank characters with the normal display attribute (0720h) directly to monochrome text video memory at segment address B000h.

4. The video display is enabled in the text mode by writing the value 28h to port 3B8h.

GraClear

Using GraClear   The function **GraClear**, which has the prototype

```
int GraClear
     (int Attr)
```

clears the entire screen by filling the screen with the requested display attribute, **Attr**. Since the current implementation of the graphics package supports only two-color graphics modes, you can specify either 0 (OFF) to create a dark background, or 1 (ON) to create a light background. When you then call graphics display functions, you can request a contrasting attribute so that the drawing will be visible against either type of background.

Actually, any non-zero value of **Attr** will result in a light background. This feature is useful in case the module has been expanded to include multi-colored modes; for example, if **Attr** is assigned a value to produce a red background, the function call will still work properly in a two-color graphics mode, simply translating the color red into the single light color that is available.

How GraClear Works

Like most of the high-level functions (that is, those that are called directly by the user of the module and are not declared **static**), **GraClear** begins by testing **CurrMode** to verify that a graphics mode is active and returns NOGRAPH if it is not. It then simply uses the function **UtySetFar** to fill either the 16K of CGA graphics memory or the 32K of Hercules graphics memory with the requested attribute. Note that the expression

```
Attr ? 0xffff : 0
```

which is used to pass the attribute to **UtySetFar**, results in an attribute of all 1's (which will light all pixels on the screen) for *any* nonzero attribute value, so that attribute values other than 0 and 1 are translated properly.

GraSetCoord and GraGetCoord

Using GraSetCoord and GraGetCoord

The functions **GraSetCoord** and **GraGetCoord** are used to set and obtain the current ranges of world coordinate values that specify the positions of points on the screen.

When you use the graphics display functions, the horizontal and vertical locations of points on the screen are specified in terms of floating point numbers known as *world coordinates*, rather than in terms of the actual pixel numbers. When the system is initialized, the default ranges of world coordinate values are as follows: horizontal values range from 0.0 at the left edge of screen to 8.0 at the right edge of the screen, and vertical values range from 0.0 at the *bottom* of the screen to 6.0 at the *top* of the screen (top and bottom are emphasized because the direction of increasing values is the opposite from that used for pixel numbers). Therefore, the default world coordinate values for the four corners and the center of the screen are as shown in Figure 7.6, where the horizontal (or X) coordinate in each pair is given first, and the vertical (or Y) coordinate second.

The values of 8.0 and 6.0 are not arbitrary, but rather are approximately equal to the physical dimensions (in inches) of the display area of a typical 12-inch monitor. Therefore, the following command will display a box in the center of the screen, with sizes approximately 2" long:

```
GraBox (3.0,2.0,5.0,4.0,ON);
```

The first two parameters give the X (horizontal) and Y (vertical) coordinates of the lower left corner of the box, the second two parameters give the coordinates of the upper right corner, and the last parameter gives the display attribute (the **GraBox** function is described later in the chapter). Note that for the functions in the graphics module, the X coordinate is always given first and the Y coordinate second.

The function **GraSetCoord** allows you to specify new world coordinate ranges. The prototype is

```
int GraSetCoord
    (float XMinNew,
     float YMinNew,
     float XMaxNew,
     float YMaxNew)
```

where the first two parameters are the new X and Y values for the lower left corner of the screen, and the second two coordinates are the new values for the upper right corner. The only restriction is that the first X value must be less than the second X value, and the first Y value less the second Y value. If this condition is not met, the function returns the error code BADCOORD.

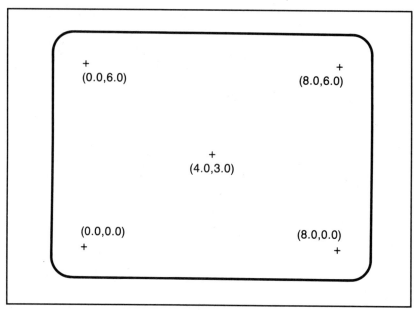

Figure 7.6: The default world coordinate values

The function **GraGetCoord** allows you to obtain the current world coordinate limits. Its prototype is

```
void GraGetCoord
     (float *XMinPtr,
      float *YMinPtr,
      float *XMaxPtr,
      float *YMaxPtr)
```

and it assigns the current world coordinate values to the variables pointed to by the four parameters.

There are several important benefits to using world coordinates rather than physical pixel numbers to specify points on the screen. First, world coordinates allow the graphics display functions to work uniformly over different types of adapters and graphics modes. For example, the box displayed by the function call above will retain its approximate position and dimensions regardless of the video mode. If pixel numbers were used instead, the box would be smaller in the Hercules mode than the CGA mode, and also its center would be closer to the lower left corner of the screen.

Second, by using world coordinates you can specify the position and size of objects in terms of their approximate physical measurements in a chosen unit. With the default ranges (0.0 to 8.0 in the horizontal dimension, and 0.0 to 6.0 in the vertical dimension), world coordinates approximate distances in inches. Since, however, the world coordinate ranges can be changed by calling **GraSetCoord**, other units, such as centimeters, could be used instead.

Another advantage of using world coordinates is that this system allows you to specify positions according to the standard Cartesian coordinate system, in which the coordinates increase moving from left to right and from bottom to top (in contrast, pixel row numbers increase moving from top to bottom).

A final benefit of world coordinates is that this system allows you to change the size or proportions of all objects subsequently displayed on the screen simply by redefining the coordinate limits (through **GraSetCoord**) *without* changing the display function calls. For example, the program in Figure 7.7 demonstrates how **GraSetCoord** can be used to zoom in on an object without modifying the call to the display function (**GraBox**). This program first sets the world coordinate ranges so that the values (–10.0,–10.0) are at the lower left corner of the screen and the values (10.0, 10.0) are at the upper right corner. Note that these ranges place the origin of the coordinate system at the midpoint of the screen and make it easy to center an object. The program then goes into a loop that repeatedly displays a box in the center of the screen, decreasing the world coordinate ranges with each pass to expand the size of the box. The coordinates are initialized and incremented in such as way that as the box increases in size, it remains centered on the screen and square in shape.

Figures 7.8 and 7.9 provide the customary MAKE file and QuickC program list.

How GraSetCoord and GraGetCoord Work

GraSetCoord first checks to make sure that the minimum values are not greater than or equal to the maximum values. This precaution prevents negative ratio values and attempted divisions by zero. Note that after assigning the new values to the internal variables **XMin**, **XMax**, **YMin**, and **YMax**, which store the current world coordinate limits, the function must recalculate the X and Y pixel to world coordinate ratios (**XRatio** and **YRatio**) so that these values remain valid. (As you will see later, these variables are used to convert world coordinate values to pixel numbers.)

The function **GraGetCoord** is so simple that you might wonder why the variables **XMin**, **XMax**, **YMin**, and **YMax** were not simply declared

```
#include <STDIO.H>
#include <PROCESS.H>

#include "GRA.H"
#include "SCR.H"
#include "KBD.H"
#include "UTY.H"

void main ()
    {
    int i;
    float X1,Y1,X2,Y2;                /* Store world coordinate values.  */
    int AdapterTypes;                 /* Stores modes supported.         */
    int Choice;                       /* Stores user mode selection.     */

    AdapterTypes = ScrTypes ();       /* Determine adapter(s) present.   */

    /* Select graphics mode and initialize graphics module.             */

    if (AdapterTypes & VCGA && AdapterTypes & VHGC)  /* Both adapters.   */
        {
        printf ("Which graphics adapter would you like to use?\n");
        printf ("     (1) Color Graphics Adapter.\n");
        printf ("     (2) Hercules Graphics Card.\n");
        printf ("Enter 1 or 2: ");
        do
            {
            Choice = (KbdGetC () & 0x00ff) - '0';
            }
        while (Choice < 1 || Choice > 2);

        if (Choice == 1)
            GraInit (CGAHIRES);
        else
            GraInit (HERC);
        }

    else if (AdapterTypes & VCGA)                    /* Only CGA adapter. */
        GraInit (CGAHIRES);

    else if (AdapterTypes & VHGC)                    /* Only HGC adapter. */
        GraInit (HERC);

    else                              /* No graphics adapter.  Therefore */
        {                             /* terminate gracefully.           */
        printf ("Must have either CGA or Hercules graphics adapter\n");
        exit (0);
        }

    /* First, redefine world coordinate range.                          */
    GraSetCoord (X1 = (float)-10.0,Y1 = (float)-10.0,
             X2 = (float) 10.0,Y2 = (float) 10.0);

    for (i=1; i<=10; ++i)
        {                                  /* Display a centered square: */
        GraBox ((float)-1.5,(float)-2.0,(float)+1.5,(float)+2.0,ON);
        UtyPause ((float)1.0);             /* Delay.                      */
        GraClear (OFF);                    /* Clear entire screen.        */
        }
```

Figure 7.7: GRADEMO2.C: Using **GraSetCoord** to zoom in on an object

```
           /* Reset the world coordinate range to make objects on screen    */
           /* appear larger:                                                 */
           GraSetCoord (X1 += (float)1.0,Y1 += (float)1.0,
                        X2 -= (float)1.0,Y2 -= (float)1.0);
        }

     GraQuit ();                              /* Return to text mode.        */

  } /* end main */
```

Figure 7.7: GRADEMO2.C: Using **GraSetCoord** to zoom in on an object (continued)

```
GRADEM02.OBJ : GRADEM02.C GRA.H SCR.H KBD.H
     cl /c /W2 /Zp GRADEM02.C

GRA.OBJ : GRA.C GRA.H
     cl /c /Zp GRA.C

SCR.OBJ : SCR.C SCR.H
     cl /c /W2 /Zp SCR.C

SCRA.OBJ : SCRA.ASM
     masm /MX SCRA.ASM;

KBDA.OBJ : KBDA.ASM
     masm /MX KBDA.ASM;

UTY.OBJ : UTY.C UTY.H
     cl /c /W2 /Zp UTY.C

UTYA.OBJ : UTYA.ASM
     masm /MX UTYA.ASM;

GRADEM02.EXE : GRADEM02.OBJ GRA.OBJ SCR.OBJ SCRA.OBJ KBDA.OBJ UTY.OBJ UTYA.OBJ
     link /NOI /NOD GRADEM02+GRA+SCR+SCRA+KBDA+UTY+UTYA,,NUL,SLIBCER;
```

Figure 7.8: GRADEMO2.M: A MAKE file for GRADEMO2.C

```
GRADEM02.C
GRA.C
SCR.C
SCRA.OBJ
KBDA.OBJ
UTY.C
UTYA.OBJ
```

Figure 7.9: A QucikC program list for preparing GRADEMO2.C

as external variables within the header file so that you could access them directly. The reason is that these variables must *not* be modified without also updating the world coordinate ratios. Therefore, in the spirit of data encapsulation (discussed in Chapter 1), these variables remain accessible only within the module.

GraPoint and GraGetPoint

*Using GraPoint
and GraGetPoint*

GraPoint has the prototype

```
int GraPoint
      (float X,
      float Y,
      int Attr)
```

and plots a single point at the horizontal position specified by **X** and the vertical position given by **Y**, using the display attribute **Attr**. The **X** and **Y** parameters must be given in world coordinate values, explained in the previous section.

The display attribute parameter **Attr** demands some explanation. If it is given a value of 0 (OFF), then the pixel will be turned *off* at that location. Thus is it possible to plot dark points on a light background (remember that a light background can be created using the command **GraClear (ON)** explained earlier in the chapter, as well as by other methods that will be described later). The following command plots a dark point:

```
GraPoint (1.5, 3.25, OFF);
```

If **Attr** is given a nonzero value (for example, ON, which equals 1) *and bit 7 of Attr is off*, then the pixel will be turned *on*, creating a light point against a dark background; for example,

```
GraPoint (X, Y, ON);
```

If, however, bit 7 of **Attr** is on *and* the low-order 7 bits of **Attr** contain a nonzero value, then the pixel will be *toggled*: if the pixel was on it will be turned off, and if it was off it will be turned back on. **GraPoint** achieves this by exclusive-ORing the current pixel value with 1. For example the following command reverses the pixel at X,Y:

```
GraPoint (X, Y, ON | XOR);
```

The constant XOR has the value 0x80, which turns on bit 7 of **Attr**. Note that if bit 7 is set and the low-order 7 bits are zero, **GraPoint** will have no effect (the current pixel value will be unaltered). If the same point is plotted repeatedly using the exclusive-OR feature, the pixel at that point is simply toggled on and off; therefore, an even number of function calls will cause no net change.

There are two primary benefits to the exclusive-OR feature. First, if a figure is drawn by using the exclusive-OR operator on the existing screen pixels, then the entire figure will be visible regardless of the background attribute. For example, you can superimpose a circle over a background consisting of both light and dark areas. Second, using the exclusive-OR operator provides a simple method for erasing a figure from the screen, while automatically restoring the previous data and leaving other screen areas unaffected. This feature is useful for creating animation effects. Using a set of display functions with exclusive-OR enabled, a figure can be drawn on top of an existing design (without saving the current data), and then can be quickly erased and the screen restored simply by calling the same set of display functions a second time. Subsequently, the figure can be drawn in a new location. In the example program of Figure 6.7, the boxes could have been erased from the screen using exclusive-OR, rather than by erasing the entire screen, as follows:

```
GraBox (-1.5,-2.0,+1.5,+2.0,ON);      /* Draw  a box.  */
UtyPause (1);                          /* Admire it     */
                                       /* for a while.  */
GraBox (-1.5,-2.0,+1.5,+2.0,ON | XOR); /* Erase         */
                                       /* the box       */
```

If a graphics mode is not active, **GraPoint** will return the error code NOGRAPH. Otherwise, it returns NOERROR. If the requested point is outside the current range of world coordinates, the command is simply ignored and no error code is returned. Thus, it is possible to draw a figure which is only partially contained on the screen, since points outside the screen area are automatically clipped.

The function **GraGetPoint**, which has the prototype

```
int GraGetPoint
       (float X,
        float Y)
```

simply returns the current pixel attribute at the specified location. Again, the parameters must be given as world coordinates, and for this version of the graphics package, the only attribute values that can be returned are 0 or 1 (OFF or ON). If, however, a graphics mode is not active, the function returns NOGRAPH, and if the specified point is outside the current range of world coordinates, then the it returns the error OUTOFRANGE.

How GraPoint and GraGetPoint Work

Like most of the functions in this module, **GraPoint** begins by testing the global variable **CurrMode** for a valid graphics mode, immediately returning the error message NOGRAPH if a graphics mode has not been established. The function then converts the world coordinate parameters to pixel values using the macros XPIX for the X value and YPIX for the Y value. These macros are defined at the beginning of the source file (Figure 7.1), and use the current pixel to world coordinate ratios (**XRatio** and **YRatio**) to calculate the nearest pixel number corresponding to the world coordinate value for the current graphics mode. The value is rounded by adding 0.5 before casting to an integer (conversion to an integer results in truncation of the value, not rounding).

Once the coordinates are converted to pixel numbers, the routine calls the low-level function **_Point**, which uses the true pixel numbers, rather than world coordinates, to perform the actual plotting. Note that **_Point** is declared **static** so that it is hidden from the user of the module; the module is designed so that the user never deals with absolute pixel numbers, but rather calls functions that invisibly perform the required translations. The reason for having a separate lower-level function for actually plotting the point is that other functions in the module (such as **GraLine**) can call **_Point** directly, avoiding the overhead of converting coordinates.

The function **_Point** first checks that the requested point is within the range of pixel numbers for the current graphics mode, using the macros BADX and BADY defined at the beginning of the file, and immediately returns if the value is out of range, with no harm done. The function now branches to the appropriate routine for the current graphics mode.

Both of these routines plot the point by directly altering the appropriate bit in video memory; for both modes, each pixel is encoded by a single bit. First, the **far** pointer **Video** is set to the address of the byte containing the desired bit. The expression for calculating the offset is a bit complex, because in both the Hercules and CGA adapters, adjacent lines of pixels on the screen are not adjacent in video memory. For example, the 16 kilobytes of video memory in the CGA adapter is divided into two 8-kilobyte blocks; line 0 of pixels is mapped at the beginning of the first block, line 1 at the beginning of the second block, line 2 following line 0 in the first block, and so on. Thus, all even pixel lines are mapped into the first block, and odd pixel lines into the second block. The 32 kilobytes of Hercules video memory is similarly organized, except that there are four 8-kilobyte blocks rather than two.

Once **Video** has been initialized to the appropriate byte, both routines use the same method for accessing and modifying the specific bit. The expression

```
0x80 >> (_X & 7)
```

is used to form a bit mask consisting of all 0's with a single 1 bit corresponding to the position of the selected pixel. Next, based upon the value of the requested attribute (**Attr**), and depending upon whether the exclusive-OR bit is on, the isolated bit is either turned off, turned on, or toggled in value using the C exclusive-OR operator.

The reason that the **far** pointer **Video** is declared externally will become evident in the description of **GraFill**, later in the chapter. In the CGA graphics mode (*not* in the Hercules mode), you could also plot the point using a BIOS service (interrupt 10h, function 0 Ch). The function does not use this method since it is less efficient; however, if you add support for other graphics modes to the module, the BIOS method is quite convenient since it works uniformly for all of the standard IBM graphics modes, and obviates the need to develop separate algorithms for accessing video memory for each mode.

The function **GraGetPoint** also converts the world coordinate parameters to pixel values and then calls a low-level function that performs the actual task, **_GetPoint**. Before calling this function, however, it checks that the pixel numbers are within the valid ranges for the specific video mode; this test is accomplished by means of the macros BADX and BADY, defined at the beginning of the source file. **_GetPoint** uses the same expressions as **_Point** to initialize the **far** pointer **Video** for the appropriate video mode. The routines for both modes then return the value of the expression

```
(*Video & 0x80 >> (_X & 7)) != 0
```

which is 1 if the pixel is on, and 0 if the pixel is off.

GraLine

Using GraLine

The **GraLine** function has the prototype

```
int GraLine
     (float X1,
      float Y1,
      float X2,
      float Y2,
      int Attr)
```

and draws a line from the point specified by the first two parameters to the point specified by the second two parameters, using the attribute given by **Attr**. The X and Y parameters must be supplied as world coordinate values, and if a portion of the requested line falls off the screen, that section will simply be clipped and the visible part (if any) will be drawn without an error message. **Attr** may be assigned either ON to draw a light line on a dark background, or OFF to draw a dark line on a light background. Also, if **Attr** is assigned the value ON | XOR, the line will be drawn by toggling the current values of the pixels on the screen (as described in the section "Using GraPoint and GraGetPoint"). If a graphics mode has not been established, the function returns NOGRAPH; otherwise, it returns NOERROR.

How GraLine Works

Following the same design as the two functions above, **GraLine** first verifies that a valid graphics mode has been established, converts the world coordinate parameters to physical pixel numbers, and then calls a low level function to perform the actual plotting of points. The low-level function, **_Line**, uses the well-known Bresenham algorithm to draw the line.

The most obvious way to draw a line would be to simply calculate the Y value corresponding to each X value and round the result to the nearest integer, using floating-point operations as follows:

```
float Slope;
int x;
int DeltaY;

Slope = (float)(Y2 - Y1) / (float)(X2 - X1);
                                    /* Slope of line    */


for (x = X1; x <= X2; ++x)      /* Calculate Y for  */
                                /* each X value.    */

    {
    DeltaY = (x - X1) * Slope + 0.5;   /* Rounded    */
                                /* change in Y. */

    _Point (x, Y1 + DeltaY);
    }
```

Although conceptually simple, this method is inefficient since it must perform a slow floating-point multiplication for each point plotted.

The advantage of Bresenham's algorithm is that it uses only fast integer operations. Many of the details of the implementation of this algorithm in the function **_Point** are necessary to properly handle lines having slopes of any possible magnitude and direction. These details will require close study of the code and a little contemplation; the basic principle, however, may be explained as follows.

Consider the line shown in Figure 7.10, which has a positive slope less than 45°, and provides the simplest example of the application of the algorithm. The variable **DeltaX** contains the total change in horizontal dimension over the length of the line, and **DeltaY** contains the total change in the Y dimension. For this line, the variable **Delta** is set equal to **DeltaX**. The main **for** loop plots a point at each X value from **_X1** to **_X2** (prove this for yourself), and the first point has a Y value of **_Y1**. The question that must now be decided with each iteration of the loop is whether or not to increment the Y value. The goal is to choose the pixel that is *closest* to the desired line (the ideal line often falls between pixel values.) The basic technique, therefore, is to increment the Y value by +1 (that is, to the next highest pixel) only when the distance between the current Y value and the correct Y value (that is, the "Y error") becomes more than 1/2. Following this rule assures that the pixel that is turned on will be the one closest to the desired line. Each time the X value is incremented by one, the "Y error" increases by **DeltaY / DeltaX**, and therefore theoretically this value should be added to the Y error with each loop iteration until the sum is greater than 1/2; this condition could be expressed as follows:

Y-error + Y-error + . . . + Y-error > 1/2

or,

$$\frac{DeltaY}{DeltaX} + \frac{DeltaY}{DeltaX} + \ldots \frac{DeltaY}{DeltaX} > \frac{1}{2}$$

Note that this expression involves addition and comparison of floating point numbers. However, by multiplying both sides of the inequality above by **DeltaX**, the following expression results:

DeltaY + DeltaY + . . . + DeltaY > DeltaX / 2.

This final relationship involves only integers and is the one used directly by the algorithm. Since the sum of all the **DeltaY**'s is no longer the true Y error, it is named **ErrNumY** (for the error *numerator* in the Y direction). **DeltaY** is added to **ErrNumY** with each pass of the loop. The value on the right side of the inequality, **DeltaX/2**, is assigned to the variable appropriately named **HalfDelta**. Therefore, whenever **ErrNumY** exceeds **HalfDelta**, Y is incremented and **ErrNumY** is decreased by the amount necessary to compensate for the increase in Y. You are invited to work through an example with slope greater than 45°, and also an example with a negative slope.

A final point: the astute reader is probably already wondering why the first point is plotted twice. The reason is that the **GraLine** function is most frequently used to draw connected lines, such as a triangle:

```
GraLine (3,2,4,4,ON);
GraLine (4,4,5,2,ON);
GraLine (5,2,3,2,ON);
```

Note that this typical series of function calls would cause the initial point of each line segment to be plotted twice. If, however, the exclusive-OR feature has been selected, the triangle would be missing its corner pixels. Therefore, **_Line** plots the initial point twice, which produces the

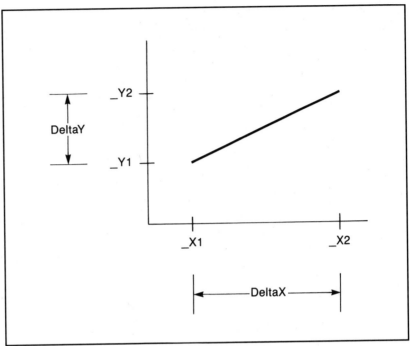

Figure 7.10: A line to be plotted using the Bresenham algorithm

expected result if exclusive-OR is selected (except for a nonconnected line), and is harmless if exclusive-OR is not selected.

GraBox

Using GraBox

The function **GraBox**, which has the prototype

```
int GraBox
     (float X1,
      float Y1,
      float X2,
      float Y2,
      int Attr)
```

draws a rectangle on the screen. The first two parameters must specify the location of one of the corners of the box in world coordinates, and the second two parameters must give the location of the corner that is diagonally opposite from this corner. The last parameter, **Attr**, is the display attribute to be used for drawing the box, and supports the exclusive-OR feature described above (under **GraPoint**) if bit 7 is on. Sections of the box that fall outside of the current range of world coordinates are clipped, while the visible portions are drawn. The function returns NOGRAPH if no graphics mode is active, and NOERROR otherwise.

How GraBox Works

GraBox could have drawn the box simply by calling the **_Line** function four times. However, horizontal and vertical lines do not require Bresenham's algorithm and can be drawn more efficiently by calling the **_Point** function directly, within one loop that draws the horizontal lines, and another loop that draws the vertical lines. Note that the macros MIN and MAX are used to establish the loop limits since it is not known which of **_X1** and **_X2** (or **_Y1** and **_Y2**) is the smallest.

GraCircle

Using GraCircle

The function **GraCircle** has the prototype

```
int GraCircle
    (float X,
    float Y,
    float R,
    int Attr,
    float Aspect)
```

It plots a circle or ellipse having a center given by the first two parameters, **X** and **Y**, and a radius given by the third parameter, **R**. It is drawn using the display attribute specified by **Attr** and the aspect ratio given by **Aspect**. The attribute parameter was explained above under **GraPoint**. **Aspect** specifies the ratio of the vertical dimensions of the points on the circle to the horizontal dimensions. If **Aspect** is set to 1, then a round circle will be drawn, provided that the current ratio of vertical world coordinates to horizontal world coordinates approximates the aspect ratio of the monitor (the default world coordinate ranges of 8 and 6 units match the 4:3 aspect ratio of most monitors). If **Aspect** is greater than 1, then an ellipse will result with the long axis vertical (that is, the vertical dimension of the figure will be greater than the horizontal dimension); the long axis will be equal to twice the requested radius. If **Aspect** is less than 1, then an ellipse will be drawn with long axis horizontal and equal to twice the requested radius. Thus, although the value of **Aspect** changes the overall shape, the longest dimension always equals twice the specified radius.

How GraCircle Works

GraCircle creates the illusion of a circle by drawing an 80-sided polygon. A simple but inefficient approach to this task would be to simply divide the 360 degree circle into 80 equal angles, and then use the old school formulas illustrated in Figure 7.11 to find the X and Y coordinates of the end points of each line segment. The X coordinate would equal the X coordinate of the center plus **R * cos (Theta)** and the Y coordinate would equal the Y coordinate of the center plus **R * sin (Theta)**, where **Theta** is the angle θ shown in the diagram, in radians. The problem with this technique is that it mandates calling two time consuming trigonometric functions with each pass of the loop (the functions **cos** and **sin** are in the Microsoft C math library).

The algorithm used by **GraCircle** uses two more school formulas to eliminate the need to call trigonometric functions from the math library. These formulas are as follows:

```
cos (α + β) = cos β cos  β - sin α sin β
sin (α + β) = sin α cos β + cos α sin β
```

GraCircle uses these formulas to find the cosine and sine of the angle θ (**CosTheta** and **SinTheta**) as θ is incremented around the circle, from the previous cosine and sine values of this angle and the sine and cosine values of the fixed angular increment. The current value of the angle θ is always equal to the old value of θ plus the amount by which θ is incremented. Since the increment is a fixed quantity (equal to $2\pi/80$), its sine and cosine values can be assigned to constants (SINDELTA and COSDELTA) and need not be calculated at runtime.

Once **CosTheta** and **SinTheta** have been found, the X and Y distances of the endpoints of the current line segment from the center of the circle are calculated using the formulas shown in Figure 7.11. Next, these distances are converted to pixel numbers using the ratios **XRat** and **YRat**, which are based on the global ratios **XRatio** and **YRatio**, but have been adjusted according to the requested aspect ratio (**Aspect**). Finally, the line segments are drawn using the low-level **_Line** function; note that once the position of one line segment is laboriously calculated, the position of three additional segments can be found through quick arithmetic conversions. Thus, 80 line segments can be drawn with only 20 iterations of the loop.

GraFill

Using GraFill

The function **GraFill** has the prototype

```
int GraFill
      (float X,
       float Y,
       int Attr,
       int Bound)
```

It fills the area surrounding the point specified by the parameters **X** and **Y** with the display attribute given by **Attr**, until a boundary having the attribute given by **Bound** is encountered. **X** and **Y** must be supplied in world coordinates.

For example, if a light box is drawn on a dark screen as follows

```
GraClear (OFF);
GraBox (3,2,5,4,ON);
```

the box can be filled with light pixels using the following function call:

```
GraFill (4,3,ON,ON);
```

Any point inside of the boundaries of the box could have been specified with equal effect. The function simply turns on pixels in all directions until a continuous boundary of lit pixels is met. If there are any gaps in

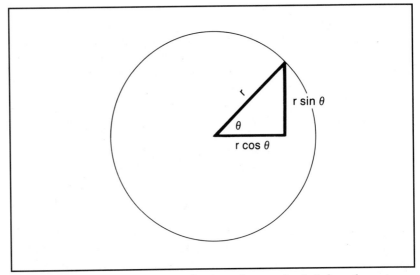

Figure 7.11: Distances of a point on the circumference of a circle from the center

the lines that form the box (even if only a single pixel wide), the "filling" will leak out and encompass the entire screen. Any irregular shaped figure can be filled with this function, provided that the boundary is continuous.

The function can be used equally well to darken the inside of a box or other figure drawn on a light background; for example,

```
GraClear (ON);         /* Creates a light screen   */
                       /* background.              */
GraBox (3,2,5,4,OFF);  /* Dark box on light        */
                       /* screen.                  */
GraFill (4,3,OFF,OFF); /* Fills box with dark      */
                       /* pixels.                  */
```

Since the graphics module currently supports only two-color graphics, **GraFill** will have no effect if the last two parameters are not equal. Both of these parameters are included, however, as a provision for an enhanced version of the package that supports multi-color graphics modes. This function returns NOGRAPH if a graphics mode has not been initialized, OUTOFRANGE if the requested point is out of the current range of world coordinates, and NOERROR if it is successful.

How GraFill Works

GraFill begins by verifying that a valid graphics mode is active and then converts the world coordinate parameters to pixel numbers. After checking that the resulting pixel numbers are within the boundaries for the current graphics mode, it calls the low-level function **_Fill**. **_Fill** performs the actual plotting of points, and is written as a separate function because it calls itself recursively. It would be inefficient to have to convert world coordinates and perform error checking with each call.

The function **GraFill** performs its task in three distinct stages. First, it fills the entire line containing the specified point, moving left until the boundary attribute or edge of the screen is encountered, and then moving right until the boundary or screen edge is met again. **GraFill** determines the attribute of a given point on the screen by calling **_GetPoint**, which, in the process of obtaining the value of the appropriate bit, sets the **far** pointer **Video** to point to the byte containing this bit. Since **Video** is an external variable, **_GetPoint** may now examine the byte it points to, and if this byte is completely unfilled, it is filled in a single operation and the function skips to the next byte boundary. Large unfilled areas are thus rapidly filled byte by byte rather than a single bit at a time.

Second, after filling the single line, **_Fill** now calls itself recursively to fill two intermediate lines on the screen (if other unfilled lines are available). The purpose of this stage is to effectively branch out and begin filling many smaller areas, rather than starting at a single point and moving out line by line to fill the entire area (which would require many levels of recursion and would tend to create stack overflows).

In the final stage, the function begins moving out line by line by recursively calling itself, first for all unfilled sections of the line above, and then for all unfilled sections of the line below. It is fun to watch **GraFill** work as it performs its recursive divisions of the screen. The default Microsoft C stack is large enough so that an entire blank screen can be filled without a stack overflow. However, there might be certain shapes that could cause stack overflows (namely, those that are short in the center of the screen, which would defeat the second stage described above, but tall toward the edges). If you encounter any crashes while using the **_Fill** function, make sure that stack checking is enabled when you compile the program. (The compiler automatically inserts a call to a stack-check routine at the beginning of each function, unless you defeat this feature by specifying the **/Gs** command line flag or the **check_stack (off)** pragma. The stack-check routine will print an error message and terminate the application if it detects a stack overflow. Note, however, that you can read the error message only if you are in the CGA graphics mode, and not in the Hercules mode.)

ENHANCEMENTS TO THE GRAPHICS MODULE

Several suggestions for enhancements have already been offered in the function descriptions. This section briefly summarizes the two basic types of enhancements you might make: first, additional graphics primitives, and second, support for other graphics modes.

Additional Graphics Primitives

Among the many graphics primitives that might be added to this package are the following:

- Functions for copying blocks of graphics data from one area of the screen to another (such as GET and PUT in BASICA).

- A command to define a *viewport*, which is a subset of the total area of the screen into which the display of graphics data is confined (such as the BASICA VIEW statement).

- A function to set the color used for the pixels in high resolution CGA graphics.

- An option for the **GraFill** function that would allow filling an area with a pattern rather than a solid color (that is, *tiling*, as provided by the BASICA command PAINT).

- An option for the **GraCircle** command that would allow drawing a partial ellipse (that is, an arc specified by the associated angle.)

- A graphics definition language to draw a figure by moving a point around the screen (such as DRAW in BASICA), or a set of turtle graphics commands.

Any new graphics display function added to the module should accept X and Y positions as world coordinates, in order to maintain graphics-device and mode independence.

Support for Other Graphics Modes

The graphics module is designed to facilitate adding support for other graphics modes. As new modes are added, the basic programmer interface will remain unchanged, and only a subset of the functions in the module need to be modified. The following functions contain code that is specific to the current graphics mode or adapter type and will need to be altered to accommodate new modes:

- **GraTypes**
- **GraInit** and **GraQuit**
- **GraClear**
- **_Point** and **_GetPoint**
- **_Fill**

For most of these functions, the only requirement will be the addition of a new branch to the main **switch** statement for each new mode supported. See the summary of standard IBM video modes at the beginning of Chapter 5. Also, as mentioned above, the routines for plotting and reading pixels can be greatly simplified and made more uniform by using the BIOS services rather than directly accessing video memory. (For a description of the BIOS services, see either the IBM PC or AT technical reference or the *BIOS Interface Technical Reference* cited in the Bibliography.)

Interrupt Handlers

CHAPTER 8

The interrupt mechanism is one of the most important resources in an MS-DOS machine. There are two general ways that your program can benefit from this mechanism. First, the hardware constantly generates interrupts that allow your program to perform useful subsidiary tasks concurrently with the main flow of logic. Second, the operating system invokes several software interrupts that permit you to install custom handlers for break-key and critical-error conditions. This chapter begins by summarizing the primary features of the interrupt mechanism in MS-DOS computers. The remainder of the chapter then presents a collection of functions that make it simple for you to take advantage of interrupts generated both by the hardware and by the operating system. Interrupt handlers have traditionally been written in assembly language; however, using some of the advanced features of Microsoft C, it is possible to write them entirely in C, as the functions in this chapter illustrate. Using these functions you can do the following:

▌ Install and remove a routine that is invoked with each clock interrupt (**IntClockInstall**, **IntClockRemove**). An example application is presented that displays the current time on the screen, while the main program continues to run in the foreground.

▌ Install and remove control-break routines. Default routines are provided that offer the user the choice of returning to the program, branching to a main menu, or gracefully terminating the application. You can install and remove a routine that is activated at virtually any time the user presses Ctrl-Break (**IntBBInstall**, **IntBBRemove**), or a routine that is activated only when DOS is active and it is safe to interrupt the process (**IntDBInstall**, **IntDBRemove**). Not only do these routines provide a useful mechanism for the user, but they also prevent uncontrolled program exit.

▌ Install and remove a routine that allows your program to handle critical DOS errors (**IntCEInstall**, **IntCERemove**). A default routine is provided that displays an error message and provides a controlled exit if the user chooses to abort the program.

The module of interrupt related functions is listed in Figure 8.1, and the header file for this module in Figure 8.2.

```
#include <STDIO.H>
#include <IO.H>
#include <DOS.H>
#include <PROCESS.H>
#include <STRING.H>
#include <CONIO.H>

#define MODFILE
#include "INT.H"
#include "KBD.H"
#include "SCR.H"

#pragma check_stack (off)        /* Turn off stack checks so that functions */
                                 /* can be called from interrupt routines.  */

#define ULR 6                    /* Position of centered window.            */
#define ULC 20

/*************************** clock interrupt 08h ***************************/

static void (interrupt far *OldClock) (void);
static void interrupt far NewClock (void);
static void (*UserClockRtn) (void);

void IntClockInstall (void (*FPtr) (void))
/*
    This function installs the function pointed to by the parameter 'FPtr'
    to be called each time the clock tick interrupt (08h) occurs.
*/
    {
    OldClock = _dos_getvect (0x08); /* Get address of old int 08 handler. */

    UserClockRtn = FPtr;            /* Set global function pointer.       */

    _dos_setvect (0x08,NewClock);   /* Initialize interrupt 08h vector.   */

    } /* end IntClockInstall */


void IntClockRemove (void)
/*
    This function restores the former clock tick interrupt service routine.
*/
    {
    _dos_setvect (0x08,OldClock);   /* Restore saved interrupt vector.    */

    } /* end IntClockRemove */


static void interrupt far NewClock (void)
/*
    This is the clock tick interrupt service routine.
```

Figure 8.1: INT.C: The module of interrupt handling functions

```
    */
        {
        (*OldClock) ();                    /* First call the former routine.     */

        _enable ();                        /* Make sure interrupts are enabled.  */

        (*UserClockRtn) ();                /* Call the user routine.             */

        return;                            /* Interrupt return.                  */

        } /* end NewClock */


/*************************** control-break routines ************************/
static void (interrupt far *OldKBHand)(void);/* Pointer to old 09h handler. */
static void (interrupt far *Old1BHand)(void);/* Pointer to old int 1Bh hand.*/
static void interrupt far NewKBHand (void);  /* New int 09h handler.        */
static void interrupt far New1BHand (void);  /* New interrupt 1Bh handler.  */
static void (*BBRtn) (void);                 /* Pointer to service function.*/
static void DefaultBBRtn (void);             /* Default service function.   */
static void (*BBWrapup) (void);              /* Pointer to wrapup routine.  */

static void (interrupt far *OldDBHand)(void);/* Pointer to old 23h handler. */
static void interrupt far NewDBHand (void);  /* New int 23h handler.        */
static void (*DBRtn) (void);                 /* Pointer to service function.*/
static void DefaultDBRtn (void);             /* Default service function.   */
static void (*DBWrapup) (void);              /* Pointer to wrapup routine.  */

static void DefaultWrapup (void);            /* Listed under crit-error.    */
static void Dummy (void);                    /* Disables DOS control break. */
static int OldRow, OldCol;                   /* Save cursor positions.      */
static unsigned char BreakFlag = 0;          /* Flag indicates Ctrl-Break.  */


void IntBBInstall (void (*UserRtn)(void),void (*UserWrapup)(void))
/*
    This function installs the BIOS control-break routine specified by
    'UserRtn', or uses the default routine if this parameter is NULL.  If
    the default routine is requested, a user wrapup routine can be
    specified by the parameter 'UserWrapup'.  If the second parameter is
    NULL, then the default wrapup routine will be used.
*/
    {
                    /* Get address of existing interrupt 1Bh handler:    */
    Old1BHand = _dos_getvect (0x1b);
                    /* Get address of existing keyboard interrupt handler: */
    OldKBHand = _dos_getvect (0x09);

    if (UserRtn == NULL)            /* Use default BIOS break routine.     */
        {
        BBRtn = DefaultBBRtn;            /* Default break routine addr. */
        if (UserWrapup == NULL)
            BBWrapup = DefaultWrapup;     /* Use default wrapup routine. */
        else                              /* Use the requested wrapup    */
```

Figure 8.1: INT.C: The module of interrupt handling functions (continued)

```
            BBWrapup = UserWrapup;        /* routine.                      */
        }
    else                                 /* Use requested break routine.  */
        BBRtn = UserRtn;

    IntDBInstall (Dummy,NULL);   /* Disable DOS control-break handler!      */

                             /* Install the new interrupt 1Bh handler:      */
    _dos_setvect (0x1b,New1BHand);

                             /* Set the keyboard interrupt vector:          */
    _dos_setvect (0x09,NewKBHand);

    } /* end IntBBInstall */


void IntBBRemove (void)
/*
    This function restores the former keyboard vector, thus removing the
    requested BIOS control-break handler.
*/
    {
    _dos_setvect (0x1b,Old1BHand);  /* Restore interrupt 1Bh address.      */

    _dos_setvect (0x09,OldKBHand);  /* Restore interrupt 09h address.      */

    IntDBRemove ();                 /* Remove the dummy DOS break routine! */

    } /* end IntBBRemove */


static void interrupt far NewKBHand (void)
/*
    This is the new keyboard hardware interrupt handler (int 09h).
*/
    {
    (*OldKBHand) ();                    /* Call former service routine.    */

    if (BreakFlag)                      /* Examine BIOS break flag.        */
        {
        BreakFlag = 0;                  /* Reset BIOS break flag.          */

        _disable ();                    /* Disable hardware interrupts     */
                                        /* while testing and setting the   */
                                        /* Busy flag.                      */
        if (Busy)                       /* Prevent recursive invocations.  */
            return;
        Busy = 1;                       /* Set busy flag.                  */

        _enable ();                     /* Reenable hardware interrupts now */
                                        /* that it's safe.                 */

        (*BBRtn) ();                    /* Call the service routine.       */

        Busy = 0;                       /* Reset busy flag.                */
```

Figure 8.1: INT.C: The module of interrupt handling functions (continued)

```
            }

        return;                              /* Interrupt return.          */

    } /* end NewKBHand */


static void interrupt far New1BHand (void)
    {
    BreakFlag = 1;

    } /* end New1BHand */


static void DefaultBBRtn (void)
/*
    This is the default BIOS-level control-break routine.
*/
    {
    ScrPush ();                          /* Display the window with menu.   */
    ScrGetCur (&OldRow,&OldCol,0);
    ScrClear (ULR,ULC,ULR+11,ULC+39);
    ScrPutBox (ULR,ULC,ULR+11,ULC+39,2);
    ScrPutS ("BIOS CONTROL BREAK HANDLER",0x0f,ULR+2,ULC+6);
    ScrPutS ("R    Return to program",0x0f,ULR+4,ULC+7);
    ScrPutS ("M    go to Main menu",0x0f,ULR+6,ULC+7);
    ScrPutS ("E    Exit to DOS",0x0f,ULR+8,ULC+7);
    ScrPutS ("enter letter of choice:",0x0f,ULR+10,ULC+7);
    ScrSetCur (ULR+10,ULC+31,0);

    for (;;)                             /* Obtain user's decision.         */
        switch (KbdGetC () & 0x00ff)
            {
            case 'r':                    /* Return to former state.         */
            case 'R':
                ScrPop (1);                      /* Restore screen.         */
                ScrSetCur (OldRow,OldCol,0);  /* Restore cursor.            */
                return;                          /* Return to program.      */

            case 'm':
            case 'M':                    /* Go to top menu.                 */
                ScrPop (1);                      /* Restore screen.         */
                ScrSetCur (OldRow,OldCol,0);  /* Restore cursor.            */
                Busy = 0;                        /* Reset busy flag.        */
                longjmp (Mark,1);                /* Back to the top.        */

            case 'e':
            case 'E':                    /* Exit to DOS.                    */
                (*BBWrapup) ();                  /* Last duties.            */
                IntBBRemove ();                  /* Restore interrupt 09h!  */
                exit (1);                        /* ERRORLEVEL = 1.         */
            }

    } /* end DefaultBBRtn */
```

Figure 8.1: INT.C: The module of interrupt handling functions (continued)

```
void IntDBInstall (void (*UserRtn)(void),void (*UserWrapup)(void))
/*
      This function installs a service routine for the DOS-level control-break
      (interrupt 23h).  See IntBBInstall for an explanation of the parameters.
*/
      {
      OldDBHand = _dos_getvect (0x23);    /* Save former int 23h handler.   */

      if (UserRtn == NULL)                /* Use default DOS break routine. */
           {
           DBRtn = DefaultDBRtn;                 /* Default break routine addr. */
           if (UserWrapup == NULL)               /* Use default wrapup routine. */
                DBWrapup = DefaultWrapup;
           else                                  /* Use the requested wrapup    */
                DBWrapup = UserWrapup;           /* routine.                    */
           }
      else                                /* Use requested break routine.   */
           DBRtn = UserRtn;

      _dos_setvect (0x23,NewDBHand);      /* Set DOS control-break vector.  */

      } /* end IntDBInstall */


void IntDBRemove (void)
/*
      This function restores the former DOS control-break handler.
*/
      {
      _dos_setvect (0x23,OldDBHand);

      } /* end IntDBRemove */


static void interrupt far NewDBHand (void)
/*
      This is the actual interrupt routine, which simply passes control to the
      requested DOS control-break handler.
*/
      {
      _disable ();                        /* Make sure interrupts are disabled*/

      if (Busy)                           /* Prevent recursive invocations.  */
           return;

      Busy = 1;                           /* Set busy flag.                  */

      _enable ();                         /* Reenable hardware interrupts.   */

      (*DBRtn) ();                        /* Call break routine.             */

      Busy = 0;                           /* Reset break flag.               */

      } /* end NewDBHand */
```

Figure 8.1: INT.C: The module of interrupt handling functions (continued)

```
        static void DefaultDBRtn (void)
        /*
              This is the default DOS-level control-break routine.
        */
              {
              ScrPush ();                                /* Display the window with menu.    */
              ScrGetCur (&OldRow,&OldCol,0);
              ScrClear (ULR,ULC,ULR+11,ULC+39);
              ScrPutBox (ULR,ULC,ULR+11,ULC+39,2);
              ScrPutS ("DOS CONTROL BREAK HANDLER",0x0f,ULR+2,ULC+6);
              ScrPutS ("R    Return to program",0x0f,ULR+4,ULC+7);
              ScrPutS ("M    go to Main menu",0x0f,ULR+6,ULC+7);
              ScrPutS ("E    Exit to DOS",0x0f,ULR+8,ULC+7);
              ScrPutS ("enter letter of choice:",0x0f,ULR+10,ULC+7);
              ScrSetCur (ULR+10,ULC+31,0);

              for (;;)                              /* Obtain user's decision.            */
                    switch (KbdGetC () & 0x00ff)
                          {
                          case 'r':              /* Return to former state.            */
                          case 'R':
                                ScrPop (1);                     /* Restore screen.            */
                                ScrSetCur (OldRow,OldCol,0);  /* Restore cursor.            */
                                return;

                          case 'm':
                          case 'M':              /* Go to top menu.                    */
                                ScrPop (1);                     /* Restore screen.            */
                                ScrSetCur (OldRow,OldCol,0);  /* Restore cursor.            */
                                Busy = 0;                       /* Reset busy flag.           */
                                longjmp (Mark,1);               /* Back to the top.           */

                          case 'e':
                          case 'E':
                                (*DBWrapup) ();                 /* Call wrap-up routine.      */
                                exit (1);                       /* ERRORLEVEL = 1.            */
                          }

              } /* end DefaultDBRtn */


        static void Dummy ()
        /*
              This routine simply returns, and serves to disable the DOS control-
              break facility.
        */
              {

              } /* end Dummy */

/*************************** critical-error handler ************************/

                                            /* Pointer to old critical-error handler: */
        static void (interrupt far *OldCEHand) (void);
```

Figure 8.1: INT.C: The module of interrupt handling functions (continued)

```
                               /* New critical-error handler:          */
static void interrupt far NewCEHand (unsigned ES, unsigned DS, unsigned DI,
                                     unsigned SI, unsigned BP, unsigned SP,
                                     unsigned BX, unsigned DX, unsigned CX,
                                     unsigned AX);

                               /* Pointer to critical-error service routine: */
static int (*CERtn) (int ErrorCode, int AX, int BP, int SI);

                               /* Default critical-error service routine:    */
static int DefaultCERtn (int ErrorCode, int AX, int BP, int SI);

static void (*CEWrapup) (void);              /* Pointer to wrapup routine.   */
static void DefaultWrapup (void);            /* Default wrapup routine.      */
char TempBuf [9];                            /* Holds character device name.*/

void IntCEInstall (int (*UserRtn) (),void (*UserWrapup) (void))
/*
    This function installs a critical-error service routine.  See
    IntBBInstall for an explanation of the parameters.
*/
    {
    OldCEHand = _dos_getvect (0x24);   /* Save former int 24h handler.    */

    if (UserRtn == NULL)               /* Use default crit-error routine. */
        {
        CERtn = DefaultCERtn;              /* Critical-error routine addr.*/
        if (UserWrapup == NULL)           /* Use default wrapup routine. */
            CEWrapup = DefaultWrapup;
        else                              /* Use the requested wrapup     */
            CEWrapup = UserWrapup;        /* routine.                     */
        }
    else                               /* Use requested crit-error routine.*/
        CERtn = UserRtn;

    _dos_setvect (0x24,NewCEHand);     /* Set DOS critical-error handler. */

    } /* end IntCEInstall */


void IntCERemove (void)
/*
    This function restores the former DOS critical-error handler.
*/
    {
    _dos_setvect (0x24,OldCEHand);     /* Restore interrupt 24h address.  */

    } /*  end IntCERemove */


static void interrupt far NewCEHand (unsigned ES, unsigned DS, unsigned DI,
                                     unsigned SI, unsigned BP, unsigned SP,
                                     unsigned BX, unsigned DX, unsigned CX,
                                     unsigned AX)
/*
    This is the DOS critical-error, interrupt 24h, handler.
*/
```

Figure 8.1: INT.C: The module of interrupt handling functions (continued)

```
        {
        _enable ();                              /* Make sure interrupts are enabled.*/

        AX = (*CERtn) (DI&0x00ff,AX,BP,SI);   /* Call the requested service  */
        return;                                 /* routine.                    */

        } /* end NewCEHand */


static int DefaultCERtn (int ErrorCode, int AX, int BP, int SI)
/*
        This is the default critical-error routine.
*/
        {
        char far *DevAttPtr;              /* Points to attribute in device header. */
                                          /* Far pointer to local buffer:          */
        static char far *FarPtrCh = (char far *)TempBuf;

        static char *Errors [] =        /* DOS critical-error table.           */
             {
             "write-protected diskette   ",
             "unknown unit               ",
             "device not ready           ",
             "unknown command            ",
             "data error (CRC)           ",
             "bad request structure length ",
             "seek error                 ",
             "unknown media type         ",
             "sector not found           ",
             "printer out of paper       ",
             "write fault                ",
             "read fault                 ",
             "general failure            "
             };

        static char *Areas [] =         /* DOS 'areas' for disk errors.        */
             {
             "DOS area",
             "FAT",
             "directory",
             "data area"
             };

        ScrPush ();                             /* Display window, critical-error */
        ScrGetCur (&OldRow,&OldCol,0);          /* information, and menu.          */
        ScrClear (ULR,ULC,ULR+11,ULC+39);
        ScrPutBox (ULR,ULC,ULR+11,ULC+39,2);
        ScrPutS ("C R I T I C A L   E R R O R",0x0f,ULR+1,ULC+6);
        ScrPutS (Errors [ErrorCode],0x70,ULR+2,ULC+5);

        if (AX & 0x8000)     /* Character device OR bad FAT.                    */
             {
             FP_SEG (DevAttPtr) = BP;           /* Set pointer to device       */
             FP_OFF (DevAttPtr) = SI + 5;       /* attribute.                  */

             if (*DevAttPtr & 0x80)             /* Character device.           */
                  {
                  ScrPutS ("error accessing device ",0x0f,ULR+3,ULC+5);
```

Figure 8.1: INT.C: The module of interrupt handling functions (continued)

```
                                        /* Load device name into local buffer. */
                movedata (BP,SI + 10,
                          FP_SEG (FarPtrCh),FP_OFF (FarPtrCh),8);
                TempBuf [8] = '\0';
                                             /* Display local buffer.      */
                ScrPutS (TempBuf,0x0f,ULR+3,ULC+28);
                }
            else                                /* Bad memory image of FAT.   */
                (
                ScrPutS ("Bad memory image of FAT",0x0f,ULR+3,ULC+5);
                }
            }
        else                     /* Disk error.                   */
            (
            if (AX & 0x0100)     /* Write error.                     */
                ScrPutS ("write error:",0x0f,ULR+3,ULC+5);

            else                     /* Read error.                  */
                ScrPutS ("read error:",0x0f,ULR+3,ULC+5);

            sprintf (TempBuf,"drive %c",'A' + AX&0x00ff);     /* Display drive. */
            ScrPutS (TempBuf,0x0f,ULR+3,ULC+18);

            ScrPutS ("area:",0x0f,ULR+4,ULC+5);                      /* Display area. */
            ScrPutS (Areas [(AX & 0x0600) >> 9],0x0f,ULR+4,ULC+12);
            }

        ScrPutS ("action:",0x0f,ULR+5,ULC+5);
        ScrPutS ("R  Retry operation",0x0f,ULR+6,ULC+8);
        ScrPutS ("A  Abort program",0x0f,ULR+7,ULC+8);
        ScrPutS ("I  Ignore error",0x0f,ULR+8,ULC+8);
        ScrPutS ("enter R, A, or I:",0x0f,ULR+10,ULC+5);
        ScrSetCur (ULR+10,ULC+23,0);

        for (;;)                         /* Obtain user's decision.        */
            switch (KbdGetC () & 0x00ff)
                (
                case 'r':                               /* Retry.             */
                case 'R':
                    ScrSetCur (OldRow,OldCol,0);  /* Restore state.     */
                    ScrPop (1);
                    return (1);                   /* 1 => retry.        */

                case 'a':                               /* Abort.             */
                case 'A':
                    ScrSetCur (OldRow,OldCol,0);  /* Restore state.     */
                    ScrPop (1);
                    (*CEWrapup) ();               /* Call wrapup routine. */
                    exit (1);                     /* Exit & set ERRORLEVEL. */

                case 'i':                               /* Ignore.            */
                case 'I':
                    ScrSetCur (OldRow,OldCol,0);  /* Restore state.     */
                    ScrPop (1);
                    return (0);                   /* 0 => ignore.       */
                }

        } /* end DefaultCERtn */
```

Figure 8.1: INT.C: The module of interrupt handling functions (continued)

```
void DefaultWrapup (void)
/*
        This is the default wrapup routine, which prepares for program
        termination by clearing the screen and closing all open streams.
*/
        {
        ScrClear (0,0,24,79);
        fcloseall ();                           /* Close all open file streams.       */

        } /* end DefaultWrapup */
```

Figure 8.1: INT.C: The module of interrupt handling functions (continued)

```
#ifndef NULL
#if defined(__TINY__) || defined(__SMALL__) || defined(__MEDIUM__)
#define NULL 0
#else
#define NULL 0L
#endif
#endif

#include <setjmp.h>
#if (defined MODFILE)
    jmp_buf Mark;
    int Busy = 0;
#else
    extern jmp_buf Mark;
    extern int Busy;
#endif

void IntClockInstall (void (*FPtr) (void));
void IntClockRemove (void);
void IntBBInstall (void (*UserBBRtn)(void),void (*UserWrapup)(void));
void IntBBRemove (void);
void IntDBInstall (void (*UserDBRtn)(void),void (*UserWrapup)(void));
void IntDBRemove (void);
void IntCEInstall (int (*UserRtn) (),void (*UserWrapup) (void));
void IntCERemove (void);
```

Figure 8.2: INT.H: The header file you must include in your program to call functions in the module INT.C

INTERRUPTS AND MS-DOS MACHINES

An *interrupt* in the 8086 family of processors is an event that temporarily suspends the current program and branches to a service routine to perform some required task. Interrupts can be divided into two categories: hardware interrupts and software interrupts.

Hardware interrupts are generated when a device sends a request signal directly to the processor. For example, the programmable timer generates a hardware interrupt 18.2 times each second. This particular interrupt causes the processor to branch to the routine at the address stored in entry number 08h of the *interrupt vector table*. (The interrupt vector table occupies the first kilobyte of memory and stores the addresses of all interrupt service routines. Each entry contains a four byte segment:offset address.) The service routine for this interrupt updates the time-of-day information maintained by the BIOS.

Another example of a hardware interrupt is the one generated by the keyboard. Each time the user presses or releases a key, the keyboard causes an interrupt that branches to the routine stored at entry 09h of the interrupt vector table. The service routine for this interrupt stores the entered key and performs other keyboard tasks.

Software interrupts are generated by a program. In Microsoft C you can generate software interrupts by calling library functions such as **int86** and **int86x**. The interrupt number you pass to these functions is the index of the interrupt table entry that contains the address of the routine you want to invoke. For example, many of the functions in this book generate interrupt number 10h, as in the following example:

```
int86 (0x10, &Reg, &Reg);
```

This instruction causes branching to the address stored in entry number 10h of the interrupt vector table, which is normally the address of the BIOS video services. Note that if the address in the interrupt vector table is replaced by the address of an alternate routine, all subsequent invocations of interrupt 10h will branch to the alternate routine. Thus, you may either replace or patch into an existing interrupt service routine, as will be demonstrated by the examples in this chapter.

MS-DOS also generates several software interrupts. Specifically, when it detects that the user has pressed a break key (Ctrl-C or Ctrl-Break), it invokes interrupt number 23h. Also, when it encounters a critical error, it invokes interrupt 24h. Several functions presented in this chapter demonstrate how you can place the addresses of custom routines in the interrupt vector table so that your program gains control when either of these interrupts occurs.

The primary advantage of the interrupt mechanism is that once your program has installed an interrupt service routine, this routine will be activated automatically at the appropriate time. Your program is now freed from the task of monitoring for a given event and calling the proper function. For example, if a clock tick interrupt routine is installed, your program does not need to periodically check the time of day and update the clock display. Also, if a break-key handler is installed, you do not need to imbed function calls within your code to determine whether the user has pressed a break key. Finally, if you have installed a critical-error handler, DOS will automatically invoke your routine whenever the need arises, obviating the need for your program to test for errors and explicitly call an error procedure.

CLOCK TICK INTERRUPT FUNCTIONS

The clock tick functions and example program use the hardware interrupt (number 08h) that is generated by the programmable timer approximately 18.2 times per second (the exact number is 1193180/65536 times per second).

IntClockInstall and IntClockRemove

*Using
IntClockInstall
and
IntClockRemove*

The function **IntClockInstall** has the prototype

```
void IntClockInstall
    (void (*FPtr) (void))
```

and installs the function specified by **FPtr** as a clock tick service routine. Once **IntClockInstall** is called, the routine pointed to by **FPtr** will be called 18.2 times per second. Note that **FPtr** does not replace the current clock tick handler, but rather is called *after* the current handler returns control.

The function **IntClockRemove**, which has the prototype

```
void IntClockRemove
       (void)
```

removes the clock tick handler previously installed by **IntClockInstall**.

Note that either calling **IntClockRemove** without a prior call to **IntClockInstall**, or terminating the program without removing an installed clock handler will result in certain disaster. (You should use both a break-key handler and a critical-error handler to assure a controlled program exit that can properly remove any installed interrupt routines. The techniques for writing and installing such routines are described later in the chapter.) Note also that the routine installed by **IntClockInstall** should be a normal C function and not a Microsoft C *interrupt* function (described in Chapter 1).

When your clock tick routine receives control, the hardware interrupts are in an enabled state. Your routine should manage the enabled state of the interrupts as required. You can call the Microsoft C function **_enable** (or the function **UtyEnable**, given in Chapter 12) to enable hardware interrupts, and the function **_disable** (or the function **UtyDisable**, in Chapter 12) to disable hardware interrupts. Note, however, that a clock tick routine does not need to save and restore the previous state of the interrupts (belonging to the interrupted foreground program), since this task is performed automatically when the interrupt handler returns. (The function that activates your routine, **NewClock**, is a Microsoft C interrupt function and therefore returns with an IRET machine instruction, which restores the former value of the machine flags register; the enabled state of hardware interrupts is determined by the interrupt flag bit within this register.) See the example program in Figure 8.3, described later in the chapter, for an illustration of how interrupts can be managed within a clock tick routine.

How IntClockInstall and IntClockRemove Work

IntClockInstall first calls the Microsoft C function **_dos_getvect** to obtain the address of the current clock interrupt handler. This address is saved in the global interrupt function pointer **OldClock**, which will be used by the other two routines in this section of the module. Next, the address of the user's function is stored in the global function pointer **UserClockRtn**. Finally, the new clock interrupt handler, **NewClock**, is installed by calling the Microsoft C function **_dos_setvect**, which places the address of this handler directly in the interrupt vector table. Subsequently, each clock interrupt will immediately invoke **NewClock**.

NewClock is a Microsoft C interrupt function; see Chapter 1 for a description of the special features of this type of function. **NewClock** *first* calls the former interrupt handler and *then* calls the user routine. This procedure illustrates an important rule for writing interrupt handlers: you should save the address of the former routine and call this routine at the beginning of your handler to avoid eliminating other important services. In this case, if you do not call the original clock tick handler, the BIOS time keeping routine would never receive control and the BIOS timing data would become invalid. (The BIOS routine also performs another important task: sending an end-of-interrupt signal to the programmable interrupt controller, which reenables interrupts of a equal or lower priority.) Note that immediately before calling the user routine, **NewClock** calls the Microsoft C function **_enable** to make sure that the hardware interrupts are enabled.

An Example Clock Program

The example program in Figure 8.3 installs a clock tick routine to continuously display the current time in a window on the screen. This program first saves the current screen contents and places a simple window in the center of the screen. It then places a small window for displaying the time in the upper left corner. Next, it installs the local function **Clock** as a clock tick routine by calling **IntClockInstall**. Once **Clock** is installed, it will automatically maintain the current time display without any further attention from the main program. The main program in this example would have no difficulty maintaining the time itself, since it simply sits in a loop waiting for a key. A typical application, however, would be busy with other tasks and it would be difficult and messy to embed frequent function calls to update the clock.

The function **Clock** is called approximately 18.2 times each second. Since only the hours and minutes are displayed, this function first determines whether the current number of minutes since midnight is greater than the number of minutes that is displayed (stored in the variable **Minutes**). If another minute has elapsed, the function must update the clock display; otherwise, it returns immediately.

Since the function **Clock** is called so frequently, it must be written efficiently. Therefore, it determines the current time by directly reading the clock tick count maintained by the BIOS (at address 0040h:006Ch, accessed through the **far** pointer **CntPtr**), rather than by invoking an MS-DOS or BIOS interrupt service. This count is set to 0 at midnight and is incremented with each clock tick. Since there are approximately 1092 ticks per minute, the correct number of minutes since midnight is determined by dividing the count by 1092 (using integer division, which appropriately truncates the result to the largest whole number of minutes). If the display requires updating, the flag **Active** is set to prevent the function from being recursively reentered while performing the relatively slow task of updating **Minutes** and formatting the values. The remainder of the function calculates the number of hours and minutes, and displays the results. (Note that the number of minutes obtained by the division at the beginning of this function is not saved, in order to minimize overhead in the most frequently used section of this code. The division is repeated and the value saved in the portion of code that is called 1092 times less often.)

Before accessing the memory location containing the BIOS clock tick count, the function **Clock** calls **_disable** to disable the hardware interrupts. This precaution prevents another process from accessing this memory location at the same time. (If, for example, another clock tick interrupt were to occur, the BIOS clock routine might modify the clock count while **Clock** was attempting to read this value. Note that the clock tick count is a four byte value; accessing such a value requires two machine instructions. If interrupts are not disabled, a hardware interrupt could occur between these two instructions, possibly invalidating the value that is read.) Disabling the interrupts also allows **Clock** to test and set the **Active** flag without the possibility of recursive reentry into the code occurring (if a second clock tick interrupt occurred after the routine tested the **Active** flag but before it set this flag, two instances of the clock routine could become active at the same time).

Once **Clock** has completed accessing the BIOS clock count area and setting the **Active** flag, it immediately calls **_enable** to reenable hardware interrupts. A program should minimize the amount of time the interrupts are disabled to prevent blocking other elements of the system.

Figure 8.4 provides a MAKE file, and Figure 8.5 a QuickC program list.

```
#include <STDIO.H>
#include <DOS.H>

#include "SCR.H"
#include "KBD.H"
#include "INT.H"

#pragma check_stack (off)

#define ULR 6                              /* Position of centered window.       */
#define ULC 20

void Clock (void);                         /* Clock tick routine.                */
void IntToString (int Source,char *Target);

void main (void)
    {
    ScrPush ();                            /* Display program window.            */
    ScrClear (ULR,ULC,ULR+11,ULC+39);
    ScrPutBox (ULR,ULC,ULR+11,ULC+39,2);
    ScrPutS ("C L O C K   D E M O",0x0f,ULR+3,ULC+9);
    ScrPutS ("Press any key to terminate program.",0x0f,ULR+6,ULC+3);

    ScrClear (0,0,3,24);                   /* Display clock window.              */
    ScrPutBox (0,0,3,24,3);
    ScrPutS ("Current Time",0x0f,2,3);
    ScrPutS (":",0x8f,2,19);               /* Blinking colon.                    */

    IntClockInstall (Clock);         /* Install the clock routine.        */

    while (!KbdReady ())              /* Wait for a keystroke.             */
            ;

    IntClockRemove ();           /* Restore old clock interrupt handler.   */
    ScrPop (1);                  /* Restore the original screen.           */

    }    /* end main    */

int Active = 0;                     /* Flag to avoid recursive calls.        */
int Minutes = -1;                   /* Counter for minutes since midnight.   */
long far *CntPtr = (long far *)0x0040006c; /* Pointer to BIOS clock count. */
int TempMinutes;                       /* Temporary hold areas:             */
unsigned char Hours;
char HourStr [3];
char MinuteStr [3];

void Clock (void)
    /*
    This routine is installed so that it is invoked each time the clock
    tick interrupt (0x09h) occurs.  It displays the current time in
    hours and minutes.
    */
    {
    _disable ();                       /* Turn off interrupts before reading    */
                                       /* BIOS clock tick count.                */

                                  /* Return immediately if a minute has     */
                                  /* not elapsed, or if function is busy.   */
    if (*CntPtr/1092 <= Minutes || Active)
        return;
    Active = 1;                        /* Set busy flag.                        */
```

Figure 8.3: INTDEM01.C: An example program that installs a clock interrupt routine to display
        the current time

```
                        /* Calculate number of minutes since midnight.  */
        Minutes = (int)(*CntPtr/1092);

        _enable ();                        /* Turn interrupts back on.   */

                        /* Calculate hours since midnight.               */
        Hours = (unsigned char)(Minutes/60);

        TempMinutes = Minutes%60;       /* Calculate minutes since last hour  */

        IntToString (Hours,HourStr);          /* Format hours and minutes.  */
        IntToString (TempMinutes,MinuteStr);

        ScrPutS (HourStr,0x0f,2,17);             /* Display values.       */
        ScrPutS (MinuteStr,0x0f,2,20);

        Active = 0;                    /* Reset busy flag and return.     */
        return;

        }    /* end clock    */

void IntToString (int Source,char *Target)
        {
        Target [0] = Source / 10 + '0';
        Target [1] = Source % 10 + '0';
        Target [2] = '\0';
        return;
        }    /* end IntToString    */
```

Figure 8.3: INTDEM01.C: An example program that installs a clock interrupt routine to display the current time (continued)

```
    INTDEM01.OBJ : INTDEM01.C SCR.H KBD.H INT.H
        cl /c /W2 /Zp INTDEM01.C

    INT.OBJ : INT.C INT.H
        cl /c /W2 /Zp INT.C

    SCR.OBJ : SCR.C SCR.H
        cl /c /W2 /Zp SCR.C

    KBDA.OBJ : KBDA.ASM
        masm /MX KBDA.ASM;

    INTDEM01.EXE : INTDEM01.OBJ INT.OBJ SCR.OBJ KBDA.OBJ
        link /NOI /NOD INTDEM01+INT+SCR+KBDA,,NUL,SLIBCER;
```

Figure 8.4: INTDEM01.M: A MAKE file for preparing INTDEM01.C

```
    INTDEM01.C
    INT.C
    SCR.C
    KBDA.OBJ
```

Figure 8.5: A QuickC program list for preparing INTDEM01.C

BIOS CONTROL-BREAK FUNCTIONS

The purpose for installing a BIOS control-break routine is to allow the user to interrupt the current process at any time. Many programs contain long sections of code that do not read input from the keyboard, such as routines for recalculating a spreadsheet, redrawing an involved graphics display, sorting a large data structure, or compiling a program. The user should be able to interrupt the process at any time and either return to the main menu or terminate the program. One approach is to embed frequent function calls within the code to determine if a key has been pressed (such as the function **KbdReady**). This tactic, however, complicates programming, slows program execution, and provides a sluggish response. A more felicitous method is to install a BIOS control-break routine that responds instantly to a break key, and requires no further function calls.

Note that if you are running a program within the QuickC integrated environment, a break-key handler installed at the BIOS level will generally never receive control, since QuickC itself intercepts the Ctrl-Break keystroke and stops program execution. Therefore, if you are using QuickC to prepare the example programs given in this section, you should run them from the DOS prompt. (DOS-level break-key handlers, discussed in the next section, generally function correctly within QuickC.)

IntBBInstall and IntBBRemove

Using
IntBBInstall and
IntBBRemove

The function **IntBBInstall** has the following prototype

```
void IntBBInstall
    (void (*UserRtn) (void),
    void (*UserWrapup) (void))
```

This function installs the C function specified by **UserRtn** so that it will be called whenever the user presses Ctrl-Break (it will not be activated by Ctrl-C). If you pass a value of NULL for the first parameter, a default control-break routine will be used instead (NULL is defined in INT.H and in STDIO.H). If you request this default control-break routine, you may then supply, as the second parameter, the address of a "wrapup" routine to be called immediately before program termination. You may also pass NULL as the second parameter to specify a default wrapup routine. Note that if you supply a function address for the first parameter, this function is presumed to contain its own wrapup routine and the second parameter is ignored. For example, the following function call installs both the default control-break routine and the default wrapup routine:

```
IntBBInstall (NULL, NULL);
```

The following line requests the default Ctrl-Break routine, but installs a custom routine that will be called immediately before program exit if the user chooses to abort:

```
void MyWrapupRtn (void);
    .
    .
    .
IntBBInstall (NULL, MyWrapupRtn);
```

Finally, the following call requests the installation of a custom control-break routine, and the second parameter is ignored (however, it must be supplied to prevent the compiler from complaining):

```
void MyCtrBrkRoutine (void);
    .
    .
    .
IntBBInstall (MyCtrBrkRoutine, NULL);
```

The procedure for using **IntBBInstall** depends upon whether the default routine is used or you supply your own routine. These two cases are treated separately.

Using the Default Control-Break Routine

The default control-break routine displays a window in the center of the screen, and offers the user the choice of returning to the current process, going to the main menu, or terminating the program. If the user chooses to return, the screen display is restored and the program resumes where it was interrupted by Ctrl-Break (the user might select this option if the break key had been pressed unintentionally). If the user opts to terminate the program, then the wrapup routine is called to perform any required last duties, and the program is terminated. If, however, the user chooses to return to the main menu, then control passes to the point in your program that you have marked by using the following statement:

```
setjmp (Mark);
```

Each time the user requests returning to the main menu, the program is reentered at the instruction immediately following the above statement. The function **setjmp** is in the C library and **Mark** is an array for holding the current state information. The file INT.C includes the header file for **setjmp** (SETJMP.H) and defines the variable **Mark**. Note that if you use the default break routine, it is mandatory to issue a **setjmp** statement *before* installing the routine.

The default wrapup routine simply clears the screen and closes all open streams by calling **fcloseall ()**. If your program requires any other last minute tasks (such as closing file handles or restoring interrupt vectors) then you should provide a custom wrapup routine and pass its address as the second argument to **IntBBInstall**.

Providing a Custom Control-Break Routine

If you decide to supply a custom control-break routine, you can model it after the default routine described in the next section, including whatever features you desire. The following are some important rules that you should follow when writing a control-break routine:

▌ Remove the control-break routine by calling **IntBBRemove** before terminating the program (if the user decides to abort).

▌ Avoid using function calls that employ MS-DOS services unless you are going to terminate the program. If the program happens to be inside a DOS service when the break key is pressed, DOS can become corrupted. You may perform necessary I/O using BIOS services or the functions in the **Scr** module.

▌ Since the default wrapup routine described above is *not* called if you have installed a custom break function, you must close all open files and perform any other required final tasks if the user opts to abort the program.

▊ If your function jumps to some other point in the code using **longjmp**, *you must first reset the **Busy** flag to 0*. This flag notifies the keyboard interrupt handler that the break routine is no longer active (this mechanism is described in the next section). **Busy** is defined in INT.H so that it may be directly modified by your program.

▊ The control-break routine must be a normal C function and not a Microsoft C interrupt function (since, as you will see, it is not directly activated by an interrupt, but rather invoked by a call instruction from an interrupt handler).

▊ When your control-break routine receives control, hardware interrupts are enabled. You can explicitly set the enabled state of the interrupts by calling the Microsoft C functions **_enable** or **_disable** as described in the section on using **IntClockInstall**, earlier in the chapter.

The function **IntBBRemove**, which has the prototype

```
void IntBBRemove
      (void)
```

removes the break handler that was installed by **IntBBInstall**. If you have installed a control-break routine with **IntBBInstall**, you *must* remove this routine before program termination by calling **IntBBRemove**. Note also that it a grievous error to call **IntBBRemove** without a prior call to **IntBBInstall**.

The function **IntBBInstall** was designed primarily to provide a break mechanism for long, non-interactive portions of a program; its chief benefit is that the routine responds at virtually any time (except for the rare times when interrupts are disabled). If, however, your program frequently performs I/O through MS-DOS services, then it would be almost as effective and somewhat safer to install a break handler at the DOS level instead, using the function **IntDBInstall** described later in the chapter. (A DOS-level break handler, although less responsive than a BIOS handler, is slightly safer since DOS will never invoke the break handler at an inconvenient time, such as in the middle of a timing sensitive disk operation.) Note, however, that you *must not install both handlers at the same time in the same program*, since these handlers would interfere with each other.

The use of the two functions described in this section is illustrated by the example program in Figure 8.6, described later in the chapter. Since many rules are associated with these two functions, the following list is provided to summarize the most important ones:

▪ If you select the default break routine (by passing NULL to **IntBBInstall**), you must issue the instruction **setjmp (Mark)** *before* installing the routine.

▪ If you have installed a break routine, you must remove it before program termination using **IntBBRemove** (but be careful not to call this function if no break routine is installed).

▪ Do not install both a BIOS level break handler (**IntBBInstall**) and a DOS level handler (**IntDBInstall**) concurrently in the same program.

How IntBBInstall and IntBBRemove Work

To effect break-key handling at the BIOS level, **IntBBInstall** installs routines for intercepting three distinct interrupts. First, it calls **IntDBInstall** (described in the next section) to install the function **Dummy** for handling interrupt 23h, the software interrupt invoked by MS-DOS when it detects a break key. As you will see in the next section, **Dummy** simply returns control and effectively disables break handling by MS-DOS. If the DOS break handler were not disabled, it could abort the program even if the user opted to continue, or it could abort before the wrapup routine had finished its tasks.

Second, **IntBBInstall** installs the routine **New1BHand** to process interrupt 1Bh. (Before installing this routine, it saves the address of the former interrupt 1Bh handler in the variable **Old1BHand**, so that **IntBBRemove** can restore this vector.) The BIOS keyboard routine (which is activated through the hardware keyboard interrupt, 09h, to be described shortly) invokes interrupt 1Bh whenever it detects a Ctrl-Break keystroke. The function **New1BHand** simply sets the global program flag, **BreakFlag**, to indicate that the break key has been pressed, and immediately returns control. Note that since **New1BHand** is invoked by an interrupt instruction, it is declared as a Microsoft C interrupt function.

Although an interrupt 1Bh handler can be used to perform a simple task such as setting a flag, the actual break-key routine should *not* be placed within this handler. When the BIOS invokes interrupt 1Bh, it has not yet completed processing the current keystroke; it is important to allow the BIOS routine to complete before executing a routine that reads the keyboard and possibly jumps back to the main program without returning. One specific problem with placing the break-key routine within an interrupt 1Bh handler is that when this interrupt is invoked, the end-of-interrupt signal has not yet been sent to the interrupt controller, and therefore hardware interrupts 09h and higher are disabled. It is thus not possible to read the keyboard unless your routine itself sends the end-of-interrupt signal.

The third and final interrupt handler installed by **IntBBInstall** is **NewKBHand**, which is activated through interrupt 09h and calls the actual break key routine. Interrupt 09h is the hardware interrupt generated by the keyboard each time a key is pressed or released. (Note that before installing the new keyboard interrupt handler, **IntBBInstall** saves the former contents of this vector in the pointer **OldKBHand**; as you will see, **NewKBHand** uses this pointer to invoke the former keyboard routine, and **IntBBRemove** uses it to restore the keyboard interrupt vector.)

Finally, **IntBBInstall** assigns the function pointers for the break routine (**BBRtn**) and for the wrapup routine (**BBWrapup**) based on the values of the two parameters.

NewKBHand is declared as a Microsoft C interrupt function. It first invokes the original BIOS keyboard handler through the function pointer **OldKBHand**. The BIOS routine places the input key in the keyboard buffer and performs a myriad of important checks and tasks. As described previously, if the BIOS routine detects a Ctrl-Break key, it invokes interrupt 1Bh, which causes the function **New1BHand** to receive control and to set the break key flag (**BreakFlag**). When the BIOS routine returns control, if the break flag has been set, **NewKBHand** resets it back to 0 and calls the break routine through the function pointer **BBRtn** (remember that this pointer was set by **IntBBInstall** to the address of either the default routine or the user-requested routine). Note that before the break routine is called, the **Busy** flag is set to 1 and is reset to 0 on return from the break routine. This flag prevents recursive reentries into the break routine if the user presses the break key while the routine is active. Note also that interrupts are disabled while the **Busy** flag is tested and set, and are reenabled immediately before calling the break routine; see the section "An Example Clock Program" for an explanation of this precaution.

The workings of the default break routine, **DefaultBBRtn**, are straightforward. It first saves the screen and cursor position, and displays a menu. If the user chooses to return, the screen and cursor are restored and the function returns (to **NewKBHand**, which then resets the **Busy** flag and performs an interrupt return back to the application). If the user chooses to go to the main menu, then the **Busy** flag is reset to 0 and **longjmp** is called, which transfers control to the statement immediately after the call to **setjmp** in the application program. Finally, if the user opts to abort the program, the appropriate wrapup routine is called through the function pointer **BBWrapup**, the interrupt handler is removed by calling **IntBBRemove**, and the program exits, setting the DOS ERRORLEVEL flag to 1 (**exit (1)**).

The function **IntBBRemove** works by replacing the former interrupt 1Bh vector (stored in the function pointer **Old1BHand**) and the former keyboard vector (stored in the function pointer **OldKBHand**). If you forget to call this function, then after the program terminates, pressing or releasing a key will transfer control to a point in memory containing random data!

An Example BIOS Control-Break Application

The program in Figure 8.6 illustrates the use of a BIOS-level break key handler. The program first calls **setjmp** to mark the position in the code that is to receive control if the user opts to return to the main menu from the break routine. Next, the default break routine and the default wrapup routine are installed with a call to **IntBBInstall**. Since the code can be repeatedly reentered at this point, using the flag **FirstPass** assures that **IntBBInstall** is called only on the first pass. (It would have been simpler to place the call to **IntBBInstall** above the **setjmp** command; however, this ordering creates a small probability that the break routine could be activated *before* the long jump address is defined.)

The program now displays a menu, and allows the user to select one of two demonstration programs or to exit the program. The demonstration routines are designed to simulate long, non-interactive processes. These routines use the function **BiosPutS** (defined at the end of the program) to display a string repeatedly in an infinite loop. If a break handler were not installed, the only way to terminate this process would be by rebooting the computer (**BiosPutS** displays characters using the BIOS services and since no MS-DOS functions are used, the operating system does not have an opportunity to test for a break key). Note that if the user chooses to exit through the main menu, the break routine is removed by calling **IntBBRemove**.

Figures 8.7 provides a MAKE file, and Figure 8.8 a QuickC program list.

```
#include <PROCESS.H>
#include "INT.H"
#include "SCR.H"
#include "KBD.H"

void Menu (void);
void Demo1 (void);
void Demo2 (void);
void BiosPutS (char *String);

void main (main)
    {
    static int FirstPass = 1;      /* Flag to mark first entry into program.*/

    setjmp (Mark);                 /* Mark position prior to main menu.   */
                                   /* Control returns here with 'longjmp'. */

    if (FirstPass)                 /* Install BIOS break handler only on   */
        {                          /* first pass.                          */
        FirstPass = 0;
        IntBBInstall (NULL,NULL);/* Select both default routines.        */
        }

    Menu ();                       /* Display main menu.                   */

    for (;;)                       /* Branch on key typed by user.         */
        switch (KbdGetC () & 0x00ff)
            {
            case '1':                        /* First demo.              */
                Demo1 ();
                break;

            case '2':                        /* Second demo.             */
                Demo2 ();
                break;

            case 'e':
            case 'E':                        /* Terminate program.       */
                ScrClear (0,0,24,80);
                IntBBRemove ();              /* Important! Remove the BIOS */
                exit (1);                    /* break handler before exit. */
            }

    } /* end main */


void Menu ()
    {
    ScrClear (0,0,24,80);
    ScrPutBox (0,0,11,39,3);
    ScrPutS ("M A I N   M E N U",0x0f,2,11);
    ScrPutS ("1   Demo One",0x0f,4,7);
    ScrPutS ("2   Demo Two",0x0f,6,7);
    ScrPutS ("E   Exit to DOS",0x0f,8,7);
    ScrPutS ("enter letter of choice:",0x0f,10,7);
    ScrSetCur (10,31,0);

    } /* end Menu */
```

Figure 8.6: INTDEM02.C: A program demonstrating the use of a BIOS-level break key handler

```
void Demo1 (void)
    {
    ScrClear (0,0,24,79);

    for (;;)              /* Infinite loop displaying a string using the BIOS*/
        BiosPutS ("THIS IS DEMO 1     ");

    } /* end Demo1 */

void Demo2 (void)
    {
    ScrClear (0,0,24,79);

    for (;;)              /* Infinite loop displaying a string using the BIOS*/
        BiosPutS ("THIS IS DEMO 2     ");

    } /* end Demo2 */


#include <DOS.H>

void BiosPutS (char *String)
/*
    This function prints 'String' on the screen, in teletype fashion,
    beginning at the current cursor position.
*/
    {
    union REGS Reg;

    Reg.h.bl = 1;         /* Specifies foreground color 1, if in a graphics. */
    Reg.h.bh = 0;         /* Active page; required for PC BIOS versions       */
                          /* dated 4/24/81 through 10/19/81.                  */
    while (*String)
        {
        Reg.h.al = *String++;   /* Next character to print.            */
        Reg.h.ah = 14;          /* BIOS teletype printing service.     */
        int86 (0x10,&Reg,&Reg); /* BIOS video services.                */
        }

    } /* end BiosPutS */
```

Figure 8.6: INTDEM02.C: A program demonstrating the use of a BIOS-level break key handler
(continued)

DOS CONTROL-BREAK FUNCTIONS

Both the BIOS keyboard handler and the MS-DOS service routines
check for the arrival of a break key. There are three important differences,
however, in the manner that a break key is handled at these two levels.

First, the BIOS can detect the presence of a break key at virtually any
time the user presses Ctrl-Break (except for those infrequent instances when interrupts are disabled). MS-DOS, however, can sense a

```
INTDEM02.OBJ : INTDEM02.C SCR.H KBD.H INT.H
     cl /c /W2 /Zp INTDEM02.C

INT.OBJ : INT.C INT.H
     cl /c /W2 /Zp INT.C

SCR.OBJ : SCR.C SCR.H
     cl /c /W2 /Zp SCR.C

KBDA.OBJ : KBDA.ASM
     masm /MX KBDA.ASM;

INTDEM02.EXE : INTDEM02.OBJ INT.OBJ SCR.OBJ KBDA.OBJ
     link /NOI /NOD INTDEM02+INT+SCR+KBDA,,NUL,SLIBCER;
```

Figure 8.7: INTDEM02.M: A MAKE file for INTDEM02.C

break key only when one of the DOS service routines is active. If the DOS BREAK condition is on, then MS-DOS checks for the break key during any MS-DOS service (except functions 06h and 07 h); otherwise, it checks only during services that perform I/O to the standard character devices (the console, printer, and serial port). See any DOS manual for an explanation of the BREAK flag (which can be modified from the DOS command line by means of the BREAK command, or by a program through interrupt 21h, function 33h). Therefore, you should use a BIOS-level break routine to allow the user to interrupt long sequences of instructions that do not call the operating system. Note that most I/O functions in the standard C library, such as **printf** and **read**, use MS-DOS service routines. (However, most of the routines presented in this book, such as those in the **Scr** module, do *not* use DOS.)

Second, by default the BIOS Ctrl-Break handler does *nothing*; you must install a routine if you want any action to be taken when a break key is detected at this level. However, when MS-DOS detects a break key its default action is to immediately terminate the program. This action might better be called a disservice than a service, since the program is given no opportunity to prepare for its untimely demise. There are two

```
INTDEM02.C
INT.C
SCR.C
KBDA.OBJ
```

Figure 8.8: A QuickC program list for preparing INTDEM02.C

specific problems with such an uncontrolled program exit. First, data written to any unclosed files are lost, since the directory entry for the file length is not updated until the file is properly closed. Second, the program is unable to restore any interrupt vectors it may have assigned, likely resulting in a system crash. Therefore, you should install a DOS-level break handler if your program has any important tasks to perform before it terminates. Note that when a BIOS control break handler is installed (using the function **IntBBInstall**), the DOS-level break handler is automatically disabled, so that you do not need to worry about uncontrolled program exit through MS-DOS.

Third, a BIOS-level break routine responds only to the Ctrl-Break key; the DOS level handler, however, responds identically to either Ctrl-Break or Ctrl-C.

IntDBInstall and IntDBRemove

*Using
IntDBInstall
and
IntDBRemove*

The functions **IntDBInstall** and **IntDBRemove** allow you to install and remove a routine that is called whenever MS-DOS detects a break key. **IntDBInstall** has the prototype

```
void IntDBInstall
    (void (*UserRtn) (void),
    void (*UserWrapup) (void))
```

The parameters work in exactly the same manner as **IntBBInstall**, and allow you either to install your own break or wrapup routine, or to select the default break or wrapup routine by passing a NULL pointer. For a full explanation of the use of these parameters, see the description of **IntBBInstall** earlier in this chapter.

The default break routine performs the same functions as that installed by **IntBBInstall**. If you use this routine, you must likewise call **setjmp** to mark the jump address in your program. The default wrapup routine also performs the same tasks as the one used by **IntBBInstall** (in fact, both these routines call the same wrapup function).

If you decide to write your own break routine, you should follow the same set of rules described for **IntBBInstall** earlier in the chapter. The only exception to these rules is that you do not need to remove the break routine before terminating the program, since this task is performed automatically by MS-DOS when you call the function **exit**. (Note, however, that if a memory-resident program installs a DOS-level break handler when it is activated, it should restore the original handler before returning control to the interrupted application; see Chapter 9 for more information on writing memory resident utilities.)

The function **IntDBRemove**, which has the prototype

```
void IntDBRemove
     (void)
```

removes a break handler that was installed by **IntDBInstall**. Since you do not need to remove a DOS-level break routine before program termination, you would call **IntDBRemove** only if for some reason you want to disable the break routine during a portion of your program (or to replace the original break handler when a memory-resident utility exits). Be sure, however, that you do not call **IntDBRemove** without a prior call to **IntDBInstall**.

There are two primary uses for a DOS-level break routine. One use, of course, is to provide a convenient method for interrupting the current process (and provide a controlled program exit if the user opts to abort); the default routine supplied by **IntDBInstall** is ideal for this purpose. Another use for a DOS break routine is simply to disable the DOS break facility in order to prevent uncontrolled program exit (remember that if you do *not* install a break handler, DOS will summarily abort the program if it detects a break key). The following line of code disables break handling at the DOS level:

```
IntDBInstall (Dummy, NULL);
```

The function **Dummy** is defined as follows:

```
void Dummy ()
     {
     }
```

If this empty break handler is installed, when the user presses Ctrl-C or Ctrl-Break, nothing will happen (except possibly the echoing of the characters ^C).

As a final note, remember that you must not install both a BIOS and a DOS break handler in the same program at the same time. The use of a DOS break handler is illustrated by the program in Figure 8.9, discussed later in the chapter.

How
IntDBInstall and
IntDBRemove
Work

When MS-DOS detects a break key during the execution of a program, it generates interrupt 23h. If the current interrupt 23h handler simply issues an interrupt return instruction (IRET in assembly language), then DOS continues the program rather than aborting it. The function **IntDBInstall** first saves the address of the existing interrupt 23h service routine in the variable **OldDBHand** and installs a new interrupt 23h routine (**NewDBHand**). **IntDBInstall** also assigns the address of the appropriate break routine to the function pointer **DBRtn**. After the installation is complete, **NewDBHand** is invoked whenever DOS detects a break key. **NewDBHand** is a Microsoft C interrupt function that simply calls the appropriate service routine through the function pointer **DBRtn**.

The default DOS break routine, **DefaultCBRtn**, is almost identical to the default BIOS routine (**DefaultBBRtn**) described earlier in this chapter. However, it does not need to remove the break handler before program exit, since this job is performed automatically by DOS.

The function **IntDBRemove** sets interrupt vector 23h back to the former value, which was saved in the variable **OldDBHand**.

An Example DOS Control-Break Application

The program in Figure 8.9 begins by opening and writing a line of data to a test file. This file can be used to test whether the program terminates normally, or aborts without closing open files. If a control break routine were *not* installed and the user pressed Ctrl-C or Ctrl-Break, the program would immediately abort, and a directory listing would show the test file to have a length of 0 since the file was never explicitly closed. If, however, a DOS break routine is installed, as in this example program, and the user presses a break key, control is routed through the routine and the file is closed before program termination. In this case, a directory listing will show the file to have a nonzero length.

This program is similar to the program illustrating a BIOS-level break routine in Figure 8.6, described earlier in the chapter. There are, however, two differences worth mentioning since they illustrate some of the basic differences in the manner that these two types of break routines function. First, the **setjmp** instruction can be conveniently placed *after* the call to **IntDBInstall**, since there would be no opportunity for a DOS-level handler to become activated between these two instructions. Second, the two demonstration routines display a string using **printf**, a function that uses an MS-DOS service. If a display function were used that does not employ MS-DOS (such as **ScrPutS**, or **BiosPutS** in Figure 8.6), then a break key would never be detected.

Figures 8.10 and 8.11 provide a MAKE file and a QuickC program list for the example DOS break program.

CRITICAL-ERROR FUNCTIONS

The MS-DOS services use two different strategies for handling error conditions. First, for many errors such as a bad file path or a full disk, the service returns an error code to the program, which must then take the appropriate action. For the class of errors known as *critical errors*, however, DOS uses a different strategy. Critical errors are typically those that can be corrected by the user at runtime, such as a disk door that is left open or a printer that is left off-line. When a critical error occurs, DOS invokes interrupt 24h. The default routine that DOS installs for this interrupt prints the familiar *Abort, Retry, Ignore?* message and then returns a code to DOS specifying which of these actions to take. There are three good reasons for replacing this default interrupt routine with a custom error handler.

First, if the user opts to abort the program, control returns immediately to DOS, without allowing the application to close files or perform other final duties. As explained in the treatment of break handlers, such an uncontrolled program exit can result in data loss and other disasters. A custom interrupt 24h handler can almost always perform any required last-minute tasks before the program ends.

Second, the default routine displays little information. More detailed error information, however, is available to a custom error handler, which can display this information for the benefit of the user.

Third, the error message printed by the default routine simply overwrites the screen at the current cursor position, giving the user the impression that the program has lost control (which it has). A custom interrupt 24h handler can save the current screen data and display the error message in a carefully formatted window.

```
        #include <STDIO.H>
        #include <PROCESS.H>
        #include "INT.H"
        #include "SCR.H"
        #include "KBD.H"

        void Menu (void);
        void Demo1 (void);
        void Demo2 (void);

        void main ()
            {
            FILE *FPtr;                     /* File pointer for test file.        */

            /* Create and write to a test file to check for proper termination.   */
            FPtr = fopen ("DUMMY.DUM","w");
            fprintf (FPtr,"These data will be lost if the program aborts.\n");

            IntDBInstall (NULL,NULL);       /* Install the DOS-level control-break */
                                            /* handler.                           */

            setjmp (Mark);                  /* Control returns to this point on a  */
                                            /* subsequent 'longjmp.'              */

            Menu ();                        /* Display main menu.                 */

            for (;;)                        /* Branch on key pressed by user.     */
                switch (KbdGetC () & 0x00ff)
                    {
                    case '1':                       /* First demo.                */
                        Demo1 ();
                        break;

                    case '2':                       /* Second demo.               */
                        Demo2 ();
                        break;

                    case 'e':
                    case 'E':                       /* Terminate program.         */
                        ScrClear (0,0,24,80);
                        exit (0);
                    }

            } /* end main */


        void Menu ()
            {
            ScrClear (0,0,24,80);
            ScrPutBox (0,0,11,39,3);
            ScrPutS ("M A I N   M E N U",0x0f,2,11);
            ScrPutS ("1   Demo One",0x0f,4,7);
            ScrPutS ("2   Demo Two",0x0f,6,7);
            ScrPutS ("E   Exit to DOS",0x0f,8,7);
            ScrPutS ("enter letter of choice:",0x0f,10,7);
            ScrSetCur (10,31,0);

            } /* end Menu */
```

Figure 8.9: INTDEM03.C: A program demonstrating the installation and use of a DOS break routine

```
void Demo1 (void)
    (
    ScrClear (0,0,24,79);

    for (;;)              /* Infinite loop displaying a string using DOS.    */
        printf ("THIS IS DEMO 1     ");

    } /* end Demo1 */

void Demo2 (void)
    (
    ScrClear (0,0,24,79);

    for (;;)              /* Infinite loop displaying a string using DOS.    */
        printf ("THIS IS DEMO 2     ");

    } /* end Demo2 */
```

Figure 8.9: INTDEM03.C: A program demonstrating the installation and use of a DOS break
    routine (continued)

```
INTDEM03.OBJ : INTDEM03.C SCR.H KBD.H INT.H
    cl /c /W2 /Zp INTDEM03.C

INT.OBJ : INT.C INT.H
    cl /c /W2 /Zp INT.C

SCR.OBJ : SCR.C SCR.H
    cl /c /W2 /Zp SCR.C

KBDA.OBJ : KBDA.ASM
    masm /MX KBDA.ASM;

INTDEM03.EXE : INTDEM03.OBJ INT.OBJ SCR.OBJ KBDA.OBJ
    link /NOI /NOD INTDEM03+INT+SCR+KBDA,,NUL,SLIBCER;
```

Figure 8.10: INTDEM03.M: A MAKE file for preparing INTDEM03.C

```
INTDEM03.C
INT.C
SCR.C
KBDA.OBJ
```

Figure 8.11: A QuickC program list for preparing INTDEM03.C

IntCEInstall and IntCERemove

**Using
IntCEInstall and
IntCERemove**

The functions **IntCEInstall** and **IntCERemove** provide the means for installing or removing a critical-error handler. The prototype for **IntCEInstall** is

```
void IntCEInstall
     (int (*UserRtn) (),
      void (*UserWrapup) (void))
```

Like the two installation functions just presented in this chapter, the parameters allow you to specify your own critical error or wrapup routine, or to install the default critical error or wrapup routine by passing a NULL pointer. See the detailed general discussion of these parameters given in the description of **IntBBInstall** earlier in the chapter.

The default critical-error handler saves the contents of the screen and then displays a window containing more detailed error information than that shown by the usual DOS routine. The following information is displayed:

- The general error message specified by DOS. Some of the more common of these messages are the following:

    ```
    device not ready
    seek error
    sector not found
    write fault
    read fault
    ```

- If the error is associated with a character device, then the routine displays the name of the device; for example, PRN.

- If the error is associated with a disk device, then the following information is provided:

    1. Whether the error is a read error or a write error.
    2. The letter of the offending drive.
    3. The disk area where the error occurred, such as *DOS area*, or *directory*.

The routine then offers the user the usual three choices: retry, abort, or ignore. If the user chooses to retry the operation or ignore the error, then the routine restores the screen display and signals DOS to perform the appropriate action. If, however, the user decides to abort the program, then the handler calls the selected wrapup function to perform any necessary final duties, such as closing files, and then terminates the program through the standard C library function **exit**. The default wrapup function is the same as that used by the break functions described earlier: the screen is cleared and all open streams are closed.

If you write and install your own critical-error handler, your function will be passed four parameters. To receive these parameters, you should define your function to conform to the following prototype:

```
int MyCritErrorHand
    (int ErrorCode,
    int AX,
    int BP,
    int SI)
```

The parameter **ErrorCode** will contain a code for the specific critical error, and the parameters **AX**, **BP**, and **SI** will contain the values of the corresponding registers assigned by DOS when it invoked the critical-error interrupt. Your routine must also return an integer value that informs DOS of the action to take in response to the critical error. See the description of the default critical-error routine in the next section for an explanation of the parameters and the return value.

Note also that if you write your own critical-error or wrapup handler you should not use any interrupt 21h DOS functions other than numbers 01h through 0 Ch (I/O to the character devices), 30h (get DOS version number), or 59h (get extended error information, available only with DOS 3.0 or later and called by the Microsoft C function **dosexterr**). Using DOS services other than these can corrupt the operating system, and therefore you should *not* use the standard C library I/O functions such as **printf** and **read**, which employ forbidden DOS functions. Instead, use low-level display functions such as those in the **Scr** module presented in Chapter 5. An exception to this rule is that you should go ahead and call any functions required to close open files, but only *immediately before program termination*. Note that the critical-error function you install must be a normal C function and not a Microsoft C interrupt function. Also, as with a DOS break handler, there is no need to remove the routine before program exit, since DOS performs this task automatically. (Note, however, that DOS does *not* automatically restore the original critical-error handler when a memory resident application returns control to the interrupted foreground application; in this case, you must explicitly restore the original handler. See Chapter 9 for more information on writing memory resident programs.)

The function **IntCERemove** has the prototype

```
void IntCERemove
     (void)
```

and removes a critical error function that was previously installed by **IntCEInstall**. Call this function if you want to remove your critical-error handler during some part of the program (or to restore the original handler when a memory resident program returns control). Note that you will cause serious problems if you call **IntCERemove** without a prior call to **IntCEInstall**.

Note that it is possible (and advisable) to install both a break handler, at either the BIOS or DOS level, *and* a critical-error handler. An example program that installs a critical-error handler is given in Figure 8.12, to be described following the next section.

How IntCEInstall and IntCERemove Work

IntCEInstall begins by saving the current interrupt 24h address in the variable **OldCEHand**. This value is saved so that **IntCERemove** will later be able to remove the handler by restoring the former interrupt vector. The function now assigns the appropriate addresses to the function pointers for the critical error routine (**CERtn**) and the wrapup routine (**CEWrapup**). Finally, it installs the new interrupt 24h routine, **NewCEHand**.

The interrupt function **NewCEHand** calls the critical-error routine through the function pointer **CERtn**. It passes to this function the low-order byte of register DI (containing the error code that DOS supplies to the interrupt handler), and the values of registers AX, BP, and SI, which contain further error code information. **NewCEHand** also loads the value returned from **CERtn** into register AX, since the value placed in AX tells DOS how to handle the error.

The default critical-error routine, **DefaultCERtn**, first saves the current screen contents and displays a window in the center of the screen.

The function next prints several of the items of error information that DOS makes available to an error handler. This information is obtained as follows. The **ErrorCode** parameter contains the basic DOS error code; the corresponding messages are stored in the table **Errors** so that they may be indexed by this code. Register AX contains the following information:

■ If bit 15 is 1, then the error is associated with either a character device (such as the console or printer), or with a bad memory image of the FAT (*file allocation table* on a disk).

■ If bit 15 is 0, then the error is associated with a disk device (but is *not* a bad FAT image). In this case, if bit 8 is 0, then the error occurred on a read operation and if it is 1, then it occurred on a write operation. Bits 10 and 9 contain the number of the affected disk area (such as *DOS area* or *directory*); the table **Areas** contains the descriptions of these areas. Finally, register AL contains the number of the offending drive, where 0 refers to drive A, 1 to B, and so on.

If bit 15 of AX is one, then the routine must first determine whether the error is associated with a character device or a bad memory image of the FAT. This information is obtained by directly accessing bit 15 of the attribute word contained in the header of the device driver belonging to the offending device. The segment:offset address of the device header is contained in registers BP:SI, and the high-order byte of the attribute word is at offset 5. These values are used to initialize the **far** pointer **DevAttPtr**. If the high-order bit (bit 15 of the attribute word) is 0, then the device is a block (that is, disk) device and a FAT image error is indicated. If, however, the bit is 1, then the error is connected with a character device, and the routine prints the name of the device, which is contained in the device header at offset 10.

Finally **DefaultCERtn** displays the three action choices (retry, abort, and ignore) and obtains the user's response. If the user chooses to retry, then the screen state is restored and a code of 1 is returned, which tells DOS to retry the failed operation. If the user opts to ignore the error, then the returned code is 0. If, however, the user wants to terminate the program, then the screen is restored, the wrapup routine is called through the function pointer **CEWrapup**, and the program is ended by calling **exit**.

An Example Critical Error Application

The program in Figure 8.12 demonstrates the installation and use of a critical-error handler. This program first installs the handler, specifying the default error routine and the default wrapup routine. It then opens a file and writes a line of data to demonstrate one of the benefits of a critical-error handler. This file will have a nonzero length after the program is aborted through the critical-error handler, indicating that the wrapup routine was called and the file successfully closed. Without a critical error handler, the data would have been lost and the file would have a length of 0.

The program then generates two excellent opportunities for critical errors: first, it writes to the printer and then it attempts to open a file on

```
#include <STDIO.H>
#include <STRING.H>
#include <IO.H>

#include "INT.H"

void main (void)
    {
    FILE *FPtr;                     /* File pointer for test disk file.  */
                                    /* Line of test data for printer:    */
    static char *Message = "This is a line to be written to the printer\r\n";

    IntCEInstall (NULL,NULL);       /* Install critical error handler,   */
                                    /* specifying both default routines. */

    /* Create and write to a test file to test for proper termination.   */
    FPtr = fopen ("DUMMY.DUM","w");
    fprintf (FPtr,"These data will be lost if the program aborts.\n");

    /* Create some critical errors:                                      */

    /* Write to the printer;  leave the printer off line to create error. */
    write (4,Message,strlen (Message));

    /* Open a file on drive A;  leave drive A door open to create error. */
    fopen ("A:CRITICAL.ERR","r");          /* Note: leave drive A door open! */

    printf ("Program terminated normally.");
    fcloseall ();                          /* Close file.                */

    } /* end main */
```

Figure 8.12: INTDEM04.C: A program demonstrating the installation of a critical-error handler

drive A. When you run this program, first turn the printer off-line and then leave the door to drive A open.

Figure 8.13 provides a MAKE file and Figure 8.14 contains a QuickC program list.

```
INTDEM04.OBJ : INTDEM04.C SCR.H KBD.H INT.H
     cl /c /W2 /Zp INTDEM04.C

INT.OBJ : INT.C INT.H
     cl /c /W2 /Zp INT.C

SCR.OBJ : SCR.C SCR.H
     cl /c /W2 /Zp SCR.C

KBDA.OBJ : KBDA.ASM
     masm /MX KBDA.ASM;

INTDEM04.EXE : INTDEM04.OBJ INT.OBJ SCR.OBJ KBDA.OBJ
     link /NOI /NOD INTDEM04+INT+SCR+KBDA,,NUL,SLIBCER;
```

Figure 8.13: INTDEM04.M: A MAKE file for processing INTDEM04.C

```
INTDEM04.C
INT.C
SCR.C
KBDA.OBJ
```

Figure 8.14: A QuickC program list for preparing INTDEM04.C

Memory
Resident Programs

C HAPTER 9

A memory resident program, or TSR (terminate and stay resident application), is one that permanently establishes itself in memory and then returns control to MS-DOS so that the user can run other programs. The TSR remains dormant in the background until the user presses a designated hotkey, whereupon it springs to life, temporarily suspending the current application and providing instant access to the services it offers.

The module of functions presented in this chapter allows you to convert a normal Microsoft C program into a TSR through a single function call. You can specify the hotkey that is to activate your TSR, and the C function in your program that is to receive immediate control when the hotkey is pressed. You can also specify a unique code to prevent the same resident program from being installed more than once. All of the details of installing and activating the program as a TSR are handled invisibly by the functions in this module.

THE TSR FUNCTIONS

The TSR functions written in C are listed in Figure 9.1, and the functions written in assembly language are listed in Figure 9.2. The header file that you must include in your C program to call these functions is given in Figure 9.3.

Writing a TSR under MS-DOS is a complex task. The primary challenge is to design a resident program that will peacefully coexist with the foreground program, with any other TSRs that are currently installed, and with the operating system. It is especially important that a TSR written in the C language be able to freely call MS-DOS functions, since many of the standard library routines make use of these services. This chapter presents only one of the many approaches that can be used to achieve these design goals. For a general discussion of the issues of designing a memory resident program, see Chapter 11 of the book *Inside DOS: A Programmer's Guide* (cited in the Bibliography).

There are only two functions in the TSR module that can be called directly by your program: **TsrInstall** and **TsrInDos**. The chapter begins by discussing these two functions and then presents an example program that uses **TsrInstall** to install itself as a memory resident program. The example program is activated with the Alt-Shift keys and displays a pop-up window that allows you to send control codes to the printer.

```
#include <DOS.H>
#include <STDLIB.H>
#include <MALLOC.H>
#include "TSR.H"
#include "KBD.H"

#pragma check_stack (off)          /* Turn off stack checks so that functions  */
                                   /* can be called from interrupt routines.   */

#define HEAPSIZE 1024              /* Memory allowed for C heap, in 16-byte     */
                                   /* paragraphs.                               */

typedef void (interrupt far *VIFP) ();   /* Void Interrupt Function Pointer.    */

                                   /* Declarations used internally by C program: */

static void (*UserRtn) (void);          /* Pointer to user's start routine.     */
static int HotKeyMask;                  /* Hot key shift mask.                  */
static unsigned int CDtaSeg;            /* C Disk Transfer Area segment.        */
static unsigned int CDtaOff;            /* C Disk Transfer Area offset.         */
static char far *PtrInDos;              /* Pointer to DOS 'indos' flag.         */
static void (interrupt far *OldInt9) (void);    /* Old int 09h vector.          */
static void interrupt far NewInt9 (void);       /* New int 09h handler.         */
static void (interrupt far *OldInt23) (void);   /* Old int 23h vector.          */
static void interrupt far NewInt23 (void);      /* New int 23h handler.         */
static void (interrupt far *OldInt24) (void);   /* Old int 24h vector.          */
                                                /* New int 24h handler:         */
static void interrupt far NewInt24 (unsigned ES, unsigned DS, unsigned DI,
                                    unsigned SI, unsigned BP, unsigned SP,
                                    unsigned BX, unsigned DX, unsigned CX,
                                    unsigned AX);
static void (interrupt far *OldInt1B) (void);   /* Old int 1Bh vector.          */
static void interrupt far NewInt1B (void);      /* New int 1Bh handler.         */
static void (interrupt far *OldInt28) (void);   /* Old int 28h vector.          */
static void (interrupt far *OldRTInt9) (void);  /* Old int 09h vector at        */
                                                /* TSR runtime.                 */
static void interrupt far NewInt28 (void);      /* New int 28h handler.         */
static int Busy = 0;                    /* Flag indicates TSR is active.        */
static void InitPSP (void);             /* Saves DOS PSP storage locations.     */
static unsigned GetPSP (void);          /* Gets current PSP address from DOS.   */
static void SetPSP (unsigned PSP);      /* Sets DOS's record of PSP address.    */

extern unsigned _atopsp;                /* Predefined C variable: offset of end */
                                        /* of C stack.                          */
void _ctermsub (void);                  /* Restores divide-by-zero interrupt    */
                                        /* vector; defined in the C startup code.*/

                                   /* Declarations shared with assembler module: */

unsigned int CSS;                       /* C stack segment.                     */
unsigned int CSP;                       /* C stack pointer.                     */
void (interrupt far *OldInt10) (void);  /* Old int 10h vector.                  */
void interrupt far NewInt10 (void);     /* New int 10h handler (in ASM mod.).   */
void (interrupt far *OldInt13) (void);  /* Old int 13h vector.                  */
void interrupt far NewInt13 (void);     /* New int 13h handler (in ASM mod.).   */
void far PreActivate (void);            /* Pre-activate routine (in ASM mod.)   */
extern int Int13Flag;                   /* Flag:  BIOS interrupt 13h active.    */
extern int Int10Flag;                   /* Flag:  BIOS interrupt 10h active.    */
```

Figure 9.1: TSR.C: C functions for converting a Microsoft C program into a TSR

```
int TsrInstall (void (*FPtr) (void),int HotKey,unsigned long Code)
/*
    This routine terminates the C program, but leaves the code resident in
    memory.  It installs interrupt handlers so that when the shift key
    combination specified by 'HotKey' is pressed, the function pointed to
    by 'FPtr' receives control, provided that conditions are safe.
*/
    {
    unsigned int i;                     /* Loop index.                    */
    int Found = 0;                      /* Flag:  free vector found.      */
    struct SREGS SReg;                  /* Gets segment registers.        */
    union REGS Reg;                     /* Holds registers for 'int86'.   */
    char huge *TopStack;                /* Top of MSC stack.              */
    char huge *BottomProg;              /* Bottom of MSC program.         */
    unsigned TSRSize;                   /* Amount of memory to leave.     */

    for (i = 0x60; i <= 0x67; ++i)      /* Search 'user' interrupt vectors */
        if (_dos_getvect (i) == (VIFP)Code) /* to see if Code is present  */
            {                           /* indicating that the TSR is     */
            Found = 1;                  /* already installed.             */
            break;
            }

    if (Found)                          /* Already installed, therefore   */
        return (INSTALLED);             /* return error message.          */

    for (i = 0x60; i <= 0x67; ++i)      /* Not already installed, therefore */
        if (_dos_getvect (i) == (VIFP)0)  /* search for a free (== 0)     */
            {                           /* user interrupt vector.         */
            _dos_setvect (i,(VIFP)Code); /* Found a free vector;  place   */
            Found = 1;                  /* special code in vector.        */
            break;
            }

    if (!Found)                         /* No free vectors;  therefore    */
        return (NOINT);                 /* return error code.             */

    if (_osmajor < 2)                   /* Test that OS version is >= 2.0. */
        return (WRONGDOS);              /* Wrong DOS version.             */

    HotKeyMask = HotKey;                /* Save hotkey shift mask.        */

    UserRtn = FPtr;      /* Save address of the routine that is activated */
                         /* when the hotkey is pressed.                   */

    Reg.h.ah = 0x2f;                    /* Invoke MS-DOS function to get   */
    int86x (0x21,&Reg,&Reg,&SReg);      /* current Disk Transfer Address.  */
    CDtaSeg = SReg.es;
    CDtaOff = Reg.x.bx;
    Reg.h.ah = 0x34;                    /* Get pointer to INDOS flag       */
    int86x (0x21,&Reg,&Reg,&SReg);      /* using the undocumented DOS      */
    FP_SEG (PtrInDos) = SReg.es;        /* function 34h.                   */
    FP_OFF (PtrInDos) = Reg.x.bx;

    InitPSP ();                         /* Find and save table of PSP      */
                                        /* addresses from DOS.             */
```

Figure 9.1: TSR.C: C functions for converting a Microsoft C program into a TSR (continued)

```
        OldInt28 = _dos_getvect (0x28);     /* Save old interrupt vectors.      */
        OldInt13 = _dos_getvect (0x13);
        OldInt10 = _dos_getvect (0x10);
        OldInt9 = _dos_getvect (0x9);

        _dos_setvect (0x28,NewInt28);       /* Initialize new interrupt vectors.*/
        _dos_setvect (0x13,NewInt13);
        _dos_setvect (0x10,NewInt10);
        _dos_setvect (0x9,NewInt9);

                                            /* Calculate memory to keep.        */
        FP_SEG (BottomProg) = _psp;         /* Set far address of bottom of TSR.*/
        FP_OFF (BottomProg) = 0;

        segread (&SReg);                    /* Set far address of top of stack. */
        FP_SEG (TopStack) = SReg.ss;
        FP_OFF (TopStack) = _atopsp;

        CSS = SReg.ss;             /* Save the C stack segment and offset.      */
        CSP = _atopsp;
                                   /* Calculate TSR size:                       */
        TSRSize = ((TopStack - BottomProg + 15) >> 4) + HEAPSIZE;

        _dos_keep (0,TSRSize);     /* Terminate and stay resident.              */

        return (ERROR);           /* '_dos_keep' should not return;  therefore  */
                                  /* something has gone terribly wrong.  Return */
                                  /* the general error code.                    */

    } /* end TsrInstall */


static void interrupt far NewInt9 (void)
/*
    This is the new handler for interrupt 09, the hardware interrupt
    activated by the keyboard.
*/
    {
    (*OldInt9) ();          /* Chain to prior interrupt 09 handler.            */

    _disable ();            /* Disable interrupts to test and set 'Busy'       */
    if (Busy)               /* semaphore.                                      */
        return;
    Busy = 1;
    _enable ();             /* Enable interrupts.                              */
    if ((KbdGetShift () & HotKeyMask) != HotKeyMask)  /* Test if hot key       */
        {                                             /* is pressed.           */
        Busy = 0;
        return;
        }
                            /* Test if EITHER a BIOS service OR DOS is active: */
    if (Int10Flag || Int13Flag || *PtrInDos)
        {
        Busy = 0;
        return;
        }
```

Figure 9.1: TSR.C: C functions for converting a Microsoft C program into a TSR (continued)

```
        PreActivate ();         /* Conditions are safe, therefore activate TSR*/

        Busy = 0;               /* Reset the active semaphore.              */

        return;

        } /* end NewInt9 */


static void interrupt far NewInt23 (void)
/*
        This is the new handler for interrupt 23h, which DOS activates when it
        detects a control-break key.  The function replaces the default DOS
        control-break handler, which aborts the process;  by simply returning,
        this function prevents DOS from attempting to terminate the TSR.
*/
        {

        } /* end NewInt23 */


static void interrupt far NewInt24 (unsigned ES, unsigned DS, unsigned DI,
                                    unsigned SI, unsigned BP, unsigned SP,
                                    unsigned BX, unsigned DX, unsigned CX,
                                    unsigned AX)
/*
        This is the new handler for interrupt 24h, which DOS invokes when a
        critical error occurs.  It assigns a value of 0 to AX, which informs
        DOS that the error should be ignored.  The function prevents DOS from
        attempting to abort the TSR.
*/
        {
        AX = 0;

        } /* end NewInt24 */


static void interrupt far NewInt1B (void)
/*
        This is the new handler for interrupt 1Bh, which is invoked by the BIOS
        keyboard routine when it detects the Ctrl-break keystroke.  While the
        TSR is active, this function replaces any BIOS-level break handler that
        might have been installed by the interrupted program.
*/
        {

        } /* end NewInt1B */


static void interrupt far NewInt28 (void)
/*
        This is the new interrupt 28h, the 'DOS idle interrupt', handler.
*/
        {
        (*OldInt28) ();         /* Chain to previous interrupt 28 handler.   */
```

Figure 9.1: TSR.C: C functions for converting a Microsoft C program into a TSR (continued)

```
        _disable ();                /* Disable interrupts to test and set    */
        if (Busy)                    /* 'Busy' semaphore.                     */
            return;
        Busy = 1;
        _enable ();                 /* Re-enable interrupts.                  */

        if ((KbdGetShift () & HotKeyMask) != HotKeyMask)  /* Test if hot key   */
            {                                             /* is pressed.       */
            Busy = 0;
            return;
            }
        if (Int13Flag || Int10Flag)        /* Test if BIOS service is active. */
            {
            Busy = 0;
            return;
            }

        PreActivate ();             /* Conditions are safe, therefore activate TSR*/

        Busy = 0;                   /* Reset the active semaphore.            */
        return;

        } /* end NewInt28 */


static unsigned int OldPsp;
static unsigned int OldDtaSeg;
static unsigned int OldDtaOff;

void far Activate (void)
/*
        This function is called either by 'NewInt9' or by 'NewInt29', when
        conditions are safe, to activate the user's TSR entry routine.
*/
        {
        union REGS Reg;                 /* Passes values to 'int86x'.        */
        struct SREGS SReg;              /* Passes values to 'int86x'.        */
        unsigned OldPSP;                /* Stores PSP address of             */
                                        /* interrupted process.              */

                                        /* Set new interrupt vectors:        */
        OldInt23 = _dos_getvect (0x23); /* Save old break-key vector.        */
        OldInt24 = _dos_getvect (0x24); /* Save old critical-error vector.   */
        OldInt1B = _dos_getvect (0x1b); /* Save old BIOS break vector.       */
        OldRTInt9 = _dos_getvect (0x09); /* Save runtime int 9 handler.      */
        _dos_setvect (0x23,NewInt23);   /* Set new break-key handler.        */
        _dos_setvect (0x24,NewInt24);   /* Set new critical-error handler.   */
        _dos_setvect (0x1b,NewInt1B);   /* Set new BIOS break handler.       */
        _dos_setvect (0x09,OldInt9);    /* Set old int 9 handler.            */

        Reg.h.ah = 0x2f;                /* Save old Disk Transfer Address.   */
        int86x (0x21,&Reg,&Reg,&SReg);
        OldDtaSeg = SReg.es;
        OldDtaOff = Reg.x.bx;
```

Figure 9.1: TSR.C: C functions for converting a Microsoft C program into a TSR (continued)

```
        Reg.x.dx = CDtaOff;              /* Set C Disk Transfer Address.    */
        SReg.ds = CDtaSeg;
        Reg.h.ah = 0x1a;                 /* DOS set DTA service.            */
        int86x (0x21,&Reg,&Reg,&SReg);

        OldPSP = GetPSP ();              /* Get PSP address of interrupted  */
                                         /* process.                        */
        SetPSP (_psp);                   /* Set PSP for C program.          */

        (*UserRtn) ();                   /* Call the user's C function.     */

        SetPSP (OldPSP);                 /* Restore PSP for the interrupted */
                                         /* process.                        */

        Reg.x.dx = OldDtaOff;            /* Restore Old Disk Transfer Address*/
        SReg.ds = OldDtaSeg;
        Reg.h.ah = 0x1a;
        int86x (0x21,&Reg,&Reg,&SReg);

                                         /* Restore old interrupt vectors:  */
        _dos_setvect (0x23,OldInt23);    /* Restore old break-key handler.  */
        _dos_setvect (0x24,OldInt24);    /* Restore old crit-error handler. */
        _dos_setvect (0x1b,OldInt1B);    /* Restore old BIOS break handler. */
        _dos_setvect (0x09,OldRTInt9);   /* Restore run time int 9 handler. */

        return;

        } /* end Activate */


int TsrInDos (void)
/*
    This function returns zero if DOS is not currently active, and a
    non-zero value otherwise.
*/
        {
        return (*PtrInDos);         /* Uses the 'indos' flag maintained by DOS.  */

        } /* end TsrInDos */


/*** PSP Functions. ***************************************************************/


static unsigned far *PtrPSPTable [2]; /* Table of pointers to DOS PSP values*/
static int PSPCount;                  /* Number of pointers in PtrPSPTable. */


static void InitPSP (void)
/*
    This function saves the addresses of the locations in the MS-DOS segment
    where DOS saves the current PSP value.
*/
        {
        union REGS Reg;
        struct SREGS SReg;
        unsigned char far *PtrDos;      /* Points to locations in DOS segment.    */
        unsigned char far *PtrEndDos;   /* Points to the end of DOS segment.      */
        unsigned far *PtrMCB;           /* Points to the location where the       */
                                        /* segment address of end of DOS is kept.*/
```

Figure 9.1: TSR.C: C functions for converting a Microsoft C program into a TSR (continued)

```
         PSPCount = 0;                      /* Initialize counter of valid entries  */
                                            /* in PtrPSPTable.                       */

                                            /* Assign PtrDos the address of the      */
         FP_SEG (PtrDos) = 0;               /* BEGINNING of the DOS segment.         */
         FP_OFF (PtrDos) = FP_SEG (PtrInDos) << 4;

                                            /* Assign PtrEndDos the address of the   */
         Reg.h.ah = 0x52;                   /* END of the DOS segment.               */
         int86x (0x21,&Reg,&Reg,&SReg);
         FP_SEG (PtrMCB) = SReg.es;
         FP_OFF (PtrMCB) = Reg.x.bx - 2;
         FP_SEG (PtrEndDos) = 0;
         FP_OFF (PtrEndDos) = *PtrMCB << 4;

                                            /* Obtain addresses where DOS stores the */
                                            /* PSP of the current process.           */
         while (PtrDos < PtrEndDos && PSPCount < 2)
             {
             if (*(unsigned far *)PtrDos ==  _psp)
                 {
                 Reg.h.ah = 0x50;
                 Reg.x.bx = _psp + 1;
                 int86 (0x21,&Reg,&Reg);
                 if (*(unsigned far *)PtrDos == _psp + 1)
                     PtrPSPTable [PSPCount++] = (unsigned far *)PtrDos;
                 Reg.h.ah = 0x50;
                 Reg.x.bx = _psp;
                 int86 (0x21,&Reg,&Reg);
                 }
             ++PtrDos;
             }

     } /* end InitPSP */
static unsigned GetPSP (void)
/*
     This function gets current PSP address from DOS.

*/
     {
     return *PtrPSPTable [0];

     } /* end GetPSP */


static void SetPSP (unsigned PSP)
/*
     This function sets DOS's record of PSP address.
*/
     {
     int i;

     for (i = 0; i < PSPCount; ++i)
         *PtrPSPTable [i] = PSP;

     } /* end SetPSP */
```

Figure 9.1: TSR.C: C functions for converting a Microsoft C program into a TSR (continued)

```
.MODEL MEDIUM

.DATA

PUBLIC _Int10Flag                          ;Flag indicating int 10h active.
       _Int10Flag    DW   0
PUBLIC _Int13Flag                          ;Flag indicating int 13h active.
       _Int13Flag    DW   0
EXTRN  _OldInt10 : DWORD                    ;Defined in TSR.C.
EXTRN  _OldInt13 : DWORD                    ;Defined in TSR.C.
EXTRN  _CSS      : WORD                     ;Defined in TSR.C.
EXTRN  _CSP      : WORD                     ;Defined in TSR.C.
       _OldSS       DW   ?                  ;Stores old stack segment.
       _OldSP       DW   ?                  ;Stores old stack pointer.


.CODE

EXTRN _Activate : FAR

PUBLIC _NewInt10
;
;     Prototype:
;          void interrupt far NewInt10
;                (void)
;     This is the new handler for interrupt 10h, the BIOS video services.
;     This function maintains a flag of interrupt 10h invocations, Int10Flag.
;     Each time interrupt 10h is invoked, the flag is incremented, and each
;     time control returns from this interrupt, the flag is decremented.  A
;     zero value of Int10Flag indicates that interrupt 10h is not active.
;
_NewInt10 PROC

        push ds                            ;Temporarily load the C data segment
        push ax                            ;address into DS.
        mov  ax, DGROUP
        mov  ds, ax
        pop  ax

        inc  _Int10Flag                    ;Increment the interrupt 10h active flag.

        pushf                              ;Simulate an interrupt to the old
        call _OldInt10                     ;handler.
        pushf
        dec  _Int10Flag                    ;Decrement the interrupt 10h active flag.
        popf
        pop  ds                            ;Restore the DS register.
        ret  2                             ;Return from interrupt, preserving the
                                           ;flags.
_NewInt10 ENDP


PUBLIC _NewInt13
;
;     Prototype:
;          void interrupt far NewInt13
;                (void)
;
```

Figure 9.2: TSRA.ASM: Assembly language functions for converting a Microsoft C program into
         a TSR

```
;       This is the new handler for interrupt 13h, the BIOS disk services.
;       This function maintains a flag of interrupt 13h invocations, Int13Flag.
;       Each time interrupt 13h is invoked, the flag is incremented, and each
;       time control returns from this interrupt, the flag is decremented.  A
;       zero value of Int13Flag indicates that interrupt 13h is not active.
;
_NewInt13 PROC

        push ds                         ;Temporarily load the C data segment
        push ax                         ;address into DS.
        mov  ax, DGROUP
        mov  ds, ax
        pop  ax

        inc  _Int13Flag                 ;Increment the interrupt 10h active flag.

        pushf                           ;Simulate an interrupt to the old
        call _OldInt13                  ;handler.
        pushf
        dec  _Int13Flag                 ;Decrement the interrupt 10h active flag.
        popf
        pop  ds                         ;Restore the DS register.
        ret  2                          ;Return from interrupt, preserving the
                                        ;flags.
_NewInt13 ENDP


PUBLIC _PreActivate
;
;       Prototype:
;           void far PreActivate
;                   (void)
;       This is the first routine called to activate the TSR.  It performs
;       initial activation tasks and then calls the C routine Activate to
;       complete activation of the TSR.
;
_PreActivate PROC

        cli                             ;Disable interrupts.
        mov  _OldSS, ss                 ;Save the old SS and SP.
        mov  _OldSP, sp
        mov  ss, _CSS                   ;Switch to the C stack.
        mov  sp, _CSP
        sti                             ;Reenable interrupts.

        call _Activate                  ;Call C function to activate TSR.

        cli                             ;Disable interrupts.
        mov  ss, _OldSS                 ;Restore the old stack.
        mov  sp, _OldSP
        sti                             ;Reenable interrupts.
        ret                             ;Return control.

_PreActivate ENDP

END
```

Figure 9.2: TSRA.ASM: Assembly language functions for converting a Microsoft C program into a TSR (continued)

```
/* Error codes returned by 'TsrInstall' if it cannot install the TSR.    */

#define ERROR      1        /* General, undefined error.                 */
#ifndef WRONGDOS
    #define WRONGDOS 2       /* Version of DOS prior to 2.0.              */
#endif
#define INSTALLED  3        /* TSR has already been installed in memory. */
#define NOINT      4        /* No free user interrupts are available.    */

int TsrInstall (void (*FPtr) (void),int HotKey, unsigned long Code);
int TsrInDos (void);
```

Figure 9.3: TSR.H: Header file you must include in your program to call the functions in the **Tsr** module

The TSR functions not only provide a useful addition to your collection of software tools, but they are also furnish an excellent demonstration of the advanced features of Microsoft C. Normally it would be quite difficult to write memory resident interrupt handlers in the C language; however, using Microsoft C language extensions such as **interrupt** functions (provided with versions 5.0 and later), it was possible to write the module in C, with the exception of three short assembly language subroutines.

TsrInstall and TsrInDos

Using TsrInstall and TsrInDos

The function **TsrInstall** has the prototype

```
int TsrInstall
    (void (*FPtr) (void),
    int HotKey
    unsigned long Code)
```

and performs the following primary tasks:

▌ It checks to make sure that the program has not already been installed in memory. Each program that is installed by this routine should be identified with a unique value of the parameter **Code**.

▌ It stores all values that will be required by the interrupt handlers after the TSR is installed.

▌ It installs the appropriate interrupt handlers so that when the user presses the shift-key combination specified by the **HotKey** parameter, the function given by the **FPtr** parameter receives immediate control.

▌ It terminates the C program, leaving the entire block of code and data resident in memory.

When you develop a memory resident program using the **Tsr** module, your program should consist of two parts. The first part is the **main** function (plus any functions called by **main**). The function **main** receives control when the user types the name of the program on the command line, and serves to *install* the TSR. This function should perform any required initialization tasks, print any desired messages to the user, and finally call **TsrInstall** to install the program as a TSR. After the call to **TsrInstall**, control returns to the DOS command line just as if the program had exited normally; however, the program's code and data are not released, but rather remain resident in memory.

The second part of your memory resident program is the portion of the code that is subsequently activated whenever the user presses the designated hotkey. This part of the program consists of the TSR entry routine—the function that receives initial control when the hotkey is pressed—plus any subroutines called by this function.

The first parameter passed to **TsrInstall** (that is, **FPtr**) should be assigned the address of the TSR entry routine. The second parameter (**HotKey**) gives the shift-key combination that is used to activate the program. Note that this parameter does *not* specify either an ASCII code or an extended keyboard code, but rather some combination of shift keys. These combinations may be specified by combining the constant identifiers contained in the header file KBD.H (Figure 2.3). For example, the combination of the Alt key and Left-Shift key could be specified by the following expression:

```
ALT | LEFTSHIFT
```

The meanings of each bit of the **HotKey** parameter are the same as those contained in the integer returned by the function **KbdGetShift**, and are listed under the description of **KbdGetShift** in Chapter 2.

The parameter **Code** is of type **unsigned long**. It should be a number between the values 0x00000001 and 0xffffffff that is unique for each separate program you convert to a TSR. Once a TSR is installed, no other program having the same ID number may subsequently be installed. By means of this parameter, **TsrInstall** avoids loading redundant copies of the same program.

Since **TsrInstall** terminates the current program, it should obviously never return. If the function does return, an error has occurred and the program has *not* been installed. In this case, one of the following error codes is passed back to the calling program:

▪ INSTALLED: This error code indicates that a TSR bearing the same identification code has already been installed.

▪ NOINT: This value means that there are no free "user" interrupts available. The interrupt vectors in the range from 60h to 67h are designated as available for user programs. The first of these vectors that is free (that is, containing zero) is used to store the identifying code (the parameter **Code**) assigned to the TSR. If all of these vectors are occupied, **TsrInstall** returns NOINT.

▪ WRONGDOS: The TSR functions require DOS version 2.0 or later. If the version is prior to 2.0, this error code is returned. (Note that the TSR can be successfully installed in the DOS-compatibility environment of OS/2, which returns a version number of 10.0 or higher.)

▪ ERROR: This general code is returned if the installation procedure failed for some unknown reason.

The function **TsrInDos** has the prototype

```
int TsrInDos
    (void)
```

This function returns a nonzero value if an MS-DOS service was active when your TSR received control, and it returns 0 if MS-DOS was not active. The purpose of this function is to allow you to determine which DOS functions your program may safely call. Specifically, if **TsrInDos** returns a value of 0, you may directly call almost any MS-DOS service or almost any C library function that invokes MS-DOS (exceptions are noted later in this section). However, if **TsrInDos** returns a non-zero value, then *you must not use DOS functions 01h through 0Ch*. This set of forbidden functions manage input and output to the basic character devices (console, printer, and serial port). The following C library functions, which are defined in the CONIO.H header file, employ these services: **cgets**, **cputs**, **cprintf**, **cscanf**, **getch**, **getche**, **kbhit**, **putch**, and **ungetch**. Fortunately, it is almost always possible to obtain the services offered by this set of procedures through the standard C file functions, or through the lower-level functions presented in this book. Either you can call **TsrInDos** before using any of the restricted functions, or you can simply eliminate them from your TSR program. The reasons that you may not call this set of MS-DOS services are explained in the next section.

In most respects, a program destined to become a TSR can be written like any other C program. However, there are five additional guidelines that you should follow when developing your memory resident program.

The first guideline is that your program—and all the C modules that are linked with it—must be compiled using the *small* or *medium* memory model (both of these models place all data within a single segment and use **near** data pointers by default). You may *not* compile the program using either the *compact, large,* or *huge* model. As you will see, the code in the **Tsr** module (specifically, TSR.C) uses techniques that require the small or medium memory model.

The second guideline is that if your program writes to the screen or alters the cursor, you must carefully save and restore the complete video state of the interrupted program. The functions in the TSR module automatically save and restore almost all of the machine state of the suspended program; the task of preserving the video state, however, is left to the application program. You can use the routines **ScrGetCur**, **ScrSetCur**, **ScrGetStyle**, **ScrSetStyle**, **ScrGetMode**, and **ScrSetMode** (presented in Chapter 5) to save and restore the cursor parameters and the video mode. See the example programs in Figures 5.4 and 5.7.

If the interrupted program is in text mode, then you can use **ScrPush** and **ScrPop** to save and restore the screen data. If, however, the interrupted program is in a graphics mode, preserving an entire graphics screen in a program buffer would require transferring and storing 16 or more kilobytes of data. If the TSR uses only text mode output, it might seem that it would be necessary to save and restore only the 4,000 bytes of video memory actually overwritten by the program. The problem, however, is that changing video modes through the standard PC and AT BIOS (employed by the **ScrSetMode** function) causes erasing of all video data. As an alternative to saving the entire contents of video memory, you could save only the portion of video memory actually modified by the TSR, and then write an alternative low-level routine for switching video modes *without* erasing data. This routine would have to directly program the video controller registers, and would be similar to the routine presented in Figure 7.1 for switching modes in a Hercules compatible adapter. For more information, see the BIOS video service listings in the IBM PC or AT technical manual, or the CGA section of the *Options and Adapters Technical Reference*, Volume 2 (both manuals appear in the Bibliography).

The third guideline is that a resident program should not attempt to allocate memory from DOS. A transient application (that is, a program that does not remain resident in memory) can normally obtain additional memory blocks by dynamically allocating them from DOS. A TSR, however, should restrict its use of memory to the block explicitly reserved for the program when it terminated and remained resident. Consequently, a TSR should not invoke the MS-DOS services for allocating, releasing, or changing the size of memory blocks (namely, services 48h, 49h, and 4Ah, accessed through interrupt 21h); likewise, it should not call any of the functions provided by Microsoft C that rely upon these DOS services (namely, **_dos_allocmem**, **_dos_freemem**, and **_dos_setblock**). Note, however, that a TSR can call the standard C memory allocation functions, such as **malloc** and **calloc**, since these functions obtain memory from within the block reserved at the time the program became resident. (However, as you will see in the next section, the TSR module places a fixed upper bound on the amount of memory that can be dynamically allocated through functions such as **malloc**.)

A corollary to the third guideline is that a TSR must not attempt to execute a child process, since doing so entails allocation of additional memory blocks. Consequently, a TSR must not call the DOS service for executing a child process (namely, function 4Bh of interrupt 21h); nor should it call any of the C library functions for starting new processes (namely, the **exec...** and **spawn...** families of functions).

The fourth guideline is that the TSR should not use floating-point numbers. Specifically, it should not declare variables of type **float** or **double**, and it should not call functions in the C math library (which are those declared in the header file MATH.H). The inclusion of floating-point code causes the C startup code to set certain interrupt vectors; floating-point operations require that these interrupt vectors remain intact. As long as these vectors remain unaltered as various programs run in the foreground, the TSR can successfully execute floating-point instructions; however, if a foreground application alters one or more of the vectors, any floating-point calculations performed by the TSR will fail. Therefore, a robust TSR must avoid floating-point operations performed by the math library. (Note that several functions within the UTY.C file presented in Chapter 12 use floating point math; therefore, you should not link the entire **Uty** module with a memory resident program. However, you can use any of the functions in UTY.C that do *not* employ floating-point parameters or operations by placing the required functions in a separate source file and linking your application with the resulting object module. You can also safely use any of the assembly language functions in the file UTYA.ASM.)

The fifth and final guideline is that your TSR must always *return* from the function that was initially activated (the function specified by the **FPtr** parameter). *You must not use the* **exit** *function to terminate the program.* The **exit** function is designed to terminate a non-resident program and return to the parent process (usually the MS-DOS command interpreter).

Note that when your TSR entry function receives control in response to the user pressing the hotkey, the **Tsr** module has temporarily disabled any control-break or critical-error handlers that may have been installed by the suspended foreground application. (Specifically, during the execution of your TSR code, interrupt vectors 1Bh, 23h, and 24h point to routines that simply return without performing any action; these vectors are restored to their former values before control returns to the suspended application.) If your TSR program needs to handle control-break keys or critical-error conditions, you can install appropriate handlers as described in Chapter 8; however, you do not need to restore the former values for these vectors since this task is performed automatically by the **Tsr** module code that receives control when your TSR issues its final return statement.

Note also that even if the TSR is properly installed, the program may not always receive immediate control when the hotkey is pressed. There are times when it is not safe to interrupt the current process (such as when DOS or the BIOS are engaged in disk activity). The **Tsr** module senses these conditions and simply ignores the hotkey until it is safe to trigger the resident program.

The program in Figure 9.4 demonstrates the use of **TsrInstall** and **TsrInDos**. This program consists of two functions: **main** and **Test**. The function **main** calls **TsrInstall** to convert the program to a TSR, specifying **Test** as the function to receive control when the user presses the hotkey. The selected hotkey is Ctrl-Left Shift, and the identifying code is 0x11111111. If another TSR is developed that might be installed at the same time as this program, a different hotkey combination and identifying code should be chosen. If **TsrInstall** is successful, it will never return; however, if an error occurs in the installation process, control

```
#include <STDIO.H>
#include <PROCESS.H>

#include "TSR.H"
#include "SCR.H"
#include "KBD.H"

#define ULR 6                               /* Position of centered window.   */
#define ULC 20

static void Test (void);                    /* The TSR demo routine.          */

void main (void)
    {
    /* Install 'Test' as TSR function;  Ctrl-Left Shift is hotkey.            */
    switch (TsrInstall (Test,CONTROL | LEFTSHIFT,0x11111111))
        {
        case WRONGDOS:
            printf ("Cannot install TSR;  must have DOS version 2.0 "
                    "or higher.\n");
            exit (1);

        case INSTALLED:
            printf ("TSR already installed.\n");
            exit (1);

        case NOINT:
            printf ("Cannot install;  no free user interrupts.\n");
            exit (1);

        case ERROR:                         /* General error case.            */
        default:
            printf ("Error installing TSR function.\n");
            exit (1);
        }

    } /* end main */


static void Test (void)
/*
    This routine is called when the hotkey is pressed.  It displays a
    window and indicates whether DOS is currently active.
*/
    {
    ScrPush ();
    ScrClear (ULR,ULC,ULR+11,ULC+39);
    ScrPutBox (ULR,ULC,ULR+11,ULC+39,2);
    ScrPutS ("T S R    D E M O",0x0f,ULR+3,ULC+11);
    if (TsrInDos ())
        ScrPutS ("Now in DOS",0x0f,ULR+6,ULC+13);
    else
        ScrPutS ("NOT in DOS",0x0f,ULR+6,ULC+13);
ScrPutS ("press any key to continue",0x0f,ULR+9,ULC+6);

KbdGetC ();
ScrPop (1);

    } /* end Test */
```

Figure 9.4: TSRDEM01.C: A simple memory resident program

returns to **main**, which then prints the appropriate error message and terminates with an ERRORLEVEL setting of 1.

If **TsrInstall** is successful, control returns to DOS. Subsequently, each time the user presses Ctrl-Left Shift (and it is safe to interrupt the current process), the function **Test** receives control. This function saves and restores the current screen contents using **ScrPush** and **ScrPop**, displays a window, and pauses for user input by calling **KbdGetC**. Note that this program, written to provide a simple example, will work properly only if the system is in an 80-column text mode when interrupted by the TSR; it will fail if either a 40-column or graphics mode happens to be active. Since **Test** does not alter the cursor, it does not need to preserve the cursor parameters.

A note to QuickC users: You should not attempt to load a TSR from within the QuickC integrated environment (the TSR should be loaded directly from the DOS command line so that it is given the lowest possible position in memory). Therefore, if you prepare the program within QuickC version 1.0, you should select the Exe item in the Output Options column of the Compile menu; this option will produce a freestanding .EXE file that can be run from DOS. QuickC version 2.0 will automatically produce such a file.

Figure 9.5 provides a MAKE file for preparing the example program, and Figure 9.6 gives a QuickC program list.

```
TSRDEM01.OBJ : TSRDEM01.C TSR.H SCR.H KBD.H
     cl /c /W2 /Zp TSRDEM01.C

TSR.OBJ : TSR.C TSR.H
     cl /c /W2 /Zp TSR.C

TSRA.OBJ : TSRA.ASM
    masm /MX TSRA.ASM;

SCR.OBJ : SCR.C SCR.H
     cl /c /W2 /Zp SCR.C

KBD.OBJ : KBD.C KBD.H
     cl /c /W2 /Zp KBD.C

KBDA.OBJ : KBDA.ASM
    masm /MX KBDA.ASM;

UTYA.OBJ : UTYA.ASM
    masm /MX UTYA.ASM;

TSRDEM01.EXE : TSRDEM01.OBJ TSR.OBJ TSRA.OBJ SCR.OBJ KBD.OBJ KBDA.OBJ UTYA.OBJ
     link /NOI /NOD TSRDEM01+TSR+TSRA+SCR+KBD+KBDA+UTYA,,NUL,SLIBCER;
```

Figure 9.5: TSRDEM01.M: A MAKE file for preparing the program TSRDEM01.C

```
TSRDEM01.C
TSR.C
TSRA.OBJ
SCR.C
KBD.C
KBDA.OBJ
UTYA.OBJ
```

Figure 9.6: A QuickC program list for preparing TSRDEM01.C

How TsrInstall and TsrInDos Work

The General Strategy

Before discussing the details of the individual functions in the TSR module, this section provides an overview of the basic tasks required to install and activate a memory resident program, and the general strategies that the **Tsr** module uses to accomplish these tasks.

The most fundamental task required to install a TSR is to load the program into a safe area of memory that will not be overwritten by subsequent applications. Fortunately, MS-DOS provides a service that allows a program to terminate *without* relinquishing the memory it occupies. MS-DOS reserves this area of memory by removing it from its list of free memory blocks, and loads all subsequent applications at higher memory addresses. The **Tsr** module accesses this DOS service through the Microsoft C library function **_dos_keep**. The only complication in using this function is that it is necessary to specify the size of the program that is to be kept resident. The details of using **_dos_keep** are discussed in the next section.

The next task required to create a TSR is to establish some means for activating the program through a hotkey. The basic strategy used by the **Tsr** module is to replace the current keyboard interrupt (09h) handler with a Microsoft C interrupt function. Each time a key is pressed or released, the interrupt function receives control. This function first calls the former interrupt handler, and then simply tests the BIOS shift status flag to see whether the designated hotkey is pressed. If the hotkey is pressed, the routine performs several additional tests and possibly activates the TSR entry function.

Another important duty of the TSR code is to prevent the resident program from being activated at a time when it is not safe to interrupt the current process. The first such dangerous time is when the BIOS is engaged in disk activity. Therefore, the TSR module also installs a handler for interrupt 13h, which is the entry point for the BIOS disk services used by MS-DOS and by some application programs. The interrupt 13h function (in the assembly language file TSRA.ASM) first increments a global flag indicating that BIOS disk activity is in progress, calls the original interrupt 13h routine, and then decrements the flag when the original routine returns. Therefore, before the keyboard interrupt handler activates the TSR entry function, it checks this flag and returns immediately if the flag is greater than zero, indicating that the disk services are currently in progress.

Another time it is unwise to interrupt the current process is while the BIOS video services are active. These services are invoked through interrupt 10h. The **Tsr** module provides an interrupt routine and a global flag for this interrupt that works in exactly the same fashion as the interrupt routine and flag for the BIOS disk services.

It is also unsafe to activate a TSR when most MS-DOS services are active. The danger of suspending an MS-DOS service is that the TSR itself may subsequently invoke an MS-DOS function, which would most likely corrupt the stack used by the original invocation of DOS. In general, the MS-DOS kernel cannot be interrupted at an arbitrary point and have its code reused by another process (since the code cannot be recursively reentered, it is termed *nonreentrant*). MS-DOS, however, provides a partial solution to this problem. Whenever DOS is active, it sets an internal flag to a non-zero value; the address of this INDOS flag is returned by the undocumented, but often used, function 34h. Therefore, in addition to checking the BIOS disk activity and video services flags, the keyboard interrupt handler needs to check the INDOS flag, and return immediately if any one of these flags is nonzero.

This technique for avoiding interrupting MS-DOS, however, has a serious problem. While the command interpreter is waiting for input at the DOS prompt, the INDOS flag is set to 1, since DOS uses one of its own services to read characters. While DOS is waiting at the command prompt, however, it is relatively safe to activate a TSR; in fact, all DOS function calls (accessed through interrupt 21h) can be used at this time except those in the range 01h to 0Ch. Therefore, the TSR needs some way of knowing that although the INDOS flag is not 0, DOS is simply waiting at the command line and the TSR function may be safely called. Again, MS-DOS provides a solution: while DOS waits for user input at the prompt, it continually invokes interrupt 28h (which is used to activate background processes such as print spooling, and is known as the DOS *idle interrupt*). Therefore, the occurrence of interrupt 28h is a *sufficient indication* (regardless of the state of the INDOS flag) that the TSR may be activated. Accordingly, the TSR module installs a fourth and final interrupt handler, which intercepts interrupt 28h and provides a second door to the TSR.

In summary, there are two parallel mechanisms for activating the TSR when the hotkey is pressed. First, the TSR may be activated through the keyboard interrupt handler, which must first check both the BIOS flags *and* the INDOS flag. Second, it may be activated through the interrupt 28h handler, which needs to check only the BIOS flags.

Your TSR program can determine whether it was activated through the interrupt 28h handler by calling the function **TsrInDos**, as described in the previous section. If this function returns TRUE, the INDOS flag is nonzero and the TSR must have been activated through the interrupt 28h handler; in this case, your program must not call DOS functions 01h through 0Ch, since these functions use the *same* operating system stack that DOS was using when it was interrupted. The parallel mechanism for activating a TSR is illustrated in Figure 9.7.

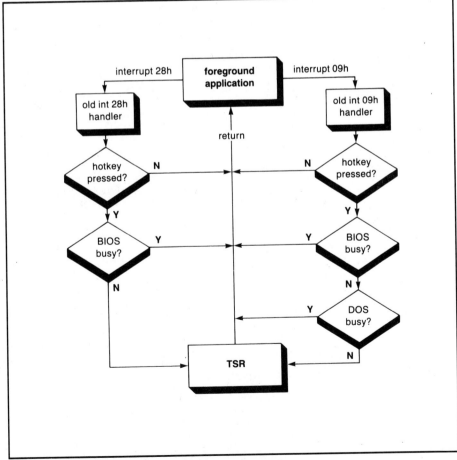

Figure 9.7: The parallel mechanism for activating a TSR

Once it has been determined that it is safe to activate the TSR, the final major task is to save the complete machine state of the interrupted program, setup the runtime environment for Microsoft C, and call the TSR entry function that was specified at installation time. When the entry function returns, the machine state must be restored before returning to the suspended application.

Details of the Implementation

The installation function, **TsrInstall** (which is located in the C file of Figure 9.1), begins by testing to see if the TSR has already been installed in memory, by searching through the user interrupts (numbers 60h to 67h) for the identification number passed in the parameter **Code**. If the code is not found, indicating that the program has *not* already been installed, then the function proceeds to place the code value in the first unused (that is, equal to 0) interrupt vector within this range. **TsrInstall** next checks that it is running under DOS version 2.0 or later, since prior versions do not support some of the functions required to install a memory resident program.

Next, **TsrInstall** saves the following important data items that will be used by the interrupt handlers, which are installed later in the function:

- The hotkey shift mask is saved in the variable **HotKeyMask**. The handlers for interrupts 09h and 28h will use this flag to determine whether the hotkey is pressed.

- The address of the TSR entry routine, given by the parameter **FPtr**, is stored in the function pointer **UserRtn**. The handlers for interrupts 09h and 28h will use this pointer to invoke your TSR program.

- The segment and offset values of the current disk transfer area (DTA) are saved so that the C DTA can be assigned before the TSR receives control. (The DTA is briefly discussed in Chapter 4 in the description of the function **FilGetVolid**.)

- The address of the INDOS flag, discussed in the previous section, is obtained through DOS service 34h, and is stored in the **far** pointer **PrtInDos**. As explained, the interrupt 09h handler will test this flag to determine whether it is safe to activate the TSR.

- Next, **TsrInstall** calls the function **InitPSP** to initialize the functions that obtain and set the value of the current program segment prefix (PSP) maintained by DOS. The PSP, and the functions that manage the system's record of the PSP, will be explained later in this section.

- Finally, **TsrInstall** saves the current contents of the four interrupt vectors that will subsequently be replaced.

- The values of the C stack segment and stack pointer must also be saved, so that the TSR can use the C stack rather than borrowing the stack belonging to the interrupted program. These values, however, are not stored until the necessary data are obtained in the course of calculating the size of the program, later in **TsrInstall**.

Once the required data have been stored, **TsrInstall** installs handlers for interrupts 28h (the DOS "idle" interrupt), 13h (the BIOS disk services), 10h (the BIOS video services), and 09h (the hardware keyboard interrupt).

The last task performed by **TsrInstall** is to calculate the size of the memory block occupied by the program and then to call the Microsoft C function **_dos_keep** to terminate the program while leaving the specified block resident in memory. The size of the memory block passed to **_dos_keep** must be given as the number of 16-byte paragraphs, and is calculated through the following sequence of steps:

1. The *far* address of the bottom of the program is assigned to the *huge* pointer **BottomProg**. The segment portion of this pointer is obtained from the predefined C variable **_psp**, and the offset is 0.

2. The *far* address of the top of the program's stack is assigned to the *huge* pointer **TopStack**. The segment portion of this pointer is obtained from the stack segment register (SS; this value is derived by calling the C library function **segread**, which reads the current values of the segment registers). The offset portion is obtained from the predefined C variable **_atopsp**.

3. The segment and offset addresses of the C stack are also assigned to the variables **CSS** and **CSP**, respectively, so that the module can later switch to the C stack when the TSR is activated (within the function **PreActivate**, in the file TSRA.ASM, Figure 9.2).

4. The function then obtains the size of the program in bytes by subtracting the *huge* pointer **BottomProg** from the *huge*

pointer **TopStack**. (With *huge* pointers, pointer subtraction returns the correct number of bytes even if the segment portions of the pointers are different.)

5. The size of the program in bytes is converted to 16-byte paragraphs (rounding up). The size of the heap in paragraphs (HEAPSIZE, defined in TSR.C) is added to this value to obtain the final number of paragraphs that should be kept in memory. The result is assigned to the variable **TSRSize**, which is passed to the C library function **_dos_keep**.

The first parameter passed to **_dos_keep** is the process return code, which is assigned to the DOS variable ERRORLEVEL when the program terminates.

Note that you can adjust the amount of memory reserved for the program's heap by assigning various values to the identifier HEAPSIZE (defined at the beginning of the C source file, TSR.C). Once you have developed a TSR, you can experiment to find the appropriate value for this constant. If the value is too large, the TSR will consume an undue amount of memory. If the value is too small, C memory allocation functions will overwrite memory that does not belong to the process, resulting in the DOS error message

```
Memory Allocation Error. System Halted.
```

Note that even if your program does not explicitly allocate memory from the heap, C library functions that your program calls may allocate such memory.

Figure 9.8 provides a map of the block of code and data that remains resident in memory, and illustrates the values used to calculate the size of the program.

The function **NewInt13**, located in the assembly language file of Figure 9.2, is the new handler for interrupt 13h, which is used to access the BIOS disk services. **NewInt13** increments the value of **Int13Flag** (which is initialized to zero), calls the original handler (the address of which was stored by **TsrInstall**), and then decrements **Int13Flag** upon return from the original handler. The flag **Int13Flag** therefore has a nonzero value only when one of the BIOS disk services is active. The program uses a counter instead of a simple true or false flag because of the small possibility that the disk services may call themselves recursively. (Note that to access **Int13Flag**, which is contained in the C data segment, the DS register is temporarily assigned the address of the C data segment, DGROUP.)

The function **NewInt10**, also in the assembly language module, is the new handler for interrupt 10h, which is used for invoking the BIOS video services. **NewInt10** manages the flag **Int10Flag**, and works in same manner as the function **NewInt13**.

The function **NewInt09** (in the C file of Figure 9.1) is the keyboard interrupt handler. This function first calls the former interrupt handler

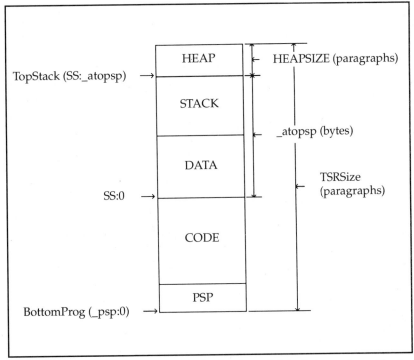

Figure 9.8: A memory map of the block of code and data that remain resident in memory

through the function pointer **OldInt09**. It then disables the interrupts so that it will not be interrupted in the middle of testing and setting the **Busy** flag. This flag serves to prevent the TSR from being recursively reentered while it is active. (Note that since the TSR switches to a fixed location in a local stack, and uses static and external variables to store data, the code is *not* reentrant.) **NewInt09** next calls **KbdGetShift** to see if the hotkey is pressed. If the hotkey is currently pressed, the function tests whether the BIOS disk or video services are active through the **Int13Flag** and **Int10Flag** variables, and whether DOS is busy through the **far** pointer to the INDOS flag, **PrtInDos**. If all tests are passed, the function **PreActivate** is called, which performs the initial steps necessary to activate the TSR entry function. Upon return from **PreActivate**, the **Busy** flag is switched off and the interrupt handler returns.

The function **NewInt28** (also in the C file of Figure 9.1) is the interrupt 28h handler and performs the same tasks as **NewInt09** except that it does *not* check whether MS-DOS is active, for reasons described in the previous section.

The function **PreActivate** is located in the assembly language file of Figure 9.2, and is called by **NewInt09** or **NewInt28**, when either one of these interrupt handlers has detected that the hotkey is pressed and that it is safe to invoke the TSR. **PreActivate** performs the following tasks:

■ It saves the existing values of the stack segment and stack pointer registers.

■ It switches to the C stack by assigning SS and SP the values saved by **TsrInstall** in the variables CSS and CSP during installation.

■ It calls the C function, **Activate**, which performs some additional preparations and invokes the TSR entry routine.

■ Upon return from the TSR code, **PreActivate** restores the stack belonging to the interrupted program.

Note that the interrupts are disabled while the program manipulates the stack registers, to prevent possible problems if a hardware interrupt were to occur before both registers have been assigned appropriate values. There are two important reasons for switching to the C stack.

First, the current stack may be quite small. Switching to the C stack provides the TSR with the full stack space that is normally allocated to a Microsoft C program.

Second, under the small data models, the C compiler assumes that the stack segment is equal to the data segment. Specifically, when an address is passed to a function, only the offset portion is used. The offset, however, may be relative either to the data segment (for external and static variables) or to the stack segment (for automatic variables). The function simply uses the offset in conjunction with the data segment register, assuming that this register is *equal* to the stack segment register. If the TSR did not switch to the C stack, this assumption would be false and C functions would be unable to access automatic data through addresses passed as parameters.

The function **Activate**, in the C file of Figure 9.1, completes the task of saving the machine state of the interrupted program and setting up the runtime environment for the TSR program, and then calls the TSR entry function.

Activate first saves the current values of the control-break interrupt vectors (numbers 23h and 1Bh) and the critical-error interrupt vector (number 24h). It then sets the control-break vectors to point to routines (**NewInt23** and **NewInt1B**) that simply return without performing any action. This precaution is taken to prevent a break handler belonging to the interrupted foreground process from receiving control if the user presses Ctrl-C or Ctrl-Break. The critical-error vector is pointed to a routine (**NewInt24**) that simply assigns the value 0 to register AX, and then returns; this value signals DOS that the error is to be ignored. Installing this critical-error handler prevents inadvertently activating the critical-error handler belonging to the interrupted foreground program, or activating the default DOS critical-error handler. (In the event of a critical error, the default DOS handler would overwrite the screen with the familiar "Abort, Retry, Ignore, Fail?" message, and then possibly attempt to abort the TSR.)

Installing these dummy control-break and critical-error handlers prevents the certain disaster of activating an inappropriate interrupt routine; however, as mentioned previously in the chapter, a robust TSR may need to install custom handlers using the methods described in Chapter 8. These handlers should be installed at the beginning of the

TSR entry function (replacing the dummy routines installed by the **Tsr** module).

Activate also temporarily restores the original keyboard interrupt handler that was active when the TSR was installed from the DOS command line (**OldInt9**). This step is necessary because a foreground program may have installed a keyboard handler that is incompatible with the TSR.

Activate next saves the old disk transfer address and switches to the C disk transfer address that was saved by the installation function.

Before calling the TSR entry routine, **Activate** must inform MS-DOS that a new process is active by setting the system's record of the current program segment prefix (PSP) to the correct value for the C program. The PSP is a 256-byte segment located immediately preceding a program in memory (see Figure 9.8); it contains important system information regarding the associated process. DOS maintains a record of the segment address of the PSP of the currently active process. (Among other uses for the PSP, DOS stores a file table within this area, which contains an entry for each open file handle belonging to the process.)

When a new program is started from the command line, or through the DOS service for executing a child process, DOS automatically updates its record of the current PSP. However, when a TSR is activated through a hotkey, DOS is unaware of the change in process, and therefore you must explicitly change the system's record of the current PSP. DOS provides two undocumented functions for managing its record of the PSP. These functions are accessed through interrupt 21h; function 51h *gets* the current PSP, and function 50h *sets* it. The problem with these two functions, however, is that under certain versions of DOS, they are unreliable if called when DOS is active (that is, when the INDOS flag is nonzero). Accordingly, the **Tsr** module provides its own functions for getting and setting the PSP: **InitPSP**, **GetPSP**, and **SetPSP** (in the C file of Figure 9.1).

The function **InitPSP** is called by **TsrInstall** during installation of the TSR. **InitPSP** obtains a table (which has one or two entries) of the addresses within the operating system code and data segment where the values of the current PSP are stored. Once these addresses are known, **GetPSP** can obtain the current PSP by simply reading one of these addresses, and **SetPSP** can set the PSP by writing the specified value directly to each of the stored addresses.

InitPSP works by searching the MS-DOS code and data for bytes that match the current PSP (which is contained in the predefined C variable **_psp**). When it finds a byte that contains the value of the current PSP, it then calls function 50h to set the PSP to some other value; if the DOS memory location changes to the new value after function 50h is called, it must be one of the addresses where DOS stores the PSP, and therefore this address is placed in the table (**PtrPSPTable**). The routine then calls function 50h once again to restore the former PSP value. (Note that **InitPSP** may safely call DOS function 50h, since **InitPSP** is called only from the installation routine, which is run from the DOS command line.)

InitPSP obtains the segment address of the *beginning* of the MS-DOS segment from the address of the INDOS pointer obtained during installation. It obtains the segment address of the *end* of DOS by calling another undocumented function, number 52h (this function supplies the address of the first DOS memory control block, which immediately follows the DOS segment). Note that these two **far** addresses are converted to a common format in which the segment portion of the address is zero, so that the addresses may be numerically compared in the loop (this technique is possible since the DOS code is located entirely within the first 64 kilobytes of memory).

Accordingly, the function **Activate** calls **GetPSP** and saves the current value of the PSP in the variable **OldPSP**.

Finally, the TSR entry function is called through the function pointer **UserRtn** that was defined in the installation procedure. Upon return from the TSR routine, **Activate** restores all values that it saved before calling the routine: the PSP, the disk transfer address, and the control-break and critical-error vectors. **Activate** then returns control to **Pre-Activate**, which switches back to the previous stack and then returns to the interrupt handler that called it (**NewInt9** or **NewInt28**).

The function **TsrInDos** simply returns the current value of the INDOS flag, which is obtained through the pointer **InDosPtr**.

A MEMORY RESIDENT PROGRAM FOR CONTROLLING THE PRINTER

The program in Figure 9.9 provides an example of a C program that is converted to a TSR, is activated through a hotkey, and displays a popup window. The program is designed to send control codes to the printer at any time they are required. The actual control code values are for the Okidata 192 printer; you should replace any codes that are different for your printer with the correct values. Figures 9.10 and 9.11 provide the usual MAKE file and QuickC program list.

```
#include <STDIO.H>
#include <PROCESS.H>
#include <CTYPE.H>
#include <DOS.H>

#include "TSR.H"
#include "SCR.H"
#include "KBD.H"
#include "PRT.H"

#define ULR 6                              /* Position of centered window.   */
#define ULC 20

static void SetPrtCodes (void);            /* The TSR entry routine.         */
static int SendCode (char *ControlString); /* Sends control string to PRN   */
static int ErrorRtn (void);                /* Printer error routine.         */

static int OldRow, OldCol;                 /* Saves old cursor position.     */

void main (void)
    {
    /* Install 'SetPrtCodes' as TSR function; Alt-Left Shift is hotkey.       */
    switch (TsrInstall (SetPrtCodes,ALT | LEFTSHIFT,0x22222222))
        {
        case WRONGDOS:
            printf ("Cannot install TSR;  must have DOS version 2.0 "
                    "or higher.\n");
            exit (1);

        case INSTALLED:
            printf ("Program already installed.\n");
            exit (1);

        case NOINT:
            printf ("Cannot install;  no free user interrupts.\n");
            exit (1);

        case ERROR:
        default:
            printf ("Error installing TSR function.\n");
            exit (1);
        }

    } /* end main */


static void SetPrtCodes ()
/*
    This is the function activated when the hot key is pressed.
*/
    {
    static char *CodeTable [] =            /* Table of printer control codes  */
```

Figure 9.9: TSRDEM02.C: A TSR for sending control codes to the printer

```
                 {                                  /* corresponding to menu items 'a'  */
                 "\x1b\x49\x01",                     /* through 'r' below.               */
                 "\x1b\x49\x03",
                 "\x1b\x49\x01\x1b\x45",
                 "\x1b\x46",
                 "\x1b\x49\x01\x1b\x47",
                 "\x1b\x48",
                 "\x12",
                 "\x1b\x3a",
                 "\x0f",
                 "\x1b\x57\x31",
                 "\x1b\x57\x30",
                 "\x1b\x41\x0c\x1b\x32",
                 "\x1b\x30",
                 "\x1b\x31",
                 "\x1b\x4e\x0b",
                 "\x1b\x4f",
                 "\x1b\x58\x10\x96",
                 "\x1b\x58\x01\x96"
                 };
        unsigned char Row;         /* Row counter for displaying strings.       */
        int Quit = 0;              /* Flag to break out of outer loop.          */
        int Key;                   /* Key typed by user.                        */
        int Selected;              /* The current highlighted control code.     */

        ScrGetCur (&OldRow,&OldCol,0);     /* Save current cursor position.    */
        ScrPush ();                        /* Save current screen.             */
        ScrSetCur (25,80,0);               /* Hide the cursor.                 */
        ScrClear (0,0,24,37);              /* Display window.                  */
        ScrPutBox (0,0,24,37,2);
        PrtTimeout (1);                            /* Set minimum printer timeout count*/
        Row = 1;                                   /* Display window data.             */
        ScrPutS ("       Send Codes to Printer",0x0f,Row++,1);
        Row++;
        ScrPutS ("              characters:  *(a) UTILITY",  0x0f,Row++,1);
        ScrPutS ("                           (b) NLQ",       0x0f,Row++,1);
        ScrPutS ("     emphasized print:     (c) ON",        0x0f,Row++,1);
        ScrPutS ("                          *(d) OFF",       0x0f,Row++,1);
        ScrPutS ("      enhanced print:      (e) ON",        0x0f,Row++,1);
        ScrPutS ("                          *(f) OFF",       0x0f,Row++,1);
        ScrPutS ("     character width:     *(g) 10 CPI",    0x0f,Row++,1);
        ScrPutS ("                           (h) 12 CPI",    0x0f,Row++,1);
        ScrPutS ("                           (i) 17.1 CPI",  0x0f,Row++,1);
        ScrPutS ("        double width:      (j) ON",        0x0f,Row++,1);
        ScrPutS ("                          *(k) OFF",       0x0f,Row++,1);
        ScrPutS ("        line spacing:     *(l) 6 LPI",     0x0f,Row++,1);
        ScrPutS ("                           (m) 8 LPI",     0x0f,Row++,1);
        ScrPutS ("                           (n) 10.2 LPI",  0x0f,Row++,1);
        ScrPutS ("skip bottom of form:       (o) ON",        0x0f,Row++,1);
        ScrPutS ("                          *(p) OFF",       0x0f,Row++,1);
        ScrPutS ("              indent:      (q) ON",        0x0f,Row++,1);
        ScrPutS ("                          *(r) OFF",       0x0f,Row++,1);
        Row++;
        ScrPutS ("press <Enter> to send selected code", 0x0f,Row++,1);
        ScrPutS ("press <Esc> to quit program",         0x0f,Row++,1);
        Selected = 0;                              /* Initialize 'selected' and display*/
                                                   /* initial highlight on item (a).   */
        ScrPutAttr (0x70,Selected+3,23,Selected+3,36);
```

Figure 9.9: TSRDEM02.C: A TSR for sending control codes to the printer (continued)

```
                    while (!Quit)
                    {
                    while (!KbdReady ())
                        ;
                    switch (Key = KbdGetC ())      /* Get key from user.                */
                        {
                        case 0x1c0d:                  /* Carriage return.                */
                            if (SendCode (CodeTable [Selected]))
                                Quit = 1;
                            break;
                        case 0x4800:                  /* Up arrow.                       */
                            if (Selected > 0)   /* Update 'Selected' and move           */
                                {               /* highlight.                           */
                                ScrPutAttr (0x0f,Selected+3,23,Selected+3,36);
                                --Selected;
                                ScrPutAttr (0x70,Selected+3,23,Selected+3,36);
                                }
                            break;
                        case 0x5000:                  /* Down arrow.                     */
                            if (Selected < 17)  /* Update 'Selected' and move           */
                                {               /* highlight.                           */
                                ScrPutAttr (0x0f,Selected+3,23,Selected+3,36);
                                ++Selected;
                                ScrPutAttr (0x70,Selected+3,23,Selected+3,36);
                                }
                            break;
                        case 0x011b:                  /* Escape.                         */
                            Quit = 1;             /* Terminate the TSR.              */
                            break;
                        default:        /* If user entered a letter, set 'Selected'     */
                                        /* and move highlight to appropriate item.      */
                            Key = toupper (Key & 0x00ff);
                            if (Key >= 65 && Key <= 82)
                                {
                                ScrPutAttr (0x0f,Selected+3,23,Selected+3,36);
                                Selected = Key - 65;
                                ScrPutAttr (0x70,Selected+3,23,Selected+3,36);
                                }

                        } /* end switch */
                    }

            PrtTimeout (20);      /* Restore 20 sec. default printer timeout.           */
            ScrPop (1);           /* Restore screen.                                    */
            ScrSetCur (OldRow,OldCol,0);       /* Restore old cursor position.          */
            return;

            } /* end SetPrtCodes */
static int SendCode (char *ControlString)
/*
    This function sends a null-terminated string of control codes to the
    printer using the BIOS printer services.
*/
        {
        union REGS Reg;

        while (*ControlString)
            {
            Reg.x.dx = 0;                     /* Specifies the first printer port.     */
            Reg.h.ah = 0;                     /* BIOS print character function.        */
```

Figure 9.9: TSRDEM02.C: A TSR for sending control codes to the printer (continued)

```
                Reg.h.al = *ControlString;    /* The character to print.      */
                int86 (0x17,&Reg,&Reg);   /* BIOS printer services interrupt.  */
                if (Reg.h.ah & 0x29)      /* Operation status is returned in AH. */
                    {                     /* Test if one of the error bits is on. */
                    if (ErrorRtn ())      /* An error bit is on, call error routine*/
                        return (1);       /* User wants to abort the program.     */
                    else
                        continue;         /* User wants to retry the operation.   */

                    }
                ++ControlString;          /* Succesfully printer character, go on */
                }                         /* to the next one.                     */
            return (0);

        } /* end SendCode */


    static int ErrorRtn ()
    /*
        This is the error routine called when the BIOS returns an error code to
        'SendCode'.
    */
        {
        ScrPush ();
        ScrClear (0,0,9,37);
        ScrPutBox (0,0,9,37,3);
        ScrPutS ("Error Writing to Printer",0x0f,1,7);
        ScrPutS ("Action?",0x0f,3,7);
        ScrPutS ("R  Retry operation",0x0f,5,7);
        ScrPutS ("A  Abort program",0x0f,6,7);
        ScrPutS ("enter R or A:",0x0f,8,10);
        ScrSetCur (8,24,0);
        for (;;)
            {
            switch (KbdGetC () & 0x00ff)
                {
                case 'r':        /* User wants to retry the operation.       */
                case 'R':
                    ScrSetCur (25,80,0);
                    ScrPop (1);
                    return (0);
                case 'a':        /* User wants to abort the TSR.             */
                case 'A':
                    ScrPop (1);
                    return (1);
                }
            }

        } /* end ErrorRtn */
```

Figure 9.9: TSRDEM02.C: A TSR for sending control codes to the printer (continued)

If the program is loaded successfully, it returns to the DOS command line without comment. If an error occurs, the program is not installed as a TSR, and an appropriate error message is displayed. Once the program is installed, any time you press the Alt-Left Shift keys, a window will appear offering you a selection of control codes. Each of the default values is marked with an asterisk (these are the values in effect when the printer is first turned on and are *not* necessarily the current

```
TSRDEM02.OBJ : TSRDEM02.C TSR.H SCR.H KBD.H
    cl /c /W2 /Zp TSRDEM02.C

TSR.OBJ : TSR.C TSR.H
    cl /c /W2 /Zp TSR.C

TSRA.OBJ : TSRA.ASM
    masm /MX TSRA.ASM;

SCR.OBJ : SCR.C SCR.H
    cl /c /W2 /Zp SCR.C

KBD.OBJ : KBD.C KBD.H
    cl /c /W2 /Zp KBD.C

KBDA.OBJ : KBDA.ASM
    masm /MX KBDA.ASM;

PRT.OBJ : PRT.C PRT.H
    cl /c /W2 /Zp PRT.C

UTYA.OBJ : UTYA.ASM
    masm /MX UTYA.ASM;

TSRDEM02.EXE : TSRDEM02.OBJ TSR.OBJ TSRA.OBJ SCR.OBJ KBD.OBJ KBDA.OBJ \
        PRT.OBJ UTYA.OBJ
    link /NOI /NOD TSRDEM02+TSR+TSRA+SCR+KBD+KBDA+PRT+UTYA,,NUL,SLIBCER;
```

Figure 9.10: TSRDEM02.M: A MAKE file for preparing TSRDEM02.C

values). To send a control code to the printer, place the highlight on the appropriate item and press Enter. To move the highlight you can either use the arrow keys or type the letter of the desired line. Pressing Esc will terminate the utility. If an error occurs while accessing the printer, an error message window will pop up and you will have the choice of retrying the operation or terminating the TSR.

The **main** function simply installs the program as a TSR by calling **TsrInstall**, and prints an error message if the installation fails. The specified TSR entry function is **SetPrtCodes**. **SetPrtCodes** saves and restores the cursor parameters and screen data, and displays the text for

```
TSRDEM02.C
TSR.C
TSRA.OBJ
SCR.C
KBD.C
KBDA.OBJ
PRT.C
UTYA.OBJ
```

Figure 9.11: A QuickC program list for preparing TSRDEM02.C

the menu, using the functions in the **Scr** module. The actual control codes are pointed to by the array of character pointers, **CodeTable**. The integer **Selected** is an index to this array, and always indexes the currently highlighted control code. The main keyboard loop must adjust the value of **Selected** and move the highlight if the user presses an arrow key or presses a letter from *a* to *r* to select one of the menu items. If Esc is typed, the TSR is terminated, and if Enter is pressed, the currently selected control code is sent to the printer through the local function **SendCode**.

SendCode sends each character in the control string to the printer by invoking the BIOS print character service accessed through interrupt 17h, with 0 in register AX. Since the characters are not printed through MS-DOS, a standard critical-error handler would be ineffectual in handling printer errors. Rather, the function uses its own error handler. The BIOS service returns a status byte in register AH; if bit 0, 3, or 5 is set, then an error occurred when printing the character. If any of these bits is set, the error-handling routine **ErrorRtn** is called, which displays window and offers the user the choice of retrying the operation or aborting the program. If the user chooses to retry, **ErrorRtn** returns 0, which causes **SendCode** to return to the top of the printing loop without incrementing the character pointer, **ControlString**; consequently, the BIOS routine is again requested to print the *same* character that resulted in the error. If the user chooses to abort the program, then a value of 1 is ultimately returned to the entry function **SetPrtCodes**, causing this function to terminate.

Note that **SetPrtCodes** uses the function **PrtTimeout** (in the **Prt** module presented in Chapter 3) to temporarily reduce the BIOS timeout count from its default value of 20 seconds to 1 second. If this step were not taken, certain errors (such as the Select button on the printer being turned off) would cause the BIOS to wait 20 seconds before returning an error code. Since a TSR normally performs its functions quickly, this long a delay will cause most users to attempt to abort the TSR and will lead many users to reboot the computer.

The following are some useful enhancements that might be added to this program:

■ An option that would allow the user to install control codes for a specific printer.

■ An option that would allow switching of the active printer on a system that uses more than one printer port. This procedure could be accomplished through the function **PrtSwap** given in Chapter 3.

▮ A procedure that would read a mailing address directly off the screen of another program and use this data to print an envelope. The return address could be installed through a separate option. Additionally, if a graphics printer were installed, a wide envelope could be printed sideways.

▮ A facility for accessing the DOS PRINT queue if the DOS version is 3.0 or above (see Chapter 3 for functions to access the PRINT queue).

An Expanded
Memory Interface

C HAPTER 10

The mechanism defined by the expanded memory specification (EMS) is currently the most successful and popular means for increasing the amount of memory available to applications running on the 8086/88 family of processors. The functions presented in this chapter provide a simplified interface that allows a Microsoft C program to detect the presence of expanded memory and access its basic features.

The chapter begins with a brief overview of the mechanics of expanded memory and a summary of the relevant terminology. Next, each function belonging to the expanded memory module is described in detail. The final section discusses how these functions are used together in a Microsoft C program, and presents a brief demonstration application.

AN OVERVIEW OF EXPANDED MEMORY

The 8086/88 processors are capable of directly addressing only 1024 kilobytes of memory (*conventional memory*). Furthermore, under MS-DOS only the first 640 kilobytes are available for the operating system and for user programs (*user memory*); memory above 640 kilobytes is normally reserved for adapter cards and for the system BIOS. Expanded memory cards, however, allow applications to access up to 32 megabytes of additional memory through an indirect paging process. The expanded memory mechanism consists of the following basic elements:

1. *Expanded memory*. Expanded memory consists of up to 32 megabytes (8 megabytes under versions prior to 4.0) of memory on one or more adapter cards. Unlike conventional memory, expanded memory *cannot* be directly addressed by a program.

2. The *page frame*. The page frame is a block of conventional memory addresses, typically located above user memory. It is generally 64 kilobytes long and is used as a window into expanded memory. Although this area of memory is normally reserved for the ROM BIOS and adapter cards, it is usually possible to find a 64 kilobyte contiguous block that is unused. The address of the page frame is designated when installing an expanded memory board. Your program accesses expanded memory by directly reading or writing to addresses within the page frame; these reads and writes are

automatically rerouted by the hardware to the appropriate portion of expanded memory. Which portion of expanded memory is actually accessed through a given address within the page frame depends upon the next element: the mapping.

3. The *mapping*. Since the size of expanded memory is typically much larger than the size of the page frame, you must specify which portions of expanded memory are to be addressable through the page frame. You specify this relationship by defining a mapping. Conceptually, the current mapping determines which sections of expanded memory are visible through the page frame window. To access additional areas of expanded memory, you must change the mapping.

4. A *physical page*. The conventional memory that constitutes the page frame is divided into physical pages. There are normally four physical pages, each of which is 16 kilobytes long. The physical pages are numbered in sequence beginning with 0.

5. A *logical page*. The expanded memory on the EMS cards is divided into logical pages, each of which is usually 16 kilobytes long. When you specify a mapping, you can associate any logical page of expanded memory with any physical page within the page frame. The logical pages that have been allocated are numbered in sequence beginning with 0.

Figure 10.1 illustrates the basic elements of the expanded memory mechanism. Note that the logical pages currently mapped to the physical pages can be located anywhere in expanded memory and are not necessarily contiguous. Your program, however, can map and access only those logical pages that it has been allocated. The primary purpose of the functions presented in this chapter is to allocate and map expanded memory pages.

The functions in this chapter are compatible with the expanded memory specification versions 3.2 through 4.0. The specification for version 3.2 was published in September of 1985; the most recent version of the specification is 4.0, published in August of 1987. Version 4.0 increased the upper limit of expanded memory from 8 megabytes to 32 megabytes, and added many sophisticated features useful for writing multitasking operating environments. For example, under version 4.0, the page frame can be larger than 64 kilobytes, and it is also possible to map expanded memory into areas of memory below 640 kilobytes, to provide fast context switching between conventional MS-DOS applications. Although the functions presented here do not *depend* upon any of

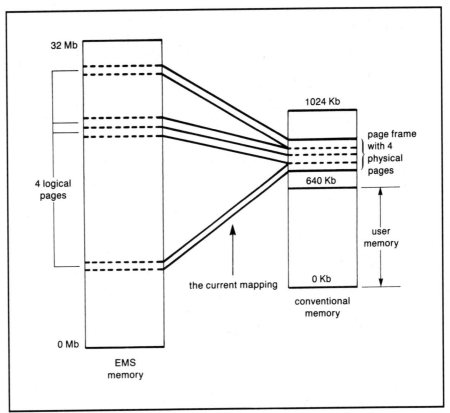

Figure 10.1: Elements of the expanded memory mechanism

the features of the latest version, they can certainly take advantage of the additional memory capacity. For information on the advanced features of version 4.0, see the handbook *Lotus/Intel/Microsoft Expanded Memory Specification, Version 4.0*, cited in the Bibliography.

The term *expanded memory* should not be confused with *extended memory*. Extended memory is the portion of the address space above 1024 kilobytes, which *can* be directly addressed by the 80286 and 80386 processors when they are in the *protected mode* (the protected mode is a processor state that provides a large address space and supports multitasking). MS-DOS, however, cannot run in the protected mode, and therefore DOS applications cannot directly address extended memory (MS -DOS must run in the *real mode*, a processor state that supports applications written for the 8086/88 processors). Consequently, expanded memory is still an important mechanism for machines using the 286 and 386 processors.

THE FUNCTIONS

The purpose of the functions in this chapter is to provide a simple interface for accessing the basic features of expanded memory from a Microsoft C program. The functions were designed to be few in number, to be similar to standard C memory allocation functions, and to hide from the calling program many of the details required to manage expanded memory. If you use this interface in your C program, you should not bypass the functions by directly calling the expanded memory manager (explained in the next section). The functions form an integrated set; by circumventing them you could invalidate some of the internal information they maintain. The functions are listed in Figure 10.2; Figure 10.3 contains the header file you must include in your program to call these functions.

All of the functions in this module (except **EmsInstalled** and **EmsErrorMsg**) assign a status code to the global variable **EmsError** before they return. The header file in Figure 10.3 defines this variable and provides constant definitions for the 16 possible error values that may be assigned. Additionally, each function directly returns some special value to indicate that an error has occurred (the actual value varies, since it must be within the range of the return type, but outside the range of valid return values). The special error return value, as well as the possible codes that may be assigned to **EmsError**, are documented for each function in the descriptions that follow.

Using the functions in the expanded memory module, you can perform the following basic tasks:

- Determine if expanded memory is installed (**EmsInstalled**).
- Obtain the expanded memory manager version (**EmsVersion**).
- Ascertain the number of expanded memory logical pages that are available for allocation (**EmsPagesAvail**).
- Allocate logical pages of expanded memory for your program (**EmsAlloc**).
- Free expanded memory logical pages (**EmsFree**).
- Map logical pages onto the four physical pages (**EmsMap**).
- Save and restore the current mapping (**EmsSave** and **EmsRestore**).
- Obtain a string containing a description for a given error code (**EmsErrorMsg**).

```
#include <DOS.H>

#define MODFILE
#include "EMS.H"

#pragma check_stack (off)        /* Turn off stack checks so that functions */
                                 /* can be called from interrupt routines.  */

static int MapError (int EmmErr);  /* Maps EMM error to module error no.    */
static int Allocated = 0;          /* Flag indicates EMS memory allocated.  */
static int Handle;                 /* The EMM handle.                       */

int EmsInstalled (void)
/*
    This function returns a non-zero value if the expanded memory manager
    is installed, and zero if it is not installed.
*/
    {
    char *EmmName = "EMMXXXX0";      /* EMM code in device name field.   */
    char far *EmmPtr;                /* Pointer to device header.        */

    EmmPtr = (char far *)_dos_getvect (0x67);
    FP_OFF (EmmPtr) = 0x000a;

    while (*EmmName)                 /* Test if name field matches the   */
          if (*EmmName++ != *EmmPtr++)   /* EMM code.                    */
              return (0);            /* Mismatch:  return false.         */

    return (1);                      /* All characters matched.          */

    } /* end EmsInstalled */


int EmsVersion (void)
/*
    This function returns the EMM version number.
*/
    {
    union REGS Reg;

    if (!EmsInstalled ())            /* First test if EMM is installed.  */
        {
        EmsError = NOTINSTALLED;
        return (0);
        }

    Reg.h.ah = 0x46;                 /* EMM function to return version.  */
    int86 (0x67,&Reg,&Reg);          /* The EMM services interrupt.      */

    if (Reg.h.ah)                    /* Test for error.                  */
        {                            /* Assign module error number to    */
        EmsError = MapError (Reg.h.ah);   /* global error variable.      */
        return (0);                  /* 0 return indicates an error.     */
        }
```

Figure 10.2: EMS.C: Module of functions for accessing expanded memory

```
        EmsError = NOERROR;                 /* Function successful.        */
        return (Reg.h.al);                  /* AL contains the version number. */

        } /* end EmsVersion */


int EmsPagesAvail (void)
/*
        This function returns the number of free pages of EMS memory that can
        be allocated.
*/
        {
        union REGS Reg;

        if (!EmsInstalled ())               /* First test if EMM installed. */
                {
                EmsError = NOTINSTALLED;
                return (-1);
                }

        Reg.h.ah = 0x42;                    /* EMM function to return number of */
        int86 (0x67,&Reg,&Reg);             /* free pages.                 */

        if (Reg.h.ah)                       /* Test for error.             */
                {                           /* Assign module error number to */
                EmsError = MapError (Reg.h.ah);   /* global error variable.  */
                return (-1);                /* -1 return indicates an error. */
                }

        EmsError = NOERROR;                 /* Function successful.        */
        return (Reg.x.bx);                  /* BX contains the number of pages. */

        } /* end EmsPagesAvail */


char far *EmsAlloc (int Pages)
/*
        This function allocates the number of logical EMS pages specified by
        the parameter 'Pages'.
*/
        {
        char far *FarPtrCh;                 /* Temporarily holds return value. */
        union REGS Reg;

        if (!EmsInstalled ())               /* First test if EMM installed. */
                {
                EmsError = NOTINSTALLED;
                return (NULL);
                }

        if (Allocated)                      /* Make sure that pages have not */
                {                           /* already been allocated.     */
                EmsError = ALLOCATED;
                return (NULL);
                }
```

Figure 10.2: EMS.C: Module of functions for accessing expanded memory (continued)

```
        Reg.x.bx = Pages;              /* BX specified number of pages.  */
        Reg.h.ah = 0x43;              /* EMM function to allocate pages. */
        int86 (0x67,&Reg,&Reg);

        if (Reg.h.ah)                  /* Test for error.                */
            {                          /* Assign module error number to  */
            EmsError = MapError (Reg.h.ah);   /* global error variable.  */
            return (NULL);             /* NULL return indicates error.   */
            }

        Handle = Reg.x.dx;             /* Store EMM handle in DX.        */
        Allocated = 1;                 /* Set flag to indicate that EMS  */
                                       /* memory has been allocated.     */

        Reg.h.ah = 0x41;               /* EMM function to return segment */
        int86 (0x67,&Reg,&Reg);        /* address of EMS page frame.     */

        if (Reg.h.ah)                  /* Test for error.                */
            {                          /* Assign module error number to  */
            EmsError = MapError (Reg.h.ah);   /* global error variable.  */
            return (NULL);             /* NULL return indicates an error. */
            }

        EmsError = NOERROR;            /* Successful completion of both  */
                                       /* functions.                     */

        FP_SEG (FarPtrCh) = Reg.x.bx;  /* Segment address is in BX.      */
        FP_OFF (FarPtrCh) = 0;

        return (FarPtrCh);

        } /* end EmsAlloc */


int EmsFree (void)
/*
    This function frees all pages of EMS memory that have been allocated by
    a prior call to 'EmsAlloc'.
*/
        {
        union REGS Reg;

        if (!EmsInstalled ())          /* First test if EMM installed.   */
            {
            EmsError = NOTINSTALLED;
            return (NOTINSTALLED);
            }

        if (!Allocated)                /* Test that EMS memory has been  */
            {                          /* successfully allocated.        */
            EmsError = NOTALLOCATED;
            return (NOTALLOCATED);
            }
```

Figure 10.2: EMS.C: Module of functions for accessing expanded memory (continued)

```
        Reg.x.dx = Handle;                /* EMM handle goes in DX.        */
        Reg.h.ah = 0x45;                  /* EMM function to free pages.   */
        int86 (0x67,&Reg,&Reg);

        if (Reg.h.ah)                     /* Test for error.               */
            {                             /* Assign module error number to */
            EmsError = MapError (Reg.h.ah);  /* global error variable.     */
            return (EmsError);            /* Return actual error code.     */
            }

        Allocated = 0;                    /* Function successful.          */
        EmsError = NOERROR;
        return (NOERROR);

        } /* end EmsFree */


int EmsMap (int Page0,int Page1,int Page2,int Page3)
/*
    This function maps the four logical pages specified by the parameters
    onto the (first) four physical pages.
*/
        {
        register int i;
        register int Page;
        union REGS Reg;

        if (!EmsInstalled ())             /* First test if EMM installed.  */
            {
            EmsError = NOTINSTALLED;
            return (NOTINSTALLED);
            }

        if (!Allocated)                   /* Test that EMS memory has been */
            {                             /* successfully allocated.       */
            EmsError = NOTALLOCATED;
            return (NOTALLOCATED);
            }

        for (i = 0; i < 4; ++i)           /* Four pages to map.            */
            {
            if (i == 0)                   /* Select one parameter with each */
                Page = Page0;             /* iteration of the loop.        */
            else if (i == 1)
                Page = Page1;
            else if (i == 2)
                Page = Page2;
            else if (i == 3)
                Page = Page3;
            if (Page == -1)
                continue;
```

Figure 10.2: EMS.C: Module of functions for accessing expanded memory (continued)

```
          Reg.x.bx = Page;                /* Logical page number.        */
          Reg.x.dx = Handle;              /* EMM handle.                 */
          Reg.h.al = (unsigned char) i;   /* Physical page number.       */
          Reg.h.ah = 0x44;                /* EMM function to map logical */
          int86 (0x67,&Reg,&Reg);         /* pages onto physical pages.  */

          if (Reg.h.ah)                    /* Test for error.            */
                 {                         /* Assign module error number to */
                 EmsError = MapError (Reg.h.ah); /* global error variable. */
                 return (EmsError);        /* Return actual error code.  */
                 }
          }

      EmsError = NOERROR;                 /* Function successful.        */
      return (NOERROR);

      } /* end EmsMap */


int EmsSave (void)
/*
     This function saves the contents of the page mapping registers in an
     internal EMM save area associate with the current EMM handle.
*/
     {
     union REGS Reg;

     if (!EmsInstalled ())               /* First test if EMM installed.  */
            {
            EmsError = NOTINSTALLED;
            return (NOTINSTALLED);
            }

     if (!Allocated)                      /* Test that EMS memory has been  */
            {                             /* successfully allocted.         */
            EmsError = NOTALLOCATED;
            return (NOTALLOCATED);
            }

     Reg.x.dx = Handle;                   /* EMM handle.                    */
     Reg.h.ah = 0x47;                     /* EMM function to save page map. */
     int86 (0x67,&Reg,&Reg);

     if (Reg.h.ah)                         /* Test for error.               */
            {                              /* Assign module error number    */
            EmsError = MapError (Reg.h.ah); /* to global error variable.    */
            return (EmsError);             /* Return actual error code.     */
            }

     EmsError = NOERROR;                  /* Function successful.          */
     return (NOERROR);

     } /* end EmsSave */
```

Figure 10.2: EMS.C: Module of functions for accessing expanded memory (continued)

```
int EmsRestore (void)
/*
    This function restores the page mapping that was saved by a prior call
    to 'EmsSave'.
*/
    {
    union REGS Reg;

    if (!EmsInstalled ())               /* Test if EMM installed.           */
        {
        EmsError = NOTINSTALLED;
        return (NOTINSTALLED);
        }

    if (!Allocated)                     /* Test that EMS memory has been    */
        {                               /* successfully allocated.          */
        EmsError = NOTALLOCATED;
        return (NOTALLOCATED);
        }

    Reg.x.dx = Handle;                  /* EMM handle.                      */
    Reg.h.ah = 0x48;                    /* EMM service to restore page map. */
    int86 (0x67,&Reg,&Reg);

    if (Reg.h.ah)                               /* Test for error.              */
        {                                       /* Assign module error number   */
        EmsError = MapError (Reg.h.ah);         /* to global error variable.    */
        return (EmsError);                      /* Return actual error code.    */
        }

    EmsError = NOERROR;                 /* Function successful.             */
    return (NOERROR);

    } /* end EmsRestore */


char *EmsErrorMsg (int ErrorNum)
/*
    This function returns a pointer to an error message corresponding to
    the module error number given by 'ErrorNum'.
*/
    {
    static char *MessageTable [] =
        {
        "No error.",
        "Expanded memory not installed.",
        "No free expanded memory pages.",
        "Software malfunction.",
        "Hardware malfunction.",
        "EMS memory already allocated by this program.",
        "No EMM handles free.",
        "Insufficient EMS pages to fill request.",
        "Attempt to allocate 0 pages.",
        "EMS memory not allocated.",
        "'EmsSave' called without subsequent 'EmsRestore'.",
```

Figure 10.2: EMS.C: Module of functions for accessing expanded memory (continued)

```
                    "Logical page out of range allocated to process.",
                    "No room in EMM save area.",
                    "'EmsSave' already called by program.",
                    "'EmsRestore' called without prior 'EmsSave'.",
                    "General error."
                    };

        if (ErrorNum < 0 || ErrorNum > 15)      /* Invalid error number.      */
            return (NULL);

        return (MessageTable [ErrorNum]);

        } /* EmsErrorMsg */


static int MapError (int EmmErr)
/*
    This function returns the module error number corresponding to the EMM
    error number specified by the parameter 'EmmErr'.
*/
        {
        static int ErrorTable [] =
             {
             SOFTERROR,
             HARDERROR,
             EMSERROR,
             EMSERROR,
             EMSERROR,
             NOHANDLES,
             NORESTORE,
             NOPAGES,
             NOPAGES,
             ALLOCERROR,
             RANGE,
             EMSERROR,
             NOSAVEAREA,
             SAVECALLED,
             NOSAVE
             };

        if (EmmErr < 0x80 || EmmErr > 0x8e)     /* Return general error code   */
            return (EMSERROR);                  /* for out of range EMM errors.*/

        return (ErrorTable [EmmErr & 0x000f]);  /* EMM error is within range.  */

        } /* end MapError */
```

Figure 10.2: EMS.C: Module of functions for accessing expanded memory (continued)

```
#if (defined(M_I86SM) || defined(M_I86MM))
#define  NULL    0
#elif (defined(M_I86CM) || defined(M_I86LM) || defined(M_I86HM))
#define  NULL    0L
#endif
                            /* Error codes:  assigned to EmsError.    */
                            /* Values in '()' are the EMM error numbers. */
#if !defined (NOERROR)
#define NOERROR         0   /* (00h) No EMS error.                    */
#endif
#define NOTINSTALLED    1   /* Expanded memory not installed.         */
#define NOFREEPAGES     2   /* No free EMS pages available.           */
#define SOFTERROR       3   /* (80h) EMM software error.              */
#define HARDERROR       4   /* (81h) EMS hardware error.              */
#define ALLOCATED       5   /* EMS memory already allocated by program. */
#define NOHANDLES       6   /* (85h) No EMM handles free.             */
#define NOPAGES         7   /* (87h/88h) Insufficient pages available to */
                            /* fill request.                          */
#define ALLOCERROR      8   /* (89h, versions < 4.0) Attempt to allocate */
                            /* 0 pages.                               */
#define NOTALLOCATED    9   /* EMS memory has not been allocated by prog. */
#define NORESTORE      10   /* (86h)  EmsSave called without subsequent */
                            /* call to EmsRestore.                    */
#define RANGE          11   /* (8Ah)  Logical page out of range allocated */
                            /* to program.                            */
#define NOSAVEAREA     12   /* (8Ch)  No room in save area.           */
#define SAVECALLED     13   /* (8Dh)  Attempt to call EmsSave twice   */
                            /* without an intermediate call to EmsRestore.*/
#define NOSAVE         14   /* (8Eh)  EmsRestore called without prior call*/
                            /* to EmsSave.                            */
#define EMSERROR       15   /* General EMS error.                     */


#if defined (MODFILE)
int EmsError = NOERROR;
#else
extern int EmsError;
#endif

int EmsInstalled (void);
int EmsVersion (void);
int EmsPagesAvail (void);
char far *EmsAlloc (int Pages);
int EmsFree (void);
int EmsMap (int Page0,int Page1,int Page2,int Page3);
int EmsSave (void);
int EmsRestore (void);
char *EmsErrorMsg (int ErrorNum);
```

Figure 10.3: EMS.H: Header file you should include in your program to call the functions in
EMS.C

EmsInstalled

Using
EmsInstalled

The function **EmsInstalled** has the prototype

```
int EmsInstalled
      (void)
```

This function returns a nonzero value if expanded memory is installed, and returns 0 if expanded memory is not installed. **EmsInstalled** neither returns an error message nor sets the global error variable **Ems-Error**. Your program should receive a nonzero return value from this function before calling other functions in the module (the other functions, however, all test for the presence of expanded memory and will convey the error message NOTINSTALLED if they detect that expanded memory is not installed). This function is demonstrated in Figures 10.4 and 10.7, described later in the chapter.

How
EmsInstalled
Works

To make use of the hardware features of expanded memory cards, the user must install a memory resident program called the *expanded memory manager* (or EMM). This program is installed as a device driver by placing an appropriate line in the configuration file, CONFIG.SYS; for example:

```
device=c:emm.sys M2 I5 d
```

All of the services of the EMM are accessed through interrupt 67h. The segment portion of this vector therefore contains the correct segment address of the EMM in memory (and the offset portion contains the offset of the code entry point). Since the EMM is installed as a device driver, it must have a name field at offset 0Ah within this segment. The string that the EMM assigns to the name field is "EMMXXXX0."

EmsInstalled first calls the Microsoft C function **_dos_getvect** to assign the **far** address (segment and offset) contained in interrupt vector 67h to the **far** pointer **EmmPtr**. The segment portion of this address contains the segment address of the EMM; the offset portion, however, must now be assigned the offset of the device header. Accordingly, **EmsInstalled** uses the Microsoft C macro FP_OFF to assign **EmmPtr**

the correct device header offset, 0x000a. The correct EMM name is pointed to by the variable **EmmName**; this string is then compared to the contents of memory pointed to by **EmmPtr**. The presence of the device name at the appropriate location in memory is considered sufficient proof that the expanded memory manager is installed.

This technique is one of the two methods recommended by the *Lotus/Intel/Microsoft Expanded Memory Specification.* The other method involves attempting to open the EMM as a file, and is not only more complicated, but is also a dangerous procedure to perform from an interrupt handler or device driver.

EmsVersion

*Using
EmsVersion*

The function **EmsVersion** has the prototype

```
int EmsVersion
    (void)
```

and returns the version number of the expanded memory manager that is currently installed. The major version number is returned in bits 4 through 7, and the minor version number in bits 0 through 3. For example, if the version is 3.2, the integer returned by this function would have the following binary value:

```
0000 0000 0011 0010
```

If successful, **EmsVersion** returns the version number and sets the global error variable **EmsError** to NOERROR. If, however, an error occurs, it returns 0 and sets **EmsError** to one of the following values:

NOTINSTALLED   Expanded memory is not installed.

SOFTERROR   Expanded memory manager software error.

HARDERROR   Expanded memory hardware error.

EmsVersion is demonstrated in Figure 10.4, described later in the chapter.

How EmsVersion Works

EmsVersion first calls **EmsInstalled** to make sure that the expanded memory manager is installed. If the EMM were *not* installed, the subsequent invocation of interrupt 67h would have unpredictable and probably fatal results.

EmsVersion, as well as the remainder of the functions in this module, performs its primary task by invoking the expanded memory manager through interrupt 67h. All EMM services are requested through this single interrupt; the individual services are specified by placing the appropriate value in register AH. **EmsVersion** invokes the EMM "get version" service, which has the following calling protocol:

EMM Function 7: Get Version

Entry:

AH   46h

Return:

AH   Error code

AL   Version number; the high order 4 bits contain the major version number, and the low order 4 bits the minor version number

In the descriptions of the calling protocols in this chapter, the *Entry* section lists the values that must be loaded into registers before generating the interrupt, and the *Return* section lists the values that are returned in registers by the requested service. The following descriptions often refer to loading various machine registers and obtaining return values from registers; remember that in Microsoft C the registers are accessed through the **union REGS** variable that is passed to the function **int86** to invoke the interrupt.

All of the EMM services return an error code in register AH. The functions in this chapter, however, do *not* simply pass this error code to the calling program, since they use their own set of error codes. Therefore, if an EMM service returns an error (indicated by a nonzero value in register AH), this error must be mapped to the correct error code for the module. This mapping is performed by the function **MapError**, which accepts an EMM error code and returns the appropriate module error code. Constants for all of the module error codes are defined in Figure 10.3, and the comments following the error codes give the corresponding EMM error values. Note that there are several module errors that do not have equivalent EMM errors. Also, there are more than twice as many EMM error codes as module error codes; to simplify the interface, the module eliminates error codes for conditions that should not occur when calling the EMM through the module. There is, however, a catchall code to cover unexpected error values: EMSERROR.

EmsPagesAvail

Using EmsPagesAvail

The prototype for **EmsPagesAvail** is

```
int EmsPagesAvail
    (void)
```

This function returns the current number of 16-kilobyte logical pages of expanded memory that are available for allocation. A program can call this function to determine whether a sufficient number of pages is available for its memory needs, and to gauge how many pages to allocate.

If **EmsPagesAvail** is successful, it returns the number of pages and sets **EmsError** to NOERROR. If an error is encountered, it returns –1 and sets **EmsError** to one of the following values:

NOTINSTALLED   Expanded memory is not installed.

SOFTERROR   Expanded memory manager software error.

HARDERROR   Expanded memory hardware error.

Note that a return value of 0 does not indicate an error, but simply means that all EMS pages have already been allocated.

The program in Figure 10.4 demonstrates the three functions that have been described so far: **EmsInstalled**, **EmsVersion**, and **EmsPagesAvail**. This program simply prints the current status of expanded memory installed in the machine, namely:

■ Whether expanded memory is installed.

■ If expanded memory is present, the major and minor version numbers of the expanded memory manager.

▌ The number of logical pages of expanded memory that are currently free.

Note that the call to each function in the expanded memory module tests for an error condition, and prints the appropriate error message before terminating. The messages corresponding to given error codes are obtained by calling the function **EmsErrorMsg**, described later in the chapter.

Figure 10.5 supplies a MAKE file, and Figure 10.6 a QuickC program list.

```c
#include <STDIO.H>
#include <PROCESS.H>

#include "EMS.H"

void main (void)
    {
    int Version;                    /* Stores version number.              */
    int Pages;                      /* Free EMS pages.                     */

    printf ("\nSTATUS OF LIM-EMS MEMORY\n\n");

    if (!EmsInstalled ())           /* Test if EMS installed.              */
        {
        printf ("Expanded memory not installed.\n");
        exit (1);
        }
    printf ("Expanded memory is installed.\n");

                                    /* Determine EMM version number.       */
    if ((Version = EmsVersion ()) == 0)
        {
        printf (EmsErrorMsg (EmsError));
        exit (1);
        }
                                    /* Format and print version number.    */
    printf ("EMM Version:  %1d.%1d\n",Version >> 4, Version & 0x000f);

                                    /* Determine number of free EMS pages. */
    if ((Pages = EmsPagesAvail ()) == -1)
        {
        printf (EmsErrorMsg (EmsError));
        exit (1);
        }
    printf ("EMS Pages Free:  %d\n",Pages);

    } /* end main */
```

Figure 10.4: EMSDEM01.C: A program that returns the status of expanded memory

```
EMSDEM01.OBJ : EMSDEM01.C EMS.H
    cl /c /W2 /Zp EMSDEM01.C

EMS.OBJ : EMS.C EMS.H
    cl /c /W2 /Zp EMS.C

EMSDEM01.EXE : EMSDEM01.OBJ EMS.OBJ
    link /NOI /NOD EMSDEM01+EMS,,NUL,SLIBCER;
```

Figure 10.5: EMSDEM01.M: A MAKE file for EMSDEM01.C

How EmsPagesAvail Works

EmsPagesAvail makes use of the EMM "get unallocated page count" service. This service has the following calling protocol:

EMM Function 3: Get Unallocated Page Count

Entry:

AH   42h

Return:

AH   Error code

BX   Number of expanded memory logical pages currently available for allocation

DX   Total number of expanded memory pages installed

Note that **EmsPagesAvail** returns only the number of unallocated pages returned in register BX, and discards the total number of memory pages returned in register DX.

```
EMSDEM01.C
EMS.C
```

Figure 10.6: A QuickC program list for preparing EMSDEM01.C

EmsAlloc and EmsFree

Using EmsAlloc and EmsFree

The function **EmsAlloc**, which has the prototype

```
char far *EmsAlloc
    (int Pages)
```

allocates the number of 16 kilobyte logical pages specified by the parameter **Pages**, and returns a **far** pointer to the base of the expanded memory page frame. This function is analogous to standard C library allocation functions such as **malloc**, except that it returns a **far** address in any memory model, and the size of the block is specified as the number of 16-kilobyte pages rather than the number of bytes. Another important difference between **EmsAlloc** and functions such as **malloc** is that you are not free to use the memory you have allocated until this memory is mapped onto the page frame using the function **EmsMap**, to be described next.

A program may call **EmsAlloc** only once (unless there has been an intermediate call to **EmsFree**). Typically, an application calls **EmsAlloc** once, at the beginning of the program, to allocate *all* expanded memory required, and then calls **EmsFree** once, at the end of the program, to free this memory. Note that this pattern differs from the usual procedure for using dynamic heap memory, in which functions such as **malloc** and **free** are called repeatedly throughout the course of the program.

If **EmsAlloc** is successful, it returns the **far** address of the base of the expanded memory page frame and sets **EmsError** to NOERROR. If an error occurs, it returns the value NULL (defined in STDIO.H and EMS.H) and sets **EmsError** to one of the following values:

NOTINSTALLED	Expanded memory is not installed.
SOFTERROR	Expanded memory manager software error.
HARDERROR	Expanded memory hardware error.
ALLOCATED	Expanded memory has already been allocated to this program.
NOHANDLES	No free EMM handles are available.
NOPAGES	Insufficient pages are available to fill the request.

The function **EmsFree** has the prototype

```
int EmsFree
        (void)
```

and frees all expanded memory that was allocated to the program with the last call to **EmsAlloc**. You should call this function before program termination since expanded memory pages are *not* automatically freed on program exit; if you do not call this function, the expanded memory pages allocated by your program will remain unavailable to other programs.

EmsFree assigns the error status to the variable **EmsError** and also directly returns the error status to the calling program. The following are the possible error status values:

NOERROR	The operation was successful.
NOTINSTALLED	Expanded memory is not installed.
SOFTERROR	Expanded memory manager software error.
HARDERROR	Expanded memory hardware error.
NOTALLOCATED	Expanded memory was not allocated to the program.
NORESTORE	**EmsSave** was called without a subsequent call to **EmsRestore** (explained later in the chapter).

The functions **EmsAlloc** and **EmsFree** are both demonstrated in Figure 10.7, described later in the chapter.

How EmsAlloc and EmsFree Work

After determining whether expanded memory is installed, **EmsAlloc** tests the internal flag **Allocated** to verify that expanded memory has not already been allocated by the calling program. When the expanded memory manager allocates a set of logical pages, it returns a handle that is used to refer to this set of pages in subsequent service requests. The functions in this chapter store this handle internally (in the variable **Handle**) to simplify the interface to the calling program. Although the EMM allows a single program to allocate pages more than once, and therefore hold multiple handles, the functions presented here further simplify the interface by allowing the program to allocate expanded memory only *once*. Therefore, the module needs to store only a single handle. (This is not a severe constraint, since it is best to allocate all required expanded memory at the beginning of a program; one reason for this procedure is that a memory resident interrupt handler or child process could gain control while your program is running and steal needed expanded memory.)

When **EmsAlloc** successfully allocates expanded memory, it sets **Allocated** to 1; when **EmsFree** subsequently frees this memory, it resets **Allocated** back to 0. The **Allocated** flag serves two purposes: first, other functions in the module can use this flag as an indication that the variable **Handle** currently holds a valid EMM handle. Second, the flag is used to prevent an attempt to allocate memory more than once, without intermediate calls to **EmsFree**.

EmsAlloc next performs the actual expanded memory allocation through the EMM "allocate pages" service. This service has the following calling protocol:

EMM Function 4: Allocate Pages

Entry:

AH   43h

BX   Number of 16-kilobyte pages to allocate

Return:

AH   Error code

DX   EMM handle

On successful return from this service, **EmsAlloc** saves the EMM handle in the variable **Handle**, and sets the flag **Allocated** to 1. Next, the segment address of the page frame is obtained by invoking the EMM "get page frame address" service. This service is called as follows:

EMM Function 2: Get Page Frame Address

Entry:

AH   41h

Return:

AH   Error code

BX   Segment address of the page frame

Finally, **EmsAlloc** uses the Microsoft C macros FP_SEG and FP_OFF to assign the **far** address of the base of the page frame to **FarPtrCh**, combining the segment value returned in BX with an offset of 0. The resulting value in **FarPtrCh** is then returned to the calling program.

The function **EmsFree** first checks that the expanded memory manager is installed, and then tests the flag **Allocated** to verify that expanded memory has been allocated to the program. The memory is then released by calling the EMM "deallocate pages" service, which has the following protocol:

> **EMM Function 9: Deallocate Pages**
>
> **Entry:**
>
> AH   45h
>
> DX   EMM handle
>
> **Return:**
>
> AH   Error code

Once the expanded memory has been successfully released, **EmsFree** resets the **Allocated** flag to 0, and returns the code NOERROR.

EmsMap

Using EmsMap

The **EmsMap** function has the prototype

```
int EmsMap
      (int Page0,
       int Page1,
       int Page2,
       int Page3)
```

This function maps the logical pages specified by the four parameters onto the four physical pages. The logical page given by **Page0** is mapped onto physical page 0, the logical page given by **Page1** is mapped onto physical page 1, and so on. Note that the logical pages that have been allocated to your program are numbered in sequence beginning with 0. If any of the parameters is assigned a value of −1, then the mapping for the corresponding physical page is left unchanged.

You must call **EmsMap** *after* allocating pages through **EmsAlloc** but *before* writing data to these pages. You can also call this function any time you want to change the current mapping, to access other areas of expanded memory. Since an application typically allocates more than four logical pages, expanded memory is normally accessed through a cycle of mapping, reading or writing data, and then remapping. **EmsMap** is demonstrated in the program of Figure 10.7, described later in the chapter.

EmsMap assigns the error status to **EmsError** and also returns it directly to the calling program. The possible error status values for this function are the following:

NOERROR	The operation was successful.
NOTINSTALLED	Expanded memory is not installed.
SOFTERROR	Expanded memory manager software error.
HARDERROR	Expanded memory hardware error.
NOTALLOCATED	Expanded memory was not allocated to the program.
RANGE	The logical page is out of the range allocated to the program.

How EmsMap Works

EmsMap first calls **EmsInstalled** to verify that the expanded memory manager is installed, and then examines the **Allocated** flag to make sure that expanded memory has been properly allocated and that the handle value stored in the global variable **Handle** is valid. It then invokes the EMM "map handle pages" service for each of the four parameters that does not equal −1. This service is requested as follows:

EMM Function 5: Map/Unmap Handle Pages

Entry:

AH	44h
AL	Physical page number
BX	Logical page number
DX	EMM handle

Return:

AH	Error code

Note that in EMS version 4.0 this service also allows *unmapping* a given physical page. A physical page is unmapped by mapping it to logical page number FFFFh. Once a page is unmapped, then none of your data in expanded memory can be accessed through that page. Unmapping all four physical pages might be a good precaution before calling another program, to insure the integrity of your data. Page unmapping is not supported by the module, but might be a useful enhancement (before using this feature, call **EmsVersion** to make sure version 4.0 is installed).

EmsSave and EmsRestore

Using EmsSave and EmsRestore

The function **EmsSave** has the prototype

```
int EmsSave
    (void)
```

This function saves the current contents of the *page mapping registers*. The page mapping registers are a hardware feature of the expanded memory board for holding the current page mapping. If your program is a memory resident utility, device driver, or other program that can receive control while another process is running and that uses expanded memory, you should call **EmsSave** to save the page mapping registers. The reason for saving the current mapping is that your program could interrupt another application that is using expanded memory, and you must preserve the page register contents belonging to the interrupted program. Note that **EmsSave** must be called *after* allocating pages through **EmsAlloc**, but *before* mapping expanded memory pages via **EmsMap**. You must then call **EmsRestore** to restore the saved contents of the page mapping registers before your application terminates *and* before freeing expanded memory through **EmsFree**. If you forget to call **EmsRestore**, **EmsFree** will return the error code NORESTORE. **EmsRestore** has the prototype

```
int EmsRestore
    (void)
```

EmsSave returns the error status to the calling program and also sets the global variable **EmsError**. The following are the possible error status values:

NOERROR	The operation was successful.
NOTINSTALLED	Expanded memory is not installed.
SOFTERROR	Expanded memory manager software error.
HARDERROR	Expanded memory hardware error.
NOTALLOCATED	Expanded memory was not allocated to the program.
NOSAVEAREA	There is no room in the save area to store the state of the page mapping registers.
SAVECALLED	Indicates an attempt to call **EmsSave** more than once.

The function **EmsRestore** also returns the error status to the calling program as well as assigning it to **EmsError**. The following are the possible error status values generated by **EmsRestore**:

NOERROR	The operation was successful.
NOTINSTALLED	Expanded memory is not installed.
SOFTERROR	Expanded memory manager software error.
HARDERROR	Expanded memory hardware error.
NOTALLOCATED	Expanded memory was not allocated to the program.
NOSAVE	**EmsRestore** called without a prior call to **EmsSave**.

How EmsSave and EmsRestore Work

The functions **EmsSave** and **EmsRestore** both begin by verifying that the expanded memory manager is installed, and that expanded memory pages have been allocated (the EMM allocation service must be called before calling **EmsSave**, since **EmsSave** requires a valid EMM handle).

EmsSave invokes the EMM "save page map" service, which is called through the following protocol:

EMM Function 8: Save Page Map

Entry:

AH   47h

DX   EMM handle

Return:

AH   Error code

EmsRestore employs the EMM "restore page map" service, which is invoked as follows:

EMM Function 9: Restore Page Map

Entry:

AH   48h

DX   EMM Handle

Return:

AH   Error code

EmsErrorMsg

Using EmsErrorMsg

EmsErrorMsg has the prototype

```
char *EmsErrorMsg
        (int ErrorNum)
```

This function returns a pointer to a string containing an error message; the error message corresponds to the error number specified by the parameter **ErrorNum**. Since the expanded memory module uses 16 error codes numbered from 0 to 15, **ErrorNum** should be a value within this range. For example, the following lines of code will print an appropriate error message and terminate the program if the function **EmsAlloc** fails:

```
if ((PageFramePtr = EmsAlloc (PagesRequired)) = =
    NULL)
```

```
{
printf (EmsErrorMsg (EmsError));
exit (1);
}
```

If you pass **EmsErrorMsg** an invalid error number, it returns the value NULL.

How
EmsErrorMsg
Works

EmsErrorMsg first checks that the value of the parameter **ErrorNum** is within the valid range, and then returns the pointer to the appropriate error message from the array **MessageTable**.

USING EXPANDED MEMORY FROM A MICROSOFT C PROGRAM

The program in Figure 10.7 demonstrates most of the functions presented in this chapter. Although this program performs only a trivial task, it illustrates a typical sequence of function calls for allocating and managing expanded memory from a C program. The program performs the following series of actions:

1. **EmsInstalled** is called to determine whether expanded memory is installed. If expanded memory is not present, the program terminates with an appropriate error message.

2. **EmsAlloc** is called to allocate four logical pages of expanded memory, and the pointer to the base of the page frame is stored in the variable **PageFrame**. This demonstration program *requires* four pages of expanded memory, and therefore it terminates if this request cannot be filled. A program that could use a variable amount of expanded memory might first call **EmsPagesAvail**, and then base its allocation request upon the number of pages actually available.

3. The program maps the four logical pages it has allocated onto the four physical pages of the page frame, by calling the function **EmsMap**. Note that logical page 0 is mapped onto physical page 0, logical page 1 onto physical page 1, and so on.

4. The program can now access expanded memory. It writes an identifying string to the beginning of each of the four logical pages, using the standard C library function **strcpy**. Note that the pointer used to access expanded memory, **PageFrame**, must be a **far** pointer; also, the C library functions such as **strcpy** and **printf** must be able to accept **far** pointers to the data strings they manipulate. Therefore *you must compile the program using a large data model* (that is, the compact, large, or huge memory model). The MAKE file in Figure 10.8 specifies the large model; if you are using QuickC version 1.0, you must compile the program from the command line as described later in this section.

5. **EmsMap** is called again, this time reversing the order of the four logical pages within the page frame.

6. The identifying strings are printed from the beginning of each physical page, demonstrating that the logical pages have successfully been reordered in memory through the second mapping.

7. Finally, **EmsFree** is called before program termination so that the expanded memory used by the program is made available to subsequent applications.

Figure 10.8 supplies the usual MAKE file; as mentioned previously in this section, this file specifies the *large* memory model. Therefore, if the object file EMS.OBJ—prepared under another memory model—is present on your disk, it should be deleted. Also, since the program requires a large data model, you cannot prepare it in the QuickC version 1.0 integrated environment (which uses the medium memory model). Rather, if you want to use this version of QuickC, you should prepare the program using the MAKE file of Figure 10.8, substituting each occurrence of **cl** with **qcl**. If you are preparing the program within the integrated environment of QuickC version 2.0 or later, be sure to specify the compact, large, or huge memory model (set through the Options/Make/Compiler Flags/Memory Model menu item). Figure 10.9 provides a list which you can use with QuickC version 2.0 or later.

```
#include <STDIO.H>
#include <PROCESS.H>
#include <STRING.H>

#include "EMS.H"

#define PAGE0 0                      /* Offsets of physical pages in EMS    */
#define PAGE1 0x4000                 /* page frame.                         */
#define PAGE2 0x8000
#define PAGE3 0xC000

void main ()
    {
    char *PageFrame;                 /* Far pointer to access EMS page frame. */

/*** (1)   Test whether expanded memory is installed ************************/

    if (!EmsInstalled)
        {
        printf ("Expanded memory not installed.\n");
        exit (1);
        }

/*** (2)   Allocate expanded memory logical pages ***************************/

    if ((PageFrame = EmsAlloc (4)) == NULL)
        {                                   /* Error allocating pages.      */
        printf (EmsErrorMsg (EmsError));
        exit (1);
        }

/*** (3)   Map logical pages onto physical pages ***************************/

    if (EmsMap (0,1,2,3))
        {                                   /* Mapping error.               */
        printf ("EmsMap: %s\n",EmsErrorMsg (EmsError));
        exit (1);
        }

/*** (4)   Access expanded memory ******************************************/

    strcpy (PageFrame+PAGE0, "Logical page 0\n");   /* Label the 4 logical  */
    strcpy (PageFrame+PAGE1, "Logical page 1\n");   /* pages by writing a   */
    strcpy (PageFrame+PAGE2, "Logical page 2\n");   /* string to the start  */
    strcpy (PageFrame+PAGE3, "Logical page 3\n");   /* of each page.        */

/*** (5)   Remap pages *****************************************************/

    if (EmsMap (3,2,1,0))                   /* Reverse the mapping.         */
        {                                   /* Mapping error.               */
        printf ("EmsMap: %s\n",EmsErrorMsg (EmsError));
        exit (1);
        }
```

Figure 10.7: EMSDEM02.C: A program demonstrating the use of expanded memory from a
Microsoft C program

```
/*** (6)   Access expanded memory *********************************************/

        printf (PageFrame+PAGE0);     /* Print strings from the 4 physical   */
        printf (PageFrame+PAGE1);     /* pages, demonstrating the reversal   */
        printf (PageFrame+PAGE2);     /* of the mapping.                     */
        printf (PageFrame+PAGE3);

/*** (7)   Free expanded memory *********************************************/

        if (EmsFree ())
            {                                    /* Error freeing memory.    */
            printf ("EmsFree:  %s\n",EmsErrorMsg (EmsError));
            exit (1);
            }

        } /* end main */
```

Figure 10.7: EMSDEM02.C: A program demonstrating the use of expanded memory from a
Microsoft C program (continued)

```
EMSDEM02.OBJ : EMSDEM02.C EMS.H
      cl /c /W2 /AL /Zp EMSDEM02.C

EMS.OBJ : EMS.C EMS.H
      cl /c /W2 /AL /Zp EMS.C

EMSDEM02.EXE : EMSDEM02.OBJ EMS.OBJ
      link /NOI /NOD EMSDEM02+EMS,,NUL,LLIBCER;
```

Figure 10.8: EMSDEM02.M: A MAKE file for preparing EMSDEM02.C

```
EMSDEM02.C
EMS.C
```

Figure 10.9: EMSDEMO2.TXT: A program list for preparing EMSDEMO2.C
with QuickC version 2.0 or later

The example program typifies expanded memory use by a transient application. A memory resident application should use a slightly different technique. The salient differences in procedure are as follows:

▌ All required expanded memory should be allocated when the program is installed, not when it is activated through the hotkey.

▌ Each time the memory resident code is activated, it should first save the current expanded memory mapping by calling **EmsSave**, perform the required mapping of its own pages, and then call **EmsRestore** before it returns control to the interrupted program.

▌ If the memory resident program is released from memory, it should first free all expanded memory it has been allocated.

A Mouse Interface

This chapter presents a complete set of functions for managing a mouse. These functions can be called from a Microsoft C program, and allow you to add a full mouse interface to your application. To use the functions, you must have a Microsoft, Logitech, or compatible mouse, and you must have installed the driver that is provided with the mouse hardware. (The Microsoft mouse driver, for example, is installed by running the program MOUSE.COM, which is furnished with the mouse.) You do *not*, however, need any additional software tools (such as the software utilities and function libraries included with the *Microsoft Mouse Programmer's Reference Guide*—see the Bibliography).

The Mouse Functions

The functions in this chapter allow you to perform the following tasks:

- Determine whether a mouse driver is installed (**MouInstalled**).

- Initialize the mouse driver and determine the number of buttons on the mouse (**MouReset**).

- Display or hide the mouse pointer (**MouShowPointer, MouHidePointer**).

- Read the current state of the mouse buttons and the position of the mouse pointer on the screen (**MouGetButtons**).

- Set the position of the mouse pointer on the screen (**MouSetPointer**).

- Ascertain the number of times a given mouse button has been pressed or released, and the position of the mouse pointer when the button was pressed or released (**MouGetButtonPress, MouGetButtonRelease**).

- Define an area on the screen inside of which the mouse pointer is confined (**MouSetPointerHorizArea, MouSetPointerVertArea**).

- Define the mouse pointer used in graphics or text mode (**MouSetGraphPointer, MouSetTextPointer**).

- Determine the distance the mouse has been moved on the desk surface (**MouGetMickeys**).

- Install an interrupt handler that is invoked when any one of a specified set of mouse events occurs (**MouSetIntHandler**).

- Set the distance the mouse pointer moves on the screen for a given amount of movement of the mouse on the desk surface (**MouSetRatio**).

- Save and restore the complete existing mouse state (**MouGet-Storage, MouSaveState, MouRestoreState**).

Note that the C interface presented in this chapter provides access to almost all of the services offered by the standard Microsoft mouse driver. For information on additional services available under a specific mouse driver, see the technical documentation supplied by the vendor of the mouse (the Microsoft mouse driver is documented in the *Microsoft Mouse Programmer's Reference Guide,* cited in the Bibliography).

The collection of mouse functions is contained in the C source file listed in Figure 11.1; the header file you must include in your program to call these functions is listed in Figure 11.2.

MouInstalled

Using MouInstalled

The function **MouInstalled** has the prototype

```
int MouInstalled
    (void)
```

It returns a nonzero value if a mouse driver is installed, or zero if a mouse driver is not installed. You should call this function before calling any of the other **Mou** functions to make sure that a mouse driver is installed (all the other functions in this module depend upon the mouse driver). Note that all of the functions described subsequently in this chapter return an error code if a mouse driver is not installed; **Mou-Installed**, however, allows you to explicitly test for the presence of a mouse driver without performing any other actions. As you will see, all of the example programs presented in this chapter make a call to **Mou-Installed** at the beginning of the code, and terminate the program if a mouse driver is not present.

```
#include <DOS.H>

#include "MOU.H"

#pragma check_stack (off)       /* Turn off stack checks so that functions  */
                                /* can be called from interrupt routines.   */

int MouInstalled (void)
/*
     This function returns TRUE if a mouse driver is installed, and FALSE
     if no driver is installed.  You must call this function to make sure that
     a mouse driver is installed before calling any other functions in the
     Mou module.
*/
     {
     unsigned char far *FarPtrMouDriver;    /* Points to mouse driver.      */

     /* Get contents of the mouse interrupt vector (number 0x33).           */
     FarPtrMouDriver = (unsigned char far *)_dos_getvect (0x33);

     /* If int 33 vector is 0 or points to an IRET instruction (0xcf), then */
     /* mouse driver is not installed.                                      */
     if (FarPtrMouDriver == 0 || *FarPtrMouDriver == 0xcf)
          return (0);
     else
          return (1);

     } /* end MouInstalled */


int MouReset (int *NumButtons)
/*
     This function resets the mouse driver to the set of default values, and
     assigns the number of mouse buttons to *NumButtons.  The function
     returns zero if successful, or a nonzero value if the mouse hardware or
     software are not properly installed.  You should call this function at
     the beginning of your program to set the mouse to a known state.
*/
     {
     union REGS Reg;

     if (!MouInstalled ())          /* Test to make sure that mouse is    */
          return (1);               /* installed.                         */

     Reg.x.ax = 0;                  /* Mouse reset and status function.   */
     int86 (0x33,&Reg,&Reg);        /* Invoke mouse services.             */

     *NumButtons = Reg.x.bx;        /* BX contains the number of buttons. */

     return (Reg.x.ax ? 0 : 1);     /* AX = -1 if mouse properly installed, */
                                    /* or 0 if mouse NOT installed.         */

     } /* end MouReset */
```

Figure 11.1: MOU.C: The mouse management functions

```
int MouShowPointer (void)
/*
    This function increments the internal pointer flag;  if this flag becomes
    0, the mouse pointer is displayed on the screen.  The function returns
    zero if successful, or a nonzero value if the mouse driver is not
    installed.
*/
    {
    union REGS Reg;
    if (!MouInstalled ())          /* Test to make sure that mouse is    */
        return (1);                /* installed.                         */

    Reg.x.ax = 1;                  /* Show mouse pointer function.       */
    int86 (0x33,&Reg,&Reg);        /* Invoke mouse services.             */

    return (0);

    } /* end MouShowPointer */

int MouHidePointer (void)
/*
    This function decrements the internal pointer flag and makes the pointer
    invisible on the screen.  The function returns zero if successful, or a
    nonzero value if the mouse driver is not installed.
*/
    {
    union REGS Reg;

    if (!MouInstalled ())          /* Test to make sure that mouse is    */
        return (1);                /* installed.                         */

    Reg.x.ax = 2;                  /* Hide mouse pointer function.       */
    int86 (0x33,&Reg,&Reg);        /* Invokes mouse services.            */

    return (0);

    } /* end MouHidePointer */


int MouGetButtons (int *ButtonStatus, int *PointerCol, int *PointerRow)
/*
    This function assigns the status of the mouse buttons to *ButtonStatus,
    the column number of the mouse pointer to *PointerCol, and the row number
    to *PointerRow.  The function returns zero if successful, or a nonzero
    value if the mouse driver is not installed.
*/
    {
    union REGS Reg;

    if (!MouInstalled ())          /* Test to make sure that mouse is    */
        return (1);                /* installed.                         */

    Reg.x.ax = 3;                  /* Get button status and pointer      */
                                   /* position function.                 */
    int86 (0x33,&Reg,&Reg);        /* Invokes mouse services.            */

    *ButtonStatus = Reg.x.bx;      /* BX contains button status.         */
    *PointerCol = Reg.x.cx;        /* CX contains pointer column.        */
    *PointerRow = Reg.x.dx;        /* DX contains pointer row.           */
```

Figure 11.1: MOU.C: The mouse management functions (continued)

```
            return (0);

            } /* end MouGetButtons */
    int MouSetPointer (int PointerCol, int PointerRow)
    /*
            This function places the mouse pointer at the column and row position
            specified by PointerCol and PointerRow.  The function returns
            zero if successful, or a nonzero value if the mouse driver is not
            installed.
    */
            {
            union REGS Reg;

            if (!MouInstalled ())            /* Test to make sure that mouse is     */
                return (1);                  /* installed.                          */

            Reg.x.ax = 4;                    /* Set pointer function.               */
            Reg.x.cx = PointerCol;           /* CX specifies horizontal position.   */
            Reg.x.dx = PointerRow;           /* DX specifies vertical position.     */
            int86 (0x33,&Reg,&Reg);          /* Invokes mouse services.             */

            return (0);

            } /* end MouSetPointer */


    int MouGetButtonPress (int Button,int *ButtonStatus,int *NumberPresses,
                           int *PointerCol, int *PointerRow)
    /*
            This function assigns *NumberPresses the number of times the button
            specified by Button (0 is the left button and 1 the right button) has
            been pressed since the last time MouGetButtonPress was called.  It also
            assigns the column and row position of the specified button -- the last
            time it was pressed -- to *PointerCol and *PointerRow.  Finally, the
            function assigns *ButtonStatus the current status of all buttons.  The
            function returns zero if successful, or a nonzero value if the mouse
            driver is not installed.
    */
            {
            union REGS Reg;

            if (!MouInstalled ())            /* Test to make sure that mouse is     */
                return (1);                  /* installed.                          */
            Reg.x.ax = 5;                    /* Get button press information service.*/
            Reg.x.bx = Button;               /* BX specifies the button.            */
            int86 (0x33,&Reg,&Reg);          /* Invokes mouse services.             */

            *ButtonStatus = Reg.x.ax;        /* AX contains the button status.      */
            *NumberPresses = Reg.x.bx;       /* BX contains the number of presses.  */
            *PointerCol = Reg.x.cx;          /* CS contains the pointer column.     */
            *PointerRow = Reg.x.dx;          /* DX contains the pointer row.        */

            return (0);

            } /* end MouGetButtonPress */
```

Figure 11.1: MOU.C: The mouse management functions (continued)

```
int MouGetButtonRelease (int Button,int *ButtonStatus,int *NumberReleases,
                         int *PointerCol, int *PointerRow)
/*
    This function assigns *NumberReleases the number of times the button
    specified by Button (0 is the left button and 1 the right button) has
    been released since the last time MouGetButtonRelease was called.  It
    also assigns the column and row position of the specified button -- the
    last time it was released -- to *PointerCol and *PointerRow.  Finally,
    the function assigns *ButtonStatus the current status of all buttons.
    The function returns zero if successful, or a nonzero value if the mouse
    driver is not installed.
*/
    {
    union REGS Reg;

    if (!MouInstalled ())          /* Test to make sure that mouse is     */
        return (1);                /* installed.                          */

    Reg.x.ax = 6;                  /* Get button release info. service.   */
    Reg.x.bx = Button;             /* BX specifies the button.            */
    int86 (0x33,&Reg,&Reg);        /* Invokes mouse services.             */

    *ButtonStatus = Reg.x.ax;      /* AX contains the button status.      */
    *NumberReleases = Reg.x.bx;    /* BX contains the number of releases.  */
    *PointerCol = Reg.x.cx;        /* CS contains the pointer column.     */
    *PointerRow = Reg.x.dx;        /* DX contains the pointer row.        */

    return (0);

    } /* end MouGetButtonRelease */


int MouSetPointerHorizArea (int MinCol, int MaxCol)
/*
    This function sets the minimum horizontal pointer coordinate to MinCol,
    and the maximum horizontal coordinate to MaxCol.  The function returns
    zero if successful, or a nonzero value if the mouse driver is not
    installed.
*/
    {
    union REGS Reg;

    if (!MouInstalled ())          /* Test to make sure that mouse is     */
        return (1);                /* installed.                          */

    Reg.x.ax = 7;                  /* Set horizontal pointer range function*/
    Reg.x.cx = MinCol;             /* CX specifies the minimum range value.*/
    Reg.x.dx = MaxCol;             /* DX specifies the maximum range value.*/
    int86 (0x33,&Reg,&Reg);        /* Invokes mouse services.             */

    return (0);

    } /* end MouSetPointerHorizArea */
```

Figure 11.1: MOU.C: The mouse management functions (continued)

```
    int MouSetPointerVertArea (int MinRow, int MaxRow)
    /*
        This function sets the minimum vertical pointer coordinate to MinRow,
        and the maximum vertical coordinate to MaxRow.  The function returns
        zero if successful, or a nonzero value if the mouse driver is not
        installed.
    */
        {
        union REGS Reg;

        if (!MouInstalled ())         /* Test to make sure that mouse is    */
            return (1);               /* installed.                         */

        Reg.x.ax = 8;                 /* Set vertical pointer range function. */
        Reg.x.cx = MinRow;            /* CX specifies the minimum range value.*/
        Reg.x.dx = MaxRow;            /* DX specifies the maximum range value.*/
        int86 (0x33,&Reg,&Reg);       /* Invokes mouse services.            */

        return (0);

        } /* end MouSetPointerVertArea */


    int MouSetGraphPointer (int HotSpotHoriz, int HotSpotVert,
                            unsigned far *FarPtrMasks)
    /*
        This function causes the mouse driver to use the graphics pointer
        specified by the bit masks *FarPtrMasks, with the hotspot given by the
        horizontal and vertical coordinates HotSpotHoriz and HotSpotVert.  The
        function returns zero if successful, or a nonzero value if the mouse
        driver is not installed.
    */
        {
        union REGS Reg;
        struct SREGS SReg;

        if (!MouInstalled ())         /* Test to make sure that mouse is    */
            return (1);               /* installed.                         */

        Reg.x.ax = 9;                 /* Set graphics pointer function.     */
        Reg.x.bx = HotSpotHoriz;      /* BX specifies horizontal hotspot coord*/
        Reg.x.cx = HotSpotVert;       /* CX specifies vertical hotspot coord. */
        Reg.x.dx = FP_OFF (FarPtrMasks); /* DX specifies offset of masks.   */
        SReg.es = FP_SEG (FarPtrMasks);  /* ES specifies segment of masks.  */
        int86x (0x33,&Reg,&Reg,&SReg); /* Invokes mouse services.           */

        return (0);

        } /* end MouSetGraphPointer */


    int MouSetTextPointer (int PointerType, int SMaskScanStart,
                           int PMaskScanStop)
    /*
        This function selects the text mouse pointer type according to the value
        passed in PointerType (0 is the software pointer, and 1 is the hardware
        cursor).  If the software pointer is selected, SMaskScanStart and
        PMaskScanStop give the screen mask and the pointer mask;  if the
```

Figure 11.1: MOU.C: The mouse management functions (continued)

```
                   hardware cursor is chosen, SMaskScanStart and PMaskScanStop give the
                   start and stop scan lines used to form the cursor.  The function returns
                   zero if successful, or a nonzero value if the mouse driver is not
                   installed.
      */
               {
               union REGS Reg;

               if (!MouInstalled ())        /* Test to make sure that mouse is     */
                  return (1);               /* installed.                          */

               Reg.x.ax = 10;               /* Set text pointer function.          */
               Reg.x.bx = PointerType;      /* BX specifies the pointer type.      */
               Reg.x.cx = SMaskScanStart;   /* CX specifies the screen mask or     */
                                            /* starting scan line.                 */
               Reg.x.dx = PMaskScanStop;    /* DX specifies the pointer mask or    */
                                            /* stoping scan line.                  */
               int86 (0x33,&Reg,&Reg);      /* Invokes mouse services.             */

               return (0);

               } /* end MouSetTextPointer */


      int MouGetMickeys (int *HorizCount, int *VertCount)
      /*
               This function assigns *HorizCount and *VertCount the number of mickeys
               the mouse has moved in the horizontal and vertical directions since the
               last time it was called.  The function returns zero if successful, or a
               nonzero value if the mouse driver is not installed.
      */
               {
               union REGS Reg;

               if (!MouInstalled ())        /* Test to make sure that mouse is     */
                  return (1);               /* installed.                          */
               Reg.x.ax = 11;               /* Read mouse motion function.         */
               int86 (0x33,&Reg,&Reg);      /* Invokes mouse services.             */

               *HorizCount = Reg.x.cx;      /* CX contains the horizontal count.   */
               *VertCount = Reg.x.dx;       /* DX contains the vertical count.      */

               return (0);

               } /* end MouGetMickeys */


      int MouSetIntHandler (int CallMask, void (far *FarPtrHandler)(void))
      /*
               This function installs the function *PtrHandler so that it will be called
               each time an event specified by CallMask occurs.  The function returns
               zero if successful, or a nonzero value if the mouse driver is not
               installed.
      */
               {
               union REGS Reg;
               struct SREGS SReg;
```

Figure 11.1: MOU.C: The mouse management functions (continued)

```
            if (!MouInstalled ())          /* Test to make sure that mouse is    */
                return (1);                 /* installed.                         */

            Reg.x.ax = 12;                  /* Set interrupt subroutine function. */
            Reg.x.cx = CallMask;            /* CX specifies the call mask.        */
            Reg.x.dx = FP_OFF (FarPtrHandler);  /* DX specifies routine offset.  */
            SReg.es  = FP_SEG (FarPtrHandler);  /* ES specifies routine segment. */

            int86x (0x33,&Reg,&Reg,&SReg);  /* Invokes mouse services.           */

            return (0);

            } /* end MouSetIntHandler */


    int MouSetRatio (int HorizRatio, int VertRatio)
    /*
            This function sets the horizontal and vertical ratios of mickeys to
            pixels to the values HorizRatio and VertRatio.  The function returns
            zero if successful, or a nonzero value if the mouse driver is not
            installed.
    */
            {
            union REGS Reg;

            if (!MouInstalled ())          /* Test to make sure that mouse is    */
                return (1);                 /* installed.                         */
            Reg.x.ax = 15;                  /* Set mickey/pixel ratio function.   */
            Reg.x.cx = HorizRatio;          /* CX specfies horizontal ratio.      */
            Reg.x.dx = VertRatio;           /* DX specifies vertical ratio.       */

            int86 (0x33,&Reg,&Reg);         /* Invokes mouse services.            */
            return (0);

            } /* end MouSetRatio */


    int MouGetStorage (int *BufferSize)
    /*
            This function assigns *BufferSize the size of the buffer required to
            store the current state of the mouse driver.  The function returns zero
            if successful, or a nonzero value if the mouse driver is not installed.
    */
            {
            union REGS Reg;

            if (!MouInstalled ())          /* Test to make sure that mouse is    */
                return (1);                 /* installed.                         */

            Reg.x.ax = 21;                  /* Get storage requirements function. */
            int86 (0x33,&Reg,&Reg);         /* Invokes mouse services.            */

            *BufferSize = Reg.x.bx;         /* BX contains storage size in bytes. */

            return (0);

            } /* end MouGetStorage */
```

Figure 11.1: MOU.C: The mouse management functions (continued)

```
int MouSaveState (unsigned char far *FarPtrBuffer)
/*
    This function saves the current state of the mouse driver in the buffer
    *FarPtrBuffer.  The function returns zero if successful, or a nonzero
    value if the mouse driver is not installed.
*/
    {
    union REGS Reg;
    struct SREGS SReg;

    if (!MouInstalled ())            /* Test to make sure that mouse is   */
        return (1);                  /* installed.                        */

    Reg.x.ax = 22;                   /* Save mouse state function.        */
                                     /* ES:DX specifies address of buffer. */
    Reg.x.dx = FP_OFF (FarPtrBuffer);
    SReg.es = FP_SEG (FarPtrBuffer);

    int86x (0x33,&Reg,&Reg,&SReg); /* Invokes mouse services.             */

    return (0);

    } /* end MouSaveState */


int MouRestoreState (unsigned char far *FarPtrBuffer)
/*
    This function restores the state of the mouse driver formerly saved in
    the buffer *FarPtrBuffer through the MouSaveState function.  The function
    returns zero if successful, or a nonzero value if the mouse driver is
    not installed.
*/
    {
    union REGS Reg;
    struct SREGS SReg;

    if (!MouInstalled ())            /* Test to make sure that mouse is   */
        return (1);                  /* installed.                        */

    Reg.x.ax = 23;                   /* Restore mouse state function.     */
                                     /* ES:DX specifies address of buffer. */
    Reg.x.dx = FP_OFF (FarPtrBuffer);
    SReg.es = FP_SEG (FarPtrBuffer);

    int86x (0x33,&Reg,&Reg,&SReg); /* Invokes mouse services.             */

    return (0);

    } /* end MouRestoreState */
```

Figure 11.1: MOU.C: The mouse management functions (continued)

```
int MouInstalled (void);
int MouReset (int *NumButtons);
int MouShowPointer (void);
int MouHidePointer (void);
int MouGetButtons (int *ButtonStatus, int *PointerCol, int *PointerRow);
int MouSetPointer (int PointerCol, int PointerRow);
int MouGetButtonPress (int Button,int *ButtonStatus,int *NumberPresses,
                       int *PointerCol, int *PointerRow);
int MouGetButtonRelease (int Button,int *ButtonStatus,int *NumberReleases,
                         int *PointerCol, int *PointerRow);
int MouSetPointerHorizArea (int Minimum, int Maximum);
int MouSetPointerVertArea (int Minimum, int Maximum);
int MouSetGraphPointer (int HotSpotHoriz, int HotSpotVert,
                        unsigned far *PrtMasks);
int MouSetTextPointer (int PointerType, int ScrMaskScanStart,
                       int ScrMaskScanStop);
int MouGetMickeys (int *HorizCount, int *VertCount);
int MouSetIntHandler (int CallMask, void (far *FarPtrHandler)(void));
int MouSetRatio (int HorizRatio, int VertRatio);
int MouGetStorage (int *BufferSize);
int MouSaveState (unsigned char far *FarPtrBuffer);
int MouRestoreState (unsigned char far *FarPtrBuffer);

#define LEFTBUTTONDOWN    0x0001
#define RIGHTBUTTONDOWN   0x0002
#define CENTERBUTTONDOWN  0x0004
```

Figure 11.2: MOU.H: The header file you must include in your program to call the functions in MOU.C

How MouInstalled Works

MouInstalled is the only function in the mouse module that does not directly call the mouse driver. All of the other functions in the module work by invoking interrupt 33h, which the mouse driver sets at installation time to point to its entry routine. If interrupt vector 33h is 0, or if it points to a simple interrupt return instruction (IRET), a mouse driver has not been installed.

Accordingly, **MouInstalled** uses the Microsoft C function **_dos_getvect** to obtain the contents of interrupt vector 33h. If the value stored in this vector is 0, *or* if the vector points to a simple IRET instruction (which has the numeric value 0xcf), then **MouInstalled** returns 0 to indicate that a mouse driver is not installed; otherwise, it returns 1, indicating that a mouse driver is present.

MouReset

Using MouReset

MouReset has the prototype

```
int MouReset
    (int *NumButtons)
```

This function initializes the mouse driver and assigns the number of mouse buttons to the variable pointed to by the parameter **Num-Buttons**. (Many of the functions in this module return values by assigning them to variables whose addresses are passed as parameters; throughout the remainder of the discussion, expressions such as "the variable pointed to by the parameter **NumButtons**" will be replaced with the succinct C expression, in this case "***NumButtons**.") If a Microsoft mouse is installed, ***NumButtons** should receive the value 2, and if a Logitech mouse is present, it should be assigned 3.

MouReset returns zero if successful, and a nonzero value if a mouse driver is not properly installed.

Initializing the mouse driver sets all parameters to their default values; these values are listed in Table 11.1. Note that for each default value, this table also gives the function within the chapter that is used to alter the value. The meaning of each value is explained in the section that presents the corresponding function.

You should call **MouReset** at the beginning of your application, to set the mouse driver to a known state before using the mouse and adjusting the mouse parameters to suit your program. You should also call **MouReset** immediately before your application terminates; this final call to **MouReset** is a convenient method for removing the mouse pointer from the screen, and for deactivating a mouse interrupt handler installed by **MouSetIntHandler** (described later in the chapter). **MouReset** is demonstrated in the example program of Figure 11.3 (described later), as well as in the remaining example programs given in this chapter.

Note that when a memory resident program becomes active, it may interrupt a foreground application that is currently using the mouse. Therefore, the memory resident code should save the existing mouse state before calling **MouReset**, and it should restore the former state

Table 11.1: The default mouse parameters assigned by **MouReset**

Mouse Parameter	Default Value Set by MouReset
Interrupt call mask	0 (see **MouSetIntHandler**)
Mickey/pixel ratio, horizontal	8 : 8 (see **MouSetRatio**)
Mickey/pixel ratio, vertical	16 : 8 (see **MouSetRatio**)
Pointer, graphics	Upward-slanted arrow (see **MouSetGraphPointer**)
Pointer, text	Reverse-video rectangle (see **MouSetTextPointer**)
Pointer flag	−1 (pointer is hidden; see **MouShowPointer** and **MouHidePointer**)
Pointer position	Center of the screen (see **MouSetPointer**)
Pointer range on screen	Full screen (see **MouSetPointerHorizArea** and **MouSetPointerVertArea)**

rather than calling **MouReset** at program termination. The techniques for saving and restoring the current mouse state are explained later in the chapter, in the section on **MouGetStorage**, **MouSaveState**, and **MouRestoreState**.

How MouReset Works

The function **MouReset** (as well as the remaining functions in this chapter), works by invoking the mouse driver through interrupt vector 33h. Before issuing the interrupt instruction, however, **MouReset** calls **MouInstalled** to make sure that a mouse driver is installed. (This precaution is important because it is unlikely that interrupt vector 33h will point to valid code unless a mouse driver has been installed; invoking such an interrupt vector would probably lock up the machine.)

If a mouse driver is absent, **MouReset** immediately returns a value of 1, indicating an error. All of the functions in this chapter—except **MouInstalled**—directly return an error status code, where zero indicates that the function was successful and a nonzero value means that an error occurred. The only error condition reported by these functions is the absence of a mouse driver.

All of the mouse driver services described in this chapter are accessed through interrupt 33h; the desired service is specified by placing a code in register AX before generating the interrupt. Other registers are used to pass values to the mouse driver or to receive returned values (a given service may use one of more of these registers: AX, BX, CX, DX, and ES). The service for resetting the mouse driver is invoked through the following protocol:

Mouse Function 0: Mouse Reset

Entry:

    AX   0

Return:

    AX   Mouse status, where −1 indicates that the mouse hardware and software are properly installed, and 0 indicates that the hardware or the software is *not* properly installed

    BX   Number of mouse buttons

In the list describing the calling protocol for each mouse service in this chapter, the Entry section lists the values that must be loaded into registers before generating the interrupt, and the Return section lists the values that are returned in registers by the requested service.

MouReset invokes interrupt 33h by calling the Microsoft C function **int86**. On return from the interrupt, it assigns the number of mouse buttons (in register BX) to the address given by the parameter **NumButtons**. Finally, **MouReset** returns an error status code based on the value of the mouse status supplied in the AX register. If AX equals −1 (indicating that the hardware and software are properly installed), **MouReset** returns 0, which informs the calling program that the function was successful. If AX equals 0 (indicating that the hardware or the software is *not* properly installed), **MouReset** returns 1, signaling an error.

MouShowPointer and MouHidePointer

*Using
MouShowPointer
and
MouHidePointer*

The mouse driver maintains an internal counter associated with the mouse pointer. When this counter is 0, the mouse pointer is displayed on the screen, and when the counter is less than 0, the mouse pointer is hidden. The function **MouReset** sets the counter to −1; thus, the pointer is initially invisible. The function **MouShowPointer**, which has the prototype

```
int MouPointer
     (void)
```

increments the counter, and causes the system to make the pointer visible if the resulting value is 0. Thus, calling **MouShowPointer** immediately after calling **MouReset** makes the pointer visible. Note that once the counter has reached a value of 0, subsequent calls do *not* increment it, and have no effect on the mouse pointer (0 is the *maximum* counter value).

The function **MouHidePointer**, which has the prototype

```
int MouHidePointer
     (void)
```

decrements the pointer counter, and always causes the mouse to be hidden. Repeated calls to this function (without intermediate calls to **Mou-ShowPointer**) continue to decrement the counter. Thus, if the pointer is initially visible, three calls to **MouHidePointer** will demand three subsequent calls to **MouShowPointer** to make the pointer reappear.

Both **MouShowPointer and MouHidePointer** return zero if successful, or a nonzero value if a mouse driver is not installed.

Because **MouShowPointer** and **MouHidePointer** employ a counter rather than setting the mouse visibility to an absolute state, a program subroutine can temporarily hide the mouse pointer (by calling **Mou-HidePointer**) and then restore the former pointer state—visible or invisible—by calling **MouShowPointer**.

Note that once the pointer becomes visible, the system automatically draws the pointer on the screen and moves the pointer image in response to movements of the mouse on the desktop. Although your program can explicitly move the pointer to a given location on the screen (by calling **MouSetPointer**, described later), generally it will simply *read* the current pointer position and state of the mouse buttons, and respond appropriately to these values.

In some of the technical documentation, you may see the mouse pointer referred to as the mouse *cursor*. This book, however, reserves the word *cursor* for the blinking cursor generated by the video hardware (although, in text mode you can optionally use the hardware cursor for the mouse pointer; see the description of **MouSetTextPointer**, later in the chapter).

Figure 11.3 lists a short program that demonstrates the functions that have been described so far in this chapter. The program first makes the mouse pointer visible and allows you to move it on the screen; it then hides the pointer and terminates. These actions are performed through the following specific steps, which illustrate the basic method for initializing and displaying a mouse pointer:

■ The function **MouInstalled** is called to make sure a mouse driver is installed before calling other mouse management functions.

■ **MouReset** is called to initialize the mouse driver and to set all mouse parameters to their default values, and the number of mouse buttons returned by this function is displayed.

■ Next, **MouShowPointer** is called to make the mouse pointer visible. The program now pauses until you press a key; during this time, you can move the pointer to any spot on the screen by moving the mouse on the desk surface.

■ After a key is pressed, the program calls **MouHidePointer** to make the pointer invisible again, and terminates. The mouse pointer will not reappear until another application requests the mouse driver to make it visible.

Note that if the program did not call **MouHidePointer** (or **MouReset**, which also hides the pointer), the mouse pointer would remain on the screen as subsequent applications are run. Figure 11.4 provides a MAKE file, and Figure 11.5 a QuickC program list.

```
/*
       This program demonstrates the functions:

               MouInstalled
               MouReset
               MouShowPointer
               MouHidePointer
*/
#include <STDIO.H>
#include <STDLIB.H>

#include "MOU.H"
#include "KBD.H"
#include "SCR.H"

void main (void)
       {
       int NumButtons;

       ScrClear (0,0,24,79);
       ScrSetCur (0,0,0);

       /* Test whether mouse driver is installed.                    */
       if (!MouInstalled ())
               {
               printf ("Sorry, a mouse must be installed.\n");
               exit (1);
               }

       /* Reset mouse driver and get number of buttons.              */
       if (MouReset (&NumButtons))
               {
               printf ("Mouse reset failed.\n");
               exit (1);
               }
       printf ("Number of mouse buttons:   %d\n",NumButtons);

       /* Display the mouse pointer.                                 */
       if (MouShowPointer ())
               {
               printf ("Mouse pointer show failed.\n");
               exit (1);
               }

       /* Pause...                                                   */
       printf ("Press any key to hide pointer...");
       KbdGetC ();

       /* Hide the mouse pointer.                                    */
       if (MouHidePointer ())
               {
               printf ("MouHidePointer failed.\n");
       exit (1);
               }

       } /* end main */
```

Figure 11.3: MOUDEM01.C: A program demonstrating the functions **MouInstalled**, **MouReset**, **MouShowPointer**, and **MouHidePointer**

```
MOUDEM01.OBJ : MOUDEM01.C MOU.H KBD.H SCR.H
    cl /c /W2 /Zp MOUDEM01.C

MOU.OBJ : MOU.C MOU.H
    cl /c /W2 /Zp MOU.C

KBDA.OBJ : KBDA.ASM
    masm /MX KBDA.ASM;

SCR.OBJ : SCR.C SCR.H
    cl /c /W2 /Zp SCR.C

MOUDEM01.EXE : MOUDEM01.OBJ MOU.OBJ KBDA.OBJ SCR.OBJ
    link /NOI /NOD MOUDEM01+MOU+KBDA+SCR,,NUL,SLIBCER;
```

Figure 11.4: MOUDEM01.M: A MAKE file for preparing MOUDEM01.C

How MouShowPointer and MouHidePointer Work

In the same manner as **MouReset**, **MouShowPointer** works by directly invoking the mouse driver. The service for showing the mouse pointer is requested through the following protocol:

Mouse Function 1: Show Pointer

Entry:

AX   1

Return:

None

```
MOUDEM01.C
MOU.C
KBDA.OBJ
SCR.C
```

Figure 11.5: A QuickC program list for preparing MOUDEM01.C

MouHidePointer invokes the following mouse driver service:

Mouse Function 2: Hide Pointer

Entry:

AX   2

Return:

None

MouGetButtons

*Using
MouGetButtons*

The function **MouGetButtons** has the prototype

```
int MouGetButtons
     (int *ButtonStatus,
     int *PointerCol,
     int *PointerRow)
```

It assigns the current mouse button status to ***ButtonStatus**, the current column position of the mouse pointer to ***PointerCol**, and the current row position to ***PointerRow**. **MouGetButtons** returns zero if successful, and a nonzero value if a mouse driver is not installed.

The value representing the button status is encoded as follows: if bit 0 is set the left button is down, if bit 1 is set the right button is down, and if bit 2 is set the center button is down (on a three-button mouse, such as the one from Logitech). You can easily test the button status by using the bit masks LEFTBUTTONDOWN, RIGHTBUTTONDOWN, and CENTERBUTTONDOWN, defined in MOU.H, as in the following example:

```
if (ButtonStatus & LEFTBUTTONDOWN)
        /* then left button is currently pressed */
```

The method the mouse driver uses to specify the pointer position depends upon the current video mode, and requires some explanation.

In a text mode, the screen is conceptually divided into 640 horizontal units by 200 vertical units, which are numbered beginning with 0. Since the pointer occupies a character cell, it cannot be displayed at an arbitrary position on the screen, but rather is contained within one of the 80 by 25 character cells present in an 80-column text mode (the pointer, therefore, does not move smoothly on the screen, but rather jumps from cell to cell). The position of the pointer is specified as the coordinates (in conceptual units) of the upper left corner of the character cell in which it is displayed. Since each character cell is eight units wide (640/80), the column position of the pointer must be a multiple of eight in the range from 0 to 632. Likewise, since each character cell is eight units high (200 /25), the row position must be a multiple of eight in the range from 0 to 192. For example, if the pointer is located in the upper-left corner of the screen, it has the coordinates (column 0, row 0); if the pointer is in the next character cell to the right, it has the coordinates (column 8, row 0).

To obtain the standard coordinates of the pointer—specified as a column from 0 to 79 and a row from 0 to 24—you must divide the values assigned to ***PointerRow** and ***PointerCol** by eight. See Figure 11.6, described later in this section, for an example program that uses these values.

In graphics modes, the position of the mouse pointer is specified as the coordinates of a specially designated pixel known as the *hot spot*; for the standard arrow pointer, the hot spot is at the tip of the arrow. For all graphics modes except modes 04h, 05h, 0Dh, and 13h, the location of the pointer is specified by the actual pixel numbers of the hot spot. For example, in CGA high-resolution graphics (mode 06h), the screen consists of 640 pixels in the horizontal direction, and 200 pixels in the vertical direction. The position of the pointer is specified by a horizontal coordinate from 0 to 639 and a vertical coordinate from 0 to 199. (For graphics modes 04h, 05h, 0Dh, and 13h the screen consists of only 320 horizontal pixels by 200 vertical pixels. The mouse driver, however, conceptually divides the screen into 640 by 200 units; therefore, each physical pixel is two conceptual units wide. Accordingly, a physical pixel at the left of the screen is given the horizontal coordinate 0, the next pixel to the right is given the horizontal coordinate 2, and so on. As a result, only even coordinate values are used.) See the description of graphics modes in Table 5.1.

Note that unlike a text pointer, a graphics pointer (that is, its hot spot) can be placed at any pixel location on the screen. Thus, the motion of a graphics pointer is much smoother than that of a text pointer.

Figure 11.6 lists an example program that allows you to move the mouse pointer on the screen, and provides a continuous display of the values returned by **MouGetButtons**. Note that since the program runs in text mode, the pointer coordinates returned by **MouGetButtons** are divided by eight to obtain the standard row and column position of the character cell containing the pointer.

Figure 11.7 provides a MAKE file, and Figure 11.8 a QuickC program list.

How MouGetButtons Works

MouGetButtons invokes the following mouse driver service:

Mouse Function 3: Get Button Status and Mouse Position

Entry:

AX   3

Return:

BX   Button press status

CX   Pointer horizontal coordinate

DX   Pointer vertical coordinate

MouSetPointer

Using MouSetPointer

The function **MouSetPointer** has the prototype

```
int MouSetPointer
     (int PointerCol,
     int PointerRow)
```

and places the mouse pointer at the specified position on the screen. **PointerCol** gives the horizontal coordinate, and **PointerRow** gives the vertical coordinate. If successful, the function returns zero, and if a mouse driver is not installed, it returns a nonzero value.

```
/*
      This program demonstrates the function:
            MouGetButtons
*/

#include <STDIO.H>
#include <STDLIB.H>

#include "MOU.H"
#include "KBD.H"
#include "SCR.H"

void main (void)
      {
      int NumButtons;
      int ButtonStatus;
      int PointerCol;
      int PointerRow;
      char NumBuf [3];

      if (!MouInstalled ())
            {
            printf ("Sorry, a mouse must be installed.\n");
            exit (1);
            }

      ScrClear (0,0,24,79);
      ScrSetCur (25,80,0);

      MouReset (&NumButtons);

      MouShowPointer ();

      ScrPutS ("Pointer Column: xx    Row: xx      |"
            "   Left Button:           Right Button:           ",0x70,0,0);

      ScrPutS ("Press any key to end program.",0x70,24,25);

      for (;;)
            {
            if (KbdReady ())
                  {
                  KbdGetC ();
                  MouReset (&NumButtons);
                  ScrClear (0,0,24,79);
                  ScrSetCur (0,0,0);
                  exit (0);
                  }

            MouGetButtons (&ButtonStatus,&PointerCol,&PointerRow);

            sprintf (NumBuf,"%2d",PointerCol/8);
```

Figure 11.6: MOUDEM02.C: A program demonstrating the function **MouGetButtons**

```
        ScrPutS (NumBuf,0x70,0,16);

        sprintf (NumBuf,"%2d",PointerRow/8);
        ScrPutS (NumBuf,0x70,0,27);

        ScrPutS (ButtonStatus & LEFTBUTTONDOWN  ? "down" : "up  ",
                0x70,0,50);
        ScrPutS (ButtonStatus & RIGHTBUTTONDOWN ? "down" : "up  ",
                0x70,0,72);
        }

} /* end main */
```

Figure 11.6:MOUDEM02.C: A program demonstrating the function **MouGetButtons** (continued)

```
    MOUDEM02.OBJ : MOUDEM02.C MOU.H KBD.H SCR.H
          cl /c /W2 /Zp MOUDEM02.C

    MOU.OBJ : MOU.C MOU.H
          cl /c /W2 /Zp MOU.C

    KBDA.OBJ : KBDA.ASM
          masm /MX KBDA.ASM;

    SCR.OBJ : SCR.C SCR.H
          cl /c /W2 /Zp SCR.C

    MOUDEM02.EXE : MOUDEM02.OBJ MOU.OBJ KBDA.OBJ SCR.OBJ
          link /NOI /NOD MOUDEM02+MOU+KBDA+SCR,,NUL,SLIBCER;
```

Figure 11.7: MOUDEMO2.M: A MAKE file for preparing MOUDEM02.C

```
    MOUDEM02.C
    MOU.C
    KBDA.OBJ
    SCR.C
```

Figure 11.8: A QuickC program list for preparing MOUDEM02.C

Note that the horizontal and vertical pointer coordinates passed to **MouSetPointer** must conform to the conventions discussed in the previous section ("Using **MouGetButtons**"). Therefore, in an 80-column text mode, you should specify a horizontal coordinate that is a multiple of eight in the range from 0 to 632, and a vertical coordinate that is a multiple of eight in the range from 0 to 192. If you pass a value that is not a multiple of eight, **MouSetPointer** will round the value *down* to the nearest multiple of eight. For example, the following command would place the pointer in the approximate center of the screen:

```
MouSetPointer (39 * 8, 12 * 8);
```

In a graphics mode (except modes 04h, 05h, 0Dh, and 13h), you should specify the actual pixel numbers of the point where the pointer hot spot is to be located. (In modes 04h, 05h, 0Dh, and 13h, multiply the physical pixel coordinates by two to obtain the appropriate screen units for the mouse driver. If you pass an odd coordinate value, **MouSetPointer** rounds the value down to the next even integer.) For example, in CGA high-resolution mode (06h) the following call to **MouSetPointer** places the hot spot at the approximate center of the screen:

```
MouSetPointer (319,99);
```

How MouSetPointer Works

MouSetPointer invokes the following service of the mouse driver:

Mouse Function 4: Set Mouse Pointer Position

Entry:

　　AX　　4

　　CX　　New horizontal pointer position

　　DX　　New vertical pointer position

Return:

　　None

MouGetButtonPress and MouGetButtonRelease

*Using
MouGetButton-
Press and
MouGetButton-
Release*

MouGetButtonPress has the prototype

```
int MouGetButtonPress
    (int Button,
    int *ButtonStatus,
    int *NumberPresses,
    int *PointerCol,
    int *PointerRow)
```

This function returns information on the button specified by the parameter **Button**, which should be assigned one of the following values:

Value of Button	**Indicated mouse button**
0	Left button
1	Right button
2	Center button on a 3-button mouse

MouGetButtonPress assigns ***NumberPresses** the number of times the specified button was pressed since the last time this function was called. It assigns ***PointerCol** and ***PointerRow** the position of the mouse pointer *at the time the mouse button was last pressed*. The pointer position coordinates supplied by **MouGetButtonPress** follow the same conventions described for the previous functions; however, unlike the previous functions, they do *not* give the current position.

MouGetButtonPress also assigns the *current* status of all the mouse buttons to ***ButtonStatus**. The value returned through this parameter is the same as that supplied by **MouGetButtons**; see the description of **MouGetButtons** for an explanation of the encoding of the button status.

MouGetButtonPress is useful for detecting that a mouse button has been pressed, and for determining the exact position of the pointer at the time the button was pressed. It can thus be used to determine which item on the screen the user has selected by clicking the mouse button. Note that you could also detect a mouse button press by repeatedly calling **MouGetButtons** to obtain the current button status, and noting when a change in this status occurs. However, the mouse pointer may be moved between the time the button is pressed and the time **MouGetButtons** is called, which would prevent the program from obtaining the correct pointer position at the time the button was pressed.

The example program in Figure 11.9 demonstrates the use of **MouGet-ButtonPress**. This program first displays a menu containing three items at the top of the screen. It then enters a loop that repeatedly calls **Mou-GetButtonPress**, specifying the left mouse button. After each call to **MouGetButtonPress**, the program displays at the bottom of the screen the button status and pointer coordinates returned by this function. When you run this program, you will notice that the coordinate values are updated only when the left button is pressed (unlike the program in Figure 11.6, which calls **MouGetButtons** and continuously updates the pointer coordinates as the mouse is moved).

After each call to **MouGetButtonPress**, the program also tests the number of button presses returned in the variable **NumberPresses**. If this value is greater than 0, indicating that the left button was pressed at least once since the last time the function was called, the program then examines the pointer coordinates to determine the location of the mouse pointer when the button was pressed. If the pointer was within the area occupied by the first menu item (labeled "MENU 1") or the second item ("MENU 2"), it displays a simple pull-down menu box. If the pointer was within the area of the third menu item ("QUIT"), the application is terminated. If the pointer was not contained in any of these areas, the button press is ignored and the program loop continues.

Figure 11.10 contains a MAKE file, and Figure 11.11 provides a Quick C program list.

The function **MouGetButtonRelease** has the prototype

```
int MouGetButtonRelease
    (int Button,
    int *ButtonStatus,
    int *NumberReleases,
    int *PointerCol,
    int *PointerRow)
```

This function assigns ***NumberReleases** the number of times the mouse button specified by **Button** was *released* since the last time the

```
/*
      This program demonstrates the function:
           MouGetButtonPress or MouGetButtonRelease
*/

#include <STDIO.H>
#include <STDLIB.H>

#include "MOU.H"
#include "SCR.H"
#include "UTY.H"

void Menu1 (void);
void Menu2 (void);

void main (void)
      {
      int NumButtons;
      int ButtonStatus;
      int NumberPresses;
      int PointerCol;
      int PointerRow;
      char NumBuf [3];

      if (!MouInstalled ())
           {
           printf ("Sorry, a mouse must be installed.\n");
           exit (1);
           }

      ScrClear (0,0,24,79);
      ScrSetCur (25,80,0);

      MouReset (&NumButtons);

      MouShowPointer ();

      ScrPutS ("+----------------------------------------------+",0x0f,0,0);
      ScrPutS ("|    MENU 1    |    MENU  2    |    QUIT      |",0x0f,1,0);
      ScrPutS ("+----------------------------------------------+",0x0f,2,0);
      ScrPutS ("Pointer Column: xx      Row: xx      |"
               "   Left Button:          Right Button:         ",0x70,24,0);

      for (;;)
           {
           MouGetButtonPress           /* Try replacing with MouGetButtonRelease. */
                (0,
                &ButtonStatus,
                &NumberPresses,
                &PointerCol,
                &PointerRow);
                PointerCol /= 8;
                PointerRow /= 8;

                sprintf (NumBuf,"%2d",PointerCol);
                ScrPutS (NumBuf,0x70,24,16);
```

Figure 11.9: MOUDEM03.C: A program demonstrating the function **MouGetButtonPress**

```
            sprintf (NumBuf,"%2d",PointerRow);
            ScrPutS (NumBuf,0x70,24,27);

            ScrPutS (ButtonStatus & LEFTBUTTONDOWN  ? "down" : "up  ",
                     0x70,24,50);
            ScrPutS (ButtonStatus & RIGHTBUTTONDOWN ? "down" : "up  ",
                     0x70,24,72);

            if (NumberPresses > 0 && PointerRow == 1)
                {
                if (PointerCol >= 1 &&
                    PointerCol <= 14)
                   Menu1 ();
                else if (PointerCol >= 16 &&
                         PointerCol <= 29)
                   Menu2 ();
                else if (PointerCol >= 31 &&
                         PointerCol <= 44)
                   {
                   MouReset (&NumButtons);
                   ScrClear (0,0,24,79);
                   ScrSetCur (0,0,0);
                   exit (0);
                   }
                }  /* end if NumberPresses > 0 */

           }  /* end for */

        }  /* end main */


void Menu1 (void)
    {
    MouHidePointer ();
    ScrPush ();
    ScrPutBox (2,0,10,15,3);
    ScrPutS ("PULL-DOWN",0x07,5,3);
    ScrPutS ("MENU 1",0x07,7,4);
    UtyPause (1.0);
    ScrPop (1);
    MouShowPointer ();

    }  /* end Menu1 */


void Menu2 (void)
    {
    MouHidePointer ();
    ScrPush ();
    ScrPutBox (2,15,10,30,3);
    ScrPutS ("PULL-DOWN",0x07,5,18);
    ScrPutS ("MENU 2",0x07,7,19);
    UtyPause (1.0);
    ScrPop (1);
    MouShowPointer ();

    }  /* end Menu1 */
```

Figure 11.9: MOUDEM03.C: A program demonstrating the function **MouGetButtonPress** (continued)

```
MOUDEM03.OBJ : MOUDEM03.C MOU.H KBD.H SCR.H
     cl /c /W2 /Zp MOUDEM03.C

MOU.OBJ : MOU.C MOU.H
     cl /c /W2 /Zp MOU.C

SCR.OBJ : SCR.C SCR.H
     cl /c /W2 /Zp SCR.C

KBDA.OBJ : KBDA.ASM
     masm /MX KBDA.ASM;

UTY.OBJ : UTY.C UTY.H
     cl /c /W2 /Zp UTY.C

UTYA.OBJ : UTYA.ASM
     masm /MX UTYA.ASM;

MOUDEM03.EXE : MOUDEM03.OBJ MOU.OBJ SCR.OBJ KBDA.OBJ UTY.OBJ UTYA.OBJ
     link /NOI /NOD MOUDEM03+MOU+SCR+KBDA+UTY+UTYA,,,NUL,SLIBCER;
```

Figure 11.10: MOUDEM03.M: A MAKE file for preparing MOUDEM03.C

function was called. ***PointerCol** and ***PointerRow** are assigned the
coordinates of the mouse pointer *at the time the button was last released,*
and ***ButtonStatus** is given the current button status.

Note that **MouGetButtonRelease** is exactly analogous to the function **MouGetButtonPress**. You might try substituting the call to the
function **MouGetButtonPress** in the example program of Figure 11.9
with a call to **MouGetButtonRelease** to observe the difference between
these two functions. In general, **MouGetButtonPress** produces a faster
response, since the program need not wait for the button to be released.

```
MOUDEM03.C
MOU.C
KBDA.OBJ
SCR.C
UTY.C
UTYA.OBJ
```

Figure 11.11: A QuickC program list for preparing MOUDEM03.C

How MouGetButton- Press and MouGetButton- Release Work

The function **MouGetButtonPress** uses the following service of the mouse driver:

Mouse Function 5: Get Button Press Information

Entry:

AX 5

BX Code for the button; 0 is left button, 1 is the right button, and 2 is the center button

Return:

AX Button press status

BX Number of button presses since last call to service

CX Pointer column coordinate when button was last pressed

DX Pointer row coordinate when button was last pressed

MouGetButtonRelease invokes the following mouse driver service:

Mouse Function 6: Get Button Release Information

Entry:

AX 6

BX Code for the button; 0 is left button, 1 is the right button, and 2 is the center button

Return:

AX Button press status

BX Number of button releases since last call to service

CX Pointer column coordinate when button was last released

DX Pointer row coordinate when button was last released

MouSetPointerHorizArea and MouSetPointerVertArea

Using MouSetPointer-HorizArea and MouSetPointer-VertArea

MouSetPointerHorizArea has the prototype

```
int MouSetPointerHorizArea
     (int MinCol,
      int MaxCol)
```

and allows you to restrict the horizontal motion of the mouse pointer. After calling this function, the pointer will not move to the left of the position specified by **MinCol** nor to the right of the position given by **MaxCol**.

The function **MouSetPointerVertArea** has the prototype

```
int MouSetPointerVertArea
     (int MinRow,
      int MaxRow)
```

This function is analogous to **MouSetPointerHorizArea**, but allows you to define the vertical limits of the travel of the mouse pointer. Note that these functions use the same coordinate conventions as the mouse functions discussed previously in the chapter. Both of these functions return zero if successful, or a nonzero value if a mouse pointer is not installed.

The example program in Figure 11.12 demonstrates the effect of **MouSetPointerHorizArea** and **MouSetPointerVertArea**. This program draws a box on the screen, and then calls these two functions to set the limits of travel of the mouse pointer to area of the box. The program then goes into a loop that repeatedly calls **MouGetButtons**; after each call, it displays the position of the pointer and the status of the mouse buttons returned by this function. When you run this program, you will see that it is impossible to move the mouse pointer outside of the area of the box.

A MAKE file is supplied in Figure 11.13, and a QuickC program list in Figure 11.14.

```
/*
     This program demonstrates the functions:
          MouSetPointerHorizArea
          MouSetPointerVertArea
*/

#include <STDIO.H>
#include <STDLIB.H>

#include "MOU.H"
#include "KBD.H"
#include "SCR.H"

void main (void)
     {
     int NumButtons;
     int ButtonStatus;
     int PointerCol;
     int PointerRow;
     char NumBuf [3];

     if (!MouInstalled ())
          {
          printf ("Sorry, a mouse must be installed.\n");
          exit (1);
          }

     ScrClear (0,0,24,79);
     ScrSetCur (25,80,0);

     MouReset (&NumButtons);

     MouShowPointer ();

     ScrPutS ("Pointer Column: xx     Row: xx    |"
          "   Left Button:          Right Button:          ",0x70,0,0);

     ScrPutS ("Press any key to end program.",0x70,24,25);

     ScrPutBox (5,10,19,69,0);

     MouSetPointerHorizArea (10 * 8, 69 * 8);
     MouSetPointerVertArea  (5  * 8, 19 * 8);

     for (;;)
          {
          if (KbdReady ())
               {
               KbdGetC ();
               MouReset (&NumButtons);
               ScrClear (0,0,24,79);
               ScrSetCur (0,0,0);
          exit (0);
               }

     MouGetButtons (&ButtonStatus,&PointerCol,&PointerRow);
```

Figure 11.12: A program demonstrating the functions **MouSetPointerHorizArea** and **MouSetPointerVertArea**

```
        sprintf (NumBuf,"%2d",PointerCol/8);
        ScrPutS (NumBuf,0x70,0,16);

        sprintf (NumBuf,"%2d",PointerRow/8);
        ScrPutS (NumBuf,0x70,0,27);

        ScrPutS (ButtonStatus & LEFTBUTTONDOWN  ? "down" : "up  ",
            0x70,0,50);
        ScrPutS (ButtonStatus & RIGHTBUTTONDOWN ? "down" : "up  ",
            0x70,0,72);
        }

} /* end main */
```

Figure 11.12: A program demonstrating the functions **MouSetPointerHorizArea** and
MouSetPointerVertArea (continued)

```
MOUDEM04.OBJ : MOUDEM04.C MOU.H KBD.H SCR.H
     cl /c /W2 /Zp MOUDEM04.C

MOU.OBJ : MOU.C MOU.H
     cl /c /W2 /Zp MOU.C

KBDA.OBJ : KBDA.ASM
     masm /MX KBDA.ASM;

SCR.OBJ : SCR.C SCR.H
     cl /c /W2 /Zp SCR.C

MOUDEM04.EXE : MOUDEM04.OBJ MOU.OBJ KBDA.OBJ SCR.OBJ
     link /NOI /NOD MOUDEM04+MOU+KBDA+SCR,,NUL,SLIBCER;
```

Figure 11.13: MOUDEM04.M: A MAKE file for preparing MOUDEM04.C

```
MOUDEM04.C
MOU.C
KBDA.OBJ
SCR.C
```

Figure 11.14: A QuickC program list for preparing MOUDEM04.C

*How
MouSetPointer-
HorizArea and
MouSetPointer-
VertArea Work*

The function **MouSetPointerHorizArea** uses the following mouse driver service:

Mouse Function 7: Set Minimum and Maximum Horizontal Pointer Position

Entry:

AX   7

CX   Minimum horizontal pointer position

DX   Maximum horizontal pointer position

Return:

None

MouSetPointerVertArea invokes the following service of the mouse driver:

Mouse Function 8: Set Minimum and Maximum Vertical Pointer Position

Entry:

AX   8

CX   Minimum vertical pointer position

DX   Maximum vertical pointer position

MouSetGraphPointer

*Using
MouSetGraph-
Pointer*

The function **MouSetGraphPointer** has the following prototype:

```
int MouSetGraphPointer
     (int HotSpotHoriz,
      int HotSpotVert,
      unsigned far *FarPtrMasks)
```

This function is used to set the shape and color of the mouse pointer displayed in graphics modes, and to define the position of the pointer hot spot. Once you have called this function, the mouse driver will automatically use the custom pointer you have defined whenever the system is in a graphics mode; this new pointer will replace the default mouse pointer (the northwest sloping arrow) set by **MouReset**. If successful, **MouSetGraphPointer** returns zero, and if a mouse driver is not installed, it returns a nonzero value.

To specify the shape and color of the mouse pointer, you must define two contiguous bit masks and pass the starting address of these masks as the third parameter, **FarPtrMasks**. The pointer on the screen is contained in an area 16 pixels wide by 16 pixels high (graphics modes 04h and 05h are exceptions, as noted later in this section). Each of the two bit masks that you define should consist of an array of sixteen 16-bit values, where each bit corresponds to a pixel within the pointer (in C, a mask can consist of 16 integers). The first 16 bits in a mask correspond to the first row of pixels in the pointer, the second 16 bits correspond to the second row of pixels, and so on.

The first bit mask is termed the *screen mask,* and the second mask the *pointer mask.* The ultimate color of each screen pixel within the area occupied by the pointer is generated by combining the corresponding bit from the first mask, the corresponding bit from the second mask, and the existing color of the pixel on the screen, according to the following table:

Screen mask bit	Pointer mask bit	Resulting Pixel on Screen
0	0	black
0	1	white
1	0	unchanged from existing value
1	1	inverted from existing value

Note that the mouse driver supports only two colors. Figure 11.15 illustrates the bit masks used to form a simple cross-shaped pointer that has a black border and a white center (this is the pointer defined in the example program of Figure 11.16, described later in this section).

A technical note: The cursor of the pixels within the area occupied by the pointer are produced by combining the existing bits within video memory with the bits of the screen mask using the logical AND operator, and then combining the result of the AND operation with the bits of the pointer mask using the logical exclusive-OR operator.

Note also that in graphics modes 04h and 05h, the mouse pointer is only 8 bits wide by 16 bits high. For these modes, you must define the same 16 by 16 bit masks as for the other modes, and the bit masks are combined with the bits in video memory in the same manner described in the previous paragraph. However, in these modes, 2 bits in video

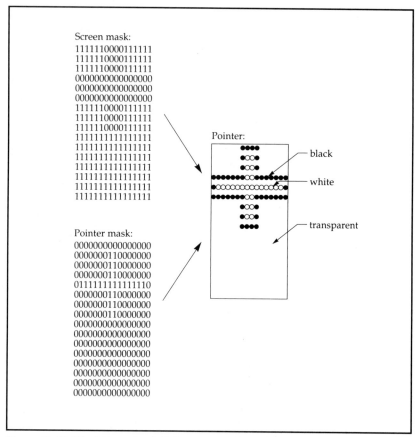

Figure 11.15: The bit masks defining a cross-shaped graphics pointer

memory correspond to a single pixel on the screen, and each screen pixel can therefore be displayed in one of 4 colors (the actual colors depend upon the current color palette). Thus, each pair of bits in a given bit mask corresponds to a single pointer pixel. For further information on creating a pointer for graphics modes not discussed in this section, see the *Mouse Programmer's Reference Guide* and the technical documentation for the specific video adapter.

The horizontal and vertical positions of the pixel that serves as the pointer hot spot are specified by the first two parameters passed to **MouSetGraphPointer**: **HotSpotHoriz** and **HotSpotVert** (the hot spot was explained previously, in the section on **MouGetButtons**). These variables can be assigned values in the range from −16 to +16, and specify the pixel position of the hot spot with respect to the pixel at the upper left corner of the matrix containing the pointer. The values (0,0) would place the hot spot at the upper left corner; positive values place the hot spot to the right of or below the upper-left corner, and negative values place the pixel to the left or above the upper left corner. (Thus, the hot spot can be placed at a point *outside* of the pointer matrix. Using a pointer with such a hot spot would have a "remote control" feel.)

Note that since the pointer in graphics modes 04h, 05h, 0Dh, and 0Eh is only 8 bits wide, the mouse driver divides the value assigned to **HotSpotHoriz** by two to obtain the actual pixel number.

The program in Figure 11.16 demonstrates the technique for defining a graphics mouse pointer. This program switches into the CGA high-resolution graphics mode (number 06h) and draws a filled box in the center of the screen using the graphics functions presented in Chapter 7. Before showing the pointer, it calls **MouSetGraphPointer** to define a custom graphics pointer.

The shape of the pointer is defined in the array **PointerMasks** (at the beginning of the program); the binary value of each of the integers assigned to this array is provided as a comment to show the actual pattern of the bits. Note that the hot spot is assigned to a pixel near the center of the cross (there is no pixel at the exact center). The resulting pointer (which is illustrated in Figure 11.15) has a black border and a white interior, and is thus visible over either a light or a dark background (the filled rectangle is provided so that you can verify this feature).

Figure 11.17 provides a MAKE file, and Figure 11.18 a QuickC program list.

*How
MouSetGraph-
Pointer Works*

MouSetGraphPointer works through the following mouse driver function:

Mouse Function 9: Set Graphics Pointer

Entry:

    AX   9

    BX   Horizontal hot spot position

    CX   Vertical hot spot position

    DX   Offset address of beginning of masks defining pointer

    ES   Segment address of beginning of masks defining pointer

Return:

    None

```
/*
     This program demonstrates the function:
         MouSetGraphPointer
*/

#include <STDIO.H>
#include <STDLIB.H>

#include "MOU.H"
#include "KBD.H"
#include "SCR.H"
#include "GRA.H"

void BiosPutS (char *String);

unsigned PointerMasks [32] =
     {                        /* Binary values:          */

                             /* Screen mask:             */
     0xfc3f,                 /* 1111110000111111         */
     0xfc3f,                 /* 1111110000111111         */
     0xfc3f,                 /* 1111110000111111         */
     0x0000,                 /* 0000000000000000         */
     0x0000,                 /* 0000000000000000         */
     0x0000,                 /* 0000000000000000         */
     0xfc3f,                 /* 1111110000111111         */
     0xfc3f,                 /* 1111110000111111         */
     0xfc3f,                 /* 1111110000111111         */
     0xffff,                 /* 1111111111111111         */
     0xffff,                 /* 1111111111111111         */
     0xffff,                 /* 1111111111111111         */
     0xffff,                 /* 1111111111111111         */
     0xffff,                 /* 1111111111111111         */
     0xffff,                 /* 1111111111111111         */
     0xffff,                 /* 1111111111111111         */

                             /* Pointer mask:            */
     0x0000,                 /* 0000000000000000         */
     0x0180,                 /* 0000000110000000         */
     0x0180,                 /* 0000000110000000         */
     0x0180,                 /* 0000000110000000         */
     0x7ffe,                 /* 0111111111111110         */
     0x0180,                 /* 0000000110000000         */
     0x0180,                 /* 0000000110000000         */
     0x0180,                 /* 0000000110000000         */
     0x0000,                 /* 0000000000000000         */
     0x0000,                 /* 0000000000000000         */
     0x0000,                 /* 0000000000000000         */
     0x0000,                 /* 0000000000000000         */
     0x0000,                 /* 0000000000000000         */
     0x0000,                 /* 0000000000000000         */
     0x0000,                 /* 0000000000000000         */
     0x0000                  /* 0000000000000000         */
     };
```

Figure 11.16: MOUDEM05.C: A program demonstrating the function **MouSetGraphPointer**

```
      void main (void)
          {
          int NumButtons;

          if (!MouInstalled ())
              {
              printf ("Sorry, a mouse must be installed.\n");
              exit (1);
              }

          if (!(ScrTypes () & VCGA))
              {
              printf ("Sorry, must have a CGA compatible graphics adapter.\n");
              exit (1);
              }

          GraInit (CGAHIRES);

          GraBox ((float)1.0,(float)1.0,(float)7.0,(float)5.0,ON);
          GraFill ((float)4.0,(float)3.0,ON,ON);

          ScrSetCur (24,25,0);

          BiosPutS ("Press any key to end program.");

          MouReset (&NumButtons);

          MouSetGraphPointer
              (7,
              4,
              PointerMasks);

          MouShowPointer ();

          KbdGetC ();

          MouHidePointer ();

          GraQuit ();

          } /* end main */


      #include <DOS.H>

      void BiosPutS (char *String)
      /*
          This function prints 'String' on the screen, in teletype fashion,
          beginning at the current cursor position.
      */
          {
          union REGS Reg;
```

Figure 11.16: MOUDEM05.C: A program demonstrating the function **MouSetGraphPointer**
(continued)

```
        Reg.h.bl = 1;         /* Specifies foreground color 1, if in a graphics. */
        Reg.h.bh = 0;         /* Active page; required for PC BIOS versions       */
                              /* dated 4/24/81 through 10/19/81.                  */
        while (*String)
            {
            Reg.h.al = *String++;   /* Next character to print.          */
            Reg.h.ah = 14;          /* BIOS teletype printing service.   */
            int86 (0x10,&Reg,&Reg); /* BIOS video services.              */
            }

        } /* end BiosPutS */
```

Figure 11.16: MOUDEM05.C: A program demonstrating the function **MouSetGraphPointer**
(continued)

```
MOUDEM05.OBJ : MOUDEM05.C MOU.H KBD.H SCR.H GRA.H
        cl /c /W2 /Zp MOUDEM05.C

MOU.OBJ : MOU.C MOU.H
        cl /c /W2 /Zp MOU.C

KBDA.OBJ : KBDA.ASM
        masm /MX KBDA.ASM;

SCR.OBJ : SCR.C SCR.H
        cl /c /W2 /Zp SCR.C

SCRA.OBJ : SCRA.ASM
        masm /MX SCRA.ASM;

GRA.OBJ : GRA.C GRA.H
        cl /c /Zp GRA.C

UTYA.OBJ : UTYA.ASM
        masm /MX UTYA.ASM;

MOUDEM05.EXE : MOUDEM05.OBJ MOU.OBJ KBDA.OBJ SCR.OBJ SCRA.OBJ GRA.OBJ UTYA.OBJ
        link /NOI /NOD MOUDEM05+MOU+KBDA+SCR+SCRA+GRA+UTYA,,NUL,SLIBCER;
```

Figure 11.17: MOUDEM05.M: A MAKE file for MOUDEM05.C

```
MOUDEM05.C
MOU.C
KBDA.OBJ
SCR.C
SCRA.OBJ
GRA.C
UTYA.OBJ
```

Figure 11.18: A QuickC program list for preparing MOUDEM05.C

Note that this mouse service must be supplied both the segment address and offset address of the beginning of the bit masks. Accordingly, the bit mask address parameter, **FarPtrMasks**, is declared as a **far** pointer, and the function must invoke the interrupt through the Microsoft C **int86x** function, which allows specification of the segment registers.

MouSetTextPointer

*Using
MouSetText-
Pointer*

MouSetPointer has the following prototype:

```
int MouSetTextPointer
    (int PointerType,
    int SMaskScanStart,
    int PMaskScanStop)
```

This function sets the pointer used in text modes. **PointerType** specifies the type of pointer—either hardware or software—and **SMaskScanStart** and **PMaskScanStop** specify the shape of this pointer. **MouSetTextPointer** returns zero if successful, or a nonzero value if a mouse driver is not installed.

To select a software text mode pointer, you should assign the parameter **PointerType** a value of 0. A software pointer is one that alters either the character or the video attributes (or both) of the character cell in which it is displayed. If you select a software pointer, the next two parameters—**SMaskScanStart** and **PMaskScanStop**—specify the appearance of this pointer; **SMaskScanStart** is the screen mask and **PMaskScanStop** is the pointer mask (these two masks are analogous to the masks supplied to **MouSetGraphPointer**; however, their size and the information they contain are quite different). You can give these parameters one of the following values:

SMaskScanStart	PMaskScanStop	Effect
0x77ff	0x7700	Reverses the display attributes of the cell in which it is displayed (this is the default text pointer)

SMaskScanStart	PMaskScanStop	Effect
0x0000	0x07*nn*	Replaces the existing screen character with the character specified by the ASCII value *nn*

The first of these pointer options simply reverses the video display attributes of the entire character cell in which it is located, without altering the existing character in this cell; this is the default pointer style set by **MouReset**. The second option causes the pointer to *replace* the existing character in its cell with a specified character. For example, if **PMaskScanStop** is given the value 0x0718, the mouse pointer will be displayed as a small up-arrow character (which has the ASCII value 18h in the IBM character set) that replaces the existing character at the pointer location.

A technical note: Each character cell on the screen is represented by a 16-bit value in video memory, which consists of a one-byte character code followed by a one-byte display attribute. The text pointer is generated by combining this 16-bit value with the screen mask using the logical AND operator, and then combining the result of the AND operation with the pointer mask using the logical exclusive-OR operator. See the discussions on video memory and display attributes in Chapter 5, or the more complete treatment of video programming in Chapter 8 of *MS-DOS Advanced Programming* (cited in the Bibliography).

If you assign the parameter **PointerType** the value 1, the mouse driver will use the blinking, hardware-generated cursor for the mouse pointer. Each time the user moves the mouse, the mouse driver will place the hardware cursor at the appropriate new location of the mouse pointer. If you choose this pointer type and your program requires a cursor to mark the text insertion point, you must explicitly create and maintain your own software cursor.

If your program explicitly moves the cursor (by invoking the BIOS interrupt 10h function 02h), or if it calls a function that updates the cursor position as a side effect (such as **printf** or interrupt 10h function 0Dh) the hardware cursor is temporarily moved away from the correct position of the mouse pointer. (The mouse driver does not restore the cursor to the correct location until the next time the mouse is moved.) Therefore, if you have chosen the hardware pointer, you should write screen data directly to video memory, or display each character using interrupt 10h function 09h or 0Ah; these methods do not move the cursor.

If you select the hardware cursor for the mouse pointer, then the second two parameters passed to **MouSetTextPointer** specify the cursor shape. **SMaskScanStart** gives the scan line where the cursor begins, and **PMaskScanStop** gives the scan line where the cursor ends. The available scan lines depend upon the video mode; see the discussion of the functions **ScrGetStyle** and **ScrSetStyle** in Chapter 5 for an explanation of the scan lines used to form the hardware cursor.

How MouSetText-Pointer Works

MouSetTextPointer invokes the following mouse driver service:

Mouse Function 10: Set Text Pointer

Entry:

AX   10

BX   Pointer type (0 is software and 1 is hardware)

CX   Screen mask for software pointer, or starting scan line for hardware cursor

DX   Pointer mask for software pointer, or ending scan line for hardware cursor

Return:

None

MouGetMickeys

Using MouGetMickeys

The function **MouGetMickeys** has the prototype

```
int MouGetMickeys
    (int *HorizCount,
     int *VertCount)
```

and supplies the distance the mouse has moved on the desktop since the last call to this function. **MouGetMickeys** returns zero if successful, or a nonzero value if an error occurs.

The movement of the mouse on the desktop is reported in units termed *mickeys*. A mickey is approximately 1/120 of an inch. The amount of horizontal motion is assigned to ***HorizCount**; a positive value indicates motion of the mouse on the desk that moves the pointer toward the right of the screen, and a negative value indicates motion that moves the pointer toward the left of the screen. The amount of vertical motion is assigned to ***VertCount**; a positive value indicates motion of the mouse that moves the pointer toward the bottom of the screen, and a negative value indicates motion that moves the pointer toward the top of the screen.

The first call to **MouGetMickeys** reports the motion of the mouse relative to its initial position assigned by **MouReset**. Subsequent calls to **MouGetMickeys** report motion of the mouse relative to its position when this function was last called. See the description of **MouSetInt-Handler**, later in the chapter, for another method of determining the mouse position and for an example program that displays the mouse position in mickeys.

*How
MouGetMickeys
Works*

MouGetMickeys uses the following service of the mouse driver:

Mouse Function 11: Read Mouse Motion Counters

Entry:

AX   11

Return:

CX   Horizontal count in mickeys

DX   Vertical count in mickeys

MouSetIntHandler

*Using
MouSetIntHandler*

The function **MouSetIntHandler** has the prototype

```
int MouSetIntHandler
    (int CallMask,
     void (far *FarPtrHandler) (void))
```

and causes the mouse driver to call the function specified by **FarPtr-Handler** whenever one of the events specified by **CallMask** occurs. **MouSetIntHandler** returns zero if successful, and a nonzero value if a mouse driver is not installed.

MouSetIntHandler allows you to install a function that is automatically called by the mouse driver whenever an event occurs that you have specified in the call mask parameter, **CallMask**. **CallMask** is a 16-bit value; you can specify one or more events by turning on the appropriate bits, according to the following table:

Call Mask Bit	Event
0	Pointer position has changed
1	Left button pressed
2	Left button released
3	Right button pressed
4	Right button released
5	Center button pressed
6	Center button released
7–15	Not used

For example, if you assign **CallMask** the value 0x0003, the function you install will be called whenever the pointer changes position on the screen *or* the left mouse button is pressed.

The parameter **FarPtrHandler** should be the address of the function within your program that you want the mouse driver to call each time one of the specified events occurs. If the name of your function is **Handler**, for example, it should have the following prototype:

```
void far Handler
     (void)
```

Note that the function must be declared as **far** (that is, it is called using both a segment and offset address, and it returns using a **far** return instruction). Also, as you will see, the function should be able to directly access the machine registers to obtain the values passed to it from the mouse driver. Accordingly, this function should be written in assembly language (declared using the PROC FAR statement). Figure 11.20, described later in the chapter, provides an example of a mouse event handler written in assembler. (Note that you cannot use a Microsoft C

interrupt function, since the resulting code overwrites the AX register and returns with an IRET instruction rather than a far RET instruction.)

When the mouse driver calls the function installed by **MouSetInt-Handler**, it passes it the following information through machine registers:

· Register	Information
AX	A bit mask indicating the event that occurred (the bits are encoded in the same manner as the bits of the call mask)
BX	Button press status
CX	Pointer column coordinate
DX	Pointer row coordinate
SI	Horizontal mouse count in mickeys
DI	Vertical mouse count in mickeys

The bits of the value placed in register AX are encoded exactly as the bits in the call mask passed to **MouSetIntHandler**, except that only a *single* bit is turned on to indicate the event that occurred. For example, the value 0x0002 indicates that the left button was pressed.

The mouse count values in registers DI and SI describe the motion of the mouse on the desktop since the driver was initialized with the call to **MouReset**. If the motion in a given direction exceeds the capacity of an integer (–32,768 to +32,767) the mouse driver ignores the resulting overflow, and the value passed to your routine no longer reflects the total distance the mouse has moved.

Note that the mouse driver receives control—and subsequently calls the routine you have installed—in response to a hardware interrupt from the mouse controller. (The routine installed by **MouSetIntHandler** is thus termed a mouse *interrupt handler*.) Such a hardware interrupt can suspend the execution of your program at almost any time; control temporarily passes to the installed handler, and when this routine completes, your program continues execution at the point it was interrupted. As a consequence, you must be careful not to call a non-reentrant routine from both the main program *and* from the mouse interrupt handler. A nonreentrant routine is a body of code that cannot be temporarily suspended and have its code reentered; examples include many of the C library routines, the MS-DOS functions, and the BIOS services. Accordingly, the interrupt handler you install should not make use of these routines. Rather, it should simply save the required information and return quickly (as in the example program of Figure 11.20).

Before your program terminates, it must deactivate the interrupt handler installed by **MouSetIntHandler**. This can be done either by calling **MouSetIntHandler** and specifying a call mask value of 0, or by simply calling **MouReset** (which also conveniently hides the mouse pointer). If you fail to deactivate the interrupt handler, the mouse driver will continue to pass control to the specified address in response to mouse events even after the application has terminated and relinquished the memory it occupied.

Note that when a memory resident program becomes active, it may suspend a foreground application that is using the mouse and has installed a mouse interrupt handler. Therefore, if you are writing a memory-resident program, you should save the existing mouse state before installing a mouse interrupt handler for the resident program, and you should restore the state before returning control to the foreground application. See the section of **MouGetStorage**, **MouSaveState**, and **MouRestoreState** for an explanation of the method for saving and restoring the mouse state.

Figures 11.19 and 11.20 provide an example program that installs a mouse interrupt handler. The C program in Figure 11.19 calls **MouSetIntHandler** to install the interrupt handler **IntHandler**, which is located in the assembly language program of Figure 11.20. The program passes a call mask value of 0x001f, which causes the driver to call **IntHandler** for any of the first five events listed earlier in this section (in other words, all events except pressing or releasing the center button on a three button mouse). Subsequently, each time **IntHandler** receives control, it simply saves all the information it is passed (except the event code in register AX) in the structure **MouseInfo** and returns control. **MouseInfo** is declared as an external data item so that it can be accessed by both the assembler module and the C program.

After installing the interrupt handler, the C program of Figure 11.19 enters a loop that repeatedly displays the information contained in the **MouseInfo** structure, which is kept up to date by the interrupt handler. Note that by installing an interrupt handler, the main program does not need to explicitly poll the mouse driver to obtain the current state of the mouse; rather, it need only perform a rapid test of a memory variable.

A more sophisticated interrupt handler could save an entire series of mouse events in a queue; when the main application was ready to process one or more mouse events, it could extract elements from this queue in the same order in which they were inserted. By using such an event queue, the program would not miss important mouse events

```
/*
    This program demonstrates the function:
        MouSetIntHandler
*/

#include <STDIO.H>
#include <STDLIB.H>

#include "MOU.H"
#include "KBD.H"
#include "SCR.H"

struct
    {
    int ButtonState;
    int PointerCol;
    int PointerRow;
    int HorizMickeys;
    int VertMickeys;
    }
MouseInfo;

void far IntHandler (void);

void main (void)
    {
    int NumButtons;
    int ButtonStatus;
    char NumBuf [7];

    if (!MouInstalled ())
        {
        printf ("Sorry, a mouse must be installed.\n");
        exit (1);
        }

    ScrClear (0,0,24,79);
    ScrSetCur (25,80,0);

    MouReset (&NumButtons);

    MouSetIntHandler (0x001f,IntHandler);

    MouShowPointer ();

    ScrPutS ("   Pointer Column:       Row:         |"
             "   Left Button:       Right Button:   ",0x70,0,0);
    ScrPutS ("   Horizontal Mickeys:                |"
             "   Vertical Mickeys:                   ",0x70,1,0);

    ScrPutS ("Press any key to end program.",0x70,24,25);
        for (;;)
            {
            if (KbdReady ())
                {
                KbdGetC ();
                MouReset (&NumButtons);
                ScrClear (0,0,24,79);
                ScrSetCur (0,0,0);
                exit (0);
                }
```

Figure 11.19: MOUDEM06.C: A program demonstrating the function **MouSetIntHandler**

4

```
        ScrPutS (MouseInfo.ButtonState & LEFTBUTTONDOWN  ? "down" : "up  ",
                0x70,0,56);
        ScrPutS (MouseInfo.ButtonState & RIGHTBUTTONDOWN ? "down" : "up  ",
                0x70,0,76);

        sprintf (NumBuf,"%2d",MouseInfo.PointerCol/8);
        ScrPutS (NumBuf,0x70,0,19);

        sprintf (NumBuf,"%2d",MouseInfo.PointerRow/8);
        ScrPutS (NumBuf,0x70,0,30);

        sprintf (NumBuf,"%6d",MouseInfo.HorizMickeys);
        ScrPutS (NumBuf,0x70,1,23);

        sprintf (NumBuf,"%6d",MouseInfo.VertMickeys);
        ScrPutS (NumBuf,0x70,1,61);
        }

    } /* end main */
```

Figure 11.19: MOUDEM06.C: A program demonstrating the function **MouSetIntHandler** (continued)

while it was busy performing other tasks. (In a similar manner, the BIOS keyboard interrupt handler saves keystrokes in a circular queue until an application is ready to read and process them.)

Figure 11.21 provides a MAKE file, and Figure 11.22 a QuickC program list.

How MouSetIntHandler Works

MouSetIntHandler invokes the following mouse driver service:

Mouse Function 12: Set Interrupt Subroutine Call Mask and Address

Entry:

AX   12

CX   Call mask

DX   Offset address of interrupt routine to be installed

ES   Segment address of interrupt routine

Return:

None

```
.MODEL SMALL

InfoType      STRUC
ButtonState   DW  ?
PointerCol    DW  ?
PointerRow    DW  ?
HorizMickeys  DW  ?
VertMickeys   DW  ?
InfoType      ENDS

.DATA

EXTRN   _MouseInfo : WORD

.CODE

PUBLIC _IntHandler

_IntHandler PROC FAR

    push ds                             ;Temporarily load the C data segment
    push ax                             ;address into DS.
    mov  ax, DGROUP
    mov  ds, ax

    mov  _MouseInfo.ButtonState, bx
    mov  _MouseInfo.PointerCol, cx
    mov  _MouseInfo.PointerRow, dx
    mov  _MouseInfo.HorizMickeys, si
    mov  _MouseInfo.VertMickeys, di

    pop  ax
    pop  ds
    ret

_IntHandler ENDP

END
```

Figure 11.20: MOUDEM6A.ASM: The assembler mouse interrupt handler installed by MOUDEM06.C

```
MOUDEM06.OBJ : MOUDEM06.C MOU.H KBD.H SCR.H
     cl /c /W2 /Zp MOUDEM06.C

MOUDEM6A.OBJ : MOUDEM6A.ASM
     masm /MX MOUDEM6A.ASM;

MOU.OBJ : MOU.C MOU.H
     cl /c /W2 /Zp MOU.C

KBDA.OBJ : KBDA.ASM
     masm /MX KBDA.ASM;

SCR.OBJ : SCR.C SCR.H
     cl /c /W2 /Zp SCR.C

MOUDEM06.EXE : MOUDEM06.OBJ MOUDEM6A.OBJ MOU.OBJ KBDA.OBJ SCR.OBJ
     link /NOI /NOD MOUDEM06+MOUDEM6A+MOU+KBDA+SCR,,NUL,SLIBCER;
```

Figure 11.21: MOUDEM06.M: A MAKE file for MOUDEM06.C

```
MOUDEM06.C
MOUDEM6A.OBJ
MOU.C
KBDA.OBJ
SCR.C
```

Figure 11.22: A QuickC program list for preparing MOUDEM06.C

MouSetRatio

Using
MouSetRatio

The function **MouSetRatio** has the prototype

```
int MouSetRatio
    (int HorizRatio,
    int VertRatio)
```

and sets the ratio of the mouse movement on the desktop to the pointer movement on the screen; **HorizRatio** gives the ratio in the horizontal direction and **VertRatio** gives the ratio in the vertical direction. The function returns zero if successful, or a nonzero value if a mouse driver is not installed.

MouSetRatio adjusts the sensitivity, or relative speed, of the mouse pointer movement. The ratio values passed to this function should specify the number of mickeys the mouse must move on the desktop in order to move the pointer a distance of 8 pixels on the screen (remember that a mickey is approximately 1/120 of an inch). The default value for horizontal movement is 8 mickeys to 8 pixels, which requires that the user move the mouse approximately 6.4 inches to move the pointer horizontally across the entire screen. The default value for vertical movement is 16 mickeys to 8 pixels, which requires that the user move the mouse approximately 4 inches to move the pointer vertically across the entire screen.

*How
MouSetRatio
Works*

MouSetRatio employs the following mouse driver function:

Mouse Function 15: Set Mickey to Pixel Ratio

Entry:

AX   15

CX   Horizontal mickey-to-pixel ratio

DX   Vertical mickey-to-pixel ratio

Return:

None

MouGetStorage, MouSaveState, and MouRestoreState

*Using
MouGetStorage,
MouSaveState,
and
MouRestoreState*

The three functions presented in this section allow a program to save and restore the complete existing state of the mouse driver (including the current call mask and the address of any mouse interrupt handler that has been installed). These functions are especially useful for a memory resident program, which may interrupt a foreground application that uses the mouse. The memory resident program should employ these functions to save the mouse state before calling **MouReset**, installing an interrupt handler (**MouSetIntHandler**), or altering any mouse parameters; it should then use these functions to restore the mouse state before returning control to the interrupted foreground application.

The function **MouGetStorage**, which has the prototype

```
int MouGetStorage
        (int *BufferSize)
```

assigns ***BufferSize** the number of bytes required to save the mouse state.

The function **MouSaveState** has the prototype

```
int MouSaveState
        (unsigned char far *FarPtrBuffer)
```

and saves the existing mouse state in the buffer specified by the parameter **FarPtrBuffer**.

Finally, the function **MouRestoreState**, which has the prototype

```
int MouRestoreState
        (unsigned char far *FarPtrBuffer)
```

restores the mouse state saved in the buffer **FarPtrBuffer** by a prior call to **MouSaveState**. All three of these functions return zero if successful, or a nonzero value if a mouse driver is not installed.

As an example, the following instructions save the state of the mouse driver, and would typically be placed near the beginning of the routine that receives initial control when a memory resident program is activated:

```
#include <MALLOC.H>
#include "MOU.H"
.

.

.

int BufferSize;
unsigned char *PtrBuffer;
.

.

.

MouGetStorage (&BufferSize);
PtrBuffer = malloc (BufferSize);
MouSaveState (PtrBuffer);
```

The following instructions would be executed before the memory resident code returns control to the suspended foreground application, and serve to restore the former state of the mouse driver:

```
MouRestoreState (PtrBuffer);
free (PtrBuffer);
```

*How
MouGetStorage,
MouSaveState,
and
MouRestoreState
Work*

MouGetStorage uses the following mouse driver service:

Mouse Function 21: Get Mouse Driver State Storage Requirements

Entry:

AX   21

Return:

BX   Size of buffer in bytes required to store the mouse driver state

MouSaveState uses the following mouse driver service:

Mouse Function 22: Save Mouse Driver State

Entry:

AX   22

DX   Offset address of buffer for storing the mouse state

ES   Segment address of buffer for storing the mouse state

Return:

None

Finally, **MouRestoreState** employs the following function:

Mouse Function 23: Restore Mouse Driver State

Entry:

AX   23

DX   Offset address of buffer in which the mouse state was stored by Function 22

ES   Segment address of buffer in which the mouse state was stored by Function 22

Return:

None

Utility Functions

CHAPTER **12**

This last chapter presents a diverse collection of functions that you can call from a Microsoft C program. These functions fall into the following two categories: (1) supporting functions called by other modules in the book (you have already seen how these functions are used; in this chapter you will see their source code); and (2) additional utility functions you have not seen before, which extend the capabilities of the Microsoft C library, but do not fit into any of the larger categories presented in previous chapters.

The module of utility functions presented in this chapter comprises the following groups: string functions, time and date functions, file path functions, numeric functions, and miscellaneous functions. The C source code for this module is listed in Figure 12.1, and the assembly language source code is in Figure 12.2. The header file you must include in your program to call these functions is given in Figure 12.3.

STRING FUNCTIONS

The functions in this group manipulate strings and other blocks of memory, and allow you to perform the following tasks:

- Test whether a string contains only blank characters (**UtyAllBlank**).
- Initialize a string with blanks (**UtyBlank**).
- Display the contents of a sequence of memory locations in hexadecimal format (**UtyDump**).
- Copy data from or to **far** memory locations in any memory model C program (**UtyFarNearCopy** and **UtyNearFarCopy**).
- Fill a block of **far** memory with given byte or word of data (**UtyFarSetByte** and **UtyFarSetWord**).
- Obtain a string filled with a specified number of a given character (**UtyRepeat**).
- Remove the trailing blanks from a string (**UtyRightTrim**).

```
#include <STDIO.H>
#include <PROCESS.H>
#include <DOS.H>
#include <STDLIB.H>
#include <CTYPE.H>
#include <DIRECT.H>
#include <STRING.H>
#include <CONIO.H>

#include "UTY.H"
#include "KBD.H"
#include "SCR.H"

#define ULR 6                   /* Position of centered window.        */
#define ULC 20

#pragma check_stack (off)       /* Turn off stack checks so that functions */
                                /* can be called from interrupt routines.  */

/*** string and memory data functions *************************************/

int UtyAllBlank (char *String)
/*
    This function returns a non-zero value if the null-terminated string
    pointed to by the parameter 'String' consists entirely of blank
    characters.  If the string contains any non-blank characters, the
    function returns 0.
*/
    {
    while (*String)
        if (*String++ != ' ')
            return (0);

    return (1);

    } /* end UtyAllBlank */


void UtyBlank (char *String,int Length)
/*
    This function writes 'Length' - 1 blank characters to 'String', and
    places a null character at the end of the string.
*/
    {
    register int i;             /* Loop index.                         */

    if (Length < 1)             /* If 'Length' is less than 1, no blanks */
        return;                 /* are written.                        */

    for (i = 0; i < Length - 1; ++i)    /* Write 'Length' - 1 blanks.  */
        String[i] = ' ';

    String[i] = '\0';           /* Null termination.                   */

    } /* end UtyBlank */
```

Figure 12.1: UTY.C: The C utility functions

```
void UtyDump (char *Source, int Count)
/*
    This function prints 'Count' bytes of data in hexadecimal, beginning at
    the address given by 'Source'.
*/
    {
    while (Count--)
        printf ("%.2x ",*Source++);

    } /* end UtyDump */


char *UtyRepeat (int Number, char Ch)
/*
    This function returns a pointer to a null terminated static string
    consisting of 'Number' copies of character 'Ch'.  The string is changed
    with subsequent calls.  Maximum value of 'Number' is 255.
*/
    {
    register int i = 0;            /* Loop index.                       */
    static char Buf [256];         /* Stores the repeated characters.   */

    while (Number-- && i < 255)    /* Write characters to 'Buf'.        */
        Buf [i++] = Ch;

    Buf [i] = '\0';                /* Add NULL termination.             */

    return (Buf);                  /* Return address of 'Buf'.          */

    } /* end UtyRepeat */


void UtyRightTrim (char *String,int Length)
/*
    This function removes all trailing blank characters from 'String'.  The
    parameter 'Length' must give the length of 'String'.
*/
    {
    char *ChPt;                    /* Points to characters in the string. */

    if (Length < 1)               /* Must be at least 1 character.       */
        return;

    ChPt = String + Length - 1;   /* Points to last character of string. */

    /* Scan backwards in string until first non-blank, non-null character: */
    while (ChPt > String && (*ChPt == '\0' || *ChPt == ' '))
        --ChPt;
    if (*ChPt == '\0' || *ChPt == ' ')        /* String all blank or NULL.  */
        *ChPt = '\0';                         /* Place NULL at first position*/
    else if (ChPt < String + Length - 1)      /* String contains non-blank,  */
        *(++ChPt) = '\0';                     /* non-NULL character(s).       */
                                              /* Place NULL after last char. */
    } /* end UtyRightTrim */
```

Figure 12.1: UTY.C: The C utility functions (continued)

```
/*** time and date functions ***********************************************/

int UtyClockCount (long *Count)
/*
    This function assigns the current count of clock ticks since midnight to
    the variable 'Count'.  It returns the value of the 'rollover' flag;  if
    this flag is 1, midnight has passed since the last time the clock count
    was read through interrupt 1Ah.
*/
    {                                         /* Pointer to BIOS tick count: */
    static long far *CntPtr = (long far *)0x0040006c;
                                              /* Pointer to rollover flag:   */
    static unsigned char far *RolPtr = (unsigned char far *)0x0040006c;
    int Enabled;                              /* Interrupts are enabled.     */
    int Rollover;                             /* Midnight has passed.        */

    Enabled = UtyEnabled ();     /* Test if interrupts currently enabled. */
    UtyDisable ();               /* Unconditionally disable interrupts.   */

    *Count = *CntPtr;            /* Fetch clock count.                    */
    Rollover = *RolPtr;          /* Fetch rollover flag.                  */

    if (Enabled)                 /* Preserve the original condition of    */
        UtyEnable ();            /* the interrupt flag.                   */

    return (Rollover);           /* Return rollover flag.                 */

    } /* end UtyClockCount */


int UtyGetDateString (char *Target)
/*
    This function writes the current system date to the string given by
    'Target', in the format mm/dd/yyyy.  'Target' must therefore be at least
    11 bytes long.
*/
    {
    union REGS Reg;
    int Month;                   /* Variables for storing numeric values: */
    int Day;
    int Year;

    Reg.h.ah = 0x2a;             /* DOS "get date" service.               */
    int86 (0x21,&Reg,&Reg);

    Month = Reg.h.dh;            /* Store returned month, day, and year   */
    Day = Reg.h.dl;              /* values.                               */
    Year = Reg.x.cx;

                                 /* Format values into target string.     */
    sprintf (Target,"%02d/%02d/%04d",Month,Day,Year);

    return (Reg.h.al);           /* Return day-of-week code.              */

    } /* end UtyGetDateString */
```

Figure 12.1: UTY.C: The C utility functions (continued)

```
    void UtyGetTimeString (char *Target)
    /*
        This function obtains the system time and writes it to the string
        'Target', in the format 'hh:mm:ss.hh". 'Target' must be at least 12
        bytes long.
    */
        {
        union REGS Reg;
        int Hours,Minutes,Seconds,Hundredths;

        Reg.h.ah = 0x2c;                        /* DOS get time service.              */
        int86 (0x21,&Reg,&Reg);

        Hours = Reg.h.ch;                       /* Assign values returned by DOS.     */
        Minutes = Reg.h.cl;
        Seconds = Reg.h.dh;
        Hundredths = Reg.h.dl;

        sprintf (Target,"%02d:%02d:%02d.%02d",Hours,Minutes,Seconds,Hundredths);

        } /* end UtyGetTimeString */


    int UtyPackDate (char *Target,char *Source)
    /*
        This function performs two services:
        (1)  It checks the validity of the date contained in 'Source', which
             must be in the format 'mm/dd/yyyy'. It returns NOERROR (0) if the
             date in 'Source' is valid, or the nonzero value BADDATE if the date
             is invalid.
        (2)  If the date is valid, it copies it to the string 'Target' in the
             format 'yyyymmdd'; 'Target' must be at least 9 bytes long. (If
             the date is invalid, 'Target' is not modified.)
    */
        {
        char Year[5], Month[3], Day[3];    /* Temporary storage for date.      */
        int i = 0;                         /* Index for 'Source'.              */
        int j;                             /* Loop index.                      */
        int Leap;                          /* Flag indicates a leap year.      */
        static int DayTable[2][13] =       /* Numbers of days in each month.   */
                {
                {0,31,28,31,30,31,30,31,31,30,31,30,31},    /* Normal year. */
                {0,31,29,31,30,31,30,31,31,30,31,30,31}     /* Leap year.   */
                };
        if (isdigit (Source[i]))                            /* Extract month.    */
            Month[0] = Source[i++];
        else
            return (BADDATE);                               /* Invalid date.     */
        if (isdigit (Source[i]))
            {
            Month[1] = Source[i++];
            Month[2] = '\0';
            }
        else
            Month[1] = '\0';
```

Figure 12.1: UTY.C: The C utility functions (continued)

```
        if (Source[i] != '-' && Source[i] != '/')    /* Test for valid        */
            return (BADDATE);                          /* separator character.  */
        else
            ++i;                                       /* Scan past separator.  */

        if (isdigit (Source[i]))                       /* Extract day.          */
            Day[0] = Source[i++];
        else
            return (BADDATE);
        if (isdigit (Source[i]))
            {
            Day[1] = Source[i++];
            Day[2] = '\0';
            }
        else
            Day[1] = '\0';

        if (Source[i] != '-' && Source[i] != '/')      /* Test for valid        */
            return (BADDATE);                          /* separator character.  */
        else
            ++i;                                       /* Scan past separator.  */

        for (j = 0; j <= 3; ++j)                       /* Extract year.         */
            if (!isdigit (Source [i]))
                return (BADDATE);
            else
                Year [j] = Source [i++];

        Year [4] = '\0';

                                                       /* Test for leap year.   */
        Leap = atoi(Year)%4 == 0 && atoi(Year)%100 != 0 || atoi(Year)%400 == 0;

        if (atoi (Month) < 1 || atoi (Month) > 12)     /* Test month.           */
            return (BADDATE);                          /* Bad month.            */

        if (atoi(Day) > DayTable[Leap][atoi(Month)])   /* Test day.             */
            return (BADDATE);                          /* Bad day.              */

                                                       /* Date must be valid, therefore */
                                                       /* assign it to 'Target'.        */

        Target[0] = Year[0];                           /* Assign year.          */
        Target[1] = Year[1];
        Target[2] = Year[2];
        Target[3] = Year[3];

        if (Month[1] != '\0')                          /* Assign month.         */
            {
            Target[4] = Month[0];
            Target[5] = Month[1];
            }
        else
            {
            Target[4] = '0';
            Target[5] = Month[0];
            }
```

Figure 12.1: UTY.C: The C utility functions (continued)

```
        if (Day[1] != '\0')                    /* Assign day.                    */
            {
            Target[6] = Day[0];
            Target[7] = Day[1];
            }
        else
            {
            Target[6] = '0';
            Target[7] = Day[0];
            }

        Target [8] = '\0';                      /* Assign terminating NULL.       */

        return (NOERROR);                       /* Return NOERROR (0), indicating */
                                                /* valid date.                    */

        } /* end UtyPackDate */


void UtyUnpackDate (char *Target,char *Source)
/*
    This function copies the date from the string 'Source' (in the format
    'yyyymmdd') to the string 'Target' (in the format 'mm/dd/yyyy');
    'Target' must be at least 11 bytes long.  No validity checking is
    performed, since the validity was presumably checked when the date was
    originally packed using 'UtyPackDate'.
*/
        {
        Target[0] = Source[4];                  /* Month.                         */
        Target[1] = Source[5];

        if (UtyAllBlank (Source))               /* Separators.                    */
            Target[2] = Target[5] = ' ';        /* Don't write separators if      */
        else                                    /* source date is blank.          */
            Target[2] = Target[5] = '/';

        Target[3] = Source[6];                  /* Day.                           */
        Target[4] = Source[7];

        Target[6] = Source[0];                  /* Year.                          */
        Target[7] = Source[1];
        Target[8] = Source[2];
        Target[9] = Source[3];

        Target[10] = '\0';                      /* Terminating NULL.              */

        } /* end UtyUnpackDate */


void UtyPause (double Seconds)
/*
    This function delays for the number of seconds specified by 'Seconds'.
*/
        {
        long CurrentCount,FinalCount;           /* Current and final BIOS clock   */
                                                /* tick counts.                   */

        UtyClockCount (&CurrentCount);          /* Get current BIOS clock count.  */
```

Figure 12.1: UTY.C: The C utility functions (continued)

```
        /* Calculate the final value of the BIOS clock tick count:        */
        FinalCount = CurrentCount + (long)(Seconds * 18.206482);

        do                                    /* Loop until current count has    */
            {                                 /* reached or exceeded final count. */
            UtyClockCount (&CurrentCount);
            }
        while (CurrentCount < FinalCount);

        } /* end UtyPause */


int UtySetDateString
        (char *Date)
/*
        This function sets the system date as specified by the string 'Date',
        which must by in the format mm/dd/yyyy (a '-' character can replace
        any '/' separator).  If the function is successful, it returns NOERROR
        (0);  if, however, 'Date' is invalid, it returns the nonzero value
        BADDATE.
*/
        {
        union REGS Reg;
        char PackedDate [9];

        if (UtyPackDate (PackedDate, Date))     /* Pack the date.           */
            return (BADDATE);
                                                /* Extract the day.         */
        Reg.h.dl = (unsigned char)atoi (PackedDate + 6);

        PackedDate [6] = '\0';                  /* Extract the month.       */
        Reg.h.dh = (unsigned char)atoi (PackedDate + 4);

        PackedDate [4] = '\0';                  /* Extract the year.        */
        Reg.x.cx = atoi (PackedDate);
        Reg.h.ah = 0x2b;                        /* DOS set date service.    */
        int86 (0x21, &Reg, &Reg);

        if (Reg.h.al == 0)                      /* AL = 0 means success.    */
            return (NOERROR);
        else                                    /* AL = 0xff means invalid date.*/
            return (BADDATE);

        } /* end UtySetDateString */


int UtySetTimeString
        (char *Time)
/*
```

Figure 12.1: UTY.C: The C utility functions (continued)

```
            This function sets the system time as specified by the string 'Time',
            which must be in the format hh:mm:ss.cc (where cc is hundredths).
            You can omit '.cc', or ':ss.cc', but must include 'hh:mm'.  If 'Time'
            is invalid,  the function returns BADTIME;  if successful, it returns
            NOERROR.
*/
            {
            union REGS Reg;
            static char Buf [3] = {'\0','\0','\0'};

                                            /* Test for hh digits:           */
            if (!isdigit (Time [0]) || !isdigit (Time [1]))
                return (BADTIME);

            Buf [0] = Time [0];             /* Extract hours.                */
            Buf [1] = Time [1];
            Reg.h.ch = (unsigned char)atoi (Buf);
            if (Reg.h.ch < 0 || Reg.h.ch > 23)   /* Test range of hours.    */
                return (BADTIME);

            if (Time [2] != ':')            /* Test for separator.           */
                return (BADTIME);

                                            /* Test for mm digits:           */
            if (!isdigit (Time [3]) || !isdigit (Time [4]))
                return (BADTIME);

            Buf [0] = Time [3];             /* Extract minutes.              */
            Buf [1] = Time [4];
            Reg.h.cl = (unsigned char)atoi (Buf);
            if (Reg.h.cl < 0 || Reg.h.cl > 59)   /* Test range of minutes.  */
                return (BADTIME);

            if (Time [5] == '\0')
                {                           /* No seconds or hundredths.     */
                Reg.h.dh = 0;               /* Set seconds to 0.             */
                Reg.h.dl = 0;               /* Set hundredths to 0.          */
                }
            else                            /* Seconds specified.            */
                {
                if (Time [5] != ':')        /* Test for separator.           */
                    return (BADTIME);
                                            /* Test for ss digits:           */
                if (!isdigit (Time [6]) || !isdigit (Time [7]))
                    return (BADTIME);

                Buf [0] = Time [6];         /* Extract seconds.              */
                Buf [1] = Time [7];
                Reg.h.dh = (unsigned char)atoi (Buf);
                                            /* Test range of seconds:        */
                if (Reg.h.dh < 0 || Reg.h.dh > 59)
                    return (BADTIME);
```

Figure 12.1: UTY.C: The C utility functions (continued)

```
            if (Time [8] == '\0')
                (                               /* No hundredths.              */
                Reg.h.dl = 0;                   /* Set hundredths to 0.        */
                )
            else
                (                               /* Hundredths specified.       */
                if (Time [8] != '.')            /* Test for separator.         */
                    return (BADTIME);
                                                /* Test for cc digits:         */
                if (!isdigit (Time [9]) || !isdigit (Time [10]))
                    return (BADTIME);

                Buf [0] = Time [9];             /* Extract hundredths.         */
                Buf [1] = Time [10];
                Reg.h.dl = (unsigned char)atoi (Buf);

                                                /* Test for hundredths range:  */
                if (Reg.h.dl < 0 || Reg.h.dl > 99)
                    return (BADTIME);

                )
            )

        Reg.h.ah = 0x2d;                        /* DOS set time service.       */
        int86 (0x21, &Reg, &Reg);

        if (Reg.h.al == 0)                      /* AL = 0 means success.       */
            return (NOERROR);
        else                                    /* AL = 0xff means invalid time. */
            return (BADTIME);

        ) /* end UtySetTimeString */


/*** file path functions ***************************************************/


char *UtyExtension (char *FileName)
/*
    Returns a pointer to the beginning of the extension contained in
    'FileName';  if 'FileName' does not contain an extension, the address
    returned by this function points to the NULL character at the end of
    'FileName'.
*/
    (
    while (*FileName)                   /* Search for first '.' or end of string.*/
        if (*FileName++ == '.')
            return (FileName);

    return (FileName);

    ) /* end UtyExtension */
int UtyQualify (char *Qual, char *Unqual, int Size)
/*
    Converts the file name 'Unqual' (a simple, partially, or fully qualified
    file name) into a fully qualified name, supplying all missing elements
    of 'Unqual' with the current default values.  The resulting NULL
    terminated string is copied into 'Qual'; 'Size' specifies the total
    size of the receiving buffer pointed to by 'Qual'.  If 'Size' is too
```

Figure 12.1: UTY.C: The C utility functions (continued)

```
            small for the resulting string, the function returns SIZETOOSMALL;  if
            an error occurs when calling DOS, it returns DOSERR;  and if
            successful, it returns NOERROR.
*/
            {
            union REGS Reg;
            int SizeNeeded = 2;          /* Size requried to hold qualified name.   */
            int Drive;                   /* Stores drive number:  1 = A:, 2 = B:, etc. */
            char CurDir [65];            /* Stores current directory.               */
            char *PtrCurDir = CurDir;    /* Pointer to 'CurDir'.                    */

            if (Size < SizeNeeded)       /* Test for required size.                 */
                return (SIZETOOSMALL);

            if (Unqual [1] == ':')       /* Test for presence of drive spec.        */
                {                        /* 'Unqual' contains drive spec.           */
                Drive = toupper (Unqual [0]) - 64;  /* Save drive number.           */
                *Qual++ = *Unqual++;     /* Copy drive spec. to 'Qual'.             */
                *Qual++ = *Unqual++;
                }
            else                         /* No drive spec.                          */
                {
                Reg.h.ah = 0x19;                      /* Get current drive from DOS.*/
                int86 (0x21, &Reg, &Reg);
                Drive = Reg.h.al + 1;                 /* Save drive number.         */
                *Qual++ = (char)(65 + Reg.h.al);      /* Copy drive spec. to 'Qual'.*/
                *Qual++ = ':';
                }

            if (*Unqual != '\\')         /* Test for full directory spec.           */
                {                        /* No full directory spec.                 */
                Reg.h.ah = 0x47;                      /* Obtain current directory    */
                Reg.x.si = (unsigned)PtrCurDir;       /* from DOS.                   */
                Reg.h.dl = (unsigned char)Drive;
                int86 (0x21, &Reg, &Reg);
                if (Reg.x.cflag)
                    return (DOSERR);
                if (*PtrCurDir != '\0')
                    {
                    if (Size < ++SizeNeeded)          /* Test for required size.     */
                        return (SIZETOOSMALL);
                    *Qual++ = '\\';                   /* Copy '\' for root.          */
                    }
                                                      /* Test for required size:     */
                SizeNeeded += strlen (PtrCurDir) + 1;
                if (Size < SizeNeeded)
                    return (SIZETOOSMALL);

                while (*Qual++ = *PtrCurDir++)        /* Copy current directory to   */
                    ;                                 /* 'Qual'.                     */
                *(Qual - 1) = '\\';
                }

            SizeNeeded += strlen (Unqual) + 1;        /* Test again for required     */
            if (Size < SizeNeeded)                    /* size.                       */
                return (SIZETOOSMALL);

            while (*Qual++ = *Unqual++)               /* Copy partial file spec.     */
                ;                                     /* to 'Qual'.                  */
```

Figure 12.1: UTY.C: The C utility functions (continued)

```
        return (NOERROR);

        } /* UtyQualify */


char *UtyUnqualify (char *Qual)
/*
        Returns a pointer to the simple file name within the string 'Qual',
        which contains a partially or fully specified file path, and converts the
        unqualified file name to upper case.
*/
        {
        char *PtrCh;                      /* Points to characters in the string. */

        PtrCh = Qual + strlen (Qual);     /* Point to terminating NULL.          */

        while (PtrCh       != Qual &&     /* Scan backward until beginning,       */
                *(PtrCh-1) != '\\' &&     /* '\' character, or                    */
                *(PtrCh-1) != ':')        /* ':' character.                       */
            --PtrCh;

        strupr (PtrCh);                   /* Convert to upper case.               */

        return (PtrCh);

        } /* end UtyUnqualify */

/*** numeric functions ****************************************************/

double UtyRound (double Value,int Digits)
/*
        This function rounds the floating point number 'Value' to the number
        of decimal places specified by 'Digits'.
*/
        {
        long John;                 /* Temporary long integer storage.        */
        double Bubble = 1.0;       /* Stores 10 to the 'Digits' power.        */

        while (Digits--)           /* 'Bubble' is assigned the value of 10    */
            Bubble *= 10;          /* raised to the 'Digits' power.           */

        /* Truncate unwanted decimal places and assign to temporary integer:  */
        John = (long)(Value * Bubble + (Value > 0.0 ? 0.5 : -0.5));
```

Figure 12.1: UTY.C: The C utility functions (continued)

```
        return ((double) (John / Bubble));        /* Convert back to a double    */
                                                  /* and return.                 */
        } /* end UtyRound */


double UtyRound5 (double Value)
/*
        This function rounds 'Value' to the nearest 0.05 decimal value.  It is
        typically used to round a dollar value to the nearest 5 cents.
*/
        {
        long John;                      /* Temporary integer storage.            */
        int Mod;                        /* Stores the value of 'John' modulo 5.   */

        John = (long)UtyRound (Value * 100.0,0);/* Temporarily store as a long    */
                                                /* integer.                       */
        Mod = (int)(John % 5);                  /* Calculate the modulus.         */
        if (Mod > 2)                            /* Adjust 'John' to the           */
                John += 5 - Mod;                /* nearest multiple of 5.         */
        else
                John -= Mod;
        return (double)(John / 100.0);          /* Convert back to a double.      */

        } /* end UtyRound5 */


/*** miscellaneous functions ***************************************************/


int UtyGetMachine (void)
/*
        This function returns the IBM model of the runtime machine.  The model
        return values are defined in the file UTY.H.
*/
        {
        register int i;                         /* Loop index.                   */
        union REGS Reg;                         /* General registers.            */
        struct SREGS SReg;                      /* Segment registers.            */
        static unsigned char far *IdPtr;        /* Far pointer for accessing BIOS. */
        static char Logo [] = "IBM";            /* Value of IBM logo in ROM.     */
        unsigned char Code;                     /* Return value from int 15h.    */

        FP_SEG (IdPtr) = 0xf000;                /* Point 'IdPtr' to location of  */
        FP_OFF (IdPtr) = 0xe00e;                /* IBM logo in the ROM BIOS.     */

        for (i = 0; i < 3; ++i)                 /* Compare ROM value to "IBM".   */
                if (*IdPtr++ != Logo [i])
                        return (NONIBM);        /* Logo not found.               */

        FP_SEG (IdPtr) = 0xf000;                /* Point to model byte.          */
        FP_OFF (IdPtr) = 0xfffe;
```

Figure 12.1: UTY.C: The C utility functions (continued)

```
        switch (*IdPtr)                /* Branch according to value of  */
            {                          /* model byte.                   */
            case 0xf8:
                return (MODEL80);      /* Model 80.                     */

            case 0xf9:
                return (CONV);         /* Convertible.                  */

            case 0xfa:
                return (MODEL30);      /* Model 30.                     */

            case 0xfb:
            case 0xfe:
                return (XT);           /* PC XT.                        */

            case 0xfc:                 /* All machines using the 80286. */

                Reg.h.ah = 0xc0;            /* Invoke BIOS return system */
                int86x (0x15,&Reg,&Reg,&SReg);  /* configuration service. */

                Code = Reg.h.ah;            /* Save return code.         */

                FP_SEG (IdPtr) = SReg.es;    /* Point to system descriptor. */
                FP_OFF (IdPtr) = Reg.x.bx + 3;

                if (Code == 0x86)      /* FCh model and 0x06 code indicates*/
                    return (AT);       /* an AT dated 1/10/84.          */

                else if (Code == 0)    /* Another 80286 machine.        */
                    switch (*IdPtr)    /* Branch on submodel byte in    */
                        {              /* system descriptor.            */
                        case 0:        /* An AT dated 6/10/85 or 11/15/85. */
                        case 1:
                            return (AT);

                        case 2:                /* Other 80286 machines: */
                            return (XT286);    /* PC XT 286.            */

                        case 4:
                            return (MODEL50);  /* Model 50.            */

                        case 5:
                            return (MODEL60);  /* Model 60.            */

                        default:               /* An unexpected submodel */
                            return (UKIBM);    /* byte value.          */
                        }
                else
                    return (UKIBM);    /* An unexpected 'Code' value.   */

            case 0xfd:
                return (JR);           /* Junior.                       */

            case 0xff:
                return (PC);           /* IBM PC.                       */

            default:
                return (UKIBM);        /* An unexpected model byte value. */

            } /* end switch */

    } /* end UtyGetMachine */
```

Figure 12.1: UTY.C: The C utility functions (continued)

```
void UtyQuit (char *Message,char *File,int Line)
/*
      This function displays the string 'Message', the C source file name
      given by 'File', and the source file line number given by 'Line';    it
      then terminates the program.  It is typically called for a fatal error
      condition.
*/
      {
      char Buffer [30];

      ScrClear (ULR,ULC,ULR+11,ULC+39);
      ScrPutBox (ULR,ULC,ULR+11,ULC+39,1);
      ScrPutS (Message,0x0f,ULR+2,ULC+2);
      sprintf (Buffer,"File: %s",File);
      ScrPutS (Buffer,0x0f,ULR+4,ULC+2);
      sprintf (Buffer,"Line: %d",Line);
      ScrPutS (Buffer,0x0f,ULR+5,ULC+2);
      ScrPutS ("Press any key to return to DOS ",0x0f,ULR+7,ULC+2);
      ScrSetCur (ULR+7,ULC+35,0);
      KbdGetC ();                        /* Pause for keyboard input.        */
      ScrSetCur (23,0,0);
      exit (1);                          /* Terminate program setting DOS    */
                                         /* 'errorlevel' to 1.               */

      } /* end UtyQuit */


void UtySound (unsigned Frequency, unsigned Duration)
/*
      This function generates a sound from the computer speaker, which has
      a frequency specified by 'Frequency' (in cycles per second, or Hz) and
      a duration of 'Duration';  like the BASICA SOUND command, the duration
      is specified in clock ticks, which are approximately 1/18.2 seconds
      each.
*/
      {
      unsigned NoteValue;                /* Value to load into timer port 42h */
                                         /* to specify the frequency.         */
      long FinalCount;                   /* Holds final clock.                */
      long Count;                        /* Used for getting clock counts.    */

      outp (0x43, 0xb6);                 /* Initialize programmable timer.    */

                                         /* Calculate 'NoteValue'.            */
      NoteValue = (unsigned)(1193180 / (long)Frequency);

      outp (0x42, NoteValue & 0x00ff);   /* Write LSB of 'NoteValue' to timer */
                                         /* port 42h.                         */
      outp (0x42, NoteValue >> 8);       /* Write MSB to port 42h.            */

      outp (0x61, inp (0x61) | 3);       /* Enable sound.                     */

      UtyClockCount (&FinalCount);       /* Create a pause for the requested  */
      FinalCount += Duration;            /* sound duration.                   */
```

Figure 12.1: UTY.C: The C utility functions (continued)

```
            do
                {
                UtyClockCount (&Count);
                }
            while (Count < FinalCount);

            outp (0x61, inp (0x61) & 0xfc);  /* Disable sound.           */

            } /* end UtySound */


    void UtyWarmBoot (void)
    /*
            This function generates a "warm" reboot (that is, it avoids the lengthy
            memory check);  the function obviously does not return a value.
    */
            {
            /* Pointer to BIOS reset flag:                               */
            unsigned far *PtrBootFlag = (unsigned far *)0x00000472;
            void (far *PtrReboot) (void);   /* Function pointer to BIOS reset code.*/

            *PtrBootFlag = 0x1234;               /* Value 1234h causes the BIOS to skip */
                                                 /* the memory check.                   */

                                                 /* Set to address of BIOS reset code:  */
            PtrReboot =  (void (far *) (void))0xffff0000;

            (*PtrReboot) ();

            } /* end UtyWarmBoot */
```

Figure 12.1: UTY.C: The C utility functions (continued)

UtyAllBlank

Using
UtyAllBlank

The function **UtyAllBlank** has the prototype

```
        int UtyAllBlank
            (char *String)
```

and returns a nonzero value if the string pointed to by the parameter **String** consists of only blank characters. If the string contains any non-blank characters, the function returns 0. The string must be NULL -terminated and is tested up to the first NULL character. **UtyAllBlank**

```
        .MODEL LARGE
        .CODE

        Frame       equ     [bp]                    ;Base for accessing stack frame.
        PUBLIC _UtyFarNearCopy
        ;
        ;       Prototype
        ;               void far UtyFarNearCopy
        ;                   (char far *TargetAddr,
        ;                   unsigned SourceSeg,
        ;                   unsigned SourceOff,
        ;                   unsigned Count);
        ;
        ;               This function copies 'Count' bytes from the far memory location
        ;               that has the segment address 'SourceSeg' and the offset address
        ;               'SourceOff' to the program target buffer specified by 'TargetAddr'.
        ;               It is useful for copying data from another segment to a program
        ;               buffer in a small data model C program (the compiler automatically
        ;               converts a near pointer passed as the first parameter to a far
        ;               pointer).
        ;
        _UtyFarNearCopy PROC

        fncFrame        struc                       ;Template to access stack frame.
        fncBasePtr      dw      ?                   ;Position of saved BP register.
        fncRetAd        dd      ?                   ;Return address.
        fncTargetOff    dw      ?                   ;Target offset.
        fncTargetSeg    dw      ?                   ;Target segment address.
        fncSourceSeg    dw      ?                   ;Source segment.
        fncSourceOff    dw      ?                   ;Source offset.
        fncCount        dw      ?                   ;Number of copies.
        fncFrame        ends

                                                    ;Standard initialization.
            push    bp                              ;Set up base pointer to access frame.
            mov     bp, sp
            push    di                              ;Save C register variables.
            push    si
            push    ds                              ;Save the C data segment register.

            mov     ax, Frame.fncSourceSeg          ;Place source segment in DS.
            mov     ds, ax
            mov     si, Frame.fncSourceOff          ;Place source offset in SI.

            mov     ax, Frame.fncTargetSeg          ;Place target segment in ES.
            mov     es, ax
            mov     di, Frame.fncTargetOff          ;Place target offset in DI.

            mov     cx, Frame.fncCount              ;Place number of bytes to move in CX.

            cld                                     ;Move from low to high addresses.
            rep     movsb                           ;Byte-by-byte string transfer.

            pop     ds
            pop     si                              ;Restore registers.
            pop     di
            mov     sp, bp
            pop     bp
            ret                                     ;Return to C program.
```

Figure 12.2: UTYA.ASM: The assembly language utility functions

```
PUBLIC _UtyNearFarCopy
;
;       Prototype
;           void far UtyNearFarCopy
;               (unsigned TargetSeg,
;               unsigned TargetOff,
;               char far *SourceAddr,
;               unsigned Count);
;
;           This function copies 'Count' bytes from the program source buffer
;           specified by 'SourceAddr' to the far memory location that has the
;           segment address 'TargetSeg' and the offset address 'TargetOff'.  It
;           is useful for copying data from a small data model C program to a
;           memory location in another segment (the compiler automatically
;           converts a near pointer passed as the third parameter to a far
;           pointer).
;
_UtyNearFarCopy PROC

nfcFrame       struc                      ;Template to access stack frame.
nfcBasePtr     dw       ?                 ;Position of saved BP register.
nfcRetAd       dd       ?                 ;Return address.
nfcTargetSeg   dw       ?                 ;Target segment address.
nfcTargetOff   dw       ?                 ;Target offset.
nfcSourceOff   dw       ?                 ;Source offset.
nfcSourceSeg   dw       ?                 ;Source segment.
nfcCount       dw       ?                 ;Number of copies.
nfcFrame       ends

                                          ;Standard initialization.
       push  bp                           ;Set up base pointer to access frame.
       mov   bp, sp
       push  di                           ;Save C register variables.
       push  si
       push  ds

       mov   ax, Frame.nfcSourceSeg       ;Place source segment in DS.
       mov   ds, ax
       mov   si, Frame.nfcSourceOff       ;Place source offset in SI.

       mov   ax, Frame.nfcTargetSeg       ;Place target segment in ES.
       mov   es, ax
       mov   di, Frame.nfcTargetOff       ;Place target offset in DI.

       mov   cx, Frame.nfcCount           ;Place number of bytes to move in CX.

       cld                                ;Move from low to high addresses.

       rep   movsb                        ;Byte-by-byte string transfer.

       pop   ds
       pop   si                           ;Restore registers.
       pop   di
       mov   sp, bp
       pop   bp
       ret                                ;Return to C program.

_UtyNearFarCopy ENDP
```

Figure 12.2: UTYA.ASM: The assembly language utility functions (continued)

```
PUBLIC _UtyFarSetByte
;
;       Prototype:
;           void far UtyFarSetByte
;                   (unsigned TargetSeg,
;                   unsigned TargetOff,
;                   unsigned char Byte,
;                   unsigned Number);
;
;       This function fills memory beginning at the segment:offset address
;       given by 'TargetSeg' and 'TargetOff' with 'Number' copies of the 1-byte
;       value 'Byte'.
;
_UtyFarSetByte PROC

fsbFrame        struc                   ;Template to access stack frame.
fsbBasePtr      dw      ?               ;Position of saved BP register.
fsbRetAd        dd      ?               ;Return address.
fsbTargetSeg    dw      ?               ;Target segment address.
fsbTargetOff    dw      ?               ;Target offset.
fsbByte         dw      ?               ;Byte to use to fill memory.
fsbNumber       dw      ?               ;Number of copies.
fsbFrame        ends

                                        ;Standard initialization.
        push    bp                      ;Set up base pointer to access frame.
        mov     bp, sp
        push    di                      ;Save C register variable.

        mov     ax, Frame.fsbByte       ;Value to store in memory.
        mov     cx, Frame.fsbNumber     ;Number of copies to store.
        mov     es, Frame.fsbTargetSeg  ;The target address.
        mov     di, Frame.fsbTargetOff
        cld                             ;Fill from low to high addresses.
        rep     stosb                   ;Rapid string instruction.

        pop     di                      ;Restore registers.
        mov     sp, bp
        pop     bp
        ret                             ;Return to C program.

_UtyFarSetByte ENDP

PUBLIC _UtyFarSetWord
;
;       Prototype:
;           void far UtyFarSetWord
;                   (unsigned TargetSeg,
;                   unsigned TargetOff,
;                   unsigned Word,
;                   unsigned Number);
;
;       This function fills memory beginning at the segment:offset address
;       given by 'TargetSeg' and 'TargetOff' with 'Number' copies of the 2-byte
;       value 'Word'.
;
_UtyFarSetWord PROC
```

Figure 12.2: UTYA.ASM: The assembly language utility functions (continued)

```
fswFrame        struc                   ;Template to access stack frame.
fswBasePtr      dw      ?               ;Position of saved BP register.
fswRetAd        dd      ?               ;Return address.
fswTargetSeg    dw      ?               ;Target segment address.
fswTargetOff    dw      ?               ;Target offset.
fswWord         dw      ?               ;Word to use to fill memory.
fswNumber       dw      ?               ;Number of copies.
fswFrame        ends

                                        ;Standard initialization.
        push    bp                      ;Set up base pointer to access frame.
        mov     bp, sp
        push    di                      ;Save C register variable.

        mov     ax, Frame.fswWord       ;Value to store in memory.
        mov     cx, Frame.fswNumber     ;Number of copies to store.
        mov     es, Frame.fswTargetSeg  ;The target address.
        mov     di, Frame.fswTargetOff
        cld                             ;Fill from low to high addresses.
        rep     stosw                   ;Rapid string instruction.

        pop     di                      ;Restore registers.
        mov     sp, bp
        pop     bp
        ret                             ;Return to C program.

_UtyFarSetWord ENDP


PUBLIC _UtyDisable
;
;       Prototype:
;           void far UtyDisable
;                   (void)
;
;       This function disables hardware interrupts.
;
_UtyDisable PROC
        cli
        ret

_UtyDisable ENDP


PUBLIC _UtyEnable
;
;       Prototype:
;           void far UtyEnable
;                   (void)
;
;       This function enables hardware interrupts.
;
_UtyEnable PROC
        sti
        ret

_UtyEnable ENDP
```

Figure 12.2: UTYA.ASM: The assembly language utility functions (continued)

```
PUBLIC _UtyEnabled
;
;       Prototype:
;               int far UtyEnabled
;                       (void)
;
;       This function returns a non-zero value if the interrupts are currently
;       enabled, and returns 0 if they disabled.
;
_UtyEnabled PROC
        pushf
        pop     ax
        and     ax, 0200h
        ret

_UtyEnabled ENDP


PUBLIC _UtyGetCpu
;
;       Prototype:
;               int far UtyGetCpu
;                       (void)
;
;       This function returns one of the following codes indicating the type of
;       processor installed in the machine:
;
;
P86             equ     00              ;Intel 8086, 8088, or compatible.
P186            equ     01              ;80186.
P286            equ     02              ;80286.
P386            equ     03              ;80386.
;
_UtyGetCpu PROC

                pushf                   ;Save flags.

                                        ;** Test for the 8086/88. **
                xor     ax, ax          ;Place 0 in AX.
                push    ax              ;Try to load FLAGS with 0.
                popf
                pushf                   ;Now test contents of FLAGS.
                pop     ax              ;Place FLAGS in AX.
                and     ax, 0f000h      ;Isolate 4 high-order bits.
                cmp     ax, 0f000h      ;Test whether high-order bits are set.
                jne     a01
                mov     ax, P86         ;Bits set indicates 86/88 processor.
                jmp     a04
a01:                                    ;** Test for the 80186. **
                push    sp              ;Test whether SP is decremented before
                pop     ax              ;or after it is written to stack;
                cmp     ax, sp          ;186 decrements BEFORE, 286/386
                je      a02             ;decrement AFTER SP is written.
                mov     ax, P186        ;Must be the 80186.
                jmp     a04
```

Figure 12.2: UTYA.ASM: The assembly language utility functions (continued)

```
a02:                                          ;** Test for the 80286. **
           mov      ax, 0f000h               ;Attempt to set 4 high-order bits of
           push     ax                        ;FLAGS.
           popf
           pushf                              ;Test the 4 high-order bits.
           pop      ax
           and      ax, 0f000h
           jnz      a03
           mov      ax, P286                 ;No bits set, must be the 80286.
           jmp      a04
a03:                                          ;** Must be the 80386. **
           mov      ax, P386
a04:                                          ;Exit point.
           popf                               ;Restore flags.
           ret

_UtyGetCpu ENDP

           END
```

Figure 12.2: UTYA.ASM: The assembly language utility functions (continued)

is used in the example program of Figure 12.13, described later in the chapter; see also the description of **UtyBlank** for an example of the use of **UtyAllBlank**.

How UtyAllBlank Works

UtyAllBlank is contained in the C source file of Figure 12.1. This function simply scans through the string, character by character. If a nonblank character is encountered before the terminating NULL, then it returns 0; otherwise, it returns 1.

UtyBlank

Using UtyBlank

UtyBlank, which has the prototype

```
void UtyBlank
     (char *String,
      int Length)
```

```
/*** string and memory data functions ************************************/

int UtyAllBlank (char *String);
void UtyBlank (char *String, int Length);
void UtyDump (char *Source, int Count);
char *UtyRepeat (int Number, char Ch);
void UtyRightTrim (char *String, int Length);
                                                 /* Assembler functions:  */
void far UtyFarNearCopy (char far *TargetAddr, unsigned SourceSeg,
                         unsigned SourceOff, unsigned Count);
void far UtyFarSetByte (unsigned TargetSeg, unsigned TargetOff,
                        unsigned char Byte, unsigned Number);
void far UtyFarSetWord (unsigned TargetSeg, unsigned TargetOff,
                        unsigned Word, unsigned Number);
void far UtyNearFarCopy (unsigned TargetSeg, unsigned TargetOff,
                         char far *SourceAddr, unsigned Count);

/*** time/date ***********************************************************/

int UtyClockCount (long *Count);
int UtyGetDateString (char *Target);
void UtyGetTimeString (char *Target);
int UtyPackDate (char *Target, char *Source);
void UtyPause (double Seconds);
int UtySetDateString (char *Date);
int UtySetTimeString (char *Time);
void UtyUnpackDate (char *Target, char *Source);

/*** file path ***********************************************************/

char *UtyExtension (char *FileName);
int UtyQualify (char *Qual, char *Unqual, int Size);
char *UtyUnqualify (char *Qual);

/*** numeric *************************************************************/

double UtyRound (double Value, int Digits);
double UtyRound5 (double Value);

/*** miscellaneous functions *********************************************/

int UtyGetMachine (void);
void UtyQuit (char *Message, char *File, int Line);
void UtySound (unsigned Frequency, unsigned Duration);
void UtyWarmBoot (void);

void far UtyDisable (void);                       /* Assembler functions:  */
void far UtyEnable  (void);
int  far UtyEnabled (void);
int  far UtyGetCpu  (void);

/*** constant definitions ************************************************/
```

Figure 12.3: UTY.H: The header file you must include in your program to call the functions in
       UTY.C

```
                                /* Codes returned by UtyGetMachine:      */
#define NONIBM      0           /* No IBM logo.                          */
#define PC          1           /* IBM PC.                               */
#define XT          2           /* IBM PC XT.                            */
#define JR          3           /* IBM PCjr.                             */
#define AT          4           /* IBM AT.                               */
#define XT286       5           /* IBM PC XT 286.                        */
#define CONV        6           /* IBM Convertible.                      */
#define MODEL30     7           /* IBM PS/2 Model 30.                    */
#define MODEL50     8           /* IBM PS/2 Model 50.                    */
#define MODEL60     9           /* IBM PS/2 Model 60.                    */
#define MODEL80     10          /* IBM PS/2 Model 80.                    */
#define UKIBM       11          /* Unknown IBM model.                    */

                                /* Contants for processor types returned by */
                                /* UtyGetCpu.                            */
#define P86         0           /* Intel 8086, 8088, or compatible.      */
#define P186        1           /* 80186.                                */
#define P286        2           /* 80286.                                */
#define P386        3           /* 80386.                                */

                                /* Error return codes:                   */
#define NOERROR     0           /* Function successful.                  */
#define BADDATE     1           /* Passed bad date.                      */
#define BADTIME     2           /* Passed bad time.                      */
#define DOSERR      3           /* Error occurred calling DOS function.  */
#define SIZETOOSMALL 4          /* 'UtyQualify' size parameter too small. */
```

Figure 12.3: UTY.H: The header file you must include in your program to call the functions in
UTY.C (continued)

fills the string pointed to by the parameter **String** with blank characters,
and places a terminating NULL character at the end of the string. The
parameter **Length** specifies the *total* resulting length of the string, including the terminating NULL. There is no return value. The following
code fragment illustrates the use of **UtyBlank** and **UtyAllBlank** to initialize a string with blank characters, and then to test whether any non-
blank data were entered by the user.

```
char Name [25];
        .
        .
        .
UtyBlank (Name, sizeof (Name));
ScrGetS (Name, 0x70, 10, 15, sizeof (Name), NOFEAT);
if (UtyAllBlank (Name))
        /* then no data were entered  */
else
        /* process the data entered  */
```

UtyBlank is called by the screen designing utility of Figure 6.1 to initialize the strings used to contain file names; it is also used in the example program of Figure 12.13, described later in the chapter.

How UtyBlank Works

UtyBlank, contained in the C source file of Figure 12.1, first checks the validity of the requested string length; if the value of **Length** is less than 1, the function returns immediately. Next, **UtyBlank** writes **Length** − 1 blanks to the target string, and then places a NULL character at the last position in this string.

UtyDump

Using UtyDump

The function **UtyDump**, which has the prototype

```
void UtyDump
    (char *Source,
     int Count)
```

displays in hexadecimal format the sequence of memory locations beginning at the address given by **Source**, and extending for the number of bytes specified by the parameter **Count**. There is no return value. This function is used primarily for debugging programs and examining file data. The following lines demonstrate its use:

```
char *ChPt = "ABCD";
  .
  .
  .
UtyDump (ChPt, 5);
```

These lines of code would result in the following output:

```
41 42 43 44 00
```

How UtyDump
Works

UtyDump is contained in the C source file of Figure 12.1. This function prints each of the **Count** characters starting at the address given by **Source**, using the standard C **printf** function. The **x** conversion type is specified to cause the characters to be printed in lowercase hexadecimal format, and the *precision* field is given a value of 2 so that each character will be printed uniformly with two digits.

UtyFarNearCopy and UtyNearFarCopy

Using
UtyFarNearCopy
and
UtyNearFarCopy

UtyFarNearCopy has the prototype

```
void far UtyFarNearCopy
    (char far *TargetAddr,
    unsigned SourceSeg,
    unsigned SourceOff,
    unsigned Count);
```

and allows you to copy a block of data *from* a **far** memory location, which has the segment address specified by **SourceSeg** and the offset given by **SourceOff**, *to* the program buffer specified by **TargetAddr**. The parameter **Count** gives the number of bytes that are to be transferred.

UtyFarNearCopy allows you to easily obtain data from a **far** memory segment (that is, a memory address outside of the default C program data segment) in *any* memory model C program. For example, the following code copies the current contents of video memory into a program array (thus, saving the screen in a local buffer):

```
unsigned char SavedScreen [4000];
    .
    .
    .
UtyFarNearCopy
    (SavedScreen, /* Address of program buffer   */
                  /* to receive the data.        */
    0xb800,       /* Segment address of source   */
                  /* of data (color video memory. */
```

```
          0x0000,        /* Offset address of source.   */
          4000);         /* Number of bytes to transfer. */
```

Note that although the target address passed as the first parameter is a **far** pointer, the compiler will automatically convert a **near** pointer to the appropriate **far** address (provided that you have included the header file UTY.H, which is a requirement for using the module).

The function **UtyNearFarCopy** has the prototype

```
void far UtyNearFarCopy
    (unsigned TargetSeg,
    unsigned TargetOff,
    char far *SourceAddr,
    unsigned Count);
```

and copies **Count** bytes of data *from* the program buffer specified by **SourceAddr** *to* the **far** memory location that has the segment address **TargetSeg** and the offset address **TargetOff**.

UtyNearFarCopy is thus the complimentary function to **UtyFarNearCopy**. For instance, you could restore the contents of the screen saved in the previous example through the following function call:

```
UtyNearFarCopy
    (0xb800,       /* Segment address to receive   */
                   /* data (color video memory).   */
     0x0000,       /* Receiving offset address.     */
     SavedScreen   /* Address of source of data.    */
     4000);        /* Number of bytes to transfer.  */
```

Note that the Microsoft C library function **movedata** can also be used to effect intersegment data transfers; **movedata**, however, requires you to specify the segment address of the program buffer that supplies or receives the data. Obtaining the segment address of a buffer in a small model C program requires an extra step (you can either call the function **segread**, or you can cast the **near** pointer to a **far** pointer and then extract the segment using the FP_SEG macro). **UtyFarNearCopy** and **UtyNearFarCopy** are thus more convenient, and work uniformly in any memory model.

How
UtyFarNearCopy
and
UtyNearFarCopy
Work

UtyFarNearCopy and **UtyNearFarCopy** are located in the assembly language source file of Figure 12.2. These functions both use the REP MOVSB machine instruction, which rapidly transfers an entire block of data. Before calling the REP MOVSB instruction, you must specify the source and target addresses, and the number of bytes to move, by loading the required values into registers as follows:

Register	Value
DS	Segment of source block
SI	Offset of beginning of source block
ES	Segment of target block
DI	Offset of beginning of target block
CX	Number of bytes to transfer

Note that before invoking REP MOVSB, both functions also issue the CLD machine instruction, which clears the *direction flag*. When the direction flag is clear, the processor first copies the byte from the offset given by SI to the offset given by DI, then copies the byte from the next higher source offset to the next higher target offset, and so on until the ends of the blocks are reached. (This direction is necessary because the function places the addresses of the *beginnings* of the source and target blocks in SI and DI. If the direction flag is set—through the STD instruction—each subsequent byte copied is obtained from the next lower source address and is written to the next lower target address; in this case, SI and DI must contain the offsets of the *ends* of the source and target blocks. If the source and target blocks overlap in memory, you should choose a direction, by setting the direction flag and assigning SI and DI appropriately, so that data are not overwritten as the block is transferred.)

UtyFarSetByte and UtyFarSetWord

*Using
UtyFarSetByte
and
UtyFarSetWord*

UtyFarSetByte has the prototype

```
void UtyFarSetByte
    (unsigned TargetSeg,
    unsigned TargetOff,
    unsigned char Byte,
    unsigned Number)
```

This function is used to fill a block of **far** memory (that is, memory outside the C data segment) with a given byte value. The segment:offset address of the block of memory is given by the parameters **TargetSeg** and **TargetOff**, the byte used to fill this block is placed in the parameter **Byte**, and the size of the block in bytes is specified by the parameter **Number**. There is no return value. For example, the function call

```
UtyFarSetByte
    (0xb000,    /* Target segment: video memory.   */
    0x0000,     /* Target offset: start of video   */
                /* memory.                         */
    0,          /* Byte to fill memory with.       */
    0x8000);    /* Number of bytes: 32 kilobytes.  */
```

fills the 32-kilobyte block of memory beginning at address B000h:0000h with the value 0. (This call initializes the block of video memory used for Hercules graphics).

The function **UtyFarSetWord** has the prototype

```
void far UtyFarSetWord
    (unsigned TargetSeg,
    unsigned TargetOff,
    unsigned Word,
    unsigned Number)
```

and fills the block of memory that has the segment address given by **TargetSeg** and the beginning offset address given by **TargetOff**, with **Number** copies of the two-byte value **Word**.

UtyFarSetWord is the same as **UtyFarSetByte**, except that it fills memory with a given *word* value (16 bits) rather than a byte value, and the parameter **Number** specifies the number of words rather than the number of bytes. For example, the following function call fills the 4,000 byte block of memory beginning at address B0000h:0000h with 2,000 copies of the word value 0x0720:

```
UtyFarSetWord
      (0xb000,    /* Target segment: mono. video   */
                  /* memory.                        */
       0x0000,    /* Target offset: start of video  */
                  /* memory.                        */
       0x0720,    /* Word to fill memory with.      */
       2000);     /* Number of words.               */
```

This function call serves to fill monochrome video memory with space characters (0x20), having the normal white on black video attribute (0x07). **UtyFarSetWord** is used to initialize video memory in the file GRA.C, of Figure 7.1.

How UtyFarSetByte and UtyFarSetWord Work

UtyFarSetByte and **UtyFarSetWord** are located in the assembly language source file of Figure 12.2. **UtyFarSetByte** uses the machine instruction REP STOSB, which causes the processor to fill an entire block of memory with a given number of copies of a specified byte value. Before issuing this instruction, you must load the registers as follows:

Register	Value
AL	Byte value to be used to fill memory
ES	Segment address of block to be filled
DI	Offset of beginning of block
CX	Size in *bytes* of block to be filled

Note that you must also issue the CLD instruction before invoking REP STOSB to make sure that the direction flag is clear. When the direction flag is clear, memory is filled beginning with the offset initially loaded into DI, and then moving toward higher addresses (this direction is required because the function loads DI with the address of the *beginning* of the destination block).

The function **UtyFarSetWord** uses the instruction REP STOSW, which is similar to the instruction REP STOSB, except that it fills a block of memory with a specified number of a *word* value. The registers are loaded as follows:

Register	Value
AX	Word value to be used to fill memory
ES	Segment address of block to be filled
DI	Offset of beginning of block
CX	Size in *words* of block to be filled

The function also invokes the CLD instruction prior to the block transfer, for the same reason just discussed.

UtyRepeat

Using UtyRepeat

The function **UtyRepeat** has the prototype

```
char *UtyRepeat
      (int Number,
      char Ch)
```

and returns the address of a NULL-terminated string consisting of **Number** repetitions of the character **Ch**. Note that you must use the resulting string *before* you call the function again, since the area reserved for this string is reused with each call to **UtyRepeat**. The maximum string length is 255; if **Number** is larger than this value, the resulting string will be only 255 characters long (not including the NULL termination). This function is similar to the BASICA command STRING$. The following lines demonstrate its use:

```
int Row;
 .
 .
 .
PrtPosition ("Sign on the dotted line:", Row, 0);
PrtPosition (UtyRepeat (54,'.'), Row++, 27);
```

UtyRepeat is used in the screen designing utility of Figure 6.1.

*How UtyRepeat
Works*

UtyRepeat, listed in the C file of Figure 12.1, reserves a 256-byte static buffer (**Buf**). Each time the function is called, it writes the requested number of copies of the specified character to this buffer, and terminates the string with a NULL. It then returns the address of **Buf** to the calling program.

UtyRightTrim

*Using
UtyRightTrim*

UtyRightTrim has the prototype

```
void UtyRightTrim
    (char *String,
    int Length)
```

This function removes all trailing blank characters from the string specified by the parameter **String**. The parameter **Length** should contain the total length of the string (including the terminating NULL character, if present.) There is no return value.

As an example, consider the following lines of code:

```
char Name [41];
    .
    .
    .
ScrGetS (Name, 0x70, Row, Col, sizeof (Name),
        NOFEAT);
UtyRightTrim (Name, strlen (Name));
printf (":%s:", Name);
```

The function **ScrGetS** reads a string from the user, which it places in the buffer **Name**, padding with blanks on the right so that the resultant string has a length equal to **sizeof (Name)**. (Remember that **ScrGetS** is used primarily for reading data into fixed-length fields belonging to data files, which are often blank-padded for uniformity). The function

UtyRightTrim then removes this blank-padding. Therefore, if the user enters the name Henrietta, the following output would result:

```
:Henrietta:
```

Thus, **UtyRightTrim** can be used in conjunction with **ScrGetS** to obtain variable length strings from the user. Also, since the length of the string is specified by a separate parameter, the string passed to **UtyRightTrim** need not be NULL-terminated. The resulting string, however, will be assigned a NULL termination if there is room for it past the last non-blank character (the function will not write beyond the length specified by the **Length** parameter). **UtyRightTrim** is demonstrated in Figure 12.13.

How UtyRightTrim Works

UtyRightTrim (in the C source file of Figure 12.1) first verifies that the specified string length is greater than 0. The function then scans through the string using the character pointer **ChPt**. It starts at the end of the string and moves toward the beginning until it reaches a non-blank, non-NULL character, or until it reaches the first character in the string. If it does not find a nonblank, non-NULL character, it places a NULL in the first position, causing the string to have a length of 0. If a nonblank, non-NULL character is found, the function places a NULL immediately following this character, provided that the next position does not extend past the string length given by the parameter **Length**.

TIME AND DATE FUNCTIONS

The functions presented in this section deal with the time and date information maintained by the system, and allow you to accomplish the following tasks:

- Obtain the number of clock counts since midnight, to efficiently determine the time of day, or to accurately measure an elapsed period of time (**UtyClockCount**).
- Obtain the current system date formatted as a string (**UtyGetDateString**).

■ Obtain the current system time formatted as a string (**UtyGetTimeString**).

■ Validate a date string entered by the user, and convert it to a packed format that may be sorted and compared chronologically (**UtyPackDate**).

■ Convert a date in packed format to a normal date string (**UtyUnpackDate**).

■ Suspend program execution for a given number of seconds, specified as a floating point number (**UtyPause**).

■ Set the system date or system time by passing a string containing the desired new value (**UtySetDateString** and **UtySetTimeString**).

UtyClockCount

Using UtyClockCount

The function **UtyClockCount** has the prototype

```
int UtyClockCount
    (long *Count)
```

and returns the time keeping information maintained by the BIOS. First, the function sets the variable pointed to by **Count** to the current count of clock interrupts since midnight. Second, it returns the value of the BIOS *rollover* flag, which indicates whether the count has gone past midnight.

The BIOS time-keeping routine increments the clock count with each clock interrupt (hardware interrupt 08h). The count is set to 0 at midnight, or can be set to the correct value by a program through interrupt 1Ah (the BIOS time of day services). The clock interrupt occurs approximately 18.2 times per second (the exact number is 1193180/65536). You can therefore calculate the number of seconds that have elapsed since midnight by multiplying the current clock count times the reciprocal of this frequency (the reciprocal equals 0.054925 seconds per count).

Each time the clock count reaches the value for midnight, the BIOS not only adjusts the count back to 0, but also sets the rollover flag to 1. When a program obtains the current time information through interrupt 1Ah, the BIOS automatically resets this flag to 0. Therefore, if the flag equals 1, the program knows that midnight has gone by since the time was last read. A program that maintains the current date, such as MS-DOS, must then increment its record of the date. Note that **UtyClockCount** does *not* invoke interrupt 1Ah, and therefore does not cause the rollover flag to be reset to 0 (the values are read directly from memory). Calling this function, therefore, will not interfere with the date maintained by MS -DOS.

The example program in Figure 12.4 demonstrates the use of **Uty-ClockCount**. This program goes into a loop that repeatedly obtains the current clock count from **UtyClockCount**, calculates the time of day, and then displays the results in a window in the upper left corner of the screen. Pressing a key terminates this loop. Note that the program derives the current time by first calculating the number of seconds since midnight, using a floating-point multiplication, and then breaks down this value into the number of hours, minutes, and seconds. The routine in the function **Clock** in Figure 8.3 (which must be very efficient since it is called 18.2 times per second) calculates the time using only fast, integer operations; however, the routine in **Clock** does *not* need to calculate and display the number of seconds.

Figure 12.5 provides a MAKE file and Figure 12.6 contains a QuickC program list.

The function **UtyClockCount** is also used by the utility functions **UtyPause** and **UtySound**. The function **UtyGetTimeString** provides a convenient method for obtaining the current time already formatted as a string. These functions are described later in the chapter.

How
UtyClockCount
Works

UtyClockCount is listed in the C source file of Figure 12.1; it obtains its information directly from the BIOS data area in low memory. The **far** pointer **CntPtr** is used to read the clock count at address 0040h:006Ch, and the **far** pointer **RolPtr** is used to read the rollover flag at address 0040h:0070h. These two pointers are initialized at the beginning of the function. Before they are used to read the BIOS data, however, interrupts must be disabled. This precaution is necessary because the clock count is four bytes long and therefore requires two machine-level transfer operations; if a clock interrupt occurred *between* transfers and the BIOS routine modified the clock count, the value obtained by **UtyClockCount** could become invalid. Note that the function saves and restores the current value of the interrupt flag, so that the interrupt status of the calling program is not altered. The function

```
#include <STDIO.H>
#include <BIOS.H>

#include "UTY.H"
#include "SCR.H"
#include "KBD.H"

void main (void)
    {
    long Count;
    long TotSeconds;
    int Hours;
    int Minutes;
    int Seconds;
    char TimeBuf [9];

    ScrClear (0,0,2,11);
    ScrPutBox (0,0,2,11,0);

    while (!KbdReady ())
        {
        UtyClockCount (&Count);
        TotSeconds = (long)(Count * 0.054925);
        Hours = (int)(TotSeconds / 3600);
        TotSeconds %= 3600;
        Minutes = (int)(TotSeconds / 60);
        Seconds = (int)(TotSeconds % 60);
        sprintf (TimeBuf,"%02d:%02d:%02d",Hours,Minutes,Seconds);
        ScrPutS (TimeBuf,0x70,1,2);
        }

    } /* end main */
```

Figure 12.4: UTYDEM01.C: A program demonstrating the use of **UtyClockCount** to obtain the time of day

```
UTYDEM01.OBJ : UTYDEM01.C UTY.H
    cl /c /W2 /Zp UTYDEM01.C

UTY.OBJ : UTY.C UTY.H
    cl /c /W2 /Zp UTY.C

UTYA.OBJ : UTYA.ASM
    masm /MX UTYA;

SCR.OBJ : SCR.C SCR.H
    cl /c /W2 /Zp SCR.C

KBDA.OBJ : KBDA.ASM
    masm /MX KBDA.ASM;

UTYDEM01.EXE : UTYDEM01.OBJ UTY.OBJ UTYA.OBJ SCR.OBJ KBDA.OBJ
    link /NOI /NOD UTYDEM01+UTY+UTYA+SCR+KBDA,,NUL,SLIBCER;
```

Figure 12.5: UTYDEM01.M: A MAKE file for processing UTYDEM01.C

```
UTYDEM01.C
UTY.C
UTYA.OBJ
SCR.C
KBDA.OBJ
```

Figure 12.6: A QuickC program list for preparing UTYDEM01.C

UtyEnabled, described later in this chapter, is used to determine whether the interrupts are currently enabled.

UtyGetDateString and UtyGetTimeString

Using
UtyGetDateString
and
UtyGetTimeString

The function **UtyGetDateString** has the prototype

```
int UtyGetDateString
    (char *Target)
```

and writes the current system date to the string pointed to by the parameter **Target**, in the format mm/dd/yyyy, with a NULL termination. The function also returns a code indicating the day of the week, where 0 indicates Sunday, 1 Monday, and so on. The receiving string **Target** must be at least 11 bytes long (to accommodate the 10 characters plus the terminating NULL).

The program in Figure 12.7 demonstrates the use of **UtyGetDateString** to obtain and print the current date and day of the week. Figure 12.8 provides a MAKE file, and Figure 12.9 a QuickC program list.

The function **UtyGetTimeString** has the prototype

```
void UtyGetTimeString
    (char *Target)
```

and writes the current system time to the string indicated by the parameter **Target**. The time is written in the format hh:mm:ss.cc, giving the hours, minutes, seconds, and hundredths of seconds since midnight, plus a NULL termination. The receiving string **Target** must be at lease 12 bytes long. There is no return value.

```
#include <STDIO.H>

#include "UTY.H"

void main (void)
    {
    char DateBuf [9];
    int Day;
    static char *DaysOfWeek [] =
        {
        "Sunday",
        "Monday",
        "Tuesday",
        "Wednesday",
        "Thursday",
        "Friday",
        "Saturday"
        };

    Day = UtyGetDateString (DateBuf);
    printf ("Today is %s %s.\n",DaysOfWeek [Day],DateBuf);

    } /* end main */
```

Figure 12.7: UTYDEM02.C: A program that uses the function **UtyGetDate-String** to obtain the current time

```
UTYDEM02.OBJ : UTYDEM02.C UTY.H
    cl /c /W2 /Zp UTYDEM02.C

UTY.OBJ : UTY.C UTY.H
    cl /c /W2 /Zp UTY.C

UTYA.OBJ : UTYA.ASM
    masm /MX UTYA;

SCR.OBJ : SCR.C SCR.H
    cl /c /W2 /Zp SCR.C

KBDA.OBJ : KBDA.ASM
    masm /MX KBDA.ASM;

UTYDEM02.EXE : UTYDEM02.OBJ UTY.OBJ UTYA.OBJ SCR.OBJ KBDA.OBJ
    link /NOI /NOD UTYDEM02+UTY+UTYA+SCR+KBDA,,NUL,SLIBCER;
```

Figure 12.8: UTYDEM02.M: A MAKE file for preparing UTYDEM02.C

```
UTYDEM02.C
UTY.C
UTYA.OBJ
SCR.C
KBDA.OBJ
```

Figure 12.9: A QuickC program list for preparing UTYDEM02.C

The program in Figure 12.10 uses **UtyGetTimeString** to provide a continuous display of the time in a window in the upper left corner of the screen. The seconds display rolls by too rapidly to be read, but provides an interesting effect. The usual MAKE file and QuickC program list are given in Figures 12.11 and 12.12.

```
#include <STDIO.H>
#include <DOS.H>

#include "UTY.H"
#include "SCR.H"
#include "KBD.H"

void main (void)
    {
    char TimeBuf [12];

    ScrClear (0,0,2,16);
    ScrPutBox (0,0,2,16,3);
    while (!KbdReady ())
        {
        UtyGetTimeString (TimeBuf);
        ScrPutS (TimeBuf,0x70,1,3);
        }

    } /* end main */
```

Figure 12.10: UTYDEM03.C: A program that uses **UtyGetTimeString** to provide a continuous display of the time

```
UTYDEM03.OBJ : UTYDEM03.C UTY.H
    cl /c /W2 /Zp UTYDEM03.C

UTY.OBJ : UTY.C UTY.H
    cl /c /W2 /Zp UTY.C

UTYA.OBJ : UTYA.ASM
    masm /MX UTYA;

SCR.OBJ : SCR.C SCR.H
    cl /c /W2 /Zp SCR.C

KBDA.OBJ : KBDA.ASM
    masm /MX KBDA.ASM;

UTYDEM03.EXE : UTYDEM03.OBJ UTY.OBJ UTYA.OBJ SCR.OBJ KBDA.OBJ
    link /NOI /NOD UTYDEM03+UTY+UTYA+SCR+KBDA,,NUL,SLIBCER;
```

Figure 12.11: UTYDEM03.M: A MAKE file for preparing the program
UTYDEM03.C

```
UTYDEM03.C
UTY.C
UTYA.OBJ
SCR.C
KBDA.OBJ
```

Figure 12.12: A QuickC program list for preparing UTYDEM03.C

Note that this chapter has provided two distinct methods for obtaining the system time:

1. You can call **UtyClockCount** and convert the clock count to the number of hours, minutes, and seconds since midnight.

2. You can obtain the system time, already formatted as a string, by calling **UtyGetTimeString**.

The second method is obviously the most convenient means for obtaining the complete time of day. There are two situations, however, where it is preferable to use the function **UtyClockCount**. First, using **UtyClockCount** is more efficient than calling **UtyGetTimeString** (it directly reads the time data from memory rather than calling the operating system). Therefore, this function is more suitable for procedures where speed is important, such as the function **UtyPause** (described later in the chapter) or the function **Clock** in Figure 8.3. Second, unlike **UtyGetTimeString**, **UtyClockCount** does not invoke MS-DOS; therefore, it can safely be called from routines that are not free to use the DOS services, such as hardware interrupt handlers, device drivers, and critical-error handlers.

How UtyGetDateString and UtyGetTimeString Work

UtyGetDateString and **UtyGetTimeString** are both listed in the C source file of Figure 12.1.

UtyGetDateString invokes the MS-DOS "get date" service (interrupt 21h, function 2Ah), which returns the current year, month, day, and day of the week as numeric values. **UtyGetDateString** uses **sprintf** to format the month, day, and year values onto the target string, and then returns the code of the day of the week.

UtyGetTimeString calls the DOS "get time" service (interrupt 21h, function 2Ah) to obtain the number of hours, minutes, seconds, and hundredths of seconds since midnight. It then uses **sprintf** to format these numeric values onto the target string.

UtyPackDate and UtyUnpackDate

*Using
UtyPackDate
and
UtyUnpackDate*

The function **UtyPackDate** has the prototype

```
int UtyPackDate
      (char *Target,
       char *Source)
```

and performs the following two tasks:

1. **UtyPackDate** checks the validity of the date contained in the string pointed to by the parameter **Source**. The date must be in the format mm/dd/yyyy; you may use either the / character or the – character as a separator. The year field must contain four digits; however, the month and day fields may contain either one or two digits. If the date is valid, **UtyPackDate** returns NOERROR (0); otherwise, it returns the nonzero value BADDATE.

2. If the date contained in **Source** is valid, it is now written to the string given by the **Target** parameter, in the packed format yyyymmdd, plus a NULL termination (this format always contains all eight digits, so that the month March, for example, is encoded as 03). Note that if the date in **Source** is invalid, then **Target** is *not* modified. **Target** must be at least 9 bytes long.

The following lines of code demonstrate using **UtyPackDate** to validate a date and pack it into a date field belonging to a data file record:

```
char DateBuf [11];
    .
    .
    .
UtyBlank (DateBuf, sizeof (DateBuf));
do
      {
      ScrGetS (DateBuf,0x70,Row,Col,sizeof
            (DateBuf),NOFEAT);
      }
while (UtyPackDate (Record.Date,DateBuf));
```

The packed date format requires fewer bytes of storage than the normal format, and also has the advantage that if date strings are sorted in simple dictionary order they will automatically be in chronological order. Dates in packed format can also be compared using standard string comparison functions. For example, in the following lines, all dates are in packed format, and string comparisons can be used to determine whether a date is within a given range:

```
if (strcmp (Date, FirstDate) >= 0 &&
    strcmp (Date, LastDate)  <= 0)
       /* then date is within range */
```

UtyUnpackDate has the prototype

```
void UtyUnpackDate
     (char *Target,
      char *Source)
```

This function copies the date from the string **Source**, which must be in the packed format yyyymmdd, to the string **Target**, which is given the format mm/dd/yyyy, plus a NULL termination. **UtyUnpackDate** performs no validity checking, since the validity of the date is normally checked when it is originally packed using **UtyPackDate**. If the date contained in **Source** is blank, then the resulting unpacked version will also be blank, and will contain no separators. There is no return value. The following lines demonstrate using **UtyUnpackDate** to convert a date stored in packed format (**Record.Date**) to a normal format so that the date can be printed on a report:

```
char DateBuf [11];
    .
    .
    .
PrtPosition ("Date:", Row, 0);
UtyUnpackDate (DateBuf, Record.Date);
PrtPosition (DateBuf, Row++, 8);
```

How
UtyPackDate
and
UtyUnpackDate
Work

UtyPackDate, listed in the C file of Figure 12.1, first scans through the source string, extracting and storing the month, day, and year in separate temporary strings (**Month**, **Day**, and **Year**). If any unexpected characters are encountered during this process, the function returns immediately, passing back a value of BADDATE to the calling program to indicate an error. Next, **UtyPackDate** tests the validity of the numeric values of the **Month** and **Day** strings. First, the month is tested to verify that it is in the range from 1 to 12. The day value is then tested by comparing it with the appropriate entry in the array **DayTable**, which contains two subarrays, one for normal years and one for leap years. The function uses the following expression to detect a leap year:

```
atoi (Year) % 4   = = 0    &&
atoi (Year) % 100 ! = 0    ||
atoi (Year) % 400 = = 0
```

This expression evaluates to TRUE if the year meets the criterion for a leap year: the year is a multiple of 4 but not of 100, *or* the year is a multiple of 400.

Once the validity of the date is established, **UtyPackDate** transfers the month, day, and year values to the target string. The month and day values are padded with a leading zero, if necessary, so that they consist of two digits, and the year field must contain four digits (or the function would have returned an error code); accordingly, the resulting string always has a length of 8. Finally, the string is NULL terminated and the value NOERROR (0) is returned to indicate that the function was successful.

The function **UtyUnpackDate** directly transfers each byte from the packed string **Source** to the appropriate position in the unpacked string **Target**, inserting the separator character / between fields. The function does not check the validity of the transferred data, and writes blanks instead of separators to the target string if the source string is completely blank.

UtyPause

Using UtyPause

The function **UtyPause** has the prototype

```
void UtyPause
    (double Seconds)
```

and simply returns control to the calling program after a delay equal to the number of seconds specified by the parameter **Seconds**. The function does not return a value. For example, the following function call suspends program execution for 1.5 seconds:

```
UtyPause (1.5);
```

UtyPause is used in the programs of Figures 2.7, 2.10, 5.27, 7.7, and 11.9.

How UtyPause Works

UtyPause (in the C file Figure 12.1) determines the elapsed time by repeatedly obtaining the BIOS clock tick count through the function **UtyClockCount**, explained earlier in the chapter. Note, however, that the function does not convert the clock count to seconds with each pass of the loop, which would involve repeated, slow, floating-point operations and decrease the accuracy of the function (a faster loop provides a finer-grained timing mechanism). Rather, the number of seconds that is passed as a parameter is converted to clock counts, and the final clock count value (**FinalCount**) is calculated before the loop begins. With each subsequent iteration of the loop, only a single integer comparison is required (**CurrentCount < FinalCount**).

UtySetDateString and UtySetTimeString

Using
UtySetDateString
and
UtySetTimeString

The function **UtySetDateString** has the prototype

```
int UtySetDateString
    (char *Date)
```

and sets the system date according to the string passed as the parameter **Date**. **Date** must have the format mm/dd/yyyy; as with the function **UtyPackDate**, you may use either the / character or the – character as a separator. The year field must contain four digits; the month and day fields, however, may contain either one or two digits. Also, the date must be in the range from 1980 through 2099. If the function is successful, it returns NOERROR (0); if, however, **Date** is invalid, it returns the nonzero value BADDATE.

UtySetTimeString has the following prototype:

```
int UtySetTimeString
    (char *Time)
```

This function sets the system time according to the string pointed to by the parameter **Time**. **Time** must have the format hh:mm:ss.cc, indicating the number of hours, minutes, seconds, and hundredths of seconds since midnight. You can omit either the :ss.cc portion of the date, or just the .cc portion; the function will supply a zero value for a missing field. You must, however, include the hour and minute fields, and each of the fields you specify must contain both digits (therefore, for example, 3 hours must be written as 03). If successful, **UtySetTimeString** returns the value NOERROR (0); if, however, you pass an invalid time format, it returns the nonzero error code BADTIME.

The program in Figure 12.13 demonstrates the use of **UtySetDate-String** and **UtySetTimeString**. This program displays a pop-up window, and allows the user to enter a new system date and time; the date string that the user enters is passed directly to **UtySetDateString**, and the time string is passed directly to **UtySetTimeString**. If either of these functions returns a nonzero value—indicating a bad date or time format—the

```
#include <PROCESS.H>
#include <STRING.H>

#include "UTY.H"
#include "SCR.H"

#define ULR 6                    /* Position of centered window.          */
#define ULC 20

void main (void)
    {
    int OldRow, OldCol;      /* For saving old cursor position.       */
    char Buffer [12];        /* For receiving strings.                */
    int ReturnCode;          /* Saves 'ScrGetS' return code.          */

    /*** Display a temporary window. ****************************************/
    ScrPush ();                             /* Save screen data.           */
    ScrGetCur (&OldRow,&OldCol,0);          /* Save the cursor position.   */
    ScrClear (ULR,ULC,ULR+11,ULC+39);       /* Clear inside of box.        */
    ScrPutBox (ULR,ULC,ULR+11,ULC+39,3);    /* Draw a box.                 */
                                            /* Print titles:               */
    ScrPutS ("Modify System Date and Time",0x0f,ULR+2,ULC+6);
    ScrPutS ("New Date:",0x0f,ULR+4,ULC+3);
    ScrPutS ("mm/dd/yyyy",0x70,ULR+4,ULC+18);
    ScrPutS ("New Time:",0x0f,ULR+6,ULC+3);
    ScrPutS ("hh:mm:ss.cc",0x70,ULR+6,ULC+18);
    ScrPutS ("Press Enter to accept current value,",0x0f,ULR+8,ULC+2);
    ScrPutS ("or type new value and then press Enter",0x0f,ULR+9,ULC+1);
    ScrPutS ("Press Esc to Exit",0x0f,ULR+10,ULC+10);

    /*** Read the date field until a valid (or blank) string is entered. ***/
    UtyBlank (Buffer, sizeof (Buffer));
    do
        {                                   /* Read string:                */
        ReturnCode = ScrGetS (Buffer,0x70,ULR+4,ULC+18,11,NOFEAT);
        if (ReturnCode == -1)               /* User pressed Esc.           */
            {
            ScrSetCur (OldRow,OldCol,0);    /* Terminate the program.      */
            ScrPop (1);
            exit (0);
            }
        if (UtyAllBlank (Buffer))           /* Do not set date if user     */
            break;                          /* enters a blank date.        */
        }
    while (UtySetDateString (Buffer));      /* Set system date.            */

    /* Read the time field until the user enters a valid (or blank) date. **/
    UtyBlank (Buffer, sizeof (Buffer));
    do
        {
        ReturnCode = ScrGetS (Buffer,0x70,ULR+6,ULC+18,12,NOFEAT);
        if (ReturnCode == -1)               /* User pressed Esc.           */
            {
            ScrSetCur (OldRow,OldCol,0);    /* Terminate the program.      */
            ScrPop (1);
            exit (0);
            }
```

Figure 12.13: UTYDEM04.C: A program demonstrating the functions **UtyGetDateString** and **UtyGetTimeString**

```
       if (UtyAllBlank (Buffer))          /* Do not set time if user    */
           break;                         /* enters a blank time.       */

       UtyRightTrim (Buffer, strlen (Buffer));  /* Remove trailing blanks*/
       }
   while (UtySetTimeString (Buffer));

   ScrSetCur (OldRow,OldCol,0);           /* Restore the cursor position*/
   ScrPop (1);                            /* Restore the screen data.   */

   } /* main */
```

Figure 12.13: UTYDEM04.C: A program demonstrating the functions **UtyGetDateString** and
UtyGetTimeString (continued)

program loops back to allow the user to reenter the string. If a blank
string is entered, the corresponding value (date or time) is unaltered, and
if the Esc key is pressed (indicated by a –1 return code from **ScrGetS**), the
program is terminated.

Figure 12.14 provides a MAKE file, and Figure 12.15 a QuickC
program list.

*How
UtySetDateString
and
UtySetTimeString
Work*

UtySetDateString and **UtySetTimeString** are both listed in the C file
of Figure 12.1.

UtySetDateString first calls **UtyPackDate** to convert the date string it
has been passed (**Date**) to the packed format; if **UtyPackDate** returns an
error code, indicating that the date format is invalid, **UtySetDateString**
immediately returns the error code BADDATE. Next, the function converts the day, month, and year fields of the packed date to numeric
values, and assigns these numbers to the appropriate register fields.
Finally, it invokes the DOS "set date" service (interrupt 21h, function
2Bh). This DOS service returns a value of FFh in register AL if the requested year is outside of the range from 1980 through 2099 (DOS supports only dates that fall within this range). In this case,
UtySetDateString returns the error code BADDATE; otherwise it
returns NOERROR.

The **UtySetTimeString** function first converts the hour and minute
fields from the string **Time** (passed as a parameter) to numeric values,
and assigns these values to the appropriate registers (through the REGS
structure). If either the hour or minute field contains a nonnumeric
character, or if the resulting numeric value of either field is outside the
valid range, **UtySetTimeString** immediately returns the error code
BADTIME. The function next proceeds to extract the optional seconds

```
UTYDEM04.OBJ : UTYDEM04.C UTY.H
     cl /c /W2 /Zp UTYDEM04.C

UTY.OBJ : UTY.C UTY.H
     cl /c /W2 /Zp UTY.C

UTYA.OBJ : UTYA.ASM
     masm /MX UTYA;

SCR.OBJ : SCR.C SCR.H
     cl /c /W2 /Zp SCR.C

KBDA.OBJ : KBDA.ASM
     masm /MX KBDA.ASM;

UTYDEM04.EXE : UTYDEM04.OBJ UTY.OBJ UTYA.OBJ SCR.OBJ KBDA.OBJ
     link /NOI /NOD UTYDEM04+UTY+UTYA+SCR+KBDA,,NUL,SLIBCER;
```

Figure 12.14: UTYDEM04.M: A MAKE file for preparing the program
UTYDEM04.C

```
UTYDEM04.C
UTY.C
UTYA.OBJ
SCR.C
KBDA.OBJ
```

Figure 12.15: A QuickC program list for preparing UTYDEM04.C

and hundredths fields. If both of these fields are missing—or if just
the seconds field is missing—the function supplies the value 0. Finally,
UtySetTimeString invokes the DOS "set time" service (interrupt 21h,
function 2Dh). If DOS returns an error code in register AL, the value
BADTIME is returned; otherwise, the value NOERROR (0) is returned.

▌FILE PATH FUNCTIONS

The functions in this section allow you to accomplish the following
operations:

▐ Extract the file extension from a file name (**UtyExtension**).

▌ Convert a simple file name to a fully qualified path name
(**UtyQualify**).

▌ Extract the simple file name from a qualified name
(**UtyUnqualify**).

UtyExtension

Using
UtyExtension

The function **UtyExtension** has the prototype

```
char *UtyExtension
      (char *FileName)
```

and returns a pointer to the beginning of the file extension within the
file name pointed to by the parameter **FileName**; **FileName** must be a
NULL-terminated string. If **FileName** does not contain an extension,
the address returned by **UtyExtension** points to the NULL character
at the end of **FileName**.

For example, the lines

```
char *FileName = "ZOUNDS.C";
      .

      .

      .
printf ("File extension: %s", UtyExtension
      (FileName));
```

would print the line

```
File extension: C
```

How
UtyExtension
Works

UtyExtension (in the C file of Figure 12.1) simply scans through the
file name until it encounters the first '.' character or until it reaches
the end of the string. If the function reaches a '.' character, it returns the
address of the next character; if it does not find the '.', it returns the address of the terminating NULL.

UtyQualify and UtyUnqualify

*Using
UtyQualify and
UtyUnqualify*

UtyQualify has the following prototype

```
int UtyQualify
    (char *Qual,
    char *Unqual,
    int Size)
```

This function converts the file name pointed to by **Unqual** to the fully qualified file name version, which is written to the buffer pointed to by **Qual** (as a NULL-terminated string). The fully qualified name includes the complete drive and directory path specification. **Size** specifies the size of the receiving buffer **Qual**. If the buffer length given by **Size** is too small to receive the fully qualified file name (including the terminating NULL), **UtyQualify** returns SIZETOOSMALL; if an error is encountered when invoking an MS-DOS service, it returns DOSERR; if successful, it returns NOERROR (0). **UtyQualify** does not check the validity of the file name passed in **Unqual**.

The source string **Unqual** can contain a simple file name, such as

```
ACME.TXT
```

a partially qualified file name, such as

```
\COMPANY\ACME.TXT
```

or

```
C:ACME.TXT
```

or it can contain a fully qualified file name such as

```
B:\BRANDS\ACME.TXT
```

In all of these cases, **UtyQualify** would write a fully qualified file name to **Qual**. Any portions of the fully qualified name not contained in

Unqual are given the *current default values*. For example, if **Unqual** contains

```
FELIX.TXT
```

and if the current drive is C: and the current directory for drive C: is \PETS\CATS, **UtyQualify** would write the following string to **Qual**:

```
C:\PETS\CATS\FELIX.TXT
```

Note that if **Unqual** contains a drive specification, **UtyQualify** will insert—if necessary—the current directory *for that drive*. For example, if **Unqual** is

```
B:CARDS\ACE.TXT
```

and the current directory for drive B: is \GAMES, **UtyQualify** will write the following string to **Qual**:

```
B:\GAMES\CARDS\ACE.TXT
```

In general, **UtyQualify** fills in a partially qualified file name in the same manner as an MS-DOS service when it is passed a file name parameter. Note that if **Unqual** already contains a fully qualified name, this name is simply copied without modification to **Qual**.

The function **UtyUnqualify** has the prototype

```
char *UtyUnqualify
     (char *Qual)
```

and returns a pointer to the simple file name contained within the fully or partially qualified file name pointed to by **Qual**. This function also converts the simple file name within **Qual** to uppercase letters. **UtyUnqualify** does not check the validity of the file name contained in **Qual**. For example, the code

```
char *FileName = "\games\checkers.c";
     .
     .
     .
printf ("Current File: %c", UtyUnqualify (FileName));
```

would print the line

Current File: CHECKERS.C

The program in Figure 12.16 demonstrates the functions **UtyQualify** and **UtyUnqualify**. This program accepts a file name from the command line, which can be a simple name, or a partially or fully qualified name. It then calls **UtyQualify** to obtain the fully qualified version of this file name, and it calls **UtyUnqualify** to obtain the simple version. Finally, it displays the original file name, the simple version, and the fully qualified version.

Figure 12.17 provides a MAKE file, and Figure 12.18 a QuickC program list.

```
#include <STDIO.H>
#include <PROCESS.H>

#include "UTY.H"

void main (int argc, char *argv [])
    {
    int Error;
    char Qual [61];

    if (argc < 2)
        {
        fprintf (stderr, "usage:  UTYDEM05 file_name\n");
        exit (1);
        }

    Error = UtyQualify (Qual, argv [1], sizeof (Qual));
    switch (Error)
        {
        case SIZETOOSMALL:
            fprintf (stderr, "Receiving buffer too small.\n");
            exit (0);

        case DOSERR:
            fprintf (stderr, "Error calling DOS.\n");
            exit (0);
        }

    printf ("Name entered:      %s\n", argv [1]);

    printf ("Unqualified name:  %s\n", UtyUnqualify (argv [1]));

    printf ("Qualified name:    %s\n", Qual);

    } /* end main */
```

Figure 12.16: UTYDEM05.C: A program demonstrating the functions **UtyQualify** and **UtyUnqualify**

*How UtyQualify
and
UtyUnqualify
Work*

UtyQualify and **UtyUnqualify** are both contained in the C source file of Figure 12.1.

UtyQualify copies the unqualified file name from the parameter **Unqual** to the buffer pointed to by **Qual**, inserting any missing elements using the current default values. If **Unqual** is missing the drive specification, the function inserts the current default drive designation obtained from the DOS "get disk" service (interrupt 21h, function 19h). If **Unqual** is missing the full directory specification (in other words, the directory specification does not begin with the \ character), **UtyQualify** inserts the directory name obtained from the DOS "get current directory" service (interrupt 21h, function 47 h) for the appropriate drive. Note that each time before it writes to **Qual**, **UtyQualify** tests to make sure that the size of the receiving buffer (indicated by the **Size** parameter) is large enough to contain the characters about to be written. **UtyQualify** makes no test for a valid file name.

```
UTYDEM05.OBJ : UTYDEM05.C UTY.H
    cl /c /W2 /Zp UTYDEM05.C

UTY.OBJ : UTY.C UTY.H
    cl /c /W2 /Zp UTY.C

UTYA.OBJ : UTYA.ASM
    masm /MX UTYA;

SCR.OBJ : SCR.C SCR.H
    cl /c /W2 /Zp SCR.C

KBDA.OBJ : KBDA.ASM
    masm /MX KBDA.ASM;

UTYDEM05.EXE : UTYDEM05.OBJ UTY.OBJ UTYA.OBJ SCR.OBJ KBDA.OBJ
    link /NOI /NOD UTYDEM05+UTY+UTYA+SCR+KBDA,,NUL,SLIBCER;
```

Figure 12.17: UTYDEM05.M: A MAKE file for preparing UTYDEM05.C

```
UTYDEM05.C
UTY.C
UTYA.OBJ
SCR.C
KBDA.OBJ
```

Figure 12.18: A QuickC program list for preparing UTYDEM05.C

The function **UtyUnqualify** finds the beginning of the simple file name by scanning the string pointed to by the parameter **Qual**, starting from the terminating NULL and moving toward the beginning of the string. It stops when it encounters the first \ character, the first : character, or the beginning of the string. Before returning the address of the start of the simple file name, it calls the Microsoft C library function **strupr** to convert this portion of the file name to upper case letters. Note that **UtyUnqualify** assumes that **Qual** contains a valid file name.

NUMERIC FUNCTIONS

This section presents two functions for rounding the values stored in floating-point numbers. Using these functions, you can perform the following operations:

- Round a floating point number to a specified number of decimal places (**UtyRound**).

- Round a floating point number to the nearest 0.05 (**UtyRound5**).

UtyRound

Using UtyRound

UtyRound has the prototype

```
double UtyRound
        (double Value,
         int Digits)
```

This function returns the floating point value passed in the parameter **Value**, rounded to the number of decimal places given by the parameter **Digits**. For example, the lines

```
double FPValue = 123.456789;
```

.
.

```
FPValue = UtyRound (FPValue, 2);
printf ("%f", FPValue);
```

would print the result 123.460000. If the parameter **Digits** is given the value 0, then the result is rounded to the nearest whole number. (Note that when a floating point number is converted to an integer, automatically or through a cast operation, the result is *truncated,* not rounded.)

Although functions such as *printf* and *sprintf* conveniently round floating point numbers while converting them to strings, it is often important that the internal representation of a floating point number also be rounded. For example, consider an accounting application in which a series of floating point variables are printed to 2 decimal places (representing dollars and cents), and then the total of these numbers is printed. If each of the variables is not internally rounded to 2 decimal places *before* the variables are added by the program, the total could be a penny or two off from the result obtained by manually adding the printed numbers (a situation that most programmers can understand, but most accountants find disturbing). **UtyRound** offers a convenient method for rounding the stored versions of such numbers.

How UtyRound Works

UtyRound (in the C source file of Figure 12.1) rounds the floating point number passed in the parameter **Value** through the following steps:

1. **Value** is multiplied by the appropriate power of 10 (contained in the variable **Bubble**) so that all the digits to be preserved are positioned to the *left* of the decimal point.

2. The value 0.5 is added to the result of the multiplication to round the whole number portion of this value (0.5 is *subtracted* if the number is negative).

3. The result is now truncated to eliminate the unwanted digits by assigning the value to a **long** variable (**John**).

4. Finally, the decimal place is restored and the value converted back to a **double** by dividing the number by the same power of ten used in the first step (contained in **Bubble**).

UtyRound5

Using UtyRound5

The prototype for **UtyRound5** is

```
double UtyRound5
        (double Value)
```

This function returns the floating point number passed in the parameter **Value**, rounded to the nearest 0.5.

The primary use for this function is to round monetary values to the nearest 5 cents. For example, the lines

```
double FPValue = 123.456789;
        .
        .
        .
FPValue = UtyRound5 (FPValue, 2);
printf ("%f", FPValue);
```

will print the result 123.450000. You can modify this function to perform rounding to other nearest values (rounding to nearest values that are negative powers of 10 such as 0.1 and 0.01 is easily accomplished through **UtyRound**).

How UtyRound5 Works

UtyRound5 (in the C source file of Figure 12.1) rounds the floating point number passed in the parameter **Value** by performing the following steps:

1. The quantity passed in **Value** is multiplied by 100, rounded to a whole number, and stored as a long integer in the variable **John**.

2. The integer value is adjusted to the nearest multiple of 5. The required adjustment is determined by using the modulus operator.

3. The adjusted result is now divided by 100 to restore its former magnitude, and is converted back to a floating point number. This value is returned.

MISCELLANEOUS FUNCTIONS

The functions presented in this last section allow you to perform the following tasks:

- Disable or enable hardware interrupts (**UtyDisable**, **UtyEnable**).
- Determine the current status of the hardware interrupts (**UtyEnabled**).
- Determine the processor model (**UtyGetCpu**).
- Determine the computer model (**UtyGetMachine**).
- Display a window containing error information and terminate the program (**UtyQuit**).
- Produce a sound from the computer speaker having a specified frequency and duration (**UtySound**).
- Perform a warm reboot (**UtyWarmBoot**).

UtyDisable and UtyEnable

*Using
UtyDisable and
UtyEnable*

The function **UtyDisable** has the prototype

```
void far UtyDisable
        (void)
```

and disables hardware interrupts. The function **UtyEnable** has the prototype

```
void far UtyEnable
        (void)
```

and enables hardware interrupts. If you want to preserve the original enabled status of the interrupts when using either of these two functions, you can employ the function **UtyEnabled**, described next.

How UtyDisable and UtyEnable Work

Both **UtyDisable** and **UtyEnable** are in the assembly language file of Figure 12.2. The function **UtyDisable** disables hardware interrupts by invoking the CLI machine instruction, and **UtyEnable** enables interrupts through the STI machine instruction.

UtyEnabled

Using UtyEnabled

The function **UtyEnabled** has the prototype

```
int UtyEnabled
    (void)
```

It returns a nonzero value if the interrupts are currently enabled, or 0 if the interrupts are disabled.

Sometimes it is necessary to explicitly enable or disable the interrupts during the execution of a section of code. **UtyEnabled** allows you to save and restore the interrupt status belonging to the calling or interrupted program. Examples of using **UtyEnabled** for this purpose can be seen in the function **KbdInsert**, listed in Figure 2.1, and in the function **UtyClockCount**, listed in Figure 12.1 and described earlier in this chapter.

How UtyEnabled Works

UtyEnabled, contained in the assembly language file of Figure 12.2, returns the status of the interrupts by placing the contents of the FLAGS register in register AX, and masking off all bits *except* the interrupt flag (IF). This (1 bit) flag has a value of 1 when the interrupts are enabled, and 0 when they are disabled.

UtyGetCpu

Using UtyGetCpu

UtyGetCpu has the prototype

```
int far UtyGetCpu
    (void)
```

and returns a code indicating the processor model. The function returns one of the following codes:

Code	Processor
P86	Intel 8086, 8088, or compatible
P186	80186
P286	80286
P386	80386

UtyGetCpu is demonstrated in the program of Figure 12.19, presented in the section on Using **UtyGetMachine**.

How UtyGetCpu Works

The function **UtyGetCpu** is in the assembly language file of Figure 12.2. It uses the following sequence of tests to discriminate among a small set of possible processors: the 8086/88, the 80186, the 80286, and the 80386.

First, it tests for the 8086/88 processor by attempting to clear the 4 high-order bits of the FLAGS register. If all 4 of these bits remain set, the processor must be an 8086/88 (only in the 8086 or 8088—from among the processors that are being tested—do these bits always remain set).

Next, the routine tests for an 80186 processor by determining whether the PUSH machine instruction decrements the stack pointer (SP) *before* or *after* the value is written to the stack. If the stack pointer is decremented before its value is written to the stack, then the processor must be an 80186 since the 80286 and 80386 both decrement SP after it is written to the stack.

Finally, the 80286 and 80386 processors are distinguished by attempting to set the 4 high-order bits of the FLAGS register. If none of these bits can be set, then the processor must be an 80286; in the 80286 these bits are always clear, while in the 80386 the bits may be set.

UtyGetMachine

*Using
UtyGetMachine*

The function **UtyGetMachine** has the prototype

```
int UtyGetMachine
     (void)
```

and returns a code indicating the current computer model. The following are the codes that can be returned:

Code	Computer model
NONIBM	Non-IBM machine
PC	IBM PC
XT	IBM PC XT
JR	IBM PC jr
AT	IBM PC AT
XT286	IBM PC XT 286
CONV	IBM Convertible
MODEL 30	IBM PS/2 Model 30
MODEL 50	IBM PS/2 Model 50
MODEL 60	IBM PS/2 Model 60
MODEL 80	IBM PS/2 Model 80
UKIBM	Unknown IBM model

Note that **UtyGetMachine** supports only IBM models, ranging from the original IBM-PC to the PS/2 models 30 through 80. If the machine is not an IBM model, the value NONIBM is returned. Note that many IBM "clones" will be detected as IBM machines, since the manufactures of IBM- compatible BIOS chips often place the IBM logo and model numbers at the appropriate addresses in the BIOS (see the next section). Also note that even if the value NONIBM is returned, the machine may still be closely IBM-compatible (for example, a Compaq computer). Further tests are required to detect IBM compatibility.

The program in Figure 12.19 demonstrates the functions **UtyGetCpu** and **UtyGetMachine**. Figure 12.20 furnishes a MAKE file, and Figure 12.21 supplies a QuickC program list.

*How
UtyGetMachine
Works*

UtyGetMachine, which is in the C source file of Figure 12.1, first determines whether the machine is an IBM model by looking for the string "IBM" that is placed in the BIOS of all IBM machines at the address F000h:E00Eh; if this string is not found it returns NONIBM. Next, the function tests the "model byte" at address F000h:FFFEh, which in all

```
#include <STDIO.H>

#include "UTY.H"

void main (void)
     {
     static char *Machines [] =
          {
          "non-IBM",
          "IBM-PC",
          "IBM-XT",
          "IBM-JR",
          "IBM-AT",
          "IBM-XT 286",
          "IBM Convertible",
          "IBM PS/2 Model 30",
          "IBM PS/2 Model 50",
          "IBM PS/2 Model 60",
          "IBM PS/2 Model 80",
          "unrecognized IBM model"
          };

     static char *Processors [] =
          {
          "8086 or 8088",
          "80186",
          "80286",
          "80386"
          };

     printf ("My computer is:   %s.\n", Machines [UtyGetMachine ()]);
     printf ("My processor is:  %s.\n", Processors [UtyGetCpu ()]);

     } /* end main */
```

Figure 12.19: UTYDEM06.C: A program demonstrating the functions **UtyGetCpu** and
UtyGetMachine

```
UTYDEM06.OBJ : UTYDEM06.C UTY.H
     cl /c /W2 /Zp UTYDEM06.C

UTY.OBJ : UTY.C UTY.H
     cl /c /W2 /Zp UTY.C

UTYA.OBJ : UTYA.ASM
     masm /MX UTYA;

SCR.OBJ : SCR.C SCR.H
     cl /c /W2 /Zp SCR.C

KBDA.OBJ : KBDA.ASM
     masm /MX KBDA.ASM;

UTYDEM06.EXE : UTYDEM06.OBJ UTY.OBJ UTYA.OBJ SCR.OBJ KBDA.OBJ
     link /NOI /NOD UTYDEM06+UTY+UTYA+SCR+KBDA,,NUL,SLIBCER;
```

Figure 12.20: UTYDEM06.M: A MAKE file for preparing UTYDEM06.C

```
UTYDEM06.C
UTY.C
UTYA.OBJ
SCR.C
KBDA.OBJ
```

Figure 12.21: A QuickC program list for preparing UTYDEM06.C

IBM machines contains a code for the specific model. Each of the possible code values indicates a specific IBM model with one exception: the value FCh is used for *all* models employing the 80286 processor. Therefore, if the model byte equals FCh, the following tests are performed to distinguish among the various 80286 machines:

■ The BIOS "return system configuration" service is invoked (interrupt 15h, function C0h).

■ If this service returns 86h in register AH, then the machine must be either a PC XT (dated 11/08/82) or a PC AT (dated 1/10/84). If the machine were a PC XT, however, the function would already have returned through the FEh branch of the case statement; therefore, the machine must be a PC AT and the value AT is returned.

▌ If interrupt 15h returns a 0, then the machine must be a PC AT (dated *after* 1/10/84), a PC XT-286, a model 50, or a model 60. In this case, the address of a *system descriptor* is contained in registers ES:BX. A *submodel byte* is located at offset of 3 within this descriptor, and is used to identify the specific model.

▌ If the submodel byte does not contain a meaningful code, or if interrupt 15h fails to return a sensible value, then the code UKIBM is returned to the calling program to indicate an unknown IBM model.

UtyGetMachine could be enhanced to include non-IBM machines. For example, Compaq computers store the string "COMPAQ" in the BIOS at address F000h:FFEAh, and AT&T systems contain "OLIVETTI" at address F000h:C050h.

UtyQuit

Using UtyQuit   The prototype for **UtyQuit** is

```
void UtyQuit
    (char *Message,
    char *File,
    int Line)
```

This function performs the following actions:

▌ A window is displayed in the center of the screen.

▌ The information passed by the three parameters is displayed within the window: the error message contained in the string **Message**, the C source file name in **File**, and the source code line number in **Line**.

▌ The function pauses until the user presses a key.

▌ The program is terminated, and an ERRORLEVEL value of 1 is returned to DOS.

UtyQuit is typically called when a fatal error occurs. The values for the source file and line number are easily obtained from the Microsoft C predefined macros __FILE__ and __LINE__ , as in the following line:

```
UtyQuit ("Out of heap memory.",__FILE__,__LINE__);
```

If there are any critical tasks that must be performed before program termination, you can either execute them before calling **UtyQuit**, or add them to the **UtyQuit** function. Note that the screen is not cleared on program exit, so that the user will have further opportunity to contemplate the error messages.

How UtyQuit Works

UtyQuit (in the C source file, Figure 12.1) uses the screen functions presented in Chapter 5. However, since the function never returns, it does not need to save and restore the underlying screen data.

UtySound

Using UtySound

UtySound is in the C source file of Figure 12.1, and has the following prototype:

```
void UtySound
    (unsigned Frequency,
    unsigned Duration)
```

This function generates a sound from the computer speaker having the tone given by **Frequency** and the duration given by **Duration**. **Frequency** is specified in cycles per second (or Herz), and **Duration** is specified as the number of clock ticks; a clock tick is approximately 1/18 of a second, since the machine generates 18.2 clock ticks per second (see the section on **UtyClockCount**, earlier in the chapter). For example, the function call

```
UtySound
        (262,           /* Frequency: 262 Hz.        */
        18);            /* Duration: 18 clock ticks. */
```

generates a middle C tone (262 Hz.) lasting for approximately 1 second (18 clock ticks).

The program in Figure 12.22 demonstrates the use of **UtySound**, and turns the numeric keys on the keyboard into a very primitive piano. The main program loop calls **KbdGetC** to read the keyboard. Each time it receives a numeric key, it calls **UtySound** to generate a sound with a frequency obtained from a table of tones, which range from the note F below middle C to the note G above middle C.

Figure 12.23 supplies the usual MAKE file, and Figure 12.24 the QuickC program list.

```
#include "UTY.H"
#include "KBD.H"

int Notes [9] =          /* Table of frequencies (Hz) for notes:    */
        {                /* Note              Number on keyboard     */
        175,             /* F                 1                      */
        196,             /* G                 2                      */
        220,             /* A                 3                      */
        247,             /* B                 4                      */
        262,             /* C (middle)        5                      */
        294,             /* D                 6                      */
        330,             /* E                 7                      */
        349,             /* F                 8                      */
        392              /* G                 9                      */
        };

void main (void)
        {
        int Ch;
        int Index;

        while ((Ch = KbdGetC () & 0x00ff) != 27)
                {
                Index = Ch - '1';
                if (Index >= 0 && Index <= 8)
                        UtySound (Notes [Index], 6);

                } /* end while */

        } /* end main */
```

Figure 12.22: UTYDEM07.C: A program demonstrating the use of the function **UtySound**

```
UTYDEM07.OBJ : UTYDEM07.C UTY.H
    cl /c /W2 /Zp UTYDEM07.C

UTY.OBJ : UTY.C UTY.H
    cl /c /W2 /Zp UTY.C

UTYA.OBJ : UTYA.ASM
    masm /MX UTYA;

SCR.OBJ : SCR.C SCR.H
    cl /c /W2 /Zp SCR.C

KBDA.OBJ : KBDA.ASM
    masm /MX KBDA.ASM;

UTYDEM07.EXE : UTYDEM07.OBJ UTY.OBJ UTYA.OBJ SCR.OBJ KBDA.OBJ
    link /NOI /NOD UTYDEM07+UTY+UTYA+SCR+KBDA,,NUL,SLIBCER;
```

Figure 12.23: UTYDEM07.M: A MAKE file for preparing UTYDEM07.C

```
UTYDEM07.C
UTY.C
UTYA.OBJ
SCR.C
KBDA.OBJ
```

Figure 12.24: A QuickC program list for preparing UTYDEM07.C

How UtySound Works

UtySound (in the C source file of Figure 12.1) generates a sound of the desired frequency by activating the programmable timer chip that drives the speaker in IBM-compatible machines. The sound is generated through the following three steps:

1. The timer is initialized by writing a value of B6h to port 43h.
2. The desired frequency is set by writing the following 2-byte value to port 42h:

$$1193180 \ / \ frequency$$

where *frequency* is the desired frequency in cycles per second. The program first writes the low-order byte of this word, and then the high-order byte (an I/O port can receive only an 8-bit value).

3. The signal to the speaker is enabled by setting on the two lowest order bits of port 61h.

The sound begins as soon as step 3 has been performed. **UtySound** then executes a loop until the specified number of clock ticks have occurred (the count of clock ticks is read by calling the function **UtyClockCount**). Finally, the sound is switched off by resetting the two lowest-order bits of port 61h back to 0.

UtyWarmBoot

Using UtyWarmBoot

The function **UtyWarmBoot**, which has the prototype

```
void UtyWarmBoot
        (void)
```

generates a *warm boot*, which means that BIOS resets the computer without executing the lengthy memory check that normally occurs when the computer is first powered on. The function obviously does not return a value.

How UtyWarmBoot Works

The function **UtyWarmBoot**, listed in the C file of Figure 12.1, first sets the BIOS reset flag at address 0000h:0472h to the value 1234h, which causes the BIOS to bypass the memory check when resetting the computer. The function then assigns the address of the BIOS reset routine to the **far** function pointer **PtrReboot**. Finally, it issues a function call through this pointer, which transfers control directly to the BIOS code that resets the computer.

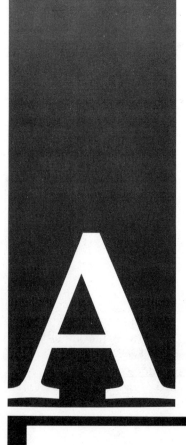

PPENDICES

APPENDIX A:
ALPHABETICAL SUMMARY OF THE FUNCTIONS

This appendix provides a brief alphabetical summary of all of the functions presented in the book. The functions are grouped according to the modules that contain them.

For each module, the following information is given:

- *Purpose:* A general description of the use of the functions in the module.

- *Source File(s):* The figure or figures in the book containing the source code for the module.

- *Header File:* The file you must include in your program to call the functions in the module.

- *Object Files:* The object files that must be linked to your program if you call a function contained in the specified source file. For example, the following files are listed for the **Kbd** module:

```
KBD.C: KBD.OBJ, UTYA.OBJ
KBDA.ASM: KBDA.OBJ
```

Accordingly, if you call a function located in the KBD.C source file, you must link your program with the KBD.OBJ and the UTYA.OBJ object files. Likewise, if you call a function located in the assembler file KBDA.ASM, you need to link the program with KBDA.OBJ.

These object files may be linked individually (as in the MAKE files and QuickC program lists given in the book), or they may be placed in a single library file (see Appendix B) that is specified on the LINK command line.

- *Error Variable:* The name of the global variable (if any) set by the functions in the module to communicate the error status to the calling program.

For each function, the following facts are provided:

- *Purpose:* A brief statement of the service provided by the function.

▌ *Prototype:* A full prototype for the function. Alongside of this is a description of each parameter passed to the function (if any).

▌ *Return Value:* An explanation of the value returned by the function (if any).

▌ *Source File:* The figure in the book containing the function.

▌ Buf... : VIDEO BUFFER FUNCTIONS

Purpose:	This module of functions allows you to collect video output in a buffer, and then display it a portion at a time through a window on the screen.
Source File:	BUF.C, Figure 5.32
Header File:	BUF.H, Figure 5.33
Object Files:	BUF.C:
	BUF.OBJ, SCR.OBJ and KBDA.OBJ
Error Variable:	**BufError**

BufFree

Purpose   Frees the memory occupied by the video output buffer.

Prototype   **void BufFree
    (void)**

Source File   BUF.C, Figure 5.32

BufGetLine

Purpose   Returns the address of a line in the video output buffer.

Prototype	char *BufGetLine	
	(int Line)	Number of the buffer line.

Return Value If successful, it returns the address of the buffer line specified by **Line** and assigns the value NOERROR (0) to **BufError**. If **Line** is out of the range of lines currently contained in the buffer, it returns NULL and assigns LINEOUTOFRANGE to **BufError**.

Source File BUF.C, Figure 5.32

BufInit

Purpose Initializes the module of buffer functions.

Prototype	void BufInit	
	(int StartRow,	Top line of the window to be used to view the buffer on the screen.
	int StartCol,	Left column of the window.
	int StopRow,	Bottom line of the window.
	int StopCol)	Right column of the window.

Source File BUF.C, Figure 5.32

BufNextLine

Purpose Adds a line to the video output buffer, and returns the address of this line.

Prototype	char *BufNextLine
	(void)

Return Value If successful, it returns the address of the line added to the buffer and assigns the value NOERROR (0) to **BufError**. If an error occurs, it returns the value NULL and assigns to **BufError** one of the following error codes:

TOOMANYLINES	The number of lines in the buffer has exceeded MAXLINES.
OUTOFMEMORY	No more heap memory is available.

Source File   BUF.C, Figure 5.32

BufShow

Purpose   Displays a section of the video output buffer through the window on the screen defined by **BufInit**.

Prototype   **void BufShow (int StartLine)**   Number of the buffer line to be displayed at the top of the window; the function will display as many subsequent lines as will fit in the window.

Source File   BUF.C, Figure 5.32

■ Ems... : EXPANDED MEMORY FUNCTIONS

Purpose:	These functions serve to manage the allocation and use of expanded memory.
Source File:	EMS.C, Figure 10.2
Header File:	EMS.H, Figure 10.3
Object Files:	EMS.C: EMS.OBJ.
Error Variable:	All functions except **EmsInstalled** and **EmsErrorMsg** assign an error code to the global variable **EmsError**. The header file EMS.H contains the definition of this variable, as well as constant definitions for all possible error codes.

EmsAlloc

Purpose	Allocates logical pages of expanded memory to the calling program.
Prototype	**char far *EmsAlloc** **(int Pages)** The desired number of 16-kilobyte logical pages of expanded memory.
Return Value	If successful, it returns the **far** address of the base of the expanded memory page frame. If an error occurs, it returns NULL and assigns to **EmsError** one of the error codes defined in EMS.H.
Source File	EMS.C, Figure 10.2

EmsErrorMsg

Purpose	Returns a pointer to a string containing an error message describing a given module error code.
Prototype	**char *EmsErrorMsg** **(int ErrorNum)** The module error number (that is, the value that is assigned to **EmsError**).
Return Value	If successful, it returns a pointer to a string containing the error description. If **ErrorNum** is invalid, it returns NULL. It does not assign a value to **EmsError**.
Source File	EMS.C, Figure 10.2

EmsFree

Purpose	Releases expanded memory pages that have been allocated to the program by a prior call to **EmsAlloc**.

Prototype	**int EmsFree** **(void)**
Return Value	If successful, it returns and assigns to **EmsError** the value NOERROR (0). If an error occurs, it returns and assigns to **EmsError** one of the error codes defined in EMS.H.
Source File	EMS.C, Figure 10.2

EmsInstalled

Purpose	Reports whether the expanded memory manager is currently installed.
Prototype	**int EmsInstalled** **(void)**
Return Value	If the expanded memory manager is currently installed it returns a nonzero value. If the expanded memory manager is *not* installed, it returns zero. It does not return an error code or assign an error status to **EmsError**.
Source File	EMS.C, Figure 10.2

EmsMap

Purpose	Maps up to four expanded memory logical pages onto the four expanded memory physical pages.
Prototype	**int EmsMap**

	(int Page0,	Logical page number to be mapped to physical page 0.
	int Page1,	Logical page mapped to physical page 1.
	int Page2,	Logical page mapped to physical page 2.
	int Page3)	Logical page mapped to physical page 3

Note: A parameter value of −1 causes the current mapping for the corresponding physical page to be left unchanged.

Return Value   If successful, it returns and assigns to **EmsError** the value NOERROR (0). If an error occurs, it returns and assigns to **EmsError** one of the error codes defined in EMS.H.

Source File   EMS.C, Figure 10.2

EmsPagesAvail

Purpose   Returns the number of free logical pages of expanded memory.

Prototype   **int EmsPagesAvail**
(void)

Return Value   If successful, it returns the number of expanded memory pages available for allocation and assigns the value NOERROR (0) to **EmsError**. If an error occurs, it returns −1 and assigns to **EmsError** one of the error codes defined in EMS.H.

Source File   EMS.C, Figure 10.2

EmsRestore

Purpose   Restores the expanded memory page mapping that was saved by a prior call to **EmsSave**.

Prototype   **int EmsRestore**
(void)

Return Value   If successful, it returns and assigns to **EmsError** the value NOERROR (0). If an error occurs, it returns and assigns to **EmsError** one of the error codes defined in EMS.H.

Source File   EMS.C, Figure 10.2

EmsSave

Purpose   Saves the current expanded memory page mapping, which can be restored at a later point by calling **EmsRestore**.

Prototype   **int EmsSave**
                  (void)

Return Value   If successful, it returns and assigns to **EmsError** the value NOERROR (0). If an error occurs, it returns and assigns to **EmsError** one of the error codes defined in EMS.H.

Source File   EMS.C, Figure 10.2

EmsVersion

Purpose   Returns the expanded memory manager version number.

Prototype   **int EmsVersion**
                  (void)

Return Value   If successful, it returns an integer containing the minor version number in bits 0 through 3, and the major version number in bits 4 through 7, and it assigns the value NOERROR (0) to **EmsError**. If an error occurs, it returns 0 and assigns to **EmsError** one of the error codes defined in EMS.H.

Source File   EMS.C, Figure 10.2

Fil... : FILE MANAGEMENT FUNCTIONS

Purpose: These functions serve to manage directory and volume names, and file modification dates. Also included are functions for opening up to 255 simultaneous file handles.

Source File: FIL.C, Figure 4.1

Header File: FIL.H, Figure 4.2

Object File: FIL.C: FIL.OBJ

Error Variable: **FilError**; the header file FIL.H contains the definition of this variable, as well as constant definitions for all possible error codes.

FilDelVolid

Purpose   Deletes a volume label.

Prototype   **int FilDelVolid**
                     (unsigned char Drive)   The drive containing the volume label to be deleted, where 0 signifies the default drive, 1 refers to drive A, 2 to drive B, and so on.

Return Value   If successful, it returns and assigns to **FilError** the value NOERROR (0). If an error occurs, it returns and assigns to **FilError** one of the following error codes:

      NOVOL   No volume label exists.

      NODEL   The deletion operation failed.

Source File   FIL.C, Figure 4.1

FilGetTime

Purpose   Obtains the modification date and time of a file.

Prototype	**int FilGetTime**	
	(char *FilePath,	The file name, which can include a full path specification.
	char *Date,	The address of the string to receive the file modification date.
	char *Time)	The address of the string to receive the file modification time.

Return Value If successful, it returns and assigns to **FilError** the value NOERROR (0). If an error occurs, it returns and assigns to **FilError** one of the following error codes:

NOOPEN	The function could not open the specified file.
NOACC	The function could not access the file date and time.

Source File FIL.C, Figure 4.1

FilGetVolid

Purpose Obtains the volume label for a given disk.

Prototype	**char *FilGetVolid**	
	(unsigned char Drive)	The disk drive, where 0 means the default drive, 1 means drive A, 2 drive B, and so on.

Return Value If successful, it returns the address of a string containing the volume label for the specified drive, and assigns to **FilError** the value NOERROR (0). If a volume label does not exist, it returns NULL and assigns to **FilError** the value NOVOL.

Source File FIL.C, Figure 4.1

FilHandle

Purpose Prepares a file for access by a low-level C file function. This function is used in conjunction with **FilOpen** to circumvent the 20 file handle limit under MS-DOS.

Prototype **int FilHandle**
      (int FileNumber) The *file* number of the file to be accessed (the file number is the value returned by the **FilOpen** function).

Return Value This function returns the integer 5, so that the function call can serve as the file handle parameter to a low-level C library file function such as **write** (when using **FilOpen** and **FilHandle**, all files are accessed through file handle 5). It does not return a special error value or assign an error status code to **FilError**.

Source File FIL.C, Figure 4.1

FilOpen

Purpose Opens a file and returns a file number that can subsequently be passed to **FilHandle**, as a mechanism for opening up to 255 simultaneous file handles.

Prototype **int FilOpen**
      (char *FilePath, The file name, which can include a full path specification.
      int Access, The type of operations allowed on the file; the same as the second parameter to the C **open** function.
      int Permiss) File permissions; the same as the third parameter to the **open** function, and required only if a new file is to be created.

Return Value If successful, it returns the *file number* (not file handle) for the opened file; this value must be saved and later passed to **FilHandle** to access the file. It also assigns the value NOERROR (0) to **FilError**. If it is unable to open the specified file, it returns −1 and assigns to **FilError** the value NOOPEN.

Source File	FIL.C, Figure 4.1

FilReadFar

Purpose   This function reads file data directly into a **far** buffer (that is, a buffer located outside the default C data segment).

Prototype   **int FilReadFar**
        (int Handle,   The handle of the file to read.

        char far *Buf,   The **far** address of the buffer to receive the file data.

        int Number)   The number of bytes to read.

Return Value   If successful, it returns and assigns to **FilError** the value NOERROR (0). If it is unable to read the file, it returns and assigns to **FilError** the value READERROR.

Source File   FIL.C, Figure 4.1

FilRenameDir

Purpose   Renames a directory.

Prototype   **int FilRenameDir**
        (char *OldDir,   The existing directory name.

        char *NewDir)   The new directory name.

Return Value   If successful, it returns and assigns to **FilError** the value NOERROR (0). If the specified directory does not exist, it returns and assigns to **FilError** the value NODIR.

Source File   FIL.C, Figure 4.1

FilSetTime

Purpose   Sets the modification date and time of a file.

Prototype   **int FilSetTime**
                  (char *FilePath,   The file name, which can include a full path specification.

                  char *Date,   The new modification date to be assigned.

                  char *Time)   The new modification time to be assigned.

Return Value   If successful, it returns and assigns to **FilError** the value NOERROR (0). If an error occurs, it returns and assigns to **FilError** one of the following error codes:

NOOPEN   Could not open the file to get the required handle.

BADDATE   Invalid date format.

BADTIME   Invalid time format.

NOACC   Cannot access file to set time.

Source File   FIL.C, Figure 4.1

FilSetVolid

Purpose   Sets the volume label for a given disk.

Prototype   **int FilSetVolid**
                  (unsigned char Drive,   The drive for the volume label, where 0 indicates the default drive, 1 drive A, and so on.

                  char *Volid)   The volume label to be assigned the specified drive.

Return Value If successful, the function returns and assigns to **FilError** the value NOERROR (0). If an error occurs, it returns and assigns to **FilError** one of the following error codes:

NOCREAT	Unable to create a new volume label.
NOREN	Unable to rename an existing volume label.

Source File FIL.C, Figure 4.1

FilWriteFar

Purpose This function writes data to a file directly from a **far** buffer (that is, a buffer located outside the default C data segment).

Prototype **int FilWriteFar**

(int Handle,	The handle of the file to which the data is to be written.
char far *Buf,	The **far** address of the buffer containing the data to write to the file.
int Number)	The number of bytes to write.

Return Value If successful, it returns and assigns to **FilError** the value NOERROR (0). If it is unable to write to the file, it returns and assigns to **FilError** the value WRITEERROR.

Source File FIL.C, Figure 4.1

■ Gra... : GRAPHICS FUNCTIONS

Purpose:	These functions provide a basic set of device independent graphics primitives for Microsoft C.
Source File:	GRA.C, Figure 7.1
Header File:	GRA.H, Figure 7.2

Object Files: GRA.C: GRA.OBJ, SCR.OBJ, SCRA.OBJ, UTYA.OBJ

Error Variable: None. All of the functions (except **GraGetCoord** and **GraTypes**) directly return one of the error codes defined in the header file GRA.H.

GraBox

Purpose   Draws a box.

Prototype

int GraBox	
(float X1,	The horizontal world coordinate of one corner of the box.
float Y1,	The vertical world coordinate of this corner.
float X2,	The horizontal world coordinate of the corner *opposite* the corner given by X1 and Y1.
float Y2,	The vertical world coordinate of this opposite corner.
int Attr)	The display attribute to be used to draw the box.

Return Value   If successful, this function returns the value NOERROR (0). If the graphics module has not been properly initialized, it returns NOGRAPH.

Source File   GRA.C, Figure 7.1

GraCircle

Purpose   Draws a circle or ellipse.

Prototype	**int GraCircle**	
	(float X,	The horizontal world coordinate of the center of the ellipse.
	float Y,	The vertical world coordinate of the center of the ellipse.
	float R,	The radius for a circle, or 1/2 the longer dimension for an ellipse.
	int Attr,	The display attribute.
	float Aspect)	The aspect ratio to be used when drawing the ellipse (ratio of vertical to horizontal dimensions).

Return Value   If successful, this function returns the value NOERROR (0). If the graphics module has not been properly initialized, it returns NOGRAPH.

Source File   GRA.C, Figure 7.1

GraClear

Purpose   Clears the screen when in graphics mode, filling the screen with the requested display attribute.

Prototype	**int GraClear**	
	(int Attr)	The display attribute to be used to fill the screen (use the value OFF to make a dark screen, or ON to make a light screen).

Return Value   If successful, this function returns the value NOERROR (0). If the graphics module has not been properly initialized, it returns NOGRAPH.

Source File   GRA.C, Figure 7.1

GraFill

Purpose   Fills a bounded area of the screen with the specified display attribute.

Prototype	int GraFill	
	(float X,	The horizontal world coordinate of a point inside the area to be filled.
	float Y,	The vertical world coordinate of this point.
	int Attr,	Display attribute to be used for filling the area.
	int Bound)	Display attribute of the boundary that defines the area to be filled.

Return Value   If successful, this function returns the value NOERROR (0). If an error occurs, it returns one of the following error codes:

	NOGRAPH	The graphics module has not been properly initialized.
	OUTOFRANGE	The specified point is beyond the boundaries of the screen.

Source File   GRA.C, Figure 7.1

GraGetCoord

Purpose   Obtains the current maximum and minimum world coordinate values.

Prototype	void GraGetCoord	
	(float *XMinPtr,	Address of variable to receive the minimum horizontal world coordinate value.
	float *YMinPtr,	Address of variable to receive the minimum vertical world coordinate value.
	float *XMaxPtr,	Address of variable to receive the maximum horizontal world coordinate value.
	float *YMaxPtr)	Address of variable to receive the maximum vertical world coordinate value.

Source File   GRA.C, Figure 7.1

GraGetPoint

Purpose	Returns the display attribute of a point on the screen.

Prototype

int GraGetPoint
    (float X,   The world coordinate values of the point.

    float Y)

Return Value   This function returns ON if the pixel at the specified point is on, or OFF if it is off. If an error occurs, it returns one of the following error codes:

NOGRAPH	The graphics module has not been properly initialized.
OUTOFRANGE	The specified point is outside the current range of world coordinate values.

Source File   GRA.C, Figure 7.1

GraInit

Purpose   Initializes the module of graphics functions; must be called prior to calling any of the graphics display functions.

Prototype

int GraInit
    (int Mode)   The desired graphics mode (either **HIRES** for high resolution CGA graphics, or **HERC** for Hercules graphics).

Return Value   If successful, this function returns the value NOERROR (0). If an error occurs, it returns one of the following error codes:

WRONGMODE	The requested mode is not supported by the hardware.

	BADMODE	The requested mode is not supported by the graphics module.

Source File GRA.C, Figure 7.1

GraLine

Purpose Draws a line.

Prototype	**int GraLine**	
	(float X1,	World coordinates of the starting point
	float Y1,	of the line.
	float X2,	World coordinates of the ending point
	float Y2,	of the line.
	int Attr)	Display attribute to be used for drawing the line.

Return Value If successful, this function returns the value NOERROR (0). If the graphics module has not been properly initialized, it returns NOGRAPH.

Source File GRA.C, Figure 7.1

GraPoint

Purpose Draws a point.

Prototype	**int GraPoint**	
	(float X,	World coordinates of the point.
	float Y,	
	int Attr)	Display attribute to be used for the point.

Return Value If successful, this function returns the value NOERROR (0). If the graphics module has not been properly initialized, it returns NOGRAPH.

Source File   GRA.C, Figure 7.1

GraQuit

Purpose   Ends the graphics mode and returns to text mode.

Prototype
int GraQuit
(void)

Return Value   If successful, this function returns the value NOERROR (0). If the graphics module has not been properly initialized, it returns NOGRAPH.

Source File   GRA.C, Figure 7.1

GraSetCoord

Purpose   Sets the minimum and maximum world coordinate values for the screen.

Prototype
int GraSetCoord
(float XMinNew,   Minimum horizontal value.
float YMinNew,   Minimum vertical value.
float XMaxNew,   Maximum horizontal value.
float YMaxNew)   Maximum vertical value.

Return Value   If successful, this function returns the value NOERROR (0). If the coordinates you have passed are invalid (that is, a minimum value is greater than or equal to a maximum value), it returns the value BADCOORD.

Source File   GRA.C, Figure 7.1

Int... : INTERRUPT HANDLING FUNCTIONS

Purpose:	A set of functions for installing hardware and software interrupt handlers.
Source File:	INT.C, Figure 8.1
Header File:	INT.H, Figure 8.2
Object Files:	INT.C: INT.OBJ, KBD.OBJ, SCRA.OBJ
Error Variable:	None.

IntBBInstall

Purpose   Installs a control-break routine at the BIOS level.

Prototype

void IntBBInstall (void(*UserRtn) (void),

Address of the function to be invoked when Ctrl-Break is detected by the BIOS. If NULL is passed, a default routine will be installed.

void (*UserWrapup) (void))

Address of a routine to be called before program termination if the break routine aborts the program. If NULL is passed, then a default routine will be called.

Source File   INT.C, Figure 8.1

IntBBRemove

Purpose   Removes the control-break handler installed by **IntBBInstall**, and restores the former handler.

Prototype   **void IntBBRemove (void)**

Source File   INT.C, Figure 8.1

IntCEInstall

Purpose   Installs a critical-error service routine.

Prototype

void IntCEInstall
(int (*UserRtn)(),   Address of the function to be installed
as a critical-error routine. If NULL is
passed, then a default function will be
installed.

void (*UserWrapup)   Address of the function to be called
(void))   before program termination if the
critical-error routine aborts the
program. If NULL is passed, then a
default function will be called.

Source File   INT.C, Figure 8.1

IntCERemove

Purpose   Removes the critical-error function installed by **IntCEInstall**, and restores the former routine.

Prototype   **void IntCERemove**
(void)

Source File   INT.C, Figure 8.1

IntClockInstall

Purpose   Installs a function to be called each time the clock hardware interrupt
(08h) occurs.

Prototype   **void IntClockInstall**
(void (*FPtr) (void))   The address of the function that is to be
invoked with each clock interrupt.

Source File   INT.C, Figure 8.1

IntClockRemove

Purpose   Removes the clock interrupt routine installed by **IntClockInstall**, and restores the former service routine.

Prototype   **void IntClockRemove
(void)**

Source File   INT.C, Figure 8.1

IntDBInstall

Purpose   Installs a function that is called by MS-DOS when it detects a break key.

Prototype

void IntDBInstall (void (*UserRtn) (void),	Address of the function to be installed as a DOS-level break routine. If NULL is passed, then a default function will be installed.
void (*UserWrapup) (void))	Address of the function to be called before program termination if the break routine aborts the program. If NULL is passed, then a default function will be called.

Source File   INT.C, Figure 8.1

IntDBRemove

Purpose   Uninstalls the break routine installed by **IntDBInstall**.

Prototype	**void IntDBRemove (void)**
Source File	INT.C, Figure 8.1

■ Ioc... : CONSOLE I/O CONTROL FUNCTIONS

Purpose:	These functions place the console device in the raw (binary) or cooked (ASCII) mode.
Source File:	IOC.C, Figure 2.25
Header File:	IOC.H, Figure 2.26
Object File:	IOC.C: IOC.OBJ
Error Variable:	None.

IocCookMode

Purpose	Places the console device in the cooked (ASCII) mode.
Prototype	**void IocCookMode (void)**
Source File	IOC.C, Figure 2.25

IocRawMode

Purpose	Places the console device in the raw (binary) mode.
Prototype	**void IocRawMode (void)**
Source File	INT.C, Figure 8.1

Kbd... : KEYBOARD FUNCTIONS

Purpose:	These functions manage the keyboard at the BIOS level.
Source Files:	KBD.C, Figure 2.1
	KBDA.ASM, Figure 2.2
Header File:	KBD.H, Figure 2.3
Object Files:	KBD.C: KBD.OBJ, UTYA.OBJ
	KBDA.ASM: KBDA.OBJ
Error Variable:	None.

KbdFlush

Purpose   Removes all characters waiting in the BIOS keyboard buffer.

Prototype   **void far KbdFlush**
     (void)

Source File   KBDA.ASM, Figure 2.2

KbdGetC

Purpose   Reads a character from the keyboard.

Prototype   **int far KbdGetC**
     (void)

Return Value   The integer returned by this function contains the ASCII value of the key in the low order byte, and the extended code for the key in the high order byte. (See Appendix C for the extended keyboard codes.)

Source File   KBDA.ASM, Figure 2.2

KbdGetShift

Purpose	Returns the BIOS shift status word.
Prototype	**int KbdGetShift** **(void)**
Return Value	The function returns the BIOS shift status word, encoded as shown in Table 2.1.
Source File	KBD.C, Figure 2.1

KbdInsert

Purpose	This function places the specified key within the BIOS keyboard buffer as if the key were typed by the user.	
Prototype	**int KbdInsert** **(char AscCode,**	The ASCII code of the key to be inserted.
	char ExtCode)	The extended code of the key to be inserted (see Appendix C).
Return Value	If successful, the function returns 0. If the keyboard buffer is full, it returns a nonzero value indicating that the key could not be inserted.	
Source File	KBD.C, Figure 2.1	

KbdReady

Purpose	Indicates whether a key has been typed and is available for reading (through **KbdGetC**).

Prototype	**int far KbdReady (void)**

Return Value	This function returns a nonzero value if a key is ready, or zero if a key is not ready.

Source File	KBDA.ASM, Figure 2.2

KbdSetShift

Purpose	Sets the BIOS shift status word.

Prototype	**void KbdSetShift (int ShiftStat)**	The desired value for the BIOS shift status word, encoded as shown in Table 2.1.

Source File	KBD.C, Figure 2.1

Mou... : MOUSE FUNCTIONS

Purpose:	These functions manage the mouse, and allow a C program to implement a complete mouse interface.
Source File:	MOU.C, Figure 11.1
Header File:	MOU.H, Figure 11.2
Object File:	MOU.C: MOU.OBJ
Error Variable:	None. All of the functions in this module, except **MouInstalled**, directly return zero if successful, or a nonzero value if an error occurs.

MouGetButtonPress

Purpose	Reports the number of times the specified mouse button has been pressed since the last time the function was called.

Prototype

int MouGetButtonPress

(int Button,	Button for which press information is to be supplied (0 is the left button, 1 is the right, and 2 is the center).
int *ButtonStatus,	Address of the integer variable to receive the current status of all mouse buttons (encoded as explained in Chapter 11).
int *NumberPresses,	Address of the integer variable to receive the number of times the button has been pressed since the last call to this function.
int *PointerCol,	Address of the integer variable to receive the horizontal position of the mouse pointer.
int *PointerRow)	Address of the integer variable to receive the vertical position.

Return Value	If successful, the function returns zero. If a mouse driver is not installed, it returns a nonzero value.
Source File	MOU.C, Figure 11.1

MouGetButtonRelease

Purpose	Reports the number of times the specified mouse button has been released since the last time the function was called.

Prototype

int MouGetButtonRelease

(int Button,	Button for which release information is to be supplied (0 is the left button, 1 is the right, and 2 is the center).

int *ButtonStatus,	Address of the integer variable to receive the current status of all mouse buttons (encoded as explained in Chapter 11).
int *NumberReleases,	Address of the integer variable to receive the number of times the button has been released since the last call to this function.
int *PointerCol,	Address of the integer variable to receive the horizontal position of the mouse pointer.
int *PointerRow)	Address of the integer variable to receive the vertical position.

Return Value   If successful, the function returns zero. If a mouse driver is not installed, it returns a nonzero value.

Source File   MOU.C, Figure 11.1

MouGetButtons

Purpose   Obtains the status of the mouse buttons and the position of the mouse pointer.

Prototype   **int MouGetButtons**

(int *ButtonStatus,	Address of the integer variable to receive the mouse button status (encoded as explained in Chapter 11).
int *PointerCol,	Address of the integer variable to receive the current horizontal position of the mouse pointer.
int *PointerRow)	Address of the integer variable to receive the current vertical position.

Return Value   The function returns zero if successsful, or a nonzero value if a mouse driver is not installed.

Source File   MOU.C, Figure 11.1

MouGetMickeys

Purpose   Reports the distance the mouse has moved on the desktop since the last time the function was called.

Prototype   **int MouGetMickeys**
        (int *HorizCount,   The horizontal distance the mouse has moved in mickeys (a mickey is approximately 1/120").

        int *VertCount)   The vertical distance the mouse has moved.

Return Value   If successful, the function returns zero. If a mouse driver is not installed, it returns a nonzero value.

Source File   MOU.C, Figure 11.1

MouGetStorage

Purpose   Reports the size of the buffer required to save the mouse state through the function **MouSaveState**.

Prototype   **int MouGetStorage**
        (int *BufferSize)   Address of an integer variable to receive the required buffer size in bytes.

Return Value   If successful, the function returns zero. If a mouse driver is not installed, it returns a nonzero value.

Source File   MOU.C, Figure 11.1

MouHidePointer

Purpose	Makes the mouse pointer invisible on the screen and decrements the internal pointer counter.
Prototype	**int MouHidePointer** **(void)**
Return Value	If successful, the function returns zero. If a mouse driver is not installed, it returns a nonzero value.
Source File	MOU.C, Figure 11.1

MouInstalled

Purpose	This function allows you to determine whether a mouse driver is installed.
Prototype	**int MouInstalled** **(void)**
Return Value	The function returns one if a mouse driver is installed, or zero if no driver is installed.
Source File	MOU.C, Figure 11.1

MouReset

Purpose	Resets the mouse driver to its default state, and reports the number of mouse buttons available.
Prototype	**int MouReset** **(int *NumButtons)** Address of the variable to receive the number of mouse buttons.

Return Value	The function returns zero if successful, or a nonzero value if the mouse hardware or software is not properly installed.
Source File	MOU.C, Figure 11.1

MouRestoreState

Purpose	Restores the state of the mouse driver formerly saved by calling **MouSaveState**.

Prototype	**int MouRestoreState (unsigned char far *FarPtrBuffer)**	**far** address of the buffer in which the mouse driver state was saved by the function **MouSaveState**.

Return Value	If successful, the function returns zero. If a mouse driver is not installed, it returns a nonzero value.

Source File	MOU.C, Figure 11.1

MouSaveState

Purpose	Saves the current state of the mouse driver.

Prototype	**int MouSaveState (unsigned char far *FarPtrBuffer)**	**far** address of the buffer in which the mouse state will be stored.

Return Value	If successful, the function returns zero. If a mouse driver is not installed, it returns a nonzero value.

Source File	MOU.C, Figure 11.1

MouSetGraphPointer

Purpose   Specifies the mouse pointer to be used in graphics modes.

Prototype

int MouSetGraphPointer	
(int HotSpotHoriz,	Horizontal position of the pointer hot spot.
int HotSpotVert,	Vertical position of the pointer hot spot.
unsigned far *FarPtrMasks)	**far** address of the bit masks that define the shape of the mouse pointer.

Return Value   If successful, the function returns zero. If a mouse driver is not installed, it returns a nonzero value.

Source File   MOU.C, Figure 11.1

MouSetIntHandler

Purpose   Installs a function that is called each time a specified event occurs.

Prototype

int MouSetIntHandler	
(int CallMask,	A bitmask that specifies which events should result in calling the function that is to be installed (the bitmask is encoded as described in Chapter 11).
void (far *FarPtrHandler) (void))	**far** address of the function that is to be installed.

Return Value   If successful, the function returns zero. If a mouse driver is not installed, it returns a nonzero value.

Source File   MOU.C, Figure 11.1

MouSetPointer

Purpose   Places the mouse pointer at a specified position on the screen.

Prototype   **int MouSetPointer**
    (int PointerCol,   Horizontal pointer position.
    int PointerRow)   Vertical pointer position.

Return Value   If successful, the function returns zero. If a mouse driver is not installed, it returns a nonzero value.

Source File   MOU.C, Figure 11.1

MouSetPointerHorizArea

Purpose   Sets the limits of horizontal motion of the mouse pointer on the screen.

Prototype   **int MouSetPointerHorizArea**
    (int MinCol,   The minimum horizontal mouse coordinate.
    int MaxCol)   The maximum horizontal mouse coordinate.

Return Value   If successful, the function returns zero. If a mouse driver is not installed, it returns a nonzero value.

Source File   MOU.C, Figure 11.1

MouSetPointerVertArea

Purpose   Sets the limits of vertical motion of the mouse pointer on the screen.

Prototype	int MouSetPointerVertArea (int MinRow,	Minimum vertical mouse coordinate.
	int MaxRow)	Maximum vertical mouse coordinate.

Return Value   If successful, the function returns zero. If a mouse driver is not installed, it returns a nonzero value.

Source File   MOU.C, Figure 11.1

MouSetRatio

Purpose   Sets the ratio of mouse movement on the desktop to pointer movement on the screen.

Prototype	int MouSetRatio (int HorizRatio,	The number of mickeys the mouse must move in the horizontal direction to move the pointer a distance of 8 pixels on the screen.
	int VertRatio)	The number of mickeys the mouse must move in the vertical direction to move the pointer a distance of 8 pixels on the screen.

Return Value   If successful, the function returns zero. If a mouse driver is not installed, it returns a nonzero value.

Source File   MOU.C, Figure 11.1

MouSetTextPointer

Purpose   Sets the mouse pointer to be used in text modes.

Prototype	int MouSetTextPointer (int PointerType,	Specifies whether the pointer is to be implemented as a software character (0), or by using the blinking hardware cursor (1).
	int SMaskScanStart,	For a software pointer, the screen mask defining the pointer shape; for a hardware pointer, the beginning horizontal scan line of the cursor.
	int PMaskScanStop)	For a software pointer, the pointer mask defining the pointer shape; for a hardware pointer, the ending horizontal scan line of the cursor.

Return Value   If successful, the function returns zero. If a mouse driver is not installed, it returns a nonzero value.

Source File   MOU.C, Figure 11.1

MouShowPointer

Purpose   Increments the internal mouse pointer counter, and shows the pointer on the screen if this counter reaches 0.

Prototype   int MouShowPointer
              (void)

Return Value   If successful, the function returns zero. If a mouse driver is not installed, it returns a nonzero value.

Source File   MOU.C, Figure 11.1

Prt... : PRINTER FUNCTIONS

Purpose:	This modules provides low-level printer control functions, as well as functions for formatting printed reports.
Source File:	PRT.C, Figure 3.1
Header File:	PRT.H, Figure 3.2
Object File:	PRT.C: PRT.OBJ
Error Variable:	None.

PrtInit

Purpose   Initializes the port for the primary printer (LPT1).

Prototype   **void PrtInit
(void)**

Source File   PRT.C, Figure 3.1

PrtInstalled

Purpose   Reports the number of printers installed.

Prototype   **int PrtInstalled
(void)**

Return Value   This function returns the number of printers installed.

Source File   PRT.C, Figure 3.1

PrtNewPage

Purpose	Initializes a new page; used in conjunction with the printer formatting function **PrtPosition**.

Prototype **void PrtNewPage**
(int FormFeed)   If this parameter is nonzero, a formfeed is generated when the new page is initialized.

Source File PRT.C, Figure 3.1

PrtPosition

Purpose	Prints a string at a specific starting position on the page.

Prototype **int PrtPosition**
(char *String,   The string to be printed.
int Row,   The starting row on the page.
int Col)   The starting column on the page.

Return Value If successful, the function returns zero. If an error occurs, it returns a nonzero value.

Source File PRT.C, Figure 3.1

PrtPutC

Purpose	Sends a character to the printer; the character is printed at the current position of the printer head.

Prototype **void PrtPutC**
(int Ch)   The character to be printed.

Source File   PRT.C, Figure 3.1

PrtPutS

Purpose   Sends a string to the printer; the string is printed starting at the current position of the printer head.

Prototype   **void PrtPutS**
              (char *String)   The NULL-terminated string to be printed.

Source File   PRT.C, Figure 3.1

PrtQueCancel

Purpose   Removes a file from the DOS PRINT queue (files are placed in the queue by means of the DOS PRINT command, or through the function **PrtQueSubmit**).

Prototype   **int PrtQueCancel**
              (char *FileName)   A string containing the full name of the file to be removed from the PRINT queue; global file name characters *are* allowed.

Return Value   If successful, the function returns NOERROR (0). If an error occurs, it returns one of the error codes defined in PRT.H.

Source File   PRT.C, Figure 3.1

PrtQueCancelAll

Purpose   Removes *all* files from the DOS PRINT queue.

Prototype	**int PrtQueCancelAll** **(void)**
Return Value	If successful, the function returns NOERROR (0). If an error occurs, it returns one of the error codes defined in PRT.H.
Source File	PRT.C, Figure 3.1

PrtQueState

Purpose	Returns the status of the DOS PRINT queue.
Prototype	**int PrtQueState** **(void)**
Return Value	The function returns NOERROR (0) if the print queue is properly installed, NOTINST if the queue is not installed, CANTINST if the queue cannot be installed, or WRONGDOS if the MS-DOS version number is less than 3.0 or if it is equal to or greater than 10.0 (OS/2 DOS compatibility box).
Source File	PRT.C, Figure 3.1

PrtQueSubmit

Purpose	Places a file in the DOS PRINT queue, to be printed in the background.
Prototype	**int PrtQueSubmit** **(char far *FileName)** The name of the file to be printed; global file name characters are *not* allowed. Under certain versions of DOS, you must specify the complete path name.
Return Value	If successful, the function returns NOERROR (0). If an error occurs, it returns one of the error codes defined in PRT.H.

Source File   PRT.C, Figure 3.1

PrtReady

Purpose   Determines whether the printer is ready to receive output.

Prototype   **int PrtReady**
(void)

Return Value   A nonzero value if the printer is ready, or zero if the printer is not ready.

Source File   PRT.C, Figure 3.1

PrtSwap

Purpose   Associates an alternate printer with the device LPT1, in a system with more than one printer attached.

Prototype   **int PrtSwap**
(int PrtNumber)   The number of the printer (2 or 3) to be "connected" to LPT1.

Return Value   The function returns zero if successful, or a nonzero value if an error occurs.

Source File   PRT.C, Figure 3.1

PrtTimeout

Purpose   Sets the BIOS timeout count, that is, the number of seconds the BIOS waits before returning an error code when certain errors occur while writing to the primary printer.

Prototype	void PrtTimeout	
	(unsigned char Seconds)	The new timeout count, in seconds.

Source File	PRT.C, Figure 3.1

Scr... : VIDEO FUNCTIONS

Purpose:	These functions provide fast, controlled video output in text modes, and manage the display of screens and windows created with the interactive designer of Chapter 6.
Source Files:	SCR.C, Figure 5.1
	SCRA.ASM, Figure 5.2
Header File:	SCR.H, Figure 5.3
Object Files:	SCR.C: SCR.OBJ and KBDA.OBJ
	SCRA.ASM: SCRA.OBJ
Error Variable:	None.

ScrClear

Purpose	Clears a section of the screen.

Prototype	void ScrClear	
	(unsigned char StartRow,	Upper row of area to be cleared.
	unsigned char StartCol,	Left column.
	unsigned char StopRow,	Bottom row.
	unsigned char StopCol)	Right column.

Source File	SCR.C, Figure 5.1

ScrColorCard

Purpose   Activates the color adapter in a system with both a monochrome and a color monitor.

Prototype   **void ScrColorCard (void)**

Source File   SCR.C, Figure 5.1

ScrGetCur

Purpose   Obtains the current cursor position for the specified video page.

Prototype

void ScrGetCur (int *Row,	Address of variable to receive cursor row.
int *Col,	Address of variable to receive cursor column.
int Page)	The video page.

Source File   SCR.C, Figure 5.1

ScrGetMode

Purpose   Obtains the current video mode, number of display columns, and active video page.

Prototype

void ScrGetMode (struct Mode *ModePtr)	Address of a **Mode** structure (defined in SCR.H) to receive video information.

Source File   SCR.C, Figure 5.1

ScrGetS

Purpose	Reads a fixed length string from the keyboard, echoing output to a specific field on the screen.

Prototype	**int ScrGetS**	
	(char *Buffer,	Address of buffer to receive string.
	int Attr,	Display attribute to be used for echoed characters.
	int Row,	Starting row on screen for echoed characters.
	int Col,	Starting column on screen for echoed characters.
	int Length,	Size of the string to be read.
	int Mode)	Specifies special features: AUTOEXIT causes field to be exited automatically when the last character is entered, UPPER causes all entered characters to be converted to uppercase, and NOFEAT indicates no special features (the constants are defined in SCR.H).

Return Value   The function returns one of the following codes indicating the key used to exit the field:

−1	Esc
0	Return
1	Left-Arrow (←)
2	Right-Arrow (→)
3	Up-Arrow (↑)
4	Down-Arrow (↓)
5	Automatic field exit

Source File   SCR.C, Figure 5.1

ScrGetStyle

Purpose   Obtains the current cursor shape.

Prototype   **void ScrGetStyle**
(int *StartLine,   Address of variable to receive beginning line of cursor.

int *StopLine)   Address of variable to receive ending line of cursor.

Source File   SCR.C, Figure 5.1

ScrMonoCard

Purpose   Activates the monochrome adapter in a system with both a color and a monochrome monitor.

Prototype   **void ScrColorCard**
(void)

Source File   SCR.C, Figure 5.1

ScrPop

Purpose   Restores the most recently saved screen from the screen stack.

Prototype   **int ScrPop**
(int Remove)   A value of 1 causes the screen to be removed from the stack when it is restored; a value of 0 causes the screen to be left on the stack.

Return Value   If successful, the function returns NOERROR (0). If there are no screens on the stack to restore, it returns STACKEMPTY.

Source File   SCR.C, Figure 5.1

ScrPush

Purpose   Saves the current screen contents on the screen stack.

Prototype   **int ScrPush**
                 (void)

Return Value   The function returns NOERROR (0) if successful, MAXTOOSMALL if the stack has reached its maximum size, or NOHEAP if heap memory is exhausted.

Source File   SCR.C, Figure 5.1

ScrPutAttr

Purpose   Assigns a video display attribute to an area of the screen without altering the existing characters.

Prototype   **void ScrPutAttr**
                 (int Attr,   The display attribute to use.
                 int StartRow,   The top row of the area to be modified.
                 int StartCol,   The left column.
                 int StopRow,   The bottom row.
                 int StopCol)   The right column.

Source File   SCR.C, Figure 5.1

ScrPutBox

Purpose   Displays a box on the screen.

Prototype	void ScrPutBox	
	(int ULR,	The row coordinate of the upper left corner of the box.
	int ULC,	The column coordinate of this corner.
	int LRR,	The row coordinate of the lower right corner of the box.
	int LRC,	The column coordinate of this corner.
	int Style)	The box drawing character style: a value from 0 to 3 (see Figure 5.17).

Source File   SCR.C, Figure 5.1

ScrPutS

Purpose   Displays a string at a specified position on the screen.

Prototype	void ScrPutS	
	(char *String,	Address of the NULL-terminated string to be displayed.
	unsigned char Attr,	Video display attribute.
	unsigned char Row,	Starting row for the display of the string.
	unsigned char Col)	Starting column for the display of the string.

Source File   SCR.C, Figure 5.1

ScrPutWindow

Purpose   Displays a section of a screen data buffer at a specific position on the screen.

Prototype	void ScrPutWindow	
	(char *Buffer,	Address of the buffer containing the screen data.

int SourceStartRow,	Beginning row coordinate of the section of the buffer to display.
int SourceStartCol,	Beginning column coordinate of the section of the buffer to display.
int SourceEndRow,	Ending row of buffer.
int SourceEndCol,	Ending column of buffer.
int TargetRow,	Row coordinate of upper left corner of display on screen.
int TargetCol)	Column coordinate of upper left corner of display on screen.

Source File   SCR.C, Figure 5.1

ScrReadWindow

Purpose   Reads 4,000 bytes of screen data from a disk file into a program buffer.

Prototype

int ScrReadWindow (char *Buffer,	Address of 4,000 byte buffer to receive the screen data.
char *FileName)	Name of 4,000 byte screen data file (created by the screen designer of Chapter 6).

Return Value   The function returns NOERROR (0) if successful, OPENERR if an error occurred opening the file, READERR if an error occurred reading the file, or CLOSERR if an error occurred closing the file.

Source File   SCR.C, Figure 5.1

ScrSetCur

Purpose   Places the hardware cursor at a specified position on the screen.

Prototype	void ScrSetCur	
	(int Row,	Row coordinate of cursor position.
	int Col,	Column coordinate of cursor position.
	int Page)	Video page.

Source File	SCR.C, Figure 5.1

ScrSetMode

Purpose	Sets the video mode and active display page.

Prototype	void ScrSetMode	
	(struct Mode *ModePtr)	Address of a **Mode** structure containing the desired video mode and display page (defined in SCR.H).

Source File	SCR.C, Figure 5.1

ScrSetStyle

Purpose	Sets the cursor shape.

Prototype	void ScrSetStyle	
	(int StartLine,	Start row for cursor.
	int StopLine)	Ending row for cursor.

Note: Rows are numbered from the top beginning with 0, and extend to 13 on monochrome systems, and to 7 on CGA systems.

Source File	SCR.C, Figure 5.1

ScrTypes

Purpose   Reports the type or types of video adapter currently installed.

Prototype   **int far ScrTypes**
                 (void)

Return Value   An integer, the individual bits of which indicate the type or types of video adapter installed in the machine. Table 5.3 describes the meanings of each of these bits, and constants for accessing the bits are defined in SCR.H.

Source File   SCRA.ASM, Figure 5.2

Tsr... : FUNCTIONS FOR MEMORY RESIDENT PROGRAMS

Purpose: This module serves to convert a normal Microsoft C application to a memory resident popup utility, activated through a hotkey.

Source Files: TSR.C, Figure 9.1

                   TSRA.ASM, Figure 9.2

Header File: TSR.H, Figure 9.3

Object Files: TSR.C: TSR.OBJ, TSRA.ASM, KBD.C, and UTYA.OBJ

Error Variable: None.

TsrInDos

Purpose   Indicates whether MS-DOS was active when the TSR received control.

Prototype	**int TsrInDos** **(void)**

Return Value   A nonzero value if DOS was active, and 0 if DOS was *not* active.

Source File   TSR.C, Figure 9.1

TsrInstall

Purpose   Converts a Microsoft C program to a TSR, and terminates the program, leaving the code and data resident in memory.

Prototype   **int TsrInstall**

(void (*FPtr) (void),	The address of the C function that is to receive control when the hotkey is pressed.
int HotKey,	The shift key combination that is to be used to activate the TSR (see Table 2.1).
unsigned long Code)	A unique code in the range of values from 0x00000001 to 0xffffffff, used to prevent the same TSR from being installed more than once.

Return Value   If successful, the function never returns; otherwise, it returns INSTALLED if the TSR has already been installed, NOINT if there are no free user interrupts available, WRONGDOS if the DOS version is not 2.0 or later, or ERROR for any other error that prevents successful installation of the TSR.

Source File   TSR.C, Figure 9.1

▌ Uty... : UTILITY FUNCTIONS

Purpose:	A collection of functions used to support the other modules, and specialized services that do not fit into any of the other categories.
Source Files:	UTY.C, Figure 12.1
	UTYA.ASM, Figure 12.2
Header File:	UTY.H, Figure 12.3
Object Files:	UTY.C: UTY.OBJ, UTYA.OBJ, SCR.OBJ, and KBDA.OBJ
	UTYA.ASM: UTYA.OBJ
Error Variable:	None.

UtyAllBlank

Purpose   Determines whether a NULL-terminated string consists of only blank characters.

Prototype

    int UtyAllBlank
      (char *String)   The address of the NULL-terminated string.

Return Value   The function returns a nonzero value if the string consists of only blank characters (or the string has zero length), or zero if the string contains one or more non-blank characters.

Source File   UTY.C, Figure 12.1

UtyBlank

Purpose   Fills a buffer with blank characters, and places a NULL character at the end of the resulting string.

Prototype	**void UtyBlank (char *String,**	The address of the buffer to be filled with blanks.
	int Length)	The total length of the resulting string, including the NULL termination.

Source File   UTY.C, Figure 12.1

UtyClockCount

Purpose   Obtains the BIOS count of clock interrupts since midnight.

Prototype	**int UtyClockCount (long *Count)**	The address of the variable to receive the count.

Return Value   The function returns 1 if midnight has passed since the clock count was read through interrupt 1Ah, or 0 otherwise (that is, it returns the value of the BIOS *rollover* flag).

Source File   UTY.C, Figure 12.1

UtyDisable

Purpose   Disables hardware interrupts.

Prototype   **void far UtyDisable (void)**

Source File   UTYA.ASM, Figure 12.2

UtyDump

Purpose   Displays a sequence of memory addresses in hexadecimal format.

Prototype	**void UtyDump**	
	(char *Source,	Starting address of memory location to dump.
	int Count)	Number of bytes to dump.
Source File	UTY.C, Figure 12.1	

UtyEnable

Purpose	Enables hardware interrupts.
Prototype	**void far UtyEnable** **(void)**
Source File	UTYA.ASM, Figure 12.2

UtyEnabled

Purpose	Reports whether the interrupts are currently enabled.
Prototype	**int far UtyEnabled** **(void)**
Return Value	A nonzero value if the interrupts are enabled, or zero if they are disabled.
Source File	UTYA.ASM, Figure 12.2

UtyExtension

Purpose	Supplies a pointer to the beginning of the extension within a file name.

Prototype	**char *UtyExtension**	
	(char *FileName)	A NULL-terminated string containing a file name, which can include a complete path specification.

Return Value   If the file name contains an extension, the function returns a pointer to the first character of the extension. If the name does not contain an extension, it returns a pointer to the NULL character that terminates the file name.

Source File   UTY.C, Figure 12.1

UtyFarNearCopy

Purpose   Copies data from a **far** memory location to a program buffer.

Prototype	**void far**	
	UtyFarNearCopy	
	(char far *TargetAddr,	The address of the program buffer to receive the data.
	unsigned SourceSeg,	The segment address of the source of the data.
	unsigned SourceOff,	The offset address of the source of the data.
	unsigned Count);	The number of bytes to copy.

Source File   UTYA.ASM, Figure 12.2

UtyFarSetByte

Purpose   Fills a **far** memory location with a given byte value.

Prototype	**void far UtyFarSetByte**	
	(unsigned TargetSeg,	The segment address of the block of memory to be filled.
	unsigned TargetOff,	The offset address of the block.

unsigned char Byte,	The byte to be used to fill the block.
unsigned Number)	The number of bytes of memory to fill.

Source File   UTYA.ASM, Figure 12.2

UtyFarSetWord

Purpose   Fills a **far** memory location with a given word (2-byte) value.

Prototype   **void far UtyFarSetWord**

(unsigned TargetSeg,	The segment address of the block of memory to be filled.
unsigned TargetOff,	The offset address of the block.
unsigned Word,	The word value to be used to fill the block.
unsigned Number)	The number of *words* of memory to fill.

Source File   UTYA.ASM, Figure 12.2

UtyGetCpu

Purpose   Reports the type of processor in the computer.

Prototype   **int far UtyGetCpu**
(void)

Return Value   A code for the type of processor installed in the machine; constant identifiers for these codes are given in UTY.H and the codes are explained in Chapter 12.

Source File   UTYA.ASM, Figure 12.2

UtyGetDateString

Purpose   Obtains the current date formatted as a string.

Prototype   **int UtyGetDateString**
          (char *Target)   The string to receive the date. The date is written in the format mm/dd/yyyy, and therefore **Target** must be at least 11 bytes long.

Return Value   It returns the day of the week, where 0 indicates Sunday, 1 Monday, and so on.

Source File   UTY.C, Figure 12.1

UtyGetMachine

Purpose   Obtains the computer model.

Prototype   **int UtyMachineType**
          (void)

Return Value   The function returns a code indicating the computer model; descriptions and constant definitions for all model types reported by this function are contained in the header file UTY.H.

Source File   UTY.C, Figure 12.1

UtyGetTimeString

Purpose   Obtains the current time formatted as a string.

Prototype   **void UtyGetTimeString**
          (char *Target)   The string to receive the time formatted as hh:mm:ss.hh

(the   string must therefore be at
least 12 bytes long).

Source File	UTY.C, Figure 12.1

UtyNearFarCopy

Purpose	Copies data from a program buffer to a **far** memory location.

Prototype	**void far**	
	UtyNearFarCopy	
	(unsigned TargetSeg,	Segment address of location to receive the data.
	unsigned TargetOff,	Offset address of location to receive the data.
	char far *SourceAddr,	Address of the program buffer that is the source of the data.
	unsigned Count);	Number of bytes to copy.

Source File	UTYA.ASM, Figure 12.2

UtyPackDate

Purpose	Converts a date string to a packed format that can be sorted chronologically.

Prototype	**int UtyPackDate**	
	(char *Target,	The address of the string to receive the packed date. The date is written in the format yyyymmdd, and therefore this string must be at least 9 bytes long.
	char *Source)	The address of the string containing the unpacked date string, which must be in the format mm/dd/yyyy (the character- may also be used as a separator).

Return Value	This function returns zero if the date is successfully packed, and 1 if the date is invalid (if the date in **Source** is invalid, the string **Target** is not modified).
Source File	UTY.C, Figure 12.1

UtyPause

Purpose	Generates a delay for a specified number of seconds.
Prototype	**void UtyPause (double Seconds)** The length of the desired pause in seconds.
Source File	UTY.C, Figure 12.1

UtyQualify

Purpose	Supplies the full path specification corresponding to a file name.
Prototype	**int UtyQualify (char *Qual,** Address of the buffer to receive the fully qualified file name.
	char *Unqual, String containing the file name to be converted into a fully qualified name.
	int Size) The size of the receiving buffer **Qual**.
Return Value	If successful, the function returns NOERROR (0). If an error occurs, it returns one of the following error codes:
	DOSERR An error occurred calling DOS.
	SIZETOOSMALL The buffer size given by **Size** is too small for the qualified file name.
Source File	UTY.C, Figure 12.1

UtyQuit

Purpose	Displays error information in a window and terminates the program.

Prototype	**void UtyQuit**	
	(char *Message,	Error message to be displayed.
	char *File,	Source file where error occurred (easily obtained from the macro __FILE__).
	int Line)	Source file line where error occurred (easily obtained from the macro __LINE__).

Source File	UTY.C, Figure 12.1

UtyRepeat

Purpose	Provides a string containing a specified number of copies of a given character.

Prototype	**char *UtyRepeat**	
	(int Number,	The desired number of copies of the character to be placed in the string.
	char Ch)	The character.

Return Value	The address of the string consisting of the repeated characters.
Source File	UTY.C, Figure 12.1

UtyRightTrim

Purpose	Removes all trailing blanks from a string.

Prototype	**void UtyRightTrim**	
	(char *String,	The string to be modified.

	int Length)	The length of the string.
Source File	UTY.C, Figure 12.1	

UtyRound

Purpose	Rounds a floating point value to a given number of decimal places.	
Prototype	**double UtyRound** **(double Value,**	The floating point number to be rounded.
	int Digits)	The desired number of decimal places in the rounded result.
Return Value	It returns the rounded result.	
Source File	UTY.C, Figure 12.1	

UtyRound5

Purpose	Rounds a floating point number to the nearest 0.05.	
Prototype	**double UtyRound5** **(double Value)**	The floating point number to be rounded.
Return Value	The rounded result.	
Source File	UTY.C, Figure 12.1	

UtySetDateString

Purpose	Sets the system date from a string.

Prototype	**int UtySetDateString**	
	(char *Date)	A string containing the date, which must by in the format mm/dd/yyyy (a - character can replace any / separator).

Return Value   If successful, the function returns NOERROR (0). If the date contained in **Date** is invalid, it returns BADDATE.

Source File   UTY.C, Figure 12.1

UtySetTimeString

Purpose   Sets the system time from a string.

Prototype	**int UtySetTimeString**	
	(char *Time)	A string containing the time, which must be in the format hh:mm:ss.cc (where cc is hundredths). You can omit'.cc', or ':ss.cc', but must include 'hh:mm'.

Return Value   If successful, the function returns NOERROR (0). If the parameter **Time** contains an invalid time, it returns BADTIME.

Source File   UTY.C, Figure 12.1

UtySound

Purpose   Generates a sound from the computer speaker having a specified frequency and duration.

Prototype	**void UtySound**	
	(unsigned Frequency,	The desired frequency of the sound, in cycles per second (Hz).

	unsigned Duration)	The desired duration of the sound in clock ticks (approximately 1/18 second each).

Source File   UTY.C, Figure 12.1

UtyUnpackDate

Purpose   Converts a date in packed format (produced by UtyPackDate), to normal unpacked format.

Prototype

void UtyUnpackDate (char *Target,	The string to receive the unpacked date in the format mm/dd/yyyy (the string must therefore be at least 11 bytes long).
char *Source)	The string containing the packed date.

Source File   UTY.C, Figure 12.1

UtyUnqualify

Purpose   Supplies a pointer to the simple file name contained within a partially or fully qualified file name, and converts the simple file name to uppercase letters.

Prototype

char *UtyUnqualify (char *Qual)	A string containing a file name.

Return Value   A pointer to the first character of the simple file name within the string Qual.

Source File   UTY.C, Figure 12.1

UtyWarmBoot

Purpose   Resets the computer, without performing the lengthy initial diagnostic operations.

Prototype   **void UtyWarmBoot**
                 (void)

Source File   UTY.C, Figure 12.1

APPENDIX B: SETTING UP A LIBRARY FILE

As you enter and compile the functions that have been presented in this book, you will find that the most convenient method for linking them to your application programs is to place all of the object files within a single library file. Once you have created a library file, it is no longer necessary to list individual object files when linking the program; rather, you need only to specify the library file name and the linker will automatically resolve all external references by binding in the appropriate code from this file. Also, a library file will require less room on the disk than a collection of separate object files.

For example, if the library file is named MSCTOOLS.LIB, the MAKE file that was provided for the first keyboard demonstration program in Figure 2.5 can be replaced by the following one line command:

```
cl /W2 /Zp KBDDEM01.C /link /NOD SLIBCER.LIB
MSCTOOLS.LIB
```

Note that this command assumes that MSCTOOLS.LIB is located either in the current directory, or in a directory specified by the LIB environment variable (see your compiler documentation for an explanation of setting the LIB variable). Note also that if your small model C library bears the standard name, SLIBCE.LIB, you can omit the **/link /NOD SLIBCER.LIB** portion of this command line.

Figure B.1 provides a MAKE file for preparing a library file from the function modules presented in this book. If you have entered all of the module source files, running this MAKE file will create a single, small memory model library file named MSCTOOLS.LIB, which will contain the object code for all of the functions in the book. The first time you run this MAKE file, the LIB utility will warn you that the object modules do not already exist in the library; you should ignore these warnings. Note that if you are using the QuickC command line compiler rather than the Microsoft optimizing compiler, replace each occurrence of the CL command in the MAKE file with the QCL command.

If you are preparing a library file in a step-by-step manner as you work through the book and enter new function modules, you can simply eliminate the commands from Figure B.1 for the modules you have not yet entered.

Once you have prepared an initial library file, you should run the MAKE file of Figure B.1 whenever you have modified an existing function module or added a new one, in order to bring the library file up to date. The MAKE file will recompile any source file that has been

```
MSCTOOLS.LIB : BUF.OBJ EMS.OBJ FIL.OBJ GRA.OBJ INT.OBJ IOC.OBJ KBD.OBJ \
    KBDA.OBJ MOU.OBJ PRT.OBJ SCR.OBJ SCRA.OBJ TSR.OBJ TSRA.OBJ UTY.OBJ \
    UTYA.OBJ

BUF.OBJ : BUF.C BUF.H
    cl /c /W2 /Zp BUF.C
    lib MSCTOOLS -+BUF.OBJ;

EMS.OBJ : EMS.C EMS.H
    cl /c /W2 /Zp EMS.C
    lib MSCTOOLS -+EMS.OBJ;

FIL.OBJ : FIL.C FIL.H
    cl /c /W2 /Zp FIL.C
    lib MSCTOOLS -+FIL.OBJ;

GRA.OBJ : GRA.C GRA.H
    cl /c /Zp GRA.C
    lib MSCTOOLS -+GRA.OBJ;

INT.OBJ : INT.C INT.H
    cl /c /W2 /Zp INT.C
    lib MSCTOOLS -+INT.OBJ;

IOC.OBJ : IOC.C IOC.H
    cl /c /W2 /Zp IOC.C
    lib MSCTOOLS -+IOC.OBJ;

KBD.OBJ : KBD.C KBD.H
    cl /c /W2 /Zp KBD.C
    lib MSCTOOLS -+KBD.OBJ;

KBDA.OBJ : KBDA.ASM
    masm /MX KBDA.ASM;
    lib MSCTOOLS -+ KBDA.OBJ;

MOU.OBJ : MOU.C MOU.H
    cl /c /W2 /Zp MOU.C
    lib MSCTOOLS -+MOU.OBJ;

PRT.OBJ : PRT.C PRT.H
    cl /c /W2 /Zp PRT.C
    lib MSCTOOLS -+PRT.OBJ;

SCR.OBJ : SCR.C SCR.H
    cl /c /W2 /Zp SCR.C
    lib MSCTOOLS -+SCR.OBJ;

SCRA.OBJ : SCRA.ASM
    masm /MX SCRA.ASM;
    lib MSCTOOLS -+SCRA.OBJ;

TSR.OBJ : TSR.C TSR.H
    cl /c /W2 /Zp TSR.C
    lib MSCTOOLS -+TSR.OBJ;
```

Figure B.1: A MAKE file for preparing a library file containing all of the function modules in this book

```
    TSRA.OBJ : TSRA.ASM
        masm /MX TSRA.ASM;
        lib MSCTOOLS -+TSRA.OBJ;

    UTY.OBJ : UTY.C UTY.H
        cl /c /W2 /Zp UTY.C
        lib MSCTOOLS -+UTY.OBJ;

    UTYA.OBJ : UTYA.ASM
        masm /MX UTYA.ASM;
        lib MSCTOOLS -+ UTYA.OBJ;
```

Figure B.1: A MAKE file for preparing a library file containing all of the function modules in this book (continued)

modified since the last time it was compiled, and it will replace the object file within the library file with the new version; the – + command causes the LIB utility to *replace* an existing object file with the new version (if the library does not currently contain the object file, the LIB utility simply *adds* the specified file and issues the warning just described).

Note that the library file created through the MAKE file of Figure B.1 contains small model code and can therefore be linked only with small model application programs. If you wish to prepare a library file that can be linked with another memory model program, you should perform the following four steps:

1. Add one of the following command line switches to each CL (or QCL) command in the MAKE file of Figure B.1, according to the desired memory model:

Switch	Memory Model
/AM	Medium
/AC	Compact
/AL	Large

   Note that you do not need to modify the MASM commands, since, as explained in Chapter 1, the assembly language files are designed to interface with any memory model C program.

2. Replace each occurrence of the file name MSCTOOLS.LIB in the MAKE file with the name you choose for the new library file. You might, for example, name a medium memory model library file MSCTOOLM.LIB.

3. Delete all existing object files in the current directory that have the same names as the object files generated by the MAKE file. (If an object file already exists, and is up to date

with the corresponding source file, the new object file will *not* be generated and the object code will not be added to the new library file. Although this step forces the assembly language files to be unnecessarily reassembled, this process takes only seconds.)

4. Run the modified MAKE file.

Note that the companion disk set for this book includes complete library files for all memory models. Also included are separate MAKE files (similar to Figure B.1) for maintaining each memory model library; if you modify or add functions to any of the modules, you can use one or more of these MAKE files to bring the corresponding library files up to date.

Once you have started enjoying the convenience of using a library file, you might consider implementing one additional refinement that can result in considerably smaller code size for the programs you link with this library. Each object file you add to the library is stored as a discrete linkable unit; if you call a function belonging to a certain object file, *all* of the programs contained in this file are automatically linked into your program. For example, calling the function **UtyPause** causes the entire set of functions defined in UTY.C to be linked into your program (plus all functions in any additional object modules referenced by UTY.C).

The solution to this problem is to place each function in a separate source file, generate a separate object file for each function, and then place all the object files in a single library file. Of course you will need to greatly expand the MAKE file presented in this appendix; however, the basic method for preparing the library file is the same as that just described.

APPENDIX C: EXTENDED KEYBOARD CODES

Many of the keys and key combinations on an IBM-compatible keyboard do not have an ASCII value. Such keys are therefore identified by an *extended code*. The function **KbdGetC**, presented in Chapter 2, returns an integer that contains the extended code in the high-order byte, and the ASCII value in the low-order byte. If a key does not have an ASCII value, the low-order byte will contain the value 0; in this case, you should examine the extended code in the high-order byte to identify the key.

The following table lists the extended codes for the keys and key combinations reported by the BIOS that do not have ASCII values. These key codes are returned in systems with the original PC keyboard, the 84-key PC-AT keyboard, or the 101-key enhanced IBM keyboard supplied with PC-AT and PS/2 machines.

Extended Code	Key/Key-combination
3	NULL Character (Ctrl-@)
15	Shift-Tab (back tab)
16-25	Alt-Q W E R T Y U I O P
30-38	Alt-A S D F G H J K L
44-50	Alt-Z X C V B N M
59-68	F1 to F10
71	Home
72	Up-Arrow (↑)
73	PgUp
75	Left-Arrow (←)
77	Right-Arrow (→)
79	End
80	Down-Arrow (↓)
81	PgDn
82	Ins
83	Del
84-93	Shift-F1 to F10
94-103	Ctrl-F1 to F10

104-113	Alt-F1 to F10
114	Ctrl-PrtSc
115	Ctrl Left-Arrow (Ctrl ←)
116	Ctrl Right-Arrow (Ctrl →)
117	Ctrl-End
118	Ctrl-PgDn
119	Ctrl-Home
120-131	Alt-1 2 3 4 5 6 7 8 9 0 – =
132	Ctrl-PgUp

BIBLIOGRAPHY

This Bibliography provides a list of books on C and assembly language programming, and on the MS-DOS operating system. The list is not exhaustive; there are undoubtedly many other books of equal merit. These are simply the ones I have discovered and have found useful in my own programming efforts. Also included are several valuable programmer's magazines.

Ammeraal, L. *Computer Graphics for the IBM PC*. Chichester, England: John Wiley & Sons, 1987.

Ammeraal, L. *Programming Principles in Computer Graphics*. Chichester, England: John Wiley & Sons, 1986.

Angermeyer, J. and Jaeger, K. *MS-DOS Developer's Guide.*, 2nd ed.. Indianapolis, IN: Howard W. Sams, 1988.

BYTE (magazine). New York: McGraw-Hill.

Computer Language (magazine). San Francisco, CA: CL Publications Inc.

Dr. Dobb's Journal (magazine). Redwood City, CA: M & T Publishing.

Duncan, R. *Advanced MS-DOS Programming*. 2nd ed.. Redmond, WA: Microsoft Press, 1988.

Harbison, S. and Steele, G. *C: A Reference Manual*. Englewood Cliffs, NJ: Prentice-Hall, 1987.

IBM. *AT Technical Reference*, part number 6280070 (update for model 339 is part number 6280099). Boca Raton, Florida: IBM Corp., 1986.

IBM. *Disk Operating System Version 4.00 Technical Reference*. Boca Raton, Florida: IBM Corp, 1988.

IBM. *DOS Technical Reference, Version 3.30*, part number 6280059. Boca Raton, Florida: IBM Corp, 1987.

IBM. *Options and Adapters Technical Reference*, part number 6322509. Boca Raton, Florida: IBM Corp., 1984.

IBM. *PC Technical Reference*, part number 6322507. Boca Raton, Florida: IBM Corp., 1984.

IBM. *Personal System/2 and Personal Computer BIOS Interface Technical Reference*. 2nd ed., part number 68X2341. Boca Raton, Florida: IBM Corp., 1988.

Intel. *Lotus/Intel/Microsoft Expanded Memory Specification, Version 4.0.* Hillsboro, OR: Intel, 1987.

Johnson, N. *Graphics in C, Programming and Techniques*. Berkeley, CA: Osborne McGraw-Hill, 1987.

Kelly-Bootle, S. *Mastering QuickC*. Alameda, CA: SYBEX, 1989.

Kernighan, B. and Ritchie, D. *The C Programming Language*. Englewood Cliffs, NJ: Prentice-Hall, 1978.

King, R. *The MS-DOS Handbook*. Alameda, CA: SYBEX, 1986.

Lafore, R. *Assembly Language Primer for the IBM PC & XT*. New York, NY: Plume/Waite, 1984.

Microsoft. *Microsoft C Optimizing Compiler, User's Guide*. Redmond, WA: Microsoft Corporation, 1987.

Microsoft. *Microsoft C Run-Time Library Reference*. Redmond, WA: Microsoft Corporation, 1987.

Microsoft. *Microsoft Mouse Programmer's Reference Guide*. Redmond, WA: Microsoft Corporation, 1986.

Microsoft. *MS-DOS Technical Reference Encyclopedia*. Redmond, WA: Microsoft Press, 1988.

Miller, A. *Assembly Language Techniques for the IBM PC*. Alameda, CA: SYBEX, 1986.

Norton, P. *The New Peter Norton Programmer's Guide to the IBM PC & PS/2*. Redmond, WA: Microsoft Press, 1988.

PC Tech Journal (magazine). New York: Ziff-Davis Publishing Company.

Plum, T. *Notes on The Draft C Standard*. Cardiff, NJ: Plum Hall, 1987.

Programmer's Journal (magazine). Eugene, OR: Oakley Publishing Company.

Radcliffe, R. and Raab, T. *Data Handling Utilities in C*. Alameda, CA: SYBEX, 1986.

Rogers, D. *Procedural Elements for Computer Graphics*. New York: McGraw-Hill, 1985.

Systems Journal (magazine). Redmond, WA: Microsoft Corporation.

Wilton, R. *Programmer's Guide to PC & PS/2 Video Systems*. Redmond, WA: Microsoft Press, 1987.

Wirth, N. *Algorithms + Data Structures = Programs*. Englewood Cliffs, NJ: Prentice-Hall, 1976.

Young, Michael J. *Inside DOS: A Programmer's Guide*. Alameda, CA: SYBEX, 1988.

Young, Michael J. *Programmer's Guide to OS/2*. Alameda, CA: SYBEX, 1988.

Young, Michael J. *Programmer's Guide to the OS/2 Presentation Manager*. Alameda, CA: SYBEX, 1989.

Young, Michael J. *Systems Programming in Turbo C*. Alameda, CA: SYBEX, 1988.

IBM technical publications may be ordered from the following address. A catalog, the *Technical Directory*, is also available.

IBM Technical Directory
P.O. Box 2009
Racine, WI 53404
1-800-426-7282

Index

Selections from The SYBEX Library

LANGUAGES

The ABC's of GW-BASIC
William R. Orvis
320pp. Ref. 663-4

Featuring two parts: Part I is an easy-to-follow tutorial for beginners, while Part II is a complete, concise reference guide to GW-BASIC commands and functions. Covers everything from the basics of programming in the GW-BASIC environment, to debugging a major program. Includes special treatment of graphics and sound.

The ABC's of Quick C
Douglas Hergert
309pp. Ref. 557-3

This is the most unintimidating C language tutorial, designed especially for readers who have had little or no computer programming experience. The reader will learn programming essentials with step-by-step instructions for working with numbers, strings, arrays, pointers, structures, decisions, and loops. For Version 2.0.

BASIC Programs for Scientists and Engineers
Alan R. Miller
318pp. Ref. 073-3

The algorithms presented in this book are programmed in standard BASIC code which should be usable with almost any implementation of BASIC. Includes statistical calculations, matrix algebra, curve fitting, integration, and more.

Encyclopedia C
Robert A. Radcliffe
1333pp. Ref. 655-3

This is the complete reference for standard ANSI/ISO programmers using any Microsoft C compiler with DOS. It blends comprehensive treatment of C syntax, functions, utilities, and services with practical examples and proven techniques for optimizing productivity and performance in C programming.

FORTRAN Programs for Scientists and Engineers (Second Edition)
Alan R. Miller
280pp. Ref. 571-9

In this collection of widely used scientific algorithms—for statistics, vector and matrix operations, curve fitting, and more—the author stresses effective use of little-known and powerful features of FORTRAN.

Introduction to Pascal: Including Turbo Pascal (Second Edition)
Rodnay Zaks
464pp. Ref. 533-6

This best-selling tutorial builds complete mastery of Pascal—from basic structured programming concepts, to advanced I/O, data structures, file operations, sets, pointers and lists, and more. Both ISO Standard and Turbo Pascal.

Mastering C
Craig Bolon
437pp. Ref. 326-0

This in-depth guide stresses planning, testing, efficiency and portability in C applications. Topics include data types, storage classes, arrays, pointers, data structures, control statements, I/O and the C function library.

Mastering QuickBASIC
Rita Belserene
450pp. Ref. 589-1

Readers build professional programs with

this extensive language tutorial. Fundamental commands are mixed with the author's tips and tricks so that users can create their own applications. Program templates are included for video displays, computer games, and working with databases and printers. For Version 4.5.

Mastering QuickC
Stan Kelly-Bootle
602pp. Ref. 550-6

This extensive tutorial covers C language programming and features the latest version of QuickC. Veteran author Kelly-Bootle uses many examples to explain language and style, covering data types, storage classes, file I/O, the Graphics Toolbox, and the window-oriented debugger. For Version 2.0.

Mastering Turbo C
(Second Edition)
Stan Kelly-Bootle
609pp. Ref. 595-6

With a foreword by Borland International President Philippe Kahn, this new edition has been expanded to include full details on Version 2.0. Learn theory and practical programming, with tutorials on data types, real numbers and characters, controlling program flow, file I/O, and producing color charts and graphs. Through Version 2.

Mastering Turbo Pascal 6
Scott D. Palmer
650pp, Ref. 675 8

This step-by-step guide to the newest Turbo Pascal release takes readers from programming basics to advanced techniques such as graphics, recursion, object-oriented programming, efficient debugging, and programming for other environments such as Vax/VMS. Includes dozens of useful exercises and examples, and tips for effective programming.

Turbo Pascal Toolbox
(Second Edition)
Frank Dutton
425pp. Ref. 602-2

This collection of tested, efficient Turbo Pascal building blocks gives a boost to

intermediate-level programmers, while teaching effective programming by example. Topics include accessing DOS, menus, bit maps, screen handling, and much more.

Up & Running with Turbo Pascal 5.5
Michael-Alexander Beisecker
Peter Brickwede
137pp. Ref.713-4

All the basics of Turbo Pascal 5.5 in twenty time-coded "steps" taking 15, 30, 45 or 60 minutes. In addition to Pascal essentials, topics include dynamic variables, file management, graphics, systems programming, the debugger, and using the Toolboxes.

OPERATING SYSTEMS

The ABC's of DOS 4
Alan R. Miller
275pp. Ref. 583-2

This step-by-step introduction to using DOS 4 is written especially for beginners. Filled with simple examples, *The ABC's of DOS 4* covers the basics of hardware, software, disks, the system editor EDLIN, DOS commands, and more.

The ABC's of DOS 5
Alan Miller
267pp. Ref. 770-3

This straightforward guide will haven even first-time computer users working comfortably with DOS 5 in no time. Step-by-step lessons lead users from switching on the PC, through exploring the DOS Shell, working with directories and files, using essential commands, customizing the system, and trouble shooting. Includes a tear-out quick reference card and function key template.

ABC's of MS-DOS
(Second Edition)
Alan R. Miller
233pp. Ref. 493-3

This handy guide to MS-DOS is all many PC users need to manage their computer files, organize floppy and hard disks, use EDLIN, and keep their computers organized. Additional information is given about utilities like Sidekick, and there is a DOS command and program summary. The second edition is fully updated for Version 3.3.

The ABC's of SCO UNIX
Tom Cuthbertson
263pp. Re. 715-0

A guide especially for beginners who want to get to work fast. Includes hands-on tutorials on logging in and out; creating and editing files; using electronic mail; organizing files into directories; printing; text formatting; and more.

The ABC's of Windows 3.0
Kris Jamsa
327pp. Ref. 760-6

A user-friendly introduction to the essentials of Windows 3.0. Presented in 64 short lessons. Beginners start with lesson one, while more advanced readers can skip ahead. Learn to use File Manager, the accessory programs, customization features, Program Manager, and more.

DESQview Instant Reference
Paul J. Perry
175pp. Ref. 809-2

This complete quick-reference command guide covers version 2.3 and DESQview 386, as well as QEMM (for managing expanded memory) and Manifest Memory Analyzer. Concise, alphabetized entries provide exact syntax, options, usage, and brief examples for every command. A handy source for on-the-job reminders and tips.

DOS 3.3 On-Line Advisor Version 1.1
SYBAR, Software Division of SYBEX, Inc.
Ref. 933-1

The answer to all your DOS problems. The DOS On-Line Advisor is an on-screen reference that explains over 200 DOS

error messages. 2300 other citations cover all you ever needed to know about DOS. The DOS On-Line Advisor pops up on top of your working program to give you quick, easy help when you need it, and disappears when you don't. Covers thru version 3.3. Software package comes with 3½" and 5¼" disks. **System Requirements:** IBM compatible with DOS 2.0 or higher, runs with Windows 3.0, uses 90K of RAM.

DOS Instant Reference SYBEX Prompter Series
Greg Harvey
Kay Yarborough Nelson
220pp. Ref. 477-1

A complete fingertip reference for fast, easy on-line help:command summaries, syntax, usage and error messages. Organized by function—system commands, file commands, disk management, directories, batch files, I/O, networking, programming, and more. Through Version 3.3.

DOS 5 Instant Reference
Robert M. Thomas
200pp. Ref. 804-1

The comprehensive quick guide to DOS—all its features, commands, options, and versions—now including DOS 5, with the new graphical interface. Concise, alphabetized command entries provide exact syntax, options, usage, brief examples, and applicable version numbers. Fully cross-referenced; ideal for quick review or on-the-job reference.

The DOS 5 User's Handbook
Gary Masters
Richard Allen King
400pp. Ref. 777-0

This is the DOS 5 book for users who are already familiar with an earlier version of DOS. Part I is a quick, friendly guide to new features; topics include the graphical interface, new and enhanced commands, and much more. Part II is a complete DOS 5 quick reference, with command summaries, in-depth explanations, and examples.

Encyclopedia DOS
Judd Robbins

1030pp. Ref. 699-5

A comprehensive reference and user's guide to all versions of DOS through 4.0. Offers complete information on every DOS command, with all possible switches and parameters—plus examples of effective usage. An invaluable tool.

Essential OS/2
(Second Edition)
Judd Robbins

445pp. Ref. 609-X

Written by an OS/2 expert, this is the guide to the powerful new resources of the OS/2 operating system standard edition 1.1 with presentation manager. Robbins introduces the standard edition, and details multitasking under OS/2, and the range of commands for installing, starting up, configuring, and running applications. For Version 1.1 Standard Edition.

Essential PC-DOS
(Second Edition)
Myril Clement Shaw
Susan Soltis Shaw

332pp. Ref. 413-5

An authoritative guide to PC-DOS, including version 3.2. Designed to make experts out of beginners, it explores everything from disk management to batch file programming. Includes an 85-page command summary. Through Version 3.2.

Graphics Programming
Under Windows
Brian Myers
Chris Doner

646pp. Ref. 448-8

Straightforward discussion, abundant examples, and a concise reference guide to graphics commands make this book a must for Windows programmers. Topics range from how Windows works to programming for business, animation, CAD, and desktop publishing. For Version 2.

Hard Disk Instant Reference
SYBEX Prompter Series
Judd Robbins

256pp. Ref. 587-5

Compact yet comprehensive, this pocket-sized reference presents the essential information on DOS commands used in managing directories and files, and in optimizing disk configuration. Includes a survey of third-party utility capabilities. Through DOS 4.0.

Inside DOS: A Programmer's
Guide
Michael J. Young

490pp. Ref. 710-X

A collection of practical techniques (with source code listings) designed to help you take advantage of the rich resources intrinsic to MS-DOS machines. Designed for the experienced programmer with a basic understanding of C and 8086 assembly language, and DOS fundamentals.

SYSTEMS PROGRAMMING IN MICROSOFT C

▌DISK OFFER

Companion Disk Set

A *Companion Disk Set* is available for Microsoft C and QuickC programmers who would like to make immediate use of the functions and utilities presented in this book. The three disks contain the following files:

- ▌ All source code listings directly from the book, in ASCII format and ready to compile or assemble.
- ▌ All header files, MAKE scripts, and program lists from the book.
- ▌ Library files containing all of the functions in the book. A separate library file is provided for each memory model. Using a library file, you can immediately link any of the functions to your Microsoft C programs, without the need to compile or assemble the function source code.

ORDER FORM

_____	Copies of the *Companion Disk Set* @ $34.50 each	_____
_____	California residents: add 7.25% sales tax	_____
	Shipping and Handling: add $2.50 ($5.00 for foreign orders)	_____
	TOTAL ORDER	_____

_____ 5¼" disks (360K)   _____ 3½' disks (720K)

Name_____

Address _____

City/State/Zip _____

Please send a check for full payment payable to Michael J. Young (no CODs, purchase orders, or bank cards; for foreign orders, please send an international money order in U.S. dollars drawn on a U.S. bank). Your software will be shipped immediately. Mail order to:

Michael J. Young
20 Sunnyside Avenue, Suite A
Mill Valley, CA 94941

SYBEX is not affiliated with Michael J. Young and assumes no responsibility for any defect in the disk or program.

SYBEX ®

FREE BROCHURE!

Complete this form today, and we'll send you a full-color brochure of Sybex bestsellers.

Please supply the name of the Sybex book purchased.

_____

How would you rate it?

_____ Excellent   _____ Very Good   _____ Average   _____ Poor

Why did you select this particular book?

_____ Recommended to me by a friend
_____ Recommended to me by store personnel
_____ Saw an advertisement in _____
_____ Author's reputation
_____ Saw in Sybex catalog
_____ Required textbook
_____ Sybex reputation
_____ Read book review in _____
_____ In-store display
_____ Other _____

Where did you buy it?

_____ Bookstore
_____ Computer Store or Software Store
_____ Catalog (name: _____)
_____ Direct from Sybex
_____ Other: _____

Did you buy this book with your personal funds?

_____ Yes   _____ No

About how many computer books do you buy each year?

_____ 1-3   _____ 3-5   _____ 5-7   _____ 7-9   _____ 10+

About how many Sybex books do you own?

_____ 1-3   _____ 3-5   _____ 5-7   _____ 7-9   _____ 10+

Please indicate your level of experience with the software covered in this book:

_____ Beginner   _____ Intermediate   _____ Advanced

Which types of software packages do you use regularly?

_____ Accounting	_____ Databases	_____ Networks
_____ Amiga	_____ Desktop Publishing	_____ Operating Systems
_____ Apple/Mac	_____ File Utilities	_____ Spreadsheets
_____ CAD	_____ Money Management	_____ Word Processing
_____ Communications	_____ Languages	_____ Other _____

(please specify)

Which of the following best describes your job title?

_____ Administrative/Secretarial _____ President/CEO

_____ Director _____ Manager/Supervisor

_____ Engineer/Technician _____ Other _____
(please specify)

Comments on the weaknesses/strengths of this book: _____

_____

_____

_____

_____

Name _____

Street _____

City/State/Zip _____

Phone _____

PLEASE FOLD, SEAL, AND MAIL TO SYBEX

SYBEX, INC.
Department M
2021 CHALLENGER DR.
ALAMEDA, CALIFORNIA USA
94501

SYBEX ®

SEAL

THE FUNCTIONS BY CATEGORY (continued from inside front cover)